D0096827

Fodor's

CITYGUIDE
ATLANTA

2ND EDITION

FODOR'S TRAVEL PUBLICATIONS
NEW YORK • TORONTO • LONDON • SYDNEY • AUCKLAND
WWW.FODORS.COM

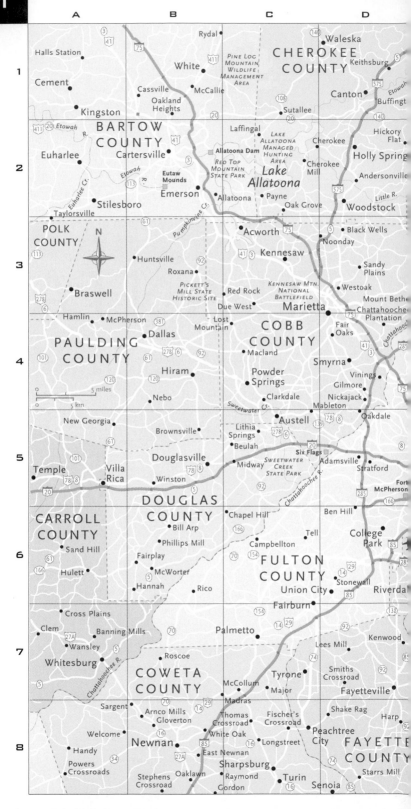

A   B   C   D

1

Halls Station
Cement
Kingston

Rydal
White
Cassville
McCallie
Oakland
Heights

*PINE LOG
MOUNTAIN
WILDLIFE
MANAGEMENT
AREA*

CHEROKEE
COUNTY

Waleska
Keithsburg
Canton
Buffingt
Etowah

Sutallee

2

Euharlee
Cartersville

BARTOW
COUNTY

Etowah R.

Allatoona Dam

*RED TOP
MOUNTAIN
STATE PARK*

Eutaw
Mounds
Emerson

Laffingal
*LAKE
ALLATOONA
MANAGED
HUNTING
AREA*

*Lake
Allatoona*

Cherokee
Cherokee
Mill

Hickory
Flat
Holly Spring
Andersonville
Little R.
Woodstock

Stilesboro
Taylorsville

Allatoona
Payne
Oak Grove

3

POLK
COUNTY

N

Braswell

Huntsville
Roxana

*PICKETT'S
MILL STATE
HISTORIC SITE*

Acworth

Kennesaw

Red Rock
Due West

*KENNESAW MTN.
NATIONAL
BATTLEFIELD*

Marietta

Black Wells
Noonday

Sandy
Plains
Westoak
Mount Beth
Chattahooche
Plantation

Hamlin
McPherson

4

PAULDING
COUNTY

Dallas

Lost
Mountain

COBB
COUNTY

Fair
Oaks

5 miles
5 km

Hiram

Nebo

Macland

Powder
Springs

Clarkdale

Sweetwater Cr.

Smyrna
Vinings
Gilmore
Nickajack
Mableton

Oakdale

5

New Georgia

Temple
Villa
Rica

Brownsville

Douglasville
Winston

Lithia
Springs
Beulah
Midway

Austell

Six Flags

*SWEETWATER
CREEK
STATE PARK*

Adamsville

Stratford

Fort
McPherson

Chattahooch R.

6

CARROLL
COUNTY

Sand Hill
Hulett

DOUGLAS
COUNTY

Bill Arp
Phillips Mill
Fairplay
McWorter
Hannah

Chapel Hill

Campbellton

Rico

Tell

FULTON
COUNTY

Union City
Fairburn

Ben Hill

College
Park

Stonewall

Riverda

7

Cross Plains
Clem
Banning Mills
Wansley
Whitesburg

Chattahoochee R.

Roscoe

COWETA
COUNTY

Palmetto

McCollum

Tyrone
Major

Lees Mill

Smiths
Crossroad

Kenwood

Fayetteville

8

Sargent
Welcome
Handy
Powers
Crossroads

Stephens
Crossroad

Arnco Mills
Gloverton
Newnan
East Newnan
Oaklawn

Madras
Thomas
Crossroad
White Oak
Sharpsburg
Raymond
Gordon

Fischer's
Crossroad
Longstreet
Turin

Shake Rag
Peachtree
City
Senoia

Harp

FAYETTE
COUNTY

Starrs Mill

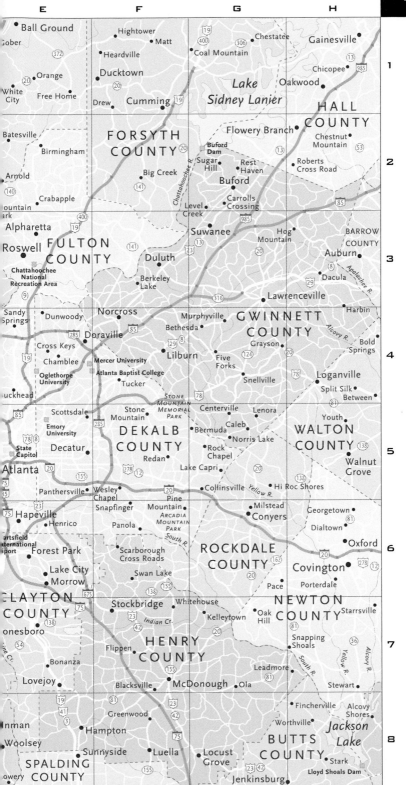

ATLANTA AREA OVERVIEW

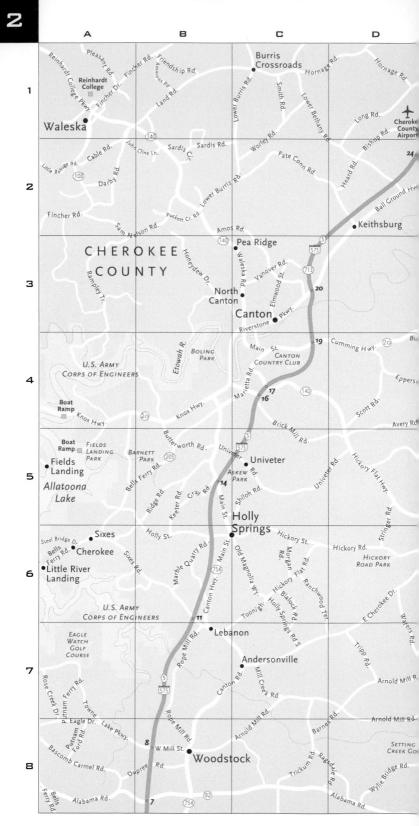

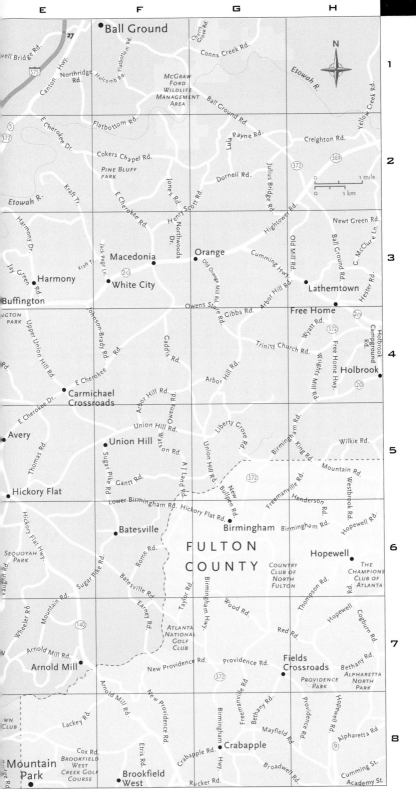

E F G H

1

● Ball Ground

well Bridge Rd.
575
27
Canton Hwy.
Northridge Rd.
Holcomb Rd.
Flatbottom Rd.
Cherry Grove Rd.
Conns Creek Rd.
McGraw Ford Wildlife Management Area
Ball Ground Rd.
Etowah R.
N

5
372
E Cherokee Dr.
Flatbottom Rd.
Cokers Chapel Rd.
Pine Bluff Park
Jones Rd.
E Cherokee Rd.
Henry Scott Rd.
Lula Payne Rd.
Dornell Rd.
Julius Bridge Rd.
Creighton Rd.
369
372
Yellow Creek Rd.
2

0 1 mile
0 1 km

Etowah R.
Kraft Tr.
Harmony Dr.
Jay Green Rd.
● Harmony
Kraft Tr.
Jack Page Ln.
● Macedonia
2C
● White City
● Orange
Old Orange Mill Rd.
Hightower Rd.
Cumming Hwy.
Old Mill Rd.
Arbor Hill Rd.
Newt Green Rd.
G. McClure Ln.
Ball Ground Rd.
● Lathemtown
Hester Rd.
3

Buffington
NGTON PARK
Upper Union Hill Rd.
Johnson-Brady Rd.
E Cherokee Dr.
● Carmichael Crossroads
Gaddis Rd.
Owens Store Rd.
Gibbs Rd.
Arbor Hill Rd.
Trinity Church Rd.
Arbor Hill Rd.
Free Home ● 20
Wyatt Rd.
Free Home Hwy.
Wrights Mill Rd.
372
Holbrook Campground Rd.
● Holbrook
20
4

Avery ●
Thomas Rd.
E Cherokee Dr.
Sugar Pike Rd.
● Union Hill
Union Hill Rd.
Watson Rd.
Arbor Hill Rd.
Owens Rd.
A J Land Rd.
Liberty Grove Rd.
Union Hill Rd.
372
New Bullpen Rd.
Birmingham King Rd.
Mountain Rd.
Wilkie Rd.
Westbrook Rd.
5

● Hickory Flat
Gantt Rd.
Lower Birmingham Rd.
Hickory Flat Rd.
● Batesville
Rome Rd.
Freemanville Rd.
Henderson Rd.
● Birmingham
Birmingham Rd.
Hopewell Rd.
6

Hickory Flat Hwy.
Sequoyah Park
uguna Rd.
Sugar Pike Rd.
Batesville Rd.
FULTON COUNTY
Country Club of North Fulton
● Hopewell
The Champions Club of Atlanta
Thompson Rd.

Wheeler Rd.
Mountain Rd.
140
Earney Rd.
Taylor Rd.
Birmingham Hwy.
Wood Rd.
Atlanta National Golf Club
Red Rd.
Providence Rd.
Hopewell Rd.
Cogburn Rd.
7

V
Arnold Mill Rd.
● Arnold Mill
Arnold Mill Rd.
New Providence Rd.
New Providence Rd.
Providence Rd.
372
● Fields Crossroads
Providence Park
Bethany Rd.
Alpharetta North Park

WN CLUB
Lackey Rd.
Cox Rd.
Brookfield West Creek Golf Course
Etris Rd.
New Providence Rd.
Birmingham Hwy.
Crabapple Rd.
Freemanville Rd.
Bethany Rd.
Mayfield Rd.
● Crabapple
Broadwell Rd.
providence Rd.
Hopewell Rd.
Alpharetta Rd.
9
8

● Mountain Park
idge Rd.
● Brookfield West
Rucker Rd.
Cumming St.
Academy St.

NORTHWEST SUBURBS: CHEROKEE COUNTY

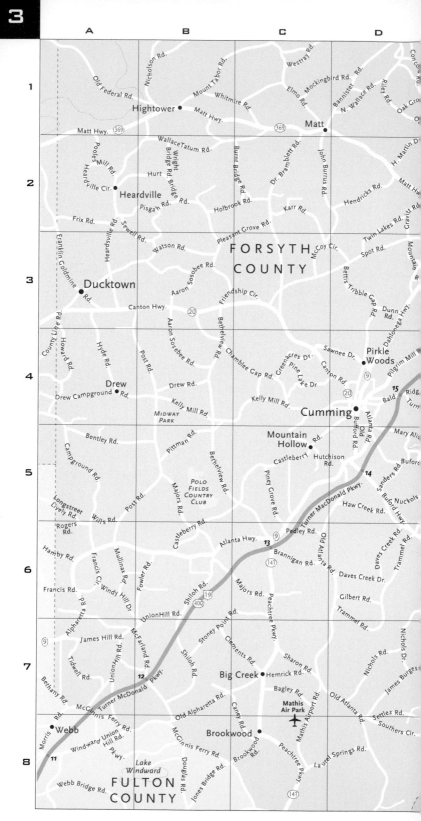

3

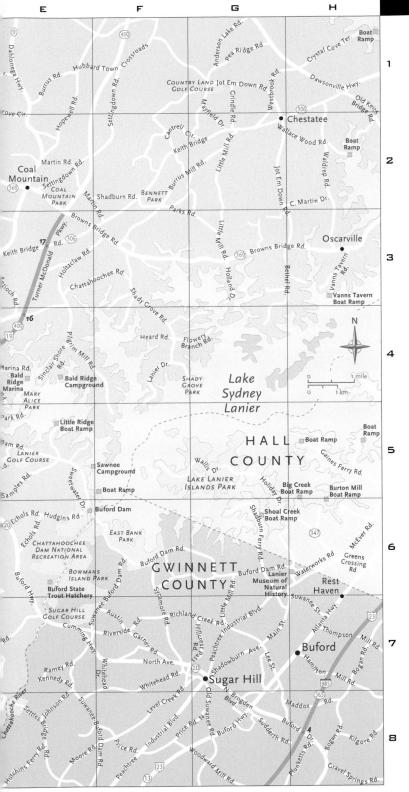

NORTHEAST SUBURBS: FORSYTH COUNTY AND LAKE LANIER

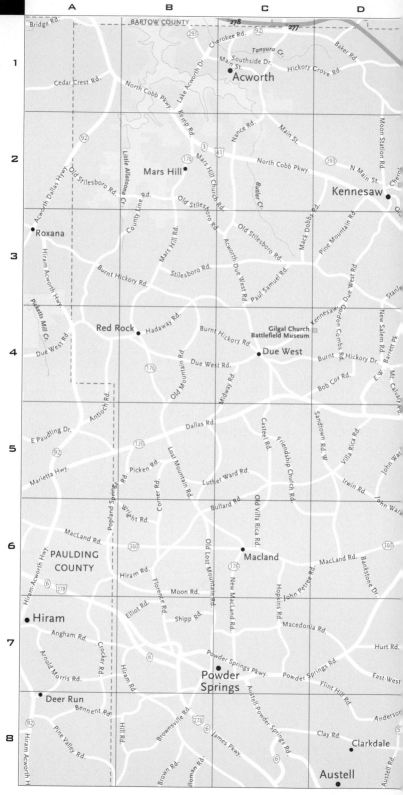

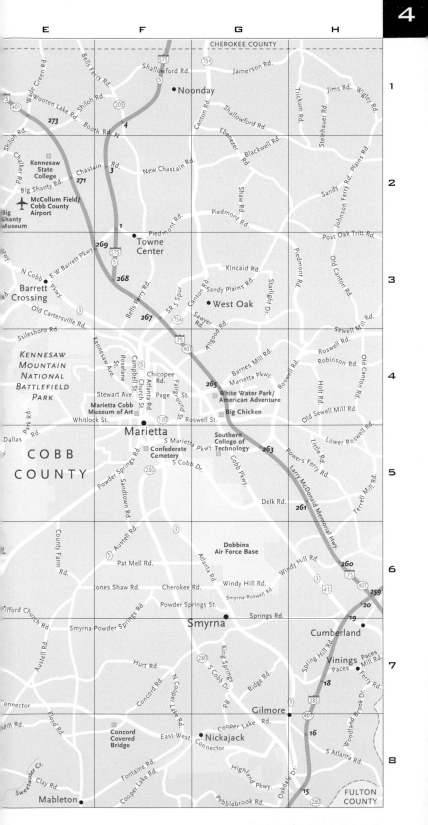

E F G H

CHEROKEE COUNTY

Shallowford Rd. 754

•Noonday Jamerson Rd.

Jims Rd. Wigley Rd.

Wade Green Rd. Bells Ferry Rd. Shiloh Rd. 205 Booth Rd.

Wooten Lake Rd. Shiloh Rd. Shallowford Rd. Trickum Rd. Steinhauer Rd.

401 273 4 N

Canton Rd. Ebenezer Rd. Blackwell Rd. Sandy Plains Rd. Johnson Ferry Rd.

Chalker Rd. Shiloh Rd.

Kennesaw State College Chastain Rd. 271 New Chastain Rd. 3 Shaw Rd.

Big Shanty Rd.

McCollum Field/ Cobb County Airport 1 Piedmont Rd. Piedmont Rd. Post Oak Tritt Rd.

Big Shanty Museum

269 Towne Center 575 Kincaid Rd. Piedmont Rd. Old Canton Rd.

N Cobb Pkwy. E.W. Barrett Pkwy. 268

Barrett Crossing 3 Bells Ferry Rd. 267 SR S Spur 754 Sandy Plains Rd. Canton Rd. •West Oak Starlight Dr.

Old Cartersville Rd.

Stilesboro Rd. Sawyer Rd. Sewell Mill Rd.

75 401 Allgood Rd.

KENNESAW MOUNTAIN NATIONAL BATTLEFIELD PARK Kennesaw Ave. Roselane St. Campbell St. Chicopee Rd. Atlanta Rd. Barnes Mill Rd. Marietta Pkwy. Roswell Rd. Robinson Rd. Holt Rd. Old Canton Rd.

Stewart Ave. Church St. Page St. Fairground St. 265 White Water Park/ American Adventure

Marietta Cobb Museum of Art Old Sewell Mill Rd.

Park Rd. Whitlock St. 120 Roswell St. Big Chicken

Dallas Marietta S Marietta Pkwy. Southern College of Technology 263 Lower Roswell Rd.

Confederate Cemetery Little Rd. Powers Ferry Rd.

COBB COUNTY Powder Springs Rd. 280 S Cobb Dr. Cobb Pkwy. Larry McDonald Memorial Hwy. Terrell Mill Rd.

Sandtown Rd. Delk Rd. 261

County Farm Rd. Austell Rd. 3 Dobbins Air Force Base Windy Hill Rd. 260 75

Pat Mell Rd. 5 Atlanta Rd. Windy Hill Rd. 3 41 401 259

Jones Shaw Rd. Cherokee Rd. Windy Hill Rd. 20

Milford Church Rd. Powder Springs St. Smyrna-Roswell Rd.

Smyrna-Powder Springs Rd. Powder Springs St. Smyrna Springs Rd. 19

Austell Rd. Hurt Rd. N Cooper Lake Rd. King Springs Rd. S Cobb Dr. Ridge Rd. Cumberland Vinings Paces Mill Rd. Paces Ferry Rd. Spring Hill Rd. 18 7

Connector Concord Rd. Gilmore 407 285

Floyd Rd. Concord Covered Bridge East-West Connector •Nickajack Cooper Lake Rd. 16 Woodland Brook Dr.

Mill Rd. Cooper Lake Rd. S Atlanta Rd. 8

Sweetwater Cr. Clay Rd. Fontaine Rd. Highland Pkwy. Oakdale Dr.

Mableton Cooper Lake Rd. Pebblebrook Rd. 15 280 FULTON COUNTY

1 2 3 4 5 6 7 8

CENTRAL COBB COUNTY, KENNESAW, AND MARIETTA

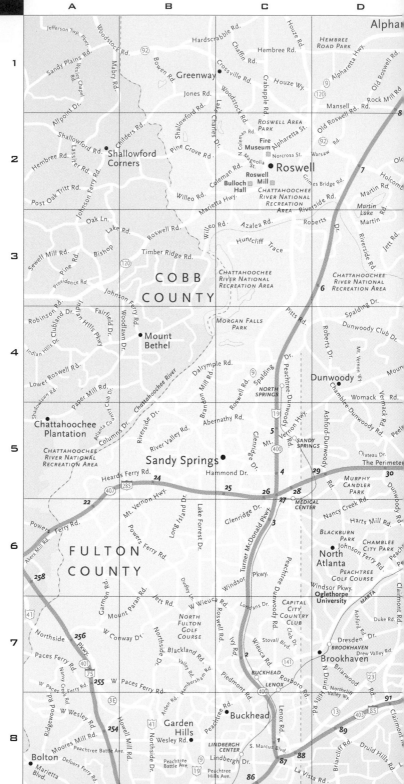

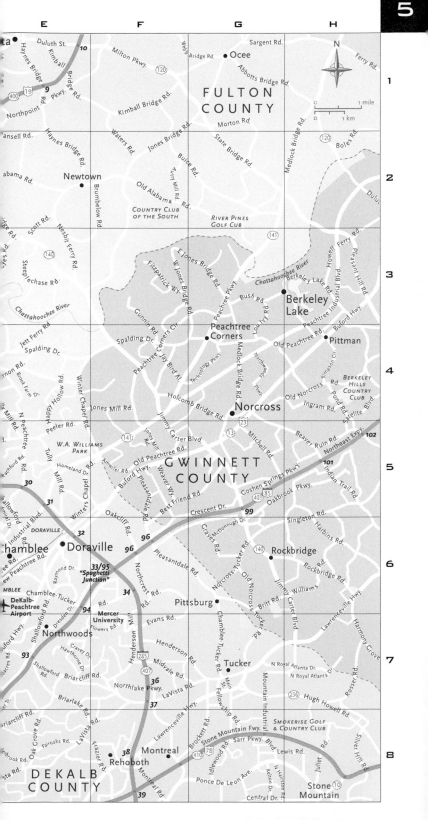

NORTHERN FULTON AND DEKALB COUNTIES

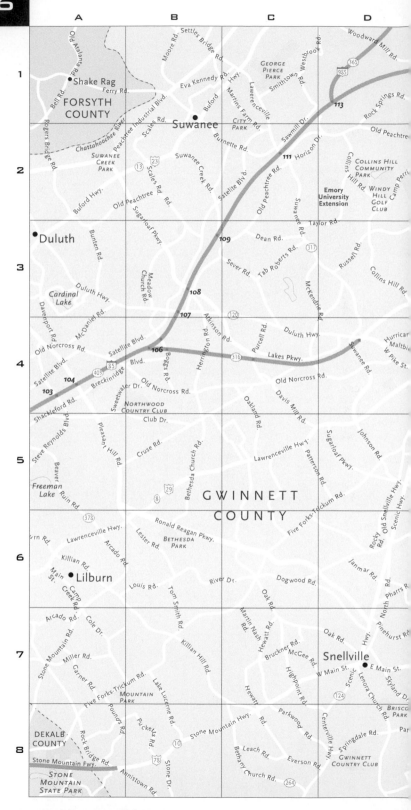

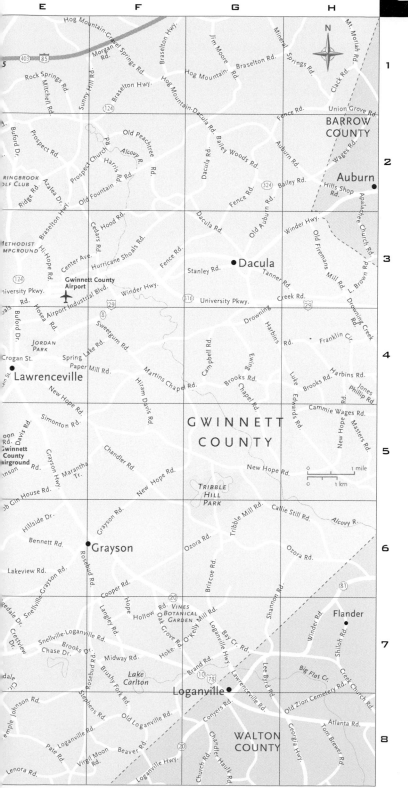

NORTHEAST SUBURBS: GWINNETT COUNTY

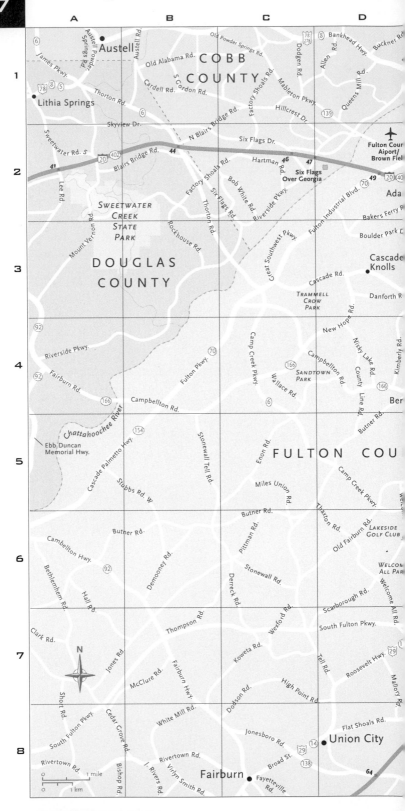

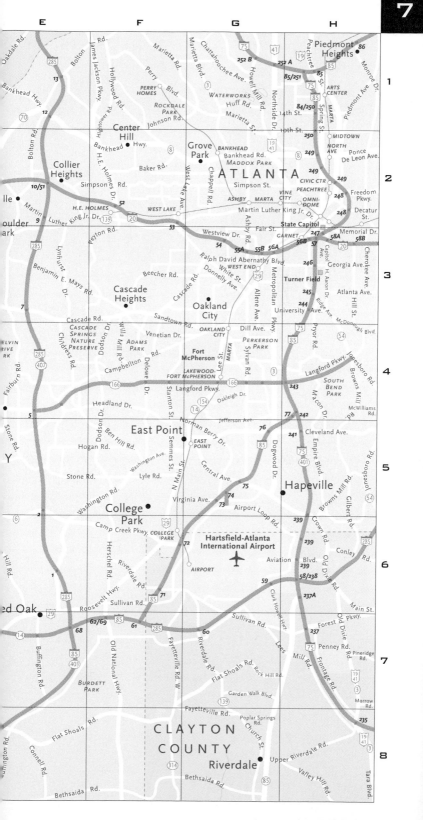

ATLANTA AND SOUTH-CENTRAL FULTON COUNTY

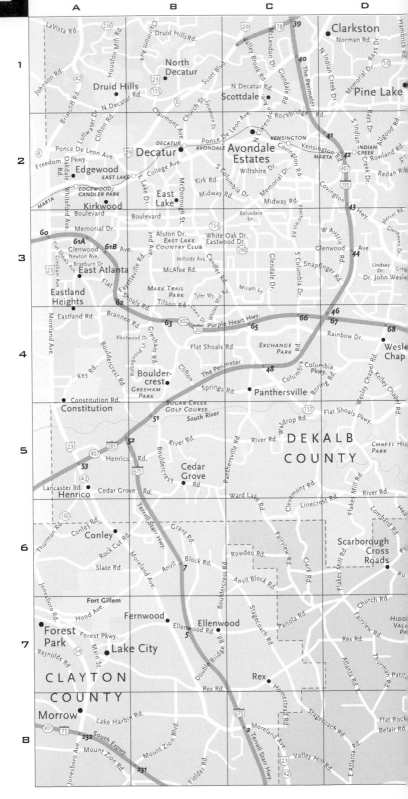

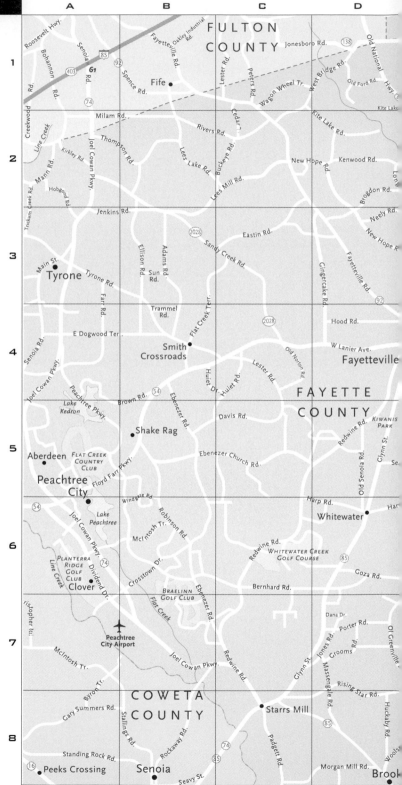

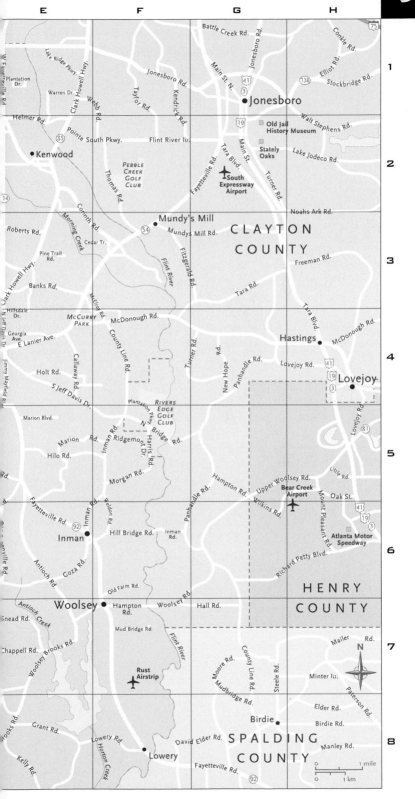

SOUTH SUBURBS: FAYETTE COUNTY, JONESBORO

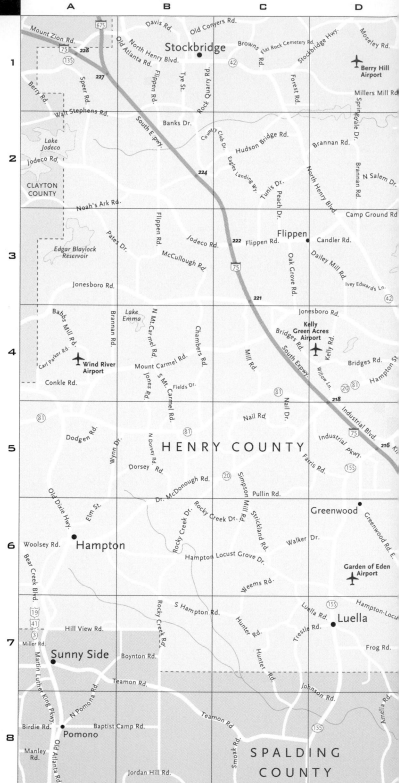

A   B   C   D

1

Mount Zion Rd.
675
75   228
135
227
Davis Rd.
Old Conyers Rd.
North Henry Blvd.
Old Atlanta Rd.
Flippen Rd.
Tye St.
Rock Quarry Rd.
Stockbridge
Browns Rd.
Flat Rock Cemetery Rd.
Stockbridge Hwy.
Moseley Rd.
✈ Berry Hill Airport
42
Forest Rd.
Berry Rd.
Speer Rd.
Millers Mill Rd.
Springdale Dr.

2

Walt Stephens Rd.
Banks Dr.
County Club Dr.
Hudson Bridge Rd.
Brannan Rd.
Lake Jodeco
South E. pwy.
224
Eagles Landing Wy.
Tunis Dr.
Peach Dr.
North Henry Blvd.
Brannan Rd.
N Salem Rd.
Jodeco Rd.
CLAYTON COUNTY
Noah's Ark Rd.
Camp Ground Rd.

3

Pates Dr.
Flippen Rd.
Jodeco Rd.
222
Flippen Rd.
Flippen
Candler Rd.
Edgar Blaylock Reservoir
McCullough Rd.
75
Oak Grove Rd.
Dailey Mill Rd.
Ivey Edwards Ln.
Jonesboro Rd.
221
42

4

Babbs Mill Rd.
Branman Rd.
Lake Emma
N Mt.Carmel Rd.
Chambers Rd.
Jonesboro Rd.
Bridges Rd.
Kelly Green Acres Airport ✈
Kelly Rd.
Carl Parker Rd.
✈ Wind River Airport
Mount Carmel Rd.
Jones Rd.
S Mt. Carmel Rd.
Fields Dr.
Mill Rd.
South Expwy.
Willow Ln.
Bridges Rd.
Hampton St.
Conkle Rd.
81
218
20
81

5

81
Dodgen Rd.
Wynn Dr.
N Dorsey Rd.
81
Nail Rd.
Nail Dr.
HENRY COUNTY
Industrial Blvd.
75
216
Dorsey Rd.
Faris Rd.
Industrial Pkwy.
153

6

Old Dixie Hwy.
Elm St.
Dr. McDonough Rd.
20
Simpson Mill Rd.
Pullin Rd.
Greenwood
Greenwood Rd. E.
Woolsey Rd.
Hampton
Rocky Creek Dr.
Rocky Creek Dr.
Strickland Rd.
Walker Dr.
Bear Creek Blvd.
Hampton Locust Grove Dr.
Weems Rd.
Garden of Eden Airport ✈

7

19
41
3
Miller Rd.
Hill View Rd.
Rocky Creek Rd.
S Hampton Rd.
Hunter Rd.
Luella Rd.
153
Hampton-Locu
Trestle Rd.
Luella
Sunny Side
Boynton Rd.
Hunter Rd.
Frog Rd.
Teamon Rd.
Johnson Rd.

8

Martin Luther King Pkwy.
N Pomona Rd.
Teamon Rd.
Amelia Rd.
Birdie Rd.
Baptist Camp Rd.
Pomono
Old Atlanta Rd.
Teamon Rd.
155
Manley Rd.
Jordan Hill Rd.
Smoak Rd.
SPALDING COUNTY

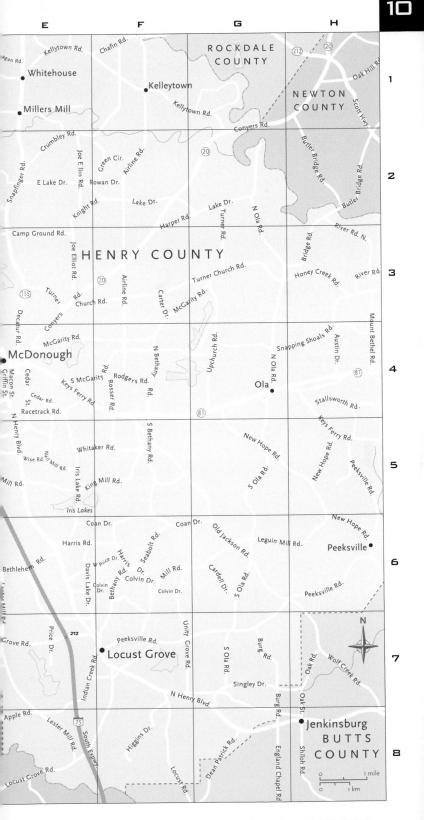

SOUTHWEST SUBURBS: HENRY COUNTY

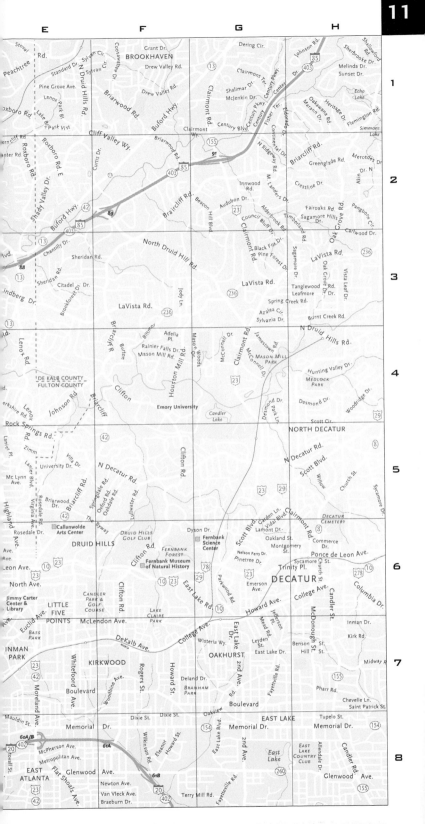

CENTRAL ATLANTA, BUCKHEAD, DECATUR OVERVIEW

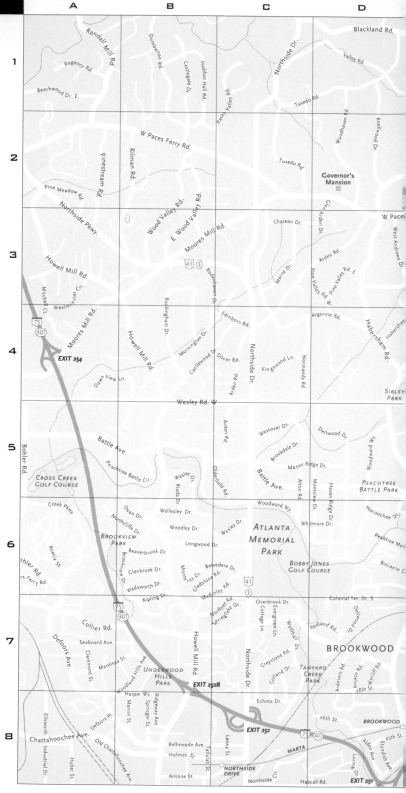

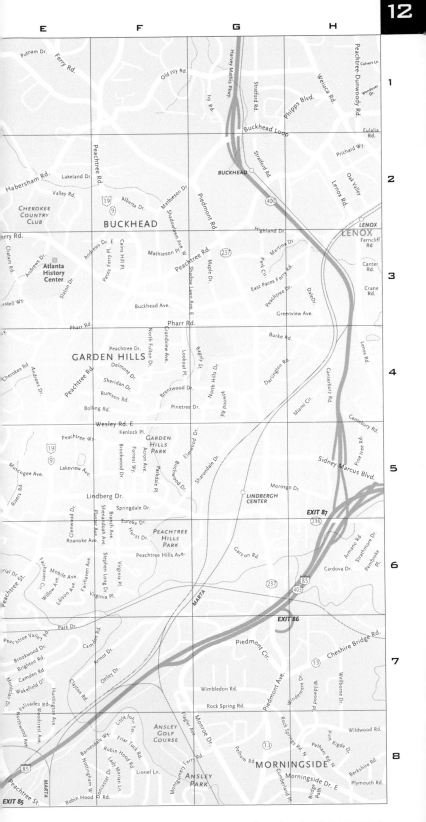

BUCKHEAD, BROOKWOOD, MORNINGSIDE

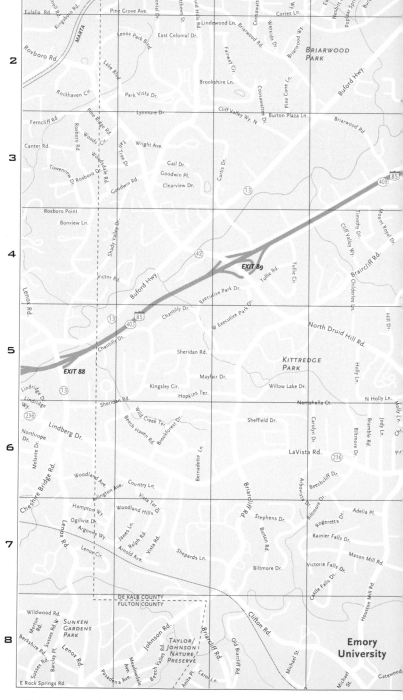

13

STREETFINDER

E   F   G   H

1

2

3

4

5

6

7

8

Cove Cir.
Skyland Dr.
Skyland Ave.
Dering Cir.
Dering Cir.
Woodacres Rd.
Capehart Cir.
Johnson Rd.
Shallowford Rd.
Clairmeade Ave.
Variations Dr.
Wentworth Dr.
Sherbrooke Dr.
Nancy Ln.
13
Drew Valley
Clairmont Valley Rd.
Jordan Ter.
85
Melinda Dr.
403
Peachwood Cir.
Clairmont Ter.
Sunset Dr.
Circlewood Rd.
Shalimar Dr.
Echo Hills Ct.
Echo Lake
Clairmont Rd.
Mcjenkin Dr.
Medflet Ter.
Meadowvale Dr.
Oakawana Rd.
Heritage Dr.
Echo Dr.
Century Pl.
Century Pkwy.
Maranin Dr.
Allaire Ln.
Briarwillow Dr.
Woodwardia Rd.
Century Blvd.
Abby Ln.
Flemington Rd.
mont Wy.
155
Continental Dr.
Eldorado Dr.
Street Deville
Valiant Dr.
Simmons Lake
Imperial Dr.
Chrysler Dr.
Lively Ter.
Cadillac Dr.
Grand Prix Dr.
EXIT 91
North Ridgeway Rd.
Fairwood Ln.
Finster Ter.
Fairwood Ter.
Mercedes Dr.
Forest Green Dr.
Briarmill Rd.
Briarcliff Rd.
Greenglade Rd.
Dogwood Ln.
Akin Dr. N
Innwood Rd.
Morris Landers Dr.
Impala Dr.
Lebaron Dr.
Chrysler Ter.
Crestline Dr.
Akin Dr. S
Woodbine Ter.
Bonnavit Ct.
Weigelia Rd.
Beacon Hill Blvd
Woodspring
Audubon Dr.
Mount Brian Rd.
Kodiak Dr.
Alderbrook Rd.
Timberland Rd.
Fairoaks Rd.
Sagamore Hills Dr.
Pangborn Cir.
Stonecliff Dr.
Montcliff Ct.
Deerfield Cir.
Bristol Dr.
28
Council Bluff Dr.
Arrowhead Ter.
Heatherwood Dr.
Tamarack Ter.
Oak Grove Rd.
Carlwood Dr.
Berkley Ln.
Clairmont Rd.
Black Fox Dr.
Pine Forest Dr.
Sagamore Dr.
LaVista Rd.
236
Amanda Cir. N
Oak Grove Dr.
Nelms Dr.
Richard Stokes Dr.
Farm Dr.
as Ln.
Merry Ln.
LaVista Rd.
236
Amanda Cir.
Wilandrew Dr.
Trailmark Dr.
Tanglewood Rd.
Leafmore Dr.
Spring Creek Rd.
Heather Dr.
Tanglewood Dr.
River Oak Dr.
Burnt Leaf Ln.
ree Cir.
TOCO HILLS
Azalea Cir.
Spring Wood Dr.
Creek Park Rd.
Burnt Creek Rd.
Willivee Dr.
Wilson Woods Dr.
Sylvania Dr.
Hill Park Ct.
North Druid Hills Rd.
W.D. THOMSON PARK
McConnell Dr.
Vissavia Cir.
Williamsburg Dr.
Jamestown Rd.
NORTH DRUID HILLS
MARTA
Asbury Ct.
Arbordale Dr.
Ridgefield Ter.
North Valley Rd.
Homewood Ct.
Dr.
Mason Mill Rd.
Clairmont Rd.
McConnell Dr.
MASON MILL PARK
Willivee Dr.
North Hills Dr.
Hastington Dr.
Pine Bluff Dr.
23
Mason Mill Rd.
MARTA
Hunting Valley Dr.
Caylemont Cir.
School Dr.
Candler Lake
NORTH DECATUR
Desmond Dr.
Park Ln.
Superior Ave.
Willivee Dr.
MEDLOCK PARK
Scott Cir.
Vistamont Dr.
Desmond Dr.
Ava Pl.
Brengare Dr.
Scott Cir.
Sunnybrook Dr.
Medlock Rd.
Wood Trail Ln.
Woodridge Dr.
Larry Ln.
McCurdy Wy.

BROOKHAVEN, TOCO HILLS

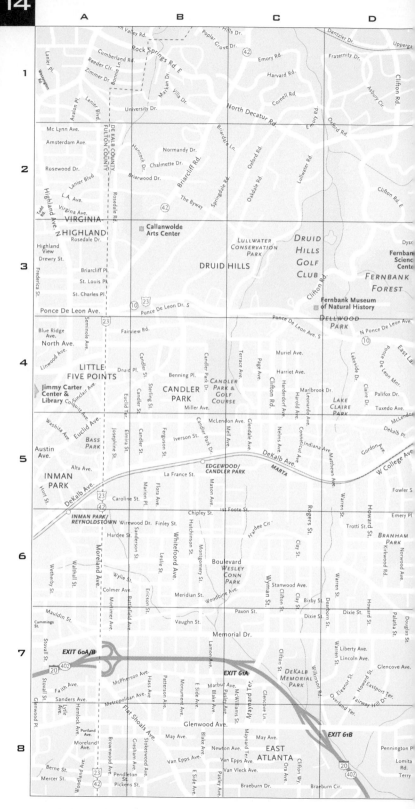

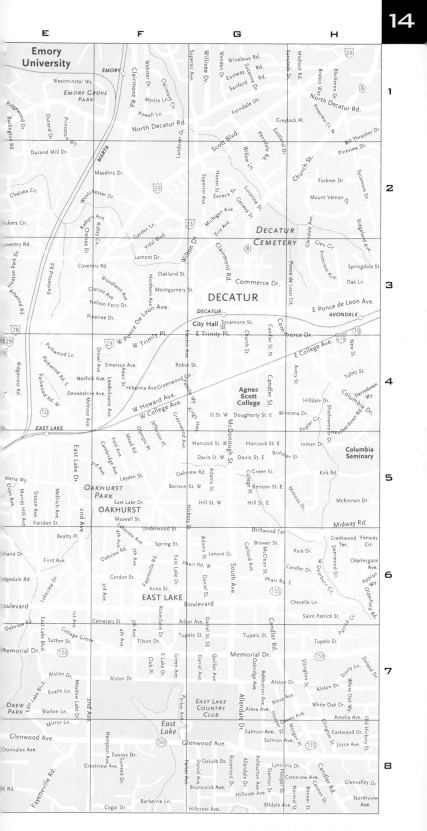

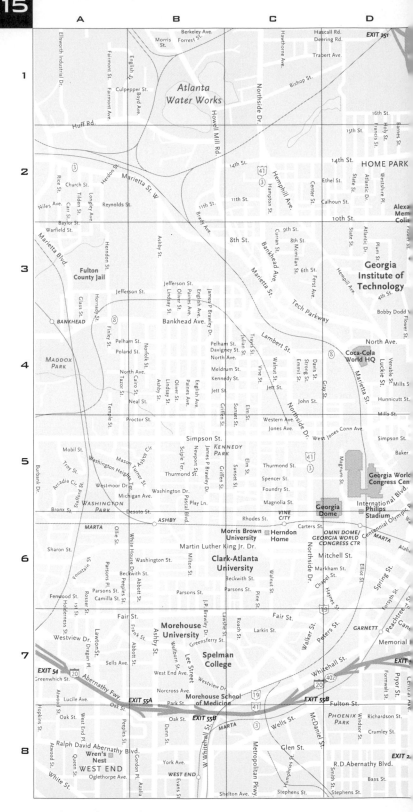

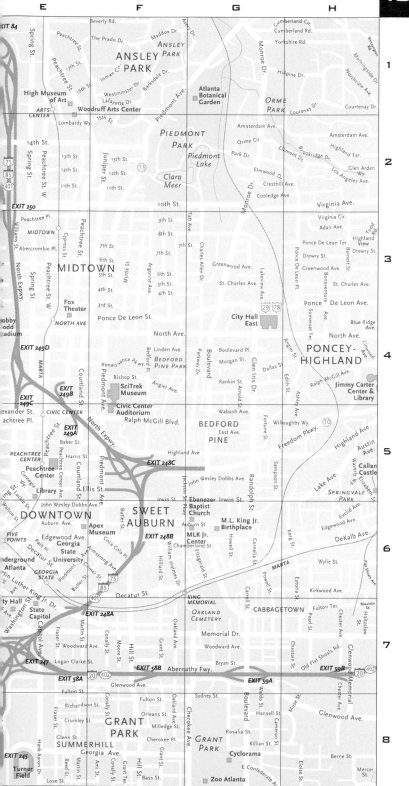

DOWNTOWN, MIDTOWN, ANSLEY PARK

The Sourcebook for Your Hometown

MANY MAPS • WHERE & HOW

FIND IT ALL • NIGHT & DAY

ANTIQUES TO ZIPPERS

BARGAINS & BAUBLES

ELEGANT EDIBLES • ETHNIC EATS

STEAK HOUSES • BISTROS

DELIS • TRATTORIAS

CLASSICAL • JAZZ • COMEDY

THEATER • DANCE • CLUBS

COCKTAIL LOUNGES

COUNTRY & WESTERN • ROCK

COOL TOURS & TRIPS

HOUSECLEANING • CATERING

GET A LAWYER • GET A DENTIST

GET A NEW PET • GET A VET

MUSEUMS • GALLERIES

PARKS • GARDENS • POOLS

BASEBALL TO ROCK CLIMBING

FESTIVALS • EVENTS

DAY SPAS • DAY TRIPS

HOTELS • HOT LINES

PASSPORT PIX • TRAVEL INFO

HELICOPTER TOURS

DINERS • DELIS • PIZZERIAS

BRASSERIES • TAQUERÍAS

BOOTS • BOOKS • BUTTONS

BICYCLES • SKATES

SUITS • SHOES • HATS

RENT A TUX • RENT A COSTUME

BAKERIES • SPICE SHOPS

SOUP TO NUTS

Fodor's

CITYGUIDE
ATLANTA

FODOR'S TRAVEL PUBLICATIONS

NEW YORK • TORONTO • LONDON • SYDNEY • AUCKLAND

WWW.FODORS.COM

FODOR'S CITYGUIDE ATLANTA

EDITOR
Chris Swiac

EDITORIAL CONTRIBUTORS
Ren Davis, Linda B. Downs, Jane Garvey, Hollis Gillespie, Michael Hagearty, Shannon Kelly, Jonathan Lerner, John Rambow, Jill Sabulis, Rennie Sloan

EDITORIAL PRODUCTION
Stacey Kulig

MAPS
David Lindroth Inc., *cartographer*; Rebecca Baer and Bob Blake, *map editors*

DESIGN
Fabrizio La Rocca, *creative director*; Guido Caroti, *art director*; Allison Saltzman, *text design*; Tigist Getachew, *cover design*; Jolie Novak, *senior picture editor*; Melanie Marin, *photo editor*

PRODUCTION/MANUFACTURING
Robert Shields

COVER PHOTOGRAPH
Chuck Pefley

COPYRIGHT

Second Edition

ISBN 0–679–00920–5

ISSN 1528–9249

SPECIAL SALES

Fodor's Travel Publications are available at special discounts for bulk purchases for sales promotions or premiums. Special editions, including personalized covers, excerpts of existing guides, and corporate imprints, can be created in large quantities for special needs. For more information, contact your local bookseller or write to Special Markets, Fodor's Travel Publications, 280 Park Avenue, New York, NY 10017. Inquiries from Canada should be directed to your local Canadian bookseller or sent to Random House of Canada, Ltd., Marketing Department, 2775 Matheson Boulevard East, Mississauga, Ontario L4W 4P7. Inquiries from the United Kingdom should be sent to Fodor's Travel Publications, 20 Vauxhall Bridge Road, London SW1V 2SA, England.

PRINTED IN THE UNITED STATES OF AMERICA

10 9 8 7 6 5 4 3 2 1

CONTENTS

METROPOLITAN LIFE

O n a bad day in a big city, the little things that go with living shoulder-to-shoulder with a few million people wear us all down. But the special pleasures of urban life have a way of keeping us out of the suburbs—and thankful, even, for every second of stress. The field of daffodils in the park on a fine spring day. The perfect little black dress that you find for half price. The markets—so fabulously well stocked that you can cook any recipe without resorting to mail-order catalogs. The way you can sometimes turn a corner and discover a whole new world, so foreign you can hardly believe you're less than a mile from home. The never-ending wealth of possibilities and opportunities.

If you know where to find it all, the city cannot defeat you. With knowledge comes power. That's why Fodor's has prepared this book. It puts phone numbers at your fingertips. It takes you to new places and reminds you of those you've forgotten. It's the ultimate urban companion—and, we hope, your **new best friend in the city.**

It's the **citywise shopaholic,** who always knows where to find something, no matter how obscure. We've made a concerted effort to bring hundreds of great shops to your attention, so that you'll never be at a loss, whether you need a special birthday present for a great friend or some obscure craft items to make Halloween costumes for your kids.

It's the **restaurant know-it-all,** who's full of ideas for every occasion—you know, the one who would never send you to Café de la Snub, because he knows it's always overbooked, the food is boring, and the staff is rude. In this book we steer you around the corner, to a perfect little place with five tables, a fireplace, and a chef on her way up.

It's a **hip barfly buddy,** who can give you advice when you need a charming nook, not too noisy, to take a friend after work. Among the dozens of bars and nightspots in this book, you're bound to find something that fits your mood.

It's the **sagest arts maven you know,** the one who always has the scoop on what's on that's worthwhile on any given night. In these pages, you can find dozens of concert venues and arts organizations.

It's also the **city whiz,** who knows how to get you where you're going, wherever you are.

It's the **best map guide** on the shelves, and it puts **all the city in your brief-case** or on your bookshelf.

Stick with us. We lay out all the options for your leisure time—and gently nudge you away from the duds—so that you can truly enjoy metropolitan living.

YOUR GUIDES

No one person can know it all. To help get you on track around the city, we've handpicked a stellar group of local experts to share their wisdom.

Linda B. Downs, a former senior editor and wine editor of *House Beautiful* magazine, updated our parks, gardens, and sports chapter. An Atlanta resident since 1992, she has written for numerous other national publications, on everything from design to tai chi to business strategies for women, and has edited three editions of the *Taste of the NFL Restaurant Guide,* which is published in connection with the Super Bowl. She also has edited for *Fodor's Road Guide USA* series.

Our "Places to Explore" and "Hotels" expert, **Hollis Gillespie** was born in Southern California but moved to Atlanta in 1989, almost immediately swapping her Valley Girl accent for a Southern drawl. A prolific travel writer and foreign-language interpreter, she pens a weekly humor column called "Mood Swings" for *Creative Loafing,* Atlanta's alternative newsweekly.

One of fewer and fewer native Atlantans, city-sources updater **Michael Hagearty** has been writing and editing for local publications since 1997 and has contributed to several Fodor's guidebooks. He splits his time evenly between sitting in traffic and rooting for the Braves.

Though story assignments for *InStyle, Delta Sky, Metropolis,* and other magazines frequently take him across the globe, **Jonathan Lerner** has called in-town Atlanta home since 1990. Lerner often covers topics ranging from architecture and urban planning to the fine arts, and he also writes the restaurant column for *Southern Voice,* Atlanta's gay and lesbian weekly newspaper. For us, he updated the restaurants, nightlife, arts, and entertainment sections.

Jill Sabulis is the Personal Shopper columnist for the *Atlanta Journal–Constitution* and has been a newspaper and magazine editor and reporter for more than 20 years. A Buckhead resident, she contributed to the shopping chapter.

For **Rennie Sloan,** researching the shopping scene (from food and drink through videos) for this book provided the perfect opportunity to become reacquainted with her hometown. A freelance writer for local and national newspapers and magazines, she is happy to be back in Atlanta after stints in Phoenix, Washington, D.C., and the metro New York area.

It goes without saying that our contributors have chosen all establishments strictly on their own merits—no establishment has paid to be included in this book.

HOW TO USE THIS BOOK

The first thing you need to know is that everything in this book is **arranged by category and alphabetically** within each category.

Now, before you go any farther, check out the **city maps** at the front of the book. Each map has a number, in a black box at the top of the page, and grid coordinates along the top and side margins. Listings throughout the CITYGUIDE are keyed to one of these maps. Look for the map number in a small black box preceding each establishment name. The grid code follows in italics. For establishments with more than one location, additional map numbers and grid codes appear at the end of the listing. To locate a museum that's identified in the text as **7** *e-6*, turn to Map 7 and locate the address within the e-6 grid square. To locate restaurants nearby, simply skim the text in the restaurant chapter for listings identified as being on Map 7.

Throughout the guide, we name the neighborhood or town in which each sight, restaurant, shop, or other destination is located. We also give you complete opening hours and admission fees for sights, and reservations, credit-card, closing hours, and price information for restaurants.

At the end of the book, in addition to an **alphabetical index,** you'll find **directories of restaurants by neighborhood.**

Chapter 7, City Sources, lists essential information and resources for residents—everything from vet and lawyer-referral services to caterers worth calling.

We've worked hard to make sure that all of the information we give you is accurate at press time. Still, time brings changes, so always confirm information when it matters—especially if you're making a detour.

Feel free to drop us a line. Were the restaurants we recommended as described? Did you find a wonderful shop you'd like to share? If you have complaints, we'll look into them and revise our entries in the next edition when the facts warrant. So send us your feedback. Either e-mail us at editors@fodors.com (specifying *Fodor's CITYGUIDE Atlanta* on the subject line), or write to the *Fodor's CITYGUIDE Atlanta* editor at Fodor's, 280 Park Avenue, New York, NY 10017. We look forward to hearing from you.

Karen Cure

Karen Cure
Editorial Director

chapter 1

RESTAURANTS

Dining in and around Atlanta can take you from the simple glories of home-style country fare to sophisticated dishes by internationally renowned chefs. In recent years, as the residential trend has shifted back toward the city center, a number of unpretentious, labor-of-love, chef-owned neighborhood eateries have arrived on the scene. And who can keep track of the latest urbane spots in Midtown? Ethnic communities add their own special grace, allowing you to sample everything from Indian vegetarian dishes to South African sosaties.

NO-SMOKING

Restaurants are free to establish their own smoking policies, as to date no metropolitan Atlanta jurisdiction has enacted a restaurant-focused no-smoking ordinance. Most establishments have well-separated no-smoking sections; some restaurants are entirely no-smoking, putting the offending puffers out on patios to smoke.

RESERVATIONS

Atlantans have gotten a reputation for making reservations all over town and then not keeping them. To combat such bad manners, many restaurants ask for your contact telephone number so they may confirm your reservation a day ahead. Still others fend off the misbehavior by not taking reservations at all, leaving patrons to wait in line for a table; in some busy places, especially those at shopping malls, the host may hand you a beeper and page you when your table is ready. Another scheduling device that's surfaced is "call-ahead" seating—you call ahead to inquire about table availability and indicate that you'll be arriving with a party in tow at a given hour. It's almost like a reservation, except it's not guaranteed.

TIPPING

How much you leave is up to you, but 15%–20% is customary and that's how much is added to the bill automatically for large parties (six or more). In very fine restaurants, if the sommelier or maître d' has taken special care to enhance your evening, an appropriate tip—15% of the value of the selected bottle for the sommelier, for instance—would be well received.

PRICE CATEGORIES

CATEGORY	COST*
$$$$	over $30
$$$	$20–$30
$$	$10–$19
$	under $10

*per person for a main course at dinner, excluding beverage, tax, and tip

restaurants by cuisine

AFRICAN

5 *b-6*
10 DEGREES SOUTH
South African cooking, which blends traditional African ingredients with elements of European and Asian cuisines, is well represented at this place, which is a piece of home for the city's South African community. Chicken livers get the peri-peri (hot-pepper) treatment; curry flavors the beef *sosaties* (kabobs). Ostrich fillet, a South African classic, is best rare. The wine list is exclusively South African. *4183 Roswell Rd., Sandy Springs, 404/705–8870. AE, D, DC, MC, V. No lunch Mon. $$–$$$*

AMERICAN

15 *g-1*
AGNES & MURIEL'S
The kitchen of this retro-look restaurant turns out 1950s home-style classics—recipes your mother might have found in a magazine, like "Bridge Club Artichoke Dip." Perhaps it's fitting, then, that the owners named the place after their moms. The turkey meat loaf, salmon patties, and buttermilk fried chicken are off the list of traditional favorites, and the magnificent chocolate chiffon pie is a perfect finale. Beer and very well chosen wines are available. *1514 Monroe Dr. NE, just past Piedmont*

Ave., near Ansley Park, 404/885–1000. Reservations not accepted. AE, D, DC, MC, V. Wine and beer only. $–$$

14 a-3
AMERICAN ROADHOUSE

For plenty of hearty, no-frills, down-home food, head to the family-friendly Roadhouse. It fills up quickly—especially for brunch on weekends—so get there early or plan to eat late. Breakfasts pile on the eggs, grits, and pancakes, plus all the trimmings. Great meat loaf with mashed potatoes and roast chicken basted with Georgia's own Red Brick Ale are lunch and dinner favorites. 842 N. Highland Ave., Virginia-Highland, 404/872–2822. AE, D, DC, MC, V. $–$$

3 h-8
AQUA TERRA BISTRO

This charming, casual bistro is devoted to inventive eclectic and American fare. The menu, which changes several times a year, may include such delectables as West Indian coconut-battered fish-and-chips, halibut with crunchy wonton salad and orange-ginger sauce, or roasted duck with couscous salad and an herb-poached pear. 55 E. Main St., Buford, 770/271–3000. Reservations not accepted. AE, D, DC, MC, V. No lunch weekends, no dinner Mon. $$

14 a-3
ATKINS PARK

A neighborhood institution since 1922, this bar-and-grill punches up American classics with Cajun and Southwestern accents. Poblano queso blends cheddar cheese and roasted chilies; the lagniappe gumbo (the classic creole soup–stew, with chicken and andouille sausage), the muffaletta (a traditional New Orleans sandwich made with deli meats, cheese, and topped with a chopped green-olive salad), and the po'boys are worthwhile, too. For dessert, check out the sweet potato–pecan pie or bananas Foster bread pudding. The wine list is good, and there are numerous on-tap brews, including Honey Brown and Caffreys. 794 N. Highland Ave., Virginia-Highland, 404/876–7249. AE, D, DC, MC, V. $$–$$$

15 e-5
ATLANTA GRILL

Breakfast, lunch, or dinner, this restaurant with a New Orleans–style interior puts an upscale spin on such down-home Southern staples as macaroni and cheese, stone-ground grits, rabbit stew, and sweet potato–corn chowder. Honey pecan pie comes with a vial of spiced bourbon syrup to pour over it. Ritz-Carlton, 181 Peachtree St., at Ellis St., Downtown, 404/659–0400, ext. 6450. AE, D, DC, MC, V. $$–$$$$

12 a-2
BLUE RIDGE GRILL

Rowing sculls hang high overhead, fishing gear forms part of the decor, and rich woods take on a warm glow in the soft lighting at this large place, which is rustic yet refined. The menu, which is seasonal, may include grilled trout, horseradish-crusted grouper, and hickory wood–grilled meats and fish. Soups change daily and are very good. 1261 W. Paces Ferry Rd., at U.S. 41 (Northside Dr.), Buckhead, 404/233–5030. AE, D, DC, MC, V. No lunch Sat. $$–$$$$

10 b-2
BUCKHEAD BREWERY & GRILL

Gleaming copper brew tanks shine through the big windows of this two-level log structure; hunt trophies set a rugged tone inside the brewpub. Game offerings, like bison, venison, elk, and quail, augment the usual meat choices. Ready to trek the bush? Have the Wild Raspberry Salad, with grilled chicken and trail mix, fresh fruit, and raspberry vinaigrette. Dessert options include peanut-butter and Snickers pies. The wheat beer and Hop Island IPA are the richest of the half dozen or so brews available. 1757 Rock Quarry Rd., Stockbridge, 770/389–8112. Reservations not accepted. AE, D, DC, MC, V. $–$$

12 g-3
BUCKHEAD DINER

Crafted by San Francisco diner designer Patrick Kuleto, this gleaming steel-sheathed structure recalls the original diners of the 1940s and 1950s. The creative menu changes frequently but sometimes includes such local specialties as rock shrimp, served as an appetizer, along with popular standbys like small pizzas, homemade potato chips, veal meat loaf, and banana cream pie. Wines are definitely not diner stuff, and many are available by the glass. 3073 Piedmont Rd., Buckhead, 404/262–3336. Reservations not accepted. AE, D, DC, MC, V. $$

15 *h-6*

CABBAGETOWN GRILL

The patio beckons in good weather, and in bad, the big stone-lined bar is a comforting spot. Lunch focuses on good sandwiches; dinner is full-blown American fare, like crab cakes and pork chops, with such Southern touches as fried green tomatoes. *727 Wylie St., Cabbagetown, 404/525–8818. Reservations not accepted. MC, V. $–$$*

3 *h-8*

CALIFORNIA CAFÉ BAR & GRILL

The wide-ranging menu of this California-based operation includes pastas, good salads, rotisserie-cooked meats, pizzas baked in a brick-lined oven, and homemade desserts. California products, such as the excellent Laura Chenel goat cheeses and California olive oil, are highlighted. For wines, it's California again, of course; the by-the-glass and half-bottle choices are good. *Mall of Georgia, 3333 Buford Dr., Buford, 770/932–6777. AE, D, DC, MC, V. $$–$$$*

14 *g-3*

CRESCENT MOON

Given the quantity and quality of the fare, a meal here is one of the best deals around. Decatur's diverse denizens crowd in for big stuffed baked potatoes, great soups, quite good barbecue, excellent chili (the specialty), and breakfast whenever you want. Urban architects could take a lesson from this clever spot, which reclaimed the ground level of a parking deck to create the street-friendly '50s-style diner. *174 W. Ponce de Leon Ave., Decatur, 404/377–5623. Reservations not accepted. AE, D, DC, MC, V. No dinner. $–$$*

15 *e-5*

DAILEY'S

Crab cakes, steaks, and roast chicken are typical of the solid American fare at this longtime downtown favorite, which is known for its bountiful dessert table. Brass fixtures, antique carousel horses, and white tablecloths bring elegance to the former warehouse. Evening wine tastings are often held downstairs in the casual bar and grill, where there's apt to be live music. *17 International Blvd., Downtown, 404/681–3303. AE, D, DC, MC, V. $$–$$$*

5 *e-3*

DICK & HARRY'S

Fresh combinations make for winning dishes at this popular, modernly elegant place in the northern suburbs. The menu is seasonal and fairly extensive—chicken, duck, pork, lamb, beef, and fish and shellfish are all likely to be represented—as is the list of daily specials. The crab cakes, lumpy and pure, are a favorite. Grilled emu with mashed potatoes and a red-wine sauce is another standout. The wine list has been carefully selected and features about a dozen half bottles. *1570 Holcomb Bridge Rd., Roswell, 770/641–8757. Reservations essential. AE, D, DC, MC, V. Closed Sun. No lunch Sat. $$–$$$$*

5 *d-7*

THE DOWNWIND

You may not think of an airport restaurant as the place to head for a good meal, but the Downwind is an exception. Kids love to view the planes taking off and landing from the outside deck, where grown-ups can relax with a beer. Salads, sandwiches, and specials such as grilled salmon (selections vary daily) are the mainstays of an uncomplicated menu. Greek specials are good, too. *2000 Airport Rd., DeKalb-Peachtree Airport, off Clairmont Rd., west of I–85 (exit 99), Chamblee, 770/452–0973. Reservations not accepted. MC, V. Closed Sun. $–$$*

15 *f-3*

EINSTEIN'S

The patio here is the main draw, especially for Sunday brunch, which could be a basic omelet or the excellent pancakes. Fish, pastas, salads, and the famous Einstein club sandwich (Swiss and cheddar cheeses, turkey, bacon, and tomato on sourdough bread that's egg-dipped and grilled) are available for lunch and dinner. Dishes take their culinary cues from around the world: chipotle-spiked tartar sauce accompanies the calamari, shrimp is coconut-crusted, and grilled chicken comes over soba noodles. *1077 Juniper St., Midtown, 404/876–7925. AE, D, DC, MC, V. $$*

14 *g-3*

FOOD BUSINESS

The menu at this friendly high-energy neighborhood place changes frequently but may include Georgia lake trout with sesame–pumpkin butter or grilled sea scallops atop potato pancake with *pico de gallo* (chunky guacamole) and cilantro cream sauce. Sandwiches, salads (the best are roasted beet, grilled chicken, and curried tuna), and fresh soups are also on offer. In addition, the kids' menu is good and the wine list is extensive, with about 65 choices, including several good by-the-glass options. *115 Sycamore St., Decatur, 404/371–9121. Reservations not accepted. AE, MC, V. Closed Sun. No lunch Sat. $$*

5 *b-6*
FOOD 101
A wall of wood-framed glass brings the outdoors in at this handsomely modern eatery, and during the warm weather, the staff slides it open. The fare, which includes crab and rock-shrimp cakes, onion rings, pork chops over mashed potatoes, and very good sea bass, draws a fairly polished crowd complete with baby-toting families. Desserts, such as banana splits and delicious waffles with toffee-crunch ice cream and caramel and chocolate sauces, are big enough for two and also tend to be of the comfort variety. The wine list is well selected, if short, and offers some unusual by-the-glass choices. *Belle Isle Square shopping center, 4969 Roswell Rd., Sandy Springs, 404/497–9700. AE, D, DC, MC, V. No lunch weekends. $$–$$$*

15 *b-3*
FOOD STUDIO
The industrial-style, high-ceilinged space in what once was a plow factory has drawn crowds to an area that no one would have thought suitable for a restaurant. But the King Plow Arts Center, with its theater and offices, has proved to be the perfect venue for this innovative restaurant's clever, witty takes on American regional cuisine. For starters, for example, salmon cured with tequila and juniper berries is served with jalapeño corn cakes, pickled tomatillo, and cilantro crème fraîche. The well-structured wine list offers selections that go well with the food. *King Plow Arts Center, 887 W. Marietta St., Downtown, 404/815–6677. AE, DC, MC, V. No lunch. $$–$$$*

1 *c-7*
FRANK'S FAMOUS FAMILY RESTAURANT
Yes, Frank's is attached to a filling station, but the food is down-home delicious and the portions outsize. Dishes

hint at a Mediterranean influence; meat loaf, for example, might come accessorized with red peppers. The prime rib is first-rate, as is the country-fried steak. The tiramisu is a top contender for best dessert here. Beer and wine selections are decent. *1188 Collinsworth Rd., Palmetto (I–85, west off exit 56/Collinsworth Rd.), south Fulton County, 770/463–5678. AE, D, DC, MC, V. Wine and beer only. Closed Sun. $$*

5 *c-2*
GREENWOODS ON GREEN STREET
A humble former residence serves as the backdrop for what's become a very popular home-style dining experience. The menu goes regional in such dishes as the outstanding crab cakes, fried chicken with mashed potatoes, duck roasted with plenty of black pepper, and luxuriously deep traditional pies. Come early or prepare to wait a long time. *1087 Green St., Roswell, 770/992–5383. Reservations not accepted. No credit cards. Wine and beer only. Closed Mon.–Tues. No lunch. $–$$*

14 *b-8*
HEAPING BOWL & BREW
This ultra-casual spot perfectly expresses the feel of its funky neighborhood. Bowls are indeed heaping—with mashed potatoes, pasta, pierogies, or some other example of the home-style cooking. Saturday and Sunday brunches are very popular. *469 Flat Shoals Ave., East Atlanta Village, 404/523–8030. Reservations not accepted. AE, MC, V. $$*

5 *f-4*
HI-LIFE KITCHEN & COCKTAILS
This lively spot proves that to turn around a seemingly dead restaurant space, all you have to do is provide good food and ambience. Hi-Life has some intriguing features on its menu, notably a wide range of lobster preparations; "Hardwood Grill" selections that focus on grilled meats, fish, and even veggies; and a four-course tasting menu that changes daily. A publike bar area gives local office workers a good spot to grab a drink after work. This is a popular venue for wine events, so be sure to ask about special dinners and tastings. *3380 Holcomb Bridge Rd., Norcross, 770/409–0101. AE, DC, MC, V. No lunch weekends. $$–$$$$*

5 *a-4*

HOUCK'S STEAK & SEAFOOD

You might find the locals and celebs depicted in the entrance murals (former U.S. House Speaker Newt Gingrich among them) supping on a tree-rimmed deck that overlooks a small pond or inside the rambling restaurant and bar. The menu emphasizes home-style cooking. Baked potatoes never see a microwave, black beans taste of slow cooking with a ham bone, and ribs are oven roasted and then grilled. The steaks and deep-fried shrimp, which are lightly battered to order, are very popular. *Paper Mill Village shopping center, 305 Village Pkwy., Marietta, 770/859–0041. Reservations not accepted. AE, D, DC, MC, V. No lunch. $$–$$$*

15 *h-3*

JAVA JIVE

Breakfast is *the* specialty at this retro spot with dinette tables and other kitsch furnishings from the 1930s to 1950s. "Peanut Butter and Jelly Goes to France" is a grilled version of that classic kids' favorite; Thanksgiving time means pumpkin pancakes. Gingerbread waffles with homemade lemon curd are weekend options, when brunch is served. Come early, or prepare to wait. The place closes at 2 PM weekdays and 2:30 PM on weekends. *790 Ponce de Leon Ave., Virginia-Highland, 404/876–6161. MC, V. Closed Mon. No lunch or dinner. $.*

12 *f-1*

LANDMARK DINER

This gleaming steel-and-neon 24-hour spot dominates the landscape at its heart-of-Buckhead location. Owner Tom Lambros hails from the Greek Island of Spespes. Greek specialties include moussaka and pastitsio; they are made from scratch, along with the meat loaf, broiled fresh fish, shrimp fettuccine, crab-stuffed flounder, and humongous desserts. Even the bread is baked on-site. Mammoth breakfasts are served around the clock. *3652 Roswell Rd., Buckhead, 404/816–9090. AE, D, DC, MC, V. $–$$*

15 *e-4*

PLEASANT PEASANT

This restaurant was done on a shoestring—brick walls and a pressed-tin ceiling are what pass for decor, and since its original owners couldn't afford printed menus, specials are scribbled on chalkboards. But that was 25 years ago, and the place has since spawned a small restaurant empire. Crab cakes, pasta dishes, excellent duck and pork, and extravagant desserts have become traditions here. *555 Peachtree St., Midtown, 404/874–3223. AE, D, DC, MC, V. No lunch weekends. $$–$$$*

5 *a-6*

RAY'S ON THE RIVER

It's little wonder that this spot snuggled along the banks of the Chattahoochee River, with a deck for fine patio dining and plenty of window-side seating, is one of the city's most popular spots. The menu changes frequently, but you can depend on the seared tuna, crab-spinach dip, grilled salmon, and crab cakes (notable for their nicely balanced flavors and textures). The key lime pie is worth leaving room for. The Sunday brunch also gets raves. Wines range from bottom-rung American choices to first-growth Bordeaux. *6700 Powers Ferry Rd., Marietta, 770/955–1187. AE, D, DC, MC, V. No lunch weekends. $$–$$$*

15 *g-7*

RIA'S BLUEBIRD

The handcrafted touches at this small breakfast-and-lunch spot include art-paper lamp shades and, on the wall, a gorgeous mosaic of a bluebird. Portions are bountiful, and the terrific, strong coffee is just the first sign that things are done right here. Innovations include tomato broth–braised brisket, shredded and topped with eggs, and sweet-potato hash browns; soysage, subbing for pork, and a fried-tempeh egg alternate are among the vegetarian choices. Lunch is a short list of sandwiches, equally artful in conception. Spicing tends not to be tame. *421 Memorial Dr., Grant Park, 404/521–3737. MC, V. No dinner. $*

14 *a-3*

THE RIGHTEOUS ROOM

Pub grub of a healthy sort is the draw here: quesadillas, excellent sandwiches, onion straws, veggie burgers and soup, and chili. Beef burgers aren't left off the menu, however. *1051 Ponce de Leon Ave., next to the Plaza Theater, Poncey-Highland, 404/874–0939. MC, V. $*

14 *g-3*

SAGE ON SYCAMORE

Remy Kerba, former owner of Le Giverny, explores the gamut of American fare, including its Italian, French, and southwestern influences, in this bustling restaurant with exposed-brick walls. Thus, there's French onion soup and mussels Provençale as well as chicken quesadillas and black bean–yucca cakes with spicy guacamole. Kerba's apricot cheesecake is the dessert winner here. The wine list is lengthy, with many by-the-glass choices. *121 Sycamore St., Decatur, 404/373–5574. AE, D, DC, MC, V. $–$$$*

5 *g-2*

SIA'S

Sia Moshk became familiar to Atlantans during his stint as manager of 103 West. Here at his own strikingly handsome restaurant, Moshk has gone all-out American but fuses influences from around the world, as demonstrated in the lemongrass-cured salmon tacos with sake-tarragon cream and enoki mushrooms. Simple dishes work well, too, such as the fried oysters with creole tartar sauce and arugula salad. Lamb chops come with a touch of cranberry and an apple-bacon-spinach strudel. Banana-ginger pound cake is a terrific finish. The wine list is very well done. *Shops of St. Ives shopping center, 10305 Medlock Bridge Rd., Duluth, 770/497–9727. AE, D, DC, MC, V. Closed Sun. No lunch Sat. $$–$$$*

8 *e-1*

THE SYCAMORE GRILL

This charming antebellum house with its wide verandas and burnished wood floors saw hospital duty during the Civil War. Today, it's an elegant place to dine well on such signature dishes as blue crab cakes, rack of lamb, roast duck, angel-food cake, and deep-dish key lime pie. There's a very good wine list as well. *5329 Mimosa Dr., Stone Mountain, 770/465–6789. AE, D, DC, MC, V. Closed Sun.–Mon. $$–$$$*

15 *g-6*

THUMBS UP DINER

This purveyor of big, yummy breakfasts and lunches—which had an earlier incarnation in Decatur—was a welcome addition to the historic Old Fourth Ward, where there aren't many places to eat. The classic breakfast fare packs 'em in on weekend mornings, so expect to wait outside for a table. The waffles and pancakes are buckwheat, the biscuits are multigrain, and the grits stone-

ground. The health-oriented kitchen also serves sandwiches, stuffed potatoes, salads, and a few Mexico-inspired items; burgers are available, too. *573 Edgewood Ave., Downtown, 404/223–0690. No credit cards. No dinner. $*

5 *c-1*

VAN GOGH'S

Brick walls serve as showcases for works by local and regional artists (one of the owners is kin to the owner of Alpha Omega Gallery in Roswell), and these artful surroundings set the stage for a menu that changes seasonally but is always enticing: crab cakes, stir fries, a daily risotto, good soups, sautéed sea bass, grilled Portobello mushroom, grilled vegetable sandwiches, and tiramisu, the house's special dessert. The wine list is very carefully crafted, and a glass of Jepson Brandy after dinner may just be the perfect finish. The restaurant often hosts wine-focused events, such as wine-maker dinners. *70 W. Crossville Rd., Roswell, 770/993–1156. AE, DC, MC, V. No lunch Sun. $$–$$$$*

11 *c-2*

WHITE HOUSE

Southern-style breakfasts come complete with grits and biscuits at this long-popular spot. At lunch, the fourth-generation Greek-American owners place Southern and Greek dishes (from pastitsio to moussaka and gyros) side-by-side on the steam table. *3172 Peachtree St., Buckhead, 404/237–7601. Reservations not accepted. No credit cards. No alcohol. No smoking. No dinner. $*

AMERICAN/CASUAL

4 *g-4*

CAREY'S PLACE

If you're passionate about burgers, the monstrous two-handers served here are such a pleasure that you probably won't mind the totally divey surroundings. Indeed, many Atlantans, from tattooed types to the suited-up, say the half-pound, hand-formed patties are the best in town. *1021 Cobb Pkwy., Marietta, 770/422–8042. Reservations not accepted. No credit cards. $*

14 *b-5*

FLYING BISCUIT CAFE

The biscuits are fluffy and justly famous at this folksy all-day eatery, which serves inventive fare with a health-food bent. Red meat isn't an option; the bacon, sausage, and meat loaf are all turkey, as are some of the burgers. The hearty, delicious breakfasts pack in the fans, so expect a wait on weekend mornings. *1655 McLendon Ave., Candler Park, 404/ 687–8888. Reservations not accepted. AE, DC, MC, V. Closed Mon. $$*

 f-2

1001 Piedmont Ave., at 10th St., Midtown, 404/874–8887.

6 *b-6*

GEORGIA DINER

Gwinnett County's reliable 24-hour dining establishment—probably its only one—serves delicious meals at any hour, plus breakfast dishes. The omelets are four-square hefty; the specials are the best meal deals, with such very well done items as stuffed roasted Cornish hen with mashed potatoes and veggies. The eye-popping desserts and more-than-decent coffee make this a good stop at the end of an evening out. *1655 Pleasant Hill Rd., Duluth, 770/806–9880. AE, D, DC, MC, V. $–$$*

5 *d-4*

HOUSTON'S

This Atlanta-founded chain draws a large lunch crowd, and wait times at peak hours can be long. Is the wait worth it? Thai chicken salad, Maryland crab cakes, grilled chicken salad with honey-lime vinaigrette, and excellent seared ahi tuna may convince you it is. Besides, the bar is a nice place to drop in for an after-work drink. *4701 Ashford-Dunwoody Rd., Dunwoody, 770/512– 7066. Reservations not accepted. AE, MC, V. $–$$$*

12 *h-2*

3321 Lenox Rd., across from Lenox Square, Buckhead, 404/237–7534.

12 *a-2*

3539 Northside Pkwy., Buckhead, 404/ 262–7130.

12 *d-8*

2166 Peachtree Rd., Brookwood (south Buckhead), 404/351–2442.

4 *h-6*

3050 Windy Hill Rd., Marietta, 770/563– 1180.

15 *f-2*

JOE'S ON JUNIPER

Nostalgia rules at this popular neighborhood bar where the retro menu includes burgers, hot dogs, and a standout homemade hash. The street-side patio is a nice place to eat or relax over a drink, or to catch some rays during weekend brunch. *1049 Juniper St., Midtown, 404/875–6634. AE, DC, MC, V. $*

14 *a-4*

MANUEL'S TAVERN

Open since 1956, Manuel's has been a gathering spot for neighbors young and old. They enjoy veggie burgers, steak sandwiches, beer-steamed hot dogs, and chicken wings (which could well be the city's best, served with house-made blue-cheese dressing) while they argue politics, watch the Braves, and schmooze with owner Manuel Maloof, himself a political leader in DeKalb County. *602 N. Highland Ave., Poncey-Highland, 404/525–3447. Reservations not accepted. AE, D, DC, MC, V. $–$$*

15 *e-5*

MAX LAGER'S AMERICAN GRILL & BREWERY

One of the city's best brewpubs is also a handy place to grab a bite before an event at the Philips Arena. The fare is casual and includes well-made sandwiches, excellent soups, pasta dishes, and salads. The brick walls and industrial atmosphere form a seemingly appropriate backdrop for a brewpub. But you can ignore the brews if you wish and perhaps savor the house-made root beer or ginger beer. Wine enthusiasts, fear not—the wine list is decent. *320 Peachtree St., Downtown, 404/525–4400. Reservations not accepted. AE, D, DC, MC, V. $–$$*

14 *a-2*

MURPHY'S

Tom Murphy's casual spot combines a restaurant, bakery, retail wine shop, and take-out operation all in one comfortable space. Soups change constantly, and all are good, but chicken and lime is the one to look for. If it's not available, console yourself with crab cakes, roast chicken, grilled tuna, or superior pasta dishes, and the "bonzo" layered brownie, cheesecake, or chocolate mousse. Outstanding egg dishes, breads, and fresh juices make this a popular brunch spot on weekends.

997 Virginia Ave., Virginia-Highland, 404/ 872–0904. Reservations not accepted. AE, D, DC, MC, V. $$

3 d-5

NORMAN'S LANDING

Family-oriented, busy, and a tad noisy, this popular place offers well-prepared home-style fare that's available all day and includes steaks, seafood, and chicken dishes. The crawfish-and-scallop cake is a tasty take on the crab cake, and the country-fried steak is made on the premises, a rare thing these days. There's a veranda for waiting, patio tables, and full bar service (but not on Sunday). You can work off your meal with a game of Ping-Pong; the $1 donation goes to a local charity, with different organizations benefiting from your largess each month. 365 Peachtree Pkwy., Cumming (at GA 400, exit 13/GA 141), 770/886–0100. AE, D, DC, MC, V. $$–$$$

13 a-6

THE ORIGINAL PANCAKE HOUSE

Apple pancakes, eggs in a blanket, "Dutch babies" (puffed pancakes with powdered sugar and lemon), waffles, all kinds of omelets, and really good sausage pack the weekend breakfast crowd into this chain. The excellent coffee is blended especially for the company, which was founded in Portland, Oregon, in 1953, about three years before IHOP came on the scene. Breakfast starts at 7 AM and goes to 3 PM during the week and to 4 PM on the weekend. 2321 Cheshire Bridge Rd., Northeast Atlanta, 404/633–5677. AE, D, DC, MC, V. No lunch or dinner. $

5 d-7

4330 Peachtree Rd. NE, Brookhaven, 404/ 237–4116.

6 b-5

3665 Club Dr., Lawrenceville, 770/925– 0065.

8 d-1

3099 Memorial Dr., Stone Mountain, 404/292–6914.

12 e-8

R. THOMAS DELUXE GRILL

The covered patio is the only place to sit, and it plays cozy to the street. But that's part of the fun, all the more so because exotic birds frolic in a nearby cage. Popular for business lunches, kids' gatherings, and late-night or early morning feasting, the place is open 9 AM–6 AM most days and around the clock from Friday until 6 AM Monday. There are excellent burgers, stuffed baked potatoes, mega-salads, omelets, malteds, and desserts—plus natural juices and smoothies. Service can sometimes be frantic and perfunctory. 1812 Peachtree Rd., Brookwood (south Buckhead), 404/872–2942. AE, D, DC, MC, V. $–$$

12 g-3

ROCK BOTTOM BREWERY

Rock Bottom brews 10 beers on the premises, ranging from seasonal beers to two cask-conditioned beers produced in the traditional British fermentation process. The menu, however, is decidedly casual American: wood-fired pizzas, sandwiches, pastas, and salads. 3242 Peachtree Rd., near Piedmont Rd., Buckhead, 404/264–0253. AE, D, DC, MC, V. $–$$

8 c-2

SKIP'S HOT DOGS

Chicago-style hot dogs—with all ingredients, right down to the bun, imported from the Windy City—are the draw, and along with the chili, milk shakes, and fries they pack in a lunchtime crowd from surrounding offices and the nearby Decatur medical-center complex. Service is brisk, but this is, after all, a Yankee operation. 48 Avondale Rd., Avondale Estates, 404/292–6703. Reservations not accepted. No credit cards. Closed Sun. $

14 f-1

TANNER'S CHICKEN ROTISSERIE

You can sit down at this Atlanta-founded chain eatery, which dispenses good rotisserie chicken and classic veggie side dishes, but takeout is the more popular option. Even your grandmother would likely approve of the traditional cornbread dressing. There's barbecue, too, but the chicken's the steal: a quarter-chicken dinner with two sides sets you back less than $6. 1371 Clairmont Rd., near N. Decatur Rd., Northeast Atlanta, 404/634–5500. AE, D, DC, MC, V. $

4 h-7

3220 Cobb Pkwy., Northwest Atlanta, 770/ 956–8866.

5 c-5

4920 Roswell Rd. NE, Sandy Springs, 404/255–4336.

5 h-7

4450 Hugh Howell Rd., Tucker, 770/621–0066.

15 e-4

THE VARSITY

Chili dogs, onion rings, frosted orange drinks, and fruit-filled fried pies are par for the course at this local institution, which has been around since 1928. During campaign gigs, politicians often pose at the Varsity, which has retained its working-class allure, as well as its curb service (downtown and in Norcross only). A "Naked Steak" is an unadorned burger, a "Bag o' Rags" is a sack of potato chips, and "Walk a Dog" means a hot dog to go. The retro-'50s Norcross and Kennesaw outlets are newer and less gritty; the Varsity, Jr., on Lindbergh, seems more frenzied and lacks the character of the real McCoy. *61 North Ave., Downtown, 404/881–1706. No credit cards. $*

13 a-6

1085 Lindbergh Dr., at Cheshire Bridge Rd., Northeast Atlanta, 404/261–8843.

5 g-6

6045 Dawson Blvd., off Jimmy Carter Blvd., east of I–85 (exit 99), Norcross, 770/840–8519.

4 f-3

2790 Town Center Dr., Kennesaw, 770/795–0802.

14 a-4

THE VORTEX

With more than 30 beers on tap and 210-plus bottled brands, this popular late-night eatery is a brew lover's paradise. It also offers 80 single-malt Scotches. Off-the-wall decor is the hallmark: an image straight from Edvard Munch's *The Scream* frames the entrance at the Little Five Points location. Burgers, made with black beans, soy beans, or turkey, are the specialty; chicken, fish, and shrimp dishes and deli sandwiches take casual fare to another level. *438 Moreland Ave., Little Five Points, 404/688–1828. AE, D, DC, MC, V. $–$$*

15 e-3

878 Peachtree St., Midtown, 404/875–1667.

14 f-3

WATERSHED

The slickly remodeled former service station sells cookbooks, scented candles, fine bottled salsas, and a superior wine inventory. But the draw is chef Scott Peacock's yummy takes on American-Southern classics that include a sharp cheddar pimento cheese sandwich, rich cauliflower soup, and New England salted cod chowder. Indeed, all the soups are off-the-charts wonderful. Desserts, such as (in season) rhubarb cobbler, are to die for. The dinner menu adds such dishes as gnocchi as well as braised pork on polenta. The by-the-glass wine list is tops, offering many unusual bottlings and poured by especially knowledgeable servers—or, pick any bottle from the bins. *406 W. Ponce de Leon Ave., Decatur, 404/378–4900. Reservations not accepted. AE, D, DC, MC, V. Closed Sun. $–$$*

15 g-4

ZESTO'S DRIVE-IN

Menus and quality vary from location to location, but all the Zesto outlets turn out reliably good milk shakes (banana, butterscotch, and coffee are slam-dunks), hamburgers, foot-long hot dogs, and ice cream desserts. The Ponce de Leon branch gets the award for the best architecture (it was redesigned in 1991 as a classic 1950s-style diner), as well as for cuisine: almond-chicken salad, grilled tuna sandwiches, and chicken fingers are excellent here. *544 Ponce de Leon Ave., Midtown, 404/607–1118. Reservations not accepted. No credit cards. $*

15 h-8

1181 E. Confederate Ave., East Atlanta, 404/622–4254.

8 a-7

151 Forest Pkwy., Forest Park, 404/366–0564.

14 a-5

377 Moreland Ave., Little Five Points, 404/523–1973.

BARBECUE

15 f-6

ACE BARBECUE BARN

This basic, no-frills spot supplies takeout for busy Auburn Avenue denizens at lunchtime and provides some tables, too. Eat in or eat out, but get ready for excellent barbecue (sliced pork sandwich, ribs, and rib tips), the most delicious baked chicken and pan dressing, and fantastic sweet-potato pie. It's open very late some nights. *30 Bell St., at Auburn Ave., Sweet Auburn, 404/659–6630. Reservations not accepted. No credit cards. Closed Tues.* $

4 *e-2*
BELL'S
To the menu classics—hickory-smoked pulled pork, Brunswick stew—Bell's adds fried chicken and shrimp, steaks, stuffed potatoes, and salads. The place is so clean you could bring your mother-in-law here, and the fried pies give the Varsity a run for its money (and that's no mean feat). *3815 Cherokee St., Kennesaw, 770/419–2626. AE, MC, V.* $–$$

5 *d-6*
BENNY'S BARBECUE
The tender, smoky ribs taste so good that it doesn't matter if the surroundings are scruffy. The pulled pork piled high on a bun isn't at all shabby, either; maybe the tart vinegar-dressed slaw is an acquired taste, but the crunchy fresh ingredients keep you reaching for more. *2150-B Johnson Ferry Rd., Chamblee, 770/454–7810. Reservations not accepted. AE, D, MC, V.* $

6 *a-5*
CORKY'S RIBS & BAR-B-Q
If you've got a taste for Memphis-style barbecue, both wet and dry, this outpost of the famous Memphis 'cue joint is about the only place in the area to get some. The dry rub is heavy on the paprika, but the meat is tender. Side dishes include very good Brunswick stew, decent baked beans, and good potato slaw. The chili is good, too, if not distinctive. *1605 Pleasant Hill Rd., Duluth, 770/564–8666. AE, D, DC, MC, V.* $–$$

15 *e-7*
DADDY D'Z
This joint serves barbecue of variable quality (but when it's good, it's downright good) and consistently good blues (Friday and Saturday nights only). Brunswick stew, macaroni and cheese, baked beans, okra, broccoli casserole, black beans and rice, and collard greens are among the adornments. *264 Memorial Dr., Downtown, 404/222–0206. Reservations not accepted. AE, MC, V.* $–$$

9 *f-1*
DEAN'S
Cooking pork the traditional way means smoking it slowly all night long and staying up to make sure the basting's done and the fire stays low. Supremely tender ribs and pulled pork are the reward, and that's what you discover at this real hole in the wall with no amenities whatsoever. *9480 S. Main St., Jonesboro, 770/471–0138. Reservations not accepted. No credit cards. Closed Sun.–Mon. No dinner Tues.* $

9 *d-4*
DU ROC CAFÉ
A south metro favorite, Du Roc ranks high for slow-smoked ribs and beef. (The "Du Roc," they say, is a breed of pig.) The pork sandwich may be had Carolina style, with the slaw on top. There's cracklin' corn bread (with sautéed crisped pork fat blended into the batter) and very good barbecue beans. *115 Marquis Dr., Fayetteville, off GA 54 toward Peachtree City, 770/719–1744. Reservations not accepted. AE, D, DC, MC, V. No alcohol. Closed Sun.* $

13 *c-7*
DUSTY'S
In a simple, rustic wood building perched on a busy corner, Dusty's dishes up North Carolina–style barbecue, the kind that comes with a thin vinegar-pepper sauce and with coleslaw on top of the meat. The hot sauce is superior, and so are the vegetable side dishes and desserts. You can order beer and wine, though not on Sunday. *1815 Briarcliff Rd., at Clifton Rd., Decatur, 404/320–6264. Reservations not accepted. AE, D, DC, MC, V. Wine and beer only.* $–$$

12 *g-7*
FAT MATT'S RIB SHACK
Folks come here for the blues as well as the barbecue—tender ribs and deeply smoky pulled-pork sandwiches. The beans are good, too, and there's beer. Go early if you plan to sit while the music's on, because after it starts, there's standing room only. *1811 Piedmont Rd., Morningside, 404/607–1622. Reservations not accepted. No credit cards.* $–$$

7 h-4

HAROLD'S

Suit types, State Patrol officers, and just about everybody else who knows good Brunswick stew heads to this quirky joint in the shadow of the Federal Penitentiary. The cracklin' corn bread is the standard against which all others are measured. The sweet, tomato-based barbecue itself is some folks' favorite and other folks' least favorite; you have to decide for yourself. The Jonesboro outlet has the same menu, but fans swear by the southeast Atlanta spot. *171 McDonough Blvd., southeast Atlanta, 404/627–9268. Reservations not accepted. No credit cards. Closed Sun. $–$$*

9 g-2

265 GA 54, Jonesboro, 770/478–5880. AE, MC, V.

6 d-8

JIMMY'S SMOKEHOUSE

Crowds from near and far flock to this mobile unit owned by Jimmy and Thelma Stokes. Your seating options are the ground or your car, but what you take away with you is tender slow-cooked pork roast, ribs, and beautiful potato casserole. The Stokes family caters private parties most of the week, which means you can find them here on Friday and Saturday only. *Corner of GA 124 and Everson Rd., Snellville, 770/972–1625. No credit cards. Closed Sun.–Thurs. $–$$*

5 f-4

J. R.'S LOGHOUSE

Good barbecue that's consistent and reliable, if not stellar, is what you get in this rambling, log-style building. Breakfast, which begins early in the morning, is Southern-style, with grits, eggs, sausage, country ham, bacon, good biscuits, and fine coffee. The barbecue omelet is an original and hearty start to the day. *6601 Peachtree Industrial Blvd., Norcross, 770/449–6426. Reservations not accepted. AE, D, DC, MC, V. $–$$*

10 d-4

O. B.'S

Smoke curls enticingly from the chimney of this squeaky-clean rustic cabin, where reliably good barbecue and sides are served in generous portions. The ribs are your best bet, and the pies aren't bad. In addition, O.B.'s claims to have the fastest to-go kitchen in town.

725 Industrial Blvd. (I–75 at exit 218), McDonough, 770/954–1234. AE, D, MC, V. $–$$

4 g-6

OLD SOUTH

One of Cobb County's best barbecue spots, this basic cabin-style place is famous for its sweet slow-smoked ribs (get the sauce on the side to dip the ribs into), vinegar-dressed coleslaw (no mayonnaise), great Brunswick stew, and beans. *601 Burbank Cir. (Windy Hill Rd.), Smyrna, 770/435–4215. Reservations not accepted. AE, D, MC, V. No alcohol. Closed Mon. $*

3 d-5

PAPPY RED'S

The single-engine plane that sits on the roof of this unassuming concrete-block eatery is a tongue-in-cheek invitation for you to drop in. Inside, the welcome doesn't quit. You could spend all day working through a menu that includes broccoli casserole, sweet-potato soufflé, and peach-blackberry cobbler—not to mention ribs, pulled pork, and Brunswick stew that 'cue lovers consider tops. *867 Buford Rd. (GA 400, exit 14), Cumming, 770/844–9446. Reservations not accepted. AE, D, DC, MC, V. Beer only. $*

2 e-7

13680 Arnold Mill Rd., Roswell, 770/475–9910.

12 f-3

THE RIB RANCH

Even sophisticated Buckhead gets down-home with the Texas-style barbecue beef ribs here. You can get baby-back pork ribs, too, but the deal is the huge beef-rib platter ($29.95) that feeds two or three people. Excellent side dishes (think onion rings, corn bread, and beans) round out the offerings. The people-watching is a plus; some real characters—a mix of working-class folk and upper-crusty types—dine at the Buckhead location. *25 Irby Ave., off Roswell Rd., 1 block north of W. Paces Ferry Rd., Buckhead, 404/233–7644. MC, V. $–$$*

4 g-3

2063 Canton Rd., near Sandy Plains Rd., Marietta, 770/422–5755.

14 *h-1*

ROCKIN' ROB'S

Hunting trophies and Marilyn Monroe and rock 'n' roll memorabilia decorate this roadhouse-style joint that covers the barbecue gamut from smoked chicken and beef brisket to sweetly tender, smoky Georgia-style ribs and pulled, sliced, and chopped pork sandwiches. The three sauces range from medium-bodied mild with a good vinegar–tomato balance to vinegar-and-hot-pepper and a mustard sauce. *1479 Scott Blvd., Decatur, 404/ 378–6041. Reservations not accepted. MC, V. Closed Sun. $–$$*

5 *c-2*

SLOPE'S

Some Atlantans swear by Slope's, especially for ribs. The sauce is a Carolina-style vinegar–pepper sauce, and the Brunswick stew reminds many folks of what their moms used to make. *34 Crossville Rd., Roswell, 770/518–7000. Reservations not accepted. AE, D, DC, MC, V. No alcohol. Closed Sun. $*

2 *b-8*

10200 GA 92, Woodstock, 770/516–6789.

5 *h-6*

SPICED RIGHT

The trophies this outstanding barbecue eatery has racked up in BBQ competitions say it all: this one's a winner. The ribs are tender and richly smoked, and in addition to the 'cue, there's a steam table with lots of good side dishes, including coleslaw, potato salad, and baked beans. The iced tea is potent and wonderful—no sugar granules on the bottom of a glass of the sweetened stuff. *5364 U.S. 29, Lilburn, 770/564– 0355. Reservations not accepted. AE, D, DC, MC, V. Closed Sun. No dinner Mon.– Wed. $–$$*

5 *c-2*

THE SWALLOW AT THE HOLLOW

Here is a place to celebrate home-style American cooking. Much of the fare is Southern style, including the pork barbecue, but it also includes smoked turkey and, for the Texans among us, beef barbecue. Alongside are macaroni and cheese, baked beans, and a unique banana pudding that's made with chocolate-chip cookies. Continuous service weekends from 11 AM to late at night makes this a handy spot to

indulge after a round of errands or shopping. There's very limited wine service. *1072 Green St., Roswell, 678/352– 1975. Reservations not accepted. No credit cards. Closed Mon. $–$$*

7 *b-1*

WALLACE BARBECUE

South Cobb County is well served by this emporium, bedecked with auto memorabilia that includes an antique gas pump and a '57 Chevy cut into a bench. You can chow down ribs, chopped or sliced pork sandwiches, barbecued chicken, and the side dishes (which, unlike the desserts, are made in house), and then take home a bottle of the tangy mustard-base sauce that's good on just about anything. *3035 Bankhead Hwy., Austell, 770/739–1686. Reservations not accepted. AE, D, DC, MC, V. Closed Sun.–Mon. $*

4 *g-4*

WILLIAMSON BROTHERS

A Cobb County favorite that also does catering, this rustic-style place is at its best when doing ribs, chopped pork, sliced pork, side dishes, and coconut cream pie (awesome!). Bottled beer is available. *1425 Roswell Rd., Marietta, 770/ 971–3201. AE, D, DC, MC, V. $–$$*

ON THE RUN

Hungry and in a hurry? These spots offer tasty fare served quickly, so you can get back to doing whatever it was you were doing.

Bajarito's (Eclectic)
Grab a tray and move down the self-service line, picking up gourmet wraps and fresh salsa. You won't break $10; you'll dine quickly; and you'll enjoy the aesthetics of the vibrant interior.

Don Taco (Mexican)
All shopping-mall food courts should be so lucky as to have food of this caliber; the burritos are especially good.

The Varsity (American/Casual)
Nothing ever came faster than a Varsity hot dog with chili, great greasy onion rings, and an orange frosty. It's a cultural experience besides.

BELGIAN

12 *f-6*

PHILIPPE'S

Chef-owner Philippe Haddad puts a contemporary spin on braised rabbit, waterzooi, beef stew, and other traditional Belgian dishes at this intimate, quietly elegant neighborhood gathering place. Mussels, for instance, might come in a coconut-curry broth. Venison with lingonberries is delicious, and the dessert of choice is the white-chocolate bread pudding. The wine list is excellent, with a good mix of European and New World bottlings, but you also have a choice of Belgian beers. There's live piano nightly, except Sunday. *10 Kings Cir., Peachtree Hills, 404/231–4113. AE, D, DC, MC, V. Closed Mon. No lunch Tues.–Sat. $$–$$$*

BRAZILIAN

12 *g-3*

FOGO DE CHAO

The salad bar is one of the city's most lavish, but it's all about meat at this *churrascaria*, or cowboy-style barbecue. Flip the little disk by your plate from red to green and phalanxes of gaucho-dressed waiters arrive bearing skewers of sizzling rump steak, sirloin, filet mignon, pork loin, lamb chops, linguiça sausage and more—the very best cuts, seared and caramelized on the outside, juicy pink within, and still burning hot from the grill. With its elaborate choreography and all-you-can-chew format, it's especially popular with large groups. *3101 Piedmont Rd., Buckhead, 404/266–9988. AE, D, DC, MC, V. No lunch weekends. $$$$*

CAFÉS

5 *b-5*

ATLANTA BREAD COMPANY

The Atlanta-based chain has about 30 metro-area outlets, with more on the drawing boards, so you don't have to look far to come by a quick and inexpensive breakfast, lunch, or snack. Pastries and cookies are baked on the premises of each shop, as is bread that accompanies soups and salads and is a prime ingredient of the sandwiches. *220 Sandy Springs Cir., Sandy Springs, 404/843–0040. Reservations not accepted. AE, D, DC, MC, V. No alcohol. $*

5 *e-1*

1056 North Point Cir., Alpharetta, 770/740–1450.

14 *g-3*

205 E. Ponce de Leon Ave., Decatur, 404/378–6600.

12 *d-7*

THE BREAD MARKET

Looking for a good sandwich? Try the curry chicken salad with almonds or shiitake mushroom with fresh mozzarella cheese. Want to indulge in a pastry to die for? Try the brownies, cookies, or cheesecake. The espresso is excellent, too; the salad bar is loaded with fresh ingredients; and a breakfast burrito stuffed with scrambled eggs and salsa is a fine way to start a day. *1927 Peachtree Rd., Buckhead, 404/352–5252. Reservations not accepted. AE, DC, MC, V. No alcohol. No dinner. $*

12 *g-3*

BUCKHEAD BREAD COMPANY & CORNER CAFÉ

Mingling aromas of coffee and freshly baked breads greet patrons, who are likely to be business folks gathering here for breakfast meetings (while enjoying the pancakes and frittatas) and shoppers who stop by at lunch time for good salads, sandwiches on house-baked bread, and cooked dishes. Baked goods are sold throughout the day. *3070 Piedmont Rd., Buckhead, 404/240–1978. Reservations not accepted. AE, D, DC, MC, V. Wine and beer only. No dinner. $–$$*

7 *g-6*

CAFÉ AT THE CORNER

It's self-service but far better than you might expect it to be. Offerings include house-made pastries, the freshest chicken and goat-cheese salads, and numerous daily specials that may well include Cajun French chili. And what a deal: a combo of a cup of soup and a half sandwich is $5. *636 S. Central Ave., Hapeville, 404/766–1155; 404/766–2255 menu-specials recording. AE, MC, V. No alcohol. Closed weekends. No dinner. $*

12 *d-7*

CAFÉ INTERMEZZO

Although there's a full menu, this Viennese-style café is best for weekend brunch (this is a great place to read the Sunday paper) or for a late-night, post-performance sweet accompanied by great coffee. The café doesn't make most of its 120 different desserts but obtains its sweets from some of the best sources—even if that means ordering from out of town or, for that matter, out of the country. *1845 Peachtree St., Buckhead, 404/355–0411. Reservations not accepted. AE, D, MC, V. $–$$*

5 *d-5*
CAFÉ NORDSTROM
Getting a bite while shopping no longer means having a lunch plate and tea; nowadays expectations have been raised to include Tuscan breads, braised chicken, grilled veggies, pastas, freshly made soups, individual pizzas, and the like, and you can find all these at the café in the Nordstrom at Perimeter Mall. You can even order wine by the glass here. *Nordstrom, Perimeter Mall, 4390 Ashford-Dunwoody Rd., Dunwoody, 770/394–1141, ext. 1610. Reservations not accepted. AE, D, DC, MC, V. $*

14 *d-2*
CAFFÈ ANTICO
If you're paying a visit to the exhibitions at Emory University's Michael C. Carlos Museum, plan on lunching at this café on the third floor. Soups and chili are house-made, the salads are excellent, and sandwiches are served on whole-grain bread. Leave room for desserts, which are first rate. *Emory University, 571 S. Kilgo St., Decatur, 404/727–0695. Reservations not accepted. AE, D, MC, V. No alcohol. $*

15 *g-6*
CARROLL STREET CAFÉ
Marvelous cakes and pastries and inventive dishes are the draws at this quirky, no-frills eatery. House-made granola, a sautéed-veggie sandwich with cumin mayonnaise, and poached eggs with toast points and creamed spinach are among the breakfast, brunch, and lunch items. In addition to the regular menu, you can choose from two or three dinner specials, priced around $15—cappellini with sautéed shrimp, spinach, mushrooms, smoked-salmon bits, and a peppery goat-cheese sauce, for instance. There's a full bar and occasional acoustic performances. *208 Carroll St., Cabbagetown, 404/577–2700. AE, MC, V. $–$$*

15 *e-4*
CHURCHILL GROUNDS
The ideal spot for a quick bite before Fox Theatre performances, this café-club opens around 6 PM and excels at light appetizers and pastries. The espresso is notable, too. Straight-ahead jazz is featured nightly beginning about 9:30 PM (the cover ranges from $5 to $25). Full bar service is available. *660 Peachtree St., Midtown, 404/876–3030. Reservations not accepted. AE, D, MC, V. Closed Sun. $*

12 *e-3*
COCA-COLA CAFÉ
Any trip to the Atlanta History Center should include a stop for lunch at this 1950s-style café packed with Coca-Cola memorabilia. Lunch is a serious treat, all the more so if it includes manager Bernard Douglas's chili, best savored atop a hot dog. Douglas also creates superb salads, but with his limited kitchen space, he relies on an outside supplier for soup, which he fine-tunes so that it tastes as if made from scratch. Malteds are outstanding, and desserts are sourced from Tuohy's Catering, one of the city's best; the Hummingbird Cake is a classic Southern layer cake not often seen these days. *Atlanta History Center, 130 W. Paces Ferry Rd., Buckhead, 404/814–4000. Reservations not accepted. No credit cards. $*

8 *a-1*
CONTINENTAL PARK CAFÉ
A great way to relax on a lazy afternoon is to perch on this outdoor dining terrace above Main Street and watch the trains come and go through the village. While here, sip a fabulous milk shake, savor a salad, or enjoy a sandwich. Then, thus fortified, check out the charming shops up and down the street. *941 Main St., Stone Mountain, 770/413–6448. MC, V. No alcohol. No dinner Sun.–Thurs. $*

13 *g-5*
FIVE SISTERS CAFÉ
Such delights as Peg's Veg, with roasted eggplant and tomatoes, mixed greens, goat cheese, and pesto, and Sylvia's Smoked Salmon, an open-face arrangement on toasted bread with horseradish crème fraîche, capers, and cucumbers, elevate sandwiches a level or two above the norm. Three cooked specials are also offered daily. The wine list is short but well selected. *Oak Grove Plaza shop-*

ping center, 2743 LaVista Rd., Decatur, 404/636–6060. Reservations not accepted. AE, D, MC, V. Closed Sun. $

14 c-5

GATO BIZCO CAFÉ/ GATO DE NOCHE

Here's a satisfying alternative if you get tired of waiting hungrily for a table across the street at the Flying Biscuit. The big biscuits, grits, soy-based sausage, *huevos rancheros* (salsa-topped fried eggs), and breakfast burrito filled with eggs, potatoes, and cheese would keep anybody going all day. The Mexican-style lunch fare of the quesadillas-burritos-tacos variety is hefty, too. Wednesday through Saturday, the place goes into Gato de Noche mode, when a different cook turns out ample, inventive dinners with the same Latin sensibility and the same good value. 1660 McLendon Ave., Candler Park, 404/371–0889. Reservations not accepted. MC, V. BYOB. Closed Tues. $–$$

15 c-2

JAQBO

If this bakery and sandwich shop, in a nondescript building just off the Georgia Tech campus, were in a ritzier neighborhood, offered table service with china, and had a patio with umbrella-shaded tables, it could triple its prices. As it is, Techies and other fans flock here to order at the counter, eat off plastic ware, and chow down the wonderful soups and sandwiches. A white wine–cream sauce binds the basil-and-shallot-studded chicken salad. Mixed vegetables are marinated, grilled, topped with provolone, and nestled between two slices of one of the house-made breads. Just try getting out the door without one of the tasty-looking cookies and pastries. 1093 Hemphill Ave., Northwest Atlanta, 404/873–1272. AE, MC, V. Closed Sun. $

15 b-2

MONDO

A newsstand occupies part of this retro-look space with a soaring ceiling—originally a 1950s-style service station—so you can catch up on current events while nibbling fresh-baked pastries, cakes, and cookies—among the very best in town—or fueling up with a salad or sandwich, all washed down with one of the specialty coffees. There's a classic diner breakfast on Saturday morning. 750 Huff Rd., Northwest Atlanta, 404/603–9995.

Reservations not accepted. AE, MC, V. No alcohol. Closed Sun. No dinner. $–$$

15 d-6

TRINITY

The Castleberry Hill neighborhood has no eateries of its own, but a short stroll toward the city center, the multipersonality Trinity does its best to serve as a local lounge and nosh nook. The room has an edgy, post-modern decor, with banquettes and low tables—which makes a stool at the full-length bar the more practical choice if you mean to make a real meal of this grazing-oriented menu. Pick from enchiladas, crab cakes, bourbon- and peppercorn-cured salmon on pita chips, and barbecued pork in egg-roll form. The scene of mostly urban hipsters is welcoming and diverse. 255 Trinity Ave., Downtown, 404/222–9925. AE, MC, V. Closed Sun.–Tues. No lunch. $

CAJUN/CREOLE

3 a-8

COMEAUX'S LOUISIANA BAR & GRILL

The crowds come for the good raw oysters, gumbo, *boudin blanc* (a pork-and-rice sausage), étouffée, and, in season, boiled crawfish. The bread pudding is worthy of New Orleans, too, and even there you wouldn't find better chicory-laced creole-style coffee. The strains of jazz from the adjacent bar add a special ambience on many evenings. *Haynes Bridge Village, 9925 Haynes Bridge Rd., Alpharetta, 770/442–2524. AE, D, DC, MC, V. $$–$$$*

12 g-7

CREOLE CAFÉ

This quirky little café with a cult following dishes out good gumbo, po'boys, and similar casual Cajun fare for lunch only. Some diners find the bread pudding heavenly. *Rock Springs Plaza, 1877 Piedmont Rd., Morningside, 404/875–6602. Reservations not accepted. AE, D, DC, MC, V. No alcohol. Closed Sun. $–$$*

5 d-6

FRENCH QUARTER, TOO

This bare-bones operation doesn't offer much in way of atmosphere, but that makes it all the more authentic. The catfish, gumbo, and bread pudding are indeed authentically Louisiana, and the fried 'gator tail and turtle soup in season are even more so. There's wine, but the beers are better, including New Orleans' Abita Turbodog on draft. *2144 Johnson Ferry Rd., Chamblee, 770/458–2148. Reservations not accepted. AE, D, DC, MC, V. Closed Sun. $$*

13 *b-4*

FUZZY'S PLACE

Longtime Atlanta restaurateur Joe Dale, now over 80, acts as consulting chef and oversees a menu of creole and Cajun specialties. His "Seafood Patsy," a creamy seafood gratin, remains one of the city's beloved dishes, and his bread pudding is the dessert standout here. A light menu is available until 11 PM, and blues and blues-based rock hum through the often-crowded, usually smoke-filled performance space to the right of the bar. *2015 N. Druid Hills Rd., Northeast Atlanta, 404/321–6166. Reservations not accepted. AE, D, DC, MC, V. $–$$*

7 *a-2*

GUMBEAUX'S: A CAJUN CAFÉ

LSU and San Francisco 49er football memorabilia decorate the upstairs dining room, where menu offerings include seafood gumbo, crawfish or shrimp étouffée, and classic bananas Foster and bread pudding. Downstairs there's an oyster bar where the bivalves are served raw, baked, and fried. Wine selections are limited, but the Louisiana beers are what you come for anyway. *6712 E. Broad St., Douglasville, 770/947–8288. AE, D, DC, MC, V. Closed Sun.–Mon. $–$$*

12 *f-1*

HAL'S

Diners come for the creole classics: the shrimp and crab rémoulade, trout fillet with crabmeat, snapper française, soft-shell crab meunière in season, and bread pudding. Of course, a lively, friendly bar scene is part of the allure. Buckhead's wine list relies heavily on chardonnay and cabernet sauvignon, but Duluth's wine cellar has 6,000 bottles. *30 Old Ivy Rd., Buckhead, 404/261–0025. AE, D, DC, MC, V. Closed Sun. $$–$$$$*

5 *g-2*

10305 Medlock Bridge Rd., Duluth, 770/418–0448. Closed Sun.–Mon. No lunch.

12 *d-7*

HUEY'S

Order a plate of beignets—those fabulous New Orleans puffed, deep-fried square doughnuts—and prepare to brush the powdered sugar off your shirt as you indulge yourself. And don't forget a cup of stiff, chicory-laced New Orleans coffee (Community brand) to go with them. Of course, there's more substantial fare to be had here, too: good gumbo, étouffée, jambalaya, and Louisiana barbecue. Creole omelets, steak and eggs, and other brunch fare are served Saturday until 3 PM and Sunday until 5 PM. There's wine and beer, including Louisiana beers. You can come after clubbing Friday and Saturday, when Huey's is open until 5 AM. *1816 Peachtree Rd., Buckhead, 404/873–2037. Reservations not accepted. AE, MC, V. Wine and beer only. $–$$*

12 *g-3*

MCKINNON'S LOUISIANE

A lot of patrons stop by Billy McKinnon's long-popular place to drink (and on Friday and Saturday nights to listen to music), but those in the know stay for dinner, too. They savor superior Cajun popcorn (deep-fried crawfish tails), perfect deep-fried shrimp and oysters, succulent soft-shell crabs, and the famous "Billy's" crab cakes, with corn relish and green-onion aioli. The wine list has a slew of reasonably priced and serviceable selections, many of which are available by the glass. *3209 Maple Dr., Buckhead, 404/237–1313. Reservations essential. AE, D, DC, MC, V. Closed Sun. No lunch. $$–$$$*

14 *f-3*

YA YA'S CAJUN CAFÉ

With its color scheme of pink and purple there's something almost mysterious about this casual café. But there's no mystery as to why it's secured a solid reputation for its food: the crawfish, gumbo, 'gator tail, po'boys, jambalaya, and red beans and rice all add up to some good eating, Cajun style. *426 W. Ponce de Leon Ave., Decatur, 404/373–9292. Reservations not accepted. AE, D, DC, MC, V. $–$$*

CARIBBEAN

14 *a-5*

BRIDGETOWN GRILL

At this rather high-energy metro-area chain, you can start with conch fritters or a vegetarian black-bean soup, finish with key-lime pie or a delectable mango bread pudding, and choose from many tempting choices for the main event. These include good jerk chicken, guava barbecue ribs that are slow-cooked and grilled before the sauce goes on, and mango pork with a house-made mango chutney and tangy habanero-mango coulis. *1156 Euclid Ave., Little Five Points, 404/653–0110. Reservations not accepted. AE, D, DC, MC, V.* $$

15 *e-4*
689 Peachtree St., Midtown, 404/873–5361.

5 *c-4*
7285 Roswell Rd., Sandy Springs, 770/394–1575.

12 *g-3*
3316 Piedmont Rd., Buckhead, 404/266–1500.

CHINESE

5 *e-6*
CANTON HOUSE
On weekends, this large, bustling emporium draws Chinese families who come for the good dim sum for breakfast. Selections of shrimp toasts, braised Chinese broccoli, barbecued pork buns, braised chicken feet, and other dishes are made from carts pushed around the room. The regular menu has tasty fare as well, including whole steamed or braised fish as well as lobster and crab with ginger-scallion flavors. If you plan to come for dim sum on the weekend, good luck getting a reservation. *4825 Buford Hwy., Chamblee, 770/936–9030. AE, D, DC, MC, V.* $–$$

5 *c-7*
CHOPSTIX
Fine Hong Kong cooking is the metier of this stylish and sophisticated spot: dumplings, pot stickers, roast-duck ravioli, black-pepper oysters (superior!), and—in season and not to be missed—soft-shell crab. The wine list sticks with standards and includes just a few choices, which actually go well with this food. *Chastain Square, 4279 Roswell Rd., Sandy Springs, 404/255–4868. Reservations essential. AE, D, DC, MC, V. No lunch weekends.* $$–$$$$

13 *f-6*
GOLDEN BUDDHA
CHINESE RESTAURANT
The extensive menu, with its familiar combination plates of well-done Chinese-American fare, has something for everybody. Some dishes, such as spicy Hunan shrimp and braised fish, reach beyond the usual sweet-and-sour drill. Service is friendly and swift. *1905 Clairmont Rd., Decatur, 404/633–5252. Reservations not accepted. AE, D, DC, MC, V.* $

5 *e-7*
HO HO
The name means "very good" in Chinese, and this homey establishment, which specializes in Mandarin, Cantonese, and Szechuan cuisines, really is. Your first move should be to check out the specials scripted on a board on the wall (the oyster pancakes are especially good). Then, move on to the Chinese specialties menu, which features such authentic dishes as steamed lion head (Chinese meatballs). Forget the wine list and settle for beer and tea. *3683 Clairmont Rd., Chamblee, 770/451–7240. Reservations not accepted. AE, D, DC, MC, V. No lunch weekends.* $

13 *a-6*
HONG KONG HARBOUR
Patrons flock to this dining room filled with Chinese art for authentic Hong Kong–style cuisine that is exceptionally well prepared and includes pot dishes with bean curd and pork belly as well as many noodle dishes. Dim sum is served weekdays at lunch, but the best time to come for this traditional meal is Saturday or Sunday morning, when the place fills with families. Other especially tasty morsels to be found on the carts wheeled around the room are the chicken feet, which are supremely sweet and tender; the shrimp wrapped in rice noodles; and the crispy fried dumplings stuffed with meat. *2184 Cheshire Bridge Rd., Northeast Atlanta, 404/325–7630. AE, DC, MC, V.* $–$$

15 *e-5*
HSU'S GOURMET
In this elegant business dining spot, the chopsticks recline on silver rests and fine objets d'art are positioned around the dining room. The Hong Kong–style cuisine delves expertly into Peking duck and myriad shrimp dishes, including an excellent one with mango and black beans. There's a good wine list, with lots of sparkling wines and champagnes to support the cuisine. *192 Peachtree Center Ave., Downtown, 404/659–2788. AE, D, DC, MC, V. No lunch weekends.* $$–$$$

5 e-6

LITTLE SZECHUAN

Starting off business as a hole in the wall in a food court, this star of Atlanta's Chinese restaurant scene has grown and expanded over the years but never lost sight of its purpose. Ask for egg rolls and you're politely advised that this is "a real Chinese restaurant." Indeed, non-Asian patrons may be invited to peruse the menu before taking a seat, just in case confrontation with pig-tripe soup is off-putting. But the spicy squid, long beans, shrimp with young garlic, and chicken rolls are anything but off-putting. It's fun to come with a group so you can share many dishes. The wine list is limited, but you can bring your own and pay a $5 corkage fee. *Northwoods Plaza, 3091-C Buford Hwy., Doraville, 770/451–0192. AE, D, MC, V. BYOB. Closed Tues. $–$$*

5 d-5

P. F. CHANG, A CHINESE BISTRO

Sculptures suggesting pieces from the ancient (11th-century) city of Xi'an adorn this stylish Americanized Chinese restaurant. But while the art may be elaborate, the dishes are straightforward and borrowed from various Chinese cuisines, especially that of Canton. Much of the fare, such as moo shu and sweet-and-sour pork, is familiar, and vegetarians can delight in the number of options available, none boring or pedestrian; furthermore, it's easy to compose a vegetarian banquet here. The wine list includes a few bottles that work well with this food, such as a riesling and a gewürztraminer. *500 Ashford-Dunwoody Rd., near Perimeter Mall, Dunwoody, 770/352–0500. Reservations not accepted. AE, D, DC, MC, V. $–$$*

5 e-1

7925 North Point Pkwy., near North Point Mall, Alpharetta, 770/992–3070.

6 d-1

Mall of Georgia, 3333 Buford Dr., Buford, 678/546–9005.

5 e-6

PUNG MIE

The kitchen of this large, elegant eatery delights a clientele of mostly Chinese Atlantans with an assortment of steamed, boiled, and fried dumplings; cold dishes that include jellyfish salad; and such authentic specialties as sea cucumber with scallops or pork. *5145 Buford Hwy., Doraville, 770/455–0435. Reservations not accepted. AE, DC, MC, V. $–$$$*

5 e-6

ROYAL CHINA

This cavernous space has a loyal following of Chinese Atlantans, who often hold weddings in the huge private room that adjoins the dining room. The first taste of salt-and-pepper squid or black-bean mussels (there may be no better preparation of this dish in town) will explain Royal China's popularity. Saturday and Sunday dim sum (served from 10 AM to 3 PM) is excellent and draws the crowds. *3295 Chamblee-Dunwoody Rd., Chamblee, 770/216–9933. Reservations not accepted. AE, DC, MC, V. $–$$*

COLOMBIAN

5 f-5

COSTA VERDE

Here is a combination of the best of Peru and Colombia: cold boiled potatoes in a very spicy cream sauce and empanadas with a hotter-than-Hades *ají* dipping sauce. Many of the house specialties (look for them especially on weekends) are seafood dishes. Fish soups, aromatic with cilantro, can come mighty hot, so be warned. *6200 Buford Hwy., Norcross, 770/449–3221. Reservations not accepted. MC, V. Beer only. Closed Mon. $*

13 a-5

FRUTII VALLE RESTAURANT & BAKERY

A television shows soap operas in Spanish at this well-regarded bakery and restaurant, which is a home away from home for local Colombianos. The food—such traditional fare as braised chicken with tomato, onions, potatoes, and yucca—is inexpensive, and you can wash it down with excellent Colombian beer. *Sun Tan shopping center, 2651 Buford Hwy., Northeast Atlanta, 404/248–1958. Reservations not accepted. MC, V. $–$$*

CONTEMPORARY

15 b-2

BACCHANALIA

Atlantans often name this restaurant their favorite in polls. The fixed-price menu changes weekly, depending on what chefs Anne Quatrano and Clifford Harrison find in the market. Count on something wonderful with foie gras, superior salads with locally grown organic greens, excellent risotto, superb fish, game, American farmstead cheeses, house-made ice creams and sorbets, and desserts that leave you awestruck. Harrison's personally selected wine list goes far beyond the usual, and the half-bottle list is amazing. Star Provision, the companion shop, sells many of the same rarefied ingredients used in the restaurant kitchen. *1198 Howell Mill Rd., Northwest Atlanta, 404/365–0410. Reservations essential. AE, DC, MC, V. Closed Sun.–Mon. $$$$*

AN EVENING TO REMEMBER

Is it ever really worth it to spend $100 or more per person for a meal? Sometimes you want to be treated royally, just because you can. And guess what? These select restaurants really do offer flawless dining, and good value for (lots of) money.

Bacchanalia (Contemporary)
The chef–owners go to any length for perfect ingredients—even growing them, organically, on their own farm and hiring an expert whose sole job is to sniff out the most exquisite cheeses.

Bluepointe (Eclectic)
The interior of this curvaceous glass box has a luminous glow, and so do the patrons who show off theirs in the lively bar and stately dining room. The food and service are superb, of course.

The Dining Room (Contemporary)
The stiff formality is gone, but this remains the last word in luxurious, beautifully paced dining.

Nikolai's Roof (Continental)
Once you reach this jewel box in the sky, the view is unsurpassed, the atmosphere deliciously romantic, and the service fit for a czar, so it won't matter that you had to pass through the downtown Hilton first.

Pano's & Paul's (Continental)
A now subdued decor is the only change at this long-revered temple of deluxe dining, where le tout Buckhead worships with regularity.

Seeger's (Contemporary)
An ocean liner–elegant interior, a 42-page wine list, and successions of dazzlingly beautiful small plates served with crisp precision make this one of the city's very top tables.

---

4 *h-7*

CANOE

When the weather's fine, sit out on the patio—probably the metro area's prettiest—by the banks of the Chattahoochee River. Inside or out, you can dine on south Georgia rock shrimp or lunch on a lamb sandwich on focaccia. Chef Gary Minnie knows how to roast a humble chicken, too. The menu changes seasonally, and Minnie prepares game superbly in the fall. The superior wine list offers unusual varietals, good reserve bottles, and many fine wines by the glass. *4199 Paces Ferry Rd., Vinings, 770/432–2663. Reservations essential. AE, D, DC, MC, V. $$–$$$*

15 *e-6*

CITY GRILL

The Hurt Building houses this posh business-lunch hot spot, which feels like a private club. Conventioneers often make up the dinner crowd, but getting a reservation for a quiet and unrushed meal in the absence of a convention isn't difficult. The menu always has certain Southern touches, such as quail, barbecue, fried green tomatoes, and crab cakes in some form or other. The cuisine also swings globally, with such dishes as cornmeal-fried veal sweetbreads and rack of lamb with preserved lemon. The grilled vegetable roulade is a great vegetarian option. The wine list is extensive, with many fine bottles and good choices by the glass. *50 Hurt Plaza, Downtown, 404/524–2489. Reservations essential. AE, D, DC, MC, V. Closed Sun. No lunch Sat. $$$$*

12 *h-2*

THE DINING ROOM, THE RITZ-CARLTON, BUCKHEAD

Long considered one of the city's top tables, the Dining Room has managed to hold its own even as competition for that status has grown. Dishes are exquisite, with a French pedigree and a trace of an Asian accent, which stems from chef Bruno Ménard's stint at the Ritz in Osaka, Japan. You can order from a set menu of seven courses, each paired with a glass of wine, or select from half a dozen choices for each of three courses. The setting extends the hotel's English–country house look, but in a light, flowery, trellised manner that suggests the conservatory of a great manor rather than a formal dining room. *3434 Peachtree Rd., Buckhead, 404/237–2700. Reservations essential. AE, D, DC, MC, V. $$$$*

5 *b-6*

HORSERADISH GRILL

Occupying a former horse barn, this supremely popular restaurant on the edge of Chastain Park has its up-to-the-minute concepts firmly rooted in authentic Southern dishes. Chef David Berry's South Carolina barbecue is right out of his dad's recipe book, but he piles it on a corn cake and tops it with coleslaw (the corn cake alludes to the hush puppies that Carolinians enjoy with their 'cue). Low-country shrimp and grits, fantastic fried chicken, quail, rabbit, and traditional Southern desserts highlight this constantly changing menu. The nearly all American wine list is extraordinarily comprehensive and offers good selections by the glass. *4320 Powers Ferry Rd., Buckhead, 404/255–7277. AE, D, DC, MC, V. $$–$$$*

12 *g-3*

MERITAGE

Minimal decor, well-spaced tables, and service that's calm, friendly, and professional make this a welcome respite from the more-buzzing Buckhead dining rooms. Tempura shrimp, as a starter, sit atop a mango-avocado salad doused with zingy, sweet-and-sour lemongrass dressing. Chicken breast is stuffed with black truffle and porcinis and served with asparagus polenta. The reverence for vegetables is impressive. The wine list is serious but accessible and amusingly organized ("light whites . . . grassy fields, cool breeze, just think Julie Andrews in lederhosen" is a category). *3125 Piedmont Rd., Buckhead, 404/231–6700. AE, D, DC, MC, V. Closed Mon. No lunch. $$–$$$*

12 *e-3*

SEEGER'S

Former Ritz-Carlton Buckhead chef Guenter Seeger creates exquisite, slightly edgy dishes in a striking, uncluttered former bungalow. He believes passionately in using the products of his adopted home state, so he pairs Geor-

gia shrimp with carrot cream and basil as well as Georgia fallow deer with beet–and–sweet potato gratin. Seeger's sequenced prix-fixe meals of three, five, or eight courses can be matched with the perfect wine for each. *111 W. Paces Ferry Rd., Buckhead, 404/846–9779. Reservations essential. AE, D, DC, MC, V. Closed Sun. No lunch. $$$$*

15 *e-2*

SOUTH CITY KITCHEN

Every day of the week, this art-filled, bright, high-energy place stays super-busy. Inspired by low-country cooking from the South Carolina and Georgia coasts, the kitchen turns out nifty versions of classic dishes, including a light but flavorful she-crab soup, fried green tomatoes, crab hash with poached eggs (a great brunch or lunch item), catfish Reuben sandwich (for lunch), and desserts that would bring Scarlett back to life, such as the chocolate pecan pie. The excellent, ever-evolving wine list has much to recommend it. *1144 Crescent Ave., between Peachtree and W. Peachtree Sts., Midtown, 404/873–7358. AE, D, DC, MC, V. $$–$$$*

15 *f-3*

SPICE

The kitchen at this see-and-be-seen scene seemed to have a revolving door in its early days, but the staff switches—and not-quite-reliable cooking—haven't dampened enthusiasm for the hot spot. The menu roams the globe, with choices such as wok-steamed mussels in hot chili–tea broth, a duck confit–and–scallion spring roll with raspberry sauce, and a "lemon assiette" of three delightful dessert treats. The skyline views from the stylishly redone 19th-century house are as fabulous as the people-watching. Too fabu *pour vous?* Come for Sunday brunch or drinks to limit your exposure. *793 Juniper St., Midtown, 404/875–4242. AE, DC, MC, V. No lunch Sat. $$–$$$*

CONTINENTAL

15 *f-4*

THE ABBEY

Stained-glass windows capture light beams and play them against walls and tablecloths in this dramatic space, which was once a church. In the choir loft, a harpist adds a celestial touch.

Equally heavenly are the foie gras, rabbit, fish, duck, and lamb that this restaurant—now more than three decades old—turns out. From time to time, game appears on the menu, which changes with seasonal rhythm. For vegetarians, there's a mille-feuille of vegetables in carrot-ginger broth. Older vintages dominate the wine list, but a good half-bottle selection, many reasonably priced bottles, and plenty of wines by the glass are included. *163 Ponce de Leon Ave., Midtown, 404/876–8532. Reservations essential. AE, D, DC, MC, V. No lunch. $$$–$$$$*

12 g-3
ANTHONY'S

Here in the antebellum Pope-Walton House, portraits of 19th-century dowagers haunt the walls of one of the 12 "dining" rooms; in another, lush romantic landscapes create a pastoral setting. Southern dishes add depth to a menu loaded with such Continental classics as chateaubriand for two. The bananas Foster deserve a try for dessert. The wine list focuses on American and French selections. *3109 Piedmont Rd., just south of Peachtree Rd., Buckhead, 404/262–7379. AE, D, DC, MC, V. Closed Sun. No lunch. $$–$$$$*

5 f-4
CHARDONNAY

The classic cuisine at this comfortable suburban spot is respectable. Sea bass, for instance, is sautéed with balsamic-soy-caper sauce and topped with shrimp; "Snapper Bayou" combines lump crabmeat with artichokes, peppers, and mushrooms in a lemon-butter sauce. Desserts are flambéed table side. The eclectic wine list ranges from moderately priced quaffs to rarities at upwards of $500 a bottle. *6325 Spalding Dr., at Holcomb Bridge Rd., Norcross, 770/263–0003. AE, D, MC, V. Closed Mon. No lunch Sat. $$–$$$*

5 h-2
KURT'S

The simple white frame structure, once a residence, seems out of place amid the surrounding business buildings. But Stuttgart native Kurt Eisele has made his restaurant an important part of the landscape with such dishes as snails baked in small potatoes and Hungarian goulash soup. Son Alexander, who has joined Kurt in the kitchen, makes superb

black-bean soup. Strudel is made on the premises, and bananas Foster are made at the table. Wines on the list represent numerous varietals and wine-growing regions, and are all priced at $23. *4225 River Green Pkwy., Duluth, 770/623–9413. AE, D, DC, MC, V. Closed Sun. No lunch Sat. $$–$$$*

5 e-4
NIKOLAI'S ROOF

One of Atlanta's truly world-class restaurants, Nikolai's, atop the Atlanta Hilton Hotel and Towers, has retained little of its former incarnation as a pseudo-Russian place complete with Cossack-garbed waiters. Today, mercifully, only the piroshki (meat-filled dumplings), caviar, blini, and similar menu items, along with the flavor-infused vodkas, reflect its past life. Chef Johannes Klapdohr concentrates on the classically French-Continental tradition, but the menu changes frequently. There are two seatings an evening, and the meal is a five-course fixed-price affair (caviar and other specialties are extra). Michel Granier keeps the fine wine list well tuned. *255 Courtland St., at Harris St., Downtown, 404/221–6362. Reservations essential. AE, D, DC, MC, V. Closed Sun. June–Aug. $$$$*

12 a-2
PANO'S & PAUL'S

The look at this special-occasion restaurant has been refreshed, but it's the classic fare that keeps drawing the crowds. Atlantans come to savor the deep-fried lobster tail served with honey mustard and drawn butter, as well as tasty preparations of foie gras, Dover sole, and sweetbreads. If all this seems rich, there's an option: "Trim Cuisine" is designed to keep the dining fine while observing dietary restrictions. The extensive wine list is administered by a sommelier who understands how to pair food and wine properly. *1232 W. Paces Ferry Rd., at Northside Dr., Buckhead, 404/261–3662. Reservations essential. AE, D, DC, MC, V. Closed Sun. No lunch. $$–$$$$*

9 a-6
PASCAL'S BISTRO

Hungry residents of the southside suburbs consider this a dining oasis. The friendly, competent servers (there's little turnover) in particular get high grades. The phyllo-wrapped Brie is a good starter; you can go on to have grilled filet mignon with a tamarind demi-glace, or shellfish with tomato sauce on linguine, and finish with honey apple tart. The luncheon buffet—of pasta, prepared to order—is a great value at $5.95. *Westpark Walk, 217 Commerce Dr., Peachtree City, 770/632–0112. AE, MC, V. Closed Sun. No lunch Sat. $$*

13 *e-6*
PETITE AUBERGE

For more than a quarter century, this neighborhood eatery in a busy but not elegant shopping mall has kept the locals well fed. Michael Gropp has the good sense to continue the family traditions his German-born parents inspired, changing the menu but not the focus on French bistro fare and German specialties. Excellent coq au vin, calves' sweetbreads in cognac cream, pork roasted in a beer sauce, smoked pork chops, and Wiener schnitzel are among the offerings. Game and other seasonal specials appear, too. *2935 N. Druid Hills Rd., Decatur, 404/634–6268. AE, D, DC, MC, V. Closed Sun. No lunch Sat. $$–$$$*

5 *f-4*
RESTO NAX

It may come off looking like a fern bar, but this suburban shopping-strip spot is surprisingly good, and the culinary offerings are more serious than the surroundings suggest. Swiss-born owner André Constantin can be cajoled into making special Swiss dishes for gatherings in the private dining room. Unfortunately, they're not on the menu, but good salmon, duck, and pasta dishes are. The mostly California wine list is quite serviceable. *6025 Peachtree Pkwy., Norcross, 770/416–9665. AE, D, DC, MC, V. Closed Sun. $$–$$$*

7 *d-8*
TEN EAST WASHINGTON

Although not within the 10-county metro area, this comfortable, casual establishment about 30 mi from Downtown warrants more than a blip on your radar screen. The location, in a historic storefront in downtown Newnan, gives it charm and makes a trip here a special excursion. The Continental cuisine includes crab cakes, lamb, fish, and excellent crème caramel (but ask for it sans the whipped cream and other needless garnishes). Beer and wine are available, and while the wine list isn't huge, it's decent. *10 E. Washington St., Newnan, 770/502–9100. AE, MC, V. Closed Sun. No lunch. $$–$$$*

CUBAN

12 *h-5*
COCO LOCO

With a firm foothold in the Spanish roots of Cuban cooking, this popular restaurant does a good job with such traditional fare as roast pork, black beans, and paella (which comes in a "big" version for at least two that requires extra prep time and a fast version you can order on the spot). Cuban sandwiches, especially the *Medianoche* (literally, midnight)—a ham-and-cheese version, on a sweetbread—are super. The wine list focuses on South American and Spanish wines, and the house make its own sangria. *Buckhead Crossing shopping center, 2625 Piedmont Rd., at Sidney Marcus Blvd., Buckhead, 404/364–0212. AE, D, DC, MC, V. $–$$*

4 *h-5*
CRAZY CUBAN

From a storefront in a suburban shopping mall, María Arce dishes up homestyle Cuban cooking. *Croquetas* (oblong croquettes made with ham or chicken and deep-fried) and empanadas make good starters, as do the *papas rellenas* (potato puffs) filled with seasoned meat and fried. Dinner options include such classics from the Spanish-Cuban kitchen as *ropa vieja* (shredded beef with tomatoes and onions) and *lechón asado* (roast pork that's been marinated in garlic-flecked mojo sauce). The house-made sangria is the beverage of choice. *1475 Terrell Mill Rd., Marietta, 770/226–0021. Reservations not accepted. AE, D, DC, MC, V. Closed Sun. $–$$*

5 *d-8*
HAVANA SANDWICH SHOP

Three generations of the Benedit family, originally from Cuba, run this operation, turning out very good black-bean soup, Medianoche sandwiches, grilled pork plates, *picadillo* (ground meat with tomatoes and spices), and, for dessert, flan and rice pudding—all made on the premises. Vegetarian offerings include empanadas with mushroom, onions, and peppers (the meat version is here, too). *2905 Buford Hwy., Northeast Atlanta, 404/636–4094. Reservations not accepted. No credit cards. $*

15 f-3

LAS PALMERAS

The cooking at this hidden neighborhood gem is mostly authentic home-style Cuban, with the addition of a few good quesadillas and burritos, in deference to the American preference for such dishes. The Cuban-style fried chicken, yucca with mojo, soup, chicken breast in salsa, chorizo-stuffed *boliche* (eye of round), house-made flan, and rice with milk are all the real thing. Alcohol isn't served, but you may bring your own or buy wine and beer at the adjoining grocery store (no corkage fee). *368 5th St., Midtown, 404/872–0846. Reservations not accepted. AE, MC, V. BYOB. Closed Sun.–Mon. $–$$*

14 a-1

MAMBO

Cuban natives Lucy Alvarez and her husband, Hilton Joseph, give their food a salsa flair, with such specials as "firecracker" steak, stuffed with chilies; paella; and black paella. Spanish, Chilean, Argentinian, and Californian wine selections are all available by the glass. *1402 N. Highland Ave., Virginia-Highland, 404/876–2626. AE, D, DC, MC, V. No lunch Sat. $$*

DELICATESSENS

13 e-6

BAGEL PALACE

For breakfast, fans fill this popular bagel bakery and deli, which opens at 6:30 AM and on weekends sells the *New York Times.* House-made spreads include superior chopped liver and assorted flavored cream cheeses. Snag a square of the dense and moist crumb cake when it's available. Lunch consists of classic deli sandwiches, grill items, and salads. *Toco Hills shopping center, 2869 N. Druid Hills Rd., Northeast Atlanta, 404/315–9016. Reservations not accepted. D, DC, MC, V. No dinner. $*

5 f-6

BALDINO'S GIANT JERSEY SUBS

Patrons line up daily for terrific sub sandwiches, made to order on good bread baked on the premises. They really are "giant," so consider getting half a sandwich. The Marietta location has an all-you-can-eat pasta bar, for only $2.99. The place is open daily 10:30–10.

5697 Buford Hwy., Doraville, 770/455–8570. Reservations not accepted. No credit cards. Wine and beer only. $

4 h-5

Harry's Crossing shopping center, 80 Powers Ferry Rd., Marietta, 770/321–1177. MC, V.

5 d-4

E. 48TH STREET ITALIAN MARKET

A shaded patio and a few tables in the store are the only dining accommodations, but the selection of eat-in and take-out fare makes this one of Atlanta's culinary treasures. Deli meats, such prepared dishes as pasta and eggplant Parmesan, cold mixed greens, espresso, and house-made Italian breads and pastries including biscotti and cookies are all fantastic. The selection of Italian beers and wines is limited but well chosen. The place stays open until 7 PM on weekdays and 6 on Saturday. *Williamsburg at Dunwoody shopping center, 2462 Jett Ferry Rd., Dunwoody, 770/392–1499. No credit cards. Closed Sun. $*

5 b-7

GOLDBERG'S

The knishes, brisket, stuffed cabbage, chopped liver, and even the bagels and breads are made in house. Still, the management has the good sense to import the best from other cities: hot dogs from Chicago, smoked sturgeon and whitefish from New York, corned beef and pastrami from New York *and* Chicago. Table seating is limited. The place stays open until 5 PM Monday through Saturday, until 3 on Sunday. *4383 Roswell Rd., Sandy Springs, 404/256–3751. AE, MC, V. $–$$*

5 d-8

Georgetown shopping center, 4520 Chamblee-Dunwoody Rd., Dunwoody, 770/455–1119.

12 a-2

West Paces Ferry shopping center, 1272 W. Paces Ferry Rd., Buckhead, 404/266–0123.

15 f-6

SALUMERIA TAGGIASCA

Tucked among the Sweet Auburn Curb Market purveyors of fish, produce, and such Southern butcher-shop items as chitterlings is this amazing Italian deli. Cheeses, dry pastas, oils, deli meats, olives, cookies, even truffled honey—everything is imported from Italy. But you can also grab a bite to eat here, putting together a made-to-order sandwich on the locally unsurpassed Bread Garden breads with anything in the deli case. You can park yourself to eat it at one of the few picnic tables near the renovated old municipal market hall. *Sweet Auburn Curb Market, 209 Edgewood Ave., Downtown, 404/524–0006. AE, MC, V. Closed Sun.* $

14 *g-3*

SONNY'S ON PONCE

This Jewish-style deli has the one classic ingredient usually missing these days: a big-mouthed proprietor with personality. Eat here once and Sonny is your friend for life. Hummus, shwarma (here it's sliced grilled turkey), falafel, and other Middle Eastern treats join such deli standards as pastrami, corned beef, salami, and other sandwiches; good slaw and redskin-potato salad; and sweet-and-sour meat-stuffed cabbage (for lunch or dinner). Sonny can't let you go away hungry, so the plates are piled high. *265 Ponce de Leon Pl., Decatur, 404/687–8881. AE, MC, V.* $

ECLECTIC

15 *g-3*

APRÈS DIEM

A featureless shopping center may seem an odd place for an eatery with this much personality—but, hey, it's Midtown, and the district's diverse populace makes tracks here for the bars (liquor and espresso), the cosmopolitan atmosphere, and the slightly wacky French–North African menu. A pasta with vegetables and salmon has a heady cream sauce laced with sambuca and thyme. Dried-fruit salad—field greens with dried cranberries, banana chips, shredded coconut, raisins, feta; and a honey-apple dressing—sounds over-the-top but makes a satisfying lunch. When the weather's cool, the well-sheltered terrace, which faces southwest, is a pleasant spot. *Midtown Promenade, 931 Monroe Dr., Midtown, 404/872–3333. AE, D, MC, V.* $–$$

12 *g-3*

ARIA

Beyond a curtain of silver metal beads is a stunningly beautiful minimalist space in shades of white. The luxurious comfort food crosses culinary cultural lines: seared pepper-crusted ahi tuna with ponzu sauce; rabbit and handmade penne pasta; meltingly tender pork that's been braised in balsamic vinegar. The desserts have flavor and flair. They change often but you might find, for example, a crème caramel with toasted coconut curls springing from its gleaming surface. *490 E. Paces Ferry Rd., Buckhead, 404/233–7673. AE, D, DC, MC, V. Closed Sun. No lunch.* $$–$$$

5 *d-7*

BAJARITO'S

The tortilla swings between simple and exotic fare with fillings as basic as shrimp or as complex as Thai curry peanut chicken and blackened salmon fillet. Regional flavors at this casual spot include barbecue and jerked chicken. For salad wraps, there's a Greek version with feta and olives. Black-and-tan beans and grilled Mediterranean veggies are good vegetarian choices. Limited alcohol is served. *Cherokee Plaza, 3877 Peachtree Rd., Brookhaven, 404/239–9727. AE, MC, V.* $

12 *h-2*

BLUEPOINTE

Soaring ceilings and abundant windows, softened with long sheers and panels that suggest shoji screens, supply the drama in this sophisticated space. The menu ranges from impeccable raw oysters to wood-grilled calamari with shiitake mushrooms and asparagus, and grilled rare duck breast with Thai-style red curry; braised beef short ribs come with a savory-sweet corn mash. The wine list presents a range of mostly American picks, with a fair by-the-glass list. *Pinnacle Building, 3455 Peachtree Rd., Buckhead, 404/237–9070. Reservations essential. AE, D, DC, MC, V. No lunch weekends.* $$$$

12 *f-3*

CAFÉ TU TU TANGO

Here's the ideal spot for an after-shopping perk-up or a talk-until-midnight date. But you can also bring the gang for rounds of tapas, or let the kids assemble their own pizzas and watch them bake in the wood-fired oven. Good house-made sangria comes both red and white; wines and beers are also available. The upper level hosts art exhibitions, so it's fitting that it resembles an artist's garret. *East Village Square, 220 Pharr Rd., Buckhead, 404/841–6222.*

Reservations not accepted. AE, DC, MC, V. $–$$

15 e-2

CHERRY

Wide-open spaces and lush textures and patterns have transformed this big old foursquare Victorian house into one of the most original dining designs in the metro area. Young folks from the nearby Midtown business towers fill the downstairs bar area for the happy-hour scene; upstairs, the dining room includes a sushi bar, and there's a shady outdoor deck with sunset views. The food—Japanese-inspired noodle recipes, South Asian fish dishes with lime and lemongrass, Latin American *churrascaria*, and such American comfort classics as pork chops and roast chicken—touches the four corners. *1051 W. Peachtree St., Midtown, 404/872–2020. AE, D, DC, MC, V. No lunch weekends. $$–$$$*

14 a-3

DISH

Once upon a time, this brick building on a busy corner housed a gas station. These days it's a popular restaurant with a neighborhood following that favors the large, covered street-side patio. Asian touches and Italian concepts coexist on the menu, where lobster and shiitake ravioli with pea shoots and ginger sauce claim a place next to molasses-roasted chicken with pappardelle. It's cooking that's both up-to-date and healthful. The wine list features interesting selections at very good prices, with many by-the-glass choices among them. *870 N. Highland Ave., Virginia-Highland, 404/897–3463. AE, DC, MC, V. No lunch. $$–$$$*

13 b-7

FLOATAWAY CAFE

Anne Quatrano of the Bacchanalia team and her partner, Clifford Harrison, staked out this territory in a funky warehouse district. The hard surfaces and high ceilings make for a rather noisy environment, but the food is completely worthwhile. Passionate about quality, Quatrano has sources for organically grown figs, tiny beets, and Georgia white shrimp. The menu responds to the seasons as a result but always offers pasta and pizza, intriguing salads, fresh fish, farmstead cheeses, and well-crafted desserts. The wine list offers unusual selections, all of which

do justice to the food. *1123 Zonolite Rd., near Johnson and Briarcliff Rds., Northeast Atlanta, 404/892–1414. Reservations essential. AE, DC, MC, V. Closed Sun.–Mon. No lunch. $$–$$$*

14 a-3

HARVEST

Occupying a former residence, Harvest invites the neighbors in for such Mediterranean-inspired dishes as ample, hearty cassoulet, as well as for Manhattan seafood chowder and maple-smoked and grilled pork chops. Creative vegetarian dishes are a house specialty, and Harvest is also known for its Sunday brunch, when low-country grits with shrimp, pork, and biscuits as well as Norwegian scramble with smoked salmon appear on the menu. *885 N. Highland Ave., Virginia-Highland, 404/876–8244. AE, D, DC, MC, V. No lunch weekends. $$–$$$*

15 e-6

MUMBO JUMBO

With a big bar scene and an upstairs dance floor, these environs can be noisy, but the food is marvelous and full of surprises. Chef Shawn Doty has been known to travel to his native southwest Virginia and come back with ramps (a kind of wild, garlicky leek), serving them with soft-shell crab for a special regional-taste sensation. The famous "Mumbo Gumbo" is lighter than most but just as flavorful. *89 Park Pl., near Woodruff Park, Downtown, 404/523–0330. Reservations essential. AE, D, DC, MC, V. No lunch weekends. $$–$$$*

7 f-6

OSCAR'S

In the shadow of Hartsfield Airport, this is the only stylish contemporary restaurant on the south side of town. White canvas–cloaked couches in the bar area, blond-wood furniture, and modernist flatware and table settings jazz up the old brick storefront. The kitchen is strongly influenced by Mediterranean tastes, but it also draws heavily on American boutique ingredients and Southern traditions. Roasted organic chicken, for instance, comes with grits, country ham, and turnip greens; sautéed fresh artichoke hearts, fennel, garlic, capers, and an intense veal reduction dress sea bass. *3725 Main St., College Park, 404/766–9688. AE, D, MC, V. Closed Sun. No lunch Sat. $$–$$$*

`15` *e-2*

PARK 75

In this spacious, elegant, and somewhat formal hotel dining room, chef Brooke Vosika offers a menu rooted in exceptional American ingredients, such as limited-production cheeses. Presentations are dramatic, and the kitchen's touch is deft. Squab, fish, steak, and lamb all are distinctive, as is the Sunday dim sum–style brunch, at which you stay put while a succession of small plates, concocted of rarefied ingredients, is brought to you. The wine list is well assembled; its final page, Last Chances, showcases unusual selections at good prices. *Four Seasons Atlanta Hotel, 75 14th St., Midtown, 404/881–9898. AE, D, DC, MC, V. $$$–$$$$*

`15` *d-5*

PRIME MERIDIAN

The Omni Hotel's dining room overlooks Centennial Olympic Park toward the downtown skyline—one of the city's most dazzling views. It gathers its culinary inspiration from around the world: Thai flavors, with ginger and lime, spike the chicken salad; creamy cèpes risotto and pancetta add a taste of Sicily to the veal chop; chestnut-chanterelle strudel and pickled Asian plums accompany the venison medallions. For lunch, pizzas emerge from a wood-burning oven, and main-course offerings lean toward stir-fries and pastas; the buffet is several cuts above your typical self-service. Breakfast includes Southern-style fare with biscuits, red-eye gravy, and grits. *Omni Hotel, 100 CNN Center, Downtown, 404/659–0000. AE, D, DC, MC, V. $$–$$$*

`7` *f-7*

SHOWCASE EATERY

This rare southside restaurant of originality and character inspires its regulars to put up with so-so service and offers live music on weekend evenings. Trombones hang from the rafters, and walls are dotted with African statuary and masks, posters of jazz stars, and old piano parts. Seafood plays a big role on the menu, which includes Caribbean fish and chicken, and champagne shrimp and mushroom linguine. Red-velvet cake, a Southern classic, is on the desserts list. *5549 Old National Hwy., College Park, 404/669–0504. AE, D, DC, MC, V. Closed Mon. $$–$$$*

`14` *a-3*

STAR

In its previous incarnation, this Texas-theme, rather corporate-feeling place for steaks and barbecue was the Indigo Coastal Grill, a longtime favorite. But following the transformation, Indigo patrons stayed away—until the owner started putting their favorites on the Star menu. It now includes those dishes, which lay Caribbean and Southwestern flavors on the freshest seafood. *1307 N. Highland Ave., Virginia-Highland/Morningside, 404/876–0676. AE, D, MC, V. No lunch. $$*

`14` *f-3*

THE SUPPER CLUB

For romance on a budget, try this funkily charming spot where gauzy hangings separate intimate seating areas. The food is sort of French, sort of Mexican. Taking advantage of what's available in the markets, the kitchen offers a wide variety of dishes that may range from an excellent oyster bisque to organic filet mignon with Gorgonzola grits. The wine tilts to thoughtfully selected California and Italian selections. Smoking isn't allowed until 10 PM. *308 W. Ponce de Leon Ave., Decatur, 404/370–1207. Reservations essential. AE, MC, V. Closed Sun.–Mon. $$–$$$*

`14` *a-2*

TIBURON GRILLE

Intriguing modern art hangs on the rough walls in the warmly lit dining room of this popular neighborhood bistro, which has hit its stride; the patio is strung with baskets of coleus and cooled by slowly twirling fans. Grilled asparagus with a peanut-based dipping sauce and good micro greens makes a perfect first course. Portion sizes are just right, to be followed by such choices as ostrich or veal tenderloin wrapped in Serrano ham. The selection of delectable desserts varies, depending on what the kitchen's made on any given day. The wine list changes often, like the menu, and has good items by the glass. *1190 N. Highland Ave., at Amsterdam Ave., behind U.S. Post Office, Virginia-Highland, 404/892–2393. Reservations essential. AE, D, MC, V. No lunch. $$–$$$*

12 *h-2*

TOMTOM, A BISTRO

Lively, art-filled, and fun, TomTom presents Asian and Southwestern fare mingled with good old-fashioned American cooking. You can have sushi, a deep-fried whole catfish with Asian seasonings, a pizza, or roast chicken or lamb with mashed potatoes. The wine list has good choices that support the eclectic menu and are reasonably priced. *Lenox Square, 3393 Peachtree Rd., Buckhead, 404/264–1163. Reservations not accepted. AE, D, DC, MC, V. $$*

12 *e-6*

TOULOUSE

At the back of a small strip center, this place started off as a French restaurant (hence the name) but slowly evolved into an American restaurant with French-accented dishes. Expect to find goat cheese in your salad and tarragon on your chicken, but you can also get good buffalo meat loaf and a hearty potato soup here. The menu includes wine recommendations for each entrée, and owner George Tice is a passionate teacher who often encourages patrons to experiment with food-wine pairings. Except for the outside patio, the restaurant is entirely no-smoking. *2293 Peachtree Rd., Buckhead, 404/351–9533. Reservations essential. AE, D, DC, MC, V. No lunch. $$–$$$*

15 *h-6*

VIRGINIA'S

You enter this slightly arrhythmic heart of the Stoveworks—an old but now stylish factory—through a well-sheltered dining terrace that leads into a soaring, two-level industrial space adorned with an enormous collection of yard-sale oil paintings and big modernist lanterns. The kitchen is like a hip-hop record producer, sampling from here and there with abandon, with dishes ranging from Hungarian mushroom soup, quesadillas, and French country pâté to satay and *gado gado* (a spicy peanut sauce) from South Asia and a vegetable version of beef Wellington. *112 Krog St., Inman Park, 404/827–9005. AE, D, MC, V. No lunch, no dinner Sun. $$*

ENGLISH

15 *f-2*

PRINCE OF WALES

Homesick Britons take comfort in this warmly lit authentic-style English pub filled with soccer trophies. The fare is the real thing, from the very good fish-and-chips to the shepherd's pie (made with beef) and the bread pudding. The 10 quaffs on tap include Strongbow Cider, otherwise hard to come by. The Sunday brunch special—a basic English breakfast, here called the "Union Jack," of two eggs, fried bread, Irish bacon and baked beans, grilled tomato, mushrooms, chips, and Scottish bangers—could keep you going all week. *1144 Piedmont Ave., Midtown, 404/876–0227. Reservations not accepted. AE, D, DC, MC, V. $–$$*

4 *h-6*

SOHO

Chef Joe Ahn manages to blend the flavors of the Southwest with those of Asia. The chicken tortilla soup is a

---

SPECIAL DATES

Whether you want to pop the question, mark an anniversary, or just get away from the kids for an evening, here are some places to enjoy a private moment.

The Abbey (Continental)
An intimate table in the corner of a former church. A harpist plucking her strings in the choir loft. Ambrosia on the plate. Who wouldn't say, "Yes"?

Meritage (Contemporary)
The cozy rooms of this former house have well-spaced tables; the service is perfectly unobtrusive; and the California-style cooking is a treat for all the senses.

The Supper Club (Eclectic)
Gauze-draped nooks and alcoves are nearly private in this dimly lighted spot. The cooking, the handwritten wine list, and the hand-dipped chocolate truffles are all labors of love.

Toulouse (Eclectic)
A wood-burning fireplace, a serious wine list, and comforting bistro cooking make this a favorite date destination.

Van Gogh's (American)
Some of the very best food north of the Perimeter, plus a classy and art-filled series of rooms, makes this the right choice for that special dinner.

Yucatecan classic, your basic *sopa de lima* with avocado, chili, and lime. Salmon is wrapped in rice paper and served with Thai pesto (a lemongrass, cilantro, basil, and mint pesto with crushed peanuts and Thai chilies), ponzu sauce, and rice. There are lots of good wines by the glass, and the list is constantly updated and enhanced. *Vinings Jubilee shopping center, 4200 Paces Ferry Rd., Vinings, 770/801–0069. AE, D, DC, MC, V. No lunch weekends. $$–$$$*

ETHIOPIAN

13 *c-3*

ETHIOPIAN ABBAY RESTAURANT

The dark yet welcoming shopping-center restaurant is a second home to Atlanta's growing Ethiopian community. Instead of using flatware, you tear off pieces of *enjera*—the traditional, slightly spongy flat bread—with which you scoop up mouthfuls of such preparations as spicy lemon chicken with boiled egg and lentil- and greens-based vegetarian dishes. Beer is the best match for this food. *Northeast Plaza shopping center, 3375 Buford Hwy., Northeast Atlanta, 404/321–5808. AE, D, DC, MC, V. $–$$*

13 *c-5*

QUEEN OF SHEBA

A full range of Ethiopian classics is served here, beginning with the traditional, lentil-stuffed turnovers called *sanbussas* and moving on to spicy beef, chicken, lamb, and vegetarian dishes. The staff is happy to guide patrons with gentle palates away from the hottest dishes. There's a full bar, but beer is the best beverage with this fare. *1594 Woodcliff Dr., near the intersection of Briarcliff and N. Druid Hills Rds., Northeast Atlanta, 404/321–1493. AE, MC, V. $–$$*

FRENCH

12 *g-2*

ANIS

Southern France comes to Atlanta in such dishes as fish stews, grilled pork chop with figs, roast chicken with cèpes, mussels, Provençale grilled vegetables, and tuna Niçoise. The list of French wines is excellent, and there's really good espresso. In addition, Anis pours some of the best iced tea in town. *2974 Grandview Ave., Buckhead, 404/233–9889. AE, D, DC, MC, V. No lunch Sun. $$*

14 *h-4*

ATLANTIC STAR

The vast series of spaces occupied by Atlantic Star is in an old ice-house building that's been converted to loft apartments. The long, low tiled bar area—where a raw bar showcases stone crab claws, cold-water oysters from both coasts, and a daily changing ceviche—is intimate and inviting. The cooking blends a strong interest in seafood with a contemporary French sensibility. Seared salmon on a bed of lentils mixed with crisp lardons and laced with white-truffle oil, and duck breast and wild mushrooms with braised parsnips and lavender honey are among the stellar entrées. *105 Sycamore Pl., Decatur, 404/377–8384. AE, MC, V. $–$$*

14 *a-5*

BANG

By far the most sophisticated space in this funkadelic neighborhood, Bang serves contemporary French cuisine in a sleekly simple redone storefront. The proprietors came from long years at the late, and much missed, Indigo Coastal Grill. Here, "pastrami-cured" tuna carpaccio with two different house-made mustards is a stellar starter, which you might follow with a classic cassoulet, or grilled duck breast with buckwheat–and–wild mushroom pancakes. *1126 Euclid Ave., Little Five Points, 404/223–5039. AE, D, MC, V. No dinner Sun.–Mon., no lunch weekdays. $$*

12 *h-2*

BRASSERIE LE COZE

The late Gilbert Le Coze and his sister Maguey, owners of Le Bernardin in New York, launched this casual, gaslight era–style bistro in Atlanta and watched its popularity grow and grow. The French fare is beautifully executed, from the white-bean soup laced with truffle oil and glorious mussels to skate wing in brown butter–caper sauce and classic crème brûlée for dessert. The wine list is French and American and offers many good by-the-glass choices. *Lenox Square, 3393 Peachtree Rd., Buckhead, 404/266–1440. AE, D, MC, V. Closed Sun. $$–$$$*

14 g-3
CAFÉ ALSACE
The hearty home-style fare here includes the inevitable (but here better than most) quiche Lorraine, but the *tarte à l'oignon* (onion tart) is the tastier choice. The meal may well move on to a very good coq au vin and end with a tart Tatin. The restaurant makes yeoman efforts to include well-priced Alsatian wines and beers on the beverage list. *121 E. Ponce de Leon Ave., Decatur, 404/373–5622. Reservations not accepted. AE, D, DC, MC, V. Closed Mon. No lunch Sat., no dinner Sun. $$*

FLEUR-DE-LIS
In this cool, bright dining room at the Spa at Château Élan, you can get around fat, sodium, cholesterol, and calories three meals a day without feeling deprived. So, you can lunch guiltlessly on ginger-marinated shrimp salad with ponzu vinaigrette, and at dinner dine on a duo of ostrich fillet and buffalo tenderloin. This is dieting? Château Élan wines are paired with the dishes. *Spa at Château Élan, 100 Tour de France, Braselton, 687/425–0900. Reservations essential. AE, D, DC, MC, V. No dinner Sun.–Tues. $$*

LE CLOS AT CHÂTEAU ÉLAN
Georgia's largest winery has several dining operations, one of which is this formal (bring your jackets, guys) dining room in the winery's chateauesque modern main building. Classic Continental and French dishes appear on the ever-changing menu, which may include butter-poached lobster with Israeli couscous, pan-seared red snapper with saffron-crawfish sauce and fingerling potato salad, or yellow gazpacho with house-smoked trout. Seven- and eight-course fixed-price dinners are paired with Château Élan wines. *Château Élan, 100 Tour de France, Braselton, 678/425–0900. Reservations essential. AE, D, DC, MC, V. Closed Sun.–Tues. No lunch. $$$$*

14 f-1
LE GIVERNY
Demand for Rémy and Milena Kerba's place has grown, so they expanded the space. But the food continues to maintain the same high standards it always has, from the rich, densely textured country pâté to the freshest fish. The wine list consists of excellent and very affordable bottles. *1355 Clairmont Rd., Decatur, 404/325–7252. AE, D, DC, MC, V. Closed Sun. No lunch Sat. $$*

4 h-4
PROVENCE
Classic French dishes from the bistro tradition are what this place does: salad with lardons (here they are crisped duck cracklings), ratatouille, steamed mussels with garlic-wine sauce, excellent fish and shellfish, and, occasionally as a special, frogs' legs with mushrooms, garlic, parsley, cream, and Calvados. Chocolate mousse and crème brûlée are the desserts to set your sights on. The wine list is entirely French. Reservations aren't taken for weekend breakfast or brunch. *4655 Lower Roswell Rd., Marietta, 770/321–5442. AE, D, DC, MC, V. Closed Mon. $$–$$$*

12 g-3
SOLEIL
Diners eager to enjoy a taste of life in a relaxed, sun-drenched part of the world throng to this former residence. The simple *grillade* and bistro dishes are well prepared, from a duck and chicken salad with lavender honey (what could be more Provençal?) to orange-glazed duck breast and coq au vin. Roast pork tenderloin with whole-grain mustard sauce is singularly tasty. The wine list packs a fair punch, with good bottles under $30 dominating the selection, and lots of them by the glass. *3081 Maple Dr., Buckhead, 404/467–1790. AE, D, DC, MC, V. $$*

13 e-3
VIOLETTE
Guy Luc, from Alsace, presents the dishes of his native land in this northeast neighborhood, where he's become a fixture. Lunch is on the order of quiche and salad; the dinner menu includes well-prepared monkfish and salmon and steaks, served au poivre or with Roquefort sauce. The wine list includes many excellent bottles at good prices. *2948 Clairmont Rd., Northeast Atlanta, 404/633–3363. AE, D, DC, MC, V. Closed Sun. No lunch Sat. $$*

GERMAN

8 *e-1*

BASKET BAKERY & CAFÉ AT THE VILLAGE CORNER

A combination bakery and restaurant, the Basket fills with yeasty aromas that may well tempt you into taking home a loaf of bread and the white chocolate chunk–macadamia nut cookies. Come for breakfast, lunch, or the popular Sunday brunch. If you stick around for dinner, you can enjoy such German specialties as sausages, schnitzels, sauerbraten, and spaetzle or Continental classics. On the second weekend of the month, local vocalist Lenny Stabile does his rendition of Frank Sinatra standards in the tavern to the rear. *6655 James Rivers Dr., Stone Mountain, 770/ 498–0329. AE, D, DC, MC, V. Closed Mon. $$*

5 *h-2*

VRENY'S BIERGARTEN

While Vreny Eisele's husband, Kurt, ably runs his eponymous restaurant up front, she oversees less formal surroundings and serves old-style German dishes. Her perennially popular standards include sauerbraten, beef rouladen, roast pork knuckle, spaetzle with black-forest ham and mushrooms, sausages, and *maultaschen* (a kind of ravioli). German wines and beers are the beverages of choice. *4225 River Green Pkwy., Duluth, 770/623–9413. AE, D, DC, MC, V. Closed Sun.–Mon. No lunch. $–$$*

GREEK

14 *f-1*

ATHENS PIZZA HOUSE

Greek-style pizza, with its thicker crust, is the draw here, but Greek specialties, such as moussaka and pastitsio, are also available. In fact, the Duluth location is called Athens Pizza Kouzzina, which means kitchen, because it offers an expanded menu with a lot more Greek dishes on the menu, such as lamb shank and eggplant with linguine. Wine and beer, including some Greek choices, are served. *1341 Clairmont Rd., Decatur, 404/ 636–1100. AE, D, DC, MC, V. $*

5 *h-5*

Pleasant Hill Square shopping center, 2205 Pleasant Hill Rd., Duluth, 770/813–1369.

7 *g-5*

GRECIAN GYRO

Nick Loulouris makes it his business to serve good, inexpensive food made in the traditional way, and he succeeds. His potato salad with homemade sauce, served with all gyros, as well as the souvlaki, chicken on pita bread, and other standards—including homemade baklava—draw raves. *855 Virginia Ave., Hapeville, 404/762–1627. Reservations not accepted. No credit cards. No alcohol. Closed weekends. $*

5 *h-7*

KALAMATA GREEK RESTAURANT & PIZZA

The building looks as though it once held a fast-food operation, but the animated patrons and the excellent cuisine more than compensate for any lack of physical charm. Octopus is seasoned with spices and char-grilled, with marinara sauce on the side; other Greek specialties include flaming cheese, spinach pie, moussaka, and baked custard with phyllo. The wine list is strongly oriented toward Greek choices. *4075 Lawrenceville Hwy., Lilburn, 770/935–9990. AE, D, MC, V. $–$$*

INDIAN

13 *c-5*

CHAT PATTI

Vegetarian dishes are the specialty at this no-frills, self-service restaurant; you won't miss the meat once you discover what assertive seasoning can do for potatoes and chickpeas. The lentil soup is delicious. *Dosai* is a crispy rice pancake filled with potatoes, onions, and lentils. *1594 Woodcliff Dr., at intersection of N. Druid Hills and Briarcliff Rds., Northeast Atlanta, 404/633–5595. MC, V. No alcohol. Closed Mon. $*

15 *e-5*

HAVELI

Many Atlantans know and enjoy Haveli, one of the metro area's first Indian restaurants, and they evidently feel very comfortable with such offerings as tandoori meats, curries, and *saag paneer* (sautéed spinach with homemade Indian cheese). Many of these appear on the lunch buffet, which is popular with businesspeople. *Gift Mart, 225 Spring St., Downtown, 404/522–4545.*

Reservations not accepted. AE, D, DC, MC, V. No lunch Sun. $–$$

 4 *f-4*

490 Franklin Rd., Marietta, 770/955–4525.

5 *e-6*

HIMALAYAS

After more than a decade at the same location, Himalayas remains a star among the city's Indian restaurants. It's filled with draped booths, Indian handicrafts, and photographs of long-ago emperors. The onion *bhajee* (deep-fried onion balls) are singularly crisp and sweet tasting here; the tandoori chicken is tender and mildly spicy; and the *chana masala*, a spicy chickpea dish, is unusually long on flavor. There's even a good wine list with gewürztraminer—the ideal wine for Indian food. *Chamblee Plaza, 5520 Peachtree Industrial Blvd., Chamblee, 770/458–6557. AE, D, DC, MC, V. $*

5 *f-7*

MAHARAJAH

South Indian cuisine is the focus here, and that means a focus on vegetarian dishes. If you crave meat, try one of the chicken dishes cooked in the tandoor oven. And whatever you have, accompany your meal with one of the delicious breads baked on the premises. Vegetarian and nonvegetarian dinners for two are an especially good bargain. *3900 LaVista Rd., Northlake, 770/414–1010. AE, D, DC, MC, V. $–$$*

6 *a-4*

POONA

Fine Indian art adorns the quiet and serene dining room—just the setting for relaxing and enjoying excellent lamb dishes (the lamb vindaloo is especially tasty), chicken tikka, and vegetarian preparations. The lunch buffet is substantial and very fairly priced, and the wine list is decent. *Wal-Mart shopping center, 1630 Pleasant Hill Rd., Duluth, 770/717–1053. AE, D, DC, MC, V. $–$$*

12 *e-4*

RAJAH

Buckhead has seen numerous changes over the past two decades, but one constant has been this tiny restaurant. The tandoor (clay oven) is used not only to bake the tender marinated chicken but

also to turn out numerous specialty Indian breads. Weekday lunch is a fantastic bargain, about $6. *2955 Peachtree Rd., Buckhead, 404/237–2661. AE, MC, V. Wine and beer only. No lunch Sun. $–$$*

5 *f-6*

SHINGAAR PALACE

The wonderfully cartoony Indian paintings on the walls are easy on the eye, and the food is heaven on the tongue. First arrives bread, wafer-thin *papadum*, and a trio of condiments, earthy-sweet tamarind sauce and fiery red-onion and green-mint chutneys. Dishes include *paneer pakoras*, patties of cottage cheese and pureed chickpea that have a yummy chewiness inside their crust; chicken tikka, with skinless chunks of marinated meat roasted in a charcoal-fired tandoor oven; and seekh kebabs, little torpedos of marvelously spiced ground lamb. *3364-H Chamblee-Tucker Rd., Chamblee, 770/458–4466. AE, D, MC, V. $–$$*

14 *h-1*

UDIPI CAFE

The huge space here almost seems like an institutional dining hall, but it's usually filled with Indian families enjoying south Indian vegetarian specialties that range from vegetable samosas to thin rice crepes with vegetables (called *dosai*) to rice specialties, called *pullavs*, that combine lentils and rice. The dinner specials assemble a variety of these dishes to provide newcomers with a tasty introduction to Indian cuisine. Reservations aren't taken for weekends. *1850 Lawrenceville Hwy., Decatur, 404/325–1933. MC, V. No alcohol. No smoking. $*

14 *h-1*

ZYKA

Cavernous Zyka is short on atmosphere but, with each dish costing $5 or less, very long on value. North Indian *chana masala*, a dish of cooked chickpeas and spicy tomatoes, makes a superfast lunch. Goat meat simmered with tomatoes and fennel and tandoori chicken so tender it's called "butter chicken" provide exotic antidotes to snack attacks. Continuous service from noon to late at night (midnight on Friday and Saturday) is available. *1677 Scott Blvd., Decatur, 404/728–4444. Reservations not accepted. AE, D, DC, MC, V. Closed Mon. $*

IRISH

12 f-3
FADÓ

The kitchen of this dark-paneled bar, popular with the Buckhead office crowd for after-work drinks, produces good pub grub, from fish-and-chips to boxty (filled Irish potato pancakes). Irish breakfast, with beans and Irish bacon, is available all day. *3035 Peachtree Rd., Buckhead, 404/841–0066. Reservations not accepted. AE, D, DC, MC, V. $–$$*

PADDY'S IRISH PUB

Traditional Irish fare at this popular attraction at Château Élan, the lavish hotel-winery-spa complex, includes shepherd's pie, fish-and-chips, and corned-beef sandwiches. Irish brews are on draft, and there's live music on weekends. *Château Élan, 100 Tour de France, Braselton, 678/425–0900. Reservations not accepted. AE, D, DC, MC, V. $*

ITALIAN

12 e-6
ABRUZZI

The setting in a nondescript shopping center won't transport you, but once owner Nico Petrucci and his staff welcome you to the formal gold–and–celery green dining room, you'll realize you have come upon one of the city's best dining experiences. The menu is excellent and focuses on seasonal dishes, including game in season. The first-class wine list is nearly all Italian, but by-the-glass selections are very limited. *Peachtree Battle shopping center, 2355 Peachtree Rd., Buckhead, 404/261–8186. Reservations essential. AE, D, DC, MC, V. Closed Sun. No lunch Sat. $$–$$$*

5 e-2
ALTOBELI'S ITALIAN RESTAURANT & PIANO BAR

Since 1988, crowds have packed this popular spot that serves classic Italian-American fare. Veal is a major feature of the menu, and a side of pasta accompanies every main dish unless its already served on pasta. Veal *a la gourmet* is a sautéed medallion with sun-dried tomatoes, asparagus, and mushrooms in a brown sauce; veal *a la romana* tops a scallopini with prosciutto, mozzarella, and mushrooms sautéed in white wine.

The wine list goes deep into Italian wines, with good Chiantis and Barolos. The piano bar is in full swing Thursday–Saturday. *3000 Old Alabama Rd., Alpharetta, 770/664–8055. AE, D, DC, MC, V. No lunch. $$*

14 a-3
ANDIAMO

There's nothing especially exotic or novel about the *cucina* here, but everything bears the mark of a loving and authentically Italian kitchen. Gnocchi in vodka–tomato cream are springy; the dense, thin crust of pizza *verde* is strewn with broccoli and two cheeses (one buttery, one sharp); sautéed grouper fillet sits in its flaky coating on garlic spinach and is sauced with lemon butter, Kalamata olives, and capers. The only drawback is the noise level, so you might opt for the tiny patio. *1044 Greenwood Ave., Virginia-Highland, 404/892–3555. AE, MC, V. Closed Sun. $$*

12 g-3
ANTICA POSTA

The taste of Tuscany came to Atlanta in 1999, when Marco Detti arrived from a little town near Florence, took over a modest house, and opened a restaurant very much like the one he ran with his brothers back home. The menu is rigorously authentic, with excellent risotto, veal dishes, gnocchi, and fish; the steak with a balsamic-vinegar reduction is outstanding. Homemade gelato finishes the meal. *519 E. Paces Ferry Rd., Buckhead, 404/262–7112. Reservations essential. AE, D, MC, V. No lunch. $$$*

15 e-3
BARAONDA

The sidewalk dining terrace is perfectly placed for people-watching at this hip spot, which manages to be simultaneously lively and mellow. The food is authentically Italian. Neapolitan-style pizzas, fired in a very hot oven, are the backbone of the menu. The smallish pies—split as a starter, or as an entrée for one—have a paper-thin crust and such simple topping combos as tomato with olives, capers, anchovies, and oregano. The menu also includes short but well-considered lists of starters and salads, pasta dishes, and a couple of entrées. *710 Peachtree St., Midtown, 404/879–9962. AE, D, MC, V. No lunch weekends. $–$$*

5 *b-5*

BROOKLYN CAFÉ

Bustling and almost always jammed (arrive early to avoid a wait), this popular Italian-American restaurant serves good food in a friendly environment. Start off with crusty, yeasty bread that you can dip in olive oil and grated Parmesan cheese, and then move on to one of the generous pastas and perhaps a fish or shrimp dish. *220 Sandy Springs Cir., Sandy Springs, 404/843–8377. Reservations not accepted. AE, D, DC, MC, V. No lunch weekends. $$*

14 *a-2*

CAMILLE'S

Even in bad weather you can dine on the sidewalk patio here (it's covered and heated), and you're likely to be all the happier if you order one of the excellent pizzas and/or wonderful mussels or calamari with marinara sauce. Whatever you plan on ordering, consider the *aroncini*, deep-fried mozzarella-stuffed rice balls, as a starter. *1186 N. Highland Ave., Virginia-Highland, 404/872–7203. Reservations not accepted. AE, MC, V. No lunch. $$*

4 *h-7*

CARRABBA'S ITALIAN GRILL

The kids are more than welcome at this chain eatery, and the food doesn't disappoint the grown-ups either. In addition to the pastas and wood-fired pizzas, the seafood, veal, and beef are excellent and satisfyingly filling. The *spiedino di mare*, for instance, is a skewer loaded with enough shrimp and sea scallops to take home for another meal. The wines are decent and very well priced. *2999 Cumberland Cir., near I–285 and U.S. 41, exits 19/20, Smyrna, 770/437–1444. Reservations not accepted. AE, D, DC, MC, V. $–$$*

4 *f-2*

1160 Ernest W. Barrett Pkwy., Kennesaw, 770/499–0338.

5 *h-4*

3580 Sweetwater Rd., east of I–85, exit 104, Duluth, 770/935–7600.

8 *c-8*

1887 Mt. Zion Rd., west of I–75, exit 222, Morrow, 770/968–3233.

12 *g-4*

CIAO BELLA

The cooking of the Italian countryside dominates this trattoria, and that means the emphasis is on hearty pasta dishes: spaghetti with quail or, a little less exotic, lasagna with béchamel sauce or cannelloni with ground veal, spinach, and cheese, to name a few. *309 Pharr Rd., Buckhead, 404/261–6013. AE, D, MC, V. No lunch. $$*

5 *g-2*

Shops of St. Ives, 10305 Medlock Bridge Rd., Duluth, 770/418–0448. Closed Sun.

5 *d-2*

DI PAOLO CUCINA

Northsiders love the great service and casual sophistication of this contemporary bistro, where the breads and pastas are made in house. There are wood oven–fired pizzas and nightly specials from lamb to venison. Walnut-encrusted trout with tomato-mashed potatoes is another winner. *8560 Holcomb Bridge Rd., Alpharetta, 770/587–1051. AE, D, MC, V. Closed Mon. No lunch. $$–$$$*

12 *e-g*

FRATELLI DI NAPOLI

Unless you plan to bring home enough food for a week, bring a gang of friends or the whole family. The space has rough-textured brick walls and high industrial ceilings; the atmosphere is high-energy. Large platters of salads, good calamari, pastas, excellent fish and chicken dishes, and a solid wine list keep you in your seat for long, leisurely meals. *2101-B Tula St., off Peachtree St., next to Brookwood Square, Buckhead, 404/351–1533. AE, D, DC, MC, V. No lunch. $$–$$$$*

5 *c-2*

928 Canton St., Roswell, 770/642–9917.

15 *h-5*

FRITTI

This adjunct to the wildly popular Sotto Sotto specializes in authentic Naples-style pizzas and soothing roasted dinners, which explains the blast-furnace-hot oven. The pies get only two minutes in the heat, just enough time to bubble and crisp their fine crusts and to heat up the top-quality topping ingredients—wild mushrooms and truffle oil, for example, or ricotta, oozy mozzarella, spinach, and tomato. A pleasant patio fronts the old industrial space. *311 N. Highland Ave., Inman Park, 404/880–0287. AE, DC, MC, V. Closed Sun. No lunch Mon. or Sat. $–$$*

4 *f-3*

IPPOLITO'S FAMILY STYLE ITALIAN RESTAURANT

The several locations of this casual place serve dishes that are straight off the Italian-American shelf—cheese-filled manicotti baked in tomato sauce, pasta shells stuffed with eggplant and ricotta, and huge calzones. Other choices include sausage and peppers, eggplant parmigiana, and good sandwiches on hoagie rolls, too. *425 Ernest Barrett Pkwy., Kennesaw, 770/514–8500. AE, D, DC, MC, V. No lunch weekends. $$*

5 *c-2*

1525 Holcomb Bridge Rd., Roswell, 770/ 998–5683.

5 *g-1*

11585 Jones Bridge Rd., Alpharetta, 770/ 663–0050.

5 *b-4*

6623 Roswell Rd., Sandy Springs, 404/ 256–3546.

5 *d-5*

LA GROTTA RAVINIA RISTORANTE ITALIANO

Different in feeling from its elder sibling in Buckhead, this La Grotta has an open kitchen and magnificent views of the landscaped grounds surrounding the Dunwoody hotel in which it's located. Some of the signature dishes presented in Buckhead, such as the excellent gnocchi, appear here, too, but others are unique to this location and include an excellent summer entrée of cold veal in sun-dried tomato sauce. The mostly Italian wine list includes many good offerings by the glass. *Ravinia Crowne Plaza Hotel, 4355 Ashford-Dunwoody Rd., Dunwoody, 770/395–9925. Reservations essential weekends. AE, D, DC, MC, V. Closed Sun. No lunch Sat. $$$*

12 *f-3*

LA GROTTA RISTORANTE ITALIANO

Classic Italian food. Period. That's what the team of Sergio Favelli and Antonio Abizanda has been doing for more than two decades, and this elegant, understated (but formal) dining room at the bottom of a posh condominium is not the place to sample the latest trends. The gnocchi are simply the best anywhere—light as a sigh and simply sauced with Swiss chard, walnuts, and cream. Risotto and pastas are, as the menu says, "like we do them in Italy." Veal, game, and seafood are outstanding, and the mostly Italian wine list, with some by-the-glass selections, reads like a novel. Linger at the bar for an after-dinner sambuca and espresso. *2637 Peachtree Rd., Buckhead, 404/231–1368. Reservations essential. AE, D, DC, MC, V. Closed Sun. No lunch. $$–$$$*

4 *h-5*

LA STRADA

Residents of East Cobb and North Fulton swarm family-owned and -oriented La Strada, where Sunday through Thursday children age 10 and under eat free 5–7 PM (one child per adult patron). The good Italian-American fare includes sausage and peppers on polenta, lasagna, linguine with clams, and veal

---

BEST BETS WITH KIDS

Determined to liberate your little mouths-to-feed from fast-food dining? Here are some of the better dining experiences they can have in Atlanta. The grown-ups won't complain about their meals either.

Café Tu Tu Tango (Eclectic)
The little ones can assemble their own pizzas and watch them bake in a wood-fired oven.

California Pizza Kitchen (Pizza)
Kid-size pizzas in familiar flavors are practical and tasty, and the kids' menu is theirs to draw on and color, with crayons supplied.

The Imperial Fez (Moroccan)
It may seem like a grown-ups' place, but the exotic atmosphere and food tend to fascinate kids eight and older. The belly dancing is tastefully done, under the watchful eye of an owner-manager who's also a parent.

La Paz (Southwestern)
There's kid-size seating at the tables, but at the Alpharetta and Woodstock locations, kids prefer to hang out without their parents in special rooms that are well supplied with toys and books.

La Strada (Italian)
Italian-American fare of good quality draws families at all hours, but get here between 5 and 7 PM, and the kids ages 10 and under (one per dining patron) eat free.

parmigiana. You can finish the meal with *zuppa inglese* (a chilled dessert of rum-soaked yellow cake layered with chocolate mousse and whipped cream) and a shot of the good espresso. *2930 Johnson Ferry Rd., Marietta, 770/640–7008. AE, D, DC, MC, V. No lunch. $–$$*

5 *c-3*

8550 Roswell Rd., Dunwoody, 770/552–1300. No lunch weekends.

14 *a-2*

LA TAVOLA

The first courses at this handsome, contemporary bistro range from superb, fat mussels in vermouth-tomato-herb broth to pappardelle (broad noodles) with duck ragù to pumpkin-stuffed sage ravioli with red-onion confit. Main courses vary daily and often include such substantial fare as spicy sausage, grilled veal chops, and traditional baked lasagna. *Panna cotta,* that custardy wonder, here served with a blood-orange sauce, is the dessert winner. At Sunday brunch, dishes such as poached eggs on toasted focaccia under a light cheese sauce are on hand. The wines are American and Italian. *992 Virginia Ave., near N. Highland Ave., Virginia-Highland, 404/873–5430. Reservations essential. AE, D, MC, V. No lunch. $$–$$$*

12 *g-1*

MAGGIANO'S LITTLE ITALY

The huge, almost cavernous dining room buzzes with animated conversation, creating a high-energy ambience that attracts families and groups eager to share dishes designed to satisfy at least two healthy appetites. The tasty baked clams, supremely moist and tender chicken with vegetables (*giardiniera*), and piccata-style veal scallopini far outshine the dishes made with the tomato sauce. The adjacent Corner Bakery sells fabulous breads and desserts. There are lots of good Italian and California wines to savor with this food. *3368 Peachtree Rd., Buckhead, 404/816–9650. Reservations essential. AE, D, DC, MC, V. $$–$$$*

5 *d-5*

MI SPIA

The Italian-inspired fare transports you to Florence. You can begin at the handsome bar, enjoying a drink with the superior fried calamari with spicy marinara sauce and smoked bacon-wrapped grilled shrimp, before moving on to the dining room for the excellent pastas, seafood,

and meats. The tiramisu is a must. The extensive wine spotlights Italian wines. *Park Place shopping center, across from Perimeter Mall, 4505 Ashford-Dunwoody Rd., Dunwoody, 770/393–1333. AE, D, DC, MC, V. No lunch weekends. $$–$$$*

12 *g-2*

NONA'S ITALIAN KITCHEN

Here, home-style comfort food means excellent saltimbocca, sirloin with parsnip–potato cake and porcini sauce, and smoked pork loin with garlic mashed potatoes and cider glaze. Pasta dishes include good gnocchi, and the cannoli and flourless chocolate torte are excellent dessert choices. The wine list is Italian and Cal-Ital, with lots of good choices by the glass. *3365 Piedmont Rd., Suite 1025 (upstairs), Buckhead, 404/261–1312. AE, D, DC, MC, V. No lunch weekends. $$–$$$*

5 *e-4*

OSCAR'S VILLA CAPRI

Argentine-born Oscar Pereyra has been doing business here since 1985, in a dining room filled with nostalgic art depicting Italian street scenes and the strains of traditional Italian music. Regulars know to rely on Oscar for excellent tiny clams baked with crumbs, herbs, and a bit of prosciutto; good veal dishes; and specials that take advantage of the day's market to include such offerings as a snapper baked with tomatoes, peppers, onions, capers, and herbs on a pasta tricolore (which, like many dishes here, can easily serve two). The wine list offers a range of Italian and American selections. *Orchard Park shopping center, 2090 Dunwoody Club Dr., between Mt. Vernon and Jett Ferry Rds., Dunwoody, 770/392–7940. AE, D, DC, MC, V. No lunch. $$–$$$*

15 *e-3*

PASTA DA PULCINELLA

The cooking is better than ever at this inexpensive favorite now in a handsomely renovated bungalow on a quiet street. The walls are hung to the ceiling with old engravings of clowns (that's what *pulcinella* means), and the brick front porch, with its sunset view, is a great spot for supper. It's not surprising that fans say Da Pulcinella serves the best pasta around: sweet-potato gnocchi and a huge half Caesar salad compose a memorable meal, and ravioli with apples, sausage, and Parmesan cheese topped with brown butter and sage is singularly tasty. *1123 Peachtree Walk, Midtown, 404/876–1114. AE, MC, V. No lunch weekends. $–$$*

 14 *b-8*

PASTIFICIO CAMELI

Thanks to the Cameli brothers, this brick-walled trattoria in an up-and-coming neighborhood has much to recommend it. The pair takes Italian cooking seriously, following fundamental Tuscan models. The handmade pastas, especially the ravioli with Gorgonzola, are worthy of a much fancier environment; entrées are simply presented, with ample but not overdone portions; and the nice, if short, wine list does a good by-the-glass job, with many Italian choices. *1263 Glenwood Ave., East Atlanta, 404/622–9926. AE, DC, MC, V. Closed Mon. No lunch. $$*

12 *g-3*

PRICCI

Don't come to this contemporary, high-energy dining room to enjoy a quiet dinner. But do come to enjoy an exceptional meal that might begin with grilled calamari accompanied by a light tomato sauce and move on to the daily risotto special or a fresh pasta dish, or one of the grilled meats or the steamed sea bass in parchment made outstanding with fresh vegetables. The wine list is heavily Italian and includes many interesting selections. *500 Pharr Rd. (Maple Dr.), Buckhead, 404/237–2941. Reservations essential. AE, D, DC, MC, V. No lunch weekends. $$$*

5 *d-5*

ROMANO'S MACARONI GRILL

These casual, Dallas-based restaurants do a good job of keeping businesspeople content at lunch while feeding families for dinner with good soups and such standbys as penne with prosciutto in a creamy sauce and grilled chicken. But the faux-stone walls don't absorb sound, so you have to put up with some noise. The wine list offers good choices (skip the house wine). *4788 Ashford-Dunwoody Rd., north of Perimeter Mall, Dunwoody, 770/394–6676. Reservations not accepted. AE, D, DC, MC, V. $–$$*

5 *h-4*

1565 Pleasant Hill Rd., east of I–85, exit 104, Duluth, 770/564–0094.

4 *e-3*

780 Cobb Place Blvd., west of I–75, exit 269, Kennesaw, 770/590–7774.

5 *c-2*

770 Holcomb Bridge Rd., ½ mi east of Alpharetta Hwy., Roswell, 770/993–7115.

5 *g-2*

Medlock Crossing shopping center, 9700 Medlock Bridge Rd. (State Bridge Rd.), Duluth, 770/495–7855.

15 *h-5*

SOTTO SOTTO

Who would have thought that the entire city would turn out and cram this tiny trattoria for such dishes as spaghetti with sun-dried mullet roe? Chef Riccardo Ullio, born in Italy but reared in Conyers, accommodates the crowds nicely and pampers them with huge antipasto platters, three special risotto dishes nightly, and such entrées as whole fish roasted on a wood plank. The panna cotta is just plain perfect and is served without needless adornment. The short wine list offers some good, well-priced Italian wines. *313 N. Highland Ave. (Elizabeth St.), Inman Park, 404/523–6678. Reservations essential. AE, MC, V. Closed Sun. $$–$$$*

15 *e-4*

TERRA DI SIENA

In the best tradition of Italian design, this stylishly modern bi-level room was carved out of a corner of the historic Fox Theatre. The owners and nearly the entire kitchen staff are from Tuscany, which explains the authentic fare and the tight focus on that region's cuisine. Braised veal shank is served with fried polenta; pappardelle has a thick, earthy duck sauce; almonds, pine nuts, and fennel adorn seared scallops. The wine list is 100% Italian. *654 Peachtree St., Midtown, 404/885–7505. AE, D, DC, MC, V. Closed Mon. No dinner Sun. $$–$$$*

15 *e-2*

VENI VIDI VICI

Marcella Hazan, the noted Italian chef and cookbook author, helped plan this menu, and her influence shows in such delectables as little plates of veal meatballs, wood-grilled shrimp with white beans, and octopus–potato salad (a satisfying first course or light luncheon). The house-made pastas are first rate, as are the rotisserie-cooked meats, braised dishes (osso buco), and seafood. The mostly Italian wine list lends superior support to this lovely fare. *41 14th St., between W. Peachtree and Spring Sts., Midtown, 404/875–8424. Reservations essential. AE, D, DC, MC, V. No lunch weekends. $$–$$$*

5 *d-6*
VILLA CHRISTINA

Contemporary artworks, painted clouds on the ceiling, and a faux-slate floor help to create an ideal setting for the beautifully presented, artful fare. But chef Darryl Evans turns out food that is not only pretty but tastes good, too. What pastas these! Clams *oreganata* top buffalo ricotta gnocchi, and local Vidalia onions grace the cappellini. Rabbit is always on the menu, sometimes prepared with lentils or maybe white beans. Pastry chef Paul Michael Bodrogi creates desserts that may incorporate a tasty chestnut mousse or roasted pear crème brûlée. The wine list is excellent, and many choices are offered by the glass. *Perimeter Summit, 43 Perimeter Summit Blvd., Dunwoody, 404/303–0133. AE, D, DC, MC, V. Closed Sun. No lunch Sat. $$$*

3 *b-8*
VINNY'S ON WINDWARD

The glow in this bright, contemporary space comes from the light that streams through the large windows. It's a splendid setting for really good Italian food, from roasted garlic–white bean soup to classic tomato-ricotta lasagna with sausage or seared duck with polenta. The menu changes often, but the dishes are always Italian to the core. Italian and California wines include wonderful choices available by the glass as well as the bottle; heaven should have this many Barbarescos and Barolos. *5355 Windward Pkwy., Alpharetta, 770/772–4644. AE, D, DC, MC, V. No lunch weekends. $$–$$$*

JAMAICAN

15 *f-6*
PARADISE PARADISE

Island music sets the tone at this modest hole-in-the-wall with red and yellow booths and tropical images. There are patties of sweet potato, beef, and chicken; main dishes include jerk chicken, curried shrimp, and stewed fish with rice and peas. A live band often entertains the Friday lunch crowd, providing the perfect office escape. *180 Auburn Ave., Downtown, 404/658–9829. AE, DC, MC, V. Closed Sun. $*

8 *e-1*
KOOL RUNNINGS

The film *Kool Runnings* tells the unlikely story of a bobsled team from Jamaica that went to find glory at the Calgary Olympics; but, thanks to the thriving community of Caribbean immigrants, finding a Jamaican eatery in eastern DeKalb County isn't at all unlikely. Traditional Jamaican breakfasts of spinachlike callaloo, ackee (a fruit that when cooked has an uncanny resemblance to scrambled eggs), and codfish, kingfish, pickled mackerel, or snapper are available here. At lunch and dinner the menu adds oxtails, brown-stewed chicken, codfish fritters, jerk chicken, and curried goat. The fruitcake is baked on the premises. *4977 Memorial Dr., Stone Mountain, 404/508–0277. AE, D, MC, V. $*

JAPANESE

12 *g-3*
KAMOGAWA

Atlanta's most elegant Japanese restaurant is a favorite with visiting Japanese businesspeople, who find pristine preparations of sashimi and sushi, as well as other classics. A very fine sake served chilled is the best beverage to accompany this exquisite fare. The experience is all the richer if you dine in one of the tatami rooms. *Grand Hyatt Atlanta Hotel, 3300 Peachtree Rd., Buckhead, 404/841–0314. Reservations essential. AE, D, DC, MC, V. Closed Sun. No lunch Sat. $$–$$$$*

12 *g-7*
NAKATO

For years this was the only Japanese restaurant Atlantans knew anything about, and Nakato—these days in a slightly Westernized Asian-style building that resembles a large house—has continued to build its following. Its several dining rooms offer a variety of dining styles; in one, patrons gather at cooking tables to watch chefs chop and cook steak, fish, chicken, and vegetables. The sushi is dependably good, and there are good traditional dishes such as shabu-shabu, for which beef and vegetables are cooked in a seasoned broth.

1776 Cheshire Bridge Rd., Northeast Atlanta, 404/873–6582. AE, D, DC, MC, V. No lunch. $$–$$$

 13 *c-3*

SA TSU KI

A favorite with the local Japanese community, Sa Tsu Ki is as comfortable as a private home. Families with children gather at the sushi bar or enjoy watching excellent shabu-shabu and sukiyaki prepared table side. Two dishes not to pass up: beef *tataki* (seared rare beef with ponzu dipping sauce) and the deep-fried shrimp heads. 3043 Buford Hwy., north of N. Druid Hills Rd., Northeast Atlanta, 404/325–5285. Reservations not accepted. AE, D, DC, MC, V. Closed Mon. No lunch. $$

12 *g-2*

SOTO

Sushi master Sotohiro Kosugi learned his art from his father, and his restaurant is mentioned in the same breath as sushi. The nightly specials feature the best dishes; they sell out quickly, so you may want to plan on an early supper. Soto is not impervious to new influences: the Cajun roll combines curry-flecked soft-shell crawfish, avocado, cucumber, spicy sesame sauce, and a dusting of smelt roe on top. Ginger ice cream, with chunks of fresh ginger bursting with hot sweetness, is a fine end-of-the-meal palate cleanser. Chilled sake is the beverage of choice, and the restaurant has a good list of it. Piedmont/Peachtree Crossing shopping center, 3330 Piedmont Rd., Buckhead, 404/233–2005. AE, D, DC, MC, V. Closed Sun. No lunch. $$–$$$

KOREAN

5 *e-6*

ASIANA GARDEN

In evidence here, the combination of Japanese and Korean cuisines works wonderfully. Everything from sushi to glass-noodle dishes with vegetables and minced seafood to *bulgogi*—Korean barbecue that's grilled at the table (chicken, beef ribs, shrimp, and salmon are prepared this way)—is here. It's open until 2 AM daily. Asian Square shopping center, 5150 Buford Hwy., Doraville, 770/452–1677. AE, DC, MC, V. $$

5 *e-5*

HAE WOON DAE

You almost have to read Korean to find this late-night restaurant tucked away in the back of a strip mall full of Korean signage. But persist, because this is one of the city's best Korean eateries. Sundry nibbles, among them a fine shredded potato salad, appear as soon as you order, and the main course of choice is the excellent barbecue done over wood charcoal. Alcohol is limited to one wine and one Korean beer. Treasure Village shopping center, 5805 Buford Hwy., Doraville, 770/458–6999. AE, D, DC, MC, V. Wine and beer only. $$

5 *d-5*

HANWOORI

There are, literally, two sides to this large, elegant restaurant adorned with gleaming woods. The Japanese side feels almost templelike and has private tatami rooms; the larger, more gregarious Korean side is filled with tables topped with gas-fired grills for barbecuing eel (so tasty even the kids want more) and other seafood and meats. Don't be intimidated by the incomprehensible-sounding "Gooksoojuhngol": it's a tasty dish of noodles, vegetables, and beef cooked in a seasoned broth spiced to suit the diner's taste buds. The staff is friendly and good with children. 4251 N. Peachtree Rd., Chamblee, 770/458–9191. AE, D, DC, MC, V. $–$$

5 *e-5*

SEOUL GARDEN

Frequented chiefly by Koreans, Seoul Garden does a rigorous job of preparing all the traditional favorites, including cold noodle dishes and what must be the best seafood pancake in town. Inexpensive "lunch boxes," available weekdays, contain both Korean and Japanese dishes and are very popular with non-Asian customers. Korean and Japanese beers, sake, and American beers and wines are available. 5938 Buford Hwy., Doraville, 770/452–0123. AE, MC, V. $–$$

KOSHER

13 *c-6*

BROADWAY CAFE

This casual restaurant is one of Atlanta's few supervised kosher dining establishments. Many of the dishes also rank with vegans, as they're made without eggs or dairy products; empanadas and pot stickers are stuffed with tempeh and veggies. Some beer and wine are available. *2166 Briarcliff Rd., Northeast Atlanta, 404/329–0888. AE, DC, MC, V. Wine and beer only. Closed Sat. No dinner Fri. $–$$*

13 *c-5*

WALL ST. PIZZA

The "pepperoni," "sausage," and "beef" at this fixture among kosher eateries and pizza joints are soy-based, and the cheeses used on the pies are made without animal rennet. Italian and Israeli items like eggplant parmigiana and falafel are also available, and soups are made fresh daily. Desserts include cheesecake and beignets. *Loehman's Plaza, 2470 Briarcliff Rd., Northeast Atlanta, 404/633–2111. MC, V. Closed Sat. No dinner Fri. $–$$*

LATIN

5 *b-6*

CASA BLANCA

Many of the dishes in this simple restaurant are Mexican, but you may want to take advantage of the hard-to-find Salvadoran cuisine. The home-style cooking produces *papusas* (corn cakes filled with cheese, meat, or beans), as well as chicken with onions and scrambled eggs with rice, beans, and pico de gallo. *5785 Roswell Rd., Sandy Springs, 404/252–3237. Reservations not accepted. AE, MC, V. $–$$*

12 *h-4*

ECLIPSE DI LUNA

The twentysomethings seeking other twentysomethings often spill out of the stylish interior onto a patio. Those who take time to notice the cuisine enjoy the tapas plates (such as thinly sliced Serrano ham shaved off the leg) before moving on to, say, delectable garlic chicken, spicy potatoes, and perfect flan. A wide range of wines is reasonably priced. *764 Miami Cir., Buckhead, 404/846–0449. AE, D, MC, V. Closed Sun. $$*

13 *c-3*

EL SALVADOR

Mexican and Salvadoran families gather to watch Spanish-language television and eat in a homey atmosphere that provides a good family-dining experience as well as an introduction to multi-

cultural cuisines. Offerings range from Salvadoran *papusas* (corn cakes) to Mexican tamales, from *campechana* (a cocktail of shrimp, octopus, and oysters) to nachos. *Northeast Plaza, 3375 Buford Hwy., Northeast Atlanta, 404/325–0482. Reservations not accepted. MC, V. $–$$*

14 *a-4*

LA FONDA LATINA

Latin in atmosphere and in cuisine, these lively restaurants serve several kinds of paella (seafood and vegetarian, as well as traditional), along with grilled pork chops and chicken, *bocadillos* (Latin sandwiches) with chorizo, and eight kinds of quesadillas. The flanlike baked custard is homemade and delicious. Chilean wines rule. *1150 Euclid Ave., Little Five Points, 404/577–8317. MC, V. $–$$*

14 *c-4*

1639 McLendon Ave., Candler Park, 404/378–5200.

12 *f-4*

2815 Peachtree Rd., Buckhead, 404/816–8311.

5 *b-6*

4427 Roswell Rd., Sandy Springs, 404/303–8201.

15 *h-3*

923 Ponce de Leon Ave., Poncey-Highland, 404/607–0665.

15 *f-3*

LOCA LUNA

Patrons stop here, at gay-disco central, to rest their feet and fuel up on authentic Spanish food before heading out again into the night. In the evening, the menu is all tapas except for paella. And, yes, the pigs'-feet vinaigrette, fried yucca, and empanada-enclosed beef in a proper lard pastry are indeed daring and delicious. *836 Juniper St. (6th St.), Midtown, 404/875–4494. AE, D, DC, MC, V. Closed Sun. No lunch weekends. $$*

14 *a-4*

PURA VIDA

Servers wear pastel guayaberas, but there's little decoration in the two simple rooms apart from a mural of Botero-esque dancing couples. The format is tapas, but the cooking is pan–Latin American rather than Spanish. And the presentation is artful. Take the ceviche of Chilean scallops, for example: three scallop shells sit on a bed of rock salt, each bearing a sweet little marinated scallop in pale green tomatillo gazpacho that's dashed with fruity olive oil and topped with fresh mint, cilantro, and oregano. Many ingredients, such as plantains and rice, are on the heavy side, and the servings are big for tapas, so order easy. *656 N. Highland Ave., Poncey-Highland, 404/870–9797. AE, D, MC, V. No lunch. $–$$*

15 *g-1*

TIERRA

Ticha and Dan Krinsky bring you the flavors of Ticha's native South America and provide a little glossary at each table to help you understand the dishes and ingredients. The daily soup, or *caldo del día,* is often based on a seafood broth and made rich with fish and shellfish; chipotle peppers infuse the mashed potatoes; and fried plantain and refried beans finish a grilled skirt steak. For dessert, it's Three Milks Cake, a light but luscious cake enriched with heavy cream, evaporated milk, and condensed milk. *1425B Piedmont Ave., Midtown, 404/874–5951. AE, MC, V. Closed Mon. No lunch. $$*

MALAYSIAN

5 *e-6*

PENANG

In addition to offering Malaysian cuisine, this attractive, wood-paneled dining room specializes in Thai fare. Many of the dishes are spicy, especially the curries, and the offerings include seafood, a wide range of soups, and traditional noodle dishes. The potables include a few beers and wines, and there's a full bar. *Orient Center shopping center, 4897 Buford Hwy., Chamblee, 770/220–0308. AE, D, DC, MC, V. $$*

12 *d-7*

SATAY RIA

The interior of this former sub shop is swathed in burnished gold, moss green, and touches of orange, with a dense motif of rampant vegetation—fitting decor for this tropical Asian cuisine. Families from the residential neighborhoods to either side of Peachtree dominate the crowd. *Roti canai* is a crispy pancake served with spicy lentil curry; *acar* is a salad with a zesty peanut-sprinkled dressing. *Nam sod* is especially fun:

you wrap minced pork spiked with ginger, ground red chili, roasted peanuts, and lime juice in a lettuce leaf, to eat by hand. The wine list is decent. *1861 Peachtree St., Buckhead, 404/609–9990. AE, D, MC, V. No lunch Sat. $–$$*

MEDITERRANEAN

15 *h-5*

BABETTE'S CAFÉ

Ensconced in a prettily redone bungalow with a pleasant dining patio, this neighborhood bistro lights up the area with a fun, casual atmosphere and good food that's consistently well prepared. Many of the offerings combine unlikely ingredients with surprising success: steamed mussels with strawberries and serrano peppers; fried oyster biscuits with cucumber sauce; grilled salmon with grapefruit; and, for dessert, espresso flan. At brunch, the best dish is "Babette's Benedict"—poached eggs perched on a fillet of beef. The coffee is good and strong, and the wine list is excellent and well priced. *573 N. Highland Ave., Poncey-Highland, 404/523–9121. Reservations not accepted. AE, D, DC, MC, V. Closed Mon. $$–$$$*

12 *g-2*

BASIL'S MEDITERRANEAN CAFÉ

The dining rooms in this former middle-class residences are somewhat small, so in good weather the best place to sit is the patio in front. Indeed, this is a great place to unwind after work or shopping trips. Indoors or out, you can savor the classics of Mediterranean fare: hummus and stuffed grape leaves; beautifully grilled fresh fish; excellent pasta with light, saffron-scented seafood; and, of course, baklava for dessert. *2985 Grandview Ave., Buckhead, 404/233–9755. AE, D, DC, MC, V. No lunch Sun. $–$$*

4 *h-4*

BASIL'S NEIGHBORHOOD CAFÉ

Bringing home-style Mediterranean fare to the northern suburbs, this Basil's does a few things differently from its older, successful sibling in Buckhead. The hummus, tabbouleh, and baba ghanouj (pureed eggplant with tahini, or sesame-seed paste) are as good as anybody else's, but the distinguishing dishes include fried calamari with tomato–leek sauce and cilantro aioli. Homemade pancakes and good turkey sausage top the lineup at Sunday brunch. *Market Plaza, 1255 Johnson Ferry Rd., Marietta, 770/578–0011. AE, D, DC, MC, V. Closed Sun. No lunch Sat. $$*

14 *f-3*

CAFÉ LILY

While most dishes in this storefront space with huge windows are Italian in inspiration, some come from Spain and Portugal. Excellent grilled lamb chops arrive with a garlic cream sauce and superior skin-on fried potatoes, and Basque eggs with pipérade sauce are a unique brunch dish. Special menus pair food with some intriguing wines. *308B W. Ponce de Leon Ave., Decatur, 404/371–9119. AE, D, MC, V. No lunch Sat. $$*

15 *f-5*

CALITERRA

Within a gloriously transformed once down-at-the-heels hotel awaits Caliterra, with its adjacent comfortable bar area and a seasonally changing menu that includes calamari appetizer with its three sauces (aioli is best), lamb shank with excellent greens, and a really good tiramisu. This top-notch restaurant is handy when you're attending events and performances at the Rialto Theatre or the Tabernacle. *Wyndham Atlanta hotel, 160 Spring St., Downtown, 678/686–3370. AE, D, DC, MC, V. $$–$$$*

12 *h-4*

CEDARS

From hummus to moussaka, the dishes at this casual restaurant explore the range of Mediterranean food. Lamb kabobs come perfectly pink and tender, and the traditional Middle Eastern *kibbeh*, a mixture of ground sirloin and cracked wheat, is set off by the tang of fine yogurt and grape leaves. Combination platters provide a good way to explore the variety of dishes. *Plantation Heights shopping center, 2770 Lenox Rd., Buckhead, 404/261–1826. AE, D, DC, MC, V. Closed Sun. No lunch Sat. $$*

15 *e-3*

ENO

Jamie Adams, formerly a chef at Veni Vidi Vici, and his partner, Doug Strickland, modeled their wine bar in the true style of an Italian enoteca. All wines are available by the taste, glass, and bottle, and the menu includes lots of small dishes that come from throughout the Mediterranean world. "Mussels Cataplana," a Portuguese dish, plops some of the sweetest and fattest of the bivalves into a broth of tomatoes, onions, paprika, prosciutto, and chorizo, then makes them aromatic with fresh cilantro; game hen on couscous is made special with the tang of preserved lemons. The hickory-smoked oysters are marvelous, but ask for them just lightly done until the edges crisp. *800 Peachtree St., at 5th St., Midtown, 404/685–3191. AE, D, DC, MC, V. Closed Sun. No lunch weekends. $$–$$$*

12 *g-3*

GRAPPA

The place is named for that incendiary Italian brandy, and first-timers are graciously offered a tasting of two of the many grappas in stock. That's just how it is at this elegant, low-lit, intimate restaurant where the service is knowledgeable and proper but utterly relaxed. The food is complex, if sometimes a bit overambitious, and gorgeously presented. A brandade of cod is formed into a chive-flecked cake and sautéed, then topped with a crisscross of peeled asparagus, crowned with a chunk of lobster meat, and set in a pool of lobster coral sauce. The signature dessert is made of caramelized bananas in a phyllo star, topped with white-chocolate mousse and strewn with crushed macadamia brittle. *3097 Maple Ave., Buckhead, 404/262–9749. Reservations essential. AE, D, DC, MC, V. No lunch. $$$–$$$$*

5 *c-2*

PASTIS

Like its Buckhead sibling, Anis, this airy, sophisticated predominantly French-accented bistro has a charming setting—here, overlooking the Historic Roswell scene. One of the starters is a roasted tomato–and–goat cheese terrine wrapped in grilled eggplant; entrées include pastas, roasted meats, and sautéed fish. There's often a jazz combo in the evening and brunch on Sunday. *936 Canton St., Roswell, 770/640–3870. AE, DC, MC, V. $$*

12 *f-3*

PORTOFINO

The big, shady brick patio provides a serene escape from the bustling Buckhead Village environs; the interior of the converted bungalow has a soothing, handsome treatment of white walls and pale natural wood. The kitchen is nominally Italian, with a wood-fired pizza oven. Pastas—such as a dish of thick rigatoni with pancetta and spinach, in a roasted garlic cream—are made with authentic ingredients from pine nuts to imported cheeses. But the menu wanders: maybe you can figure out, in between dreamy bites of the stuff, where sweet-potato risotto with cinnamon-seared chicken and Black Mission fig broth originated. *3199 Paces Ferry Pl., Buckhead, 404/231–1136. AE, D, MC, V. No lunch Sun. $$*

13 *a-6*
SOUTH OF FRANCE
In winter, a warm fire glows in the large hearth of this long-popular restaurant, which re-creates the warmth of Provence; year-round, a chanteuse adds her melodies to the atmosphere (Wednesday through Saturday). Little wonder that couples bent on romance come for dishes that include foie gras cooked correctly to the just-pink stage, a house-made terrine, duck à l'orange or with a raspberry–hazelnut sauce, and excellent lamb and fresh fish. *Cheshire Square, 2345 Cheshire Bridge Rd., at LaVista Rd., Northeast Atlanta, 404/325–6963. AE, D, DC, MC, V. Closed Sun. No lunch. $$–$$$*

MEXICAN

5 *e-7*
DON TACO
Every other sort of American is beginning to discover these well-run, mostly drive-through, operations that have long been popular with Mexican families in search of authentic home-style cooking. The house-made salsas are fresh and lively tasting, and the burritos, tacos, *tortas* (sandwiches with meat, mayonnaise, onion, jalapeños, lettuce, tomato, and avocado), quesadillas, and *huarachas* (a kind of corn patty, topped with meat, beans, and cheese) are excellent and inexpensive. Beer and wine are available. *4997 Buford Hwy., Chamblee, 770/458–8735. AE, D, DC, MC, V. $*

5 *d-5*
Perimeter Mall food court, 4400 Ashford-Dunwoody Rd., Dunwoody, 770/394–0084.

4 *f-4*
50 S. Cobb Pkwy., Marietta, 770/792–8406.

5 *e-6*
EL PESCADOR
The menu at this simple restaurant advises that preparing the food takes 30–45 minutes, so be warned: (1) this is not a fast-food joint, and (2) just about anything you order is going to be beautifully prepared. Ceviche and seafood soup are excellent starters, and they can be nicely followed with the fish tacos or crabs (*jaivas*), which come either spicy or in garlic sauce (*mojo de ajo*). Fresh shrimp is peeled for the excellent shrimp salad. A heated patio is a lovely spot for alfresco dining year-round. Good Mexican beers are available. *5768 Buford Hwy., Doraville, 770/452–1555.*

A BREATH OF FRESH AIR

You can dine alfresco nearly all year round; only the dead of summer—with its dense humidity and smoggy air—sends people fleeing indoors. Here are some spots for outside lingering.

Après Diem (Eclectic)
A relaxed European sensibility pervades, so nobody minds if you camp out in the particularly well sheltered terrace over your espresso or wine.

Atlantic Star (French)
The terrace is big, well protected, and faces southwest, and the kitchen stays open between lunch and dinner—perfect for that cool but sunny winter afternoon.

Canoe (Contemporary)
The parklike setting, among big old trees on the banks of the Chattahoochee River, is unsurpassed—and the kitchen's contemporary reverence for food nearly so.

Einstein's (American)
Tank-top alert: the food's only so-so, but the enormous streetside patio is a must-stop for muscle boys, their gal-pals, and those who only want to gawk.

Portofino (Mediterranean)
Mount the steps to the trellised, tree-shaded brick patio and you're instantly transported from the hectic buzz of Buckhead Village to the sunny Mediterranean.

Reservations not accepted. No credit cards.
$$–$$$

5 *e-6*

EL TACO VELOZ

Metro Atlanta has become dotted with these simple spots specializing in totally tasty tacos. Pick up little tacos *de lengua* (tongue), *de barbacoa* (pork), or *de carne asada* (roasted meat), and be sure to specify *"con todo"* (with everything) so you can savor your selection with great salsa verde, minced onions, and cilantro—oh, and extra jalapeños. The Chamblee and Roswell locations use the name Taco Prisa. *5084 Buford Hwy., Doraville, 770/936–9094. Reservations not accepted. No credit cards. $*

3 *h-7*

2700-C Buford Hwy. (in Chevron gas station next to Publix), Duluth, 770/622–0138.

5 *d-6*

3245 Chamblee-Tucker Rd., Chamblee, 770/458–7779.

5 *b-5*

5670 Roswell Rd., Sandy Springs, 404/252–5100.

4 *h-6*

925 Windy Hill Rd., Smyrna, 770/432–8800.

5 *c-2*

Roswell Village, 10495 Alpharetta Hwy. (Holcomb Bridge Rd.), Roswell, 770/993–2621.

5 *g-3*

2077 Beaver Ruin Rd., Norcross, 770/849–0025.

3 *h-7*

950 Jessie Jewel Rd., Gainesville, 770/503–1100.

5 *h-5*

FONDA SAN CARLOS

Authenticity reigns in this restaurant, which is appended to a fish market and serves the growing Hispanic population of south Gwinnett County. This is the place to savor freshly made pico de gallo, authentic mole that's smoky and deeply seasoned, and perhaps the city's best frozen margaritas. Given the adjoining business, seafood is big on the menu. It's open until 4 AM (if not later) on Friday and Saturday. *2077 Beaver Ruin Rd., Norcross, 770/797–2828. Reservations not accepted. AE, D, DC, MC, V. $–$$*

15 *g-3*

F.R.O.G.S. CANTINA

You can get 14 kinds of margarita, 50 brands of tequila, and better-than-average burritos, soft tacos, and other Mexican eats at this shopping-center spot with a delightful two-level terrace. Much of the fare is unsurprising, but there are some inventive menu additions, including Baja fish tacos, a pretty plate of three small soft tortillas piled with blackened fish, sautéed spinach, and a mildly spicy mango–pineapple salsa. *931 Monroe Dr., Midtown, 404/607–9967. AE, MC, V. $*

5 *g-6*

FRONTERA MEX-MEX GRILL

While all locations of this multibranch operation serve authentic Mexican specialties (such as *escabeche*, raw fish marinated in citrus juices, and *chilaquiles*, tortillas baked in a casserole), each also offers something a little different. Mexican breakfast (*desuyano*) is served at the Jimmy Carter Boulevard and Stone Mountain locations and features some 15 different dishes, including *carne asada* (roasted meat), *carnitas* (little roasted cubes of pork), and excellent *menudo* (tripe soup). The Norcross location has entertainment Wednesday through Monday, with live mariachi music Sunday and Monday. *4606 Jimmy Carter Blvd., Norcross, 770/493–8341. Reservations not accepted. AE, D, DC, MC, V. $–$$*

1 *g-6*

1820 GA 30, Conyers, 770/860–8922.

5 *e-3*

3466 Holcomb Bridge Rd., Norcross, 770/441–3488.

10 *a-1*

3607 GA 138, Stockbridge, 770/474–1540.

8 *e-1*

5070 Stone Mountain Hwy. (U.S. 78), Stone Mountain, 770/972–3366.

14 *b-5*

GRINGOS'

This former gas station and auto-repair garage rolled up its bays a few years ago and became a popular neighborhood dining spot. The authentic Mexican dishes include many vegetarian selections, outstanding among them a delicious chile relleno stuffed with farmer's cheese and fresh corn, cooked in cream and *chihuahua* cheese. The Yucatecan specialty *cochinita pibil*, tender pork cooked in banana leaves, is singularly well done here. There's a wine list, but the margaritas are the beverages of choice, while the list of fine tequilas, ranging from the basic *blanco* (silver) to *reposado* (aged 1 year) and *añejo* (aged 3 years), is unequaled in the city. *1238 DeKalb Ave., Inman Park, 404/522–8666. Reservations not accepted. AE, MC, V. Closed Mon. No lunch. $–$$*

12 *f-3*

OH! . . . MARÍA

Finally, a beautifully atmospheric Mexican restaurant worthy of any gourmet's attention has come to Atlanta, thanks to Lucero Obregón of Zócalo. Step inside and be transported to the land of aromatic spices, lively music, vivid colors, and intriguing textures. The large bar is a popular meeting place, but you'll want to take a seat at a table and begin a sampler platter of three kinds of quesadillas, garnished with great fresh guacamole and either homemade salsa verde or salsa roja. Steak sabana, a thin rib steak served with black beans and homemade tortillas, is a worthy main course; the flan is superior; and the margaritas are superb. *3167 Peachtree Rd., Buckhead, 404/261–2032. AE, D, DC, MC, V. $$*

15 *b-2*

TAQUERIA DEL SOL

The inspired folks behind Sundown Cafe have scored again with this wildly popular purveyor of Mexican cooking, which shows a touch of the classic Southern home kitchen. The couple of dinner plates include boneless fried chicken on ancho-spiked mashed potatoes with chili-zapped turnip greens. But mostly you put together your meal from a range of tacos, enchiladas, soups, and sides all priced at just $2 and $3. It's a big, simple, industrial space with a patio. You order at the counter and take a seat—usually after standing in a justifiably long line. Here's an inside tip: seats at the bar are often available without a wait. *1200-B Howell Mill Rd., Northwest Atlanta, 404/352–5811. AE, MC, V. Closed Sun. No dinner Mon. $–$$*

15 *f-2*

ZÓCALO

Owner Lucero Obregón learned to cook from her mother and also spent time

working with Mexico's queen of cuisine, Patricia Quintana. It's little wonder her dining room and enclosed patio fill quickly, even during the week, and the cuisine lives up to its reputation. Dishes feature the authentic fare of Obregón's native central Mexico, but she wends into other territory when she wishes, doing an excellent *sopa de lima* (a chicken broth–based soup with lime, pieces of chicken breast, and tortilla strips) and *cochinita pibil* (pork cooked in banana leaves) from the Yucatán. Brunch is especially popular, with a menu that includes such satisfying dishes as steak with eggs and tomatillo sauce. *187 10th St., Midtown, 404/249–7576. Reservations not accepted. AE, D, DC, MC, V. $–$$*

MIDDLE EASTERN

13 *b-4*

LAWRENCE'S CAFE

Step into this cool, dark oasis, leaving behind the bustle of Buford Highway, for good value, excellent service, and made-from-scratch food of the Eastern Mediterranean. Grape leaves, falafel, baba ghanouj, a variety of chicken- and lamb-based main courses, moussaka, and couscous are on offer, along with a modest list of wines and beers. There's a pleasant covered patio, and belly-dancing performances weekend evenings. *2888 Buford Hwy., Northeast Atlanta, 404/320–7756. AE, D, MC, V. Wine and beer only. Closed Sun. $–$$*

5 *e-8*

MEZZA

Mezze—that's the plural—are small plates, like tapas, hailing from such Eastern Mediterranean countries as Greece, Turkey, and Lebanon, and that's what you get at this pleasant storefront eatery. Some, like hummus and tabbouleh, are familiar. But most of the 50-some menu items are discoveries. They're made of ingredients like eggplant, fava beans, cracked wheat, feta cheese, ground meat, and pine nuts and spiced with basil, garlic, black pepper, thyme, parsley, and lemon. Order a selection to share, and make an evening of it. *2751 LaVista Rd., Decatur, 404/633–8833. AE, D, DC, MC, V. Closed Sun.–Mon. $–$$*

13 b-6
NICOLA'S

For more than a decade, Nicola Ayoub has been introducing Atlantans to the pleasures of the Middle Eastern table. These include his *mezza,* a platter of salads and appetizers, and *shwarma,* shredded lamb served with lemon, sesame, or spinach–mushroom sauces. If you really want to experience Ayoub's mastery, try *kibbey nayee*—a delicious dish of raw ground lamb that's available only on Saturday, must be ordered a day in advance, and is prepared for a minimum of three diners. The wine list is very small, but for a corkage fee ($6) you can bring your own bottle. *1602 LaVista Rd., near Briarcliff Rd., Northeast Atlanta, 404/325–2524. AE, D, MC, V. Closed Mon. No lunch. $$*

MOROCCAN

15 h-5
CASBAH

Draped to look like the tent of a desert sheik, this casual, pretty space offers an exotic atmosphere in which to enjoy *b'stella,* in which a Cornish hen is encased in pastry and perfumed with sweet aromatic spices. (The dish traditionally is made with pigeon, but the hen is a concession to American tastes.) Couscous with vegetables and lamb, *tagines* (traditional stews), and good baklava are the ideal follow-ups. Belly dancing begins at 8 PM every night. *465 N. Highland Ave., Poncey-Highland, 404/524–5777. AE, MC, V. No lunch. $$*

12 e-6
THE IMPERIAL FEZ

Prepare to remove your shoes before stepping into this luxuriously draped and swagged restaurant and taking a seat on one of the cushioned banquettes. After you wash your hands in water perfumed with scented oils, dishes from the fixed-price traditional meal begin to arrive: pastry-baked Cornish hen; assorted salads; lentil soup; your choice of meat, fish, or vegetarian main course; and nut pastries for a conclusion. Traditional (i.e., belly) dancing enhances the mood. The wine list is quite good and includes some Moroccan wines. *Peachtree Battle Condominium, 2282 Peachtree Rd., Buckhead, 404/351–0870. Reservations essential. AE, D, DC, MC, V. No lunch. $$$$*

PAN-ASIAN

12 b-7
MALAYA

Choose from Chinese, Indonesian, Malaysian, and other southeast Asian dishes at this simple, family-run operation; many of them, such as a *goreng* (a stir-fry of spicy string beans and tofu), can be made with or without meat or with seafood. Excellent noodle dishes and soups make fine light lunches, and *rijsttafel,* the traditional Indonesian feast based on rice, is served to a minimum of eight people (you must order it a couple of days in advance). *857 Collier Rd., Buckhead, 404/609–9991. AE, DC, MC, V. Closed Sun. No lunch Sat. $–$$*

12 f-3
NICKIEMOTO'S

Sitting on a patio at the corner of 10th Street and Piedmont Avenue in Midtown is not a bad way to pass a warm afternoon. When to that scenario you can add the taste of steamed dumplings stuffed with vegetables and chicken, a coconut broth with black mussels, a tasty stir-fry, or top-quality sushi, life really is good. This is Asian fare in the highest style. *990 Piedmont Ave., Midtown, 404/253–2010. Reservations not accepted. AE, D, MC, V. $$–$$$*

15 f-2

East Village Square, 247 Buckhead Ave., Buckhead, 404/842–0334. No lunch.

14 g-3
NOODLE

It's true: this lovely, serene room, with its quirky collection of teapots and its concrete floor painted with noodlelike shapes, was once a service station. Now it's the place to head for noodle dishes that hail from across Asia, Japan to Thailand, and the many vegetarian choices. Can't handle a wet noodle? Go for one of the rice-based plates instead. And start with cool basil rolls or a lettuce wrap: you take big leaves of lettuce and roll them yourself around a sauté of tofu or beef cubes with bell pepper, onion, and green beans in a spicy red sauce. *205 E. Ponce de Leon Ave., Decatur, 404/378–8622. AE, D, DC, MC, V. $*

15 e-5
PACIFIC RIM

Raymond and Anna Hsu (of Hsu's Gourmet) have crafted a warmly lit, wood-filled interior in which to present the dishes of Asia. Shredded green papayas and tofu moistened with lime juice zing with Thai chilies, while beef dishes offer assertive flavorings that range from Korean hot sauce to the sweet, pungent Hawaiian marinade. The little dishes and sushi work almost like Asian tapas, so it's easy to assemble a light meal. *303 Peachtree Center Ave., Downtown, 404/893–0018. AE, D, MC, V. No lunch weekends. $$–$$$$*

5 *c-5*
SAVU

Named for an island off the coast of Indonesia, the restaurant at the hip W Atlanta hotel dives coolly and with assurance into a melding of French, Chinese, Japanese, and Thai cuisines, each bringing its distinctive flavors to the dishes. Szechuan lobster pancakes recall the seafood pancakes of China and Korea, while crispy Beijing duck comes with the familiar scallion pancakes and a unique black-bean vinaigrette. Dessert returns to Occidental traditions, with "Christine's Candy Bar," a layering of dark chocolate, macadamia-nut brittle, vanilla, and raspberry. The wine list is extensive, with many bottles that pair well with a wide range of these dishes. Brunch reverts to American (Southern) standards, including Georgia pecan waffles and speckleheart grits. *111 Perimeter Center W, Dunwoody, 770/280–0700. AE, D, DC, MC, V. $$–$$$*

5 *d-2*
WOK & CHOPS

Out-of-the-ordinary dishes pepper the menu, which gathers a variety of tastes from throughout Asia. The noodle dishes run from Indonesian to Malaysian styles, and you can find many interestingly spicy seafood dishes, such as mango grouper and coconut–curry soft-shell crab. The most exotic combination is frogs' legs with black-bean sauce and sweetbreads. *Kings Market shopping center, 1425 Market Blvd., at Old Alabama and Holcomb Bridge Rds., Roswell, 770/552–8982. AE, D, MC, V. $*

PERSIAN

5 *c-3*
MIRAGE

This friendly, bright restaurant serves many good meatless dishes, beginning with appetizers that include an intriguingly tangy combination of herbed feta cheese and yogurt with a sprinkling of shallots, served with flat bread, and moving on to such pleasing but simple presentations as vegetable kabob perched on a bed of basmati rice. For meat eaters there are excellent lamb and chicken dishes. The wine list holds its own. *Abernathy Shopping Center, 6631-C Roswell Rd., Sandy Springs, 404/843–8300. AE, D, DC, MC, V. $–$$*

5 *c-5*
PERSEPOLIS

Iranian expats come here for the tastes of their homeland—kebabs, simmered stews, and meat and rice dishes flavored with dried fruits. The lunch buffet is an especially good value and an introduction to this elegant cuisine. The formerly dumpy dining room has been transformed into a bright and pleasant space. *6435 Roswell Rd., Sandy Springs, 404/257–9090. AE, MC, V. $$*

PERUVIAN

13 *c-3*
MACHU PICCHU

Stuffed toy llamas and a mannequin dressed in traditional costume set the stage for Atlanta's favorite (and just about its only) Peruvian restaurant. Peruvian patrons enjoy authentic *anticuchos* (beef-heart kabobs), *chanfainita* (beef-heart stew), and *caucau* (tripe stew), while American diners are likely to stick to more-familiar fare such as one of the ceviches of marinated seafood or mixed seafood soup. Indeed, seafood is the strong suit here, and it shows up in everything from omelets to stews. Beer and wine are served, and the traditional fruit drinks are excellent, especially those with mango. *Northeast Plaza shopping center, 3375 Buford Hwy., Northeast Atlanta, 404/320–3226. AE, D, DC, MC, V. Wine and beer only. Closed Tues. $–$$*

14 *f-5*
SWEET DEVIL MOON

The decor is homemade and low-budget, and the mellow room is crowded with tables and thrift-shop couches. The good, distinctly Latin American paintings on the walls are for sale. Pisco sours are the specialty drink, and South American bottlings dominate the wine list. The modernized Peruvian food comes in the form of tapas, perfect for making an evening of it, especially Wednesday through Saturday, when there's live music. Yucca *rellena* are croquettes of mashed yucca root with a snappy crust, creamy innards, and, at the center, a sweet and spicy treasure of diced chicken, red bell pepper, and raisins. Paella, a light chicken soup with egg, and a fantastic high-rise flan are some other options. *350 Meade Rd., Decatur, 404/371–3999. AE, D, MC, V. Closed Sun. No lunch. $–$$*

PIZZA

12 *g-2*

CALIFORNIA PIZZA KITCHEN

Lots of glass, wood, and white tile give these designer-pizza specialty restaurants a hip ambience. The pizza tends to be trendy, too, appearing with ingredients from every cuisine imaginable, from Thai to Japanese to Southern. The best, though, stick closer to the pizza's original world, the Mediterranean (the one with goat cheese and roasted peppers is especially good). Sandwiches, salads, and pastas are also available, with the last appearing in such odd international variations as Kung Pao spaghetti. The full bar includes decent wines and beers. *Lenox Square (lower level, near Macy's), 3393 Peachtree Rd., Buckhead, 404/262–9221. Reservations not accepted. AE, D, DC, MC, V. $–$$*

5 *f-1*

6301 North Point Mall, across from Sears, Alpharetta, 770/664–8246.

5 *c-5*

4600 Ashford-Dunwoody Rd., just north of Perimeter Mall, Dunwoody, 770/393–0390.

15 *h-4*

CAMELI'S GOURMET PIZZA JOINT

Cameli's is run by the same two brothers who operate Pastificio Cameli in East Atlanta. Their creations include many tasty "stuffed pizzas," including "half moon" versions that are ideal for solo diners and are filled with ingredients of your choice; the unique combinations include "Dante's Delight," with black olives. *699 Ponce de Leon Ave., Poncey-Highland, 404/249–9020. Reservations not accepted. AE, D, DC, MC, V. No lunch Sun. $–$$*

14 *d-2*

EVERYBODY'S PIZZA

The pizza with green peppers, mushrooms, and tomatoes is especially popular with Emory students at the Decatur Road location, but all the pies at both outlets are delicious; so are the pepperoni pizza crisps, especially the kind with onions and cheese, and they are a little lower in calories. Huge salads and soups are excellent, too. There's beer and wine only at Decatur Road, full bar at Highland Ave. *1593 N. Decatur Rd., Decatur, 404/377–7766. Reservations not accepted. AE, D, DC, MC, V. $–$$*

14 *a-2*

1040 N. Highland Ave., Virginia-Highland, 404/873–4545.

15 *g-8*

GRANT CENTRAL PIZZA & PASTA

This pizza–pasta outlet has operations in both the burgeoning East Atlanta and Grant Park restaurant scenes. What they have in common are excellent pies, but each has its specialties: calzones, salads, and a nightly special, along with table service, at Grant Park, and sandwiches (but counter service only) at East Atlanta. Toppings range from traditional pepperoni to black olive on the pizzas at both locations. Beer and wine are available, and the choices are quite decent. *1279 Glenwood Ave., East Atlanta, 404/627–0007. Reservations not accepted. MC, V. No lunch Sat. $*

14 *b-8*

451 Cherokee Ave., Grant Park, 404/523–8900. Closed Sun. No lunch Sat.

5 *d-5*

MELLOW MUSHROOM

The metro area has about two dozen Mellow Mushroom franchises, so sooner or later anyone in search of good pizza is bound to step into one. Even the most demanding pizza aficionado isn't going to be disappointed, with offerings that include a white pizza with garlic, olive oil, sun-dried and fresh tomatoes, onions, and cheese; pesto pizza with spinach, mushrooms, and tomatoes; and steak calzone, a sort of steak-and-cheese sandwich. Beer and wine are available. *Dunwoody Corners shopping center, 5575 Chamblee-Dunwoody Rd., Dunwoody, 770/396–1696. AE, MC, V. Wine and beer only. $*

13 c-6

1679 LaVista Rd., Northeast Atlanta, 404/325–0330.

5 h-6

331 Rockbridge Rd., at U.S. 29, Lilburn, 770/921–1612.

5 f-4

Marketplace shopping center, 6135 Peachtree Pkwy., Norcross, 770/729–1555.

4 h-6

2150 Powers Ferry Rd., at Akers Mill Rd., Marietta, 770/955–4311.

5 d-7

4058 Peachtree Rd., Brookhaven, 404/266–1661.

13 e-3

MO'S PIZZA

Area high school and college students are among the regulars who flock here for great traditional pizza, which proves they have good taste. The yeasty pizza dough is superior, the tomato sauce is earthy, and the mozzarella is rich. Other toppings are available, too, of course, and so are great hot dogs, excellent chicken wings, and sandwiches of all kinds. There's an extensive beer collection, including Haake Beck's nonalcoholic malt, plus wine and wine coolers. *3109 Briarcliff Rd., at Clairmont Rd., Northeast Atlanta, 404/320–1258. Reservations not accepted. MC, V. $–$$*

9 a-6

PARTNERS II PIZZA

Don't look for the same old toppings here—unless you consider potatoes with sour cream, cheddar cheese, green onions, and bacon or buffalo meat, mozzarella cheese, and smoked provolone to be typical toppings. Traditional pasta dishes, including homemade lasagna, and meatball subs get raves, too. Good wine is available. The weekday lunch and Monday-night buffet feature all-you-can-eat pizza and salad. *215 Northlake Dr., Peachtree City, 770/487–9393. Reservations not accepted. AE, D, DC, MC, V. $*

12 d-8

ROCKY'S BRICK OVEN PIZZA & ITALIAN RESTAURANT

There's a lot more here than just pizza, including a cioppino (at the Buckhead location only), a tomato-based seafood stew that's served in a bread bowl. But the pizzas are the draw, and they range from basic tomato and cheese to excellent white pies. The Virginia-Highland location adds huge sandwiches to the offerings. Delivery is available from both locations. *1776 Peachtree St., Buckhead, 404/876–9441. Reservations not accepted. AE, D, DC, MC, V. $–$$*

14 a-1

1395 N. Highland Ave., Virginia-Highland, 404/876–1111.

15 d-6

ROSA'S PIZZA

Transplanted New Yorkers and Chicagoans keep lining up for by-the-slice lunches at this straightforward spot. Very thin pizza crust with a good yeasty flavor comes topped with a variety of choices, but the best is the classic and simple tomato and cheese. *62 Broad St., Downtown, 404/521–2596. No credit cards. Closed weekends. $–$$*

14 a-4

SAVAGE PIZZA

The pizza combos at this place with table service and takeout walk the wild side. Mai Pai comes with spicy red-pepper sauce and fresh pineapple; chicken cordon bleu comes off a bit better, with garlic white sauce, roasted chicken, and prosciutto. Small pies, individual slices, salads, and calzone are also available. *484 Moreland Ave., Little Five Points, 404/523–0500. Reservations not accepted. AE, MC, V. $–$$*

SEAFOOD

12 f-4

ATLANTA FISH MARKET

There's no missing this place, because a huge multistory bronze fish announces its location; the dining room is distinctive, too, divided into sections that resemble railway cars. Despite these decorative excesses, the food stands on its own merit: gumbo, crab cakes, steamed sea bass Hong Kong style, and the raw oyster selection are all superb. The wine list is worthy and offers good choices by the glass. *265 Pharr Rd., Buckhead, 404/262–3165. Reservations essential. AE, D, DC, MC, V. No lunch Sun. $$$–$$$$*

12 h-2

CHEQUERS SEAFOOD GRILL

Stick to simply prepared fresh fish and other basic fare at these pub–restaurants and you'll probably be quite happy. Both Chequers are well located for an after-shopping bite, and Sunday brunch is popular. *3424 Peachtree Rd., across from Phipps Plaza, just behind Ritz-Carlton, Buckhead, 404/842–9997. AE, D, DC, MC, V. No lunch weekends. $$–$$$$*

5 c-5

236 Perimeter Pkwy., near Perimeter Mall, Dunwoody, 770/391–9383.

5 b-1

COAST 92

An entry from the team behind the much-lauded Dick and Harry's, Coast 92 has a sleek, blue, glassy, underwater feel. It's a fitting setting, as the specialty here is really fresh seafood, inventively prepared and presented. Shrimp and grits, an old Charleston classic, are perked up with bits of wonderfully meaty sweet-cured bacon and a garlicky white wine–butter sauce; thick broiled swordfish steak, latticed with asparagus spears and napped with béchamel, sits in a pool of rich lobster sauce. The custardy key-lime pie recalls the Latin standard *dulce de leche. 625 Crossville Rd., Roswell, 770/649–6739. AE, D, DC, MC, V. $$–$$$$*

5 b-5

EMBERS SEAFOOD GRILL

Rustic, wacky, casual, showing the patina of time—this seafood grill evokes the shacks you've seen at the shore. The seafood chowder, fresh grilled fish, blackened amberjack, crab cakes, and key-lime pie are as good as any you'd find at a place like that, too. *234 Hildebrand Dr., near Roswell Rd., Sandy Springs, 404/256–0977. AE, D, DC, MC, V. Closed Sun. No lunch. $$–$$$*

12 d-7

FISHBONE PIRANHA BAR

Coconut-battered deep-fried shrimp (crisp and delicious) provide a perfect nibble as you sit at the huge copper-covered bar and prepare you for a wide array of fish and shellfish dishes inspired by cuisines from around the world. Thai-style peppery calamari and wood-grilled Hawaiian wahoo capture the spirit of this inventive food. Just try to resist the Barbados rum cake for dessert. *1874 Peachtree Rd., Buckhead, 404/367–4772. AE, D, DC, MC, V. No lunch weekends. $$–$$$$*

5 b-6

FISHMONGER'S

The house soup is the Fishmonger's Stew, based on the lightest possible seafood broth, fragrant with saffron, and containing mussels, clams, fish, and shrimp. Crab and shrimp cakes with a spicy curry mayonnaise make a light but well-seasoned treat. There's also an excellent filet mignon of Argentine beef with chimichurri sauce—a blend of parsley, white vinegar, garlic, and olive oil. The wine list has a number of South African selections, a tribute to the home country of Angelo Laios, one of the two owners (the other, Zimbabwe native Nik Panagopoulos, also lived there at length). *Belle Isle shopping center, 4969 Roswell Rd., Suite 160 (lower rear level), Sandy Springs, 404/459–9003. Reservations essential. AE, D, DC, MC, V. No lunch Sat.–Thurs. $$–$$$*

5 d-5

GOLDFISH

Outside there's a dining terrace with a pretty sunken courtyard. Inside, it's of-the-moment glamour: stacked stone, reddish wood, wrought iron. The space is huge, high, and rather dark. And it can get loud—because it's a wild success. And why not? With an enormous sushi menu, as well as a range of really well done seafood dinners presented in a steak-house format—you order your sides, such as garlic spinach or baked potatoes, separately—and even a short list of chicken and top-quality beef choices, there's something here to please everybody. *Perimeter Mall, 4400 Ashford-Dunwoody Rd., Dunwoody, 770/671–0100. AE, D, DC, MC, V. $$–$$$$*

12 e-6

JIM WHITE'S HALF SHELL

Good seafood is what you get at this longtime favorite. The she-crab soup, a light version of this low-country specialty, is a classic, and this is about the only place in town where you can get scamp, a large-mouth Florida fish that yields a meaty thick fillet. Stone crab claws are a much-awaited seasonal specialty. *Peachtree Battle shopping center, 2349 Peachtree Rd., Peachtree Battle, 404/237–9924. AE, D, DC, MC, V. No lunch. $$–$$$$*

`12` h-7

MARRA'S SEAFOOD & STEAKS

The kitchen here explores American cuisine from all four corners, with such offerings as swordfish crusted with ancho peppers and served with pineapple–tomatillo salsa and jícama salad, and giant scallops encircled by house-made salmon bacon and paired with grilled yams and a roasted corn–shallot sauce. In good weather, you can dine alfresco on the large deck to the rear of the small former residence. *1782 Cheshire Bridge Rd., Northeast Atlanta, 404/874–7347. Reservations essential. AE, D, DC, MC, V. No lunch. $$–$$$$*

`5` e-6

STRINGER'S FISH CAMP

Imagine a fishing camp—you know, slightly scruffy, with worn Formica tables and plastic-covered chairs. That's Stringer's. Seafood may be ordered anyway you wish, but this is the place to spend your fried-fish calories: the deep-fried catfish, shrimp, scallops, and oysters are perfectly done. The seafood platter easily feeds two. *3384 Shallowford Rd., Chamblee, 770/458–7145. AE, D, MC, V. $$*

SOUTHERN

`15` d-2

BOBBY & JUNE'S KOUNTRY KITCHEN

Hams hang from the rafters and rockers sit on the porch, and both the hard hats and Georgia Tech students who come here for breakfast and lunch find the rustic cabin-style ambience comfortable. The sliced barbecue pork sandwich is tops in its category, and the biscuits deserve a medal. Some vegetables are frozen but prepared with taste. Breakfast is Southern style, with grits (albeit instant ones). *375 14th St., Northwest Atlanta, 404/876–3872. Reservations not accepted. MC, V. No dinner. $*

`15` b-8

CHANTERELLES

As in the typical steam-table, "meat-and-two" eatery, you order at the counter here. But then a waiter in white shirt and black bow tie delivers to your table a tray with a setting of heavy flatware and a linen napkin. The food is similarly elevated above the norm: look

for curries, Cajun-spiced fish, eggplant stewed in tomato, peas in cream sauce. The neighborhood has few eateries; this one serves as a social center of sorts and offers a warm welcome. *646 Evans St., West End, 404/758–0909. AE, MC, V. Closed Mon. $*

`12` h-7

THE COLONNADE RESTAURANT

The Southern food here is the real thing: proper biscuits, yeast rolls and corn bread, the perfect salmon patty, country ham steak that's not afraid to sport a bone, and excellent Southern-style hot and cold vegetables keep the place bustling even on weekdays. There's a separate bar and lounge opposite the dining room, and the crowd is an amusing mix of gay men and blue-haired ladies, all seeming to enjoy their martinis with equal gusto. *1879 Cheshire Bridge Rd., Northeast Atlanta, 404/874–5642. No credit cards. No lunch Sun. $–$$*

`4` f-5

1848 HOUSE

The fine Classical Revival plantation house is said to be haunted, but its grounds provide a significant buffer from surrounding urban intrusions. Chef Thomas McEachern wanders into Italian dishes, but in general, Southern food and the plantation forms of Southern cooking dominate—from the excellent she-crab soup to the buttermilk-fried quail, fried green tomatoes, trout, and sometimes game, depending on the season. (McEachern can create a vegetarian feast upon request.) The "Sweet Georgia Brown" dessert tops rhubarb with vanilla-bean ice milk, a very Southern finale. The wine list is good, and the Sunday brunch is a large, jazz-accompanied buffet. *780 S. Cobb Dr., Marietta, 770/428–1848. Reservations essential. AE, D, DC, MC, V. No lunch. $$–$$$*

`14` f-1

EVANS FINE FOODS

Down-home food is the draw at this Decatur favorite. The daily specials get raves, and breakfast is a high point, with country ham, grits, eggs, and all the trimmings. For lunch or dinner ("dinner or supper" in Southern parlance), the favorites are the fried chicken livers, the meat loaf, the country-fried steak, and the barbecue. At all meals, veggies and everything else are made from scratch. *2125 N. Decatur Rd., Decatur, 404/634–6294. Reservations not accepted. No credit cards. Closed Sun. $*

15 *e-4*

GLADYS AND RON'S CHICKEN & WAFFLES

The chicken-and-waffles combo supposedly originated during the Harlem Renaissance; that doesn't make it Southern by a strict geographic reckoning, but it has found its place in black-American culinary culture. It's a favorite treat of Gladys Knight, the Motown star (and Georgia native), who owns this popular spot with gospel crooner Ron Winans. The barbecue sauce on the fried chicken combines with the waffles' sweet syrup for the desired effect, and you're indeed meant to eat them together. Other staples of the Southern kitchen are available, including candied yams, macaroni and cheese, salmon croquettes, grits and eggs, red beans and rice, chicken omelets, and the signature dessert, sweet-potato cheesecake with whipped cream and cinnamon. *579 Peachtree St., Midtown, 404/874–9393. AE, D, MC, V. $*

8 *c-1*

LET'S EAT CAFÉ

There's enough going for this tiny place to make the effort of seeking it out on a side street in an industrial area worth your while. Whiting is dipped in cornmeal, fried, and served with good grits—an outstanding dish in the best of southeast Georgia culinary traditions. The sweet-potato pie is flat-out awesome. *780 Glendale Rd., Decatur, 404/297–9316. Reservations not accepted. No credit cards. No alcohol. Closed Sun. No dinner. $*

14 *a-3*

MAJESTIC FOOD SHOPS

For late-night fare, this classic 24-hour diner, open since 1929, is a reliable and safe haven that includes good breakfast dishes as well as dependable renditions of fried chicken and other offerings. Want a little people-watching with your grilled ham steak and coconut-cream pie? The characters who hang out here provide some splendid sightseeing—you could cast a movie. *1031 Ponce de Leon Ave., Poncey-Highland, 404/875–0276. Reservations not accepted. No credit cards. No alcohol. $*

15 *f-4*

MARY MAC'S TEA ROOM

Now in its third generation of ownership, Mary Mac's (which is not a true tearoom despite its name) has fed everyone from film stars to old-time Atlantans. When the legislature is in session, politicos hash out their differences over superior fried chicken, country-fried steak, fresh vegetables Southern style, and homemade desserts. You sit down, pick up a pencil, and write down your order. Brunch is served on weekends. Don't be surprised if everyone from the cashier to the busboy calls you "baby." *224 Ponce de Leon Ave., Midtown, 404/876–1800. No credit cards. No dinner Sun. $–$$*

5 *g-7*

MATTHEWS CAFETERIA

Founded in 1955 and said to be DeKalb County's oldest continuously operating restaurant, this time- and use-worn establishment may look like pure country, but the occasional Rolls-Royce has been known to park outside. No matter what you drive, you line up to claim a tray and select from a steam table of various specialties, depending on the day of the week, market availability, and the whim of the kitchen. Possibilities include great squash casserole, macaroni and cheese, grilled Polish sausage with sauerkraut, and corned beef and stewed cabbage. Peach cobbler is the dessert to save room for, but then there's the banana pudding, too. *2299 Main St., Tucker, 770/491–9577. No credit cards. No alcohol. $*

7 *f-3*

MRS. BEA'S KITCHEN

Within the confines of Heath's Cascade Grocery, Beatrice Heath makes superb fried chicken, fried pork chops, fresh vegetables, and cakes. Breakfast and all-day lunch to 7:30 are offered. There's takeout only. *787 Cascade Ave., Cascade Heights, 404/755–0543. Reservations not accepted. No credit cards. No alcohol. No dinner. $*

12 *a-2*

OK CAFÉ

Families love the OK's kid-friendly fare and the casual, 1950s-style atmosphere. The best meal is breakfast, with good grits, omelets, and pancakes; the savory classics of American home-style cooking that show up at other meals include meat loaf, country-fried steak, mashed potatoes and gravy, fried chicken, and pot roast. It's open very early to very late weekends. Takeout is available. *1284 W. Paces Ferry Rd., at I–75, Buckhead, 404/233–2888. Reservations not accepted. AE, D, DC, MC, V. Wine and beer only. $–$$*

7 *g-5*

ORIGINAL DWARF HOUSE

The menu mounted on a wall of this 1950s-feeling restaurant includes steak and hamburgers and—the real reason to come here—the famous chicken hot brown sandwiches (basically bacon-topped chicken casserole in white sauce). It closes at 4 AM Sunday morning and reopens 5 AM Monday morning, then is open around the clock until Sunday rolls around again. *461 Central Ave., Hapeville, 404/762–1746. Reservations not accepted. No credit cards. Closed Sun. $*

14 *g-4*

OUR WAY CAFÉ

Home cooking that is wickedly cheap and served on steam tables draws students from nearby Agnes Scott College. You line up for your tray and select your meat and sides. Choices vary daily and might include meat loaf, chicken enchiladas, and roast pork and, for veggies, green-bean or squash casserole, collard greens, sweet-potato soufflé, and macaroni and cheese. You'll get out of here with so much change from a $10 bill that you'll think you stole your lunch. *303 E. College Ave., Decatur, 404/292–9356. Reservations not accepted. No credit cards. No alcohol. Closed weekends. $*

14 *h-1*

PICCADILLY CLASSIC AMERICAN COOKING

This Baton Rouge–based outfit, founded in 1944, offers cafeteria-style Southern food at more than 20 locations around the metro area—and maintains a level of quality that is consistently high. Good étouffée and jambalaya are occasional specials, while gumbo is a regular item. Baked chicken, baked and fried fish, fried chicken, salmon patties, good veggies (only the mashed potatoes are packaged), and desserts are the popular dishes with the budget-conscious diners here. It's open until 8:30 PM, with continuous service, and on holidays except Christmas. *Suburban Plaza shopping center, 2595 N. Decatur Rd., Decatur, 404/373–5116. Reservations not accepted. AE, D, DC, MC, V. No alcohol. $*

15 *g-1*
Ansley Mall shopping center, 1452 Piedmont Ave., Ansley Park, 404/872–8091.

12 *g-5*
Lindbergh Plaza shopping center, 2581 Piedmont Rd., Buckhead, 404/364–9636.

12 *a-3*
Howell Mill Square shopping center, 1715 Howell Mill Rd., Northwest Atlanta, 404/352–1743.

5 *e-1*
891 Mansell Rd. (Alpharetta Hwy.), Roswell, 770/518–8905.

4 *g-7*
2781 S. Cobb Dr., at Windy Hill Rd., Smyrna, 770/435–6707.

13 *h-5*

QUINNIE'S

Southern-style vegetables prepared without meat or grease are what this bare-bones, family-run restaurant is known for. So, it has the right to designate some dishes "Heart Healthy," but it's not like everything is. As you move along the steam tables, you may be tempted, justifiably, by the Brunswick stew, fried chicken, macaroni and cheese, barbecue, and, on Friday, deep-fried, cornmeal-crusted whole catfish. *2860 LaVista Rd., Northeast Atlanta, 404/728–8763. Reservations not accepted. MC, V. No alcohol. Closed Sun. $*

5 *f-5*

ROY'S DINER

A native of Boston owns this classic diner, and a native of Guatemala oversees the kitchen. Nonetheless, the fare is classic Southern, with very good grits and eggs for breakfast and homemade specials that vary daily but might include stuffed peppers, meat loaf, fried pork chops, and fresh vegetables—plus shakes, malts, and classic floats. *600 Buford Hwy., Norcross, 770/242–7211. Reservations not accepted. No credit cards. No alcohol. Closed Sun. No dinner, no lunch Sat. $*

15 *e-4*

SHARK BAR

Part of a national chain, this place presents itself as an "upscale African-American" restaurant. Come not only to dive into the cooking but also to glean fashion tips from the stunningly well dressed clientele. Seafood gumbo; roast chicken with okra and andouille sausage in dark red roux; barbecued ribs; and smothered pork chops are among your entrée choices. *571 Peachtree St., Midtown, 404/815–8333. AE, D, DC, MC, V. No dinner Mon.– Tues., no lunch Sat. $$–$$$*

15 d-2
SILVER SKILLET

An authentic Southern-diner atmosphere pervades this long-standing establishment, where breakfast and lunch (aka "dinner" in the South) are the only meals served. Eggs, grits, and country ham breakfasts bring in the locals; at other meals, a mix of blue-collar workers, professionals, and students shows up for the classics of Southern home-style fare, including baked chicken and fish, meat loaf, tender grilled pork chops, chicken-fried steak, superb vegetables, and fantastic pies. *200 14th St., Midtown, 404/874–1388. Reservations not accepted. AE, D, DC, MC, V. No alcohol. No lunch weekends, no dinner. $*

15 h-5
SON'S PLACE

The late Deacon Burton—who for many years presided next door, at what almost everybody agreed was the city's top source for iron skillet–fried chicken—need not worry: his reputation is secure in the cooking of his son, Lenn Story. Along with the legendary fried chicken, vegetables, pound cake, sweet-potato pie, and light, flat cornmeal hoe cakes keep patrons very happy at this bright, cheery place. Great homemade lemonade makes you forget that there's no alcohol here. *100 Hurt St., Inman Park, 404/581–0530. No credit cards. No alcohol. $*

15 c-3
THELMA'S KITCHEN

Though Thelma Grundy was booted out of her longtime Luckie Street location by construction for the 1996 Olympics, she soon found a home in this old hotel and remains an Atlanta culinary institution. Her fans have followed her for okra pancakes (a must when they're on the menu), to be accompanied by such favorites as fried catfish, well-seasoned vegetables, macaroni and cheese, "cold" slaw, and pecan pie. *Roxy Hotel, 768 Marietta St., Downtown, 404/688–5855. No credit cards. No alcohol. Closed weekends. No dinner. $*

8 a-8
TRUETT'S GRILL

The authentic 1950s diner is named for Truett Cathy, the grandfatherly motorcycle-riding guy who founded Chick-fil-A in Hapeville. Restored antique cars dot the grounds, a thrill for car buffs. The good home-style fare includes the famous chicken sandwich, plus fresh vegetables, and steaks. You can get breakfast here, too. *2042 Mt. Zion Rd., Morrow, 770/210–0500. Reservations not accepted. MC, V. Closed Sun. $*

SOUTHWESTERN

15 g-7
AGAVÉ

The cooking has its roots in New Mexico, while the staff and clientele are about as multicultural as you can find. While you're looking at the menu, blue corn chips arrive—still hot from the fryer—along with a medium-fiery cooked red salsa. There are traditional choices, like *posole* (the stew of hominy, pork, and red chilies), and inventive ones, like black sesame–crusted seared tuna on a bed of sautéed vegetables, topped with marinated cucumber. The bar offers dozens of tequilas. Brunch is served on Sunday. *242 Boulevard Dr., Cabbagetown, 404/588–0006. AE, MC, V. No lunch. $–$$*

8 a-8
AZTECA GRILL

Some of the best examples of the kitchen's inventiveness can be found in the specials. In December Azteca's been known to make *posole*, that great, classic one-pot meal with hominy and pork (traditionally a whole pig's head) of the American Southwest. Menu staples, such as fish tacos, green-chili stew, and the chocolate chimichanga for dessert are excellent, too. *1140 Morrow Industrial Blvd., off Jonesboro Rd., near Southlake Mall shopping center, Morrow, 770/968–0907. Reservations not accepted. AE, D, DC, MC, V. $–$$*

5 c-5
CANYON CAFE

The Tex-Mex fare offered by this Dallas-based eatery is a hit. Margaritas are generous and not short in the tequila department; South Texas tortilla soup, thick with tortilla strips, is a good version of the classic; the paella is respectable; and the chicken-fried steak spills off the sides of the plate. Salad dressings are all made on the premises, including a decent fat-free sun dried–tomato vinaigrette. The spinach–and–Portobello mushroom quesadilla is out of this world and works as a vegetarian option (though carnivores love it, too). *118 Perimeter Center W, near Perimeter Mall, Dunwoody, 770/395–6605. AE, D, DC, MC, V. $–$$*

5 *e-1*

11405 Haynes Bridge Rd., near North Point Mall, Alpharetta, 770/346–0996.

12 *e-6*

GEORGIA GRILLE

The "Georgia" part of the name is a reference not to the state but to Georgia O'Keeffe. Owner Karen Hilliard is a great admirer of her art, although work by local artist Steve Penley graces the walls. The fare is artful and includes "hot shots," jalapeños stuffed with cheese, breaded in cornmeal, and fried; lobster-stuffed enchilada; and excellent flan. The short wine list is carefully chosen to go with the food, but the margaritas get the raves. *Peachtree Square shopping center, 2290 Peachtree Rd., Buckhead, 404/352–3517. Reservations not accepted. AE, MC, V. Closed Mon. No lunch. $$–$$$*

2 *a-8*

LA PAZ

The management of La Paz could give lessons in how to run a chain dining operation without sacrificing detail, authenticity, and quality. Each restaurant has its own defining architecture and personality: the original location, in Sandy Springs, evokes a cantina, while the Vinings location resembles a Mexican chapel. All are good spots to stop after work for a drink, and the menu attracts families. Vegetarian options include spinach enchiladas made with blue-corn tortillas. *250 Cinema View, Woodstock, 770/591–1073. Reservations not accepted. AE, D, DC, MC, V. $–$$*

5 *f-1*

11605 Jones Bridge Rd., Alpharetta, 770/521–0506.

5 *c-4*

6410 Roswell Rd., Sandy Springs, 404/256–3555. No lunch weekends.

4 *h-6*

2950 New Paces Ferry Rd., Vinings, 770/801–0020.

12 *f-3*

NAVA

Fine Southwestern art adorns the several levels of this high-energy restaurant, where traditional fare is enhanced by deft handling of seasonings and sophisticated presentations. Many of the appetizers, including a barbecued rabbit tostada with black beans and arugula salad, suffice as a light meal. Or, you may want to stay on the lighter side by assembling an assortment of side dishes for a vegetarian platter that could include a tamale stuffed with sweet potato or Portobello mushrooms, white-bean enchiladas, and a black-bean cake. The B&B Cube (a cube of chocolate with a B&B-flavored mousse and crushed chocolate-chip cookies enfolded within) is a chocolate attack. The good wine list offers plenty of fine by-the-glass choices. *3060 Peachtree Rd., near W. Paces Ferry Rd., Buckhead, 404/240–1984. Reservations essential. AE, D, DC, MC, V. No lunch weekends. $$–$$$*

14 *a-2*

NOCHE

Tom Catherall, a native of Scotland who owns this bustling, gleaming restaurant (as well as steak house Prime), has fallen for the flavors of chipotle, ancho, and serrano chilies; they infuse such dishes as tortilla soup with avocado and fresh cheese, as well as grilled shrimp with corn *masa*–garlic sauce. The chocolate *tres leches* (three milks, literally) is served as a sort of latte with chocolate cigarettes—clever, rich, and satisfying. There's good wine here, but the margaritas are the draw. *1000 Virginia Ave., Virginia-Highland, 404/815–9155. Reservations not accepted. AE, D, DC, MC, V. No lunch. $$–$$$*

12 *h-7*

SUNDOWN CAFE

Southwestern fare rarely gets better or more modern in execution than this: chicken-liver salad; roast pork tenderloin rubbed with Southwestern spices and served with a tomatillo-infused gravy and ancho mashed potatoes; tangy turnip greens enlivened by zippy arbol chilies. The chocolate chimichanga is a piece of pastry genius. *2165 Cheshire Bridge Rd., Northeast Atlanta, 404/321–1118. Reservations not accepted. AE, MC, V. Closed Sun. No lunch Sat. $$*

15 h-3

TORTILLAS

An energetic, hip, long-popular taquería, this student and grunge-kid hangout offers some of the best cheap food in town. Burritos and quesadillas are the main attractions, bringing in a constant stream of devotees, and the freshly made guacamole and salsas, especially the green tomatillo, are ideal accompaniments. Beer is the best quaff with this fare. *774 Ponce de Leon Ave., Virginia-Highland, 404/892–0193. Reservations not accepted. No credit cards. $*

SPANISH

15 e-3

ANDALUZ

You'd never believe that the sleek room with the stylish mural and a sunny patio sporting a stainless-steel fountain was a bleak gas station–convenience store. The food is just as much a revelation: authentic Spanish tapas, produced by a chef from Barcelona, and a few main courses, like paella. Try the *esqueixada*, salt cod and tomato with red-onion *concassé*, or a plate of tiny chorizo sausages poached in sparkling wine. For dessert there's a mind-expanding choice: toasted bread topped with warm, bitter chocolate, olive oil, and coarse salt. Wash it all down with the house sangria. *903 Peachtree St., Midtown, 404/875–7013. AE, DC, MC, V. Closed Sun. $–$$*

12 e-4

VINO!

A tapas and wine bar plus full-service restaurant, Vino! has its roots firmly planted in Spanish cuisine. Empanadas (meat-filled turnovers), octopus, olives, and chorizo are good starters, while the better dinner entrées focus on seafood. Grilled salmon with romesco, a Catalan sauce made with peppers, ground nuts, and olive oil, is straight from Barcelona. The very good wine list even has dry (truly dry) sherry by the glass and has moved these aperitif wines off the dessert list into their own category. There's a reserve list of fine Bordeaux as well. *2900 Peachtree Rd., Buckhead, 404/816–0511. AE, D, MC, V. Closed Sun. $$–$$$*

STEAK

4 h-7

BLACKSTONE

The excellent steaks here come from prime Iowa corn-fed beef. But the non-beef choices are plentiful. A grilled wild-game sausage is served with Asiago-cheese grits and cranberry-onion compote; steak tartare is still on the menu (an increasingly rare sighting these days), and fish and seafood aren't overlooked, either. Some wines are offered by the glass. *Vinings West shopping center, 4835 S. Atlanta Rd., Vinings, 404/794–6100. AE, D, DC, MC, V. Closed Sun. No lunch. $$–$$$$*

12 g-3

BONE'S

In an atmosphere conducive to gathering all the fraternity boys in town, well-established Bone's serves excellent steaks, as well as very fine lamb and veal. The lobster bisque is justifiably well regarded for its silky texture and fulsome lobster flavor, and the huge onion rings are so good they alone have been known to draw in customers. The wine list is a serious piece of work, with fine American, French, and Italian wines. *3139 Piedmont Rd., Buckhead, 404/237–2663. Reservations essential. AE, D, DC, MC, V. No lunch weekends. $$$–$$$$*

6 a-3

BUGABOO CREEK LODGE & BAR

The rustic, lodge-centered lifestyle of the Canadian Rockies provides the theme for this steak house, which also offers grilled shrimp, salmon, and chicken. Steak is the meal deal, however, and it's offered at very fair prices. For lunch, there are burgers and assorted sandwiches. The wine list is ho-hum, so pick one of the Canadian brews instead. *3505 Satellite Blvd., Duluth, 770/476–1500. Reservations not accepted. AE, D, DC, MC, V. $$*

5 e-1

CABERNET

Finally here's a restaurant equal in scale to the sprawling new homes that carpet this northside suburb. The executive class dines on prime aged beef—the rock salt–marinated rib eye for two is especially choice—and a few top-quality seafood items. Choose from the vast dining room with a view into the exhibition kitchen, or one of the more intimate spaces, which include a stone-walled wine cellar. *5575 Windward Pkwy., Alpharetta, 770/777–5955. AE, D, DC, MC, V. Closed Sun. No lunch Sat. $$$–$$$$*

13 *a-4*

THE CABIN

You may feel as though you've entered a very posh, private hunt club when you walk into this rustic structure complete with trophies and antler chandeliers. That, of course, is the whole idea. But this is a friendly, casual setting in which to enjoy serious food that includes beef, buffalo steak, wild game, and crab cakes—as well as outrageously good key-lime and pecan pies. *2678 Buford Hwy., Northeast Atlanta, 404/315–7676. Reservations essential. AE, D, DC, MC, V. Closed Sun. No lunch Sat. $$–$$$$*

4 *f-3*

CHEROKEE CATTLE CO.

Beyond steaks that run the gamut from an applewood-smoked, bacon-wrapped fillet to a 21-ounce porterhouse (many anointed with the house bourbon–peppercorn sauce), this roadhouse-style restaurant does such regional classics as chicken-fried steak and house-made chili, straight from the heart of Texas. *2710 Canton Hwy., Marietta, 770/427–0490. AE, D, DC, MC, V. No lunch weekends. $$–$$$*

12 *e-3*

CHOPS

The sleek, contemporary clublike interior of the main dining room makes this an attractive spot for businessmen (as opposed to businesspeople), which seems to be its main claim to fame. Steaks and chops are cut with the male appetite in mind, and salads and sandwiches are big, too. The downstairs Lobster Bar, where shellfish and fin critters dominate the menu, is more appropriate for a romantic dinner (it's not open for lunch). Raw Blue Points are a grand beginning in either venue, while rum-raisin bread pudding with bourbon-vanilla sauce is the ideal conclusion. The wine list has a lot to offer, with many good choices by the glass. *70 W. Paces Ferry Rd., Buckhead, 404/262–2675. Reservations essential. AE, D, DC, MC, V. No lunch weekends. $$$–$$$$*

5 *e-1*

KILLER CREEK CHOP HOUSE

Crafted with Frank Lloyd Wright designs in mind, the building is a study in natural materials, chiefly stone and wood. The steaks, rack of lamb, and Jack Daniels–marinated London broil are prepared naturally, too, grilled over hickory-wood fires. In addition, the menu includes grilled fresh fish and, occasionally, wild boar, venison, and other game, and you can begin a meal with a pot of mussels or a selection from the raw bar. The wine list is extensive and focuses on California wines with a generous number by the glass. Jazz plays every night except Sunday. *1700 Mansell Rd., Alpharetta, 770/649–0064. AE, D, DC, MC, V. No lunch. $$–$$$*

5 *b-6*

KOBE STEAKS

This Japanese steak house does superior tender beef, chicken, fish, and seafood right before your eyes—with no small amount of flourish, and with extraordinary results. There's a children's menu, so you can bring the little diners. *The Prado shopping center, 5600 Roswell Rd., Sandy Springs, 404/256–0810. AE, D, DC, MC, V. No lunch. $$–$$$*

12 *d-7*

LONGHORN STEAKS

It's almost impossible not to come upon one of these Atlanta-based steak houses, since there are 30 of them in the metro area. Families love them for steaks, ribs, chicken, and the fun of eating peanuts—and tossing the shells on the floor—while waiting for the food to come. *2151 Peachtree Rd., near Collier Rd., Buckhead, 404/351–6086. Reservations not accepted. AE, D, DC, MC, V. $$*

7 *b-1*

1355 East–West Connector, Austell, 770/941–4816.

9 *g-1*

7882 Tara Blvd., near GA 138, Jonesboro, 770/477–5365.

13 *e-6*

2892 N. Druid Hills Rd., Northeast Atlanta, 404/636–3817.

4 *h-6*

Akers Mill Square, 2973 Cobb Pkwy., Northwest Atlanta, 770/859–0341.

5 *d-5*

MCKENDRICK'S

Game, fish dishes (especially the grilled selections), buffalo steaks, and veal chops fare well at this clubby dining room, as does the steak. Side orders, even sauces, are priced separately, in the classic steak-house manner. The extensive wine list is well selected and varied. *Park Place shopping center, 4505 Ashford-Dunwoody Rd., across from Perimeter Mall, Dunwoody, 770/512–8888. AE, D, DC, MC, V. Closed Sun. No lunch. $$$–$$$$*

15 *e-5*

MORTON'S OF CHICAGO

Atlanta is blessed with two of these Chicago-based steak houses, which have plenty of clubby character despite being chain outlets. You pick your steak from a rolling trolley. Broccoli with hollandaise and good baked potatoes are ideal companions to these steaks; grilled veal and lamb chops are also available, as are fish and chicken. The American-focused wine list numbers nearly 300 selections. *Sun Trust Plaza Bldg., 303 Peachtree St., Downtown, 404/577–4366. Reservations essential. AE, D, MC, V. No lunch. $$$–$$$$*

12 *g-2*

Peachtree Lenox Bldg., 3379 Peachtree Rd., Buckhead, 404/816–6535.

5 *b-7*

OUTBACK STEAKHOUSE

This Florida-based operation with the Aussie-theme menu has numerous outlets in Atlanta, all worthwhile for their steaks and other grilled entrées. Besides steaks, there's excellent prime rib, grilled shrimp (order a double appetizer for an entrée), and chicken. The wine list is fair enough, with several Australian selections, and there are Australian beers, too, such as Foster's. Outback is popular, so expect to wait in line unless you arrive very early. *3850 Roswell Rd., Buckhead, 404/266–8000. Reservations not accepted. AE, D, DC, MC, V. $$–$$$*

4 *f-1*

810 Ernest W. Barrett Pkwy., Kennesaw, 770/795–0400. No lunch.

5 *f-4*

4015 Holcomb Bridge Rd., Norcross, 770/448–6447. No lunch.

8 *e-1*

1525 E. Park Place Blvd., Stone Mountain, 770/498–5400. No lunch.

13 *e-6*

2145 LaVista Rd., Toco Hills, 404/636–5110. No lunch.

12 *g-2*

PALM

Celebrities often patronize this classy steak house, a branch of the famous New York operation. Besides gargantuan slabs of beef and lobsters in the 3-pound range, it also has good crab cakes, grilled fresh fish, veal chops, steak, and soups, as well as pasta and other Italian dishes. The wine list presents lots of French, Italian, and American wines, with limited by-the-glass selections. *Swissôtel, 3391 Peachtree Rd., Buckhead, 404/814–1955. AE, D, MC, V. $$–$$$$*

12 *h-2*

PRIME

Forget that it's in a mall: this is one of the airiest and prettiest dining rooms in town. And Prime is not just a steak house (a very good one at that); it's also an excellent sushi restaurant. As if these two options weren't enough, Prime also does a magnificent job with veal chops and tuna steak and serves salmon on a bed of grits. The wide-ranging wine list offers a number of fine choices by the glass. *Lenox Square, 3393 Peachtree Rd., Buckhead, 404/812–0555. Reservations essential. AE, D, DC, MC, V. $$$–$$$$*

15 *d-5*

RUTH'S CHRIS STEAK HOUSE

Only hand-cut corn-fed beef is served at this posh steak house, where steaks are brought to the table on hot plates so diners may "finish" the meat as desired by cutting pieces and searing them on the plate. Fish, lobster, and lots of good side dishes round out the menu, and the wine list is excellent. Atlanta has three outposts of this New Orleans–based chain. The downtown location is an especially handsome room with a smashing park view. *Embassy Suites hotel, 267 Marietta St., at Centennial Park, Downtown, 404/223–6500. Reservations essential. AE, D, DC, MC, V. $$–$$$$*

`5` b-5

5788 Roswell Rd., Sandy Springs, 404/ 255–0035. No lunch.

`12` h-3

Atlanta Plaza, 950 E. Paces Ferry Rd., Buckhead, 404/365–0660. No lunch weekends.

`5` c-2

STONEY RIVER LEGENDARY STEAKS

With their huge bars and lively dining rooms, these steak houses fill quickly—especially on weekend nights—with hungry diners who enjoy good steaks that could easily feed two. (To avoid a wait, arrive early or grab a seat at the bar and eat there.) In addition to steaks, there are good shrimp, fish, and chicken dishes. The wine list is generous. 10542 Alpharetta Hwy., Roswell, 678/461–7900. Reservations not accepted. AE, D, DC, MC, V. No lunch Mon.–Sat. $$$

`5` f-1

5800 State Bridge Rd., Duluth, 770/476–0102.

TEA

`12` h-2

RITZ-CARLTON, BUCKHEAD

High tea is celebrated in a formal manner (and in front of a fire in wintertime) in the English country house–style lobby of this classy hotel. Full tea service includes, as it should, a good selection of small sandwiches and pastries as well as the perfectly steeped leaves in warmed pots. There's even an elegant version of peanut butter–and–jelly for the kids. 3434 Peachtree Rd., Buckhead, 404/237–2700. Reservations essential. AE, D, DC, MC, V. $$$

`12` e-3

SWAN COACH HOUSE

Very popular with the "ladies who lunch," who often stay for exhibitions at the adjacent art gallery, this tearoom also sees duty as a good place for bridal luncheons. Dishes that never change, or so it seems, are the chicken salad, Jell-O salad, and zucchini muffins. One trip to this hallowed haunt of Buckhead matrons (it's on the grounds of the Atlanta History Center) and you'll see what it means to grow old graciously, Southern style. Don't forget your white gloves. Full bar service is available. 3130

Slaton Dr., Buckhead, 404/261–0636. AE, MC, V. Closed Sun. No dinner. $–$$

TEX-MEX

`12` d-7

CASA GRANDE

This oversize eatery is meant to look like a country hacienda, and the Disneyesque presentation even includes an imaginary "Uncle Julio" who supposedly resides here. Still, it produces good fajitas, salsa, and chips, along with the freshest tortillas, made by a gas-fired tortilla press that sits in sight of the dining room. The best bets are the specials, which often include the very good shrimp with papaya pico de gallo. Premium tequilas are a specialty. 1860 Peachtree Rd., near Collier Rd., Buckhead, 404/350–6767. AE, D, DC, MC, V. $$

`12` a-8

NUEVO LAREDO CANTINA

The spirit of the Cadillac Bar in the border town of Nuevo Laredo, Mexico, comes to Atlanta in the form of this casual, family-comfy spot. The food is good—not nearly as homogenized as it is at most other Mexican restaurants—and includes freshly made guacamole, refried beans, steak, seafood, and a respectable flan. Mexican beers and Spanish wines are available, as are terrific margaritas and good sangria. Though it's in an industrial neighborhood, the restaurant is close enough to residential Buckhead to attract throngs, especially on weekend nights. 1495 Chattahoochee Ave., off Howell Mill Rd., Northwest Atlanta, 404/352–9009. AE, D, DC, MC, V. Closed Sun. $–$$

THAI

`12` f-3

ANNIE'S THAI CASTLE

Lunch at this long-popular restaurant, a converted bungalow decorated with authentic Thai artifacts, is briskly served, even a bit rushed, in deference to limited lunch hours. You may want to come here for a leisurely dinner instead, when you have time to enjoy more of a wide-ranging menu that includes red-curry duck, whole-fish dishes, and the ever-popular pad thai. The excellent specials are available only at dinner on weekends. 3195 Roswell Rd., Buckhead,

404/264–9546. AE, MC, V. No lunch weekends. $–$$

13 *a-6*
BAI TONG
The pretty restaurant derives much of its charm from the artwork that adorns its walls and the nicely diffused lighting. The fairly standard takes on Thai cuisine are appealing, too. *Larb* (an appetizer of seasoned ground sirloin) is especially tasty here, while the spicy basil lamb takes your taste buds off the planet (ask the kitchen to tone it down if you can't handle really hot fare). The curries, classically done with coconut milk, are spicy but not searingly so. *2329-C Cheshire Bridge Rd., Northeast Atlanta, 404/728–9040. AE, D, DC, MC, V. No lunch weekends. $–$$*

15 *g-1*
KING & I
One of the city's first Thai restaurants, King and I has made pad thai and other noodle dishes as popular as burgers for diners in the Ansley neighborhood. Its other Thai dishes, including the spicy basil chicken and chicken and pork satays, are popular, too, particularly with the lunch crowd. *Ansley Square, 1510-F Piedmont Ave., behind Ansley Mall, Ansley Park, 404/892–7743. AE, MC, V. $–$$*

12 *a-2*
NORTHLAKE THAI CUISINE
A singularly pretty restaurant—with Thai artwork on the walls, romantic lighting, and a subdued atmosphere that encourages conversation—Northlake Thai also turns out plates that are especially pretty. Vegetable–cream cheese crisps are a light change-of-pace approach to the egg roll, while giant sea scallops are fried in a rice batter and served in a garlic–black peppercorn sauce. The wine list isn't much, and neither are the dessert choices, but the food is so wonderful you won't mind. *3939 LaVista Rd., Tucker, 770/938–2223. AE, D, DC, MC, V. No lunch weekends. $$–$$$*

11 *e-6*
PANITA THAI KITCHEN
In addition to the huge Thai menu, there's an equally staggering list of flawlessly fresh sushi. It's all offered up with a good-natured, if slightly wacky, style— many dishes come in huge, silly foil swans—in an old bungalow that's been opened up, with arches and lacy grill-work replacing most exterior walls. (The place is high and airy, like the open-walled timber structures of Southeast Asia.) A front patio is far enough from Highland Avenue to escape the exhaust clouds but close enough to present the passing scene. *1043 Greenwood Ave., Virginia-Highland, 404/888–9228. AE, MC, V. $$*

4 *f-8*
SUKOTHAI
Pretty Sukothai is hidden in a shopping center, and those who feel they have "discovered" it would just as soon keep it a secret. The standards of Thai cooking are well prepared here, especially the soups, salads, and the coconut milk–based curries. *Windy Hill West shopping center, 1995 Windy Hill Rd., Marietta, 770/434–9276. AE, D, DC, MC, V. Closed Sun. No lunch Sat. $$*

15 *e-2*
TAMARIND
A contemporary space with a large deck for fine-weather dining, Tamarind has become the Midtown mecca for Thai fare. For those whose hotness tolerance falls on the lower end of the scale, the jumbo prawns in green curry and the panang curries are both mildly spiced and absolutely delicious. Steamed rice-paper basil rolls wrap green veggies, and steamed dumplings with minced pork make a light opener. *80 14th St., Midtown, 404/873–4888. AE, D, DC, MC, V. No lunch weekends. $$–$$$*

13 *c-6*
THAI CHILLI
One of the city's best Thai restaurants is decoratively embellished with fine Thai art. The menu is highly regarded for its authenticity and deals with fairly standard fare, while the chef's specials often include such unusual selections as spicy whole catfish and vegetarian dishes, many based on tofu. *Briarvista shopping center, 2169 Briarcliff Rd., Northeast Atlanta, 404/315–6750. AE, D, DC, MC, V. No lunch weekends. $–$$$*

5 *g-2*
9775-A Medlock Bridge Rd., Duluth, 770/476–3369.

11 *c-5*
Colony Square mall, 1197 Peachtree St., Midtown, 404/875–2275.

7 *f-7*

ZAB-E-LEE

This long-established restaurant raises standard Thai dishes to new levels of excellence. Many are vegetarian: *Mee krob* (crispy fried noodles) is made with tofu, which also appears in one of the coconut milk–based yellow-curry dishes. Spicy dishes are clearly marked, and hotness levels can be adjusted up or down. Lunch is a spread of standard Chinese dishes and Thai fare, so dinner is the best time to enjoy the kitchen's full range. Beer and wine are served. *4837 Old National Hwy., College Park, 404/768–2705. Reservations not accepted. AE, DC, MC, V. Closed Sun. No lunch Sat. $–$$*

TURKISH

14 *h-1*

CAFE ISTANBUL

Low-key and quirkily charming, this store-front offers a rare taste of intensely sea-soned Turkish cuisine, dished up in big helpings—a terrific value. You can dip the tender house-made flat bread into a starter of wonderfully smoky roasted egg-plant salad made with chopped onion and tomato, or into *jajoukh*, a dip of dill, mint, and minced cucumber in a yogurt base. Anatolian-style lamb is braised for an entrée in an earthy sauce of tomato, onion, and ground coriander seed. Baklava is the classic dessert. On week-ends, there's live music and belly danc-ing. *1850 Lawrenceville Hwy., Decatur, 404/320–0054. AE, MC, V. Closed Sun. No lunch. $–$$*

VEGETARIAN & MACROBIOTIC

12 *d-7*

CAFE SUNFLOWER

Atlanta isn't much on vegetarian restau-rants, but Cafe Sunflower has been a hit since the day it opened. Dishes come from around the world: Burritos are filled with beans, moo shu vegetables draw on Chinese culinary tradition, and tofu–peanut butter pie is outrageously good. The Brookwood Square location serves beer and wine; Roswell Road does not (guests who inquire about it could get a lecture on the evils of alco-hol) and the menus at the two locations vary slightly as well. Both offer good-

quality juices, teas, and other nonalco-holic drinks. *Brookwood Square shopping center, 2140 Peachtree Rd., Brookwood, 404/352–8859. AE, D, DC, MC, V. Closed Sun. $$*

5 *b-4*

Hammond Springs shopping center, 5975 Roswell Rd., at Hammond Dr., Sandy Springs, 404/256–1675. No alcohol.

14 *f-1*

RAINBOW GROCERY

At the rear of one of Atlanta's longest-established health-food stores, you can try meatless sandwiches and specials that include excellent soups, veggie chili and lasagna, tofu dishes, walnut loaf, and luscious desserts. Smoothies are the drinks of choice. The dinner hour ends at 8 PM. *2118 N. Decatur Rd., North-east Atlanta, 404/636–5553. No credit cards (MC, V at store). No alcohol. Closed Sun. $*

11 *f-3*

VEGAN WAY CAFE

The name tells you that the food is free of animal products. And while some of what's served is cooked, such as the hearty bean soups, the greater part of the menu isn't—an approach that may be unusual but does have its health-ori-ented adherents. Still, the "slaw dog," a smoky soy frankfurter with coleslaw on a whole-wheat bun, could fool your aver-age ball-park habitué. Some dishes are a bit strange, like the "Kinder Living Pizza," which has a moist grain base that can't really be called a crust; but all are fresh. There's no ambience to speak of in this storefront spot, which mostly does a take-away business. *1358 LaVista Rd., Northeast Atlanta, 404/325–4343. AE, MC, V. Closed Sun. $*

VIETNAMESE

5 *e-6*

BIEN THUY

The clientele consists of local Viet-namese Atlantans and others who savor such authentic traditional dishes as *hu tieu*, a soup of glass noodles with seafood; *banh xeo*, stuffed pancakes; and *cha gio*, Vietnamese spring rolls. This is a good spot for vegetarians. *Northwoods Plaza, 5095-F Buford Hwy., Doraville, 770/454–9046. AE, D, MC, V. $–$$*

chapter 2

SHOPPING

L ike to shop? Got a car? Atlanta's an eastern Los Angeles, with sprawling suburbs that have swallowed up surrounding towns. Shoppers these days are likely to zip to the nearest mall or head a few more exits down the highway to yet another shopping center more upscale than the last. Nevertheless, small, locally owned shops haven't become extinct; the huge metro area has managed to retain some good places to track down antiques (Marietta, Roswell, Crabapple) as well as old Atlanta shopping neighborhoods with one-of-a-kind boutiques (Five Points, Brookwood, Buckhead). And chances are that you'll find some genuine Southern hospitality along with whatever it is you need.

shopping areas

DEPARTMENT STORES

5 *e-1*

DILLARD'S

A relative newcomer to the Atlanta shopping scene, mid-price Dillard's has the best Carole Little selection in town, often on sale; plus-size lingerie galore; and a well-stocked men's clothing department. The costume jewelry here is worth a look. *North Point Mall, 7000 North Point Cir., Alpharetta, 770/410–9020.*

3 *h-7*

Mall of Georgia, 3333 Buford Dr., Buford, 678/482–5241.

7 *a-2*

Arbor Place Mall, 6720 Douglas Blvd., Douglasville, 770/577–4271.

8 *g-4*

The Mall at Stonecrest, 8000 Mall Pkwy., Lithonia, 770/666–0000.

5 *f-7*

JCPENNEY

This mainstay chain is the place for inexpensive, durable children's clothing, linens, and window treatments. The store-brand towels aren't the thirstiest, but for the money, they suffice. The January white sale is a good time to stock up on basics. *Northlake Mall, 4840 Briarcliff Rd., Northlake, 770/934–8111.*

5 *e-1*

North Point Mall, 2000 North Point Cir., Alpharetta, 770/475–9850.

6 *a-4*

Gwinnett Place, 2100 Pleasant Hill Rd., Duluth, 770/476–3220.

4 *e-3*

Forest Park, 5500 Old Dixie Hwy., Forest Park, 404/363–3855.

8 *a-8*

Southlake Mall, 1400 Southlake Mall, Morrow, 770/961–6211.

4 *e-3*

Town Center at Cobb, 400 Ernest W. Barrett Pkwy., Kennesaw, 770/514–7101.

12 *h-2*

LORD & TAYLOR

The venerable New York department store exports its ladies-who-lunch air to the Deep South—a perfect match in terms of gentility. The goods are of generally high quality, with the standard mid-price designer names represented, including Liz Claiborne and Polo. Atlanta women swear by the dress department; men know that conservative suits crowd the racks. *Phipps Plaza, 3500 Peachtree Rd., Buckhead, 404/266–0600. MARTA: Lenox.*

5 *e-1*

North Point Mall, 4000 North Point Cir., Alpharetta, 770/667–0665.

3 *h-7*

Mall of Georgia, 3333 Buford Dr., Buford, 770/831–0115.

12 *h-2*

MACY'S

In the Atlanta area, this New York import, which is owned by Federated Department Stores, is overshadowed by its better-run sibling, Rich's. Service is practically nonexistent here, but Macy's is worth a look for the great bargains you can find on any day (not to mention during its frequent sales). Expect good buys on housewares in the Cellar, men's and women's shoes, and accessories. (For a taste of old Atlanta, visit the downtown store, which occupies the historic Davison building on Peachtree Street.) *Lenox Square, 3393 Peachtree Rd., Buckhead, 404/231–8985. MARTA: Lenox.*

15 *e-5*

180 Peachtree St., Downtown, 404/221–7221. MARTA: Peachtree Center.

6 *a-4*

Gwinnett Place, 2100 Pleasant Hill Rd., Duluth, 770/476–6985.

5 *c-5*

Perimeter Mall, 4400 Ashford-Dunwoody Rd., Dunwoody, 770/399–4985. MARTA: Dunwoody.

4 *e-3*

Town Center at Cobb, 400 Ernest W. Barrett Pkwy., Kennesaw, 770/423–3985.

5 *f-7*

Northlake Mall, 4800 Briarcliff Rd., Northlake, 770/491–2985.

8 *a-8*

Southlake Mall, 1200 Southlake Mall Dr., Morrow, 770/961–3995.

4 *h-7*

Cumberland Mall, 1200 Cumberland Mall, Smyrna, 770/433–3975.

12 *h-2*

NEIMAN MARCUS

There's no denying this upscale Dallas-based chain first prize for its consistently high-quality merchandise. This is the place to pick up Manolo Blahnik spike heels, a Jean Paul Gaultier evening dress, and a tin of cheese straws fit for the fanciest party. N-M private-label clothing is a good buy, and the fabulous "Last Call" storewide sales are held twice a year. *Lenox Square, 3393 Peachtree Rd., Buckhead, 404/266–8200. MARTA: Lenox.*

5 *c-5*

NORDSTROM

Personal service is emphasized here, and the rather upscale selection covers the entire family. The shoe department is a winner, with a wide range of styles and sizes. *Perimeter Mall, 4400 Ashford-Dunwoody Rd., Dunwoody, 770/394–1141. MARTA: Dunwoody.*

3 *h-7*

Mall of Georgia, 3333 Buford Dr., Buford, 678/546–1122.

12 *h-2*

PARISIAN

The accent isn't French; it's from Birmingham, Alabama, where this chain is based. But Atlantans certainly have no trouble understanding it. Parisian straddles a fine line between mid-price and upscale. Designer names for men, women, and children range from Ralph Lauren to Tommy Hilfiger to Hugo Boss to Dana Buchman. The personnel set the standard for service: they know when to leave you alone, and they know the merchandise from other departments well enough to retrieve it in your size and color. The children's shoe department is well stocked with such popular brands as Elefanten, Bass, and Nina. Sales are frequent throughout. Watch for special coupons in the newspaper. *Phipps Plaza, 3500 Peachtree Rd., Buckhead, 404/814–3200. MARTA: Lenox.*

2 *b-4*

North Point Mall, 4500 North Point Cir., Alpharetta, 770/754–3200.

7 *a-2*

Arbor Place Mall, 6640 Douglas Blvd., Douglasville, 678/838–2200.

6 *a-4*

Gwinnett Place, 2100 Pleasant Hill Rd., Duluth, 770/813–7200.

4 *e-3*

Town Center at Cobb, 400 Ernest W. Barrett Pkwy., Kennesaw, 770/514–5200.

5 *f-7*

Northlake Mall, 4800 Briarcliff Rd., Northlake, 770/496–3200.

12 *h-2*

RICH'S

Founded in Atlanta in 1867, Rich's today is part of the Federated group, owner of Macy's, among other retailers. Still, this place belongs to Atlanta; the late newspaper columnist Celestine Sibley even wrote a valentine of a book, *Dear Store: An Affectionate Portrait of Rich's*. For generations, Rich's vast network of services has drawn people from throughout the region—for everything from optical supplies and a hair salon to travel planning and carpet cleaning. That's all in addition to the mid-price men's, women's, and children's apparel and shoes, fine jewelry, cosmetics, and housewares. (The Perimeter and Gwinnett Place stores include furniture; the South Cobb Drive and Greenbriar locations have furniture-clearance centers.) *Lenox Square, 3393 Peachtree Rd., Buckhead, 404/231–2611. MARTA: Lenox.*

5 *c-5*

Perimeter Mall, 4400 Ashford-Dunwoody Rd., Dunwoody, 770/396–2611. MARTA: Dunwoody.

5 e-1

North Point Mall, 5000 North Point Cir., Alpharetta, 770/410–2600.

3 h-8

Mall of Georgia, 3333 Buford Dr., Buford, 678/546–4313.

5 f-8

North DeKalb Mall, 2144 Lawrenceville Hwy., Decatur, 404/329–2600.

7 e-4

Gwinnett Place, 2100 Pleasant Hill Rd., Duluth, 770/623–2201.

7 e-4

Greenbriar Mall, 2841 Greenbriar Pkwy., Lakewood, 404/346–2600.

8 a-8

Southlake Mall, 1500 Southlake Mall, Morrow, 770/961–3301.

4 h-7

Cumberland Mall, 1300 Cumberland Mall, Smyrna, 770/434–2611.

7 c-8

Shannon Mall, 200 Shannon Mall, Union City, 770/969–2600.

5 e-1
SEARS
The national retailer strives to position itself against the discount chains that have proliferated in the metro area in recent years. In spite of the competition, however, it has managed to thrive, offering that metric wrench, a DVD player, and a beaded formal jacket all in one stop. (The Cumberland Mall store's millinery section offers fanciful creations of sequins, feathers, and bows that appeal to the church ladies.) North Point Mall, 6000 North Point Cir., Alpharetta, 770/667–6700.

4 h-7

Cumberland Mall, 1500 Cumberland Mall, Smyrna, 770/433–7400.

6 a-4

Gwinnett Place, 2100 Pleasant Hill Rd., Duluth, 770/476–6600.

5 f-7

Northlake Mall, 4800 Briarcliff Rd., Northlake, 770/493–3210.

8 a-8

Southlake Mall, 1300 Southlake Mall Dr., Morrow, 770/961–7110.

4 e-3

Town Center at Cobb, 400 Ernest W. Barrett Pkwy., Kennesaw, 770/429–4155.

7 a-2

Arbor Place Mall, 6580 Douglas Blvd., Douglasville, 770/577–5200.

DISCOUNT STORES

14 h-1
BIG LOTS
The concept is just what the name suggests: This well-represented national chain buys large shipments from manufacturers at less than wholesale, then resells at prices up to 70% below suggested retail. This closeout merchandise is first-quality and frequently brand-name, but the junk shares shelf space with the jewels. Expect a wide selection of home furnishings and housewares, pantry staples, luggage, toys, sporting goods, clothes, linens—you name it. 2617 N. Decatur Rd., Decatur, 404/378–6187.

12 g-5

Lindbergh Plaza, 2851 Piedmont Rd., Buckhead, 404/237–9298. MARTA: Lindbergh Center.

4 g-3

2745 Sandy Plains Rd., Marietta, 770/973–8947.

7 g-7

7055 Hwy. 85, Riverdale, 770/909–0824.

4 g-7

3791 S. Cobb Dr. SE, Smyrna, 770/438–8321.

6 d-7

2280 Main St. SW, Snellville, 678/344–8303.

8 d-1

6011 Memorial Dr., Stone Mountain, 770/469–7277.

7 g-5
KMART
With celebrities such as Martha Stewart lending cachet to its formerly very downscale image, Kmart (and its bigger-is-better sibling Big Kmart) has made an effort to attract shoppers with more disposable income. (The effort may not be enough; the retailer filed for bankruptcy protection in early 2002.) Some items are name-brand—particularly electronics, some housewares, household prod-

ucts, and toys—but others are inexpensive knock-offs. The Martha Stewart Everyday label includes linens, gardening products, and housewares, all of it stylish and generally well made, though of a quality you'd expect to be found in a discount chain. *230 Cleveland Ave. SW, East Point, 404/766–7543.*

2 *b-4*

1750 Marietta Hwy., Canton, 770/479–8757.

8 *d-4*

2395 Wesley Chapel Rd., Decatur, 770/808–0606.

5 *e-6*

5597 Buford Hwy., Doraville, 770/458–9506.

5 *c-2*

606 Holcomb Bridge Rd., Roswell, 770/992–9525.

8 *e-1*

1701 Mountain Industrial Blvd., Stone Mountain, 770/938–0151.

12 *g-5*
MARSHALLS
The brand names at this off-price chain are plentiful, and the savings can hit 60% off regular retail—especially if you don't mind past seasons' styles. Domestics, family apparel, accessories, toys, and giftware can yield good buys. Marshalls carries a wider selection of men's fashion than does sibling TJMaxx. The more upscale the Marshalls location, the more likely the store is to have more-upscale merchandise. *2625 Piedmont Rd., 404/233–3848. MARTA: Lindbergh Center.*

13 *e-1*

4166 Buford Hwy., Brookhaven, 404/329–0200.

12 *g-3*

3232 Peachtree Rd., Buckhead, 404/365–8155. MARTA: Buckhead.

6 *a-4*

3675 Satellite Blvd., Duluth, 770/497–1052.

4 *f-3*

425 Ernest W. Barrett Pkwy., Kennesaw, 770/424–2064.

8 *e-1*

6011 Memorial Dr., Stone Mountain, 770/469–4005.

5 *h-5*
SAM'S CLUB
With the $35 annual membership, you can shop a warehouse full of food, fine jewelry, electronics, appliances, books, clothing, automotives, and, yes, kitchen sinks. It's easy to get carried away loading up your cart; some of the bulk food packages are more than most shoppers need (and sometimes the grocery stores beat the Sam's price). In general, though, the discounts on nonfood merchandise are some of the best in town. *3450 Steve Reynolds Blvd., Duluth, 770/497–1165.*

7 *c-2*

150 Six Flags Dr., Austell, 770/739–0019.

4 *g-4*

150 Cobb Pkwy., Marietta, 770/423–7018.

8 *a-8*

7325 Jonesboro Rd., Morrow, 770/960–8228.

5 *g-8*

1940 Mountain Industrial Blvd., Tucker, 770/908–8408.

5 *c-5*
STEIN MART
Company chairman Jay Stein's grandfather founded Stein Mart at the turn of the 20th century, and the family touch is obvious throughout the national chain: well-lit, scrupulously clean stores with courteous service. The concept is a cross between a traditional department store and the typical off-price retailer. Merchandise includes moderate-to-designer brand-name apparel and shoes for the entire family, as well as accessories, gifts, and linens. Prices average about 30% off retail but can hit 60% off. Best bets here are accessories, with a wide selection of costume jewelry, handbags, and hair baubles; the well-stocked housewares department, including better crystal, Spode china, and trendy lamps; and luxury linens (think 300-thread-count sheets). *1155 Mt. Vernon Hwy., Dunwoody, 770/804–9149.*

5 *d-2*

Rivermont Plaza, 8560 Holcomb Bridge Rd., Alpharetta, 770/518–4340.

8 *c-1*

2050 Lawrenceville Hwy., Decatur, 404/329–0927.

4 *f-3*

50 Ernest W. Barrett Pkwy., Kennesaw, 770/514–8900.

5 b-4

1309 Johnson Ferry Rd., Marietta, 770/579–0940.

6 d-7

1670 Scenic Hwy., Snellville, 770/982–1670.

5 b-5

TARGET

High-design housewares from the likes of esteemed architect Michael Graves have polished the image of this discount chain: better design at a discount price has become Target's market niche. There are still good buys on laundry detergent, but don't miss the home-decor department with its Pottery Barn and Crate & Barrel knockoffs. Look for cheap, stylish clothes for men, women, and children (especially the Mossimo label). The Buckhead store is a family destination just to see the vermiport, an escalator for shopping carts. 235 Johnson Ferry Rd., Sandy Springs, 404/256–4600.

12 h-2

3535 Peachtree Rd., Buckhead, 404/237–9494.

5 h-4

2300 Pleasant Hill Rd., Duluth, 770/623–3519.

9 h-1

1940 Mt. Zion Rd., Morrow, 770/472–3355.

4 h-6

2201 S. Cobb Pkwy., Smyrna, 770/952–2241.

8 d-4

WAL-MART

These oversize general merchandise stores invaded Atlanta's suburbs long ago but have yet to make major inroads within the city. The chain offers discount shopping for the masses, with little regard for style trends but a constant emphasis on low prices. The Super Wal-Marts pack all of the standard departments plus a pharmacy, vision center, car-care, and groceries under one roof. 2496 Wesley Chapel Rd., Decatur, 770/593–3540.

5 d-5

4725 Ashford-Dunwoody Rd., Dunwoody, 770/395–0199.

4 g-5

1785 Cobb Pkwy. S, Marietta, 770/955–0626.

5 e-3

1580 Holcomb Bridge Rd., Roswell, 770/993–4103.

6 d-7

2135 E. Main St., Snellville, 770/979–2447.

7 d-8

4700 Jonesboro Rd., Union City, 770/964–6921.

MALLS & SHOPPING CENTERS

More than a dozen major malls and hundreds of mini-malls dot the 10-county Atlanta landscape.

7 a-2

ARBOR PLACE MALL

One of the newer area malls serves the western suburbs. Major anchors include Rich's and Sears, with lots of specialty shops in between. 6720 Douglas Blvd., Douglasville, 770/577–4271.

4 h-7

CUMBERLAND MALL

Macy's, Sears, Rich's, and JCPenney anchor this mall between Atlanta and Marietta. There's a wide mix of smaller specialty chains, which include Ann Taylor, the youthful Abercrombie & Fitch, and Frederick's of Hollywood. The food court offers such fast-food standbys as Wendy's, plus ethnic eateries from Mexican to Japanese. Garage and valet parking are available. I–285 and I–75 at Cobb Pkwy., Smyrna, 770/435–2206.

4 h-7

GALLERIA SPECIALTY MALL

Because this mall is adjacent to a hotel and conference and convention facilities and hosts many of the area's trade shows, the boutique-type shops here tend to cater to out-of-towners, offering resort and party wear, art, and souvenirs. Restaurants range from mid-price to fast food, and there's an eight-plex movie theater. Parking is plentiful. I–285 and I–75 at Cobb Pkwy., Smyrna, 770/989–5100.

7 e-4

GREENBRIAR MALL

Greenbriar's the "comeback kid" of area malls, due in large part to the aura of Magic Johnson, who chose this site for one of his theater complexes. Stores ↗

include Rich's, Burlington Coat Factory, and Circuit City, with a standard-issue food court and parking in a sea of asphalt. *I–285 at Arthur Langford Pkwy. (Hwy. 166), 5 mi west of I–85/I–75 S, Lakewood, 404/344–6611.*

6 *a-4*

GWINNETT PLACE

Here is the mall that ate Pleasant Hill Road. The huge complex contains anchor stores Parisian, Sears, Rich's, Macy's, and JCPenney, plus a lineup of specialty shops that includes Williams-Sonoma, Gap, and Brookstone. Shopping centers and independent stores have been popping up in the mall's shadows, putting just about any type of shopping conceivable within a few miles' drive. The food court includes the popular retro soda fountain–style restaurant Johnny Rockets. There is no deck or garage parking. *I–85 N at 2100 Pleasant Hill Rd., Duluth, 770/476–5160.*

12 *h-2*

LENOX SQUARE

The granddaddy of Atlanta malls took root in the late 1950s on a few acres of land. It's been expanded many times since then but continues to thrive on the individuality of its shops (the Waterford-Wedgwood Store, Neiman Marcus, Bally, Cartier, FAO Schwarz, and the Metropolitan Museum of Art Store are here) and the upper incomes of its shoppers. Lenox Square and the even more upscale Phipps Plaza, across the street, compose one of the city's largest shopping areas and offer a shuttle service between them. Parking is a problem only during holidays; Lenox is also on the northern MARTA route, making it one of Atlanta's few shopping centers accessible by public transportation. *3393 Peachtree Rd., Buckhead, 404/233–6767. MARTA: Lenox.*

8 *g-4*

THE MALL AT STONECREST

Dillard's, Parisian, Rich's, and JCPenney are at this celebrated mall, one of the first to make major inroads in the southern suburbs in a generation. The complex includes a multiplex and a food court. *8000 Mall Pkwy., Lithonia, 770/666–0000.*

5 *e-1*

NORTH POINT MALL

The nearly 200 stores at North Point, which reflects the tastes of the higher-income northside suburban shoppers it serves, include Lord & Taylor, Rich's, Dillards, Parisian, Sears, JCPenney, Banana Republic, Mary Engelbreit, and the Braves Clubhouse Store. In the food court, an antique carousel spins for young visitors during regular mall hours. *1000 North Point Cir. (exits 8 and 9 from GA 400), Alpharetta, 770/740–9273.*

5 *c-5*

PERIMETER MALL

Nordstrom opened its first Atlanta store here, which makes sense given the mostly traditional, upscale, family-oriented Dunwoody population. Rich's also has a major presence, with its largest furniture and interior-design center. Specialty stores include April Cornell, Brooks Brothers, Crate & Barrel, Eddie Bauer, and MAC cosmetics. There's a multiplex and, just across Hammond Drive, Home Depot's Design Expo store. The food court offers a few outlets that aren't found in other malls, including the highly rated Kameel's Cafe, which serves Middle Eastern dishes. *4400 Ashford-Dunwoody Road, off I–285 between Sandy Springs and Chamblee, Dunwoody, 770/394–4270. MARTA: Dunwoody.*

12 *h-2*

PHIPPS PLAZA

This is one of the prettiest malls in the country. Polished dark wood and rosy marbles provide a suitable setting for Saks Fifth Avenue, Lord & Taylor, Tiffany & Co., and other high-end shops, along with a wealth of boutiques and galleries. There is a modest food court on the upper level and a movie theater (the box office is on the floor below). The Pleasant Peasant restaurant is a popular meeting spot. *3500 Peachtree Rd., across from Lenox Square, 404/262–0992. MARTA: Lenox.*

4 *e-3*

TOWN CENTER AT COBB

Situated amid a sea of subdivisions and car dealerships in Cobb County, Town Center serves a solidly middle-class demographic. It's anchored by Rich's, Macy's, Parisian, Sears, and JCPenney; specialty shops include Country Clutter, Deck the Walls, It's Atlanta, Lane Bryant, Motherhood Maternity, and Zales Jewelers. *400 Ernest W. Barrett Pkwy., off I–75 north of Marietta, Kennesaw, 770/424–0915.*

15 *e-6*

UNDERGROUND ATLANTA

The below-street-level mall of more than 100 shops and restaurants is aimed squarely at visitors to Atlanta. Its six city blocks are home to the World of Coca-Cola museum, the Atlanta Convention and Visitors Bureau, and AtlanTIX, a half-price ticket service for local performing-arts venues. The corridors mimic gaslit cobblestone streets, and a historical marker denotes the spot where the original railroad marker stood for Terminus, as Atlanta was originally known. Shops include Victoria's Secret and Hats Under Atlanta. The food court leans toward ethnic choices. Lombardi's restaurant is a best bet for enjoying well-prepared Italian specialties and spying on local- and state-government officials with nearby offices. Garage parking is available. *50 Upper Alabama St., Downtown, 404/523–2311. MARTA: Five Points.*

SHOPPING NEIGHBORHOODS

12 *d-7*

BROOKWOOD

Just south of Buckhead on Peachtree Road, a small complex has grown up in response to Piedmont Hospital across the street and one of the city's loveliest neighborhoods behind it. Brookwood occupies a few blocks of early 20th-century buildings that now house galleries, antiques stores, good restaurants, and cafés. Parking is available behind the complex. *18th and 19th block of Peachtree Rd., across from Piedmont Hospital.*

12 *f-3*

BUCKHEAD

Considered the suburbs well into the 20th century, Buckhead is Atlanta to hundreds of thousands of tourists each year, and even to some locals who seldom venture beyond its northern limits. This is Atlanta's Miracle Mile—block after block of boutiques, art galleries, day spas, home-furnishings stores, antiques shops, jewelers, clubs, and restaurants—with the intersection of West Paces Ferry and Peachtree roads as its locus. Traffic can be impossible, and self-parking is frequently at a premium (though many businesses here offer valet parking). *Intersection of W. Paces Ferry and Peachtree Rds.*

12 *h-7*

CHESHIRE BRIDGE ROAD

Some of the city's best garden centers are juxtaposed with strip bars and adult-video stores on this strange strip of commercial Atlanta. Shop Cheshire Bridge for antiques, retro home decor, and flea-market finds at Tara Antiques; gourmet-food baskets at Happy Herman's; and exceptional garden fountains at Atlanta Water Gardens. Traffic is usually miserable, and parking lots here are notorious for potholes. Restaurants include Atlanta institutions the Colonnade Restaurant and Varsity Junior. *Between Buford Hwy. 23 and Piedmont Rd., Ansley Park.*

15 *d-5*

CNN CENTER

The Hawk Walk corridor, which leads to Philips Arena, is where you can comb souvenir shops for merchandise emblazoned with Atlanta memorabilia and sports-team logos. Fast-food outlets push burgers, tacos, pizza, and hot dogs. Pay parking lots are nearby, but there's a MARTA stop here. *One CNN Center, between International Blvd. and Centennial Olympic Park Dr., Downtown, 404/827–1700. MARTA: Dome/GWCC/Philips Arena/CNN Center.*

2 *g-8*

CRABAPPLE

Once a one-horse whistle-stop northwest of Roswell, this was the intersection of country roads well beyond the reach of the big city. But the big city grew bigger, and now this community is home to subdivisions and the shops that come with them. A cluster of early homes, country-store buildings, and a restored cotton gin has been converted to a few homey shops offering gifts and primitive to fine antiques. Lunch at the rustic John B's, located in a restored house. *Hwy. 372 and Broadwell Rd., 25 mi from the city center in north Fulton County.*

14 *a-4*

LITTLE FIVE POINTS

If you remember the 1960s with fondness, the intersection of Moreland and Euclid avenues is a little slice of heaven. Crystals, tattoos, incense, retro clothing, futons, piercings—it's all here. Don't miss Identified Flying Objects for toys, Flax for comfortable linen women's clothing, and Junkman's Daughter for miscellaneous funk. *Intersection of Euclid and Moreland Aves. and McLendon and Seminole Sts., east of downtown.*

4 *f-4*
MARIETTA SQUARE
Nostalgia for the good ol' days can be indulged right here, on this picture-perfect town square complete with band shell. Dozens of shops—mostly antiques dealers—border the square. Other notable stops include Theatre on the Square, one of the area's best, and the Civil War cemetery. *Marietta, west of I–75 north, 35 mins from downtown, 770/528–4653.*

12 *h-4*
MIAMI CIRCLE
This former warehouse district in Buckhead is now one of the busiest and most prosperous antiques centers in the Southeast. Eighty shops carry all you need to furnish a house, everything from Americana to fine European furniture to Zumpano tiles. House of Thebaut is a source for unusual lamps; Curran Designer Fabrics & Furniture offers decorative accessories and furniture as well as discounts on upholstery fabrics. Books & Cases has used and rare books. *Off Piedmont Rd., 1 block north of Sidney Marcus Blvd., Buckhead. MARTA: Lindbergh Center.*

5 *g-5*
NORCROSS
The lovingly restored downtown business district of this charming town is listed on the National Register of Historic Places. Most of the shops lining the blocks across from the old train depot specialize in antiques, crafts, and gifts; Lively House, A Taste of Britain, and Olde Norcross Antiques Market are worth a stop. Parking is plentiful, and a good café now occupies the old station. *Buford Hwy. 23 and Holcomb Bridge Rd., 20 mins from downtown, 770/448–2122.*

5 *e-1*
ROSWELL
Founded in 1836, Roswell survived the Civil War intact because Sherman housed his troops in the town's antebellum mansions and because the railroad lines were farther south. Dozens of these houses line the streets of old Roswell, and antiques shops now line the town square. (The Chandlery is a favorite for gifts and antiques.) Canton Street, about a mile north off Highway 120, is also lined with shops, including Bella Fiori for home and garden accents and the Wild Rose Boutique for women's apparel. For shopping sustenance, there's Swallow at the Hollow, Pastis, or Green's on Green Street. *Roswell Rd. and Hwy. 120.*

8 *f-1*
STONE MOUNTAIN VILLAGE
In the shadow of the massive Confederate memorial carved into Stone Mountain sits a quaint shopping district that does quite well with visitors and locals alike. Main Street has more than 60 shops selling antiques, gifts, quilts, accessories, toys, and jewelry, as well as ice cream parlors and small cafés. Parking is free and plentiful. *Hwy. 78 E to Silver Hill Road exit, 30 mins from downtown.*

13 *f-6*
TOCO HILLS
The borders of this North DeKalb County commercial area are generally defined by North Druid Hills, Briarcliff, and LaVista roads, all of which are lined with shopping strips and vast parking lots. But it pays to get out of the car and explore the out-of-the-ordinary stores here. The area has a large Jewish population, so Toco Hills is a best bet for Judaica and kosher foods. Bagel Palace has the city's best bagels. For women's apparel and home decor, ConsignKidz and ConsignShop are worth exploring. *North Druid Hills and LaVista Rds., 15 mins from downtown.*

15 *h-3, a-2*
VIRGINIA-HIGHLAND
Developed in the 1920s and '30s as a middle-class suburb of large cottages and bungalows, Virginia-Highland has evolved into a neighborhood of beautifully renovated houses. Its commercial strip has art galleries and stores selling hip-funky clothing, elegant home decor, antiques, jewelry, and collectibles. Intown Hardware, one of the better hardware stores anywhere, is a don't-miss. Some of the city's most popular cafés and restaurants line North Highland Avenue. *Highland Ave. between Johnson and Ponce de Leon Rds., 5 mins from downtown.*

12 *f-3*

WEST VILLAGE

The Andrews Drive area is a mix of shops selling high-end art, home decor, gifts, and clothing, with a little bargain-shopping thrown in for good measure. Cains Hill Place is home of the popular Urban Cottage, which sells distinctive furniture, accessories, art, and gifts. A few doors down is Latitudes, a discount teak store. Also in the neighborhood are Boxwoods Gardens and Gifts, an upscale garden and accessories shop, and Now and Again, a consignment shop specializing in high-end home decor. Parking can be tight. *Between W. Paces Ferry and Roswell Rds., Buckhead.*

specialty shops

ANTIQUES

antiques centers & flea markets

12 *h-7*

A FLEA ANTIQUE II

In this collection of little shops you can find everything from vintage-clothing bargains to 9th-century Korean celadon. *1853 Cheshire Bridge Rd., Midtown, 404/872–4342.*

12 *e-6*

ATLANTA DECORATIVE ARTS CENTER

It's worthwhile to find an interior designer who can take you through this to-the-trade-only complex. Genuinely fine antiques abound here, often mixed with the best in new design trends. ADAC contains especially good dealers in Oriental rugs, paintings, and furniture. Twice a year, the center opens to the public for a sample sale. *351 Peachtree Hills Ave., Buckhead, 404/231–1720.*

12 *d-7*

BENNETT STREET

More than a decade ago, this tired warehouse district near Piedmont Hospital caught the attention of artists looking for inexpensive studio space, and today it bustles with galleries and antiques shops. The street is several blocks long, the variety amazing, and the quantity huge. Interiors Market and the Stalls both have booths stocked by some of Atlanta's savviest designers. *2100 block of Peachtree Rd., Buckhead.*

5 *d-6*

BROAD STREET ANTIQUES MALL

Browse through the flotsam and jetsam of the 19th and 20th centuries at this consignment booth–style antiques mall. Old quilts, primitive oak furniture, brass beds, porcelains, Civil War relics, and collectibles of all kinds are some of the items you can find. *3550 Broad St., Chamblee, 770/458–6316. MARTA: Chamblee.*

CRABAPPLE

See Shopping Neighborhoods, *above.*

8 *c-1*

KUDZU ANTIQUES MARKET

A couple of blocks west of the famous DeKalb Farmers' Market, Kudzu's collection of dealers finds everything from vintage clothing to *Star Wars* collectibles. It's jumbled, messy, and fun, and when a really fine piece turns up among the clutter, it's gone almost immediately (as the case with a fine Cormandel screen for $250 found among a selection of not-very-good quilts). If you'd like a particular piece, put your name on the list of dealers who like to stock it. Around here, it's the only way to compete. Look beyond the clutter, too. *2874 E. Ponce de Leon Ave., Decatur, 404/373–6498. MARTA: Avondale.*

5 *b-5*

LAKEWOOD ANTIQUES GALLERY

If it's hard for you to get to the Lakewood Antiques Market on the second weekend of each month, you can shop here in climate-controlled comfort. The bargain-hunting isn't quite up to par with that at the market, but the premises are clean, neat, and well organized and house a delectable assortment of American and European furniture and bric-a-brac. *6336 Roswell Rd., Sandy Springs, 404/459–8994.*

7 *h-4*

LAKEWOOD ANTIQUES MARKET

The crumbling state fairgrounds, with art-deco buildings and an attached amphitheater, now house antiques instead of cows, rock concerts instead of bake-offs. The second weekend of each month, regardless of the weather, dealers from all over the East and Midwest assemble here with their wares. There's a certain cachet to having "found it at Lakewood," which translates to "bargain" even if it wasn't. The best buys are on silver, furniture (especially on Sunday afternoon—they don't want to take it home), china, crystal, exotica, garden furniture and ornaments, architectural oddities, comics, fabrics—well, everything. The $3 admission includes parking. *2000 Lakewood Ave., Lakewood, 404/622–4488. MARTA: Lakewood/Ft. McPherson.*

MARIETTA SQUARE
See Shopping Neighborhoods, *above.*

MIAMI CIRCLE
See Shopping Neighborhoods, *above.*

7 *h-6*
SCOTT ANTIQUES MARKET
You have to arrive just when the market opens—it runs Friday through Sunday, the second weekend of each month—to find the real bargains here, which otherwise will later turn up on Miami Circle and in other antiques emporiums. But the higher-end antiques and decorative accessories move a little less quickly. Admission is $3. *Atlanta Expo Center, 3650 Jonesboro Rd., Forest Park, 404/363–2299.*

12 *e-6*
2300 PEACHTREE
In 1987 Atlanta designer Jane Marsden built a complex based on architecture she'd fallen in love with in France, and her three buildings house some of the area's finest antiques dealers and interior designers. Not surprisingly, this is the place to find incredible French furniture, porcelains, chandeliers, silver, and estate jewelry. *2300 Peachtree Rd., at Peachtree Battle Ave., Buckhead, 404/355–1288.*

collectibles

12 *e-6*
LEVISON & CULLEN GALLERY
Deanne Levison, one of the country's foremost experts in American decorative arts, spent many years of her career at Israel Sack in New York. Her education shows up in her discerning eye for fine American antiques, especially pottery

and painted furniture. A visit here enriches your knowledge and delights your eye. *2300 Peachtree Rd., Buckhead, 404/351–3435.*

8 *c-2*
RAY'S INDIAN ORIGINALS
If you can't find the antiquities you're looking for out West, it's because they're here. The store sells an astonishing array of Native American collectibles, memorabilia, and antiques. Really good antique Navajo rugs, genuine weaponry, baskets, and pottery seem matched only by the owner's depth of knowledge and willingness to share it. *90 Avondale Rd., Avondale Estates, 404/292–4999. MARTA: Avondale.*

12 *g-4*
REGEN-LEIGH
Highly respected, savvy, and well traveled, Bobbie Culbreath locates the crème de la crème of Europe and presents it here in her little shop. *3140 E. Shadownlawn Ave., Buckhead, 404/262–9303.*

furniture

12 *d-7*
BITTERSWEET
The owners love to travel to England and Scotland, where they ferret out their furniture and unique small treasures. Part of the shop is J. B.'s Corner, which specializes in sporting antiques—fishing poles, pond boats, golf memorabilia, prints, and oddities. *45 Bennett St., 1 block north of Piedmont Hospital, Brookwood, 404/351–6594.*

12 *g-5*
FURNITURE EXCHANGE
The stock is an interesting mix of 19th- and 20th-century pieces, and some of them are really very good. Prices for most items are good, too, especially on items such as the red Chinese lacquered furniture. *646 Lindbergh Way, Buckhead, 404/233–2100. MARTA: Lindbergh Center.*

12 *h-4*
THE GABLES
The owners and managers buy in Europe several times a year, so everything in this interesting mix of French country and English period furniture, Chinese porcelains, and well-crafted reproduction pieces is handpicked for

the shop. The bookcases are especially attractive. With a 9,000-square-ft showroom and 20-plus years of experience, this shop has become a primary, worldwide source for both designers and collectors. *711 Miami Cir., Buckhead, 404/231–0734. MARTA: Lindbergh Center.*

12 *e-6*

JACQUELINE ADAMS ANTIQUES & INTERIORS

The most gorgeous armoires in the city, French country furniture, and accessories delight even the most fastidious collector. The owners scour France for the merchandise, and designers from California to Maine come to Atlanta to snap it up. *2300 Peachtree Rd., Buckhead, 404/355–8123.*

12 *h-4*

MAISON DE PROVENCE

The huge inventory of French country pieces here is chosen by the owner, who lives in France most of the year, and combines quality and beauty. *764 Miami Cir., Buckhead, 404/364–0205. MARTA: Lindbergh Center.*

14 *a-2*

20TH CENTURY ANTIQUES

You can find Heywood-Wakefield, Charles and Ray Eames, Knoll, Eero Saarinin, Bauhaus, and all the other big names in 20th-century craft and design here. *1044 N. Highland Ave., Virginia-Highland, 404/892–2065.*

quilts

12 *d-7*

GRANNY TAUGHT US HOW

You may want to visit this shop just to feel comfy. It's chock-full of antique quilts in the myriad colors and patterns of yesteryear; table linens, curtains, dresser runners, and antimacassars fall from period trunks and cover antique tables. The quilted bears from recycled quilts make lovely gifts. *1921 Peachtree Rd., Brookwood, 404/351–2942.*

ART SUPPLIES

12 *g-5*

BINDERS

One of Atlanta's best sources for art supplies is overcrowded and a little disorganized but has just about anything a graphic or fine artist or craftsperson might need. The selection of handmade paper is extraordinary, and Binders also carries clever stationery. *Lindbergh Plaza, 2581 Piedmont Rd., Buckhead, 404/233–5423. MARTA: Lindbergh Center.*

5 *c-2*

DICK BLICK

What started out as a half-pet-supplies, half-art-supplies store has blossomed into one of the city's better-stocked sources for art supplies. Crafts supplies share space, too, and there's a catalog if you can't find what you need. Prices tend to be very competitive. *1117 Alpharetta St., Roswell, 770/993–0240.*

4 *f-2*

2615 George Busbee Pkwy., Kennesaw, 770/514–8456.

5 *g-7*

6330 Lawrenceville Hwy., Tucker, 770/939–5719.

12 *h-3*

ICHIYO ART CENTER, INC.

This charming store can infuse you with serenity and excitement at the same time. Shop here for Japanese art supplies and art made of paper, or take lessons in calligraphy and other Japanese arts. *432 E. Paces Ferry Rd., Buckhead, 404/233–1846. MARTA: Lenox.*

5 *b-7*

PEARL ARTIST & CRAFT SUPPLY

An outlet of the national art-supply chain, the store carries an amazing amount of merchandise and can outfit a whole studio for whatever medium you work in (and in the rare case it doesn't have what you need, its catalog probably can). The crafts section is especially well developed, with lessons and teachers available on and off site. Some salespeople are attentive and knowledgeable, but if the person helping you really isn't, ask for somebody else. *Powers Ferry Square, 3756 Roswell Rd., Buckhead, 404/233–9400.*

12 *c-8*

SAM FLAX

Neat, orderly, and precise, this well-designed outlet of the national chain can supply you with presentation materials and portfolios, terrific graphics-design furnishings, wonderfully designed contemporary office supplies, and much more—right down to a fine selection of handmade papers. There's a great catalog, too. *1460 Northside Dr., Midtown, 404/352–7200. MARTA: Midtown.*

BEAUTY

fragrances & skin products

5 *d-5*

AVEDA LIFESTYLE STORE

Here is the ultimate shopping stop if you're an Aveda products aficionado. The store has it all: perfume, hair-care products, body care, even what the company calls "air care" (candles, etc.). *4400 Ashford-Dunwoody Rd., Dunwoody, 770/522–9972. MARTA: Dunwoody.*

6 *d-1*

Mall of Georgia, 3333 Buford Dr., Buford, 678/482–6779.

12 *f-3*

BETH ANN

Owner Beth Ann Taratoot has been a makeup professional for about three decades, and this place shows her experience. The makeup is a private label created especially for the store. *47 Irby Ave., Buckhead, 404/233–4424.*

14 *b-8*

BUBBLES BATH & CARD SHOP

A store that understands the luxury implicit in a long bath, Bubbles is redolent with hip scents and suds. Innumerable reasons never to leave the tub—or never smell anything but sumptuous, for that matter—can be found within these walls. *492 Flat Shoals Ave., East Atlanta, 404/522–5562.*

14 *a-5*

FIFI MAHONY'S

From glamorous understatement to over-the-top painted lady, you can achieve whatever look you're going for at this shop. In addition to all the cosmetics a girl could need, fun wigs and false eyelashes are also available. *1152 Euclid Ave., Little Five Points, 404/681–3434. MARTA: Inman Park.*

7 *f-3*

LINSEY COSMETICS

Linsey's cosmetics, foundations, cleansing systems, blushers, lipsticks, and other beauty products are specially created for women of color. You can also indulge in a makeover here. *2140 Martin Luther King Jr. Dr., Lakewood, 404/696–3064. MARTA: Westlake, H.E. Holmes.*

12 *h-2*

SEPHORA

A French favorite, Sephora is bound to have the elusive lipstick shade you've been looking for: It has more than 300 colors. The perfume selection is almost as vast. *Lenox Square, 3393 Peachtree Rd., Buckhead, 404/816–0123. MARTA: Lenox.*

5 *c-5*

Perimeter Mall, 4400 Ashford-Dunwoody Rd., Dunwoody, 678/731–9950. MARTA: Dunwoody.

5 *g-1*

UNCOMMON SCENTS

You won't find these bath and body essentials at your corner drugstore. This privately owned bath and body shop is patterned after ones in Europe and offers products from around the world. Its staff is extremely knowledgeable, and some of the products are exclusives. *11550 Jones Bridge Rd., Alpharetta, 770/569–7627.*

spas

5 *d-4*

BEAUTY BY NATURE

You can receive facials, massages, and other body treatments here. *1707 Mt. Vernon Rd., Dunwoody, 770/394–3795.*

12 *g-2*

JOLIE THE DAY SPA

The facials and massages—from Swedish to aromatherapy to prenatal—at this premier day spa, which opened in the mid-1980s, make you feel good all over. Hair and nail care, waxing, and makeup session are among the services offered. *3619 Piedmont Rd., Buckhead, 404/266–0060. MARTA: Lindbergh Center.*

12 *f-4*

SPA SYDELL

Treatments at this popular local chain include body scrubs, massages, wraps, and polishes; hair removal; nail and skin care; and makeup sessions. Plus, you can pick up lotions and potions galore. *3060 Peachtree Rd., Buckhead, 404/237–2505.*

`6` *a-4*

2255 Pleasant Hill Rd., Duluth, 770/622–5580.

`5` *c-5*

1165 Perimeter Center W, Dunwoody, 770/551–8999. MARTA: Dunwoody.

`4` *h-7*

Cumberland Mall, 1259 Cumberland Mall, Smyrna, 770/801–0804.

BOOKS

antiquarian

`14` *a-5*

A CAPPELLA BOOKS

One of the charms of Little Five Points, this cluttered but orderly store helps you in a search for rare books or a not-so-rare classic. One of its strongest sections focuses on underground and gay and lesbian hard-to-find books. The staff is friendly and knows its stuff. *1133 Euclid Ave., Little Five Points, 404/681–5128. MARTA: Inman Park.*

`12` *h-4*

ANTONIO RAIMO GALLERIES

Antonio's knowledge and ability to find precisely the book you want in the kind of condition you require are nothing short of encyclopedic. The shop is a fun place to browse among leather and decorative bindings, maps and globes, and thousands of antique prints (custom framing is offered for the prints). *700 Miami Cir., Buckhead, 404/841–9880. MARTA: Lindbergh Center.*

`12` *h-2*

C. DICKENS

The rare-books shop is a source for everyone from Civil War buffs to people who study incunabula to chefs looking for out-of-print cookbooks. *56 E. Andrews Dr., Buckhead, 404/231–3825. MARTA: Lenox.*

`5` *d-1*

THE NATIONAL LIBRARY BINDERY COMPANY OF GEORGIA

It's not really a shop per se, but it's one of the few places in Atlanta where you can have your family Bible rebound, your masters thesis immortalized in exotic leather with gold-tooled lettering, or your family album fashioned into a proper book. *100 Hembree Park Dr., Roswell, 770/442–5490.*

discount

`13` *e-1*

BOOK NOOK

Be warned that you may well feel swamped by the books, CDs, paperbacks, comics, magazines, videos, tapes, books on tape—all new or used—that are stacked to the ceilings here. The comic book selection is especially fabulous. *3342 Clairmont Rd., Northeast Atlanta, 404/633–1328.*

`6` *a-6*

4664 Lawrenceville Hwy., Lilburn, 770/564–9462.

`4` *g-4*

1151 Roswell St., Marietta, 770/499–9914.

`7` *g-7*

6569 Church St., Riverdale, 770/994–3444.

`12` *g-8*

CHAPTER 11

This chain deals in high-volume remainders and overstocks, and everything—including *New York Times* best-sellers—is discounted. *1544 Piedmont Ave., Midtown, 404/872–7986.*

`12` *e-6*

Peachtree Battle shopping center, 2345 Peachtree Rd., Buckhead, 404/237–7199.

`12` *c-2*

3509 Northside Pkwy., Buckhead, 404/841–6338.

`14` *f-1*

2091 N. Decatur Rd., Decatur, 404/325–1505.

`5` *b-5*

6237 Roswell Rd., Sandy Springs, 404/256–5518.

`6` *d-7*

2280A Hwy. 78, Snellville, 770/736–0502.

general

`15` *e-5*

B. DALTON BOOKSELLER

The national chain's emphasis is on popular titles. *231 Peachtree St., Downtown, 404/577–2555. Closed Sun. MARTA: Peachtree Center.*

`12` *h-2*

Lenox Square, 3393 Peachtree Rd., Buckhead, 404/231–8516. MARTA: Lenox.

`5` *c-5*

Perimeter Mall, 4400 Ashford-Dunwoody Rd., Dunwoody, 770/394–4185. MARTA: Dunwoody.

`4` *f-2*

400 Ernest W. Barrett Pkwy., Kennesaw, 770/425–2817.

`5` *f-7*

Northlake Mall, 4800 Briarcliff Rd., Northlake, 770/934–9292.

`12` *e-4*

BARNES & NOBLE

Although it seems like they've been here forever, the clean, well-lighted outlets of this national chain began opening only within the past decade, setting up shops that offer 150,000 titles, along with discounts, adjacent coffee shops, and in-house music departments. A regular program of visiting authors and comfy chairs add a touch of the old-bookstore atmosphere. *2900 Peachtree Rd., Buckhead, 404/261–7747.*

`5` *c-5*

120 Perimeter Center W, Dunwoody, 770/396–1200. MARTA: Dunwoody.

`6` *a-4*

2205 Pleasant Hill Rd., Duluth, 770/495–7200.

`8` *a-8*

1939 Mt. Zion Rd., Morrow, 770/471–2227.

`4` *h-6*

2952 Cobb Pkwy., Smyrna, 770/953–0966.

`12` *h-1*

BORDERS

Books, music, and a café work their charms on customers here. The selection is well edited and you can often find obscure titles on the shelves. *3637 Peachtree Rd., Buckhead, 404/237–0707. MARTA: Lenox.*

`4` *e-7*

1605 East–West Connector, Austell, 770/941–8740.

`6` *a-4*

Gwinnett Plaza, 3555 Gwinnett Place Dr., Duluth, 770/495–4043.

`5` *d-5*

4745 Ashford-Dunwoody Rd., Dunwoody, 770/396–0004. MARTA: Dunwoody.

`4` *h-7*

3101 Cobb Pkwy., Northwest Atlanta, 770/612–0940.

`8` *a-1*

TALL TALES BOOKSHOP

Quick-delivery special-order books, extensive children's and fiction sections, and a well-read staff are the main draws here. *2105 LaVista Rd., Toco Hills, 404/636–2498.*

special-interest

`15` *e-5*

ARCHITECTURAL BOOK CENTER

Atlanta's largest concentration of architecture and related books, more than 10,000 titles, ranges from academic monographs to lavishly illustrated coffee-table tomes. *Peachtree Center, 231 Peachtree St., Downtown, 404/222–9920. MARTA: Peachtree Center.*

`15` *g-1*

BOOKEARS

Audiobooks are big in this car town. These stores carry about 10,000 audio titles, both abridged and unabridged, and rent, trade, and sell. *1579 Monroe Dr., Midtown, 404/815–7475.*

`5` *d-2*

8465 Holcomb Bridge Rd., Alpharetta, 770/649–8273.

`13` *b-1*

3944A Peachtree Rd., Brookhaven, 404/816–2665. MARTA: Brookhaven.

`5` *c-6*

1100 Hammond Dr., Sandy Springs, 770/671–8273.

`14` *a-5*

CHARIS BOOKS & MORE

As a center for lesbian-gay literature, music, and networking, Charis has an excellent selection of books on feminism, multicultural children's books, titles on raising children with a same-sex partner, and much more. *1189 Euclid Ave., Little Five Points, 404/524–0304. MARTA: Inman Park.*

`5` *f-8*

COKESBURY BOOKSTORE

If you're looking for serious theological works, start at this well-stocked and nonsectarian store. *2495 Lawrenceville Hwy., Decatur, 404/320–1034.*

14 *d-1*

Emory University, Candler School of Theology, Bishop's Hall, 500 Kilgore Cir. NE, Decatur, 404/727–6336.

15 *f-6*

GEORGIA BOOKSTORE

Georgia State University's bookstore offers new and used textbooks (including all authorized textbooks for GSU classes, which come with a generous buy-back policy) and study aids. GSU clothing and school supplies have a place, here, too. *124 Edgewood Ave., Downtown, 404/659–0959. Closed Sun. MARTA: Georgia State.*

15 *f-2*

OUTWRITE BOOKSTORE & COFFEEHOUSE

A popular spot for gay and lesbian residents of the Midtown area, the bookstore–coffee shop stocks a good selection of books and periodicals and provides the latest information on AIDS, national and international activist issues, and gay and lesbian services. *991 Piedmont Ave., at 10th St., Midtown, 404/607–0082. MARTA: Midtown.*

15 *e-2*

U.S. GOVERNMENT BOOKSTORE

You can find about 10,000 of the hundreds of thousands of published government documents here, including the ones Al Gore wrote about how to stop wasting government money. *999 Peachtree St., Midtown, 404/347–1900. MARTA: Midtown.*

CLOTHING & SHOES FOR CHILDREN

12 *g-3*

ANIMALS

The store sells its own line of reasonably priced, practical dresses, T-shirts, onesies, and other items for babies and kids that can actually get dirty and not be ruined. *375 Pharr Rd., Buckhead, 404/816–5588.*

12 *h-2*

BABYGAP

Some of the clothes come in pinks and light blues, but many of the baby basics here are unisex; the bold stripes, bright solids, cool prints, and pale grays are great gifts for expectant moms (and dads) who haven't divulged "boy" or "girl." Prices are relatively low and sales frequent, so you can go for quantity. Hats, socks, and shoes accessorize the outfits. *Lenox Square, 3393 Peachtree Rd., Buckhead, 404/261–0395. MARTA: Lenox.*

5 *a-3*

Avenue at East Cobb, 4475 Roswell Rd., Marietta, 770/579–5678.

5 *d-4*

CHICKENLIPS

The clothes here are distinctively designed, lean toward casual styles, and fit infants to kids size 6. Handmade items, including personalized artwork for a child's room, are also available. *5484 Chamblee-Dunwoody Rd., Dunwoody, 770/395–1234. MARTA: Dunwoody.*

12 *h-2*

GAPKIDS

Preppy polos, sassy khaki skirts, swim shorts, and logo and striped Ts are some of the under-$20 basics you can pick up here. Jeans come piped, studded, patched, and screen-printed (about $30–$45). *Lenox Square, 3393 Peachtree Rd., Buckhead, 404/264–1883. MARTA: Lenox.*

5 *e-1*

North Point Mall, 1082 North Point Cir., Alpharetta, 770/751–9889.

12 *h-2*

Phipps Plaza, 3500 Peachtree Rd., Buckhead, 404/237–1898. MARTA: Lenox.

3 *h-7*

Mall of Georgia, 3333 Buford Dr., Buford, 678/482–7144.

6 *a-4*

Gwinnett Place, 2100 Pleasant Hill Rd., Duluth, 770/476–0117.

5 *c-5*

Perimeter Mall, 4400 Ashford-Dunwoody Road, off I–285 between Sandy Springs and Chamblee, Dunwoody, 770/394–6848. MARTA: Dunwoody.

4 *e-3*

Town Center at Cobb, 400 Ernest W. Barrett Pkwy., off I–75 north of Marietta, Kennesaw, 770/425–6003.

5 *a-3*

Avenue at East Cobb, 4475 Roswell Rd., Marietta, 770/579–5678.

4 *h-7*

Cumberland Mall, 1000 Cumberland Mall, I–285 and I–75 at Cobb Pkwy., Smyrna, 770/437–9261.

12 *f-3*

KANGAROO POUCH

Buckhead moms outfit their little darlings here. Many of the pieces are handmade, but the parents who shop here don't mind that their kid is likely to outgrow the outfit before they've gotten their money's worth. 56 E. Andrews Dr., Buckhead, 404/231–1616.

CLOTHING FOR MEN/GENERAL

casual

12 *h-2*

EDDIE BAUER

Easygoing, comfortable, and outdoorsy sums up this chain, where you can find outfits for camping as easily as you can for casual Fridays. Accessories range from belts and wallets to umbrellas and duffel bags. Lenox Square, 3393 Peachtree Rd., Buckhead, 404/816–4555. MARTA: Lenox.

4 *h-7*

Cumberland Mall, 1309 Cumberland Mall (I–285 and I–75 at Cobb Pkwy.), Smyrna, 770/435–8818.

classic & conservative

12 *h-2*

BROOKS BROTHERS

This classic clothier has been a favorite with each new generation of politicians, actors, and businessmen, but it's the ready-to-wear lines that have brought this New York–based store to the masses. Top-of-the-line quality and excellent service may not come cheap, but one of the custom-made suits makes you feel like a million bucks. Lenox Square, 3393 Peachtree Rd., Buckhead, 404/237–7000. MARTA: Lenox.

15 *e-5*

235 Peachtree St., Downtown, 404/577–4040. MARTA: Peachtree Center.

5 *c-5*

Perimeter Mall, 4400 Ashford-Dunwoody Rd., Dunwoody, 770/394–9051. MARTA: Dunwoody.

15 *e-5*

H. STOCKTON

Ham Stockton has been an Atlanta staple among discriminating consumers ever since he opened his first haberdashery in 1963. The shop prides itself on offering the finest products from such top-quality manufacturers as Canali, Zanella, and Bobby Jones, as well as its own custom-made, made-to-measure, and ready-made clothing. 191 Peachtree St., Downtown, 404/523–7741. MARTA: Peachtree Center.

12 *h-2*

Lenox Square, 3393 Peachtree Rd., Buckhead, 404/233–1608. MARTA: Lenox.

5 *d-5*

4505 Ashford-Dunwoody Rd., Dunwoody, 770/396–1300. MARTA: Dunwoody.

4 *h-7*

Galleria, 1 Galleria Pkwy., Smyrna, 770/984–1111.

12 *g-3*

THE MEN'S WAREHOUSE

With more than 400 stores across the country, the Men's Warehouse sets the standard for the all-under-one-roof concept in men's clothing. The chain's large retail spaces allows the stores to offer a large selection of everything from formal wear to basic business suits to office casual wear, complete with shoes and accessories. A knowledgeable and friendly staff can even help you with your tailoring needs. 3255 Peachtree Rd., Buckhead, 404/264–0421. MARTA: Buckhead.

4 *h-7*

931 Cobb Pkwy., Smyrna, 770/956–7297.

6 *a-8*

5370 Stone Mountain Hwy., Stone Mountain, 770/498–5871.

12 *h-2*

POLO/RALPH LAUREN

Is there a more recognizable logo in men's clothing than this one? A bit of overindulgence, sure, but this sizable storefront offers a complete men's collection for any dress occasion, including shoes and accessories. Lenox Square, 3393 Peachtree Rd., 404/261–2663. MARTA: Lenox.

custom

11 *c-5*

ANDREW
The men's boutique caters to the very upscale, and very fashionable. Hand-made suits made from only the richest fabrics in a European style are designed to make a fashion-forward statement. Off-the-rack luxe duds from creative and edgy designers are available, too. *1545 Peachtree St., Midtown, 404/869–1881. MARTA: Arts Center.*

designer

12 *h-2*

VERSACE
The world-renowned design house offers haute couture to Atlantans. Here, the fashion elite linger in the spare, uncluttered environment to don the season's latest trend. A good rule of thumb: If you have to check the price tags, you probably can't afford it. *Phipps Plaza, 3500 Peachtree Rd., Suite 34, Buckhead, 404/814–0664. MARTA: Lenox.*

discount & off-price

5 *e-6*

BURLINGTON COAT FACTORY
If you know what you're doing, this is a great place to find name brands at low prices. The selection of men's sports coats is especially large and ranges from shabby to something Rich's might have at twice the price. *4166 Buford Hwy., Doraville, 404/634–5566.*

7 *e-4*
Greenbriar Mall, 2841 Greenbriar Pkwy., Lakewood, 404/349–6300.

8 *a-8*
1516 Southlake Pkwy., Morrow, 770/960–7555.

5 *c-2*
608 Holcomb Bridge Rd., Roswell, 770/518–9800.

6 *a-4*

K&G MEN'S CENTER
Determined to keep overhead low, this men's retailer buys in bulk and stocks its selections in stores that resemble warehouses, using basic fixtures and offering little or no ambience for the customer. But if you're looking to get the most for your money, you can't beat the prices on the name-brand, first-quality merchandise, much of which is 30%–70% off department-store prices. It's open Friday through Sunday only. *3750 Venture Dr., Duluth, 770/623–9895. Closed Mon.–Thurs.*

12 *b-8*
1750 Ellsworth Industrial Blvd., Midtown, 404/350–2927.

4 *g-2*
2949 Canton Rd., Marietta, 770/428–9660.

8 *a-8*
1294 Mt. Zion Rd., Morrow, 678/422–2425.

unusual sizes

5 *f-8*

CASUAL MALE BIG & TALL
Men whose size limits their selection in other clothing stores can cover all the bases at this one-stop shop. The casual, business, and active wear ranges from sizes 1X to 6X and XLT to 4XLT, at reasonable prices. *3963 LaVista Rd., Tucker, 770/908–2523.*

5 *d-2*
7681 North Point Pkwy., Alpharetta, 770/642–9700.

6 *a-4*
1950 Pleasant Hill Rd., Duluth, 770/476–8112.

4 *h-6*
2778 Cobb Pkwy., Smyrna, 770/984–8050.

6 *a-8*
5370 Stone Mountain Hwy., Stone Mountain, 770/469–4002.

vintage

14 *a-5*

STEFAN'S VINTAGE CLOTHING
Atlantans have known for a long time that this is the place to find the fashion styles of generations past, located among the counterculture clothiers in Little Five Points. Stefan's is great for finding period costumes or for defining that personal sense of style. *1160 Euclid Ave., Little Five Points, 404/688–4929. MARTA: Inman Park.*

CLOTHING FOR MEN/SPECIALTY

coats & rainwear

REI

See Coats & Rainwear, in Clothing for Women/Specialties, below.

formal wear

12 h-2

GINGISS FORMALWEAR

A full-service rental and sales outfit, Gingiss offers dozens of sharp styles to suit any taste. Lenox Square, 3393 Peachtree Rd., Buckhead, 404/266–2115. MARTA: Lenox.

6 d-1

Mall of Georgia, 3333 Buford Dr., Buford, 770/932–0062.

6 a-4

Gwinnett Place, 2100 Pleasant Hill Rd., Duluth, 770/476–2100.

5 c-5

Perimeter Mall, 4400 Ashford-Dunwoody Rd., Dunwoody, 770/394–2860. MARTA: Dunwoody.

4 e-3

Town Center at Cobb, 400 Ernest W. Barrett Pkwy., Kennesaw, 770/424–0066.

5 f-7

Northlake Mall, 4800 Briarcliff Rd., Northlake, 770/934–0868.

shoes & boots

Department stores are a major source for shoes and boots, as are some of the smaller chain retailers. Nordstrom, with its broad selection of styles and sizes, takes top honors in this category.

12 g-5

BENNIE'S SHOES

Begun as a repair shop in 1909, Bennie's is a longtime Atlanta favorite for discount shoes. Footwear runs the gamut from dress to casual to golf—all top name brands. 2581 Piedmont Rd., Buckhead, 404/262–1966. MARTA: Lindbergh Center.

5 h-5

5192 Brook Hollow Pkwy., Norcross, 770/447–1577.

4 h-6

2441 Cobb Pkwy., Smyrna, 770/955–1972.

12 h-1

COLE HAAN

The woven, moccasin, and loafer styles go through endless permutations and combinations. Lately the designs have loosened up a bit; some of the shoes employ Nike Air technology, and the slides and sandals range from sporty to strappy. Phipps Plaza, 3500 Peachtree Rd., Buckhead, 404/233–6634. MARTA: Lenox.

12 h-1

KENNETH COLE

The advertisements trumpet clever, liberal sayings to match the trendy shoes. Phipps Plaza, 3500 Peachtree Rd., Buckhead, 404/261–2653. MARTA: Lenox.

CLOTHING FOR WOMEN/GENERAL

casual

12 h-2

BANANA REPUBLIC

At the most sophisticated sector of the Gap enterprise, you can depend on lightweight wool trousers, sleek suits, all-cotton little-boy tees, and the latest denim looks—plus leather bags and shoes (a good assortment under the $100 mark), soft undergarments, and scented candles and creams. Lots of things stretch here, from matte jersey skirt–shirt combos and straight-leg slacks to button-front blouses and silk shells. Frequent sales let you stretch your dollars. Lenox Square, 3393 Peachtree Rd., Buckhead, 404/231–4905. MARTA: Lenox.

5 e-1

North Point Mall, 1052 North Point Cir., Alpharetta, 770/667–8789.

3 h-7

Mall of Georgia, 3333 Buford Dr., Buford, 678/482–2855.

6 a-4

Gwinnett Place, 2100 Pleasant Hill Rd., Duluth, 770/476–4650.

5 c-5

Perimeter Mall, 4400 Ashford-Dunwoody Road, off I–285 between Sandy Springs and Chamblee, Dunwoody, 770/393–1130. MARTA: Dunwoody.

4 *e-3*

Town Center at Cobb, 400 Ernest W. Barrett Pkwy., off I—75 north of Marietta, Kennesaw, 678/290—8405.

5 *a-3*

Avenue at East Cobb, 4475 Roswell Rd., Marietta, 678/560—0597.

5 *c-5*

CHICO'S

All the clothing here is casual, and most is made of cotton—not a surprise considering that the chain is based in Florida. These easy separates can help make packing for that upcoming trip a breeze. The accessories, which include chunky bracelets and ethnic-inspired necklaces, are fun and well priced. 4505 Ashford-Dunwoody Rd., Dunwoody, 770/673—0813. MARTA: Dunwoody.

12 *f-1*

CP SHADES

The company projects a "natural fibers" image, and in a way it lives up to it. Linen and cotton crop up on the labels, but so does rayon. The reasonably priced, comfortable styles tend to be loose and drapey, with subdued colors. 3106 Roswell Rd., Buckhead, 404/816—0872.

12 *h-2*

GAP

All the basics are here: stacks of chinos, cotton Ts and tanks, button-downs, and straightforward sweaters. Finding the right pair of khakis (about $45–$55) or jeans (boy cut to boot cut, sandblasted to indigo, $30–$60) can translate into 45 minutes in the dressing room, but with patience you can emerge victorious. Larger stores include pjs, underwear, sweats, and toiletries. Sales are frequent, but don't count on being able to find your size in that great rain jacket you saw a few weeks ago—if you really want it, snap it up when you see it. Lenox Square, 3393 Peachtree Rd., Buckhead, 404/233—3229. MARTA: Lenox.

5 *e-1*

North Point Mall, 1082 North Point Cir., Alpharetta, 770/751—9889.

12 *h-2*

Phipps Plaza, 3500 Peachtree Rd., Buckhead, 404/237—1898. MARTA: Lenox.

3 *h-7*

Mall of Georgia, 3333 Buford Dr., Buford, 678/482—7144.

15 *d-6*

Underground Atlanta, 102 Lower Alabama St., Downtown, 404/522—0027. MARTA: Five Points.

6 *a-4*

Gwinnett Place Mall, 2100 Pleasant Hill Rd., Duluth, 770/476—0117.

5 *c-5*

Perimeter Mall, 4400 Ashford-Dunwoody Road, off I—285 between Sandy Springs and Chamblee, Dunwoody, 770/394—6848. MARTA: Dunwoody.

4 *e-3*

Town Center at Cobb, 400 Ernest W. Barrett Pkwy., off I—75 north of Marietta, Kennesaw, 770/426—1045.

5 *a-3*

Avenue at East Cobb, 4475 Roswell Rd., Marietta, 770/579—5678.

4 *h-7*

Cumberland Mall, 1321 Cumberland Mall (I—285 and I—75 at Cobb Pkwy.), Smyrna, 770/433—3263.

12 *h-2*

J. CREW

The national retailer has expanded its range beyond the classic prep collections it started with, to include stretchy strapless and halter dresses, ruched and wrap tops, sexy and sporty swimwear, flared and low-rise jeans, and accessories from bags to barrettes. But you can still find blazers, skirts, and trousers for the office. Lenox Square, 3393 Peachtree Rd., Buckhead, 404/237—2739. MARTA: Lenox.

3 *h-7*

Mall of Georgia, 3333 Buford Dr., Buford, 770/932—3332.

5 *c-5*

Perimeter Mall, 4400 Ashford-Dunwoody Road, off I—285 between Sandy Springs and Chamblee, Dunwoody, 770/551—8900. MARTA: Dunwoody.

classic & conservative

5 *c-5*

ANN TAYLOR

The savvy businesswoman (or the aspirant who wants to look her best for an upcoming interview) can find everything she needs here, from classic yet chic suits to belts, shoes, and accessories. Perimeter Mall, 4400 Ashford-Dunwoody Rd., Dunwoody, 770/671—8874. MARTA: Dunwoody.

5 e-1

North Point Mall, 1000 North Point Pkwy., Alpharetta, 770/664–4915.

12 h-2

Lenox Square, 3393 Peachtree Rd., Buckhead, 404/264–0450. MARTA: Lenox.

6 d-1

Mall of Georgia, 3333 Buford Dr., Buford, 770/271–8258.

12 h-2

3500 Peachtree Rd., across from Lenox Square, Buckhead, 404/264–1211. MARTA: Lenox.

6 a-4

Gwinnett Place, 2100 Pleasant Hill Rd., Duluth, 770/813–0022.

4 e-3

Town Center at Cobb, 400 Ernest W. Barrett Pkwy., Kennesaw, 770/425–7540.

4 h-7

Cumberland Mall, 1216 Cumberland Mall, Smyrna, 770/319–6363.

10 c-3

BECKY YVONNE SHOP

The apparel here includes business and casual wear and runs into cocktail dressing as well. Prices range from moderate to semi-high end. 5900 Jonesboro Rd., McDonough, 770/961–1653.

2 c-4

BELK'S

The selection here resembles what you would find in a larger department store: active wear, business attire, casual clothing, evening dress, along with accessories and shoes. 1447 River Stone Pkwy., Canton, 770/720–1125.

12 h-2

BROOKS BROTHERS

The women's clothes in this menswear bastion are often variations on old-boy standards—cotton polos, French-cuff shirts—but also include such demure separates as pleated skirts and silk or merino-wool sweater twinsets. Lenox Square, 3393 Peachtree Rd., Buckhead, 404/237–7000. MARTA: Lenox.

15 e-5

235 Peachtree St., Downtown, 404/577–4040. MARTA: Peachtree Center.

5 c-5

Perimeter Mall, 4400 Ashford-Dunwoody Rd., Dunwoody, 770/394–9051. MARTA: Dunwoody.

12 f-1

PEOPLES

This classic clothing is different and suits the upscale Southern lifestyle to a tee. 3236 Roswell Rd., Buckhead, 404/816–7292.

12 f-1

POTPOURRI

There's a fine selection of traditional women's clothing here, including wonderful sportswear, dinner dresses, and accessories. 3718 Roswell Rd., Buckhead, 404/365–0880.

12 f-3

RASSLE DAZZLE

Almost an Atlanta tradition, the shop specializes in casual clothing, including great sweaters and pants. Some dressier choices are available, too, including evening wear. You can find a designer label on most of the selections. 49 Irby Ave., Buckhead, 404/233–6940.

5 d-4

TALBOTS

A leader in sophisticated, tailored clothing, Talbots carries lines that range from casual to career wear. Personal shopping service is available. Regulars eagerly await the semiannual sales. 690 Holcomb Bridge Rd., Dunwoody, 770/642–1852.

designer

15 h-3

BILL HALLMAN

The talented Atlanta designer creates clothing for the fashion-forward woman and shows his designs in a boutique that is lively and young at heart. However, you don't have to be young to wear this clothing, and the store represents other designers as well. 792 N. Highland Ave., Virginia-Highland, 404/876–6055. MARTA: North Ave.

4 h-7

BONNIE'S BOUTIQUE

The exceptional collections include everything from elegant evening wear to prom and pageant gowns, and the service is helpful. Galleria, 1 Galleria Pkwy., Smyrna, 770/850–0595.

12 *g-2*

LUNA

Top-of-the-line merchandise is offered at this boutique, where fashions range from designer jeans to gowns and accessories. Incidentally, anything you see here is for sale, right down to the furnishings. *3167 Peachtree Rd., Buckhead, 404/233–5344.*

15 *h-3*

MITZI & ROMANO

These very cool designer clothes are geared to women who want something different but graceful. The jewelry and accessories are great, too. *1038 N. Highland Ave., Virginia-Highland, 404/876–7228.*

12 *h-2*

NEIMAN MARCUS

You know the name and what you can expect to find here—the finest in bridal gowns, shoes, and clothing for any occasion. *Lenox Square, 3393 Peachtree Rd., Buckhead, 404/266–8200. MARTA: Lenox.*

7 *h-2*

RENÉ RENÉ

If you're looking for something to wear to the club scene, you can find it here, along with accessories. Some of the designs are appropriate for business as well. *1142 Euclid Ave., Downtown, 404/522–7363.*

5 *c-5*

THE WHITE HOUSE/ BLACK MARKET

Most everything here is black and white, from chic business wear to romantic evening dresses. Accent pieces are available in contrasting colors, and the inventory extends to accessories and gifts. *4505 Ashford-Dunwoody Rd., Dunwoody, 770/395–7500. MARTA: Dunwoody.*

5 *a-3*

Avenue at East Cobb, 4475 Roswell Rd., Marietta, 770/971–7315.

discount & off-price

5 *e-1*

ALPHARETTA BARGAIN STORE

The store's a secret, at least among the moneyed set who loves the designer

clothing at as much as 70% off. When you see the Benzes, Beamers, Jags, and Lexuses parking in the lot, head in for the new shipment. You may have to pick around the polyester, and some sections may be a bit thin depending on the day, but if you're a regular shopper here, you know what you can come home with. *131 S. Main St., Alpharetta, 770/475–5062.*

13 *d-4*

LOEHMANN'S

To savvy shoppers, this name means designer closeout merchandise, anything from Donna Karen to Ralph Lauren and Gucci. (As you probably know, you won't see the label because it's been cut out.) The buys on jewelry, handbags, and shoes are also outstanding. *2480 Briarcliff Rd., Toco Hills, 404/633–4156.*

4 *g-5*

2460 Cobb Pkwy. SE, Smyrna, 770/953–2225.

5 *c-5*

SYMS

The choice of designer clothing runs from business attire through evening wear, and it's available at a fraction of the cost you'd pay elsewhere. If you don't find what you want, wait a couple of days and come back, because the merchandise changes frequently. *1803 Roswell Rd., Roswell, 770/321–3400.*

5 *g-5*

5775 Jimmy Carter Blvd., Norcross, 770/368–0200.

unusual sizes

5 *b-5*

THE PETITE PLACE

Everything for the petite woman is here, including casual, business, and evening wear. In fact, you won't find these designs in a petite section of a department store or anywhere else. *6309 Roswell Rd., Sandy Springs, 404/252–1223.*

4 *h-7*

TALL IS BEAUTIFUL

The elegant fashions for the tall woman come in luxurious fabrics and tasteful designer styles. Coordinating accessories are available, too. *Galleria, 1 Galleria Pkwy., Smyrna, 770/541–6880.*

CLOTHING FOR WOMEN/ SPECIALTY

coats & rainwear

5 c-5

REI

Beyond the province of the mere raincoat, this company has the equipment for the worst blows nature can inflict upon you, from high-tech jackets and hats to boots, gloves, and plain old umbrellas. (The Clairmont Road location has the largest inventory and best selection.) *1165 Perimeter Center W, near Perimeter Mall, Dunwoody, 770/901–9200. MARTA: Dunwoody.*

13 e-3

1800 Northeast Expwy., exit 32 at Clairmont Rd. on the access road next to I–85 S, North Atlanta, 404/633–6508.

shoes & boots

1 e-6

BOOT VILLAGE & WESTERN WEAR

You can find great values on the latest styles in name-brand boots and Western wear, along with a selection of belts and accessories. Some of the designs are of alligator and crocodile, when they are available. *1393 Mt. Zion Rd., Morrow, 770/968–0024.*

7 a-4

3221 Hwy. 5, Douglasville, 770/489–4555.

5 h-2

2131 Pleasant Hill Rd., Duluth, 770/476–1555.

COMPUTERS & SOFTWARE

5 h-4

COMP USA

Geared toward serving both the savvy user and the novice, this large outlet of the national chain is a key spot for shopping name-brand hardware, but it's the dizzying selection of software titles that makes this an essential stop. *3825 Venture Dr., Duluth, 770/813–8565.*

5 e-5

DELTA COMPUTERS

Mid-range prices, good locations, and a wide selection make this long-standing local outfit worth looking into. You can find everything from complete systems to individual components. *2633 Beacon Dr., Doraville, 770/457–9999.*

9 g-1

7147 Jonesboro Rd., Jonesboro, 770/968–8822.

4 g-4

2100 Roswell Rd., Marietta, 770/579–1212.

5 g-5

HiQ COMPUTERS

The store is a prime resource for knowledgeable, budget-conscious users who know exactly what they want under the hood. Built-to-order systems can be turned out in 24 to 48 hours—or less. *5600 Oakbrook Pkwy., Suite 260, Norcross, 404/223–3127.*

4 h-5

MICRO CENTER

Shoppers coming in from the northwest side may find that this store has many of the perks of a megastore but fewer

---

SHOPPING STRESS-BUSTERS

On your next shopping excursion, consider taking a break with one of these stress-busters.

Alon's (Bread & Pastries)
Sit down, relax, and savor some aromatic fresh-brewed coffee and a tasty pastry in this European-style café.

Fantasyland Records (CDs, Tapes & Vinyl)
The collection of records available here takes you on a nostalgic trip back through the decades and will leave you humming tunes from a prom night long forgotten.

Joe Muggs (Newspapers & Newsstands)
Catch up on the scoop from your hometown paper, find out what's going on in another part of the world, or get lost in a magazine section sure to harbor your favorite hobby or interest.

Maison Robert Fine Chocolates (Chocolates & Other Candy)
A delectable treat of marzipan or a French truffle at this quaint shop is a perfect pick-me-up during an antiques outing in Chamblee.

hassles. Macintosh users are well served here. *1221 Powers Ferry Rd., Marietta, 770/859–1540.*

COSTUMES

5 *a-2*

A COSTUME BALL

Everybody has a ball here, even if just stopping in to look. Whatever the occasion or the fantasy, whatever your size or age, you can find just the right costume, along with a good selection of masks, cosmetics, accessories, wigs, hats, and mustaches. *3101 Roswell Rd., Marietta, 770/565–5558.*

13 *c-4*

ATLANTA COSTUME

The outfit supplies many of the area's theaters, motion-picture companies, and other commercial concerns with costumes and creates custom designs should you not find something to suit you in the huge inventory. The store extends its hours in October. *2089 Monroe Dr., at I–85 N, Midtown, 404/874–7511.*

4 *f-4*

EDDIE'S TRICK & NOVELTY SHOP

These two shops have an especially fine selection of costumes for Halloween. Throughout the year students of the magical arts make their way through books and props and sit in on the ongoing courses. *70 S. Park Sq., Marietta, 770/428–4314.*

6 *a-4*

3675 Satellite Blvd., Duluth, 770/814–9700.

CRAFTS & HOBBY SUPPLIES

needlework & knitting

4 *h-4*

ABECEDARIUS

Atlanta's most committed cross-stitch shop makes sure you're taught the techniques correctly and are equipped with all the accessories and framing things you could need. *2141 Roswell Rd., Marietta, 770/977–3585.*

5 *c-2*

CAST-ON COTTAGE

In one of the old houses along these character-filled streets, the shop offers a large selection of beautiful woolen yarns. Its knitting classes are much in demand, and deservedly so. *1003 Canton St., Roswell, 770/998–3483.*

5 *d-4*

DUNWOODY NEEDLE ACCENT

If you're handy with a needle you may want to seek out this shop for the widest range of materials, and classes. The offerings include hand-painted canvases in one-of-a-kind designs and limited-edition intricacies from the country's top designers of needlepoint, crewelwork, and cross-stitch. Mail orders are accepted. *5477 Chamblee-Dunwoody Rd., Dunwoody, 770/393–9322.*

5 *e-4*

JAPANESE EMBROIDERY CENTER

In a serene environment filled with shojii screens, you can learn Japanese embroidery techniques. Beginners and advanced students can take classes in this art, taught by Japanese masters and their American colleagues; this is not for the occasional cross-stitcher. *2727 Spalding Dr., Dunwoody, 770/390–0617.*

13 *c-6*

NEEDLE NOOK

Judaic designs are the specialty at this shop, and it has some of the best you can find. There's instruction in cross-stitch, needlepoint, glass beadwork, and other media. *2165 Briarcliff Rd., at LaVista Rd., Toco Hills, 404/325–0068.*

4 *h-7*

PINTUCKS & PINAFORES

This is perhaps the only place in Atlanta where you can learn sewing techniques for flower-girl and christening gowns, bar and bat mitzvah outfits, confirmation dresses, and other children's ware. Classes are offered in heirloom sewing, smocking, embroidery, and needle lace, and you can shop here for all the attendant supplies. *Vinings Jubilee Shopping Center, 4300 Paces Ferry Rd., Suite 405, Vinings, 770/384–1216.*

5 *b-6*

STRINGS & STRANDS

Primarily focused on knitting—with an emphasis on wonderful hand-dyed yarns of every variety and expert instruction—this shop also offers yarns and instruction for crochet aficionados. *4632 Wieuca Rd., Sandy Springs, 404/252–9662.*

other categories

12 *d-6*

ART AND SOUL
ARTS & CRAFTS CAFÉ
Make your own pottery but leave the glazing and the firing to the staff here. You can sip specialty coffees and nibble pastries in the adjoining café while you wait. *2140 Peachtree Rd., Buckhead, 404/352–1222.*

ELECTRONICS & AUDIO

12 *h-1*

BANG & OLUFSEN
Still enjoying its popularity, this high-end chain offers sleek, well-designed products at prices that are not for the faint of heart. *Phipps Plaza, 3500 Peachtree Rd., Buckhead, 404/233–4199. MARTA: Lenox.*

5 *c-5*

BEST BUY
While the megastore competition gets thicker, this chain still wins points for selection and respectable quality across the board. *1201 Hammond Dr., Dunwoody, 770/392–0454. MARTA: Dunwoody.*

5 *e-1*

975 North Point Pkwy., Alpharetta, 678/339–1321.

6 *a-4*

1875 Pleasant Hill Rd., Duluth, 770/381–9494.

4 *g-5*

2460 Cobb Pkwy. SE, Smyrna, 770/859–9266.

5 *f-8*

4145 LaVista Rd., Tucker, 770/939–7660.

6 *d-7*

HIFI BUYS
For fast service on low, mid-range, or somewhat higher-priced equipment, this chain is a sound performer. Car installations are particularly quick and painless, and warranties aren't a hassle. *2059 Scenic Hwy., Suite 101, Snellville, 678/344–0007.*

EYEWEAR

12 *g-2*

THE EYE GALLERY
Three optometrists began this complete eyewear shop to compete with the major national retailers. Customers can schedule examinations, have prescriptions altered, and shop for frames all under one roof. *3330 Piedmont Rd., Buckhead, 404/231–3772. MARTA: Buckhead.*

5 *e-1*

North Point Mall, 1000 North Point Pkwy., Alpharetta, 770/475–6500.

5 *b-5*

5975 Roswell Rd., Sandy Springs, 404/252–4111.

5 *c-5*

LENS CRAFTERS
The national chain has set up shop in virtually every part of the metro area to offer full-service eye care known for its speed. *4400 Ashford-Dunwoody Rd., Dunwoody, 770/395–6717. MARTA: Dunwoody.*

5 *e-1*

North Point Mall, 1114 North Point Cir., Alpharetta, 770/667–8800.

6 *d-1*

Mall of Georgia, 3333 Buford Dr., Buford, 678/482–4491.

12 *h-2*

Lenox Square, 3393 Peachtree Rd., Buckhead, 404/239–0784. MARTA: Lenox.

7 *e-4*

Greenbriar Mall, 2841 Greenbriar Pkwy., Lakewood, 404/346–2025.

5 *f-7*

Northlake Mall, 4800 Briarcliff Rd., Northlake, 770/493–6553.

4 *h-6*

PEARLE VISION
Possibly the most well known of eye-care specialists, Pearle has more than 20 metro locations, offering a complete range of optometry services and a guarantee on the lowest prices for contact lenses. *2778 Cobb Pkwy., Smyrna, 770/859–0444.*

12 *h-2*

3425 Lenox Rd., Buckhead, 404/237–6210. MARTA: Lenox.

5 g-2

9775 Medlock Bridge Rd., Duluth, 770/622–5300.

5 c-2

10775 Alpharetta Hwy., Roswell, 770/998–9656.

6 d-7

1708 Scenic Hwy. SW, Snellville, 770/736–3006.

2 a-8

9801 Hwy. 92, Woodstock, 770/592–7100.

12 f-3

PLANET EYEWEAR

An eyeglass boutique where the stock runs from classic to funky, Planet Eyewear is for people who are superserious about their accessories. Dramatically subdued lighting showcases the merchandise, with a selection ample enough that even Elton John could find something to suit his extravagant tastes. Be sure to try one of the select beverages from the organic juice bar. 3167 Peachtree Rd., Buckhead, 404/816–4224. MARTA: Buckhead.

5 h-5

THE SUNGLASS WAREHOUSE

The selection of sunglasses and accessories—domestics and imports—is huge and suited to all budgets and tastes. You may find that many of the finer brands are 5%–15% off what the department stores charge. 5182 Brook Hollow Pkwy., Norcross, 770/729–1961.

FABRICS & NOTIONS

7 f-6

BUKOM TEXTILES STORE

Bukom is one of the only fabric shops in the city that specialize in African fabrics. Many of the materials are actually imported from Europe, where the manufacturers are located, but are used in the making of traditional African garb. 2680 Godby Rd., College Park, 404/766–1228.

12 h-4

CURRAN DESIGNER FABRICS & FURNITURE INC.

Tucked away in one of the city's antiques districts, Curran offers more than 5,000 types of fabrics in addition to furniture and home accents at wholesale. 737

Miami Cir., Buckhead, 404/237–4246. MARTA: Lindbergh Center.

15 b-2

FORSYTH FABRICS

Serving Atlanta since 1949, Forsyth Fabrics is one of the best-known and most frequented fabric suppliers in the city. Racks and racks of fabrics ranging from feather-light sheers to sumptuous tapestries fill the warehouse space. 1190 Foster St., Midtown, 404/351–6050.

15 b-2

LEWIS & SHERON TEXTILE COMPANY

With a whole room devoted just to silks, it's safe to say that Lewis & Sheron has an encompassing inventory. The selection is vast, the staff knowledgeable, the reputation long-standing (since 1945). An adjacent furniture store makes for one-stop shopping, if you're so inclined. 912 Huff Rd., Midtown, 404/351–4833.

FLOWERS & PLANTS

12 g-7

ATLANTA WILDFLOWERS

The self-styled European flower market may be a bit out of your way, but it's worth the trek. Thousands of exotic blooms greet customers in this generous space exclusively devoted to flowers, plants, and garden accessories. You can also take a six-week floral-design class here. 1893 Piedmont Rd., Midtown, 404/873–7300.

12 f-4

BROOKHAVEN-BUCKHEAD FLOWERS

Family-owned and -operated, this busy spot services most of the local area churches. The shop has developed a reputation for excellent arrangements for any event that won't break the budget and also delivers balloon bouquets, plants, and gift baskets metro-wide. 2905 Peachtree Rd., Buckhead, 404/237–6351.

4 g-5

CARITHERS

This full-service florist has been serving the local market for more than a quarter century. Messengers cover the metro area twice daily to ensure delivery of the freshest possible bouquets and arrangements, along with gourmet and gift baskets for every occasion. Carithers also offers customers with a 24-hour service line. *1708 Powers Ferry Rd., Marietta, 770/980–3000.*

12 *h-2*

FLOWERS FROM HOLLAND LIMITED

It may be small, but this shop stocks the best. Flowers from Holland eschews the more common bulbs to maximize the space for its top-quality line of exotics. *Lenox Square, 3393 Peachtree Rd., Buckhead, 404/233–0090. MARTA: Lenox.*

14 *a-3*

FOXGLOVES & IVY

Step inside the cobblestone entranceway and take in the lush English-garden setting. Given the shop's large variety of the finest tropicals and exotics, you won't find any mundane blooms in the bouquets here. The owners take great pride in creating their custom-made arrangements and in making sure that their employees are trained in the latest design techniques. This is a popular choice for wedding parties and other joyous events. *1060 St. Charles Ave., Midtown, 404/892–7272.*

14 *g-3*

MAUD BAKER FLORIST

Flowers and gifts from this shop are a Decatur landmark. Arrangements are always custom-tailored and offer the best from Holland and other locales. Maud Baker is open most major holidays and, for that last-minute affair, can oftentimes make deliveries within one hour of receiving an order. *609 Church St., Decatur, 404/373–5791. MARTA: Decatur.*

FOLK ART & HANDICRAFTS

14 *b-5*

DONNA VAN GOGH'S INTOWN ARTIST MARKET

The motto is "art for y'all" at this charming gallery, which includes an eclectic assortment of locally crafted items in a friendly atmosphere. *1165 McClendon Ave., Candler Park, 404/370–1003. MARTA: Edgewood/Candler Park.*

14 *a-2*

SIDEWALK STUDIO

This inviting enclave of high-end crafts features the work of artists who specialize in pottery, paintings, sculptures, and jewelry of the handmade as well as custom-made variety. *1050 N. Highland Ave., Virginia-Highland, 404/872–1047.*

FOOD & DRINK

A typical Atlantan's shopping list reflects the long-standing influence of newcomers: There's the balsamic vinegar alongside the black-eyed peas. Accordingly, almost anybody new to the metro area can find a taste of home these days in produce markets, fancy delis, and ethnic food shops. Locating the grits and fried chicken could take a little more effort, but they're still around, too.

breads & pastries

14 *a-2*

ALON'S

Visit this European-style bakery early on a summer Saturday for a bag of fresh pastries and a tall, strong coffee before heading across the street for the Morningside Farmers Market. Or then again, visit anytime. *1394 N. Highland Ave., Virginia-Highland, 404/872–6000.*

15 *g-2*

BREAD GARDEN

The tiny storefront in a Midtown outlet district sells what are reputed to be the best baked goods in town. The loaves of country Italian bread, fresh-fruit tarts, and homemade biscotti are heavenly. *549 Amsterdam Ave., Midtown, 404/875–1166. Closed Sun.*

12 *g-3*

BUCKHEAD BREAD

A few blocks south of the Ritz-Carlton, Buckhead. A stone's throw from a Jaguar dealership. Across the street from the gleaming Buckhead Diner. Get the picture? Amid the glitz, this large-scale baking operation turns out incredible specialty breads and jewel-like desserts. *3070 Piedmont Rd., Buckhead, 404/240–1978.*

9 *d-4*

CITY CAFÉ & BAKERY

The German owner focuses on European-style breads—about a dozen kinds each day—in addition to cakes, pies, and pastries. *215 S. Glynn St., Fayetteville, 770/461–6800. Closed Sun.*

12 *f-3*

HENRI'S

A Buckhead institution since 1929, this place still turns out superlative cheese straws, Italian cream cake, and chocolate eclairs. *61 Irby Ave., Buckhead, 404/237–0202. Closed Sun.*

5 *b-5*

6289 Roswell Rd., Sandy Springs, 404/256–7934.

15 *e-4*

KRISPY KREME

The little pillows of sweetness sold here have conquered Atlanta's suburbs, which claim several franchises, and the corner grocery, where shoppers can grab a box of the Southerner's take on a doughnut. But the city's original Krispy Kreme still flashes the red neon when the ovens are on. It's a worthy pit stop. *295 Ponce de Leon Ave. NE, Midtown, 404/876–7307.*

15 *b-2*

MONDO

In the trendy industrial section of Midtown, this bakery-café is known for such original desserts as the Maker's Mark bourbon-fig bars, as well as such basics as carrot cake and lemon love bars. *750 Huff Rd., Midtown, 404/603–9995. Closed Sun.*

8 *c-1*

SOUTHERN SWEETS

If the pecan tart and the Key lime pie at this wholesale baker's outlet store taste familiar, it's probably because they're served in some of Atlanta's best restaurants. Homemade soups and party spreads, such as smoked-salmon pâté, are also available. *186 Rio Cir., Decatur, 404/373–8752. Closed Sun.*

chocolate & other candy

12 *h-2*

KARL BISSINGER FRENCH CONFECTIONS

In May, fresh strawberries are dipped in the richest French chocolate; in July, raspberries get the treatment. Apricots, oranges, and other fruits round out the rest of the year, along with a nice selection of other chocolates and candies. *Phipps Plaza, 3500 Peachtree Rd., Buckhead, 404/237–7161.*

5 *e-6*

MAISON ROBERT FINE CHOCOLATES

From a cottage tucked on a side street in Chamblee, Robert Reeb sells the finest handmade chocolates and truffles around. This European master also turns out fruit tarts, assorted quiches, and a fantastic macaroon. *3708 N. Peachtree Rd., Chamblee, 770/454–6442. Closed Sun.*

15 *e-6*

SOUTHERN CANDY CO.

The aromatic shop in Underground Atlanta sells pecan pralines, fudge, nut brittles, taffy, candy apples, and other sweets. *Underground Atlanta, 112 Lower Alabama St., Downtown, 404/577–3697. MARTA: Five Points.*

coffee & tea

14 *a-4*

AURORA

The locally owned Aurora appeals to the anti-chain coffeehouse set. Coffees by the pound come in a seemingly endless array of roasts, grinds, and flavors. *468 Moreland Ave., Little Five Points, 404/523–6856.*

14 *a-2*

992 N. Highland Ave., Virginia-Highland, 404/892–7158.

15 *g-1*

1572 Piedmont Ave., Midtown, 404/607–9994.

5 *c-7*

BARCLAY'S FLOWER & TEA GARDEN

The unexpected location, amid offices and rental housing, adds to the charm of this cottage, where you can find a wide selection of loose leaves and tea accessories. A formal afternoon tea is served in traditional English style here, complete with bone china, scones, cream tea, and finger sandwiches. *285 W. Wieuca Rd., Sandy Springs, 404/705–5900. Closed Sun.*

12 *h-2*

TEAVANA

Whether it's oolong you seek or herbal, this tea-obsessive shop (formerly Elephant Tea Company) has it. Choose from more than 100 kinds of loose teas, or tea by the cup or pot. Tea accessories include a Chinese carved-stone teapot that would make a nice hostess gift. *Phipps Plaza, 3500 Peachtree Rd., Buckhead, 404/261–3004. MARTA: Lenox.*

`12` *h-2*

Lenox Square, 3393 Peachtree Rd., Buckhead, 404/495–0760. MARTA: Lenox.

ethnic foods

`5` *d-4*

EAST 48TH STREET MARKET

This is as Italian as it gets in Atlanta. Snap up the authentic crusty Italian bread as soon as it's brought out. There's also a good selection of imported pastas, olive oils, cheeses, and cured meats, including the perfect prosciutto. Top cooks swear by the canned tomatoes and purees here. *2462 Jett Ferry Rd., Dunwoody, 770/392–1499. Closed Sun.*

`5` *e-6*

HONG KONG SUPERMARKET

Rice vermicelli, fresh frogs' legs, galangal root—if it's an ingredient in Asian cooking, you can find it here. The full-service supermarket offers produce, meats, seafood, and all manner of grocery items imported from China, Vietnam, Thailand, Korea, Japan, and elsewhere in Asia. *4166 Buford Hwy., Doraville, 404/325–3999.*

`12` *f-7*

LOS AMIGOS TORTILLA MANUFACTURING

Latino markets line the Buford Highway corridor in North Atlanta, but they buy their corn and flour tortillas here, where they're made fresh daily. There's also a limited selection of chips, salsa, jalapeños, and other Mexican specialties. *251 Armour Dr., Midtown, 404/876–8153. Closed Sun.*

`13` *c-6*

QUALITY KOSHER EMPORIUM

The meats are of the highest quality, and the choices in canned and dry goods are plentiful. Visit the deli for heat-and-eat items. *2153 Briarcliff Rd., Toco Hills, 404/636–1114. Closed Sat.*

fish & seafood

`12` *f-4*

ATLANTA FISH MARKET

The giant metal fish sculpture created a stir in 1994, when it was first displayed, but it's a handy landmark for this restaurant-cum-market. Squeeze past the throngs of diners to choose live lobsters, Dungeness crabs, fresh grouper, or whatever else might be among the shop offerings of the day. You can also get to-go orders of most anything from the menu. *265 Pharr Rd., Buckhead, 404/262–3165.*

`15` *a-2*

INLAND SEAFOOD

This major southeastern wholesaler has no retail storefront and accepts telephone orders only. But you're guaranteed a wide selection of fish, crustaceans, bivalves, or any other edible sea creature, flown in fresh daily. *1222 Menlo Dr., Midtown, 404/350–5850. Closed weekends.*

gourmet foods

`12` *h-2*

EATZI'S MARKET & BAKERY

The Dallas-chain outpost woos Buckhead with wine and flowers, rotisserie chickens, and fresh produce. The heat-and-eat cases are jammed, and the bakery is particularly good. *3221 Peachtree Rd., Buckhead, 404/237–2266.*

`5` *c-7*

GREENWOOD ICE CREAM CO. OUTLET STORE

Here's the scoop; find the same custom-made, premium ice creams sold in restaurants across Atlanta here by the half-gallon carton or the three-gallon tub. Try the champagne sorbet, the green tea, or just plain vanilla. Flavors vary each day. *4829 Peachtree Rd., Chamblee, 770/455–6166. Closed weekends.*

`13` *a-7*

HAPPY HERMAN'S

Head here for a glimpse of Atlanta's gourmet roots. The grocery store sells fresh produce, wine, ready-to-eat foods, chocolates, and other epicurean items. *2299 Cheshire Bridge Rd., Midtown, 404/321–3012.*

15 *b-2*

STAR PROVISIONS

The top purveyor of gourmet products in the Southeast, this 4,000-square-ft store is sister and neighbor to Bacchanalia, one of the city's best restaurants. Offerings range from artisanal cheeses to Kobe beef to Petrossian caviar to 100-year-old balsamic vinegar. Don't miss the selection of unusual kitchen accessories and the library of rare cookbooks. *1198 Howell Mill Rd., Northwest Atlanta, 404/365–0410. Closed Sun.–Mon.*

8 *b-2*

WATERSHED

Fans say this trendy downtown Decatur shop sells the best egg-salad sandwich around, along with a selection of salads, sides, and desserts. *406 W. Ponce de Leon Ave., Decatur, 404/378–4900. Closed Sun.*

health food

13 *a-7*

RETURN TO EDEN

The huge vitamin and supplement section and the friendly staff are the draws at this totally vegetarian grocery. The produce is all organic and offered only in peak season (so you won't find pink strawberries in December). *2335 Cheshire Bridge Rd., Midtown, 404/320–3336.*

14 *a-4*

SEVANANDA COMMUNITY-OWNED NATURAL FOODS MARKET

From its roots as a food cooperative, this Little Five Points institution has grown into a sophisticated, well-run vegetarian grocery. The $20 annual membership provides a 5% discount each Tuesday. *467 Moreland Ave., Little Five Points, 404/681–2831.*

12 *h-2*

UNITY NATURAL FOODS

Dietary supplements, organic produce, and free-range eggs and poultry round out the offerings at this health-food store just south of the Buckhead bar district. *2955 Peachtree Rd., Buckhead, 404/261–8776.*

13 *c-6*

WHOLE FOODS MARKET

You can find a variety of vegetarian products as this organic grocery chain but also free-range chickens and eggs, quality meats and pâtés, and cheese galore. The produce, some of it from local organic farms, is superb. *2111 Briarcliff Rd., Toco Hills, 404/634–7800.*

5 *c-5*

5930 Roswell Rd., at Hammond Dr., Sandy Springs, 404/236–0810.

meat & poultry

12 *f-3*

NEW YORKER DELI & BUTCHER SHOP

Meat or seafood, New Yorker's got it or will find it for you. Call ahead for special orders such as crown roasts or aged prime rib. The deli features prepared entrées such as filet mignon and grilled salmon, as well as a selection of side dishes. *322 Pharr Rd., Buckhead, 404/240–0260. Closed Sun.*

4 *c-1*

PATAK-BOHEMIA SAUSAGE CHALET

Cold cuts, bacon, sausages—80 varieties are made at this country-lane chalet, which focuses on European processed meats. Also look for high-quality cuts of beef, pork, and veal, from roasts to chops. *4107 Ewing Rd., Austell, 770/941–7993. Closed weekends.*

11 *g-5*

SHIELD'S MARKET

An old-timey meat market in the best sense, Shield's is *the* name in aged beef in the area. *1554 N. Decatur Rd., Decatur, 404/377–0204. Closed Sun.*

14 *h-2*

143 Sycamore St., Decatur, 404/377–0204.

nuts & seeds

8 *e-1*

STONE MOUNTAIN PECAN CO.

The orchards may be in south Georgia, but the processed pecans are right here, by the pound or the case, along with an assortment of other nuts and candies. *6565 James B. Rivers Dr., Stone Mountain, 770/469–8824. Closed weekends.*

pasta & noodles

4 *f-4*

COSTA'S FRESH PASTA

Call ahead a day if you want something special—fresh tagliatelle, for instance. But from Monday through Thursday, the Costas also sell their fresh pastas, including ravioli and tortellini, over the counter. *2045 Attic Pkwy., Kennesaw, 770/514–8814. Closed weekends.*

produce

7 *h-7*

ATLANTA STATE FARMER'S MARKET

Known as the "world's largest roadside fruit stand," this market spreads across 146 acres, offering regional and imported produce, flowers, and plants. Georgia fresh crops such as pumpkin are available in winter and zucchini, okra, and beans in summer. *16 Forest Pkwy., Forest Park, 404/675–1782.*

5 *d-1*

HARRY'S FARMERS MARKET

Despite the name, all three locations are clean, well lit, and indoors—basically, they're giant supermarkets. The produce is great, but you can get anything here, from a jar of Indian chutney to a Chianti Classico. *1180 Upper Hembree Rd., Roswell, 770/664–6300.*

5 *g-5*

2025 Satellite Point, Duluth, 770/416–6900.

4 *h-5*

70 Powers Ferry Rd., Marietta, 770/578–4400.

12 *d-7*

HARRY'S IN A HURRY

Designed to appeal to commuters on the run, these stores feature fresh fruits and vegetables as well as such basics as wine, cheese, and flowers, plus a wide selection of prepared meals-to-go. *1875 Peachtree Rd., Buckhead, 404/352–7800.*

4 *h-7*

2939 Cobb Pkwy., Marietta, 770/541–9316.

14 *a-3*

1061 Ponce de Leon Ave., Virginia-Highland, 404/439–1100.

12 *f-1*

3804 Roswell Rd., Buckhead, 404/266–0800.

9 *g-1*

5380 Jonesboro Rd., Jonesboro, 404/361–7522.

5 *d-4*

1418 Dunwoody Village Pkwy., Dunwoody, 770/238–1400.

5 *e-6*

INTERNATIONAL FARMERS MARKET

You might be able to pick up cooking tips from a Thai restaurant owner as you examine the lemongrass stalks here. This full-scale farmer's market is all indoors and draws a large immigrant clientele. *5193 Peachtree Industrial Blvd., Chamblee, 770/455–1777.*

15 *g-6*

SWEET AUBURN CURB MARKET

At this renovated urban bazaar, you can get a taste of Sweet Auburn's past as the center of a bustling African-American business district. Everything from fresh meats to Caribbean jerk spices to kaolin, the edible white clay, is on offer. *209 Edgewood Ave., Sweet Auburn, 404/659–1665.*

8 *c-1*

YOUR DEKALB FARMERS MARKET

The dozens of immigrant cultures that inhabit the metro area are well represented in the exotic produce, the aisles of imported dry goods, the tanks of live fish, and on the name tags of the clerks listing all the languages they speak. *3000 E. Ponce de Leon Ave., Decatur, 404/377–6400. Closed Sun.*

wines & spirits

2 *h-8*

BEVERAGE WAREHOUSE

For practical, everyday stocking up on beer, ale, wine, and hard liquor, these warehouse-style stores offer common brands at great prices. *11005 Alpharetta Hwy., 2 blocks north of the Mansell intersection, Roswell, 770/992–0007. Closed Sun.*

5 *e-1*

10950 State Bridge Rd., Alpharetta, 770/569–2345.

5 b-6

BUCKHEAD FINE WINE

The place specializes in designing wine cellars and racking systems and then stocking them with the best vintages. If you're thinking about stocking a cellar, or just buying a great bottle of burgundy or a Bordeaux, this is the place to come. *3906 Roswell Rd., Buckhead, 404/231–8566. Closed Sun.*

8 c-1

DEKALB FARMERS' MARKET

The emphasis here is on great pricing and a wide range of wines. There's a good selection of microbrew beers, too. *3000 E. Ponce de Leon Ave., Decatur, 404/377–6400. Closed Sun.*

5 e-7

EMBRY HILLS LIQUOR WAREHOUSE

The women who own this shop know a lot about wine, how to price it, and what's going to taste good with your selection. *3503 Chamblee Tucker Rd., Chamblee, 770/455–8549. Closed Sun.*

ROADSIDE PRODUCE

Maple Drive, Buckhead
If you're looking for a tomato that really smacks your palate with dusky sweetness and summer twilight, head here.

Merchant's Walk, Hwy. 120 and Johnson Ferry Rd., East Marietta
This outdoor market has tons of fresh produce along with fun things like stacks of cane sugar and bales of pine straw. It's a great source for Halloween pumpkins and Christmas trees.

Mt. Vernon Hwy. and Sandy Springs Cir., Sandy Springs
Sweet corn is best when it's only hours old, which is why you should check out this popular truck stand for new shipments throughout summer.

Toco Hills Shopping Center, LaVista and North Druid Hills Rds., Toco Hills
The freshest produce, including great corn, tomatoes, and peaches, starts arriving in May and keeps coming until September.

---

15 d-6

HABERSHAM VINEYARDS & WINERY

The shop sells wines produced by Georgia's own vineyards at Château Élan (near Braselton, off I–85 north). *Underground Atlanta, 50 Upper Alabama St., Downtown, 404/522–9463. MARTA: Five Points.*

13 a-7

HAPPY HERMAN'S

Here's the place to find the perfect merlot for the dinner you're preparing for your boss. The selection of California, Australian, and French wines is excellent, with many wines from small, exclusive vineyards. Expect to pay for the high quality, service, and variety. *2299 Cheshire Bridge Rd., Midtown, 404/321–3012.*

7 f-7

KILROY'S PACKAGE STORE

Folks on the south of town find that this store has the best prices and largest wine selection in the area. The entire staff is knowledgeable, but ask for Bill, whose in-depth expertise can guide you to the perfect choice. *4879 Old National Hwy., College Park, 404/768–3159. Closed Sun.*

15 e-3

MAC'S

The excellent selection here is especially strong on California and French wines. Mac's offers free wine consultation and also plans special events. *929 Spring St., Midtown, 404/872–4897. Closed Sun. MARTA: Midtown.*

12 f-3

PEARSON'S

The people who shop here know their stuff, so the staff keeps up on the latest offerings in wines and spirits. The selections of single-malt scotches, liqueurs, brandies, and dessert wines are excellent, as is the variety of wines from Europe, Australia, and the United States. There's a decent cigar selection, too. *3072 Early St., Buckhead, 404/231–8752. Closed Sun.*

4 g-4

SHERLOCK'S BEER & WINE WAREHOUSE

The selection here is fine, with unusual offerings that include many German and

Italian wines. *2156 Roswell Rd., Marietta, 770/971–6333. Closed Sun.*

4 *f-3*

135 Ernest W. Barrett Pkwy., Kennesaw, 770/426–6744.

FRAMING

12 *f-3*

BA FRAMER

With more than 700 custom frames for you to choose from, BA Framer has one of the best selections in the area. An experienced staff is on hand to help you with your framing needs, including shadow boxes and preservation framing. Ready-framed pictures and mirrors adorn the walls. *3145 Peachtree Rd., Buckhead, 404/237–3135. MARTA: Buckhead.*

5 *d-5*

4780 Ashford-Dunwoody Rd., Dunwoody, 770/396–1006.

5 *h-3*

5805 State Bridge Rd., Duluth, 770/497–9850.

4 *h-2*

2960 Shallowford Rd., Marietta, 770/977–8771.

6 *d-7*

1630 W. Scenic Hwy., Snellville, 770/982–1696.

14 *a-1*

1402 N. Highland Ave., Virginia-Highland, 404/815–8771.

5 *h-2*

CARTER HOUSE GALLERY & FRAMING

In addition to custom framing, this place also sells contemporary paintings, collectibles, and glass sculpture. *10820 Abbott's Ridge Rd., Duluth, 770/495–1998. Closed Sun.*

12 *g-5*

FAST FRAME

This is the place for simple, practical frames, to display your children's artwork or to complete other basic framing projects. The quality and the prices are good. *2625 Piedmont Rd., Buckhead, 404/261–1213. MARTA: Lindbergh Center.*

5 *b-6*

4920 Roswell Rd., Sandy Springs, 404/252–9250.

8 *a-1*

2205 LaVista Rd., Toco Hills, 404/636–2787.

5 *d-2*

2300 Holcomb Bridge Rd., Roswell, 770/992–5545.

5 *d-4*

2090 Dunwoody Club Dr., Dunwoody, 770/399–5725.

6 *a-4*

2180 Pleasant Hill Rd., Duluth, 770/623–1100.

12 *e-6*

THE FRAMERS

Specializing in customizing frames for artwork, the shop also devotes a good portion of its retail space to original works of art. The knowledgeable and friendly staff has a good eye. *2351 Peachtree Rd., Buckhead, 404/237–2888. Closed Sun.*

12 *f-3*

THE GREAT FRAME UP

For do-it-yourself framing, the Great Frame Up allows you to be as involved as you want to be. Select your own frame and mat, and then move over to the workbench area to complete the job. Employees can advise and assist as necessary, or even take the job out of your hands if you're in over your head. *3085 Peachtree Rd., Buckhead, 404/231–9754. MARTA: Buckhead.*

15 *g-2*

985 Monroe Dr., Midtown, 404/892–3212.

5 *b-5*

220 Sandy Springs Cir., Sandy Springs, 404/255–1400.

14 *f-1*

2095 N. Decatur Rd., Decatur, 404/325–5225.

5 *f-4*

3466 Holcomb Bridge Rd., Norcross, 770/368–9015.

5 *f-7*

2138 Henderson Mill Rd., Northlake, 770/939–7100.

5 *d-7*

HOUSE OF 10,000 PICTURE FRAMES

Family owned and operated for nearly three decades, the shop devotes 3,500 square ft of retail space to its impressive selection of specialty frames and custom molding. Prompt service and attention to detail keep customers loyal. *3680 Clairmont Rd., Chamblee, 770/457–5862. Closed Sun.*

4 *g-5*
MARIETTA FRAME & ART
Patrons swear by this place for its excellent selection and customer service. Employing an expert staff that works with you in determining just the right form and style for presentation, Marietta Frame & Art puts an emphasis on customer satisfaction. *1171 S. Marietta Pkwy., Marietta, 678/355–1445. Closed Sun.*

5 *g-5*
REGENCY FINE ART
For more than 30 years this shop has focused on innovative custom framing for a variety of items and art, either purchased here or rescued from the attic. Regency prides itself on employing a design staff with a wealth of knowledge and experience. *6458 Dawson Blvd., Norcross, 770/840–7701.*

GIFTS

14 *a-2*
BACK TO SQUARE ONE
In a neighborhood consistently abuzz with hip vibes, Back to Square One stays blissfully low key. Here, handmade picture frames and eclectic bird feeders share store space with a cooler stashed with homemade ice cream. *1054 N. Highland Ave., Virginia-Highland, 404/815–9970.*

12 *f-3*
BOXWOODS GARDENS & GIFTS
You can get a little turned around in this maze of rooms in an endearing cottage in the heart of Buckhead. Each room is filled with a different kind of gift—one with garden-related goods and another with silver tea sets and jewelry boxes. *100 E. Andrews Dr., Buckhead, 404/233–3400. Closed Sun.*

10 *e-4*
THE COUNTRY MOUSE
The Country Mouse fits into its genteel setting on a classic town square with folksy home-decor items and collectible figurines. *10 Macon St., McDonough, 770/957–0278. Closed Sun.*

13 *c-6*
JUDAICA CORNER
Don't let its nondescript locale fool you. Judaica Corner is one of the best places in town to get quality-crafted items like handmade menorahs and exquisite seder plates as well as Jewish-related books and music. *2185 Briarcliff Rd., Toco Hills, 404/636–2473. Closed Sat.*

5 *c-5*
5968 Roswell Rd., Sandy Springs, 404/843–1933.

14 *a-2*
METROPOLITAN DELUXE
It's deluxe all right. Everything screams primo, from the clever cards and books to the eclectic picture frames, games, and martini-theme bar items. *1034 N. Highland Ave., Virginia-Highland, 404/892–9337.*

5 *h-3*
PARSONS ACE HARDWARE
Parsons has been family owned since it opened in 1924, and this heritage is reflected in attentive service and a personally selected range of the utilitarian to the aesthetic, from hardware to original art to plants. *2780 Buford Hwy., Duluth, 770/623–9976.*

12 *g-3*
PERIDOT DISTINCTIVE GIFTS
Although you can find the usual picture frame here, Peridot tries to suit the against-the-grain aesthete. For the mom-to-be, how about a baby burrito, a blanket with a baby outfit wrapped inside? Home-decor and kitchen items are especially appealing. *514 E. Paces Ferry Rd., Buckhead, 404/261–7028. Closed Sun.*

5 *b-7*
PHOENIX & DRAGON
For anyone interested in metaphysics, the spiritual, or the supernatural, this is a great place. Items range from gurgling tabletop fountains to crystals, Buddhas to Wicca books. *5531 Roswell Rd., Sandy Springs, 404/255–5207.*

14 g-3
SEVENTEEN STEPS
The fun array of items runs the gamut from bar utensils to kids' stuff. *235-M Ponce de Leon Pl., Decatur, 404/377–7564. MARTA: Decatur.*

5 b-5
VERONICA'S ATTIC
Billing itself as Atlanta's best-kept secret, Veronica's Attic has managed to become anything but. It's a favorite for its selection of unique clothing and jewelry. Look for a variety of beaded items and aromatherapy and bath products. *220 Sandy Springs Cir., Sandy Springs, 404/257–1409.*

HOME FURNISHINGS

5 c-2
BALLARD'S BACKROOM
The selected overstocks, samples, and customer returns from the Ballard Designs catalog might include beds and bedding, rugs, tables and office furniture, lighting, wall decor, and more—at prices 10%–80% below the catalog prices. *1475 Holcomb Bridge Rd., Roswell, 770/594–0102. Closed Mon.*

12 h-2
CRATE & BARREL
Don't look for Wedgwood here, but if you need well designed (elegant or casual) things for your table—or you need to buy a table—this is the place. *Lenox Square, 3393 Peachtree Rd., Buckhead, 404/239–0008. MARTA: Lenox.*

5 c-5
Perimeter Mall, 4400 Ashford-Dunwoody Rd., Dunwoody, 770/671–9797. MARTA: Dunwoody.

12 h-2
PIER ONE IMPORTS
You won't break the bank spicing up your home with the tableware, candles, and other accessories offered here. You can rack up more bargains during the seasonal sales, especially after the December holidays. *3435 Lenox Rd., Buckhead, 404/233–1080. MARTA: Lenox.*

12 g-8
1544 Piedmont Rd., Midtown, 404/881–6549.

5 e-1
6010 North Point Pkwy., Alpharetta, 770/569–1133.

12 e-6
2298 Peachtree Rd., Brookwood, 404/355–1832.

6 a-4
2131 Pleasant Hill Rd., Duluth, 770/497–0513.

5 g-5
5795 Jimmy Carter Blvd., Norcross, 770/840–9545.

12 h-2
POTTERY BARN
Wares at this home-design chain run the gamut from leather couches to lamps, picture frames to candles, and bedding to dishes. *Lenox Square, 3393 Peachtree Rd., Buckhead, 404/812–9726. MARTA: Lenox.*

6 d-1
Mall of Georgia, 3333 Buford Dr., Buford, 678/482–4261.

5 a-3
Avenue at East Cobb, 4475 Roswell Rd., Marietta, 678/560–3590.

architectural artifacts

12 g-3
ARCHITECTURAL ACCENTS
The old Sealtest dairy now houses French limestone fireplaces, wonderful doors, massive wrought-iron gates, English judge's paneling, and other European and American artifacts. *2711 Piedmont Rd., Buckhead, 404/266–8700. Closed Sun.*

5 d-7
METROPOLITAN ARTIFACTS
The variety at this 25,000-square-ft wonderland of architectural remnants is astonishing—paneled rooms in their entirety, acres of wrought iron, restaurant-hotel decor. *4783 Peachtree Rd., Chamblee, 770/986–0007. Closed Sun. MARTA: Chamblee.*

14 a-5
THE WRECKING BAR
Since 1969, the components of houses, hotels, and commercial buildings have found their way to this decaying Beaux-Arts mansion, where everything is cleaned and restored to operating condi-

tion. Prices may cause some hard swallowing, but old-fashioned quality can be priceless. *292 Moreland Ave., Little Five Points, 404/525–0468. Closed Sun.*

baskets

4 *d-4*

GARDEN RIDGE

The prices of the willow, plant, and special holiday baskets are reasonable, and you can find all kinds of creative things to do with them while strolling around this crafts store. *2875 George Busbee Pkwy., Kennesaw, 770/425–8337.*

7 *a-4*

7400 Douglas Blvd., Douglasville, 770/577–7005.

5 *h-5*

1887 Willow Trail Pkwy., Norcross, 770/921–1883.

7 *h-7*

MATTHEWS HAMPER HOUSE

A house of baskets inside the Atlanta State Farmer's Market sells hundreds of imported wicker and market models. Choose from natural colors, painted, two tones, and sizes as small as 6 inches. You can accessorize with ribbons, pull-string bows, and sachet bags. *16 Forest Pkwy., Forest Park, 404/366–7166.*

bed and bath linens & accessories

5 *g-6*

CLASSICAL BRASS & IRON BEDS ETC.

The outlet store, in business since 1972, carries 450 different bed styles, and their prices are well below those of many bed retailers. Mattresses and other pieces you might need for the bedroom are available as well. Conveniences include a layaway plan. *6624 Dawson Blvd., Norcross, 770/441–2529.*

5 *g-6*

THE GREAT FUTON STORE

The exclusive Atlanta distributor of Gold Bond futons also offers many other brands of this Japanese bedding solution, in a variety of sizes, colors, and prices. You can get futon frames here, too, even a Charleston iron-rail four-poster. *6576 Dawson Blvd., Norcross, 770/448–9200.*

12 *d-7*

THE HEIRLOOM IRON BED COMPANY

You can choose a reproduction of a classic antique design or have a bed designed and built to your tastes. Then you can outfit your choice with the finest linens, including those from Anichini, the Purists, Ygle, Lisa Galimberti, and Ann Gish. Trouble is, when you climb into your masterpiece, you might never want to get out. *2140 Peachtree Rd., Brookwood, 404/352–3132.*

5 *c-1*

10800 Alpharetta Hwy., Alpharetta, 770/993–7249.

4 *f-4*

65 Church St., Marietta, 770/514–0556.

12 *f-3*

IRISH CRYSTAL CO.

This outlet for beautiful Irish products carries linens by Ireland's major weavers, with damask tablecloths in all sizes, including banquet. Oval cloths are always in stock. Custom-order cloths of any size are also available, as are linen sheets (mostly by special order) and a large supply of flat-weave handkerchiefs and other table linens. *3168 Peachtree Rd., Buckhead, 404/266–3783. Closed Sun.*

12 *h-2*

LASSITER'S BATH & BOUDOIR

Once you've discovered the feel of Egyptian cotton with 500 threads per square inch or a loft-down comforter, a taste for top-of-the-line linens isn't likely to leave you. This is the place to indulge those tastes; fortunately, there are occasional sales. *Phipps Plaza, 3500 Peachtree Rd., Buckhead, 404/261–0765. MARTA: Lenox.*

12 *f-4*

LINENS & THINGS

These stores carry every mid-range brand of linens for bed, bath, and table, with kitchen wares and window treatments thrown in for good measure. Look here for good, solid utilitarian products in assorted colors; you can find an especially wide variety of bold colors and interesting designs in sheets, comforters, and duvets. *2900 Peachtree Rd., Buckhead, 404/816–2700.*

5 *e-1*

6200 North Point Pkwy., Alpharetta, 770/ 667–3611.

6 *a-4*

2340 Pleasant Hill Rd., Duluth, 770/418– 1074.

5 *c-5*

1711 Hammond Dr., Dunwoody, 770/698– 0374.

6 *d-4*

875 Lawrenceville–Suwanee Rd., Lawrenceville, 770/995–6413.

6 *c-8*

5370 Stone Mountain Hwy., Stone Mountain, 770/498–9566.

5 *d-2*

ORIGINAL MATTRESS FACTORY

Mattresses are made on the premises of these outlets, saving you money because you're buying direct. Most models are available immediately, and coming up with an odd size never seems to pose a problem. *1605 Mansell Rd., Alpharetta, 678/461–8755.*

6 *a-4*

3360 Satellite Blvd., Duluth, 770/232– 0770.

4 *e-3*

667 Ernest W. Barrett Pkwy., Kennesaw, 770/420–5303.

4 *g-5*

1335 Capital Cir., Marietta, 770/612–8117.

9 *g-1*

6735 Jonesboro Rd., Morrow, 678/422– 7779.

6 *a-8*

5370 Stone Mountain Hwy., Stone Mountain, 770/498–1009.

5 *e-6*

WALLBEDZZZ

In order to find the hidden-bed systems on display in these model rooms you have to look behind bi-fold doors, pull-down panels above sofas, and swing-out bookcases, and engage in some other sleuthing. The solutions are so ingenious you may be inspired to create another guest room just about anywhere in your home. *3838 Green Industrial Way, Chamblee, 770/455–7662.*

candles

5 *d-2*

ATLANTA CANDLE FACTORY

You'll say *c'est bon* to the "Afternoon in Paris" candle and highly concentrated scents such as "Vanilla Shortcake" at this Roswell candle factory. Shapes vary from votives to 32-ounce jars, with burn times of 12 to 120 hours. *619 Holcomb Bridge Rd., Roswell, 770/649–9005.*

4 *h-7*

WICKS N STICKS

Choose from a full line of pillars and tapers, home accents that are also candle holders, oil lamps and glass, collectible pieces, potpourri pots, wax angels, sun catchers and dragons, incense, and sachets. *Cumberland Mall, 1247 Cumberland Mall, Smyrna, 770/436–3924.*

carpets & rugs

8 *d-2*

CARPET MILL OUTLET

The largest selection of carpets just about anywhere in the metro area includes broadlooms for less than $5 per yard in hundreds of colors, dozens of styles, and from many mills. (You can get a list of installers.) *3805 Covington Hwy., Decatur, 404/286–5999. Closed Sun.*

7 *e-4*

Winn-Dixie shopping plaza, 2076 Headland Dr., East Point, 404/763–0776.

7 *h-7*

7659 Tara Blvd., Jonesboro, 770/472–4545.

12 *h-5*

THE HOME DEPOT

Atlanta is near the epicenter of U.S. carpet manufacturing—Dalton, Georgia— and it's also near the corporate headquarters of this national chain, in Smyrna. Combine these two facts and it's not surprising that the 30-some metro-area Home Depot outlets are excellent sources for a wide range of carpets in every price range and style, from wool sisal to custom rugs. The sales staff is extremely knowledgeable and stands behind the recommended installers. *815 Sidney Marcus Blvd., Buckhead, 404/231–1411.*

5 *f-8*

2295 Lawrenceville Hwy., Decatur, 404/ 315–0015.

5 e-5

4343 Tilly Mill Rd., Doraville, 770/452–8858.

5 c-1

870 Woodstock Rd., Roswell, 678/461–0155.

8 a-8

2034 Mt. Zion Rd., Morrow, 770/478–9990.

6 d-7

1670 Scenic Hwy., Snellville, 770/982–6166.

12 f-3

NOMADIC ART GALLERY

Come with an open mind and a free afternoon. The friendly proprietor is one of the most knowledgeable dealers around, and he can educate you with tales of the nomadic tribes from whom he buys his colorful wares, which include rugs, textiles, and jewelry. 3219 Cains Hill Pl., Buckhead, 404/261–7259.

12 f-4

SHARIAN

The Sharian family has presented Atlanta with the finest in Oriental rugs since 1931. An expert service department washes and cleans carpets with classic methods used in ancient days and matches yarns and colors to reweave them using centuries-old hand-knotting methods. Atlanta Decorative Arts Center, 351 Peachtree Hills Ave., Buckhead, 404/261–2968.

14 f-3

368 W. Ponce de Leon Ave., Decatur, 404/373–2274.

china, glassware, porcelain, pottery, silver

12 f-3

BEVERLY BREMER SILVER SHOP

Nationally acclaimed as a resource for flatware and hollowware, Bremer's shop contains floor-to-ceiling silver objects. Some of them are exotic, some ordinary, but all are polished (how they remain so is a mystery). If you're missing pieces of your pattern, Beverly Bremer will find them—or convince you to mix and match. The chance to visit with her is alone worth the trip to this shop. 3164 Peachtree Rd., Buckhead, 404/261–4009. Closed Sun.

14 g-3

BY HAND SOUTH

This quaint, eye-pleasing shop in the heart of cool and quirky downtown Decatur sells original pottery, jewelry, glass, and other handmade items. 112 E. Ponce de Leon Ave., Decatur, 404/378–0118. Closed Sun. MARTA: Decatur.

12 h-3

CHARLES WILLIS ATLANTA

Come here for a quiet, hushed atmosphere; individual service; and everything you could possibly want or need in china, crystal, and silver, from Baccarat through Waterford and Wedgwood. Add gracious return policies and a hospitable sales staff, and it's easy to see why Atlanta brides register here first. 465 E. Paces Ferry Rd., Buckhead, 404/233–9487.

5 b-5

FRAGILE

Browse to your heart's content at this warehouse-style store with a huge array of great goods at a fair price. Selections of crystal goblets and tumblers, china, and flatware are especially good. There's a section for art glass, too. The store has a bridal registry and gift-wraps for free and ships anywhere. 175 Mt. Vernon Hwy., Sandy Springs, 404/257–1323.

12 e-6

H. MOOG

If you want to know where a piece of porcelain came from, where it was made, how much it's worth, or where to repair it, the Moogs, in business since 1983, will have the answer. Plus, the exquisite and extensive selection of Chinese Export and French porcelains here will take your breath away. You can rest assured of authenticity and reliability in an increasingly scam-filled market. Weekends it's open by appointment only. 2300 Peachtree Rd., Buckhead, 404/351–2200.

12 e-6

JANE J. MARSDEN INTERIORS & ANTIQUES

Famous for their porcelains, Marsden and her family own and anchor the 2300 Peachtree complex. Mother and daughter are interior designers, too, in case you need more than just an exquisite piece of Rose Medallion. 2300 Peachtree Rd., Buckhead, 404/355–1288. Closed Sun.

`12` *h-2*

MACY'S

Watch for the frequent one-day sales in the china and crystal departments at Macy's eight Atlanta branches; you're likely to walk away with a great price on the Ralph Lauren crystal tumbler or Waterford flutes you've been craving or, since Macy's carries everything from high-end to low-end merchandise, a set of raspberry-red plastic goblets for poolside. *Lenox Square, 3393 Peachtree Rd., Buckhead, 404/231–8985. MARTA: Lenox.*

`5` *b-4*

RAINBLUE

The trove of functional and decorative pottery and gifts here is handcrafted by more than 250 local and regional American artisans. The family-owned store (since 1976) also sells candle lanterns, oil lamps, pitchers, bowls, and more. *1205 Johnson Ferry Rd., Marietta, 770/973–1091. Closed Sun.*

`12` *d-7*

VESPERMAN GALLERY

A highly respected showcase of original glass sculpture, Vesperman offers everything in glass, from one-of-a-kind masterpieces to reasonably priced, handmade jewelry and gifts. Its biannual teapot show fills the gallery with imaginative teapots of all shapes and sizes. *309 E. Paces Ferry Rd., Buckhead, 404/266–0102. Closed Sun.– Mon.*

clocks

`12` *b-7*

CLASSIC CLOCKS

Bernie Tekippe and his son have been repairing, restoring, and learning about clocks for more than two decades. Bernie loves French clocks, which exhibit some of the finest materials and craftsmanship ever found, especially in carriage clocks. He makes his own clocks, often makes his own repair tools, and has an incredible library. They'll quote you fair prices on repair and restoration and do a perfect job. *857 Collier Rd., Midtown, 404/355–5141. Closed Sun.*

`12` *h-2*

IT'S ABOUT TIME

For some people, a clock's a clock and a watch just tells time. This store can change that, with its huge selection of clocks and watches in glass, metal, acrylic, leather, and steel. *Lenox Square, 3393 Peachtree Rd., Buckhead, 404/233–0357. MARTA: Lenox.*

`5` *c-2*

ROSWELL CLOCK & ANTIQUE COMPANY

The lovely march of swinging pendulums makes itself heard and felt among a good selection of all sorts of antique clocks—mantel clocks, table clocks, grandfather and grandmother clocks, French carriage clocks. *955 Canton St., Roswell, 770/992–5232. Closed Sun.–Mon.*

flooring

`5` *b-5*

COLOR TILE

Every kind of tile and flooring alternative you could possibly need is on hand, often at very reasonable prices, along with all the attendant material and equipment you need to lay it down. Service can be uneven, but when the sales people are good, they're very good, leading you through the huge selection and instructing you on minute aspects of do-it-yourself installation. *6204 Roswell Rd., Sandy Springs, 404/256–2331. Closed Sun.*

`6` *a-4*

2131 Pleasant Hill Rd., Duluth, 770/495–1800.

`5` *c-5*

HOME DEPOT EXPO

The tile and flooring section is especially wonderful at these warehouse-style designer outlets of the popular chain. You can lose yourself in marble and limestone and easily talk yourself into redoing the floor of that little entry area. *1201 Hammond Dr., across from Perimeter Mall, Dunwoody, 770/913–0111. MARTA: Dunwoody.*

`12` *g-6*

515 Garson Dr., Buckhead, 404/442–1600.

`5` *d-1*

10700 Davis Dr., Alpharetta, 678/352–7300.

`12` *f-3*

TRADITIONS IN TILE

Traditions at these four outlets include providing an excellent product line—tiles, limestone, marble, antique terra cotta, travertine, and mosaics from Italy, Spain, and the United States—along with attentive service, including a free design service and company-backed installation and repair. *3210 Roswell Rd., Buckhead, 404/239–9186. Closed Sun.*

9 *e-3*

692 N. Glynn St., Fayetteville, 770/461–8141.

4 *g-5*

4041-B Kingston Ct., Marietta, 770/951–1416.

5 *d-2*

11350 Old Roswell Rd., Roswell, 770/343–9104.

6 *c-2*

1256 Oakbrook Dr., Suwanee, 770/448–8133.

12 *h-4*

ZUMPANO ENTERPRISES
The largest selection of ceramic tile, porcelain, and natural stone in the Southeast attracts designers, architects, and home owners looking for the best. Appliances and fixtures are available, too, so it's possible to outfit an entire kitchen or bath here. *764 Miami Cir., Buckhead, 404/237–6001. Closed Sun. MARTA: Lindbergh Center.*

9 *g-1*

7411 Tara Blvd., Jonesboro, 770/471–0666.

4 *g-4*

562 Wylie Rd., Marietta, 770/423–0599.

5 *g-6*

6354 Warren Dr., Norcross, 770/449–3528.

furniture & accessories

12 *e-6*

AXIS TWENTY
Falling somewhere between art gallery and contemporary design studio, Axis Twenty is the city's cutting-edge showcase for artists working in wood and metal furniture and accessories. Established craftspeople as well as emerging designers are represented, and the store provides a full-service interior-design service. *200 Peachtree Hills Ave., Buckhead, 404/261–4022. Closed Sun.*

5 *b-4*

BABES & KIDS FURNITURE
Some clever merchandiser realized that children grow up, and here's a store filled with furniture designed to be added to, stacked on, and rearranged to meet changing needs and interests. Accessories such as bedding, bookends, student lamps, and computer desks are at hand, too. *Parkaire Landing, 4880 Lower Roswell Rd., at Johnson Ferry Rd., Marietta, 770/565–1420.*

5 *c-6*

BELLINI
The furniture for infants, children, and teens is beautifully designed and crafted out of solid wood in the best old-world traditions. Considering the quality, prices are quite reasonable, and you can be guaranteed that the bassinet or furniture you purchase will be around long enough to become a family heirloom. *5285 Roswell Rd., Sandy Springs, 404/851–1588. Closed Sun.*

5 *d-1*

7300 North Point Pkwy., Alpharetta, 770/442–6680.

5 *d-2*

BEVERLY HALL FURNITURE GALLERIES
There's a great deal to be said about furniture that can be handed down to grandchildren, and Beverly Hall has that, and more. Upholstered pieces are endowed with trademarks of old-fashioned quality that include well-tied springs and down cushions. Fine accessories are also available, along with a great interior-design service. *740 Holcomb Bridge Rd., Roswell, 770/642–6641.*

12 *d-7*

200 Bennett St., Buckhead, 404/351–7267.

12 *g-4*

2789 Piedmont Rd., Buckhead, 404/261–7580.

5 *g-6*

BY DESIGN INTERNATIONAL FURNITURE
Even in traditional Atlanta, this company, which focuses on contemporary design, has managed to do well by virtue of its practical, clean approach to furniture and accessories and its affordable prices. Many of the pieces require assembly, but the store does it for you. The home-office departments are especially good, and the warehouse in the Norcross location supplies terrific deals on overstocks and damaged pieces—treasure hunts may yield $500 pieces marked down to $5. *6348 Dawson Blvd., Norcross, 770/840–8832.*

`12` h-7

1747 Cheshire Bridge Rd., Midtown, 404/607–9098.

`12` g-7

DOMUS
A group of architects founded Domus in 1972 with the goal of bringing great design at reasonable prices to Atlantans. The well-crafted, solid wood furniture is primarily of Italian and European design along postmodern lines, which means it references classical style without imitating it and makes you feel comfortable and avant at the same time. 1919 Piedmont Rd., Midtown, 404/872–1050.

`12` g-3

ETHAN ALLEN
You can furnish every room in the house at this national name in traditional home furnishings. Sales staff, delivery and return policies, and financing options are all customer friendly, and the store offers an in-house design service. 3221 Peachtree Rd., Buckhead, 404/816–5848.

`5` e-1

6751 North Point Mall Pkwy., Alpharetta, 770/664–9770.

`6` a-4

1630 Pleasant Hill Rd., Duluth, 770/717–7733.

`4` e-3

1005 Ernest W. Barrett Pkwy., Kennesaw, 770/795–0034.

`4` h-6

2205 Cobb Pkwy., Smyrna, 770/953–3320.

`4` g-5

FLACK'S INTERIORS
Hilda Flack carved a niche for herself by marketing her well-designed traditional furnishings to those who enjoy fine furniture but can't necessarily afford expensive designers. She carries such designers as Ralph Lauren along with her own line of accessories, and she offers 40% off manufacturers' prices. Design services come at no additional charge, and the accommodating staff happily assists you in choosing an accessory or a whole house full of furniture. 2999 Cobb Pkwy., Smyrna, 770/952–6599.

`12` h-2

Phipps Plaza, 3500 Peachtree Rd., Buckhead, 404/816–1722.

`5` d-2

1500 Holcomb Bridge Rd., Roswell, 770/992–7121.

`4` f-3

FURNITURE CRAFTSMEN
Welcome to 40,000 square ft of furniture. Top-of-the-line furniture and bottom-line discounts have kept this business in business for more than five decades. 1700 White Cir., Marietta, 770/427–4205.

`5` g-6

GEORGIA BABY & KIDS
If you don't live in Gwinnett County it's well worth the trek out to this huge warehouse filled with Atlanta's largest selection of nursery and children's furniture, including more than 6,000 bedding sets. Many of the beds are designed so they start out as cribs and can be converted into youth beds, then to kid-size couches. 130 Dawson Blvd., Lilburn, 770/448–2455.

`4` h-6

HAVERTY'S
This locally owned and operated firm has been in business for more than 115 years, keeping its products affordable and solidly in the middle of the road for design. You can find everything except the kitchen sink and wall coverings at metro stores; on-staff designers accessorize your choices with taste. 2079 Cobb Pkwy., Smyrna, 770/953–2160.

`5` c-5

132 Perimeter Center W, Dunwoody, 770/352–0901.

`5` e-1

6731 North Point Pkwy., Alpharetta, 770/442–2810.

`6` a-4

3380 Satellite Blvd., Duluth, 770/497–0567.

`5` f-8

4013 LaVista Rd., Northlake, 770/491–0536.

`6` d-7

2297 Stone Mountain Hwy., Snellville, 770/972–0564.

`15` a-1

HORIZON PACIFIC HOME
Exotic, extraordinary furnishings from Pacific Rim countries fill this store's

huge showrooms to overflowing. You expand your cultural horizons just by walking through the collection of Oriental carpets, architectural artifacts, rich leather sofas, chairs and chaises, and beautiful rattan basketry. *1611 Ellsworth Industrial Blvd., Midtown, 404/350–0884.*

5 *g-6*

HOUSE OF DENMARK

The furniture here leans toward modular bedroom, dining-room, and home-office pieces in teak and rosewood as well as in glass and metal, and it shows off the latest innovations in Danish design. Prices, and quality, range from low to high, and much of the stock comes as assemble-it-yourself kits. *6248 Dawson Blvd., Norcross, 770/449–5740.*

12 *g-3*

HUFF FURNITURE

The Huff has designed and made furniture since 1955, and the designs are dramatic and distinctive, and often wonderfully whimsical and wildly contemporary. The store's worth a visit even if you're not in the market for furnishings. *3178 Peachtree Rd., Buckhead, 404/ 261–7636. MARTA: Buckhead.*

15 *g-2*

INNOVATIONS

The sofas and chairs here are overstuffed and comfy and come in jazzy colors or muted tones; the overall look is elegant yet casual; and the prices affordable. Especially popular are the classic designs from such earlier eras as the 1940s and '50s. *1011 Monroe Dr., Midtown, 404/881–8111.*

5 *g-6*

6218 Dawson Blvd., Norcross, 770/449– 1500.

15 *b-2*

MANORISM

The hand-crafted, made-to-order furniture here is imported directly from Indonesia and includes entertainment centers, armoires, computer desks, coffee tables, dressers, and beds. Most pieces are ornately carved. *1494 Ellsworth Industrial Ave., Midtown, 404/ 603–8300.*

5 *g-6*

6410 Dawson Blvd., Norcross, 770/416– 1947.

5 *a-7*

MATTHEWS FURNITURE

The glittering Waterford chandeliers overhead and plush Oriental carpets underfoot transport you to worlds far beyond the ordinary shopping center in which this local landmark happens to reside. The collections reflect an English heritage with some French and Italian influences, and the woods are primarily mahogany and fine fruitwoods. Accessories include exquisite tapestries and paintings. If you're looking for furniture to leave to future generations, this is the place to find it. The store offers a complimentary in-home design service as well as free local delivery and installation. *West Paces Ferry Shopping Center, 1240 W. Paces Ferry Rd., Buckhead, 404/ 237–8271.*

5 *e-1*

RHODES

It's hard to imagine a home in Atlanta without at least something from this multistore chain, which showcases furnishings from such makers as Henredon, Kincaid, Broyhill, Bernhardt, and La-Z-Boy, along with bedding from Sealy and Simmons. The sturdy, good-looking furniture is available in a full range of fabrics and finishes. *6050 North Point Pkwy., Alpharetta, 770/475–1656.*

8 *c-2*

3655 Memorial Dr., Decatur, 404/289– 2136.

5 *f-6*

4363 Northeast Expwy. Access Rd., Doraville, 770/934–9350.

6 *a-4*

2340 Pleasant Hill Rd., Duluth, 770/476– 1890.

5 *d-5*

4175 Ashford-Dunwoody Rd., Dunwoody, 770/395–1812.

4 *h-7*

2540 Cumberland Blvd., Smyrna, 770/ 434–8911.

12 *h-2*

STOREHOUSE

This locally owned and operated franchise has successfully expanded throughout the Southeast for very good reasons: great looks, affordable prices, and varied styles, along with convenient locations and good management. The idea is to buy a plain bookcase or storage unit, then add moldings and accessories to suit your taste. At clearance centers in Buckhead and Norcross, overstocks, floor samples, and slightly damaged merchandise are piled on top of each other, giving you the opportunity to hunt for treasures. *Lenox Square, 3393 Peachtree Rd., Buckhead, 404/261–3482. MARTA: Lenox.*

`12` *f-3*

3106 Early St., Buckhead. MARTA: Buckhead.

`5` *b-5*

6277 Roswell Rd., Sandy Springs, 404/256–3844.

`5` *e-1*

North Point Mall, 1100 North Point Cir., Alpharetta, 770/754–5590.

`5` *g-6*

6368 Northeast Expwy. Access Rd., Norcross, 770/446–2646.

`12` *g-4*

STYLUS

If you're hooked on wild color, interesting shapes, and a great look for the year 2050, come here. These pieces may have begun with a basic shape, but somewhere along the way the lines were popped out, curved, imploded, and serpentined. No shape or function goes unexamined or taken for granted. Euro styling and a wealth of interesting fabrics and finishes help to bring these distinctive pieces from Stylus in line with your existing decor. *3097 Piedmont Rd., Buckhead, 404/231–5888.*

`5` *g-6*

6358 Dawson Blvd., Norcross, 770/409–3204.

`12` *g-3*

URBAN COTTAGE

The wide selection of furniture here—from fancy pine to French country pieces—can help you outfit your urban cottage. *3211 Cains Hill Pl., Buckhead, 404/760–1334. Closed Sun.*

lamps & lighting

`15` *c-2*

THE BIG CHANDELIER

It's the Big Showroom, too, loaded with antique chandeliers and lights. From the street, the myriad twinklings of antique crystal draw you in; once inside, you can find exactly the right lighting for your

home, whether it's old or new. *484 14th St., Midtown, 404/872–3332. Closed Sun.*

`14` *a-2*

ECLECTIC ELECTRIC

A funky palace of light, this place carries lamps of every size and shape, whether candle-powered or plugged-in. For the most imaginative illumination, pick up a unique original or a reasonably priced gift item. *1393 N. Highland Ave., Virginia-Highland, 404/875–2840. Closed Sun.*

`15` *c-2*

GEORGIA LIGHTING

If you can imagine it lit, this firm can do the job—from atmospheric outdoor illumination or lighting for your art collection. Expect to walk around the store with your neck craned, because there are hundreds of chandeliers and hanging fixtures to examine, often in a multiplicity of colors and finishes. One section in the main showroom of the Midtown store also carries fine European antiques and lighting fixtures to match. *530 14th St., Midtown, 404/875–4754. Closed Sun.*

`5` *c-2*

1207 Alpharetta St., Roswell, 770/552–5438.

`6` *d-7*

2340 Ronald Reagan Pkwy., north of Hwy. 78 outside I–285, Snellville, 770/979–0146.

`12` *h-4*

HIGHLIGHTERS

If you've been impressed with the incredible things European designers are doing with contemporary lighting, you're in luck. Highlighters can supply you with those sleek, très chic European designs from Artemide, Flos, Leucos, and others and help you create stunning lighting environments. The shop also carries many glass fixtures from Murano, the famous glass-making island in the Venetian lagoon. *690 Miami Cir., Buckhead, 404/264–1599. Closed Sun.–Mon. MARTA: Lindbergh Center.*

`12` *h-4*

HOUSE OF THEBAUT

For more than 30 years, Hedy Thebaut has led lighting trends in Buckhead and environs. She's mastered the art of making antique Chinese Export porcelain vases into lamps and created new ways to look at old dated lamps by rebuilding and restyling them. She sells antique, custom-built, and replica lamps as well as a selection of interesting shades, too. *674 Miami Cir., Buckhead, 404/261–4166. Closed Sun. MARTA: Lindbergh Center.*

15 *b-2*

LAMP ARTS

If you're missing a few crystals from your dining-room chandelier, you can probably find replacements here, along with all the other parts you need to make or repair a lighting fixture or lamp. Ask to see the back room, where slightly damaged custom shades are available for $15 to $25. *Chattahoochee Industrial District, 1199 Howell Mill Rd., Northwest Atlanta, 404/352–5211. Closed Sun.*

12 *g-3*

LIGHT BULBS UNLIMITED

Visit this store for fabulous neon extravaganzas in gorgeous colors, witty ways to install low-voltage halogen lights, and European lighting and fiber optics. The specialty is hard-to-find bulbs, so you can find any odd thing you need for fluorescent, tungsten, aquarium, marine, plant, photo, and health lighting equipment. The shop fixes neon lights, too. *3171 Peachtree Rd., Buckhead, 404/261–3023. Closed Sun. MARTA: Buckhead.*

5 *e-6*

SHARON'S HOUSE OF LAMPS & SHADES

Sharon's provides Atlantans easy access to more than 15,000 square ft of lamps, shades, chandeliers, and lighting accessories. Each store has a complete parts and repair center and a courteous staff that knows about proportion and scale when trying to find the right shade for the lamp or vice versa. *5544 Peachtree Industrial Blvd., Chamblee, 770/455–0135. Closed Sun.*

5 *d-1*

10887 Alpharetta Hwy., Roswell, 770/587–4403.

5 *b-6*

SUNLIGHTING LAMP & SHADE CENTER

Have you ever thought you could design a better lamp than the ones you see in stores? Here's your chance. The staff here makes lamp bases to your specifications, custom stains or paints them, and adds such finishing touches as gold

or silver leaf or whatever else suits your fancy. This is a great place to bring a lamp for restyling or a chandelier for retwinkling. *4990 Roswell Rd., Sandy Springs, 404/257–0043. Closed Sun.*

paint & wallpaper

5 *g-6*

JUST WALLPAPER

Although the place stocks more than 5,000 patterns from which to choose, it's blessedly well organized. Just tell the helpful staff members what you want—whether it's Grecian columns on faux marble or a cowboy theme—and they can direct you to the right section. Everything on the floor is usually in stock; you can make a decision and carry home what you need the same day. *6218 Dawson Blvd., Norcross, 770/409–1992.*

4 *h-4*

2187 Roswell Rd., Marietta, 770/509–1982.

8 *a-8*

1999 Mt. Zion Rd., Morrow, 770/477–2772.

12 *f-3*

MYRON DWOSKINS WALLCOVERINGS, INC.

The sales staff in these stores know its merchandise, and it's dedicated to helping you find the right paper in the right quantity. The salespeople also direct you to the excellent selection of discontinued and overstocked merchandise. *211 Pharr Rd., Buckhead, 404/231–5880.*

9 *e-4*

372 N. Glynn St., Fayetteville, 770/460–0593.

5 *b-4*

4880 Lower Roswell Rd., Marietta, 770/973–3955.

5 *a-7*

SHERWIN WILLIAMS

"Ask Sherwin Williams," suggests the advertising. If you do, it will answer with fine quality, good prices, and exclusive paint colors that coordinate with floor and wallcoverings. *3519 Northside Pkwy., Buckhead, 404/885–5500. Closed Sun.*

5 *d-8*

2460 N. Druid Hills Rd., Brookhaven, 404/633–6818.

5 *d-6*

5517 Peachtree Industrial Blvd., Chamblee, 770/451–0301.

6 *c-3*

2017 Lawrenceville–Suwanee Rd., Lawrenceville, 770/962–5294.

5 *f-4*

3925 Holcomb Bridge Rd., Norcross, 770/449–7993.

5 *b-5*

245 Johnson Ferry Rd., Sandy Springs, 404/257–0514.

rentals

5 *f-6*

AARON RENTS & SELLS FURNITURE

Aaron can install comfy furnishings in your new digs or office the day after you order them and make them available on short- or long-term leases. The appliances you need are here, too, along with some electronics. A rent-to-buy policy and great prices on used furniture make Aaron one of the most successful national franchises in the business. *4194-B Northeast Expwy. Access Rd., Doraville, 770/458–6131. Closed Sun.*

12 *g-6*

2173 Piedmont Rd., Buckhead, 404/873–1455.

4 *g-6*

1710 S. Cobb Pkwy., Marietta, 770/952–7444.

8 *a-8*

1115 Mt. Zion Rd., Morrow, 770/968–0810.

wicker

5 *h-6*

PARR'S

Since 1984, Parr's has offered Atlantans competitive prices on a huge selection of wicker, rattan, and outdoor furniture. The store carries some unusual styles and colors, along with sturdy, traditional fare. *3086 Lawrenceville Hwy., Lilburn, 770/923–3153.*

2 *h-8*

512 N. Main St./Hwy. 9, Alpharetta, 770/664–6291.

3 *h-6*

3022 Peachtree Industrial Blvd., Buford, 678/482–8008.

5 *d-1*

ROSWELL RATTAN

This tasteful shop arranges its product lines—all of which are top quality and available in a wide range of colors and designs—in home-style settings. *11230 Alpharetta Hwy., between Mansell and Upper Hembree Rds., Roswell, 770/442–0237.*

5 *d-1*

WICKER WAREHOUSE OUTLET

With 8,000 ft of showroom space, this wicker-and-rattan outlet can fill your house with a wide selection of dining and bedroom sets, lamps, magazine racks, and tables, all for reasonable prices. *963 N. Burnt Hickory Rd., Douglasville, 770/942–3992. Closed Sun.*

window treatments

JCPENNEY

See Department Stores, *above.*

RICH'S

See Department Stores, *above.*

SEARS

See Department Stores, *above.*

HOUSEWARES & HARDWARE

5 *c-5*

ACE HARDWARE

A few years ago, Ace found itself competing with Home Depot and determined that personal service would provide the leading edge. Ace personnel certainly know their stock and how to install and use the products they sell. They also have an excellent selection, and since the stock varies quite a bit from location to location, if one Ace doesn't have what you need, another may. *8010 Roswell Rd., Dunwoody, 404/255–2411.*

12 *g-3*

THE CONTAINER STORE

A visit to this store will no doubt convince you that your CDs should be stored more efficiently, that your kid's old toys could live in a sturdy cardboard box until the next tag sale, and that your kitchen cupboards could really benefit from a new design system. Designs for most of the products are jazzy, modern, and colorful. Look here for great back-to-school supplies and the best after-Christmas wrapping-paper sale in town. *3255 Peachtree Rd., south corner of Piedmont Rd., Buckhead, 404/261–4776. MARTA: Buckhead.*

5 *c-5*

120 Perimeter Center W, Sandy Springs, 770/351–0065.

14 *a-2*

HIGHLAND HARDWARE

It's more than a hardware store—it's a legend. People from all over the world buy woodworking tools and other merchandise from the catalog, but visiting this century-old store, with its high molded tin ceilings and wood floors, is an experience in itself. Highland stocks wonderful annuals and perennials, as well as all manner of regular hardware. *1045 N. Highland Ave., Virginia-Highland, 404/872–4466.*

12 *h-2*

RESTORATION HARDWARE

Everything in the store has a slick retro feel, from actual hardware—house numbers to shower heads—to leather couches, gardening supplies, and cool kitchen gadgetry. The best part? Much of the funky array of wares won't break the bank. *3393 Peachtree Rd., Buckhead, 404/240–2844. MARTA: Lenox.*

6 *d-1*

Mall of Georgia, 3333 Buford Dr. NE, Buford, 678/482–7691.

5 *e-5*

120 Perimeter Center W, Dunwoody, 770/804–9440. MARTA: Dunwoody.

12 *h-2*

WILLIAMS-SONOMA

All the fabulous high-quality kitchenware and other merchandise this California firm loads into its famous catalog is right here in the store. The oils, vinegars, and other ingredients included in the recipes that appear in the catalog are for sale, too. *Lenox Square, 3393 Peachtree Rd., Buckhead, 404/812–1703. MARTA: Lenox.*

5 *c-5*

Perimeter Mall, 4400 Ashford-Dunwoody Rd., Dunwoody, 770/698–8584. MARTA: Dunwoody.

6 *a-4*

Gwinnett Place, 2100 Pleasant Hill Rd., Duluth, 678/473–0766.

5 *a-3*

Avenue at East Cobb, 4475 Roswell Rd., Marietta, 678/560–3660.

JEWELRY & WATCHES

antique & collectible items

7 *h-4*

LAKEWOOD ANTIQUES MARKET

This is the place for collectible costume jewelry and fairly standard fine stuff. If you study the books on costume jewelry of the 20th century, you'll be amazed at what can turn up here for bargain prices. Some dealers, however, know a lot, so don't expect rare pieces to go completely unnoticed. Dealers often spend half the first morning of the show scouring other dealers for deals. You can do it, too, on the second weekend of each month. *2000 Lakewood Ave., 404/622–4488. MARTA: Lakewood/Ft. McPherson.*

12 *e-6*

LAURA PEARCE

Pearce was a buyer at Tiffany & Co. for five years, and she maintains her ties with estate dealers in New York. Her most popular pieces include platinum and diamonds, especially from the 1920s, though she also sells exquisite reproductions. *2300 Peachtree Rd., Buckhead, 404/350–9207. Closed Sun.*

12 *f-3*

REED SAVAGE

Reed Savage places esoteric collectibles in museums and private collections often, but for the most part, he likes to carry things that people can wear. He charges by what he has to pay for the piece, not how much the market will bear, and he trades, too. *110 E. Andrews Dr., Buckhead, 404/263–3439.*

12 *e-6*

RICHTER'S

Frederick Gray, manager of one of the oldest firms (since 1893) specializing in estate jewelry in the country, favors the "big, powerhouse pieces" for his clientele. These appear to be those with big stones and pieces that exhibit fine craftsmanship and attention to every detail. *2300 Peachtree Rd., Buckhead, 404/355–4462. Closed Sun.*

7 *h-6*

SCOTT ANTIQUES MARKET

Collectors hunting bargains on costume and real pieces from the 19th and 20th centuries can have a field day here on the second weekend of every month, when dealers from all over the country set up displays. It's worth your effort to do some comparison shopping (that amethyst necklace might have a less expensive companion in another row), and remember that while many dealers set up here month after month, others aren't so reliable. *3650 Jonesboro Rd., Forest Park, 404/363–0909.*

12 *h-2*

SKIPPY MUSKET & CO.

Make a jewelry wish and it's granted at this boutique across the way from Tiffany & Co. Diamonds, rubies, emeralds, and pearls in antique settings find their way here from estates all over the world, and small glamorous accessories—such as tortoiseshell boxes, collectible paperweights, small bronzes, and exquisite watches—command attention, too. *Phipps Plaza, 3500 Peachtree Rd., Buckhead, 404/233–3462. Closed Sun. MARTA: Lenox.*

contemporary pieces

12 *h-2*

CARTIER

The House of Cartier, in business for more than 100 years, brings Paris to Atlanta. The surroundings are quiet and tasteful, and the staff handles even the smallest purchase as though it were for the Duchess of Windsor (who wore many of the firm's designs). What's more, Cartier pieces hold their value, and many go up, so any purchase is really an investment. *Lenox Square, 3393 Peachtree Rd., Buckhead, 404/841–0840. Closed Sun. MARTA: Lenox.*

IT'S ABOUT TIME

See Clocks *in* Home Furnishings, *above.*

12 *g-3*

MAIER & BERKELE

The best in traditional fine jewelry, watches, china, silver, and crystal fills these stores. The small estate-jewelry

division is highly regarded, and the after-Christmas sales are excellent. *3225 Peachtree Rd., Buckhead, 404/261–4911. Closed Sun. MARTA: Buckhead.*

12 *h-2*

Lenox Square, 3393 Peachtree Rd., Buckhead, 404/233–8201. MARTA: Lenox.

5 *e-1*

North Point Mall, 1152 North Point Cir., Alpharetta, 770/667–1887.

6 *d-1*

Mall of Georgia, 3333 Buford Dr., Buford, 770/271–0966.

12 *h-2*

ROSS SIMONS

Atlanta's only outlet of the national chain carries perhaps the widest selection of jewelry in the city. While the designs aren't extraordinary, the pieces are solid, well crafted, and well priced. Look here for a wide range of earring jackets and studs, and especially good prices in rings, bracelets, and pearls. *Phipps Plaza, 3500 Peachtree Rd., Buckhead, 404/266–9050. MARTA: Lenox.*

4 *g-5*

THE SHANE COMPANY

These folks import their diamonds direct from Antwerp and do a fine job on selection, price, and quality. The sales staff know the stock; will educate you on the four C's of clarity, color, cut, and carat; and back Shane's reputation with good guarantees. *2365 Windy Hill Rd., Marietta, 770/984–9900.*

5 *f-1*

10885 Haynes Bridge Rd., Alpharetta, 678/393–0701.

5 *h-5*

3300 Steve Reynolds Blvd., Duluth, 770/623–3660.

4 *e-3*

735 Ernest W. Barrett Pkwy., Kennesaw, 678/355–1144.

12 *h-2*

TIFFANY & CO.

Tiffany's features designers whose names sometimes become household words—Paloma Picasso, for example, who holds sway in the contemporary design area—and who inevitably are the world's top names in jewelry, china, crystal, and silver. While you expect nothing but the best from Tiffany, it's worth noting that prices at the Atlanta store are often less expensive than they are in New York or other cities, because the overhead is lower and the market won't bear bigger-city prices. *Phipps Plaza, 3500 Peachtree Rd., Buckhead, 404/261–0074. MARTA: Lenox.*

costume jewelry

5 *e-1*

DILLARD'S

Because Dillard's doesn't have a fine-jewelry department, the store can concentrate on finding interesting costume pieces. Look here for great fine-jewelry knockoffs and less-expensive interpretations of custom designs found in pricey boutiques. *7000 North Point Cir., Alpharetta, 770/410–9020.*

6 *d-1*

Mall of Georgia, 3333 Buford Dr., Buford, 678/482–5241.

14 *g-3*

THE FAMILY JEWELS

Probably the city's most comprehensive collection of vintage costume jewelry includes all those things your aunts wore in the 1950s and '60s as well as pieces that date to Victorian times and the Roaring '20s. The collection is great for pins and necklaces, but you need to adopt the old clip-on earrings for pierced ears. The place is by appointment only. *114 E. Ponce de Leon Ave., Decatur, 404/377–3774.*

12 *h-2*

THE ICING

Every bodily accessory you can think of crams this store. The offerings are especially attractive to teenagers, because the jewelry is well priced and designed with the young set in mind. Faux body-piercing items are available here, too. *Lenox Square, 3393 Peachtree Rd., Buckhead, 404/869–0800. MARTA: Lenox.*

12 *h-2*

NEIMAN MARCUS

The "last call" sales here are absolutely the best place to buy the things you've been coveting for a while. The designs range from classic to wacky, and if you're good at spotting next year's trends, this is the place to pick them up before the rest of the world does. *Lenox Square, 3393 Peachtree Rd., Buckhead, 404/266–8200. MARTA: Lenox.*

LEATHER GOODS & LUGGAGE

12 *h-2*

BENTLEY'S

A national chain, Bentley's guarantees its prices on high-quality day planners and other leather goods are low; carries Samsonite, Hartmann, and Tumi; and takes special orders and gets them to you quickly. Plus, the Sandy Springs, Buckhead, and Decatur stores provide repair services as well. *Phipps Plaza, 3500 Peachtree Rd., Buckhead 404/841–6247. MARTA: Lenox.*

5 *e-5*

Perimeter Mall, 4400 Ashford-Dunwoody Rd., Dunwoody, 770/671–1071. MARTA: Dunwoody.

6 *d-1*

Mall of Georgia, 3333 Buford Dr., Buford, 678/482–6404.

5 *f-8*

North DeKalb Mall, 2050 Lawrenceville Hwy., Decatur, 404/633–9323.

6 *a-4*

Gwinnett Place, 2100 Pleasant Hill Rd., Duluth, 770/497–8447.

4 *e-3*

Town Center, 400 Ernest W. Barrett Pkwy., Kennesaw, 770/422–9406.

12 *h-2*

CIVILIZED TRAVELER

Whether you're a first-time traveler or a veteran, this place has the little things you never think about until you need them, like a nearly invisible money–passport belt in flexible cotton. Maps, electricity adaptors, and savvy travel guides also fill the shelves here. *Phipps Plaza, 3500 Peachtree Rd., Buckhead, 404/264–1252. MARTA: Lenox.*

5 *e-5*

Perimeter Mall, 4400 Ashford-Dunwoody Rd., Dunwoody, 770/673–0111. MARTA: Dunwoody.

12 *h-2*

MORI LUGGAGE & GIFTS

Ever since it opened in 1971, Mori's has been known for quality and price, and it prides itself on top-quality leathers, finely crafted desk accessories, collectible pens, and luggage. You can find lots of good gifts here. The Lenox Square shop has a repair service. *Lenox*

Square, 3393 Peachtree Rd., Buckhead, 404/231–0074. MARTA: Lenox.

5 c-5

Perimeter Mall, 4400 Ashford-Dunwoody Rd., Dunwoody, 770/394–3215. MARTA: Dunwoody.

5 e-1

North Point Mall, 1000 North Point Cir., Alpharetta, 770/667–9177.

8 a-8

Southlake Mall, 1000 Southlake Mall, Morrow, 770/961–7322.

5 f-7

Northlake Mall, 4800 Briarcliff Rd., Northlake, 770/934–8221.

4 h-7

Cumberland Mall, I–285 and I–75 at Cobb Pkwy., Smyrna, 770/436–6112.

12 g-3

TUESDAY MORNING

An often overlooked resource for luggage, Tuesday Morning buys overstocks and discontinued items, and there's always plenty of both. You're sure to find pieces in almost any size and price. 3145 Piedmont Rd., Buckhead, 404/233–6526. MARTA: Buckhead.

5 d-5

4502 Chamblee-Dunwoody Rd., Dunwoody, 770/457–3565.

5 b-4

736 Johnson Ferry Rd., Marietta, 770/971–0511.

5 f-4

6325 Spalding Dr., Norcross, 770/447–4692.

4 h-6

2512 Spring Rd. SE, Smyrna, 770/435–6678.

6 d-7

4051 Stone Mountain Hwy., Snellville, 770/978–3573.

MAPS

5 c-7

BRADFORD MAP

The store carries Atlanta map books, as well as a large selection of city, state, and computer-customized maps. There's a nice range of globes, too ($30 to $6,000). 1873 Lawrenceville Hwy., Decatur, 404/633–7562.

5 c-5

300 Hammond Dr., Sandy Springs, 404/843–9610.

CIVILIZED TRAVELER

See Leather Goods & Luggage, above.

11 c-5

A MAP & GRAPHICS CO.

The complete line of business and travel maps here includes postal-code maps (which can be customized); city, state, and Southeast maps; and national and world maps. Laminating, mounting, and framing are available also. 1151 W. Peachtree St., Midtown, 404/607–9178.

MINIATURES

6 d-4

MINIATURE DESIGNS

All the little furniture, mini-scale lighting, and other special touches sold at this 3,800-square-ft, family-owned store could make you want to become a dollhouse collector. 2399 Lawrenceville Hwy., Lawrenceville, 770/339–6849.

MUSIC

cds, tapes, & vinyl

8 e-2

A TO Z RECORDS

Whether you're seeking specialty R&B, jazz, gospel, reggae, or hip-hop, this shop is sure to meet your needs. Because A to Z is keyed into several distribution outlets, the staff can usually track down atypical items in one to three days. 4844 Redan Rd., Lithonia, 404/292–5115. Closed Sun.

14 g-8

4000 Glenwood Rd., Decatur, 404/286–2264.

5 e-1

BEST BUY

It's hard to beat this mega-chain in terms of the scope of the selection, and Best Buy is known for keeping prices at reasonable levels. 975 North Point Dr., Alpharetta, 678/339–1321.

15 d-4

BIG OOMP'S RECORD STORE

This South Atlanta spot has the latest in rhythm and blues and urban and down-

South rap. It sells mostly CDs, but some records and DVDs also are available. *2668 Campbellton Rd., Southwest Atlanta, 404/349–0620. Closed Sun.*

14 *a-4*

CRIMINAL RECORDS
The focus of this shop in hip Little Five Points is new CDs and an array of comic-book titles. There's also a premium supply of DVDs and music–pop culture periodicals. *466 Moreland Ave., Little Five Points, 404/215–9511.*

5 *g-6*

EAT MORE RECORDS
The emphasis on the new and used CDs and vinyl here is on U.K. rock and indie imports, but this is an indispensable resource for local collectors of all genres. The knowledgeable staff can help track down hard-to-find items. *1210 Rockbridge Rd., Lilburn, 770/717–8111.*

12 *f-4*

FANTASYLAND RECORDS
Here's sheer vinyl heaven. Collectors on the hunt relish the bins of treasures that stretch across genres and back across the decades. Collections are bought and sold. *2839 Peachtree Rd., Garden Hills, 404/237–3193. Closed Sun.*

5 *e-5*

KATEY'S CDS
Katey and her husband offer great service and low prices on new and used CDs and record albums; there's also a large DVD selection. Be sure to ask if you don't find what you're seeking; they'll help you locate it. *3352 Chamblee-Tucker Rd., Chamblee, 770/936–8554. Closed Sun.*

music boxes

11 *c-5*

SAN FRANCISCO MUSIC BOX
Whether you want a special gift box that plays the haunting melodic strains from *Dr. Zhivago* or a popular tune from *The Sound of Music*, count on finding it here. Take time to browse through the unique collectibles and nostalgic best-sellers such as the Scarlett and Mammy figurine and Wizard of Oz water globes. *400 Ernest W. Barrett Pkwy., Kennesaw, 404/438–9982. Closed Sun.*

musical instruments

5 *c-2*

ATLANTA ST. VIOLIN SHOP
The high-end distributor shop includes violin, viola, cello, and bass brands such as Rudolf Doetsch, Ivan Dunov, and Wilhelm Klier, among others. *352 S. Atlanta St., Roswell, 770/642–8111. Closed Sun.*

5 *e-5*

CARERE MUSIC
Big-band and orchestra instruments abound at this authorized dealer for a wide range of new and used items from such brands as Buffet, Emerson, Yamaha, and Allegro, among others. The place also offers rentals, repairs, accessories, and sheet music. *4947 Winters Chapel Rd., Doraville, 770/671–0517.*

4 *g-4*

KEN STANTON MUSIC
Since 1949 this family-owned store has offered a wide selection of new and used guitars, amps, drums, keyboards, and audio equipment. Take advantage of the convenient on-site repair shop. You also can rent equipment for school bands and orchestras. *777 Roswell St., Marietta, 770/427–2491. Closed Sun.*

5 *d-2*

Roswell Village shopping center, 627 Holcomb Bridge Rd., Roswell, 770/993–8334.

6 *d-7*

Scenic Square Shopping Center, 1977-B Scenic Hwy., Snellville, 770/979–0736.

2 *b-8*

1105 Parkside La., Woodstock, 770/516–0804.

sheet music

CARERE MUSIC
See Musical Instruments, *above.*

KEN STANTON MUSIC
See Musical Instruments, *above.*

5 *c-5*

SYMMES MUSIC COMPANY
Shop for scores of the latest sheet music here—for piano, guitar, and those popular tunes heard around town in karaoke clubs. The staff will gladly special-order items not found in the store. *6600 Roswell Rd., Sandy Springs, 404/255–4027. Closed Sun.*

NEWSPAPERS & MAGAZINES

Barnes & Noble and Borders (see General, in Books, above) each offer a slew of publications, and neither seems to mind if you hang out all day browsing.

5 c-7

JOE MUGGS

Sunny weekend mornings you can join the trendy throngs sipping coffee, meeting and greeting, eating pastries, and reading newspapers on the patio of this newsstand. Newspaper selections are local, national, and international, and you can choose from more than a thousand magazine titles. 3275 Peachtree Rd., Buckhead, 404/364–9290.

11 a-4

2020 Howell Mill Rd., Buckhead, 404/ 350–0461.

PET SUPPLIES

4 f-5

GEORGIA PETS

You can buy anything pet-related—from livestock and supplies to a furry new kitten and rubber toys—at this comprehensive pet store. In addition to live bait and feed for a variety of critters, most major pet-food brands are sold here. 1150 Powder Springs Rd., Marietta, 770/ 514–7387.

5 d-5

5513 Chamblee-Dunwoody Rd., Dunwoody, 770/339–5161.

4 f-5

PETS ETC.

If you need food, supplies, or grooming for cats, dogs, birds, fish, or ferrets, this place has it. The staff can help you determine which kind of food is best suited for your pet. The store also offers obedience classes. 2131 Pleasant Hill Rd., Duluth, 770/476–4749.

11 g-3

WILD SIDE

Kids enjoy the coral-reef farm and aquariums at this store, which also sells small animals and supplies for cats, dogs, snakes, and hamsters. Toco Hills Shopping Center, 2855 N. Druid Hills Rd., Toco Hills, 404/636–3333.

for birds

5 c-7

WILD BIRDS UNLIMITED

Bird and nature lovers alike should flock here for seed, garden statuaries, feeders, birdhouses, birdbaths, and wind chimes and other specialty gift ideas. 1050 E. Piedmont Rd., Buckhead, 770/ 565–9841.

5 e-1

9925 Haynes Bridge Rd., Alpharetta, 770/ 410–0799.

5 c-5

4920 Roswell Rd., Sandy Springs, 404/ 257–0084.

for fish

12 f-3

THE FISH STORE & MORE

You can find everything you need to care for fish at this place, which also offers the city's largest quality selection of marine and fresh-water organisms. 3145 Peachtree Rd., Buckhead, 404/231–5111.

5 a-3

MARINE & TROPICAL FISH

You're likely to get hooked on the incredible colors, shapes, and sizes of the fish swimming around in here. Afterward, the experts here can design and help you to maintain a custom aquarium; there's even a fish biologist on staff. 1255 Johnson Ferry Rd., Marietta, 770/321–8404.

7 h-8

PISCES PET

The staff of specialists reveals the secrets of exotic fish, sharks, and eels and can supply you with a selection of them. It builds, delivers, and installs custom aquariums, and it can help you create and populate a koi pond. 8013 Tara Blvd., Jonesboro, 770/477–0113. Closed Sun.

for reptiles

5 e-6

REPTILE WAREHOUSE

The warehouse can satisfy all of your reptile needs with an array of snakes, frogs, lizards, and turtles and the supplies to feed them. Love creepy crawlers? A tarantula can be double the fun when it sheds its skin to create the illusion of two. *2080 Peachtree Industrial Blvd., Chamblee, 770/455–3131. Closed Mon.*

PHOTO EQUIPMENT

15 *c-2*

CAMERA BUG

Both serious hobbyists and vacation snappers are likely to find what they need at this one-stop shop, which can track down replacement accessories for standard equipment or your old favorite. *1799 Briarcliff Rd., Toco Hills, 404/873–3925. Closed Sun.*

15 *c-2*

PROFESSIONAL PHOTO RESOURCES

This lifeline for working professionals provides repairs, trial rentals on high-end gear, studio resources, and digital editing. *667 11th St., Midtown, 404/885–1885. Closed Sun.*

5 *e-5*

V-PHOTO OF ATLANTA

Convenient to shutterbugs in Northeast, this shop places an emphasis on providing reasonable repair work. The services include free cleanings, checkups, and estimates. *6950 Peachtree Industrial Blvd., Norcross, 770/441–1644. Closed weekends.*

15 *d-2*

WOLF CAMERA

The big retailer in town for most of your photographic needs also has other metro-area locations. The large Midtown location carries used gear, darkroom equipment, and even telescopes. *150 14th St., Midtown, 404/892–1707.*

12 *h-2*

Lenox Square, 3393 Peachtree Rd., Buckhead, 404/237–2388. MARTA: Lenox.

6 *d-1*

Mall of Georgia, 3333 Buford Dr., Buford, 678/482–1749.

SOUVENIRS & POSTCARDS

11 *c-7*

COLLAGE

Choose from postcards, coffee mugs, key chains, and T-shirts, or go for the ubiquitous shot glass. *223 CNN Center, Omni International Blvd., Downtown, 404/525–8700. MARTA: Dome/GWCC/Philips Arena/CNN Center.*

7 *g-6*

GREAT SPORTS

Heading out of town and need some last-minute gifts? This airport shop offers a nice selection of fitted and adjustable caps, sweatshirts, and baseball and football jerseys sporting Atlanta and Georgia team logos. *Hartsfield Atlanta International Airport, Concourse C, 404/756–6300. MARTA: Airport.*

SPORTING GOODS & CLOTHING

11 *d-1*

GALYAN'S

Whether you're looking for golf balls, a yoga mat, sneakers, or a kayak, Galyan's covers all the bases. Each location has a climbing wall with instructors, but get there early if you want to climb—lines can be long. *3535 Peachtree Rd., Buckhead, 404/267–0200, www.galyans.com.*

3 *h-8*

Mall of Georgia, 3333 Buford Dr., Buford, 678/482–1200.

4 *f-3*

691 Ernest W. Barrett Pkwy., Kennesaw, 770/281–0200.

12 *h-2*

NIKETOWN

The place is an event, with huge TV screens running sports channels as you try on your shoes or T-shirt. Everything Nike is available here, so if you're swoosh-happy, this is the place for you. *Phipps Plaza, 3500 Peachtree Rd., Buckhead, 404/841–6444. MARTA: Lenox.*

5 *c-7*

PLAY IT AGAIN SPORTS

A Minneapolis entrepreneur had the bright idea that all the sports stuff people became bored with or didn't use anymore could be sold in a store instead of at a garage sale. Some of the stock here is new and discounted, but much of it has been played with and is deeply discounted. You can trade gear, too. *4279 Roswell Rd., Buckhead, 404/257–0229.*

5 *f-8*

North DeKalb Mall, 2050 Lawrenceville Hwy., Decatur, 404/329–2005.

4 *e-3*

800 Ernest W. Barrett Pkwy., Kennesaw, 770/429–8636.

5 *e-8*

2080 Henderson Mill Rd., Northlake, 770/493–8299.

5 *c-5*

REI

The chain is serious about camping, hiking, kayaking, and climbing and, judging from the hip colors and styles of the clothing, believes you can look smashing doing them. 1165 Perimeter Center W, Dunwoody, 770/901–9200. MARTA: Dunwoody.

11 *g-2*

1800 Northeast Expwy. Access Rd., Druid Hills, 404/633–6508.

12 *g-3*

SPORTS AUTHORITY

If you know what you want, aren't interested in frills, and desire a big selection of gear at reasonable prices, this is your store. Serious fitness training equipment; bowling balls; and fishing, tennis, and baseball items, in addition to seasonal stuff, have earned these stores a well-deserved reputation for outfitting all people in all sports. There are more than a dozen Atlanta locations. 3221 Peachtree Rd., Buckhead, 404/814–9873. MARTA: Buckhead.

5 *e-1*

North Point Mall, 7461 North Point Pkwy., Alpharetta, 770/518–3303.

6 *b-8*

4235 Stone Mountain Hwy., Lilburn, 770/979–7020.

4 *g-5*

50 Powers Ferry Rd., Marietta, 770/509–5700.

5 *b-5*

6690 Roswell Rd., Sandy Springs, 770/845–0727.

4 *h-3*

TEAM SPORTS

You can outfit your team with baseball, football, tennis, and soccer uniforms here. Custom lettering, embroidery, and screen printing are available, and with

fast turnaround times. 2250 E. Piedmont Rd., Marietta, 770/973–9991.

bicycles

4 *h-7*

ATLANTA CYCLING

The broad selection of high-end road bikes and mountain bikes here includes models by Trek, Schwinn, and Cannondale. Some exercise bikes are available as well. 4335 Cobb Pkwy., Vinings, 770/952–7731.

12 *f-3*

3165 Peachtree Rd., Buckhead, 404/237–1188.

15 *g-1*

1544 Piedmont Rd., Midtown, 404/873–2451.

4 *e-2*

440 Ernest W. Barrett Pkwy., Kennesaw, 770/427–1980.

6 *a-4*

3502 Satellite Blvd., Lawrenceville, 770/476–8158.

12 *f-3*

THE BICYCLE LINK

The spot for Atlanta's road-bike enthusiast specializes in Serotta, Ibis, Bianchi, and Trek. The shop offers fitting and repair services and is the starting point for weekly rides. Like many other serious shops, it's closed Sunday because everyone's out riding. 210 Pharr Rd., Buckhead, 404/233–4103. Closed Sun.

5 *b-4*

CYCLEWORKS

A full-service shop, Cycleworks provides lifetime adjustment service with the purchase of a new bike. It also rents out Trek 6500s by day or longer (helmets included). 4880 Lower Roswell Rd., Marietta, 770/509–9494.

5 *d-2*

1570 Holcomb Bridge Rd., Alpharetta, 770/993–2626.

5 *h-3*

3576 Peachtree Industrial Blvd., Duluth, 770/476–4949.

15 *g-2*

INTOWN BICYCLES

This friendly, neighborhood shop for the recreational rider carries a selection of Jamis, Raleigh, and Giant bicycles. The convenient Piedmont Park location makes this a good place to stop in for a quick patch or some air for your tires. *1035 Monroe Dr., Midtown, 404/872–1736.*

6 *a-8*
PEDAL POWER
The largest retail bike shop in the state specializes in tandem bicycles. The staff welcomes inquiries from cyclists looking to become familiar with bicycling in Georgia. *1900 Rockbridge Rd., Centerville, 770/498–2453.*

boating

5 *a-3*
GO WITH THE FLOW SPORTS
A dazzling display of canoes and kayaks fills this lovely old building in historic Roswell's shopping district. The staff is committed to providing you with the best you can get for your budget and teaching you how to use it. *4 Elizabeth Way, between Canton St. and Alpharetta Hwy., Roswell, 770/992–3200.*

7 *h-7*
MARINEMAX
For more than a quarter century, this superstore has supplied Georgians with boats, yachts, and other watercraft. The salespeople are expert, the service and repair services unsurpassed. *5840 South Expwy., Forest Park, 404/363–6910. Closed Sun.*

3 *h-7*
6069 Holiday Rd., Buford, 770/614–6968.

fishing tackle & supplies

12 *f-3*
THE FISH HAWK
Fly-fishing equipment is a specialty here, but the store also offers a high-quality selection of casting and spinning gear for fresh- and saltwater fishing—everything from trout gear to cane poles to big-game and IGFA rods and all the accessories you could dream of. *279 Buckhead Ave., Buckhead, 404/237–3473. Closed Sun.*

6 *a-5*
SPORTSMAN'S WAREHOUSE
The biggest fresh- and saltwater fishing department store in the Gwinnett

County area features a full line of Orvis products. For those unfamiliar with the lure of bass fishing, the 6,000-gallon bass tub is the place to learn how to catch these cagey, finny creatures. *3825 Shackleford Rd., at Steve Reynolds Blvd., Duluth, 770/931–1550.*

golf

12 *g-3*
EDWIN WATTS GOLF SHOP
The chain offers everything and anything to do with golf, and it'll beat any advertised price by 10%. Although the services and products meet and match those of most area stores, this place also delivers clubs to hotel rooms—great for executives and others visiting from out of town. *3141 Piedmont Rd., Buckhead, 404/816–2166. MARTA: Buckhead.*

5 *f-6*
5810 Buford Hwy., Doraville, 770/455–8809.

6 *a-4*
1645 Pleasant Hill Rd., Duluth, 770/931–1666.

4 *g-5*
1581 Cobb Pkwy., Marietta, 770/955–9500.

8 *e-1*
4961 Memorial Dr., Stone Mountain, 770/294–0818.

6 *a-4*
GOLFSMITH
The assortment of golfing equipment here goes on and on; every aisle holds ways for you to try out your technique. Plus you can use one of the computerized golf simulators to analyze your swing or learn how to deal with water features. If it's raining too hard for you to play outside, you can play in here all day. *3690 Venture Dr., Duluth, 770/623–6336.*

4 *e-3*
2500 Cobb Place La., Kennesaw, 770/421–0106.

5 *h-5*
GOLF WAREHOUSE
Since 1989, this chain has stocked clubs, shoes, bags, clothes, and accessories for anybody who swings a club, including kids and senior citizens. The prices are low and competitive, and the shop carries name brands and has a

complete club-repair facility. *5192 Brook Hollow Pkwy., Norcross, 770/447–4653.*

5 d-2

King's Market shopping center, 1425 Market Blvd., Roswell, 770/643–0061.

4 f-3

390 Ernest W. Barrett Pkwy., Kennesaw, 770/428–8700.

9 g-1

6975 Jonesboro Rd., Morrow, 770/960–1992.

5 g-5

5192-B Brook Hollow Hwy., Norcross, 770/447–4653.

4 h-7

2697 New Spring Rd., Smyrna, 770/435–1934.

7 g-5

METRO ATLANTA GOLF SHOP

Want some custom clubs? Pro owner Tom "Smitty" Smith can design them for you, sell you some new ones, or equip you with used ones for terrific prices. He's been in business since 1970, keeps his overhead low, and concentrates on the game rather than fancy clothing. *34 Cleveland Ave., near Brown's Mill Golf Course, East Point, 404/768–9146. Closed Sun.*

5 f-6

OLD SPORT GOLF

The stock at this wonderful store includes more than 25,000 used clubs, some from back when golf was a finesse game rather than a power game. Golf art and memorabilia and antique and new clubs are also available. The trained professionals on staff help you choose the clubs that best fit your skills on a buy, sell, rent, or trade basis. *4297 N. Access Rd., Doraville, 770/493–4344. Closed Sun.*

riding

2 h-8

ATLANTA SADDLERY

The emphasis here is on showing, so look for the finest in English tack—bridles, strap goods, leg and hoof wear, saddles and pads. The human wear includes boots, breeches, coats, helmets, and outerwear for dressage, show jumping, and pleasure categories. *1670 Hwy. 9, Alpharetta, 770/475–1967.*

4 g-1

HORSE TOWN

Everything you need for western saddlery—from saddles with pommels to 10-gallon hats and boots made of exotic skins—is here. A full line of English tack is also available. *1231 Shallowford Rd., Marietta, 770/926–7346.*

6 d-7

1959 Dogwood Dr. SW, Snellville, 770/736–1888.

8 h-5

INTERNATIONAL SADDLERY

When the Olympics came to Atlanta in 1996, this store won the designation "official saddlery." That recommendation, along with a convenient location at the Georgia International Horse Park, makes it a prime place to buy English tack, clothing, and gifts. Barn and stable supplies are available, too. *1960-A Centennial Olympic Pkwy., Conyers, 770/929–8832.*

running

12 g-8

PHIDIPPIDES

The staff here makes you take a little run in front of the store to make sure you're getting the right shoe with a proper fit. The store also carries some trail-running shoes and racing flats. *Ansley Mall, 1544 Piedmont Ave., Midtown, 404/875–4268. Closed Sun.*

5 b-5

220 Sandy Springs Cir., Sandy Springs, 404/255–6149.

skating

15 f-2

SKATE ESCAPE

Visitors to Piedmont Park see some incredible in-line skating, and if you're inspired to join in the fun, this nearby shop can equip you with in-lines, along with skateboards and accessories. The sales staff is dedicated to the sport and it educates beginners and talks the talk with regulars. *1086 Piedmont Ave., Midtown, 404/892–1292.*

5 g-5

SONIC BLADES

For beginners or advanced skaters, this store sells and rents ice skates, in-line skates, and skateboards. The staff is into these sports, so you can expect great advice. Repairs are available, too. *5775 Jimmy Carter Blvd., Norcross, 770/662–5665.*

5 *b-4*

736 Johnson Ferry Rd., Marietta, 770/977–0005.

5 *b-4*

SPARKLES

The emphasis is definitely below the knee—on in-lines, roller skates, and ice skates. You have to go elsewhere for the correct apparel, but you would be hard-pressed to find a better selection of equipment. *4800 Davidson Rd., Marietta, 770/565–8899.*

2 *c-3*

1153 Marietta Hwy., Canton, 770/479–9546.

4 *d-2*

1000 McCollum Pkwy., Kennesaw, 770/428–3941.

6 *f-6*

1104 Grayson Hwy. 20, Lawrenceville, 770/963–0922.

7 *g-8*

7335 Hwy. 85, Riverdale, 770/997–6363.

4 *g-7*

666 Smyrna Hill Dr., Smyrna, 770/432–6222.

skiing

5 *c-6*

ROCKY MOUNTAIN SPORTS SKI SHOP

Atlanta has one of the largest ski clubs in the country, and this store is where most of the members come to buy equipment. That's because the inventory is extensive and the sales staff is dedicated to the sport and knowledgeable about boots, skis, boards, and bindings. It's open from September through March and on Sundays from November through February. *5323 Roswell Rd., Sandy Springs, 404/252–3157. Closed Apr.–Aug.; Sun. in Sept., Oct., and Mar.*

5 *b-5*

SPORTS EXPRESS

Half the store specializes in ski equipment, half in tennis. Along with high-tech designer ski wear and tennis wear for everybody in the family, skis, snow-boards, rackets, and all the gear and accessories you need for either sport are available. Plus, skis can be tuned on a same-day basis. *6681 Roswell Rd., Sandy Springs, 404/252–7963.*

tennis

5 *e-1*

SERIOUS TENNIS

It's serious in that the stock is geared exclusively and seriously to tennis clothing and equipment. As a result, you can expect to find knowledgeable service and every brand of racket, mostly priced from $90 to $300. With this kind of focus, it's hard to leave without feeling like a serious player. *10800 Alpharetta Hwy., Roswell, 770/641–8321.*

SPORTS EXPRESS

See Skiing, above.

5 *a-4*

YOUR SERVE TENNIS & FITNESS

Since 1976, this store has brought Atlantans the newest in clothing and equipment. Its reputation for quality and service matches its desire to bring the latest in technology to your game. *1205 Johnson Ferry Rd., Marietta, 770/977–1513.*

5 *f-4*

4015 Holcomb Bridge Rd., Norcross, 770/447–9989.

6 *b-8*

5295 Stone Mountain Hwy., Stone Mountain, 770/469–2791.

STATIONERY & OFFICE SUPPLIES

office supplies

15 *e-5*

IVAN ALLEN

The family of one of Atlanta's most famous mayors founded this company in 1900, and it has managed to adapt to the city's constantly changing business environment. The selection of everything from supplies to furniture is wide, and the service is attentive. *730 Peachtree St., Midtown, 404/760–8700. MARTA: Peachtree Center.*

`12` *g-5*

OFFICE DEPOT

The Depot supplies offices with everything from storage boxes to computers and software (a good buy, but the staff doesn't always know the difference between a gig and a byte). Sometimes the stock is surprisingly extensive, such as the choice of exotic printing papers. *2581 Piedmont Rd., Buckhead, 404/261–4111. MARTA: Lindbergh Center.*

`13` *e-2*

14th St. and Centennial Olympic Park Dr., Midtown, 404/724–0584. MARTA: Midtown.

`5` *d-6*

5300 Peachtree Industrial Blvd., Chamblee, 770/452–0187.

`4` *g-4*

119 Cobb Pkwy., Marietta, 770/499–2001.

`5` *g-6*

5495 Jimmy Carter Blvd., Norcross, 770/446–6646.

`8` *e-1*

5064 Memorial Dr., Stone Mountain, 404/297–4841.

paperweights

`12` *d-7*

VESPERMAN GLASS

Atlanta's premier art-glass gallery displays dozens of gorgeous paperweights and also does a healthy business in other kinds of corporate gifts. *2140 Peachtree Rd., Brookwood, 404/359–9698. Closed Sun.*

pens & pencils

`12` *g-7*

ARTLITE

In this old-fashioned office-supply store, people who know fine pens can shop for antique instruments as well as top-of-the-line examples by Waterman, Montblanc, Cross, Sheaffer, and Parker. The fountain-pen selection is especially fine, and there are also mechanical pencils and drafting instruments. *1851 Piedmont Rd., Midtown, 404/875–7271. Closed Sun.*

`12` *h-2*

MONTBLANC

Within the black-and-white polished walls of this store are handmade papers, boxes of fine stationery, leather goods, and, of course, the famous pens, all made by this German company. You can have a $125,000 diamond pen made to order, get one in platinum for $15,500, or settle for the store's most popular item, a black rollerball with gold trim for $175. *Lenox Square, 3393 Peachtree Rd., Buckhead, 404/231–4810. MARTA: Lenox.*

stationery

`12` *f-3*

PACES PAPERS INC. BY JACKIE

Tout Buckhead comes here for engraved invitations and announcements, along with very fine laid, watermarked, and bonded papers to engrave upon. Tasteful, handmade cards are sold here as well, in case you need something fine in a hurry. *Cates Center, 110 E. Andrews Dr., Buckhead, 404/231–1111. Closed Sun.*

`12` *h-2*

PAPYRUS

Wedding invitations, birth announcements, and personalized stationery are specialties here, but the chain also offers a wide selection of cards and giftwrap. *Lenox Square, 3393 Peachtree Rd., Buckhead,, 404/233–1292. MARTA: Lenox.*

`5` *c-5*

Perimeter Mall, 4400 Ashford-Dunwoody Rd., Dunwoody, 770/677–0313. MARTA: Dunwoody.

TOBACCONISTS

`5` *d-4*

THE CIGAR MERCHANT

In addition to housing a wide array of pipes and pipe tobaccos, these stores offer state-of-the-art walk-in humidors and smoking lounges. They'll sell you hand-rolled cigars from Jamaica, Honduras, and the Dominican Republic, encouraging you to test a few before selecting. *1404 Dunwoody Village Pkwy., Dunwoody, 770/671–1777.*

`5` *e-2*

9850 Nesbit Ferry Rd., Alpharetta, 770/552–1942.

`5` *e-1*

10800 Alpharetta Hwy., Roswell, 770/642–1221.

`12` *g-3*

EDWARD'S PIPE & TOBACCO SHOPS

Since around 1963, this shop carries an in-depth selection of pipes, cigarettes, cigars, and accessories. The inventory includes thousands of premium handmade cigar brands, along with Edward's own hand-blended tobaccos. *3137 Piedmont Rd., south of Peachtree Rd. intersection, Buckhead, 404/233–8082.*

`8` *d-1*

444 North Indian Creek Dr., near the Perimeter College Central campus, Clarkston, 404/292–1721.

TOYS & GAMES

collectibles

`12` *g-7*

CLASSIC COMICS

Hard-to-find *Star Wars* collectibles, primarily from the latest iterations (since 1995), are a draw here. There's also a good selection of the female action figures that have been creeping into the once-all-male domain. (If you go to the Roswell store, don't be surprised if a Doberman pinscher pops up from behind the counter to wait on you.) *1860 Piedmont Rd., Buckhead, 404/892–4442.*

`2` *h-8*

11235 Alpharetta Hwy., between Mansell and Hembree Rds., Roswell, 770/753–9400.

`6` *d-4*

GALACTIC QUEST

The trove of *Star Wars* collectibles here, both new and old, is the largest in the metro area. In addition to action figures, new and vintage comics, collectible card games, and animated videos are also available. *155 Gwinnett Dr., Lawrenceville, 770/339–3001. Closed Sun.*

`3` *g-8*

4300 Buford Hwy., Buford, 770/614–4804.

`5` *e-6*

GANDY DANCERS

The great selection of specialty toys includes children's and adult wooden, plastic, and electric trains. You can also find horses, dolls, and model kits for cars, planes, and boats on the shelves. *5438 Peachtree Industrial Blvd., Chamblee, 770/451–7425.*

`12` *g-4*

OXFORD COMICS & GAMES

One of the best selections of comics in town is accompanied by a large section of adult magazines. It's great for heavy-metal T-shirts and some action figures. *2855 Piedmont Rd., Buckhead, 404/233–8682.*

kites

`14` *a-5*

IDENTIFIED FLYING OBJECTS

Wonderful creations in all shapes and sizes lure you into the romance of the kite. The selection includes kits and custom-built kites, and the salespeople take the time to tell you how to get your purchase aloft. Look here also for darts, disc-golf Frisbees, juggling equipment, boomerangs, and other gravity-defying gizmos. *1164 Euclid Ave., Little Five Points, 404/524–4628.*

new

`12` *h-2*

FAO SCHWARZ

Atlanta's outlet of the famous New York store is laid out according to age and gender divisions, making it easy to find just the right gift. The staff is unfailingly helpful, too, and knows what each age wants for holiday or birthday. Along with a full line of Steiff products, you can also pick up such FAO exclusives as the *Star Wars* Princess Leia–R2D2 combo. *Lenox Square, 3393 Peachtree Rd., Buckhead, 404/814–1675. MARTA: Lenox.*

`5` *e-1*

TOYS "R" US

What would we do without this paradise for kids? Well, even if you're not swept away by the vast selection of action figures and Barbie dolls, you can still have a field day studying what these stores have to tell us about American attitudes toward play, violence, and self-image. *7731 N. Point Pkwy., Alpharetta, 770/424–9100.*

`12` *g-2*

1 Buckhead Loop, Buckhead, 404/467–8697.

`8` *c-4*

2842 Whites Mill Rd., Decatur, 404/243–4333.

`6` *a-4*

2205 Pleasant Hill Rd., Duluth, 770/476–4646.

`4` *h-7*

2997 Cobb Pkwy., Smyrna, 770/951–8052.

`5` *f-8*

4033 LaVista Rd., Tucker, 770/938–4321.

`5` *b-5*

ZANY BRAINY

These colorful stores offer a thoughtful approach to play and playing with large selections of books and think-toys. Classes on a wide range of subjects teach kids how to have fun with their imaginations as well as toys. 6285 Roswell Rd., Sandy Springs, 404/252–3280.

`5` *e-1*

6551 North Point Pkwy., Alpharetta, 770/569–0679.

`4` *f-3*

50 Ernest W. Barrett Pkwy., Kennesaw, 770/590–0525.

`5` *a-3*

1100 Johnson Ferry Rd., Marietta, 770/977–3373.

`5` *f-4*

3200 Holcomb Bridge Rd., Norcross, 770/447–6222.

`6` *d-7*

1905 Scenic Hwy., Snellville, 678/344–8830.

VIDEOS

`15` *g-2*

BLOCKBUSTER

The huge chain stocks thousands of titles, and the list is growing all the time. (Still, it doesn't delve nearly deeply enough into esoterica.) The stores also carry every conceivable video game for Sega, Nintendo, and Playstation, as well as an increasingly large selection of DVDs. 985 Monroe Dr., Midtown, 404/876–0433.

`5` *e-7*

3550 Chamblee-Tucker Rd., Chamblee, 770/457–1440.

`5` *f-8*

3934 N. Druid Hills Rd., Decatur, 404/636–0064.

`6` *a-4*

2180 Pleasant Hill Rd., Duluth, 770/497–8189.

`4` *g-7*

2900 S. Cobb Dr., Smyrna, 770/431–9700.

`8` *e-1*

921 N. Hairston Rd., Stone Mountain, 404/299–3500.

`7` *g-8*

THE MOBILE VIDEO STORE

The selection isn't as big as it is at the huge chains, but then again, this place is more about convenience. 1419 Cambridge Ct., Riverdale, 770/909–8683 or 404/202–6214.

`14` *a-5*

VIDEO UPDATE

Selections at the dozen-plus metro-area locations are pretty much the same, and huge, with more than 10,000 titles in stock at each. Call ahead to reserve a copy of your selection. 299 Moreland Ave., Little Five Points, 404/658–1772.

`12` *g-8*

595 Piedmont Ave., 404/815–9616.

`5` *f-4*

3200 Holcomb Bridge Rd., Norcross, 770/449–5454.

`5` *a-3*

4400 Roswell Rd., Marietta, 770/321–5300.

`6` *d-4*

950 Herrington Rd., Lawrenceville, 770/277–0070.

chapter 3

PARKS, GARDENS, & SPORTS

Earlier Atlantans probably built their homes through, around, and among the trees for a most practical reason: the shade and breezes their branches offered in the battle against the summer heat. Their legacy was broad swaths of undeveloped land throughout the metro area as well as a fitting modern motto, "the city of trees." Amid intense regional growth and development, the untouched patches of green have become ever smaller, but private citizens and governments at all levels have created a vast array of outdoor venues for recreation and leisure. There are several big parks including a huge state park with a massive rock, two large lakes, and a long river that rambles along from fishing hole to boat ramp to duck havens—and there are delightful small and midsize parks scattered throughout every city and county in the metro area. So, too, can you find public gardens, nature preserves, sports fields and arenas, amusement parks, and the stellar zoo. It may take you a while to find the place that exactly fits your needs, but the hunt can open up a whole new view of Atlanta—beyond the cars and multiplying office towers—for you to enjoy.

parks

A tapestry of parks peppers Atlanta and the 10-county metro area with courts and ball fields for organized games, lakes for fishing and sailing, pools for sunning and swimming, trails for exploring, and playgrounds and picnic grounds for informal family gatherings. The city alone manages more than 350

ACCESS LIMITATIONS

In the aftermath of terrorist attacks in New York and Washington, D.C., in September 2001, a number of sites near dams and other water sources were closed to recreational use. Call ahead to check for restrictions before planning activities at any such locales.

---

parks, recreation centers, and other facilities, from tiny green spaces to large multipurpose parks that are major regional destinations. The region's rapid growth has created greater demand for green spaces, so counties, too, have been expanding their parks systems; DeKalb County, for example, manages 107 parks. Therefore, the parks listed here are only the most popular of the dozens around Atlanta.

park information

Some parks listed in this chapter don't have their own phone numbers; contact the appropriate parks department for information about them. If a park is known primarily for a specific activity, such as soccer or tennis, look for it under that activity heading in the Sports & Outdoor Activities section. You can get to most parks by MARTA buses or a combination of train and bus.

Atlanta Department of Parks, Recreation, and Cultural Affairs (404/817–6752 general parks information; 404/817–6766 recreation, www.ci.atlanta.ga.us/citydir/rec_info.html). **Cherokee County Parks and Recreation Authority** (770/924–7768, www.crpa.net). **Clayton County Parks and Recreational Department** (770/477–3766, www.co.clayton.ga.us/parks_and_recreation). **Cobb County Parks and Recreation Department** (770/528–8890 West Cobb; 770/591–3160 East Cobb, www.cobb-net.com/residentservices/prca.htm). **DeKalb County Parks and Recreation Department** (404/371–2631, www.co.dekalb.ga.us/dekalbfun). **Douglas County Parks and Recreation Department** (770/920–7129). **Fayette County Recreation Department** (770/461–9714, www.admin.co.fayette.ga.us/Recreation/index.html). **Forsyth County Parks and Recreation Department** (770/781–2215, www.forsythco.com/parkrec). **Fulton County Parks and Recreation Department** (404/704–6300, www.co.fulton.ga.us/parksrecreation). **Gwinnett County Parks and Recreation Department** (770/822–8840, www.co.gwinnett.ga.us/Low/parks_rec/parks). **Henry County Parks and Recreation Department** (770/954–2031, www.co.henry.ga.us).

To find Web sites for counties and municipalities—many of which have detailed lists of parks and recreational opportunities—access www.ganet.org/index/local.cgi, part of the Web site of the Georgia State Government (www.ganet.org), and select from the city or county lists. You can request brochures and lodging and camping reservations for state parks through **Georgia State Parks & Historic Sites** (770/389–7275).

city of atlanta

7 *f-4*

ADAMS PARK
A wooded and hilly area adjacent to the Alfred "Tup" Holmes Golf Course, Adams Park has four ball fields, a gymnasium and recreation center, a seasonal swimming pool, two tennis courts, and picnic pavilions around a small lake. *1620 Delowe Dr., north of Campbellton Rd., Cascade Heights, 404/756–1827.*

8 *a-2*

CANDLER PARK
The land for this popular town park was given to the city by Coca-Cola Company founder Asa Candler. The park has a ball field, four tennis courts, a basketball court, a volleyball court, and a picnic area. The 9-hole golf course is inexpensive and great for beginners. *1500 McLendon Ave., south of Ponce de Leon Ave., Candler Park, 404/817–6757.*

15 *d-5*

CENTENNIAL OLYMPIC PARK
Before the 1996 Centennial Olympic Games, decaying buildings filled this area of downtown. These days, the park glows with life. Families picnic on the 330,000 square ft of grass scattered with outdoor art and marked by a commemorative pathway of bricks bearing the names of Olympic visitors. On warm days, you can see all ages splashing in the dancing waters of the *Fountain of Rings*; from Thanksgiving through December, skaters and onlookers cluster at the ice rink. The 21-acre park also has outdoor concert areas, a casual restaurant, and a series of plazas devoted to stories of the '96 games. Parking is available in numerous private lots around the perimeter and at the Georgia World Congress Center. *285 International Blvd.bordered by Techwood Dr. on the east, Baker St. on the north, Luckie and Foundry St. on the west, Downtown, 404/223–4412, www.gwcc.com/park/park.htm. MARTA: Omni/Dome/GWCC.*

5 *b-7*

CHASTAIN PARK
Golf, tennis, and youth team sports draw many Atlantans here, but the park also has a large playground and picnic area, a 3½-mi footpath (watch out for errant golf balls), an arts-and-crafts center, and Chastain Horse Park. The outdoor amphitheater is a major summer destination for concert series featuring big-name entertainers. *140 W. Wieuca Rd. (bordered by Powers Ferry Rd. and Lake Forrest Dr.), Buckhead, 404/252–8866.*

15 *g-8*

GRANT PARK
This park is best known as the home of Zoo Atlanta and the Cyclorama. Lemuel P. Grant, who designed Atlanta's Civil War defenses, donated the land for the park to the city in 1882. The rolling, tree-shaded hilltop that once housed a Confederate artillery battery is now a splendid spot from which to view the city skyline. The park has picnic pavilions, ball fields, four tennis courts, a gym, and a swimming pool. It lends its name to the surrounding area of restored Victorian houses and Craftsman-style bungalows that make up one of Atlanta's most ethnically diverse neighborhoods. *537 Park Ave. (bordered by Cherokee Ave. on the east, Atlanta Ave. on the south), Grant Park, 404/624–0697. MARTA: West End.*

15 *f-2*

PIEDMONT PARK
Atlanta's most enduringly popular playground, Piedmont Park has been practically loved to death during its 110 years. It was the site of the first football game played in Georgia (Georgia vs. Auburn), in 1892, and, three years later, of the Cotton States Exposition, a Southern version of the World's Fair. John Philip Sousa composed his *King Cotton March* for the event. Vestiges of the exposition grounds, designed by landscape architect Frederick Law Olmsted, remain. The years have taken their toll, but the nonprofit Piedmont Park Conservancy works closely with the city on restoration and preservation. Softball and soccer teams play on the three ball fields, and tennis buffs lob balls in 12 public courts. Picnickers spread their blankets beside Lake Clara Meer; skateboarders and in-line skaters cruise park roads; and children frolic at a playground designed by Japanese artist Isamu Noguchi. The Atlanta Botanical Garden is on the

park's northern boundary. *Main entrance: 12th St. and Piedmont Ave., park bordered by Piedmont Ave., 10th St., and Monroe Dr., Midtown, 404/817–6757. MARTA: Midtown or Arts Center.*

7 *h-4*

SOUTH BEND PARK

Its location makes this 76-acre park handy for a picnic before a concert at Lakewood Amphitheatre. In addition to four picnic shelters, it has two lighted tennis courts, a public pool, and softball, baseball, and football fields. *1955 Compton Dr., east of I–75/I–85 at GA 166 (Langford Pkwy./Lakewood Fwy.), Lakewood.*

15 *e-6*

WOODRUFF MEMORIAL PARK

Surrounded by skyscrapers in the heart of the city, Woodruff Park is the ideal spot for lunchtime people-watching. Street preachers and sidewalk vendors mix with business types in this parcel of green. During spring and summer, the park hosts noontime and after-work events on outdoor stages. *Peachtree St. and Edgewood Ave., Downtown. MARTA: Five Points.*

cherokee county

2 *b-4*

BOLING PARK

Among the highlights of Cherokee County's park system, this multifacility park has four lighted tennis courts, four handball or racquetball courts, four soccer fields, three softball or baseball fields, a basketball or volleyball court, playground, jogging track, and picnic pavilions. *1279 GA 5, Canton.*

2 *a-8*

HOBGOOD PARK

Between Woodstock and Lake Allatoona, Hobgood Park has four lighted championship softball fields, four lighted tennis courts, a jogging trail, fitness courts, playground, picnic pavilions, and an outdoor amphitheater. *6688 Bells Ferry Rd., Woodstock.*

clayton county

9 *h-1*

CLAYTON COUNTY INTERNATIONAL PARK

The 200 wooded acres here include a fishing lake, beach area, concession stands, bike trails, and a miniature-golf course. The volleyball complex, built for the 1996 Olympics, hosts a concert series each summer. A meeting space adjacent to the complex presents traveling arts-and-crafts exhibitions. *Off GA 138, west of I–75 and east of Crane Rd., Jonesboro, 770/473–4005.*

9 *f-2*

INDEPENDENCE PARK

One of Clayton County's more popular parks, this green space has a paved walking trail, playground, tennis courts, ball fields, and basketball courts. *8970 Thomas Rd., Jonesboro.*

9 *h-1*

PANHANDLE PARK

In the southern part of the county, this popular park has a paved walking path, picnic pavilions, a playground, ball fields, and a basketball court. *10930 Panhandle Rd., off Autumn Forest Dr., south of Stockbridge Rd./GA 138, Jonesboro.*

cobb county

4 *e-6*

JIM MILLER PARK

The North Georgia State Fair and the Shrine Circus are held here each year, along with various rodeos. The park has two 9,000-square-ft exhibition buildings, a lake, an equestrian center, cross-country running course, a fitness trail, and picnic pavilions. *2245 Callaway Rd., south of Al Bishop Softball Complex, Marietta, 770/528–8875.*

4 *b-5*

LOST MOUNTAIN PARK

This comprehensive recreation center between Due West and Macland in west Cobb has a tournament softball complex with ball fields, playgrounds, fitness and jogging trails, ponds, and a tennis center. *4845 Dallas Rd., Powder Springs, 770/528–8885.*

4 *c-7*

WILD HORSE CREEK PARK

This multifaceted 70-acre park with a lake has softball, football, baseball, and soccer fields; tennis courts; playgrounds; fitness trails; picnic pavilions; a community center; a BMX bicycle track; and an equestrian ring. *3820 Macedonia Rd., Powder Springs, 770/528–8890.*

dekalb county

DeKalb parks with Atlanta addresses are in unincorporated areas of the county. The **DeKalb County Parks Athletics Department** (404/371–2629 youth sports; 404/508–7568 adult sports) has information about adult athletic leagues and youth sports programs, which involve about 20,000 children each year.

5 *d-6*

BLACKBURN PARK

In northeastern DeKalb, this park offers soccer and softball fields, large picnic areas, walking trails, and a full-service tennis center. *3493 Ashford-Dunwoody Rd., Dunwoody.*

8 *e-5*

BROWNS MILL PARK

With tennis courts, walking trails, a recreation center, and baseball, softball, and football fields, the emphasis here is definitely on sports. There's a picnic area, too. *5101 Browns Mill Rd., Lithonia, 770/593–5874.*

8 *c-4*

EXCHANGE PARK

A favorite destination in southeastern DeKalb, this large park has ball fields, tennis courts, playgrounds, picnic areas, a fishing lake, foot trails, and a recreation center. *2771 Columbia Dr., Decatur.*

8 *f-1*

GEORGIA'S STONE MOUNTAIN PARK

More than 800 ft high and more than 5 mi in circumference, Stone Mountain is 300 million years old. It's the largest piece of exposed granite in the world, yet geologists believe that not even $\frac{1}{1000}$ of the giant rock is above ground. Besides the epic sculpture on the north side of the mountain depicting Confederate leaders, Stone Mountain—state-owned since 1958—offers a slew of attractions. You can swim in the lake, play golf or tennis, ride an old-fashioned steam train or a modern skylift gondola, see an antebellum plantation or Civil War museum, visit the petting farm, or cruise on a paddle wheeler. Areas for biking, running, in-line skating, hiking, camping, and picnicking are scattered all around the 3,200 acres. A nightly laser show garners oohs and ahs during summer, and there are other events dur-

ing the year. Park entry is free, but admission for events and activities varies. The Rock, Stock, and Barrel Pass allows unlimited use of the facilities (excluding golf and tennis) for $25 per person a year. Family passes are available as well and include parking discounts. *Off U.S. 78, about 7½ mi east of I–285 (East Gate entered from U.S. 78, West Gate from Memorial Dr.), Stone Mountain, 770/498–5690, www. stonemountainpark.com.*

8 *b-4*

GRESHAM PARK

Youth sports are the main focus at 125-acre Gresham Park, but adults and families can enjoy the seasonal swimming pool, playgrounds, picnic areas, fishing lake, trails, and recreation center. *3113 Gresham Rd., Gresham Park, 404/244–4890.*

5 *f-7*

HENDERSON PARK

Soccer is the main draw at this large park, which has several fields for play and practice. It also has a playground, trails, picnic areas, and a small lake. *2803 Henderson Rd., Tucker.*

8 *b-3*

MARK TRAIL PARK

A short distance from I–20 in southern DeKalb, this modest 45-acre park has plenty of sports facilities, including ball fields, basketball and tennis courts, and a seasonal swimming pool, plus playgrounds, picnic areas, a recreation center, and walking trails. *2230 Tilson Rd., Decatur, 404/244–4891.*

5 *d-6*

MURPHY CANDLER PARK

Best known for its youth baseball, softball, and football programs, this 135-acre park also has a large fishing lake, picnic pavilions, hiking trails, tennis courts, playgrounds, and a swimming pool. *1551 W. Nancy Creek Rd., Dunwoody.*

8 *f-3*

REDAN PARK

A favorite spot for disc-golf players, this park in eastern DeKalb County also has ball fields, tennis courts, playgrounds, picnic areas, and walking trails. *1745 Phillips Rd., Lithonia.*

8 *e-2*

WADE-WALKER PARK

In the shadow of Stone Mountain, this 177-acre park has tennis courts, playgrounds, picnic areas, a swimming pool, a fishing lake, trails, a rink for street hockey leagues, and fields for softball, baseball and football. *5585 Rockbridge Rd., Stone Mountain.*

douglas county

 b-5

DEER LICK PARK

In addition to three softball fields and a football field, this park has an outdoor amphitheater, a playground, picnic shelters, a 3-acre lake for fishing, a sand volleyball court, a jogging track, and a 9-hole disc-golf course. *2105 Mack Rd., east of I–20 via GA 92, Douglasville.*

7 *a-2*

SWEETWATER CREEK STATE CONSERVATION PARK

Blending scenic beauty and historic heritage, this park protects the swift waters of Sweetwater Creek and preserves the historic ruins of the New Manchester Manufacturing Company, a textile mill burned by Union Army cavalry in 1864. The 2,035-acre park has more than 9 mi of hiking trails, plus picnic areas, and boat rentals and docks at 215-acre Sparks Reservoir. Each September, the Civil War mill days are commemorated with living history demonstrations, and there's a Native American Festival here every June. At park headquarters, you can obtain park maps and information, as well as fishing licenses, bait, and supplies. *Mount Vernon Rd., south of Blairs Bridge Rd. and I–20, south of Lithia Springs, 770/732–5871.*

fayette county

9 *d-5*

KIWANIS CENTER PARK

Many civic events are held at this busy park, which has tennis courts, a playground, picnic areas, a recreation center, and 10 baseball fields. *936 Redwine Rd., Fayetteville, 770/461–9714.*

9 *e-7*

LAKE HORTON

In the heart of a wooded, rural area of the county, this park has 2 mi of walking trails and a small nature preserve. The 800-acre lake is popular for sailing as well as fishing from rowboats or motorboats. *Antioch Rd., east of GA 92, south of Fayetteville.*

9 *e-4*

MCCURRY PARK

In addition to softball fields, McCurry Park has a football complex with a running track, a walking path, picnic pavilions, and a ropes course. *GA 54 E at McDonough Rd., east of Fayetteville.*

forsyth county

1 *g-1*

LAKE SIDNEY LANIER

Named in honor of the famed Georgia poet who wrote *Marshes of Glynn* and *Song of the Chattahoochee,* this 38,000-acre lake (commonly called Lake Lanier) sprawls through the scenic Appalachian foothills of northeastern Georgia. The lake was created when the Army Corps of Engineers built Buford Dam in the 1950s and is one of the busiest recreational lakes in the nation, especially on summer weekends. Along the 540 mi of shoreline are 40 day-use parks and 10 campgrounds maintained by the Corps of Engineers; 9 public parks on land leased to the county or surrounding towns; more than 60 boat launches; and 10 commercial marinas. The Lake Lanier Islands Resort has golf, tennis, biking, horseback riding, sailing, and many other activities (the Resource Manager's Office, 770/932–7000, has details). Campground reservations also may be made through the National Recreation Reservation Service (877/444–6777, www.reserve.usa.com), a Corps of Engineers–U.S. Forest Service joint venture. *Between GA 400 and I–985, about 35 mi northeast of Atlanta, between Buford and Gainesville, 770/945–9531 office; 770/945–1467 recorded information, www.sam. usace.army.mil/op/rec/lanier.*

3 *d-3*

SAWNEE MOUNTAIN PARK

The eight youth baseball fields make this park especially busy during Little League season. But it also has football, softball, and soccer fields; two tennis courts; a playground; a picnic pavilion; a community recreation building; and trails where bike rides are held in the summer. *3995 Watson Rd., off GA 20 via Tribbles Rd., Cumming, 770/886–4085.*

3 *c-6*

SHARON SPRINGS PARK

Youth and adult team sports are the emphasis at Forsyth County's largest and busiest park. There are four youth baseball or softball fields, five adult ball fields, two football or soccer fields, eight tennis courts, a playground, a paved walking and jogging path, a picnic pavilion, and tennis courts. *1950 Sharon Rd., off GA 141, south of GA 400, Cumming.*

fulton county

5 *a-5 through g-3*

CHATTAHOOCHEE RIVER NATIONAL RECREATION AREA

Stretching like a string of pearls through Atlanta's northern suburbs, this federal park protects the shoreline and wooded hills along 48 mi of the slow-moving river. The 14 units of the park stretch from Bowman's Island, south of Buford Dam in Gwinnett County, to Pace's Mill, beneath the concrete of I–75 in Northwest Atlanta. The 9 developed sections that are open to the public have rich fishing waters, recreational fields, more than 70 mi of hiking trails, and put-in points for canoes, kayaks, and powerboats; all have picnic areas. Bikes and pets are allowed (on leashes) in certain parts; maps on the park Web site note these. Trail routes generally begin near the parking areas; guided hikes are available through park headquarters. *770/952–4419, www.nps.gov/chat.*

5 *g-1*

Abbots Bridge Prized by fishermen for its trout, this small unit also has has a short trail and a picnic shelter. *Abbotts Bridge Rd./GA 120, west of GA 141, near Duluth.*

5 *a-6*

Cochran Shoals/Powers Island The Cochran Shoals and Powers Island areas face each other from opposite banks of the river, with Powers Island in between. The 3⅓-mi paved Cochran Shoals Fitness Trail winds around wetlands and an activity field. From the Floodplain Trail in the Powers Island section, you can see kayakers tackling the Atlanta Whitewater Club's slalom gates. *Interstate North Pkwy. off I–285, at New Northside Dr., between Northwest Atlanta and Marietta.*

5 *a-7, a-6*

East and West Palisades Perched on palisades along the east and west banks of the Chattahoochee, the two sections of this unit flank an area of rapids and have more than 8 mi of trails, a large recreation field, boat ramps, launching spots for canoes and rafts, and picnic areas. *West Palisades entrances: U.S. 41 at the river or Akers Dr., off Akers Mill Rd.; East Palisades entrances: Indian Trail, off Northside Dr., south of I–285, or Whitewater Creek Rd., off Harris Trail (off Northside Dr. south of I–285); between Northwest Atlanta and Marietta.*

5 *c-3*

Gold Branch From the parking area, more than 7 mi of trails wind through the woods or follow the banks of Bull Sluice Lake, created in 1904 by the construction of nearby Morgan Falls Dam. *Lower Roswell Rd., west of the Chattahoochee Nature Center and east of Mount Bethel.*

5 *c-3*

Island Ford Massive rock outcrops frame the 3-mi trail that winds along the river and into the surrounding hills. An oversize 1940s log building houses park headquarters, which has a viewing area overlooking the river; picnic tables and an activity field are nearby. *Island Ford Pkwy., off Roberts Dr., west of GA 400, south of Roswell.*

5 *b-5*

Johnson Ferry North/Johnson Ferry South Both of these sections have easy hiking trails between the river and wetlands. There's a put-in point for commercial raft trips in Johnson Ferry North. Johnson Ferry South includes several large, open fields once used for polo and now for soccer and other activities. *Columns Dr., off Johnson Ferry Rd. on the north side of the river, between Mount Bethel and Marietta.*

5 *f-3*

Jones Bridge Trails follow the riverbanks and cut through thick woodlands in this unit. There's a boat ramp just beyond the first parking area, with a canoe/raft launch at the north end of the park unit, where you can see the trusses of an old bridge and watch fishermen casting for trout in the rapids. The Geosphere Environmental Education Center—where the National Park Service conducts programs for elementary and high school teachers, Scout leaders, and adult educators—is open to the public only for special events. *Barnwell Rd., off Holcomb Bridge Rd., south of Newtown.*

5 *g-3*

Medlock Bridge The boat ramp here gives you access to several popular fishing spots. The unit also has 3 mi of trails. *Medlock Bridge Rd., off Peachtree Pkwy./GA 141, west of Duluth.*

5 *a-5*

Sope Creek Part of the Powers Ferry unit, this area has hiking and biking trails that lead past old mill ruins and Sibley Pond. *Paper Mill Rd., off Johnson Ferry Rd., between Marietta and Mount Bethel.*

RIVER OF HISTORY

Deep in the north Georgia mountains, the Chattahoochee River springs cold and clear. For the Creek and Cherokee, who gave it the name that means "river of the painted rocks" in ancient Cherokee, the river was a pathway between villages and fishing grounds. In the 1830s, the rushing waters of Vickery Creek, a tributary of the Chattahoochee, brought Roswell King to the area. King established a textile mill on the banks of the creek, and the town of Roswell grew up around it. During the Civil War, Union cavalry raided Roswell, burned the mill, and shipped about 400 women and children who worked in the mill north, never to return. The mill was rebuilt and operated for nearly a century, until the construction of Buford Dam created Lake Sidney Lanier in the 1950s and forced the mill to close for a final time. Over the years, the river became a playground for boaters and anglers, and the once remote village of Roswell grew into a thriving Atlanta suburb; many of the old mill buildings have been converted into offices and stores. By the 1970s, the pace of development in Atlanta threatened to overwhelm the river's scenic but fragile environment. In 1978, Georgia native President Jimmy Carter created the Chattahoochee River National Recreation Area to protect and preserve vestiges of the river's natural landscape for all to enjoy.

---

5 *c-3*

Vickery Creek Six miles of trails follow the Big Creek offshoot of the Chattahoochee. Trails west of the creek lead to the ruins of a textile mill burned by Union Army cavalry in 1864. The larger, eastern area has some easy paths as well as more difficult trails along Roswell Dam. *South Atlanta St./GA 9 for west area, Riverside Rd. for east area (both just beyond Roswell Rd.–Azalea Dr. intersection), Roswell.*

5 *c-3*

CHATTAHOOCHEE RIVER PARK

Extending for nearly ½ mi along the banks of the Chattahoochee, this park is a haven for boaters, picnickers, anglers, and those who want to watch the river roll by or feed the inquisitive ducks and Canada geese. The park has a boat ramp, picnic tables and two covered pavilions, a playground, and a walking trail. *203 Azalea Dr., west of Roswell Rd./GA 9, 1 mi south of Roswell, 770/740–2416.*

7 *b-8*

CLARENCE DUNCAN MEMORIAL PARK

In the southern end of Fulton County, this large park bustles with activity most of the year. It has lighted ball fields, two tennis courts, two outdoor basketball courts, a playground, hiking trails, picnic pavilions, an indoor-outdoor swimming pool with retractable roof, and a small lake. *6000 Rivertown Rd., Fairburn, 770/306–3136.*

1 *c-7*

COCHRAN MILL PARK

Large and heavily wooded, this park has several miles of trails for hiking and horseback riding, a challenging ropes course, picnic areas, and sites for primitive camping. The park shares trails with the adjacent Cochran Mill Nature Preserve. Trails meander through the thick woods to the banks of Bear and Little Bear creeks and past the ruins of 19th-century mill dams, built by Cheadle Cochran on land he received for service in the War of 1812. In the 1930s, Cochran's descendants sold the site to Hiram Evans, then the Imperial Wizard of the Ku Klux Klan, and the remote location was used for secret Klan activities. The park and preserve lands were acquired by Fulton County in the late

1970s. *6785 Cochran Mill Rd., west of South Fulton Pkwy. and Rivertown Rd., north of Palmetto, 404/730–6200.*

7 *c-5*

TOM LOWE SHOOTING GROUNDS

A delight for the sports shooter, this park has 25 skeet fields and 20 trap fields, plus other target-shooting ranges, along with a pro shop and club-house. *3070 Merck Rd., off Camp Creek Pkwy., between Enon and Butner Rds., 404/346–8382.*

7 *d-6*

WELCOME ALL PARK

Jam-packed with recreational facilities, this 37-acre park has football and soccer fields, five youth baseball fields, two lighted tennis courts, two picnic shelters, walking trails, a community center, and a multipurpose gymnasium and fitness center that includes an indoor pool. *4255 Will Lee Rd., off Welcome All Rd., north of Roosevelt Hwy./U.S. 29, College Park, 404/762–4058.*

gwinnett county

5 *g-5*

BEST FRIEND PARK

On 55 acres, the park has a tennis center, softball-baseball fields, a picnic area, and a community building with a gymnasium and volleyball courts. A swimming pool cools things down in summer. *6224 Jimmy Carter Blvd./GA 140, north of I–85, Norcross, 770/417–2200.*

3 *h-8*

BOGAN PARK

The year-round aquatic center at this popular park has both competition and zero-depth wading pools. The park also has sand volleyball courts, picnic pavilions, walking-jogging trails, playgrounds, ball fields, basketball courts, and a community building. *2723 N. Bogan Rd., west of GA 365/I–985, Buford, 770/614–2060.*

6 *b-2*

GEORGE PIERCE PARK

Forest and wetland are the setting for this multipurpose park, which has softball-baseball fields, walking trails, a small lake, picnic pavilions, a playground, and a five-field soccer complex.

55 Buford Hwy., west of I–85, near Suwanee, 770/614–2060.

5 *f-3*

JONES BRIDGE PARK

When the sun rises through the girders of the old bridge on the first days of trout season, this picturesque 30-acre park seems to have three anglers for every fish. Plan activities at the large recreation field, playground, community building, or at one of four soccer fields, or, in warm weather, join the bathers who wade through the shallow rapids to bask on the rocks. The park is across the river from the Jones Bridge unit of the Chattahoochee River National Recreation Area. *4901 E. Jones Bridge Rd., west of Peachtree Pkwy./GA 141, near Norcross, 770/417–2200.*

6 *d-8*

LENORA PARK

The 112-acre park offers a rich blend of recreational opportunities at a six-field baseball–softball complex, a gymnasium, a playground, a small fishing lake, a paved walking trail, an equestrian practice ring, and an 18-hole disc-golf course. *4515 Lenora Church Rd., at Lee Rd., east of GA 124, Snellville, 770/237–5626; 770/978–5271 youth sports.*

6 *b-7*

MOUNTAIN PARK

One of Gwinnett County's most visited parks, this spot has a seven-field softball-baseball complex, eight tennis courts, picnic pavilions, a playground, a walking trail, and a year-round aquatics center. *5050 Five Forks Trickum Rd., Lilburn, 770/237–5626.*

6 *e-4*

RHODES JORDAN PARK

The centerpiece of this park is a 22-acre fishing lake, but it also includes a seven-field softball-baseball complex, a youth football field, picnic pavilions, playgrounds, two summer swimming pools, a community center with gymnasium, and an eight-court tennis facility. *100 E. Crogan St./U.S. 29, Lawrenceville, 770/237–5626.*

6 *f-6*

TRIBBLE MILL REGIONAL PARK

On 650 wooded acres in rural Gwinnett County, this park has picnic pavilions set around two lakes—a 40-acre fishing lake and a 108-acre boating lake. It also has a group camping area, large recreation fields, and trails for hiking, jogging, and horseback riding. *2425 Ozora Church Rd., off New Hope Rd., Grayson, 770/978–5270.*

henry county

8 *d-6*

HIDDEN VALLEY PARK

This large park has four baseball-softball fields, an outdoor basketball court, a nature trail, a ¼-mi paved jogging track, two lighted tennis courts, picnic pavilions, and a horseshoe court. *1 Fairview Rd., at Spraggins Memorial Pkwy., Ellenwood, no phone.*

10 *h-5*

SANDY RIDGE PARK

Sports enthusiasts frequent this park for the mix of outdoor facilities, which include a baseball-softball field, a basketball court, tennis courts, a playground, a paved jogging track, and a volleyball court. *1200 Keys Ferry Rd., McDonough, no phone.*

10 *d-4*

WINDY HILL PARK

Baseball and soccer fields, an obstacle course, a horseshoe court, a jogging trail, tennis courts, a picnic pavilion, and a playground make this a popular outdoor destination. The park is home to the Henry County Fairgrounds and Exhibit Area. *100-A Windy Hill Rd., McDonough, no phone.*

other outdoor attractions

AMUSEMENT PARKS

4 *g-4*

AMERICAN ADVENTURES

Owned by the same company as neighboring White Water Atlanta, this park is designed for families with kids under 12. The younger kids can ride a miniature Ferris wheel, train, and planes while the slightly older crowd explores the kid-size

roller coaster and bumper cars or enjoys water-based play at Captain Kids Cove. Season passes are available, as are combination plans with Six Flags and White Water. *250 Cobb Pkwy., near I–75 exit 265, Marietta, 770/424–9283, www.sixflags. com. Children under 36″, adults, and senior citizens $4, children over 36″ (to age 18) $15. May–Labor Day; call for hours.*

7 *d-2*

SIXFLAGS OVER GEORGIA

Like its sister operations all over the world, SixFlags Over Georgia is designed to entertain all ages. Preschoolers can play in Bugs Bunny World, and older kids can try the bumper cars or rock-climbing wall. For big brothers and sisters (and moms and dads), the thrill rides await; they include the loop-de-loop-de-loop Mind Bender (the world's first triple-loop coaster), a 20-story parachute drop, and a water ride that goes over a 50-ft waterfall. Call the park or check out its Web site for information on season passes and schedules, which vary with the season and weather. *250 Riverside Pkwy., off I–20, Austell, 770/948–9290, www.sixflags. com. Adults $40, senior citizens and children (under 48″) $20; parking $9–$12. May–Labor Day; call for hours.*

BEACHES

Atlanta may be a long drive from the ocean, but the metro area has a number of beaches and water parks to slake the Atlantan thirst for shore-side fun. Thanks to the mild climate, most beaches and water parks open their doors in late spring and remain busy until mid-September.

8 *f-1*

THE BEACH AT GEORGIA'S STONE MOUNTAIN PARK

A ⅓-mi stretch of white sand along the shores of 363-acre Stone Mountain Lake, this beach has a large picnic area and twin water slides suitable for even young swimmers. Season passes are available for $25, and 12-month parking passes for $30. *Off U.S. 78, about 7½ mi east of I–285 (West Gate entered from Memorial Dr.), Stone Mountain, 770/ 498–5690, www.stonemountainpark.com. $7; parking $7. Late May–early Sept., daily 10–7.*

9 *h-1*

CLAYTON COUNTY INTERNATIONAL PARK

The 1996 Olympics volleyball teams competed at this site, which has a ½-mi sandy beach edging a 6-acre lake that's never deeper than 4½ ft. The surrounding water park has other amusements. *Off GA 138, west of I–75 and east of Crane Rd., Jonesboro, 770/473–4005. Adults $6–$8, children under 2 free; parking $2–$5. Late May–early Sept., daily 10–6 (beach and water park).*

2 *a-5*

LAKE ALLATOONA

Beach areas are scattered among the 16 Army Corps of Engineers day-use parks on the shores of 12,010-acre Lake Allatoona. If you tire of sunning or watching the boats go by, you can play at the volleyball areas or ball fields nearby. *East of I–75, between Acworth and Cartersville, 770/382–4700, www.sam.usace.army.mil/op/rec/allatoon. $1.*

3 *g-5*

LAKE LANIER ISLANDS RESORT BEACH

On a sunny day, when the sailboats are bouncing on sparkling blue water, this stretch of beach can seem a million miles from inland Atlanta. The beach is part of the complex that includes the Lake Lanier Islands Resort water park. The admission fee covers both the rough-and-tumble of the water park and the quiet basking of the beach. Two-day passes are available. *6950 Holiday Rd., west of I–985 off Friendship Rd., 770/932–7000, www.lakelanierislands.com. Adults $25, children under 42" and senior citizens $17, children 2 and under free. Memorial Day–Labor Day, Mon.–Thurs. 10–6, Fri.–Sun. 10–7; rest of May, weekends 10–6.*

BOTANICAL GARDENS

15 *g-1*

ATLANTA BOTANICAL GARDEN

Within the borders of Piedmont Park, at the northern corner, the Atlanta Botanical Garden is a 30-acre garden lover's delight. The centerpiece is the shimmering glass of the Dorothy Chapman Fuqua Conservatory, which houses 16,000 square ft of tropical and desert plants from around the world, many of them endangered species. Outside, you can view specialty gardens from herbs to roses, a delicate Japanese garden, and the whimsical Children's Garden, filled with interactive exhibits. Along the foot trails that cut through the 15-acre Storza Woods, you can explore a vestige of the hardwood forest that once covered much of this region. In the Upper Woodlands area a mountain bog has been preserved to protect its endangered plants. Events through the year present seasonal plants in bloom; the 4,000 volumes in the Sheffield Botanical Library and the ABG Hotline (404/888–4769) can help you find answers to your plant-related questions. *Piedmont Park, 1345 Piedmont Ave., Midtown, 404/876–5859, www.atlantabotanicalgarden.org. Adults $7, senior citizens $5, students $4, children under 6 free; admission free Thurs. 3–closing. Apr.–Sept., Tues.–Sun. 9–7; Oct.–Mar., Tues.–Sun. 9–6. MARTA: Arts Center.*

12 *e-3*

ATLANTA HISTORY CENTER

Around the city's premier historical institution, 33 acres of carefully cultivated gardens put Atlanta's history into a nat-

---

PICNIC PLACES

From the bloom of spring's first blossoms until the leaves drop in autumn, Atlanta's parks are a great place for spreading a picnic blanket. These spots are prime for enjoying scenery, watching people, or both.

Chattahoochee River Park
Picnic tables, sheltered pavilions, and playgrounds dot this thin ribbon of green along the river's northern bank.

Georgia's Stone Mountain Park
The meadow beneath the giant carving is an ideal spot for a picnic during a day exploring the park's many attractions.

Grant Park
One of Atlanta's oldest and most historic parks is alive with picnickers on warm-weather weekends. Pack a lunch when you come to explore Zoo Atlanta and the Cyclorama.

Piedmont Park
Tucked beneath the towering Midtown skyline, this is the city's busiest park. Spread a picnic on the grass and watch the people walk, jog, roll, and dance by.

ural context. Shaded woodland trails, a quarry garden of native Georgia plants, the Italian-inspired formal plantings at the 1928 Swan House, and the herb plots at the 1840s Tullie Smith Farm and Tullie Smith House all help tell the story of the habitats Atlantans found, planted, and lived with through the years. *130 W. Paces Ferry Rd., Buckhead, 404/814–4000, www.atlhist.org. Adults $12, students (over 18) and senior citizens $10, children (ages 3–17) $7, Atlanta History Center members and children under 3 free. Mon.–Sat. 10–5:30, Sun. noon–5:30.*

6 f-7
BONSAI BY THE MONASTERY GREENHOUSE

The monks at the Monastery of the Holy Spirit have some outdoor gardens, but most visitors come to see the nationally known bonsai greenhouse. Unusual bonsai are on display throughout, and pre-trained bonsai and special tools and pottery are available for purchase. *2621 GA 212, Conyers, 770/918–9661, www.bonsaimonk.com. Free. Tues.–Sat. 10–5, Sun. 11–4:30.*

6 f-7
VINES BOTANICAL GARDEN

Once a private estate, the elegant 18,000-square-ft manor house and its 25 acres of gardens were a gift to Gwinnett County from Charles and Myrna Adams in 1990. Today, you're welcome to stroll through lush woodlands, enjoy rich heirloom roses, savor the colors of seasonal plants, admire the elegance of the European Statuary Garden, and chuckle at the yard art in the Whimsical Garden. *3500 Oak Grove Rd., Loganville, 770/466–7532, www.vinesbotanicalgardens.com. Free (donations accepted). Tues.–Sat. 10–5, Sun. 11–5.*

NATURE PRESERVES

5 f-2
AUTREY MILL NATURE PRESERVE

Amid several upscale golf-course communities, this 45-acre preserve is the site of wild woodlands and a century-old farm. A 1½-mi nature trail meanders along a thickly wooded hillside. A small cabin houses the Tenant Museum, which depicts the rugged life of tenant farmers in the early years of the 20th century. Educational programs are offered in a restored 1880s house. *9770 Autrey Mill Rd., off Old Alabama Rd., east of Peachtree Pkwy./GA 141, Alpharetta, 770/360–8844. Free. Grounds daily dawn–dusk, visitor center and museum Thurs.–Sun. 12:30–4:30.*

7 e-4
CASCADE SPRINGS NATURE PRESERVE

More than a century ago, the pure, bubbling waters of Cascade Springs drew some of the first residents to what is now the suburb of Cascade Heights. Managed by the Outdoor Activity Center, the 120-acre preserve protects the spring waters and a small tract of forest. A network of trails is being developed. Hours vary; call ahead. *2852 Cascade Rd., east of I–285, Cascade Heights, 404/752–5385. Free. Dawn–dusk.*

5 b-3
CHATTAHOOCHEE NATURE CENTER

More than 2 mi of foot trails crisscross the wooded hillsides and marshes of this 100-acre preserve along the Chattahoochee. Since its founding in 1976, the center has become a leader in environmental education; two appealing programs are the Camp Kingfisher summer camp for children ages 5–12 and the summer-evening canoe floats on the Chattahoochee. The center has an active wildlife-rehab program and permanently houses rescued hawks, eagles, and other birds of prey that have been injured too severely to survive in the wilds. The Discovery Center has interactive displays of indigenous wildlife, taxidermic specimens, live fish, turtles, and snakes. The gift shop is impressive, with a good selection of educational toys for kids, and wildlife-theme items for adults. *9135 Willeo Rd., south of GA 120, Roswell, 770/992–2055, www.chattnaturecenter.com. Adults $3, senior citizens and children (3–12) $2, children under 3 and members free. Mon.–Sat. 9–5, Sun. noon–5.*

1 b-5
CLINTON NATURE PRESERVE

Spread over 200 acres of woods and meadows, the preserve includes a small lake for fishing, more than 5 mi of marked hiking and horse trails, a ½-mi walking track, and an amphitheater for outdoor education programs. Still on its original site is a log cabin built by the pioneer Carnes family in 1828. A three-room farmhouse built by the family in the early 20th century is now a museum, with furniture typical of the period. *Ephesus Church Rd., off Post Rd., south of I–20, Douglasville, 770/459–1849. Free. Thurs.–Tues. 9 AM–dusk.*

1 *c-7*

COCHRAN MILL NATURE PRESERVE

The thick woods of this 50-acre preserve at Cochran Mill Park wander to the banks of Bear and Little Bear creeks and past the ruins of some 19th-century mill dams. There are trails through the woods, plus a ropes course. A visitor center houses natural-history exhibits and classrooms; injured wildlife are treated in an adjacent rehabilitation facility. *6785 Cochran Mill Rd., west of South Fulton Pkwy. and Rivertown Rd., north of Palmetto, 770/306–0914. Free (donations accepted); fee for ropes course. Apr.–Oct., Mon.–Sat. 9–5, Sun. 1–5; call for winter hrs.*

8 *g-5*

DAVIDSON–ARABIA MOUNTAIN NATURE PRESERVE

Hidden away in a rural part of southeastern DeKalb County, this large preserve, designated a National Heritage Area, is a fascinating mix of forest and open rock. It's home to two endangered primitive plant species and a mix of colorful and unusual native plants and birds. Park staffers conduct guided hikes to the peak of the 140-ft-high mountain and offer a variety of outdoor educational programs. *3850 Klondike Rd., south of I–20, Lithonia, 770/484–3060. Free. Daily 7 AM–dusk.*

14 *d-3*

FERNBANK FOREST

During a 1949 visit to this natural treasure 6 mi east of downtown Atlanta, naturalist Charles Russell of the American Museum of Natural History called it a showpiece that no other American city can match. Purchased by Col. Zador Harrison in 1881, this piece of virgin forest was zealously protected by his daughter Miss Emily Harrison for more than five decades. She even bought out her siblings' interest in the property to prevent its subdivision, and she lived to see it donated to DeKalb County. Behind the Fernbank Science Center, the forest is accessible by a well-marked 1½-mi trail that winds beneath a thick canopy of pines and hardwood trees. *156*

Heaton Park Dr., off Ponce de Leon Ave., Druid Hills, 404/370–0960. Free. Sun.–Fri. 2–5, Sat. 10–5.

7 *e-4*

OUTDOOR ACTIVITY CENTER

Called Atlanta's Forest in the City, the Outdoor Activity Center preserves a slice of wilderness on the slopes of Bush Mountain, a few miles southwest of downtown. From the visitor center, 2 mi of foot trails trace a loop through 26 acres of mountain ridges, creek valleys, and towering hardwoods. Many of the center's environmental education programs reach out to children from Atlanta's inner-city schools and neighborhoods. *1442 Richland Rd., east of Cascade Rd., West End, 404/752–5385. Free. Mon.–Sat. 9–4.*

8 *e-6*

PANOLA MOUNTAIN STATE CONSERVATION PARK

More than 600 rolling acres of forest surround the exposed rock of rugged Panola Mountain, a Registered Natural Landmark. The mountain is a 125-ft-high outcrop of granite similar to Stone Mountain, but this park hasn't been commercially exploited and its fragile environment is carefully protected; several rare plants grow within its boundaries. The 3½-mi trail to the top of the mountain is open only for naturalist-guided hikes, but access to three other trails is unrestricted. *2600 Snapfinger Rd./GA 155, south of I–20 at Wesley Chapel Rd., near Stockbridge, 770/389–7801. Free; parking $2. Daily 7 AM–dusk; interpretive center Tues.–Fri. 9–5, weekends noon–5.*

10 *e-4*

RED TAIL HAWK NATURE PRESERVE

The heavily wooded park preserves an undisturbed forest of pines and hardwoods that is home to wildlife and various bird species. The park has a nature trail, a wildlife observation area, and a Boy Scout–Girl Scout campsite. *143 Henry Pkwy., McDonough, 770/954–2031. Free. Daily dawn–dusk.*

8 *a-7*

REYNOLDS NATURE PRESERVE

Before the Civil War, this 146-acre forest preserve was farmland. In the 1920s it was acquired by Judge William Reynolds, who spent years turning it into a botanical wonderland, searching

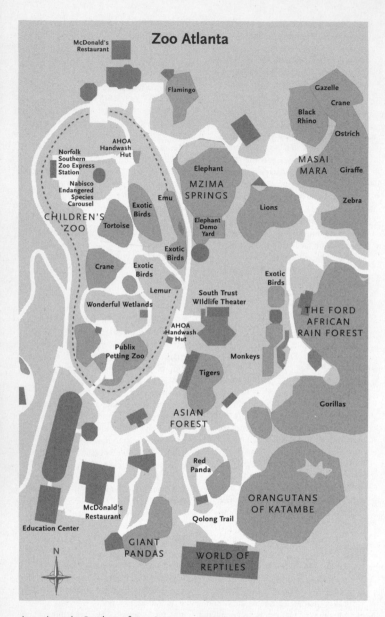

Zoo Atlanta

McDonald's Restaurant

Flamingo

Gazelle

Crane

Black Rhino

Ostrich

AHOA Handwash Hut

Norfolk Southern Zoo Express Station

Nabisco Endangered Species Carousel

CHILDREN'S ZOO

Tortoise

Emu

Elephant

MZIMA SPRINGS

Exotic Birds

Elephant Demo Yard

MASAI MARA

Giraffe

Lions

Zebra

Crane

Exotic Birds

Exotic Birds

Lemur

Wonderful Wetlands

South Trust Wildlife Theater

Exotic Birds

AHOA Handwash Hut

THE FORD AFRICAN RAIN FOREST

Publix Petting Zoo

Monkeys

Tigers

Gorillas

ASIAN FOREST

Red Panda

McDonald's Restaurant

Qolong Trail

ORANGUTANS OF KATAMBE

Education Center

GIANT PANDAS

WORLD OF REPTILES

N

throughout the Southeast for native azaleas to plant in his recovering forest. Shortly before his death in 1976, Reynolds donated the land to Clayton County as a permanent woodland preserve, where all can stroll along 4 mi of forest trails, picnic by tranquil ponds, and observe white-tail deer, raccoons, beavers, land birds, and waterfowl in their natural habitat. *5665 Reynolds Rd., near GA 54, Morrow, 770/603–4188. Free. Daily 8:30 AM–dusk, interpretive center weekdays 8:30–5:30.*

9 *h-3*

NEWMAN WETLANDS CENTER

Operated by the Clayton County Water Authority, the 32-acre park has a ½-mi-long boardwalk over a marsh and an active education program. The preserve is especially popular with birding enthusiasts seeking waterfowl and other species on their annual migrations. *2755 Freeman Rd., Hampton, 770/603–5606, www.ccwal.com. Free. Trail daily 8:30–5.*

Interpretive center Nov.–Feb., weekdays 8:30–5; Mar.–Oct., Mon.–Sat. 8:30–5.

8 g-1

YELLOW RIVER REGIONAL PARK

A short distance east of Georgia's Stone Mountain Park, Yellow River Regional Park is a woodland preserve that follows the meandering course of its namesake river. The 564-acre park has a rich variety of plants and wildlife in a mixed forest of pine and hardwood trees. Well-maintained trails are open to hikers, joggers, mountain bikers, and equestrians. *3232 Juhan Rd., off Rockbridge Rd., Stone Mountain, 770/978–5270. Free. Daily dawn–dusk.*

WATER PARKS

9 h-1

CLAYTON COUNTY INTERNATIONAL PARK

At this park you can swim in a lake bordered by water slides or watch the youngsters frolic in a children's pool with whimsical water slides. Attractions also include miniature golf ($2 per person), volleyball, and a sand soccer court. *Off GA 138, west of I–75 and east of Crane Rd., Jonesboro, 770/473–4005. Beach, adults $6–$8, children under 2 free; parking $2–$5. Late May–early Sept., daily 10–6 (beach and water park).*

3 g-5

LAKE LANIER ISLANDS RESORT WATER PARK

Even when the surface of the lake is smooth and calm, this wilder side of the Lake Lanier Islands beach and water-park complex has more than a dozen water slides to make sure your day is full of splashes and pulsing action. The Fun Dunker is a multilevel, interactive ride designed to get you wet in more than 100 ways, and Wild Waves—Georgia's largest wave pool—pounds near the beach. Young swimmers have their own Kiddie Lagoon and Wiggle Waves. The fee admits you to both the water park and the beach area; two-day passes are available. *6950 Holiday Rd., west of I–985, south of Gainesville, 770/932–7000, www. lakelanierislands.com. $27–$38, children 2 and under free. Memorial Day–Labor Day, Mon.–Thurs. 10–6, Fri.–Sun. 10–7; rest of May, weekends 10–6.*

4 g-4

WHITE WATER ATLANTA

The South's largest water park has more than 50 water attractions to beat the summer heat. Test your nerves on the Cliffhanger's 90-ft free fall, challenge the rapids on the Run-a-Way River, or body-surf in the Atlanta Ocean. When you're ready to relax, soak up some rays on Tree-house Island and then float on a raft while watching an evening movie. The season usually runs from May to Labor Day; call for schedules and information on season passes, including joint plans

---

AMAZING ANIMALS

In addition to being an entertaining place, Zoo Atlanta has become a triumphant example of civic cooperation and a leader in wildlife conservation efforts, especially in breeding at-risk species. Much of its success lies in the natural habitats it has created:

Ford African Rainforest
This is home for a family group of silverback gorillas, including Willie B. Jr. and other offspring of the beloved Willie B. Named for former Atlanta mayor William B. Harts-field, Willie B. came to the zoo in 1961, lived here until his death in 2000, and became a symbol of the zoo's climb upward.

Giant Pandas of Chengdu
When the two Chinese pandas Lun-Lun and Yang-Yang arrived in 1999, they quickly won Atlanta's heart, and they've adapted well to this surround resembling their native territory.

Masai Mara
Lions, rhinos, giraffes, ostriches, and zebras can feel almost free in Masai Mara, modeled after the African savanna.

Monkeys of Makoku
Drill baboons and mona monkeys frolic together here.

Mzima Springs
The elephants amble to their water holes here just as their ancestors likely did in the sub-Sahara regions.

Orangutans of Ketambe
These captivating primates endear themselves to visitors.

Sumatran Tiger Forest
Regal Sumatran tigers lounge and play in the shade of the trees.

with SixFlags Over Georgia and the American Adventures theme park for kids. *250 Cobb Pkwy., near I–75 exit 265, Marietta, 770/424–9283, www.whitewaterpark.com. Adults $29, senior citizens and children (under 48″) $19. Memorial Day–Labor Day, Mon.–Thurs. 10–6, Fri.–Sun. 10–7.*

ZOOS

`15` *g-8*

ZOO ATLANTA

More than 1,000 animals live in natural settings in Zoo Atlanta, which has become one of the finest such facilities in the United States and enjoys tremendous public and corporate success. Much of this is thanks to Dr. Terry Maple, who in the early 1980s was brought in to rescue the complex after the death of one of the zoo's elephants finally ignited the public's passion to revive it. Kids can see the animals up close and the Publix Petting Zoo or thrill to carousel and train rides. The zoo offers a variety of educational programs and children's camps, too. *800 Cherokee Ave., south of I–20, adjacent to Atlanta Cyclorama, Grant Park, 404/624–5600; 404/624–5822 educational programs and children's camps, www.zooatlanta.org. Adults $16, senior citizens $12, children ages 3–11 $11. Weekdays 9:30–4:30, weekends 9:30–5:30. MARTA: King Center.*

stadiums

Atlanta has three major sporting venues for pro football, baseball, basketball, and ice-hockey games or track-and-field competitions, circuses, and concerts. Event tickets are available from team box offices, event sponsors, or **Ticketmaster** (404/249–6400 or 800/326–4000, www.ticketmaster.com).

`15` *d-6*

GEORGIA DOME

A Teflon roof allows sunlight to penetrate this 71,500-seat enclosed stadium, the largest cable-supported domed stadium in the world and home to the National Football League's Atlanta Falcons. The Southeastern Conference college football championship, the annual Heritage Bowl, and the Peach Bowl games also take place here, and the dome periodically hosts the NFL Super Bowl and the NCAA's (National Collegiate Athletic Association's) regional and Final Four basketball tournaments. Part of the Georgia World Congress Center complex, along with Philips Arena, the Dome is easily reached by the adjacent MARTA station. Guided tours are given Tuesday–Saturday 10–4 and Sunday noon–4, except on game days. *One Georgia Dome Dr., off International Blvd., south of the Georgia World Congress Center, Downtown, 404/223–9200, www.gwcc.com/dome/dome.htm. MARTA: Vine City and Omni/Dome/GWCC.*

`15` *d-6*

PHILIPS ARENA

On the site of the old Omni Coliseum, Philips Arena opened in 1999 and is home to both the National Basketball Association's Atlanta Hawks (404/827–3865) and the National Hockey League's Atlanta Thrashers (404/584–7825). The arena seats 15,179 for hockey, 16,378 for basketball, and up to 17,000 for concerts. Hawk Walk, an enclosed pedestrian boulevard lined with shops and restaurants, connects the arena with the adjacent CNN Center. *1 Philips Dr., off Techwood Dr., Downtown, 404/878–3000 arena info, www.philipsarena.com. MARTA: Omni/Dome/GWCC.*

WHERE THE PROS PLAY

Atlanta fields competitive teams in nearly all major professional sports:

Atlanta Braves (Baseball)
The perennial National League leaders play their home games at Turner Field.

Atlanta Falcons (Football)
This often-maligned team has put its fans through an emotional roller-coaster ride, cresting with an appearance in the 1999 Super Bowl. The Falcons are at home in the Georgia Dome.

Atlanta Hawks (Basketball)
Always competitive, the Hawks light up the scoreboard at Philips Arena.

Atlanta Silverbacks (Soccer)
A small but loyal following roots for the United Soccer League team at DeKalb Memorial Stadium.

Atlanta Thrashers (Hockey)
The Thrashers carve the ice at Philips Arena for the NHL.

Philips Arena

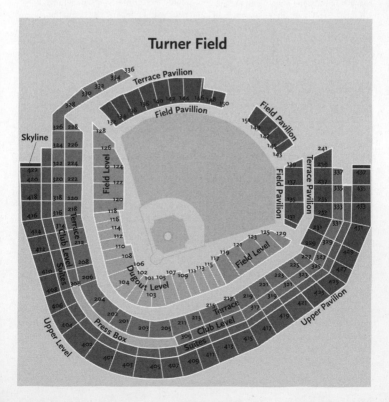

Turner Field

15 *e-8*

TURNER FIELD

Built for the 1996 Olympics as an 80,000-seat track-and-field venue, the facility was later reconfigured into the present 46,000-seat baseball stadium. The postmodern structure is home to the Atlanta Braves of Major League Baseball's National League and is named for team owner and media mogul Ted Turner. (The stadium is nicknamed "The Ted.") Turner Field is an attraction in itself: you can test your pitching and hitting skills in Scouts Alley, or view an assortment of sports-related artwork and see memorabilia—like the bat Hank Aaron swung when he hit his history-making 715th home run—in the Ivan Allen Jr. Braves Museum and Hall of Fame, named for the mayor who brought the Braves to Atlanta in 1966. During ball games, fans flock to Coca-Cola Sky Field, above the left-field stands, hoping to win $1 million by catching the first home run ever to be hit there; since the stadium's opening in 1997, no player has come close. Tours ($7) are given daily, except when day games are scheduled, and include visits to the locker rooms, press box, and museum. *755 Hank Aaron Dr., adjacent to I-85 and I-20, Grant Park, 404/522-7630 tickets; 404/614-2311 tours, www.atlantabraves.com. MARTA: Georgia State.*

sports & outdoor activities

The winds on Lanier and Allatoona don't create the kinds of waves that make for surfing, and you might get in a short sled run only a couple of times a decade, but Atlanta is generally sports-happy and sports-savvy. Go fly a kite, if that will lift your spirits. But if you prefer flyers on the wing to those on a string, you'll see that the woodlands and marshes are appealing to home-born birds and to the northern visitors who drop in during their spring and fall journeys. If your bent is toward more robust activities, you can be part of the cheering crowds at pro-sports events of many types and discover all manner of facilities where you can run, ride, row, climb, swim, hike, and hit. If you can't immediately find exactly what you want, keep

trying: someone is bound to know someone who can hook you up with just the place or group you seek.

The free monthly magazine **Atlanta Sports and Fitness** (404/843-2257, www.atlantasportsmag.com) lists all kinds of amateur sports leagues and events. The magazine is available at sporting-goods stores, fitness centers, bookstores, and other outlets around the city. The following outdoor-equipment retailers offer clinics, lessons, or guided adventures for a variety of sports and activities: **Galyan's** (404/267-0200 Buckhead; 770/281-0200 Kennesaw; 678/482-1200 Mall of Georgia, www.galyans.com), **High Country Outfitters** (404/814-0999, www.highcountryoutfitters.com), and **REI, Inc.** (404/633-6508 North Atlanta; 770/901-9200 Perimeter; www.rei.com).

ARCHERY

Local archery clubs host adult and junior competitions at fields around Atlanta, and many teach bow-hunting techniques as well as target-shooting. Archery courses are also sometimes offered in summer youth programs; check with county or city recreation departments.

FAYETTE ARCHERY ASSOCIATION
295 Old Farm Rd., Fayetteville, 770/460-0513.

GWINNETT ARCHERY ASSOCIATION
770/513-3646.

KENNESAW ARCHERY CLUB
770/640-5576.

AUTOMOBILE RACING

Auto racing in the South may have sprung from moonshiners' souping up their cars to stay a few wheel-turns ahead of the "revenooers," but it is a big business now. Nationally, it's been one of the fastest-growing sports in terms of attendance, and the Atlanta metro area has a couple of sophisticated tracks. If you've always wanted to play Paul Newman and climb into a car yourself, the tracks also offer driving schools.

9 *h-6*

ATLANTA MOTOR SPEEDWAY

A major stop on the NASCAR circuit, this 1.54-mi track has grandstand seating for 124,000 and packs in thousands more who camp in the infield or on outside lots for big race weekends. The late Dale Earnhardt set the track record at 163.633 mph in 1995. Major events include the Atlanta 500 and Napa 500 in the Winston Cup Series and the 312 in the NASCAR Busch Series. Tickets, available at the track, at retail outlets, or through Ticketmaster (404/249–6400, www.ticketmaster.com), range from $10 to $105, depending on the race. *1500 Hwy. 19/41 S, off Richard Petty Blvd., Hampton, 770/946–4211, www.atlantamotorspeedway.com.*

1 *h-2*

LANIER NATIONAL SPEEDWAY

Georgia's only sanctioned asphalt short track, this ⅜-mi oval has a busy and varied schedule that includes ministocks, truck events, and the Budweiser Pro Late-Model races. *GA 53, between I–985 and I–85, Braselton, 770/967–8600, www.lanierspeedway.com.*

1 *h-2*

ROAD ATLANTA

Many road-racing fans like to follow the European tradition of watching from lawn chairs or blankets around this 2.54-mi, 12-turn road circuit. Road Atlanta has motorcycle races and sleek open-cockpit sports-car races. Gates usually open at 7 AM the first day of big auto-race weekends and remain open until the racing is done. Driving and motor-biking instruction is offered here. *GA 53, between I–985 and I–85, Braselton, 770/967–6143 or 800/849–7243, www.roadatlanta.com.*

BASEBALL & SOFTBALL

teams to watch

ATLANTA BRAVES

Since the miraculous "worst-to-first" 1991 season that propelled the Braves into their first World Series since 1958 (back when they were the Milwaukee Braves), this team has become a perennial contender for the National League championship. It holds the record for 10 straight division titles and has played in five World Series (1991, 1992, 1995, 1996, and 1999), defeating the Cleveland Indians in 1995 to claim Atlanta's first major professional sports championship. The Braves play home games at Turner Field from April to October. Tickets are available through the stadium box office or Ticketmaster. A small number of Skyline seats go on sale for $1 three hours before each game. Braves shuttle buses run from the Five Points Marta station to the field from one hour before the game to one hour after. *404/522–7630 box office; 404/249–6400 Ticketmaster.*

GEORGIA STATE UNIVERSITY PANTHERS

The GSU Panthers play in the Atlantic Sun competition each May. Tickets are available by phone or at the GSU Athletic Department at University Plaza on the Georgia State campus. *Panthersville Stadium, 2817 Clifton Springs Rd., near Panthersville Rd., off I–20 exit 33, Panthersville, 404/651–2772, www.georgiastate.com/athletics/baseball.*

GEORGIA TECH YELLOW JACKETS

A frequent NCAA Division I national championship contender, Tech plays in the power-packed Atlantic Coast Conference each May. Games against rivals Florida State, Clemson, and Georgia frequently sell out. *Russ Chandler Stadium, 5th and Fowler Sts., Midtown, 404/894–5447. MARTA: Midtown.*

city- & county-sponsored softball leagues

Many local parks have softball fields with organized adult leagues in spring and summer. The parks listed here have especially good facilities. More information about adult softball leagues may be available from the **City of Atlanta Department of Parks, Recreation, and Cultural Affairs** (404/817–6752), the county parks department, and the individual parks.

4 *e-6*

AL BISHOP PARK

1082 Al Bishop Dr., off Powder Springs and Callaway Rds., south of Kennesaw Mountain National Battlefield Park, Kennesaw, 770/528–8860.

3 *a-8*

HOBGOOD PARK
6688 Bells Ferry Rd., Woodstock, 770/924–7768.

8 *c-5*

TRUELOVE SOFTBALL COMPLEX
3510 Oakvale Rd., Decatur, 404/371–2631.

private softball leagues

ATLANTA CLUB SPORT
The group arranges play for a number of coed teams. Annual membership is $35. *404/257–3355, www.usclubsport.com.*

ATLANTA SOUTHSIDE MEN'S SENIOR BASEBALL LEAGUE
Teams in this league are generally for men ages 30 and up. *770/487–5337.*

ATLANTA SPORT & SOCIAL CLUB
This organization sponsors several leagues and includes coed teams. *404/262–7655.*

MEN'S ADULT BASEBALL LEAGUE
Guys who cling to their diamond dreams can play in the Men's Adult Baseball League or in other privately organized groups. MABL teams compete in four age divisions, from 18 and up. Tryouts are held to match players of comparable age and ability. The 25-game season is played at local high-school and college fields from April to September. Players must furnish their own equipment and pay dues. *404/250–8075 information; 770/527–0083 league office, www.atlantamsbl.com/mabl.*

METRO ATLANTA WOMEN'S SUMMER BASEBALL LEAGUE
An NCAA-approved summer league, the group usually plays its games at Atlanta's Ben Hill Park Recreation Center (2505 Fairburn Road) from mid-June to early August. *404/752–5551.*

BASKETBALL

teams to watch

ATLANTA HAWKS
The Hawks compete in the NBA's Central Division, against such rivals as the Indiana Pacers and the Chicago Bulls. Tickets are available from the Hawks box office, from Ticketmaster, or at retail outlets. *Philips Arena, Techwood Dr., south of Marietta St., Downtown, 404/827–3865 box office; 404/249–6400 Ticketmaster, www.nba.com/hawks. MARTA: Omni/Dome/GWCC.*

GEORGIA STATE UNIVERSITY PANTHERS
The Panthers' men's and women's teams play in the Atlantic Sun Conference each May. Tickets are available by phone or at the GSU Athletic Department at University Plaza, adjacent to the arena. *GSU Sports Arena, Piedmont Ave., at Decatur St., Downtown, 404/651–3166. MARTA: Georgia State.*

GEORGIA TECH YELLOW JACKETS
Tech's men's and women's teams compete in the tough Atlantic Coast Conference. Tickets to men's games frequently sell out, but tickets to women's games are more readily available and less expensive. *Alexander Coliseum, MacDonald's Center, 10th and Fowler Sts., off I-75/I-85, Downtown, 404/894–5447. MARTA: Midtown.*

where to play
County parks departments can provide information on basketball leagues that play at many of the county recreation centers. Pickup games abound both at public gyms and at numerous outdoor courts. The following courts are especially popular.

15 *f-4*

BEDFORD–PINE PARK
White-collar professionals and in-town residents play pickup games at the courts at this inner-city public park. Some of the play is highly competitive, but most players can find a group that fits their skills. *Bedford Pl., between Angier and Linden Aves., Midtown. MARTA: North Ave. or Civic Center.*

5 *c-5*

HAMMOND PARK
This Fulton County park hosts league play on indoor courts and on two lighted outdoor courts. Evenings and weekends, the "trash talk" at the very competitive pickup games may be too strong for children. *705 Hammond Dr., at Glenridge Dr., Sandy Springs, 404/303–6176.*

7 *g-4*

RUN N' SHOOT ATHLETIC CENTER

Ranked by Hoops Nation Tour as one of the best pickup basketball courts in the United States, this private facility offers open play on seven indoor courts. Most participants take the game very seriously, and you may find yourself lining up against a few current and former NBA players (especially in summer). *1959 Metropolitan Pkwy., north of Langford Pkwy./GA 166, Southwest Atlanta, 404/767–7125, www.runnshoot.com.*

BICYCLING

Atlanta's high volume of automobile traffic and lack of bicycle lanes means that the city proper isn't the most bike-friendly of communities. But the area's combination of rolling hills, abundant trees, and scenic and historic neighborhoods can make for enjoyable riding. Several area biking clubs sponsor bike trips and competitions. *Atlanta Walks* (Peachtree Publishers, $14.95), available in bookstores, has information on biking routes in and around the city.

The advocacy group **Atlanta Bicycle Campaign** is one of the many local organizations dedicated to promoting pedal-powered transportation. ABC conducts Effective Cycling classes ($20) to teach bicyclists how to ride safely in the city and sponsors other awareness-raising events. Its annual Bike to Work Day has even Atlanta's mayor pedaling to City Hall. *404/881–1112, www.atlantabike.org.*

bicycling clubs

FULTON FLYERS
www.fultonflyers.org.

GEORGIA BICYCLE FEDERATION
770/422–4840, www.bicyclegeorgia.com.

HENRY COUNTY BMX ASSOCIATION
770/954–2031.

METRO ATLANTA CYCLING CLUB
www.macattack.org.

SOUTHERN BICYCLE LEAGUE
770/594–8350, www.bikesbl.org.

SOUTHERN OFF-ROAD BICYCLING ASSOCIATION
770/216–9745, www.sorba.org.

where to ride

Many bicycling clubs recommend specific trails or sites on their Web sites, as do the state site georgiatrails.com and the Regional Transportation Authority site, www.grta.org. For weekend or weeklong rides, see the Bicycle Rides Across Georgia site (www.brag.org). Off-road biking is restricted or not permitted at many parks and at Lake Allatoona. The Web sites www.clubmtb.org and www.trailexpress.com offer some suggestions for off-road biking.

1 *d-6*

ATLANTA/DEKALB TRAIL

Still in the early stages of development, the Atlanta/DeKalb Trail is envisioned as a 124-mi series of biking-walking paths from Greenbrier Mall to Stone Mountain Park that splinters into several pathways around downtown landmarks and neighborhoods. Small segments are now in place, linking existing streets and sidewalks along the route to extend exploring options. The PATH Foundation, set up specifically with the goal of building greenway trails throughout the metro area, oversees the project. *404/875–7284 PATH, www.pathfoundation.org.*

5 *a-5*

BLANKETS CREEK TRAIL

Mountain bikers often recommend this 7-mi trail in Woodstock. If the gate is closed, the trail is closed. *Off Aixes Rd., about 1¾ mi from I–575 exit 11, Woodstock, no phone.*

5 *a-5*

CHATTAHOOCHEE RIVER NATIONAL RECREATION AREA

A bike trail from the Cochran Shoals Fitness Trail connects with the adjacent Sope Creek section of the recreation area. Thick woods can make the going rough in some areas. The trail is open daily 7–7 and until dusk in summer. Parking is $2; annual passes are available. *Cochran Shoals entrance: Interstate North Pkwy., off I–285 at New Northside Dr., between Northwest Atlanta and Marietta; Sope Creek entrance: Paper Mill Rd., off Johnson Ferry Rd., between Marietta and Mount Bethel; 770/952–4419.*

9 *h-1*

CLAYTON COUNTY INTERNATIONAL PARK

The 8 mi of trails at the Beach, a water-park complex, are maintained by the Southside Mountain Bike Association. Trails are color-coded for beginner, intermediate, and advanced levels and include pathways beside a lake and through wooded areas. The Beach is open daily 8–8 from late May to early September; admission is $8 for adults, $6 for senior citizens and children ages 3–12, and free for children two and younger. Clayton residents can buy a season pass ($35–$44) and an annual parking pass ($20). Parking without a pass is $2–$5. *Off GA 138, west of I–75 and east of Crane Rd., Jonesboro, 770/473–5425.*

7 *f-5*

DICK LANE VELODROME

Atlanta's only permanent bicycle track, the velodrome in Sumner Park is operated by the Fulton Flyers Cycling Club. In addition to local and regional competitions for teams and individuals, the club offers classes and club races. *Lexington Ave., at Neely St., East Point, 877/835–7200, ext. 178, www.dicklanevelodrome.com.*

1 *g-6*

GEORGIA INTERNATIONAL HORSE PARK

Besides hosting equestrian events at the Olympics in 1996, this park was the site of the first Olympic mountain-biking competition, which left a legacy of some challenging biking trails. Bikers must register at the International Saddlery (770/929–8832). Trails are open Tuesday through Saturday 10–6 and Sunday 11–3. There is a $5 riding fee. *1996 Centennial Olympic Pkwy., off GA 138, Conyers, 770/602–2606.*

8 *f-1*

GEORGIA'S STONE MOUNTAIN PARK

Miles of lightly traveled roads meander through this 3,200-acre park. It's open daily 6 AM to midnight. Admission is free if you ride your bike into the park; otherwise, you must pay a daily parking fee of $7 per vehicle. *Off U.S. 78, about 7½ mi east of I–285 (East Gate entered from U.S. 78, West Gate from Memorial Dr.), Stone Mountain, 770/498–5690, www.stonemountainpark.com.*

9 *b-6, b-7*

PEACHTREE CITY

Nearly 70 mi of paved recreational paths make this planned community about 25 mi southwest of downtown Atlanta a bicyclist's dream. Visitors may access the trail system at recreation and shopping areas; just park and start riding. *Off GA 74, about 12 mi south of I–85, Peachtree City.*

3 *d-4*

RAMPAGE EXTREME SPORTS

If you're ready for some daredevil action, this extreme-sports complex has facilities for BMX stunt riding as well as for skateboarding and in-line skating. *3775 Peachtree Crest Dr., east of Peachtree Industrial Blvd., 3 mi north of GA 20, Duluth, 678/417–8700, www.rampageextremesports.com.*

4 *g-8*

SILVER COMET TRAIL

Modeled like Rails-to-Trails programs in other states, this trail is being developed by the PATH Foundation and can be used by bicyclists, joggers, and walkers. About 37 mi of the planned 57-mi route had been completed at the end of 2001. Eventually it is to run from near the Mount Paran Road–Northside Drive intersection to the Alabama state line and connect there with an Alabama trail. You can find a map of the trail, indicating the 14 open trailheads in Cobb, Paulding, and Polk counties, at www.trailexpress.com. The trail is open dawn to dusk. *Mavell Road trailhead: Mavell Rd., off Cooper Lake Rd., west of S. Cobb Dr., west of Gilmore, 404/875–7284 PATH, www.pathfoundation.org.*

8 *g-1*

YELLOW RIVER REGIONAL PARK

Primarily a nature preserve, this 564-acre park has trails for mountain bikers, hikers, joggers, and equestrians. The park is open daily from dawn to dusk. *3232 Juhan Rd., off Rockbridge Rd., Stone Mountain, 770/978–5270.*

BILLIARDS

You can take up your cue at a neighborhood hall or a sophisticated billiard parlor. Check with the hall for age rules. If you're a serious player, call **Atlanta Pool**

Leagues (404/255–4090) for information on local leagues affiliated with the American Poolplayers Association. The **Billiards Congress of America** (www.atlanta-bca.com) has a directory of leagues on its Web site. The **United States Billiards Association** (www.uscarom.org) lists local billiard rooms on-line. The extensive site also covers rules, history, and pointers, and lists tournament dates.

12 *e-5*

BARLEY'S BILLIARDS DOWNTOWN

The 32 Brunswick tables at Barley's are surrounded by an elegant atmosphere. *338 Peachtree St., Downtown, 404/522–2522, barleysatlanta.com. MARTA: Civic Center or Peachtree Center.*

9 *d-4*

CLASSIC CUE

Families are welcome at this parlor with 18 Gandy tables. Rates are discounted 30% before 6 PM on weekdays. Food and drink are available. *200 Glynn St., Fayetteville, 770/461–2496.*

5 *b-6*

CORNER POCKET

With 18 Gandy tables, a snooker table, and three dart lanes, this parlor is for serious players. It has a 15-table restaurant, a full bar, and live music on weekends. *4920 Roswell Rd., Sandy Springs, 404/255–6002.*

5 *e-6*

MR. CUE'S BILLIARDS

One of Atlanta's largest billiard parlors, Mr. Cue's has 35 Gandy tables, as well as a snooker and a three-cushion table. Light food service is available. If you lunch here, you play free until 2 PM. *3541 Chamblee–Tucker Rd., Chamblee, 770/454–7665.*

5 *c-5*

SANDY SPRINGS BILLIARDS

The 5,000-square-ft parlor in Parkside Shopping Center caters to both novice players and experienced competitors. There are 15 billiard tables and one snooker table. *Parkside Shopping Center, 5920 Roswell Rd., Sandy Springs, 404/257–0888.*

14 *g-4*

TWAIN'S BILLIARDS & TAP

The two rooms here (smoking and no-smoking) have more than 20 Brunswick tables, plus a full bar with a range of microbrews. The parlor is open from afternoon to early morning. *211 E. Trinity Pl., Decatur, 404/373–0063.*

5 *g-7*

WORLD CUP BILLIARDS

During its first year of operation, the parlor hosted a tournament of the 2000 Carom Tour of the United States Billiards Association and a few months later was the site of the group's 2001 three-cushion national championship. The place has four Verhoven tables and six smaller ones. *4308 Chamblee-Tucker Rd., Tucker, 770/492–9319.*

BIRD-WATCHING

The metropolitan area is home to more than 100 species of birds, and many more pause here on annual fall and spring migrations along the Eastern Flyway. Unless otherwise noted, admission to these areas is free.

guided walks

ATLANTA AUDUBON SOCIETY

The society offers guided field trips and seasonal migration walks at a variety of locations in the 10 counties and beyond. Destinations vary depending on season, bird migrations, nesting activities, and sightings. You can find schedules in the Audubon newsletter, *Wingbars*; in local newspapers; and on the club's Web site. *770/955–4111, www.atlaudubon.org.*

GEORGIA ORNITHOLOGICAL SOCIETY

Local birders especially value the rare-bird alerts presented on the Web site of the group, which also sponsors birding trips. *770/493–8862, www.gos.org.*

popular sites

Your own backyard may draw a surprising number of resident and migratory birds, as do many parks. Serious birders also recommend the following sites.

5 *a-5 through g-3*

CHATTAHOOCHEE RIVER NATIONAL RECREATION AREA

Along the almost 50 mi of the Chattahoochee, you can see many species of birds and waterfowl, including wood ducks, herons, and several types of woodpeckers. The Cochran Shoals section is especially recommended during spring and fall migrations, when olive-sided flycatchers and Connecticut warblers have been sighted. The park is open from dawn to dusk. Parking is $2 ($25 for an annual pass). *Cochran Shoals: Interstate North Pkwy., off I–285, at New Northside Dr., Northwest Atlanta, 770/952–4419 park headquarters, www.nps.gov/chat.*

11 *f-6*

FERNBANK FOREST

The 65-acre forest has a list of 150 species of birds sighted among its old white oaks, including six types of resident woodpeckers. During migration seasons, it also appeals to many songbirds. *156 Heaton Park Dr., off Ponce de Leon Ave., Druid Hills, 404/370–0960.*

4 *e-4*

KENNESAW MOUNTAIN NATIONAL BATTLEFIELD PARK

The first Georgia location to be designated an Important Bird Area by the Audubon Society, Kennesaw Mountain is known as the best place around Atlanta for observing migrating raptors in the fall. Other seasonal guests have included such species as the cerulean warbler, normally found in New York. The park is open dawn to dusk daily. *Old U.S. 41 southwest of I–75, via Barrett Pkwy., Marietta, 770/427–4686, www.nps.gov/kemo.*

9 *h-3*

NEWMAN WETLANDS CENTER

Warblers and Louisiana waterthrushes can be seen from the center's boardwalk through the wetlands. Or you can drive along the dikes of the E. L. Huie Land Application Facility, part of the same complex, and see numerous types of waterbirds and shorebirds. *2755 Freeman Rd., Hampton, 770/603–5606, www.ccwal.com.*

BOATING

The two big lakes north of Atlanta are excellent for power-boating. Powerboats must be registered in Georgia. Fees for boat registration vary with boat length and type; the **Boating Unit of the Georgia Department of Natural Resources** (770/414–3337, www.ganet.org/dnr) can provide more information. Boating permits must be purchased by mail or in person from the **Georgia Department of Natural Resources License Unit** (2189 Northlake Pkwy., Bldg. 10, Suite 108, Tucker 30084, 770/414–3337). Applications are also available at many bait-and-tackle shops and at Kmart and Wal-Mart stores.

where to boat

5 *a-5 through g-3*

CHATTAHOOCHEE RIVER NATIONAL RECREATION AREA

Anglers who want to test their luck—or skill—in the waters of the Chattahoochee frequently use the boat ramps of the Abbots, Medlock, and Jones bridge units of the national recreation area for their put-in points. You may want to call 770/945–1466 to find out when Buford Dam will be opened before you take any kind of watercraft near it. State licenses are required for power and fishing boats. Parking is $2 a day or $25 for an annual pass. *770/952–4419, www.nps.gov/chat.*

2 *a-5*

LAKE ALLATOONA

Although the lake lies about 30 mi northwest of Atlanta, outside the 10-county metro area, powerboaters and sailors head here from the city each weekend. Surrounded by rolling hills, the 12,010-acre lake created by the Army Corps of Engineers in 1950 has become a favorite destination for anglers in search of local game fish such as bream and largemouth bass. Public facilities include more than 30 public boat ramps, 8 commercial marinas, 16 day-use areas, and 9 campgrounds (usually open April–Labor Day) at various locations between I–75 and I–575. Campground reservations also may be made through the National Recreation Reservation Service (877/444–6777, www.reserve.usa.com), a joint venture of the Corps of Engineers and the U.S. Forest Service. Many visitors access the lake via Red Top Mountain

State Park (southeast of Cartersville), which has a lodge, cabins, campgrounds, trails, and a marina. The boat-launch fee is $2, an annual pass $25. *East of I–75, between Acworth and Cartersville, 770/688–7870 or 770/382–4700; 770/386–0549 for lake conditions, www.sam.usace.army.mil/op/rec/allatoon.*

9 *a-5*
LAKE KEDRON
The small lake just north of Peachtree City appeals to anglers and canoers as well as boaters. Facilities include a public boat ramp and modest fishing docks. If you're not a Peachtree City resident, one must accompany you here. *N. Peachtree Pkwy., off GA 74, north of Peachtree City, no phone.*

1 *g-1*
LAKE SIDNEY LANIER
With more than 540 mi of shoreline, Lake Lanier offers both wide channels for boating and waterskiing and nearly endless coves for fishing. You can access the lake via several dozen entrances—at 10 commercial marinas and at more than 60 boat-launching areas in many of the 40 day-use areas and 10 campgrounds maintained by the U.S. Army Corps of Engineers or the 9 city or county parks along the shores. Information on specific locations and fees is available from the Lake Resource Manager (770/945–9531). *Between GA 400 and I–985, about 35 mi northeast of Atlanta, between Buford and Gainesville, 770/945–1467, www.sam.usace.army.mil/op/rec/lanier.*

BOWLING

The alleys listed here are only a sampling of the many that dot the metro-area map. The individual alleys can provide league information.

city of atlanta

11 *d-4*
EXPRESS LANES
1936 Piedmont Cir., Midtown, 404/874–5703.

5 *d-8*
NORTHEAST PLAZA FUN BOWL
3285 Buford Hwy., North Atlanta, 404/636–7548.

cherokee county

2 *b-8*
WOODSTOCK LANES
108 Woodpark Blvd., Woodstock, 770/926–2200.

clayton county

7 *h-7*
EMBASSY ROW LANES
5885 Old Dixie Rd., Forest Park, 404/363–6110.

cobb county

4 *e-7*
AZALEA LANES
2750 Austell Rd., Marietta, 770/435–2120.

4 *h-5*
CEDAR CREEK LANES
2749 Delk Rd., Marietta, 770/988–8813.

4 *g-5*
MARIETTA LANES
565 Cobb Pkwy., Marietta, 770/427–4696.

4 *e-3*
U.S. PLAY
775 Cobb Place Blvd., Kennesaw, 770/427–7679.

4 *g-2*
VILLAGE LANES
2692 Sandy Plains Rd., Marietta, 770/973–2695.

dekalb county

5 *e-5*
CHAMBLEE LANES
2175 Savoy Dr., Chamblee, 770/451–8605.

8 *d-1*
STONE MOUNTAIN LANES
720 Hambrick Rd., Stone Mountain, 404/296–2400.

fulton county

5 *d-2*
ROSWELL LANES
785 Old Roswell Rd., Roswell, 770/998–9437.

7 *d-8*

UNION CITY LANES
5100 Goodson Connector Rd., Union City, 770/969–0100.

gwinnett county

5 *g-6*

GWINNETT LANES—AMF
4990 Jimmy Carter Blvd., Norcross, 770/923–5080.

6 *b-5*

GWINNETT LANES—
BRUNSWICK
3835 Lawrenceville Hwy., Lawrenceville, 770/925–2000.

5 *f-4*

PEACHTREE LANES
6345 Spalding Dr., Norcross, 770/840–8200.

6 *d-7*

SNELLVILLE LANES
2350 Ronald Reagan Pkwy., Snellville, 770/972–5300.

instruction

5 *h-5*

JOE MAXEY'S BOWLING
& TROPHY SHOP
5470 Oakbrook Pkwy., Norcross, 770/458–7050.

5 *g-7*

PRO STRIKE
BOWLING SUPPLY
4365 Cowan Rd., Tucker, 770/938–6637.

BOXING

The success of heavyweight champion Evander Holyfield, an Atlanta native, has boosted the popularity of boxing in the area. Several local venues offer boxing instruction and competition, as well as time in the ring. The **Georgia Amateur Boxing Association** (404/753–8002) can suggest venues and instructors.

15 *e-4*

BIGGS MORRISON BOXING
92 Linden Ave., Midtown, 404/872–7049.
MARTA: North Ave.

5 *e-6*

DORAVILLE BOXING CLUB
3688 King Ave., Doraville, 770/457–0003.

6 *e-4*

EAGLE BOXING
& KICK-BOXING
133 S. Clayton St., Lawrenceville, 770/682–5046.

7 *g-3*

GEORGIA AMATEUR
BOXING ASSOCIATION
& HOLYFIELD ARENA
1000 Beecher St., West End, 404/753–8002. MARTA: West End.

1 *b-5*

TOTAL PACKAGE
BOXING GYM
5848 Bankhead Hwy./Hwy. 278, Douglasville, 770/489–9100.

CROQUET

Atlanta doesn't have public croquet lawns. If you yearn to play, the **Atlanta Mallet Club** (770/242–5955), a member of the U.S. Croquet Association, can point you in the right direction.

DISC GOLF

The **Atlanta Flying Disc Club** (404/351–0914, www.afdc.com) has information about disc golf in the metro area. For discs and accessories, maps to courses, and club-membership information, stop by **Identified Flying Objects** (1164 Euclid Ave., Little Five Points, 404/524–4628), operated by disc-golf hall-of-famer Patti Kunkle and her husband, John.

disc courses

Some teams compete on the playing fields of local schools. You also can check out the disc courses at the following parks. All of the courses have 18 holes, except for the course at Deer Lick Park, which has 9.

1 *b-5*

DEER LICK PARK
2105 Mack Rd., east of I–20 via GA 92, Douglasville, no phone.

6 *d-8*

LENORA PARK

4515 Lenora Church Rd., at Lee Rd., east of GA 124, Snellville, 770/237–5626.

4 *c-4*

OREGON PARK

145 Old Hamilton Rd., Marietta, no phone.

8 *f-3*

REDAN PARK

1745 Phillips Rd., Lithonia, no phone.

2 *c-5*

SEQUOYAH PARK

7000 Vaughn Rd., Alpharetta, no phone.

5 *c-2*

WILLS PARK

11915 Wills Rd., Alpharetta, 678/297–6120.

FENCING

7 *f-5*

ATLANTA FENCERS' CLUB

The club has its own 7,000-square-ft facility. *1556 Nabell Ave., west of Hwy. 29, East Point, 404/762–7666, www.atlantafencersclub.com.*

7 *h-7*

NELLYA FENCERS

A 2000 world champion came from Nellya, which has seven full-size fencing strips at its club. *4931 Phillips Dr., off Forst Pkwy., Forest Park, 404/362–0368, www.burdanusa.com.*

FISHING

The lakes and rivers around Atlanta abound with more than 20 species of game fish, from bass and bream to trout. The **Federation of Fly Fishers** (www.fedflyfishers.org) has two affiliates here, the Atlanta Fly Fishing Club and the Georgia Women Flyfishers. The federation's Web site has a wealth of information about fly fishing.

In Georgia, a state fishing permit is required for anyone over age 16. State residents may purchase one-day licenses for $3.50 or annual licenses for $9. Nonresidents can buy the one-day license, a weekly license for $7, or a seasonal license for $24. Trout anglers pay

an additional fee ($5 residents, $13 nonresidents) for a trout stamp. You can also purchase a Sportsman's License, which covers fishing, big game, and archery. The **Georgia Department of Natural Resources License Unit** (2189 Northlake Pkwy., Bldg. 10, Suite 108, Tucker, 770/414–3337, www.permit.com) issues licenses in person or by mail. If you buy a license on-line you must pay a $3 service charge. **Georgia Sports Licensing** (888/748–6887 or 800/748–6887) issues fishing licenses by mail. Permits are also available at sporting-goods and fishing-supply stores. If you fish from a powerboat, you also need a boat license; the Georgia Department of Natural Resources Web site (www.ganet.org/dnr) has complete guidelines.

outfitters, classes, & guides

Because the area has so many good fishing holes, anglers can choose from an abundance of sources for fly-fishing ties, fresh- and saltwater accessories, instruction, guides, and tips on local hot spots. The list here includes a few of them.

5 *d-1*

ATLANTA FLY FISHING OUTFITTERS

Basic and advanced lessons, including some evening classes, are offered at this store. *11060 Alpharetta Hwy., Roswell, 770/649–9866, www.atlantaflyfishing.com.*

6 *b-3*

BASS PRO SHOPS OUTDOOR WORLD

This full-service outfitter has a Sportsman's Warehouse discount outlet at this Discover Mills Mall location. The shop offers instruction and arranges fishing trips all over the world through **Xtreme Angling** (515 Trailside Court, Roswell, 888/744–8867 or 770/998—7631). *Discover Mills Mall, 5900 Sugarloaf Pkwy., off I–985, north of GA 120, Duluth, 678/847–5500, www.outdoor-world.com or www.basspro.com.*

BILL VANDERFORD'S GUIDE SERVICE

Day trips on Lake Lanier and the Chattahoochee River are offered by this guide. *770/962–1241, www.fishinglanier.com.*

12 *f-3*

FISH HAWK

The store's three-day fly-fishing school, open April through October, is in Raben County, in north Georgia. Schedules include three- and four-day programs, as well as individual hour-long lessons. *279 Buckhead Ave., Buckhead, 404/237–3473, www.thefishhawk.com.*

5 *b-3*

FLY BOX OUTFITTERS

The store, an Orvis dealer, can arrange fishing trips and offers courses and private instruction for all skill levels. *4475 Roswell Rd., Suite 1100, Marietta, 770/971–2208, www.flyboxoutfitters.com.*

FLY FISHING WEST GEORGIA & BEYOND

This guide service leads fishing trips to lakes and rivers throughout north Georgia. Instruction is available for groups and individuals of all skill levels. *No phone, www.mindspring.com/~kje.*

GLENN MORRISON'S LAKE LANIER GUIDE SERVICE

The guide takes you out on Lake Lanier for striped-bass fishing trips. *770/962–8738, www.georgiafishing.com.*

HAROLD NASH FISHING GUIDE SERVICE

Bass-fishing trips on Lake Lanier are this guide service's specialty. *770/967–6582, www.hnashfishing.com.*

1 *h-2*

LAKE LANIER OUTFITTERS

Fly-fishing lessons as well as guided bass-fishing trips on Lake Lanier are offered by this company. *4603 Fox Forest Dr., Flowery Branch, 770/764–0191, www.lakelanieroutfitters.com.*

11 *e-1*

ORVIS ATLANTA

This outpost of the well-known national chain offers some instruction. It also can help you join up with a variety of sporting vacations arranged by the headquarters store or Georgia fishing trips conducted by Fly Box Outfitters. *3255 Peachtree Rd., Buckhead, 404/841–0093, www.orvis.com.*

where to fish

Several local and county parks have small ponds and lakes ideal for family

fishing. Serious and sport fishermen focus on the three major fishing areas: Chattahoochee River, Lake Allatoona, and Lake Sidney Lanier.

5 *a-5 through g-3*

CHATTAHOOCHEE RIVER NATIONAL RECREATION AREA

Anglers test their fly-fishing skills at many areas along the swift-flowing channels of "the Hootch," habitat to several species of game fish, including bream, catfish, and brook, brown, and rainbow trout. The national recreation area's various sections offer public access to the river below Lake Lanier; anglers often use the boat ramps of the Abbots, Medlock, and Jones Bridge units. Before you take any kind of watercraft near the Buford Dam, you can find out when it will be opened by calling 770/945–1466. State licenses are required for fishing boats. *770/952–4419, www.nps.gov/chat.*

2 *a-5*

LAKE ALLATOONA

Northwest of Atlanta, the lake is a popular destination for deep-water anglers searching for trophy-size bass, bream, and trout. You have your pick of any number of boat ramps, marinas, and day-use areas. The boat-launch fee is $2. *East of I–75, between Acworth and Cartersville, 770/688–7870 or 770/382–4700, www.sam.usace.army.mil/op/rec/allatoon.*

1 *g-1*

LAKE SIDNEY LANIER

On summer weekends, this lake north of Atlanta can become so crowded with water-skiers and powerboaters that anglers may find themselves battling boat wakes and tangled lines—but there are quiet coves away from the mob. Game fish here include large- and smallmouth bass, crappie, bream, and catfish. Some day-use areas charge a fee of $3 per vehicle, which includes use of boat ramps. *Between GA 400 and I–985, about 35 mi northeast of Atlanta, between Buford and Gainesville, 770/945–9531 office; 770/945–1467 recorded information, www.sam.usace.army.mil/op/rec/lanier.*

FLYING & SOARING

If you are an experienced pilot, you might check out volunteer opportunities with **Angel Flight of Georgia** (DeKalb Peachtree Airport, off Chamblee-Tucker Rd., between New Peachtree Rd. and Buford Hwy., Chamblee, 770/452–7958, www.angelflight-ga.org), which offers medical transport for patients in need.

You have to venture out of the city to find good currents for ultralight flight, but these clubs are nearby: **Atlanta Ultralights** (Cartersville–Bartow County Airport, 770/315–6244 or 770/331–5044, www.atlantaultralights.com), **East Atlanta Flyers** (Monroe–Walton County Airport, 770/339–8394), and **Georgia Sport Flyers Association** (3764 Halyard Ct., Acworth 30102, no phone, www. georgiasportflyers.com).

airports

1 *b-2*

CARTERSVILLE–BARTOW COUNTY AIRPORT

Hwy. 61, Cartersville, 770/382–9800.

4 *e-2*

COBB COUNTY AIRPORT–MCCOLLUM FIELD

1723 McCollum Pkwy., Kennesaw, 770/422–4300.

5 *e-6*

DEKALB PEACHTREE AIRPORT

2000 Airport Rd., off Chamblee-Tucker Rd., between New Peachtree Rd. and Buford Hwy., Chamblee, 770/936–5440.

7 *d-2*

FULTON COUNTY AIRPORT–BROWN FIELD

3952 Aviation Cir., Carol Heights, 404/699–4200.

MONROE–WALTON COUNTY AIRPORT

227 S. Broad St., Monroe, 770/267–2343.

1 *b-8*

NEWNAN COWETA COUNTY AIRPORT

115 Airport Rd., near Hwy. 29, Newnan, 770/254–8102.

clubs & schools

Most of the organizations listed here offer instruction and rental planes. Some are clubs as well, and some also give aerial tours. Contact the clubs or schools for fees, schedules, and specifics.

4 *e-2*

AERO ATLANTA FLYING CLUB

Cobb County Airport–McCollum Field, 1723 McCollum Pkwy., Kennesaw, 770/422–2376.

5 *e-6*

AVIATION ATLANTA

DeKalb Peachtree Airport, 2000 Airport Rd., Chamblee, 770/458–8034, www. aviationatlanta.com.

7 *d-2*

FULTON FLIGHT SERVICE

Fulton County Airport–Brown Field, 3952 Aviation Cir., Carol Heights, 404/691–1118.

5 *e-6*

ISLAND HELICOPTERS

DeKalb Peachtree Airport, 2000 Airport Rd., Chamblee, 770/451–2066.

5 *e-6*

PDK FLIGHT ACADEMY

DeKalb Peachtree Airport, 2000 Airport Rd., Chamblee, 770/457–1270.

5 *e-6*

PRESTIGE HELICOPTERS

DeKalb Peachtree Airport, 2000 Airport Rd., Chamblee, 770/458–6047.

5 *e-6*

QUALITY AVIATION

DeKalb Peachtree Airport, 2000 Airport Rd., Chamblee, 770/457–6215.

5 *e-6*

SAFETY AIRE FLYING ASSOCIATION

DeKalb Peachtree Airport, 2000 Airport Rd., Chamblee, 770/457–6740.

1 *b-8*

SKY'S AIRCRAFT CORPORATION

Newnan Coweta County Airport, 115 Airport Rd., near Hwy. 29, Newnan, 770/253–2774.

Georgia Dome

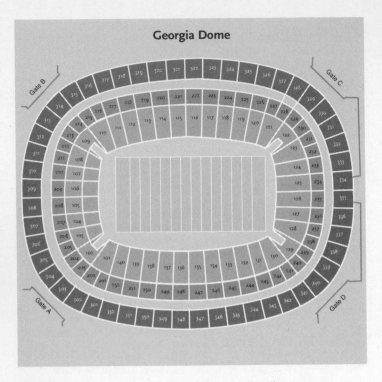

15 *d-3*

YELLOW JACKETS FLYING CLUB

Instruction and club privileges are available to Georgia Tech alumni, faculty, and students. The club meets every Tuesday when school is in session. Meeting locations vary (the Web site has details). *Georgia Tech, 10th and Fowler Sts., off I-75/I-85, Midtown, no phone, www.yjfc.org. MARTA: Midtown.*

FOOTBALL

teams to watch

ATLANTA FALCONS

Atlantans finally caught Falcon Fever when the team earned its first-ever Super Bowl berth in 1998. No matter that they lost to the Denver Broncos—the fans were just happy to be there. Hope for the future is bright, and season tickets to home games are hot. Tickets are available from the box office weekdays 9–5, via the Falcons' Web site, or from Ticketmaster. *Georgia Dome, 1 Georgia Dome Dr., off International Blvd., south of the Georgia World Congress Center, Downtown, 404/223–8000 box office;* *404/249–6400 Ticketmaster, www.atlantafalcons.com. MARTA: Vine City and Omni/Dome/GWCC.*

GEORGIA TECH YELLOW JACKETS

The four-time national champions (1917, 1928, 1952, 1990) play Atlantic Coast Conference opponents and other rivals at historic 46,000-seat Bobby Dodd Stadium, the oldest stadium in NCAA Division I football. At this writing, a $63 million expansion was expected to be completed by August 2003. The work halts in fall, however, to allow games to continue. Game tickets are available at the Edge Athletic Center at the stadium or by phone. Home games against the University of Georgia Bulldogs are always sold out, and seats are available only to season ticket holders. *Bobby Dodd Stadium, Grant Field, 220 Bobby Dodd Way, at Ferst St., Midtown, 888/832–4849, ramblinwreck.fansonly.com. MARTA: Midtown.*

where to play

You might find a pickup game of touch football at a local park, but for scheduled play, join a local league. Your county or city parks department may have information about other adult flag- and touch-football leagues.

ATLANTA CLUB SPORT
Teams at Atlanta Club Sport are coed. *404/257–3355, www.usclubsport.com.*

ATLANTA METRO FLAG & TOUCH FOOTBALL LEAGUE
Men's, women's, coed, and youth teams are divided into varsity (serious) and junior varsity (not-so-serious) competition levels. *770/281–3127, www.amaftfl. com.*

GOLF

Maybe it's the climate, which allows year-round play, or the connection with native golf legend Bobby Jones, or the proximity to pro golf's greatest tournament (the Masters in Augusta); whatever the reason, Atlanta is knee-deep in golf courses. Metro area links run the gamut from daily-fee courses that are relatively inexpensive (there is no such thing as cheap when it comes to greens fees) to country clubs with all the amenities. You can get information on more than 60 public courses throughout Atlanta and in north Georgia from **AtlantaGolfer.com** (www.atlantagolfer. com). If you suddenly feel the urge and have not called ahead for a tee time, **Last Minute Tee Times** (770/664–4653, www.lmtt.com) can check availability at several courses and book next-day reservations for you.

courses

All courses listed here are open to the public on a daily-fee basis; memberships are available at many courses. Tee-time reservations are strongly recommended for warm-weather weekends. The City of Atlanta and several county parks departments also operate golf courses. At courses managed by American Golf Inc. (Alfred "Tup" Holmes, Bobby Jones, Browns Mill, and North Fulton), you may purchase an annual membership, which gives you a discount on fees. Greens fees listed here are regular weekday or weekend rates. Some courses offer discounted rates for senior citizens and women or for early morning or twilight play; "twilight" starting times vary widely.

city of atlanta

7 *f-4*
ALFRED "TUP" HOLMES
Once part of adjacent Adams Park, the course was renamed in 1983 for Alfred "Tup" Holmes. One of the nation's premier African-American golfers, Holmes was instrumental in integrating Atlanta's public golf courses in the 1950s. This rolling, shaded 18-hole, par-72 course is suitable for both novice and experienced players. Greens fees are $27–$38. *2300 Wilson Dr., off Delowe Dr., Adams Park, 404/753–6158. MARTA: Oakland City.*

12 *c-6, c-7*
BOBBY JONES
One of Atlanta's busiest courses, this 18-hole, par-71 course is a blend of flat terrain and rugged hillside holes. Jones had a hand in its design in the 1940s. Only 4 mi north of downtown, the course is especially popular with in-town golfers and those looking to squeeze in a round after work. Greens fees are $24–$38. *384 Woodward Way, off Northside Dr. northeast of I–75, Buckhead, 404/355–1009.*

7 *h-5*
BROWNS MILL
An easily walkable 18-hole, par-72 course, Browns Mill is a favorite of southside residents. Greens fees are $24–$38. *480 Cleveland Ave., east of I–75, Lakewood, 404/366–3573.*

14 *b-4*
CANDLER PARK
This open, rolling 9-hole, par-31 course is popular with beginners, neighborhood locals, college students, and casual players who want to hit a few after office hours. Greens fees are $7–$9. *585 Candler Park Dr., off McLendon Ave., Candler Park, 404/371–1260. MARTA: Edgewood/Candler Park.*

12 *a-5*
CROSS CREEK
The semiprivate 18-hole, par-54 executive course offers a challenging blend of open fairways, water holes, and hills. Near a popular condominium complex, the course is an enjoyable walk and has a pro shop and clubhouse restaurant. Greens fees are $14–$19. *1221 Cross Creek Pkwy., off Bohler Rd., south of W. Wesley Rd., Buckhead, 404/352–5612.*

5 *b-7*

NORTH FULTON

In the heart of Chastain Park, the 18-hole, par-71 links are the city's longest and most challenging. The mix of open and tight fairways and undulating greens, crisscrossed by the meandering waters of Nancy Creek, can daunt even the most experienced golfers. Greens fees are $36–$41. *216 W. Wieuca Rd., north of Roswell Rd., at Powers Ferry Rd., Buckhead, 404/255–0723.*

cherokee county

2 *a-7*

EAGLE WATCH

Arnold Palmer designed this 18-hole, par-72 course, and it has been one of Atlanta's favorites since its opening in 1989. In a handsome layout of rolling hills, tall trees, and tight fairways, it is a challenging but fair course for players of all levels. It has a driving range, practice greens, pro shop, clubhouse, and grill. Greens fees are $58–$78. *3055 Eagle Watch Dr., east of Towne Lake Pkwy., off I–575, Woodstock, 770/591–1000.*

2 *a-7*

TOWNE LAKE HILLS

One of the metro area's most scenic places to play, this Arthur Hills–designed 18-hole, par-72 course offers views of nearby Kennesaw Mountain. The course has many elevation changes, and an abundance of trees lines the fairways. Facilities include a driving range, practice greens, pro shop, and grill. Greens fees are $55–$70. *1003 Towne Lake Hills E, west of I–575, at Town Lake Pkwy., Woodstock, 770/592–9969.*

clayton county

10 *a-2*

LAKE SPIVEY

Spread out along the shores of a lake, this older course has long been one of the most popular in Atlanta's southern crescent. It offers 27 challenging holes on three courses for golfers of all abilities (Clubside, par 36; Hillside, par 36; Lakeside, par 37). The complex has a driving range, practice greens, pro shop, and grill. Greens fees are $31–$48. *8255 Clubhouse Way, off GA 138, west of I–75, Jonesboro, 770/471–4653.*

9 *f-2*

THE LINKS

Equipped to serve golfers who have only a few hours to spare—as well as those with a full day to play—this complex has two courses: an 18-hole, par-72 championship course and a 9-hole, par-31 course suitable for junior golfers and beginners. Facilities include a driving range, practice greens, and pro shop. Greens fees are $32–$40. *340 Hewell Rd., off Tara Blvd. and GA 54, Jonesboro, 770/461–5100.*

cobb county

Cobb County residents may purchase cards good for discounts at both Cobblestone and Legacy, which are operated by the Cobb County Parks and Recreation Department.

4 *f-5*

CITY CLUB OF MARIETTA

On the grounds of the sprawling Marietta Conference Center, this challenging 18-hole, par-71 course was once part of the Marietta Country Club. The adjacent conference-center facilities make City Club a favorite venue for group and corporate outings. Greens fees are $39–$49. *510 Powder Springs Rd., south of Marietta Pkwy./GA 120, Marietta, 770/794–5611.*

4 *c-2*

COBBLESTONE

The 18-hole, par-71 course makes its ruggedly beautiful way through tall pines bordering Lake Acworth. The complex has a practice range, pro shop, and a clubhouse with a restaurant. Greens fees are $22–$59. *4200 Nance Rd., off U.S. 41 and Acworth Due West Rd., Acworth, 770/917–5151.*

4 *h-6*

FOX CREEK
EXECUTIVE COURSE

Next door to Legacy Links, this executive course offers 18 holes of par-3 golf convenient to residents of Cobb and north Fulton counties. The course lies just south of Dobbins Air Force Base; lining up a tough putt while fighter jets scream overhead is a true test of concentration. It has a practice range, pro shop, and snack bar. Greens fees are $28–$38. *1501 Windy Hill Rd., west of U.S. 41, Smyrna, 770/435–1000.*

4 *h-6*

LEGACY GOLF LINKS

The Larry Nelson—designed 18-hole, par-58 executive course evokes the craggy links of Scotland. Tight, tree-lined fairways, sand and grass bunkers, and small, rolling greens challenge shot-making skills on even the shortest par-3 hole. The complex also has a driving range, Bogey's Run (an 18-hole grass putting course), and a clubhouse with pro shop and Scottish-inspired pub. Greens fees are $24–$29. *1825 Windy Hill Rd., west of U.S. 41, Marietta, 770/434–6331.*

dekalb county

DeKalb residents may purchase an annual discount card that gives them reduced fees at county-owned golf courses Mystery Valley and Sugar Creek.

8 *f-1*

GEORGIA'S STONE MOUNTAIN PARK

Robert Trent Jones designed the 18-hole, par-72 Stonemont Course in 1969, and *Golf Digest* has consistently ranked it among the nation's premier public courses ever since. Two 9-hole courses (Lakemont, skirting the Stone Mountain Lake, and Woodmont, surrounded by trees and granite outcrops) combine for a scenic and technically challenging 18-hole, par-72 round. The magnificent natural setting helps make Stone Mountain Park one of the most popular golf destinations in the state. Facilities include a driving range, practice greens, a pro shop, and a restaurant-lounge. Greens fees are $47–$57. *1145 Stonewall Jackson Dr., off Jefferson Davis Dr., at GA 78, Stone Mountain, 770/465–3728.*

8 *f-4*

METROPOLITAN

For more than 30 years, this Rees Jones—designed course has delivered championship-caliber golf to the every-day player as well as to PGA professionals competing to join the tour. The course plays long and tight yet remains fair and fun. Metropolitan has a driving range, practice greens, a pro shop, and a grill. Greens fees are $39–$49. *3000 Fairington Pkwy., off Panola Rd., south of I–20, Lithonia, 770/981–5325.*

8 *f-2*

MYSTERY VALLEY

In the shadow of Stone Mountain, this hilly 18-hole, par-72 course of tree-lined fairways has a long-standing reputation for demanding play. Facilities include a driving range, practice greens, pro shop, and grill. Greens fees are $34–$41. *6094 Shadow Rock Rd., off Stone Mountain–Lithonia Rd., Lithonia, 770/469–6913.*

8 *b-5*

SUGAR CREEK

Extremely popular with south DeKalb golfers, this rolling, open course offers an exciting round without penalizing beginners. The 18-hole, par-72 course is bisected by I–285, so traffic noise can affect concentration on a few holes. Facilities include a pro shop, a driving range, and practice greens. Greens fees are $21–$38. *2706 Bouldercrest Rd., at I–285, Gresham Park, 404/241–7671.*

douglas county

7 *a-1*

GREYSTONE

A favorite of golfers from the Douglasville area and Atlanta's western suburbs, this 18-hole, par-72 layout, on tree-shaded rises, allows for an enjoyable day's outing at a very reasonable price. A driving range, practice greens, a pro shop, and a grill are all here. Greens fees are $22–$35. *4020 Greystone Dr., north of I–20 via Thornton Rd. and GA 78, Lithia Springs, 770/489–9068.*

fayette county

9 *f-5*

RIVER'S EDGE

On the shores of the historic Flint River, this course tests players' skills with a hilly mix of trees and water hazards. Southside Atlanta residents keep the 18-hole, par-71 course especially busy on weekends. A driving range, practice greens, a pro shop, and a grill are additional draws. Greens fees are $34–$44. *40 Southern Golf Ct., off McDonough and County Line Rds., east of Fayetteville, 770/460–1098.*

9 *d-7*

WHITE WATER

With its manicured greens and Old South–style clubhouse, this 18-hole, par-

72 course sets a genteel stage for sport. Between Peachtree City and Fayetteville, White Water satisfies players who seek a country-club golfing experience at public-course rates. It also has a driving range, practice greens, a pro shop, and a grill. Greens fees are $36–$46. *165 Birkdale Dr., off GA 74, Fayetteville, 770/ 461–6545.*

fulton county

North Fulton is the land of country-club communities and upscale semiprivate golf courses. You can expect high-caliber golf and elegant amenities at each of the dozen or more courses.

3 *a-6*

TROPHY CLUB OF ATLANTA

One of three Champions Club courses in metro Atlanta, this course is highly regarded for its hilly terrain, elevated greens, and water hazards. Players who are proficient with fairway woods and putters can score well here. Facilities include a driving range, practice greens, pro shop, and grill. Greens fees are $65–$85. *15135 Hopewell Rd., off GA 9, Alpharetta, 770/343–9700.*

2 *g-6*

WHITE COLUMNS

This Tom Fazio–designed 18-hole, par-72 course is considered by many to be one of the nation's top public courses. The expansive course features large greens and wide, tree-lined fairways, with enough challenges to keep experienced golfers coming back. Among its facilities are a driving range, practice greens, a pro shop, and a clubhouse with a restaurant. Greens fees are $85–$120. *300 White Columns Dr., Alpharetta, 770/343–9025.*

gwinnett county

1 *h-2*

HAMILTON MILL

The first of the Fred Couples Signature courses, Hamilton Mill has a local reputation for tough but enjoyable play for golfers of all levels. Its 18-hole, par-72 layout blends into the Appalachian foothills of north Georgia. The complex has a large practice facility, a pro shop, and a clubhouse with a restaurant and bar. Greens fees are $62–$79. *1995 Hamilton Mill Pkwy., south of I–85, Dacula, 770/945–4653.*

6 *g-3*

TROPHY CLUB AT APALACHEE

One of three Champions Clubs in metro Atlanta, this 18-hole, par-71 course has a challenging layout of tight fairways, bunkers, water hazards, and fast greens. The club has a driving range, practice greens, pro shop, and grill. Greens fees are $55–$65. *1008 Dacula Rd., off Cedars and Hurricane Shoals Rds., north of GA 316, Dacula, 770/822–9220.*

6 *d-8*

TROPHY CLUB OF GWINNETT

A mix of tight and open fairways comes with a healthy dose of hazards at this 18-hole, par-72 Champions Club course. Facilities include a driving range, practice greens, a pro shop, and a snack bar. Greens fees are $49–$67. *3254 Clubside View Ct., off GA 124, south of U.S. 78, Snellville, 770/978–7755, www. trophyclub-gwinnett.com.*

henry county

10 *d-5*

COTTON FIELDS & GREEN VALLEY

One of the best and most affordable daily-fee courses on metro Atlanta's south side, this 36-hole spread includes the par-71 Cotton Fields and par-72 Green Valley links. Both courses have open, gently hilly layouts that test expert players yet do not punish the beginner. The complex includes a driving range, pro shop, and pavilion for groups. Greens fees are $29–$45. *400 Industrial Blvd., between I–75 and GA 155, McDonough, 770/914–1442.*

10 *e-4*

GEORGIA NATIONAL

A superbly maintained course designed by Denis Griffeths lies in a rustic setting near a picturesque lake. Accuracy off the tee is a must on the 18-hole, par-71 course, which hides large, drive-swallowing bunkers along its wide, inviting fairways. Facilities include a driving range, practice greens, and a luxurious clubhouse with pro shop and grill. Greens fees are $50–$65. *1715 Lake Dow Rd., between GA 20 and GA 81, east of McDonough, 770/914–9994.*

lessons

Nearly every course has a pro shop staffed by PGA-certified professionals qualified to give individual or group lessons. The following commercial operations also offer lessons.

5 *f-6*

GOLF AUGUSTA

1255 Johnson Ferry Rd., Marietta, 770/509–8395.

5 *f-4*

6385 Spalding Dr., Norcross, 770/448–6920.

4 *e-8*

HERITAGE HILLS GOLF SHOP

3890 Floyd Rd., Austell, 770/431–0740.

6 *d-4*

JIMMY MOZLEY GOLF & BASEBALL CENTER

292 Oakland Rd., Lawrenceville, 770/962–4918.

4 *g-4*

MARIETTA GOLF CENTER

1701 Gresham Rd., Marietta, 770/977–1997.

GYMNASTICS

In addition to the sites listed here, you can find gymnastics classes at several city and county recreation centers.

1 *d-4*

BUCKHEAD GYMNASTICS CENTER

Parent-and-child classes are offered for children over age two. Group and private lessons, as well as team opportunities, are available for older children. *2335 Adams Dr., Buckhead, 404/367–4414.*

4 *f-5*

COBB COUNTY GYMNASTICS CENTER

This well-equipped 11,600-square-ft Cobb facility has numerous instructional and competitive programs for children ages 2 to 18. *Larry Bell Park, 542 Fairground St., Marietta, 770/528–8450.*

5 *g-4*

GYM ELITE

Little gymnasts can begin learning here at age two. Cheerleading instruction is also available. *5903 Peachtree Industrial Blvd., Norcross, 770/448–1586.*

1 *c-2*

WORLD OF GYMNASTICS

Parents can take classes with their preschool children (starting at 18 months). Classes for special-needs children are offered also, as well as a full range of classes for older boys and girls, including team training. *104 Victoria Court N, off Bells Ferry Rd., Woodstock, 770/516–6898, www.worldofgymnastics. com.*

HIKING

You can find hiking paths at parks and green spaces throughout the metropolitan area.

clubs

The following clubs sponsor daylong and/or weekend hiking excursions in the Atlanta area and beyond. Some organize longer trips to far-flung places. REI stores also organize hiking trips. Local Sierra Club affiliates include the **Atlanta Group** (678/294–6686 or 770/458–3389), the **Greater Gwinnett Group** (404/294–6686), and the **Centennial Group of Cobb, Cherokee, and North Fulton Counties** (georgia.sierraclub.org/local).

ATLANTA OUTDOOR CLUB

atlantaoutdoorclub.com.

CHEROKEE HIKING CLUB

770/720–1515, ext. 233, www.geocities. com/cherokeehike.

GEORGIA APPALACHIAN TRAIL CLUB

404/634–6495, www.georgia-atclub.org.

GEORGIA CONSERVANCY

404/876–2900, www.georgiaconservancy. org.

SIERRA CLUB, GEORGIA CHAPTER

404/607–1262, georgia.sierraclub.org.

trails

1 *d-6*

ATLANTA/DEKALB TRAIL

The PATH Foundation has an ongoing program to connect in-town sidewalks, streets, and trails into a 124-mi route from Greenbrier Mall to Stone Mountain Park. Walkers can find interesting sites, especially along existing sidewalks and new pathways through some older neighborhoods. You can find detailed maps of various areas on the PATH Web site. *404/875–7284 PATH, www. pathfoundation.org.*

⑤ *a-5 through g-3*

CHATTAHOOCHEE RIVER NATIONAL RECREATION AREA

More than 70 mi of trails crisscross the various units of the popular recreation area. Most follow wooded ridges and riverbanks, and they range from easy to difficult. Trails generally begin at the parking lots. Park headquarters has information on guided hikes. *770/952–4419, www.nps.gov/chat.*

⑤ *a-5, a-6*

Cochran Shoals Fitness Trail The 3.3-mi paved trail at Cochran Shoals is one of the most popular parts of the recreation area. Rated as moderately difficult, the hiking-biking trail connects directly with

---

A WALK ON THE WILD SIDE

Despite Atlanta's sprawling development, pockets of wilderness remain to explore. Check these out when you need a natural high.

Chattahoochee River National Recreation Area
Fortunately, the river isn't navigable—otherwise the Atlanta skyline would have banished the thousands of trees along its banks.

Cochran Mill Park and Nature Preserve
Rushing streams flow through this rolling, wooded oasis in the southern metro area.

Davidson–Arabia Mountain Nature Preserve
Winding trails lead you through a unique and nearly unspoiled wilderness.

Fernbank Forest
Find virgin wilderness 5 mi from Five Points.

Reynolds Nature Preserve
A profusion of wild azaleas and other flowering plants makes this an ideal spot for a springtime walk.

---

the Sope Creek paths. *Interstate North Pkwy., off I–285, at New Northside Dr., between Northwest Atlanta and Marietta.*

⑤ *a-7, a-6*

East and West Palisades Trails Here, just north of Atlanta city limits, there are more than 8 mi of trails. *West Palisades entrances: U.S. 41 at the river or Akers Dr., off Akers Mill Rd.; East Palisades entrances: Indian Trail, off Northside Dr. south of I–285, or Whitewater Creek Rd., off Harris Trail (off Northside Dr. south of I–285); between Northwest Atlanta and Marietta.*

⑤ *a-6*

Floodplain Trail The Powers Island unit's quiet 2-mi trail gives hikers a view of kayakers tackling the rapids. *Interstate North Pkwy., off I–285, at New Northside Dr., between Northwest Atlanta and Marietta.*

⑤ *c-3*

Gold Branch Trails More than 7 mi of trails provide some easy hiking and some difficult routes through thick woods and brush along the banks of Bull Sluice Lake. *Lower Roswell Rd., west of the Chattahoochee Nature Center and east of Mount Bethel.*

⑤ *c-3*

Island Ford Trail Huge rock outcrops surround this 3-mi trail, which winds along the river and into the hills. *Island Ford Pkwy., off Roberts Dr., west of GA 400, south of Roswell.*

⑤ *b-5*

Johnson Ferry Loop Trail The 2½-mi loop trail in Johnson Ferry North crosses several creeks and passes a large boat ramp, a put-in point for commercial raft trips. Johnson Ferry South also has easy hiking trails between the river and wetlands. To get here, take one of the three entrances on Columns Drive. *Columns Dr., off Johnson Ferry Rd., on the north side of the river, between Mount Bethel and Marietta.*

⑤ *f-3*

Jones Bridge Trails More than 5½ mi of trails lead hikers along quiet riverbanks and through thick woodlands. *Barnwell Rd., off Holcomb Bridge Rd., south of Newtown.*

⑤ *g-3*

Medlock Bridge The unit has 3 mi of trails, including a long, easy swoop beside the river and a loop that's rated moderately difficult. *Medlock Bridge Rd., off Peachtree Pkwy./GA 141, west of Duluth.*

5 *a-5*

Sope Creek Trails The 1½-mi Mill Trail, which the Parks Service considers part of the Powers Ferry unit, winds along the banks of Sope Creek past old mill ruins. The 2-mi Fox Creek loop trail connects with the Cochran Shoals paths, including the Fitness Trail. *Paper Mill Rd., off Johnson Ferry Rd., between Marietta and Mount Bethel.*

5 *c-3*

Vickery Creek Trails West of Big Creek, an offshoot of the Chattahoochee, easy trails lead to the ruins of a textile mill burned by Union Army cavalry in 1864. In the larger area east of the creek, you can choose from a scattering of easy paths or hike the more difficult trails that run beside Roswell Dam. *South Atlanta St./GA 9 for west area, Riverside Rd. for east area (both just beyond Roswell Rd.–Azalea Dr. intersection), Roswell.*

8 *f-1*

GEORGIA'S STONE MOUNTAIN PARK

With more than 15 mi of trails, this park is a walker's—and runner's—heaven. The more serious hikes include the arduous 1.3-mi Walk-Up Trail to the summit of the 800-ft-high granite monadnock and the rugged 5-mi Cherokee Trail, which winds through woods and along mountain flanks. *Off U.S. 78, about 7½ mi east of I–285 (East Gate entered from U.S. 78, West Gate from Memorial Dr.), Stone Mountain, 770/ 498–5690, www.stonemountainpark.com.*

4 *e-4*

KENNESAW MOUNTAIN NATIONAL BATTLEFIELD PARK

It's only a foothill in comparison to its Appalachian Mountains cousins to the north, but 800-ft-high Kennesaw Mountain lays out nearly 20 mi of park trails in three interconnecting loops. Trails wind through thick woods, open meadows, and across Kennesaw and Little Kennesaw mountains. *Old U.S. 41 southwest of I–75, via Barrett Pkwy., Marietta, 770/427–4686, www.nps.gov/kemo.*

4 *g-8*

SILVER COMET TRAIL

You can access the completed portions of the Silver Comet Trail at 14 points between Mavell Road, off Cooper Lake Road south of Smyrna, and Rockmart in Polk County. Eventually, the walking-jogging-biking trail being developed by the PATH Foundation is to stretch to the Alabama state line. For good directions to the trailheads and facilities, check with PATH or access www.trailexpress. com. *Mavell Road trailhead: Mavell Rd., off Cooper Lake Rd., west of S. Cobb Dr., west of Gilmore, 404/875–7284 PATH, www.pathfoundation.org.*

HOCKEY

When the NHL's Atlanta Flames took to the ice in 1972, skeptics thought that ice and grits would never mix, but the Flames developed a devoted following in the eight years before they moved to Calgary—and left a legacy of competitive amateur hockey at local rinks. Now it seems that half the population of Atlanta's suburbs hails from somewhere up north, and the ranks of fans who greeted the appearance of the Thrashers in 1999 have grown even stronger.

team to watch

ATLANTA THRASHERS

Tickets to games are available from the arena box office or from Ticketmaster, including outlets at Publix supermarkets. The Thrashers Web site lets you click on a seating section and see a view of the ice from that area. *Philips Arena, Techwood Dr., south of Marietta St., Downtown, 404/827–3865 box office; 404/249–6400 Ticketmaster, www. atlantathrashers.com. MARTA: Omni/Dome/GWCC.*

ice leagues

Most Atlanta ice rinks offer lessons, coaches, and rental skates for Gretzky wanna-bes. If you want to play on a hockey team, contact one of the leagues listed here. Young players may want to check out the Thrashers' **H.I.T.S (Hockey in the Streets) Program** (www. atlantathrashers.com). In addition, many rinks organize youth leagues. For information about ice rinks, *see* Ice-Skating, *below.*

ATLANTA AMATEUR HOCKEY LEAGUE (AAHL)
770/321–2245, www.atlantahockey.org.

ATLANTA COED HOCKEY LEAGUE (ACHL)
770/414–8950.

SOUTHERN ICE HOCKEY ASSOCIATION (SICH)
770/935–9337.

field hockey
Field hockey has transplanted well to the land of hoop skirts. The **Georgia Field Hockey Association** (770/484–7824 women's teams; 770/222–8726 men's teams, www.gfha.com) has about 25 affiliated teams around the area.

HORSEBACK RIDING

Atlanta's highways put many well-equipped stables within easy driving distance, along with parks and other open spaces where you can ride. To find fellow riders, try one of these clubs: **Cherokee County Saddle Club** (770/704–5592) in Canton; **Midway Saddle Club** (770/887–2140) in Cumming; **Saddle Up Cobb** (770/919–2944) in Kennesaw; or **Villa Rica Saddle Club** (770/537–4464) in Carrollton. The calendar at Stable Mates (www.stablemates.com) lists many related activities, as well as saddleries, tack shops, and companies that organize trail rides.

instruction & boarding

1 *a-3*
APPLEWOOD FARM
Michelle Gibson and her horse, Peron, were on the U.S. team that rode to a bronze medal in dressage at the 1996 Centennial Olympics. Now she trains future winners and their horses. *11 Apple Wood La., off Macedonia Rd., between Hwys. 278 and 411/GA 20, Taylersville, 770/663–4075 lessons; 770/684–2256 boarding, www.applewood-farm.com.*

2 *d-4*
BITS & BYTES
The husband-and-wife team Barry Guber and Elizabeth Wood take Thoroughbreds who've disappointed at racing, including many of famous lineage, and retrain

them as event or show horses. Boarders are accepted if stable space permits. *1275 Owens Store Rd., south of GA 20, east of I-575, Canton, 770/704–6595.*

5 *b-7*
CHASTAIN HORSE PARK
A $2 million rebuilding transformed this once-run-down site within Chastain Park into a source of pride for the city. It's a handy in-town location for jumper riding lessons and for boarding a horse. The program has been praised for its work with children and adults with disabilities. *4371 Powers Ferry Rd., Buckhead, 404/252–4244.*

5 *b-7*
REECE CENTER FOR THE HANDICAPPED HORSEMANSHIP
Since 1984, the center has used therapeutic riding to develop muscle tone and physical coordination in children with mental and physical disabilities, including the visually impaired. *4145 Panthersville Rd., Ellenwood, 404/241–4263.*

where to ride

8 *c-7*
CLAYTON SPRINGS FARMS
This 100-acre farm has horses for riding, gives lessons, arranges trail rides, and allows some camping on the property. *4940 Steele Rd., east of I-675 via Stagecoach Rd., Ellenwood, 770/968–0934.*

1 *g-6*
GEORGIA INTERNATIONAL HORSE PARK
You can give yourself—and your horse—a taste of glory by riding trails that Olympic equestrians used in '96. All riders must register first at the International Saddlery (770/929–8832). *1996 Centennial Olympic Pkwy., off GA 138, Conyers, 770/602–2606.*

4 *e-6*
JIM MILLER PARK
This Cobb park has an equestrian ring you can use. However, it hosts many rodeos and other events, so call ahead for availability. *2245 Callaway Rd., south of the Al Bishop Softball Complex, Marietta, 770/528–8875.*

4 b-7

SILVER COMET TRAIL

Horseback riding is allowed from the Florence Road trailhead near Powder Springs to all points west on this scenic path along onetime rail lines. *Florence Rd., off U.S. 278, Powder Springs, 404/875–7284 PATH, www.pathfoundation. org.*

4 e-1

WILD HORSE CREEK PARK

Several horse shows are held annually at this large Cobb park, which has an equestrian ring and an arena where owners can put their mounts through their paces. *3280 Macedonia Rd., Powder Springs, 770/528–8890.*

5 e-1

WILLS PARK

Horse owners are welcome to ride at the 50-acre park's equestrian center. Be sure to call ahead for availability, because the park hosts everything from dog trials to bull-riding competitions. *11915 Wills Rd., Alpharetta, 678/297–6120.*

ICE-SKATING

You won't be gliding over frozen ponds in Atlanta, but most ice rinks are open year-round for lessons, hockey leagues, and attempts at perfecting a flying camel. The **Georgia Figure Skating Club** (770/493–2595, www.gafsc.com), the local affiliate of the U.S. Figure Skating Association, has information on local events and lists rinks and clubs in the metro area.

5 d-1

ALPHARETTA FAMILY SKATE CENTER

Known as the Cooler, this large complex has three full-size rinks for recreational ice skating and competitive youth and adult hockey. The Life University and Georgia State University teams, the Atlanta Amateur Hockey League (AAHL), the Georgia Amateur Hockey Association (GAHA), and the Atlanta Fire synchronized skating team are based here. Various instruction programs are offered. There's an admission fee for open skating; skate rentals are available. *10800 Davis Dr., off Mansell Rd., Alpharetta, 770/649–6600, www.cooler.com.*

11 b-7

CENTENNIAL OLYMPIC PARK

From Thanksgiving through December, the Southern Company Amphitheater on the southern side of the park is transformed into an ice rink for ice shows and exhibitions and public skating ($5 per 1½ hours). *285 International Blvd., Downtown, 404/222–7275, www.gwcc/park. MARTA: Omni/Dome/GWCC*

6 b-2

ICEFORUM ATLANTA

The complex, which is the training and practice facility for the Atlanta Thrashers, has two NHL-regulation rinks that host youth and adult teams in AAHL and GAHA league competition. Facilities include a full-service pro shop, instructional programs, and a restaurant–sports bar. Open skating is available for a fee, and you can rent skates. *2300 Satellite Blvd., off I–85, Duluth, 770/813–1010, www.iceforum.com.*

1 e-7

ICEFORUM AT SOUTHLAKE

This southside home for men's hockey leagues also has group figure-skating classes. Open skating is available for a fee, as are skate rentals. *7130 Mount Zion Blvd., west of I–75, Jonesboro, 770/477–5112, www.iceforum.com.*

4 e-2

ICEFORUM AT TOWN CENTER

Home to the national-championship synchronized skating team Peach Frost, this IceForum offers a full range of teaching programs and hockey leagues. The rink has open skating (for a fee) and skate rentals. *3061 George Busbee Pkwy., off I–75, Kennesaw, 770/218–1010, www.iceforum.com.*

5 b-4

PARKAIRE ICE ARENA

Atlanta's oldest ice arena has a full-size rink for recreational skating and hockey competition, a pro shop, and professional instruction programs. The Atlanta Rage, Western Division winners in the Southern Youth Hockey League, call this rink home. You can pay to skate when leagues are not in play; rentals are available. *4880 Lower Roswell Rd., at Johnson Ferry Rd., Marietta, 770/973–0753, www.parkaire.com.*

IN-LINE SKATING, ROLLER SKATING & SKATEBOARDING

instruction

In addition to these skate schools, many skating rinks also have classes and private lessons, as well as affiliated speed-skating and hockey teams and leagues.

BOHEMIAN SKATE SCHOOL

The school's instructors offer group and individual lessons, generally at Piedmont Park, and the school fields a "team-in-training" for various events. Lessons range from $30 per person for group sessions to $45 for private lessons. *404/298–6378, www.bohemianskateschool.com.*

SKATE-O-ROBICS

The organization conducts skating classes intended to promote fitness. Sessions are held at various rinks and run $35 per month for eight classes if you have your own skates, $40 per month if you rent skates. *Box 47534, 30362, 404/501–0309, www.skateorobics.com.*

clubs & organizations

For information on roller-hockey leagues, contact one of the following: **Metropolitan Atlanta Street Hockey Association** (MASHA; 770/840–6952), **Kennesaw Roller Hockey Association** (770/915–0127), **Atlanta South Hockey League** (770/719–2999, www.atlantasouthhockey.com), or local rinks.

The Web site for the **International In-Line Skating Association** (www.iisa.org) may be helpful. The **Aggressive Skaters Association** (www.asaskate.com) Web site lists pro and amateur tours and tournaments; the **Asphalt Atlas** Web site (www.skating.com) suggests skating routes.

ATLANTA PEACHTREE ROADROLLERS SKATING CLUB

This club schedules a couple of group skates per week, usually at Carter Center in the evening and at Piedmont Park on Sunday morning. Many members are involved with the Atlanta Skate Patrol at the park. *404/634–9032, www.aprr.org.*

skating rinks

3 *d-5*

CUMMING SKATE CENTER

This large facility is the home rink of national and X-Games racing champion Derek Downey and of the GT Speed, one of the nation's top speed-racing teams, as well as local youth and adult roller-hockey leagues. *863 Buford Hwy., west of GA 400, Cumming, 770/887–5283.*

5 *g-6*

KUDZU HOCKEY

The official home of MASHA (Metropolitan Atlanta Street Hockey Association) has street- and roller-hockey facilities. If you'd like to see how you might fare in league play, try the "open stick" nights, held each Sunday. *4231 Northeast Expwy. Access Rd., Doraville, 770/270–0906.*

5 *d-2*

ROSWELL ROLLER RINK

The Roswell Rage, the 10-and-under 2001 Echo Roller Hockey national champions, is one of the youth groups that lace their skates here. The rink has open skating and rents quad and in-line skates. *780 Old Roswell Rd., Roswell, 770/998–9701, www.roswellrollerrink.com.*

4 *e-2*

SPARKLES ROLLER RINK

This family rink offers group teaching every Saturday, but private coaching is also available. There's a fee for open skating; you can rent quad skates, speed skates, and in-line skates. There's also a rink in Hiram (770/943–4446). *1000 McCollum Pkwy., off Cobb Pkwy., Kennesaw, 770/428–3941, www.sparklesrollerrinks.com.*

extreme parks

As a rule, extreme parks require parents to sign waivers of liability or permission agreements for skaters under 18. Outdoor ramps or courses are closed during bad weather.

3 *d-4*

RAMPAGE EXTREME SPORTS

The large complex includes a 12-ft vertical ramp and courses for in-line skating, skateboarding, and BMX stunt biking. It offers various clinics and has several affiliated clubs. You get discounts on rates with a monthly membership.

3775 Peachtree Crest Dr., east of Peachtree Industrial Blvd., 3 mi north of GA
20, Duluth, 678/417–8700, www.
rampageextremesports.com.

3 *d-5*

SLAPSHOTS SPORTSPLEX

Besides a hardwood indoor rink for public skating and youth hockey leagues,
this complex has an outdoor extreme
park that's open in warm-weather
months. Summer clinics are offered,
too. Slapshots doesn't rent skates or
equipment for the extreme park. 5065
Piney Grove Rd., off GA 9, 1 mi from GA
400 exit 13, Cumming, 770/888–5000,
www.slapshots.net.

other places to roll

8 *f-1*

GEORGIA'S STONE
MOUNTAIN PARK

Fifteen miles of trails and lightly traveled
roads alongside the park roads accommodate runners, bikers, and skaters. Off
U.S. 78, about 7½ mi east of I–285, East
Gate entered from U.S. 78, West Gate
from Memorial Dr., Stone Mountain, 770/
498–5690, www.stonemountainpark.com.

15 *f-2*

PIEDMONT PARK

Piedmont heads the "favorites" list of
many in-town skaters. On Sunday especially, you can see them rolling along the
roadways from the main entrance on.
Main entrance: 12th St. and Piedmont
Ave., park bordered by Piedmont Ave., 10th
St., and Monroe Dr., Midtown, 404/817–
6757. MARTA: Midtown or Arts Center.

4 *g-8*

SILVER COMET TRAIL

This trail being developed by the PATH
Foundation along old rail lines can be
accessed at 14 points between Mavell
Road, south of Smyrna, and Rockmart in
Polk County. Some skaters like to drive
beyond the first few trailheads to skate
where they can see more dramatic
scenery around the old railroad trestles.
Mavell Road trailhead: Mavell Rd., off
Cooper Lake Rd. west of S. Cobb Dr., west
of Gilmore, 404/875–7284 PATH, www.
pathfoundation.org or www.trailexpress.
com.

MARTIAL ARTS

Several of the organizations listed here
have multiple locations; the listed studio or Web site can direct you to other
sites. Many local recreation centers,
adult-education programs at area colleges, and YMCAs also frequently offer
classes in various disciplines.

lessons

8 *b-1*

AIKIDO CENTER
OF ATLANTA

630 Valley Brook Rd., Decatur, 404/297–
7804.

6 *a-4*

AMERICAN KARATE—
JOE CORLEY STUDIOS

2300 Pleasant Hill Rd., Duluth, 770/623–
4100, www.joecorley.com.

4 *g-3*

CHINESE
SHAO-LING CENTER

2727 Canton Rd., Marietta, 770/422–9250,
www.shaolincenter.com.

5 *d-5*

DAVE YOUNG'S
WORLD CLASS KARATE &
MARTIAL ARTS ACADEMY

5400 Chamblee-Dunwoody Rd., Dunwoody, 770/394–5425.

5 *b-5*

IMPERATORI FAMILY
KARATE CENTER

5920 Roswell Rd., Sandy Springs, 404/
252–8200, www.mindspring.com/
~karate/.

5 *e-6*

TAI CHI CH'UAN ATLANTA

After some years of teaching through
area colleges, instructor Herb Goldberg
now leads private classes through the
fundamentals of traditional tai chi.
Yeshiva High School, 3130 Raymond
Dr., Doraville, 404/881–0030, www.
taichichuanatlanta.com.

practice groups

Following the Chinese tradition of open-
air tai chi, the **Atlanta Taiji Pushing
Hands Practice Group** meets Sunday
morning at 10:30 or 11 at the gazebo off
Swanton Way behind the old courthouse

in Decatur; all practitioners are welcome. The **ROSS Practice Group of Kennesaw** (404/483–0679) and the **Bahala Na Arnis Escrima Practice Group of Smyrna** (770/732–1140) may have info about tai chi practice in other areas.

MINIATURE GOLF

where to play

 9 *h-1*

CLAYTON COUNTY INTERNATIONAL PARK

If you want to do something besides sun on the beach or squeal down the water slides, this water-park complex also has a miniature golf course. *Off GA 138, west of I–75 and east of Crane Rd., Jonesboro, 770/473–4005.*

6 *a-4*

PIRATES COVE ADVENTURE GOLF & VIDEO ARCADE

This outpost of a national chain has three courses of varying layouts, including a challenging 36-holer. *3380 Venture Pkwy., Duluth, 770/623–4184.*

PADDLING

Atlanta's white-water enthusiasts often head to the rivers of northern Georgia (Chatooga), western North Carolina (Nantahala), and eastern Tennessee (Ocoee), but the metro region's own Chattahoochee River National Recreation Area has Class I–II rapids. The river is a great place for novice and experienced paddlers alike to hone their skills and for rafters to enjoy a leisurely float down the river.

canoeing & kayaking

Several clubs listed here offer instruction and conduct outings and competitions. Retailers, too, can be sources for lessons and connections with trips. In addition to the multisport outfitters High Country Outfitters, Galyan's, and REI, check out possibilities at **Geared to Go** (4313 Northeast Expwy., 678/406–0008, www.gearedtogo.com) and **Go with the Flow** (4-A Elizabeth Way, Roswell, 888/345–3569).

ATLANTA CENTER FOR EXCELLENCE

Competitive canoers and kayakers can get training here. There is a yearly membership fee. *Box 723274, 31139, 770/937–5073, www.acecanoekayak.com.*

ATLANTA KAYAKERS

The focus of this young group is on sea kayaking—which necessarily makes for a lot of travel. Outings take place the third Saturday of each month. *Box 546, Redan 30074, www.atlantakayak.com.*

ATLANTA WHITEWATER CLUB

The club organizes canoeing and kayaking trips. *Box 11714, 30355, 404/299–3752, www.atlantawhitewater.com.*

GEORGIA CANOEING ASSOCIATION

Training and trips are available to club members. *Box 7023, 30357, 770/421–9729, www.georgiacanoe.org.*

LANIER CANOE & KAYAK CLUB

Events sponsored by this group are held at the Lake Lanier Olympics venue. *Clarks Bridge Park, 3105 Clarks Bridge Rd., Gainesville, 770/287–7888, www.lckc.org.*

8 *b-3*

WHITEWATER LEARNING CENTER OF GEORGIA

If you want to learn how to tackle the rapids in an open canoe or how to perform an Eskimo roll in a kayak, the center can give you a hand. *3437 Rockhaven Cir. NE, Buckhead, 404/231–0042, www.whitewatergeorgia.com.*

rafting

The best white-water rafting in the state is probably on the Chatooga River near the South Carolina border, about 90 mi north of Atlanta, but you can get some thrills closer to home. The **Chattahoochee River National Recreation Area** (770/952–4419, www.nps.gov/chat) has information about group rafting (12 or more people) on the Chattahoochee. Check local newspapers, too.

rowing & sculling

5 *c-2*

ATLANTA ROWING CLUB

Early mornings and late afternoons—even in cold weather—you can see ARC members training on the river near the Chattahoochee River Park. More than 1,000 members strong, the club is open to all skill levels and conducts classes and trips. Its Head of the Hooch Regatta has become a major outdoors event in fall. *500 Azalea Dr., Roswell, 770/993–1879, www.atlantarow.org.*

where to float & paddle

5 *a-7 through g-3*

CHATTAHOOCHEE RIVER

With long, relatively easy stretches for learning basic skills and Class I–II rapids for a little excitement, the Chattahoochee River is Atlanta's main paddling attraction. Several units of the Chattahoochee River National Recreation Area have public launching sites.

1 *g-1*

LAKE SIDNEY LANIER

The sometimes capricious winds on Lake Lanier can add risk to paddling sports—and might be too much for rank beginners. Call for information about launch sites and facilities. *Between GA 400 and I–985 about 35 mi northeast of Atlanta, between Buford and Gainesville, 770/945–9531 office; 770/945–1467 recorded information, www.sam.usace.army.mil/op/rec/lanier.*

PAINTBALL

where to play

4 *a-1*

ARKENSTONE PAINT BALL

Twelve playing fields here are spread across 71 acres of wooded terrain, with creeks, hills, and artificial obstacles. The complex has a clubhouse and a snack bar. *7257 Cedarcrest Rd., off GA 92, Acworth, 770/974–2535.*

3 *c-6*

PAINTBALL ATLANTA

Atlanta's first paintball facility has 10 outdoor fields on nearly 150 acres, plus two indoor arenas at 700 Holcomb Bridge Road in Roswell. There's also a pro shop and snack bar. *Stoney Point Rd., off McFarland and Shiloh Rds., east of GA 400, Alpharetta, 770/594–0912.*

WILDFIRE PAINTBALL GAMES

The operation is small, but its courses buzz with paintball excitement. *Outdoor course: 2641 Hestertown Rd., off Pannell Rd. near GA 11, Madison; Indoor course:* *3725 Stone Mountain Highway, Suite C, Snellville.; 770/982–8180, www.wildfire-paintball.com.*

RACQUETBALL, HANDBALL, & SQUASH

Some YMCAs and local recreation centers also have courts for these sports. The private clubs listed here are among the many that welcome nonmember players for a daily guest fee.

where to play

13 *b-5*

ATHLETIC CLUB NORTHEAST

Ten courts are for racquetball and handball, two for squash. *1515 Sheridan Rd., off Briarcliff Rd., Druid Hills, 404/325–2700.*

5 *c-5*

CONCOURSE ATHLETIC CLUB

Six courts are for racquetball and handball, four for squash. *8 Concourse Pkwy., off Peachtree-Dunwoody Rd., north of I–285, Dunwoody, 770/698–2000.*

9 *h-1*

SOUTHSIDE ATHLETIC CLUB

The eight courts are for racquetball and handball. *1792 Mount Zion Rd., west of I–75, Morrow, 770/968–1798.*

4 *h-6*

SPORTING CLUB AT WINDY HILL

Two courts are for racquetball, five for squash. *135 Interstate North Pkwy., east of I–75, Marietta, 770/953–1100.*

5 *g-7*

TUCKER RACQUET & FITNESS CENTER

The five courts are for racquetball, handball, and squash. *3281 Tucker–Norcross Rd., Tucker, 770/491–3100.*

ROCK CLIMBING

Traditionally, climbers drove to the north Georgia mountains to indulge their passion for scaling sheer rocks. Today, with a little instruction, young climbers and novices can feel like an Alpine mountaineer at indoor climbing walls. Climbers under 18 may be required to have their parents sign a waiver of liability. **GA Adventures** (404/630–7382, www.ga-adventures.com) can provide information about outdoor climbing. The **Atlanta Climbing Club** (770/621–2544, www.atlantaclimbingclub.org) organizes trips for adults with climbing experience; membership is $20 to $35. The **Georgia Rock Climbing** Web site (www.climbgeorgia.com) lists links to popular climbing spots.

lessons

Many of the facilities with climbing walls also offer classes or clinics.

13 *b-2*

CHALLENGE ROCK CLIMBING SCHOOL

Courses, camps, and climbing trips are offered here. *1085 Capitol Club Dr., Brookhaven, 404/237–4021, www. thechallengerock.com.*

4 *e-2*

ESCALADE

The facility functions as a private club with an 8,000-ft climbing wall, but it offers an extensive range of classes in climbing skills. Day passes are available for $10–$12. *2995-B Cobb International Blvd., near McCollum Pkwy., Kennesaw, 770/974–9817.*

where to climb

12 *a-7*

ATLANTA ROCKS!

With more than 12,000 square ft of climbing area, Atlanta Rocks! Intown is the largest facility of its type in the Southeast. Introductory classes start at $35; rental rates for harnesses and other equipment vary. Atlanta Rocks! Perimeter is smaller but has the same climbing challenges. *1019-A Collier Rd., Buckhead, 404/351–3009, www.atlantarocks.com.*

5 *e-5*

4411-A Bankers Cir., Doraville, 770/242–7625.

11 *d-1*

GALYAN'S

The climbing and gear are free at Galyan's three stores—and the trade-off is long lines. Sometimes the line is so

long that entry is closed off, so call ahead to find out. *3535 Peachtree Rd., Buckhead, 404/267–0200, www.galyans.com.*

4 *f-3*

691 Ernest Barrett Pkwy., Kennesaw, 770/281–0200.

3 *h-8*

Mall of Georgia, 3333 Buford Dr., Buford, 678/482–1200.

5 *c-1*

PROVIDENCE OUTDOOR RECREATION CENTER

The rock-climbing cliff draws many to this forest park and wildlife habitat. *13440 Providence Park Dr., off Mayfield Rd., Alpharetta, 770/740–2419.*

14 *c-5*

WALL CRAWLER ROCK CLUB

The more than 7,000 square ft of indoor climbing surfaces include a state-of-the-art climbing wall and a 1,700-square-ft bouldering cave. Memberships are available. *1522 DeKalb Ave., Candler Park, 404/371–8997, www.wallcrawlerrock.com.*

15 *d-4*

YMCA CLIMBING WALL

The Centennial Place YMCA has climbing walls up to 36 ft tall, but they are open only to groups of five or more. Various types of instruction are offered. Reservations are required. *555 Luckie St., Downtown, 404/445–7221.*

RUGBY

For years, rugby has had a small but very loyal following in the Atlanta area. If you would like to learn more about this challenging sport or find a team to join, contact one of the local rugby football clubs (RFCs).

ATLANTA HARLEQUINS WOMEN'S RFC

770/908–1526, www.atlantaharlequins. com.

ATLANTA OLD WHITE RFC

404/355–1617, www.atlantarugby.com.

ATLANTA RENEGADES RFC

No phone, www.atlantarenegades.com.

RUNNING & WALKING

Atlanta's moderate climate and varied terrain contribute to its growing popularity as a metropolitan area to be explored on foot.

running clubs

One of the largest runners' association in the United States, the **Atlanta Track Club** (404/231–9064, www.atlantatrackclub. org) has more than 11,000 members. Best known for its signature event, the Peachtree Road Race held each July 4, the club also sponsors other annual events, including the Atlanta Marathon on Thanksgiving.

ATLANTA SINGLES RUNNING ORGANIZATION
404/675–3824, www.atlanta-singles-running.org.

BUCKHEAD ROAD RUNNERS CLUB
404/816–6299, www.brrc.org.

CHATTAHOOCHEE ROAD RUNNERS
770/984–0451, www.hooochies.org.

CHEROKEE RUNNING CLUB
770/928–4239, www.hooochies.org.

GAINESVILLE ROAD RUNNERS
770/536–8322.

GREATER GWINNETT ROAD RUNNERS
770/979–6336, www.ggrr.org.

PEACHTREE CITY RUNNING CLUB
770/460–6712.

TEAM SPIRIT
404/705–4263 daytime; 404/256–8722 evenings.

YOUTH TRACK CLUB
404/817–6801 Atlanta Parks and Recreations Department.

walking clubs

Several of these clubs for serious walkers are affiliated with the American Volkssport Association (AVA), a national organization that sanctions noncompetitive 10-K walks at hundreds of locations around the United States each year.

GEORGIA WALKERS
770/914–9404.

MCINTOSH TRAIL WALKERS
770/631–8543.

ROSWELL STRIDERS
770/998–7362.

WALKING CLUB OF GEORGIA
770/593–5817, www.walkingclubofgeorgia.com.

where to walk or run

The Atlanta Track Club's Web site (www.atlantatrackclub.org) details some specific running routes, and *Atlanta Walks: A Comprehensive Guide to Walking, Running and Bicycling the Area's Scenic and Historic Locales*, 2nd Edition (Peachtree Publishers, $14.95), outlines a number of walking tours. Popular sites are listed below, but you can find many more places to beat your feet in parks and green spaces throughout the metro area.

1 d-6
ATLANTA/DEKALB TRAIL
The trail, which is to stretch as a 124-mi series of paths from Greenbrier Mall to Stone Mountain Park, is still in its early stages of development. However, it already includes many areas that make for interesting running or walking, such as in the Inman Park neighborhood. The PATH Foundation is overseeing the project. 404/875–7284 PATH, www.pathfoundation.org.

5 a-5 through g-3
CHATTAHOOCHEE RIVER NATIONAL RECREATION AREA
More than 70 mi of all kinds of trails meander along a 48-mi stretch of river, including a few paved trails for easier walking as well as more difficult paths through the woods. 770/945–1466, www.nps.gov/chat.

8 f-1
GEORGIA'S STONE MOUNTAIN PARK
Some of the park's 15 mi of trails are paved for runners and walkers. *Off U.S. 78, about 7½ mi east of I–285 (East Gate entered from U.S. 78, West Gate from Memorial Dr.), Stone Mountain, 770/498–5690, www.stonemountainpark.com.*

9 *b-7*
PEACHTREE CITY
The planned community south of
Atlanta is known for its more than 70 mi
of paved pedestrian and cycling paths,
which link residential neighborhoods,
commercial districts, and recreation
areas. Recreation and shopping areas
are good places to access the trail system. *Off GA 74, about 12 mi south of I–
85, Peachtree City.*

15 *f-2*
PIEDMONT PARK
From early morning into the evening,
you can join others out to stroll, walk
briskly, or run along the paved walks,
roads, and pathways that lace this large
city park. It's especially busy on weekends. *Main entrance: 12th St. and Piedmont Ave., park bordered by Piedmont
Ave., 10th St., and Monroe Dr., Midtown,
404/817–6757. MARTA: Midtown or Arts
Center.*

4 *g-8*
SILVER COMET TRAIL
Between Mavell Road, south of Smyrna,
and Rockmart in Polk County, 14 access
points let you start walking or running
on this paved trail developed by the
PATH Foundation along old rail lines.
*Mavell Road trailhead: Mavell Rd., off
Cooper Lake Rd. west of S. Cobb Dr., west
of Gilmore, 404/875–7284 PATH, www.
pathfoundation.org or www.trailexpress.
com*

SAILING

Winds from neighboring mountains
bring strong and sometimes tricky
breezes to Lakes Allatoona and Sidney
Lanier, making both popular with inland
sailors. The two lakes are the largest
bodies of water close to the city and
about the only places to enjoy large-
craft, open-water sailing. There are
numerous marinas at both locations.
Clubs at the two lakes are very active,
with full slates of competition, social
events, and instructional classes.

Sailboats longer than 12 ft must be registered in Georgia. The **Boating Unit of
the Georgia Department of Natural
Resources** (770/414–3337, www.ganet.
org/dnr) has details about boat registration. Sailing permits must be purchased
by mail or in person from the **Georgia
Department of Natural Resources**

License Unit (2189 Northlake Pkwy.,
Bldg. 10, Suite 108, Tucker, 770/414–
3337). Applications are also available at
many bait-and-tackle shops and at
Kmart and Wal-Mart stores.

instruction
Continuing-education programs at area
colleges and universities sometimes offer
sailing courses, as do some of the large
sporting-goods retailers. The following
commercial schools are recommended.

3 *g-5*
LANIER SAILING ACADEMY
Classes teach skills in basic coastal
cruising, bareboat chartering, coastal
navigation, and celestial navigation. Private lessons and classes for kids (ages
11–17) are available. You can rent sailboats and nautical equipment. *Holiday
Marina, 6920 Holiday Rd., Z Dock,
Buford, 800/684–9463 or 770/945–8810,
www.laniersail.com*

3 *g-5*
WINDSONG SAILING ACADEMY
At Windsong, you can learn basic
coastal cruising, bareboat chartering,
coastal navigation, celestial navigation,
and marine meteorology. Students can
participate in scheduled trips. *Holiday
Marina, 6900 Holiday Rd., Dock 6,
Buford, 770/931–9151, www.windsongsail.
com*

lake lanier clubs
BAREFOOT SAILING CLUB
*404/256–6839, www.mindspring.com/
~barefootsailing.*

KINGDOM YACHTS SAILING CLUB
770/887–7966, www.andrews.com/kysc.

1 *h-2*
LAKE LANIER SAILING CLUB
*6206 Commodore Dr., Flowery Branch,
www.llsc.com.*

lake allatoona clubs
ATLANTA YACHT CLUB
www.atlantayachtclub.org.

SOUTH WINDS SAILING CLUB
770/974–6422.

SOCCER

teams to watch

ATLANTA BEAT

The Beat capped its 2001 inaugural season here by winning the regular season championship in women's professional soccer. The team, which quickly built local interest via a lot of community appearances, will play games at the 16,000-seat Herndon Stadium at Morris Brown College. *Herndon Stadium, Morris Brown College, Martin Luther King Jr. Dr., at Vine St., Vine City, 404/249–6400 Ticketmaster; 877/762–2371 season tickets, www.theatlantabeat.com.*

ATLANTA SILVERBACKS

The team competes in the professional United Soccer League's "A" League and is affiliated with Major League Soccer's Dallas Burn. The season runs from April to September. *DeKalb Memorial Stadium, off Memorial Dr. (from I–285), Decatur, 770/645–6655, www. atlantasilverbacks.com.*

where to play

The municipal facilities listed here have multiple fields and sponsor both league and tournament play.

 5 *h-6*

HARMONY GROVE SOCCER COMPLEX

9 Harmony Grove Rd., Lilburn, 770/978–5271.

5 *f-7*

HENDERSON PARK

2803 Henderson Rd., Tucker, 404/371–2631.

9 *h-5*

LOVEJOY SOCCER COMPLEX

1935 McDonough Rd., Hampton, 770/477–3766.

5 *h-4*

PICKNEYVILLE SOCCER COMPLEX

4707 Old Peachtree Rd., Norcross, 770/417–2200.

10 *e-4*

SOCCER COMPLEX

143 Henry Pkwy., adjacent to Red Tail Hawk Nature Preserve, McDonough, 770/954–2031.

4 *d-7*

TRAMORE PARK

2150 East–West Connector, Marietta, 770/528–8800.

soccer clubs & leagues

ATLANTA CLUB SPORT

For soccer-playing members of this independent group, coed recreational leagues are an option. *404/257–3355.*

ATLANTA DISTRICT AMATEUR SOCCER LEAGUE

The league is for men only. *770/452–0505.*

ATLANTA SILVERBACKS SOCCER CLUB

The club organizes men's and women's teams. *www.silverbackssoccerclub.com.*

GREATER ATLANTA WOMEN'S SOCCER ASSOCIATION

The growing popularity of the sport among women has boosted the teams in this association. *404/687–8004.*

INTERNATIONAL SPORTS SOCCER ASSOCIATION

This recreational league draws many in-town residents. *770/279–4699.*

OVER-35 MASTERS LEAGUE

The league is for men. *770/979–9046.*

SWIMMING

You can swim in the indoor Y pools year-round, or you can find a nearby beach in summer. A number of parks in the 10-county metro area have either seasonal pools (Memorial Day through Labor Day) or year-round aquatics centers. Many of these offer lessons, swim and dive leagues, exercise and hydro-aerobics classes, and recreational swimming.

lessons

 5 *b-4*

ATLANTA SCUBA & SWIM ACADEMY

Group, private, and semiprivate instruction is offered in a range of swimming techniques, including snorkeling, underwater photography, and scuba training for certification. *932 Johnson Ferry Rd., at Lower Roswell Rd., Marietta, 770/973–3120, www.atlantascuba.com.*

5 *g-1*

DYNAMO COMMUNITY SWIM CENTERS

Dynamo Centers offers instruction and sponsors highly competitive swim teams and leagues. Lessons are available for adults and children preschool age and older. *5075 Abbots Bridge Rd., Alpharetta, 770/772–6789, www. dynamoswimamerica.com.*

5 *e-7*

3119 Shallowford Rd., Chamblee, 770/451–3272.

6 *a-6*

SWIM ATLANTA

Swim Atlanta offers instruction and competitive team training and events. *324 Holly Ridge Dr., Lilburn, 770/381–7946, www.swimatlanta.com.*

5 *d-2*

795 Old Roswell Rd., Roswell, 770/992–1778.

5 *h-1*

4050 John's Creek Pkwy., Suwanee, 770/622–1735.

public pools

CITY OF ATLANTA

Adams Park (1620 Delowe Dr., north of Campbellton Rd., Cascade Heights, 404/753–6091); **Anderson Park** (100 Anderson Ave., West Atlanta, 404/799–0317); **Candler Park** (1500 McLendon Ave., south of Ponce de Leon Ave., Candler Park, 404/817–6757); **Chastain Park** (235 W. Wieuca Rd., Buckhead, 404/255–0863); **Garden Hills Park** (355 Pinetree Dr., Buckhead, 404/848–7220); **Grant Park** (625 Park Ave., south of I-20, Grant Park, 404/622–3041, MARTA: West End); **John A. White Park** (1103 Cascade Cir., Cascade Heights, 404/755–5546); **Maddox Park** (1142 Bankhead Hwy., Grove Park, 404/892–0119); **Oakland City Park** (1305 Oakland Rd., Oakland City, 404/753–7245); **Phoenix Park** (477 Windsor St., Lakewood, 404/522–0030); **Piedmont Park** (main entrance at 12th St. and Piedmont Ave.; park bordered by Piedmont Ave., 10th St., and Monroe Dr.; Midtown; 404/892–0117, MARTA: Midtown or Arts Center); **Pittman Park** (950 Garibaldi St., South Atlanta, 404/522–0021); **Powell Park** (1690 Martin Luther King Jr. Dr., Downtown, 404/753–7156); **South Bend Park** (2000 Lakewood Ave., off Langford Pkwy., Lakewood, 404/622–3048);

Thomasville Park (1745 Thomasville Dr., Lakewood, 404/622–3045); **Tucson Trail Park** (4610 Tucson Trail Dr., Southwest Atlanta, 404/349–4342).

Aquatics centers: **John F. Kennedy Park** (225 James P. Brawley Dr., Vine City, 404/524–2858, MARTA: Ashby); **Martin Luther King, Jr. Natatorium** (70 Boulevard Dr., Downtown, 404/658–7330, MARTA: King Memorial); **Southeast Atlanta Park** (365 Cleveland Ave., East Point, 404/624–0774). **Perry Homes** (1041 Kerry Dr., Grove Park, 404/794–0161).

CLAYTON COUNTY

Bonanza Park (1620 Flicker Rd., Jonesboro, 770/477–3766).

COBB COUNTY

Powder Springs Park (3899 Brownsville Rd., Powder Springs, 770/439–6315); **Sewell Park** (2055 Lower Roswell Rd., Marietta, 770/509–2741).

Aquatics centers: **Larry Bell Park** (592 Fairground St., southeast of downtown on GA 120/Marietta Pkwy., Marietta, 770/528–8465); **Mountain View Aquatic Center** (2650 Gordy Pkwy., Marietta, 770/509–4925); **West Cobb Aquatic Center** (3675 Macland Rd., Powder Springs, 770/222–6700).

DEKALB COUNTY

Briarwood (2235 Briarwood Way, Ashford Park, 404/679–5924); **Cofer** (4259 N. Park Dr., Tucker, 770/270–6253) **Gresham** (3113 Gresham Rd., Gresham Park, 404/244–4966); **Kittredge** (2535 N. Druid Hills Rd., Druid Hills, 404/679–5925); **Lithonia** (2501 Park Dr., Lithonia, 770/484–3054); **Lynwood** (3360 Osborne Rd., Lynwood Park, 404/303–2105); **Mark Trail** (2230 Tilson Rd., Decatur, 404/244–4938); **Medlock** (874 Gaylemont Cir., Decatur, 404/679–5926); **Midway** (3181 Midway Rd., Decatur, 404/286–3313); **Murphy Candler** (1526 W. Nancy Creek Dr., Dunwoody, 770/936–5468); **Wade-Walker Park** (5584 Rockbridge Rd., Stone Mountain, 770/879–3462).

FULTON COUNTY

Aquatics centers: **Clarence Duncan Memorial Park** (6000 Rivertown Rd., Fairburn, 770/306–3136); **Welcome All Park** (4255 Will Lee Rd., off Welcome All Rd., north of Roosevelt Hwy./U.S. 29, College Park, 404/762–4058).

GWINNETT COUNTY

Dacula Park (205 Dacula Rd., Dacula, 770/822–5410); **Rhodes Jordan Park** (100 E. Crogan St./U.S. 29, Lawrenceville, 770/237–5626); **Springbrook Golf, Tennis, and Aquatics Complex** (585 Camp Ferrin Rd., Lawrenceville, 770/417–2210).

Aquatics centers: **Bogan Park** (2723 N. Bogan Rd., west of GA 365/I–985, Buford, 770/614–2060); **Mountain Park** (5050 Five Forks Trickum Rd., Lilburn, 770/237–5626).

TENNIS

Many public parks have free, first-come, first-served courts. Those listed here have a large number of courts or full-service tennis centers with professional instruction, equipment sales and rentals, and organized competition.

The **Atlanta Lawn Tennis Association** (ALTA; 770/399–5788, www.altatennis.org), which has nearly 81,000 members, organizes singles and doubles competitions. There are coed, senior-citizen, youth, men's, women's, and wheelchair-bound leagues for every skill level.

city of atlanta

12 c-7

BITSY GRANT TENNIS CENTER

The center has 20 hard courts and four clay courts, all of which are lighted. *2125 Northside Dr., Buckhead, 404/609–7193.*

5 b-7

CHASTAIN PARK TENNIS CENTER

The 9 hard courts here are lighted. *110 W. Wieuca Rd., Buckhead, 404/255–1993.*

7 g-3

MCGHEE TENNIS CENTER

The center has 9 lighted hard courts. *820 Beecher St., Cascade Heights, 404/756–1869.*

15 g-2

PIEDMONT PARK TENNIS CENTER

The park's 12 hard courts are lighted. *Bordered by Piedmont Ave., 10th St., and Monroe Dr., Midtown, 404/853–3461. MARTA: Midtown or Arts Center.*

15 a-6

WASHINGTON PARK TENNIS CENTER

The eight hard courts are lighted. *1125 Lena St., Washington Park, 404/658–6229.*

cobb county

Cobb County has a tennis Web site: www.cobbcounty.org/tennis.

4 f-5

FAIR OAKS PARK

All 12 hard courts here are lighted. *1460 W. Booth Rd., Marietta, 770/528–8480.*

5 b-2

HARRISON PARK

The park has eight lighted hard courts. *2653 Shallowford Rd., Marietta, 770/591–3151.*

4 c-1

KENNWORTH PARK

The eight hard courts here are lighted. *4100 GA 293, Acworth, 770/917–5160.*

4 b-5

LOST MOUNTAIN TENNIS CENTER

The 12 hard courts are lighted. *4845 Dallas Hwy., Powder Springs, 770/528–8525.*

4 d-8

SWEETWATER PARK

There are eight lighted hard courts at the park. *2447 Clay Rd., Austell, 770/819–3221.*

4 h-5

TERRELL MILL PARK

The eight hard courts here are lighted. *480 Terrell Mill Rd., Marietta, 770/644–2771.*

dekalb county

5 d-6

BLACKBURN TENNIS CENTER

All 18 hard courts at this center are lighted. *3493 Ashford-Dunwoody Rd., Dunwoody, 770/451–1061.*

13 f-7

DEKALB TENNIS CENTER

The 17 hard courts here are lighted. *1400 McConnell Dr., Decatur, 404/325–2520.*

5 *d-5*

DUNWOODY
TENNIS CENTER

The center has half a dozen lighted hard courts. *1850 Cotillion Dr., Dunwoody, 770/551–8578.*

14 *g-2*

GLEN LAKE
TENNIS CENTER

The 9 hard courts here are lighted. *1121 Church St., Decatur, 404/377–7231.*

8 *g-1*

LINCOLN TENNIS CENTER
AT STONE MOUNTAIN PARK

The park's tennis center includes 15 lighted hard courts. *5525 Bermuda Rd., off West Park Pl., east of Stone Mountain Park, Stone Mountain, 770/498–5600.*

8 *b-5*

SUGAR CREEK

The 12 hard courts and four clay courts are lighted. *2706 Bouldercrest Rd., Gresham Park, 404/243–7149.*

fayette county

9 *a-6*

PEACHTREE CITY
TENNIS CENTER

The center has 12 hard courts and 6 clay courts, all of them lighted. *10 Planterra Way, Peachtree City, 770/486–9474.*

fulton county

7 *e-7*

BURDETT TENNIS CENTER

The eight hard courts are lighted. *5975 Old Carriage Dr., College Park, 770/996–3502.*

5 *c-5*

NORTH FULTON
TENNIS CENTER

The center lights its eight hard courts. *5975 Old Carriage Dr., College Park, 770/996–3502.*

7 *d-7*

SOUTH FULTON
TENNIS CENTER

All 24 hard courts and 4 clay courts are lighted at this center. *5645 Mason Rd., College Park, 770/306–3059.*

gwinnett county

5 *g-5*

HUDLOW TENNIS CENTER

Sixteen hard courts are lighted here. *6224 Jimmy Carter Blvd., Norcross, 770/417–2210.*

6 *b-7*

MOUNTAIN PARK
TENNIS CENTER

The center lights eight hard courts. *5050 Five Forks Trickum Rd., Lilburn, 770/564–4651.*

henry county

8 *d-8*

GARDNER PARK

Of the 12 hard courts here, 6 are lighted. *160 E. Atlanta Rd., Stockbridge, no phone.*

VOLLEYBALL

The beach-volleyball competition held in Clayton County International Park during the 1996 Olympics sparked a wave of local interest in volleyball. The number of courts in the Atlanta area has been growing, and the Olympic site hosts a variety of regional and national volleyball competitions.

teams to watch

GEORGIA STATE
UNIVERSITY LADY
PANTHERS

Runner-up in the 1998 Trans-America Athletic Conference, the Lady Panthers play fast-paced, highly competitive volleyball. Admission is free. *GSU Sports Arena, Piedmont Ave. and Decatur St., Downtown, 404/651–2772. MARTA: Georgia State*

GEORGIA TECH
LADY JACKETS

This team is a major presence in the highly competitive Atlantic Coast Conference. *Georgia O'Keefe Gymnasium, Georgia Tech, Techwood Dr., at 6th St., Downtown, 888/832–4849. MARTA: Midtown.*

where to play

Local county parks departments may have information on league play. **Atlanta Club Sport** (404/842–0317), one of three independent organizations in the area, sponsors recreational and competitive leagues for youths and adults. The **North Atlanta Volleyball Club** (770/909–0281, www.northatlantavolleyball.org) and **Volleyball Atlanta** (770/394–7074, www.volleyballatlanta.org) send teams to tournaments sponsored by the Southern Region Volleyball Association. Listed here are some of the most popular spots around Atlanta to find a pickup game or join in a league.

15 *f-4*

BEDFORD-PINE PARK
Bedford Pl. between Angier and Linden Aves., Midtown, no phone. MARTA: Civic Center.

9 *h-1*

CLAYTON COUNTY INTERNATIONAL PARK
Olympic wanna-bes can pound the sand here, at the site of the 1996 Olympic Games beach volleyball competition. The heart of the park is the 6,200-seat volleyball stadium and 13-court volleyplex. *Off GA 138, west of I–75 and east of Crane Rd., Jonesboro, 770/473–4005.*

14 *g-3*

DECATUR RECREATION CENTER
231 Sycamore St., Decatur, 404/377–0494.

5 *c-5*

HAMMOND PARK
705 Hammond Dr., at Glenridge Dr., Sandy Springs, 404/303–6176.

15 *h-2*

HOWELL MEMORIAL PARK
Virginia Ave., at Barnett St., Virginia-Highland, 404/222–8244.

4 *g-6*

SMYRNA COMMUNITY CENTER
200 Village Green Cir., Smyrna, 770/431–2842.

WRESTLING

11 *a-4*

WWA4 PRO WRESTLING SCHOOL
Emphasis is on training professional wrestlers, but the gym has various levels of classes and competitive matches.

4375 Commerce Dr., Northwest Atlanta, 404/696–5696.

YOGA

Several private health clubs, including L.A. Fitness, also offer yoga sessions.

13 *e-6*

METAMORPHOSIS YOGA STUDIO
2931-A N. Druid Hills Rd., Toco Hills, 404/633–8484.

12 *f-3*

PEACHTREE YOGA CENTER
3130 Peachtree Rd., Buckhead, 404/467–9642.

14 *a-2*

PIERCE YOGA PROGRAM
1164 N. Highland Ave., Virginia-Highland, 404/875–7110.

15 *f-2*

STILLWATER YOGA STUDIO
270 15th St., Midtown, 404/874–7813. MARTA: Arts Center.

fitness centers & health clubs

Atlanta sweats in dozens of health clubs and gyms—in storefronts, strip malls, and office buildings. Some of the best-known clubs belong to national chains, though a number of local clubs have a loyal following. The chain outlets generally offer the same programs. Below is a sampling of what's available.

PRIVATE HEALTH CLUBS

5 *c-4*

BALLY TOTAL FITNESS
An abundance of solo strength-training equipment is what you get here, in addition to personal trainers and step-training, ballet, and tai chi classes. Bally has eight clubs in the metro area. *6780 Roswell Rd., Sandy Springs, 770/394–0090 or 800/695–8111, www.ballyfitness.com.*

5 *c-5*

CONCOURSE ATHLETIC CLUB

Besides its body-sculpting and toning equipment, the club runs a well-received aquatics program in its indoor and heated outdoor pools. *8 Concourse Pkwy., Dunwoody, 770/698–2000, www. concourseclub.com.*

4 *h-7*

CRUNCH FITNESS

Programs such as "Urban Rebounding" and "Body Pump" clue you into the hip attitude here. But Crunch maintains a vigorous gym approach at heart, with workouts of the no-pain-no-gain variety. The city has six Crunch clubs. *3101 Cobb Pkwy., Parkway Pointe, 770/955–3845, www.crunch.com.*

9 *e-2*

FIREHOUSE FITNESS

A group of Clayton County firemen turned their own quest for conditioning into a spacious, abundantly equipped fitness center. Apart from rows and rows of strength-building machines, the club has two racquetball courts, a lap pool, and a supervised child-care area. Members have key-access to the gym 24 hours a day, seven days a week. *691 Hwy. 138 SW, Riverdale, 770/991–3355, www.firehousefitness.com.*

5 *f-4*

GOLD'S GYM

Traditional weight-lifting equipment, treadmills, and stationary bikes fill this place, which also offers exercise classes based on kickboxing and jazz and hip-hop dance. There are four Gold's locations in the area. *6315 Spalding Dr., Norcross, 770/209–9955.*

15 *e-1*

L.A. FITNESS

The chain formerly known as Australian Body Works was merged into L.A. Fitness, but the 22 metro-area locations have retained most of the programs. All offer a full range of activities and classes—from racquetball and cardio kickboxing to yoga—designed to help you tone both body and spirit. *1197 Peachtree St., at Colony Square, Midtown, 404/897–1550, www.lafitness.com, MARTA: Arts Center.*

11 *d-6*

LEE HANEY'S UNIVERSAL FITNESS CENTER

Body-building star Lee Haney won the Mr. Olympia title a record eight straight years, wiping out Arnold Schwarzenegger's old mark of seven titles. Now Haney helps both men and women shape up, with a large helping of his own nutritional guidelines. *675 Ponce de Leon Ave. NE, Virginia-Highland, 404/892–6737, www.leehaney.com.*

4 *h-6*

MAIN EVENT FITNESS

With pro wrestler Lux Luger as one of the owners, this gym promises its patrons "serious workouts"—and has the equipment and personal trainers to deliver. Massage therapy and tanning are available, too. *2000 Powers Ferry Cir., just north of I–285, Marietta, 770/951–2120.*

11 *d-6*

PE MIDTOWN

This local gym draws a lot of regulars with its mix of workout equipment, tai chi and yoga classes, and a smoothie bar. *742 Ponce de Leon Pl. NE, Poncey-Highland, 404/885–1499, www. pe-midtown.com.*

7 *g-4*

RUN N' SHOOT ATHLETIC CENTER

Best known for its basketball courts, Run N' Shoot is open 24 hours and also offers a full aerobics-conditioning center and weight room—plus an on-site barber shop. *1959 Metropolitan Way, north of Langford Pkwy./GA 166, South Atlanta, 404/767–7125, www.runnshoot.com.*

PUBLIC HEALTH CLUBS

Many town and county recreation centers have some conditioning equipment or weight rooms, or they may sponsor evening exercise classes. You also might check out the class listings of the adult-education programs of area colleges and universities or hospitals with wellness programs—some have extensive fitness facilities.

5 *b-7*

CHASTAIN PARK GYMNASIUM

The weight room at Chastain isn't as posh as those at other clubs, but membership is free. *140 W. Wiuca Rd., Buckhead, 404/851–1273.*

YMCA OF METROPOLITAN ATLANTA

Known for their aquatics programs and instruction, the metro-area YMCAs offer numerous other classes, from cheerleading and gymnastics to rock-climbing and pre-school basketball, open to members and the general public. YMCA members receive discounts. The main office can guide you to facilities, programs, and rates at YMCAs throughout the city. *Main office: 100 Edgewood Ave. NE, Midtown, 404/588–9622, www.ymcaatl.org, MARTA: Five Points.*

5 *f-1*

3655 Preston Ridge Rd., Alpharetta, 770/664–1220.

5 *d-6*

3692 Ashford-Dunwoody Rd., Dunwoody, 770/451–9622.

11 *a-2*

1160 Moores Mill Rd., Buckhead, 404/350–9292.

11 *c-7*

555 Luckie St., Downtown, 404/724–9622. MARTA: Peachtree Center.

1 *h-6*

2140 Newton Dr., Covington, 770/787–3908.

14 *f-2*

1100 Clairmont Rd., Decatur, 404/377–0241.

4 *h-4*

10545 E. Piedmont Rd., near Roswell Rd., Marietta, 770/977–5991.

9 *b-5*

215 Huiet Rd., east of I–85, Fayetteville, 770/719–9622.

1 *c-8*

1755 E. GA 34, east of I–85, Newnan, 770/252–7575.

5 *f-3*

5600 W. Jones Bridge Rd., Norcross, 770/246–9622.

4 *b-3*

1700 Dennis Kemp La., off Stilesboro Rd. near Mars Hill Rd., Kennesaw, 770/423–9622.

8 *a-3*

1765 Memorial Dr., Decatur, 404/373–6561.

7 *f-4*

2200 Campbellton Rd., Adams Park, 404/753–4169.

6 *b-4*

2985 Sugarloaf Pkwy., Lawrenceville, 770/963–1313.

chapter 4

PLACES TO EXPLORE

galleries, gargoyles, museums, & more

I n 1993 you couldn't get a decent latte in this town. Now that seems like a century ago. Thanks in part to the 1996 Summer Olympic Games, which put the city at the top of the international menu, Atlanta has become a global business center. But if it's business opportunity that draws newcomers, it's Atlanta's Southern heritage that gives them a genuine taste for the place. After all, any city worth its salt must preserve its character even as new, and sometimes exotic, ingredients are added to the mix—and Atlanta's Southern flavor remains strong.

As in any other world-class metropolis, the shiny new coexists with the quirky old, so that locals can still feel at home even as they are energized by the excitement of their ever-evolving city. Old haunts and neighborhood institutions anchor the rush of the present in the grace of the past. Cheek-by-jowl with young businesses, the city's landmarks have been dusted off to glow in their own right and to lend their patina to their newly pretty environs.

neighborhoods

15 f-1
ANSLEY PARK
Because it's just north of Midtown, this community has all the convenience of city living without the bustle of foot traffic on its way to popular nightclubs and restaurants. The homes here are large and attractive, and the streetscape is surprisingly serene for being so close to downtown. *Bordered by Peachtree St. on the west, Piedmont Rd. on the east, 14th St. on the south, the Piedmont Rd.–Monroe Dr. intersection on the north.*

12 f-2
BUCKHEAD
A large percentage of the city's wealthy citizens live here. It's such a popular region that many outlying neighborhoods have virtually been incorporating themselves into it uninvited for years, at once blurring and expanding its boundaries. Its central business district is

home to trendy restaurants, elegant boutiques, and both ritzy and rough-edged nightclubs. Buckhead "proper" includes some of the oldest and biggest mansions in the state. *Bordered, roughly, by Lenox Rd. on the east, Northside Dr. on the west, the Buckhead Loop on the north, Lindberg Dr. on the south.*

14 b-4
CANDLER PARK
The renovated Craftsman bungalows here have been among the quickest to escalate in value in recent years, boosted by the young and affluent who are drawn by Candler Park's close proximity to everything: original restaurants, landscaped bike trails, colorful retail stores. And Downtown is only five minutes away. *Bordered by Ponce de Leon Ave. on the north, DeKalb Ave. on the south, Moreland Ave. on the east, Clifton Rd. on the west.*

5 b-7
CHASTAIN PARK
Known for its romantic outdoor amphitheater—which hosts both pop and classical concerts spring through fall—the park for which the area's named also has a golf course, athletic fields, and an arts center. The large, well-tended homes surrounding the park are reflective of a solid community of longtime residents. *Bordered by Roswell, Powers Ferry, and W. Wieuca Rds.*

15 e-6
DOWNTOWN
Renovated residential lofts and interesting shops and restaurants draw people to the district at all hours these days, so it's no longer just a husk of office buildings inhabited only during daylight hours. The area's become so popular that the outlying metro region has seen an exodus of sorts, with commuters abandoning the traffic jams of the suburbs for the convenience of in-town living. *Bordered by Ralph McGill Blvd. on the north, Memorial Dr. on the south, Boulevard Dr. on the east, Marietta St. on the west.*

14 c-3
DRUID HILLS
Beautiful, languid mansions with expansive lawns along sloping, wooded streets characterize Druid Hills, one of the city's best-known neighborhoods.

Bordered by Ponce de Leon Ave. on the
south, N. Decatur Rd. on the north, Briarcliff Rd. on the west, and Clifton Rd. on
the east.

15 e-8
EAST ATLANTA

Defined by a corridor along Flat Shoals
Road that was once unsavory, East
Atlanta started sprouting some of the
most inventive, inviting, and fun shops
and restaurants in the city and quickly
became a superhot real-estate spot. Its
homes were snatched up in the frenzy
and then renovated, making up one of
the most popular areas among the hip
and adventurous. Bordered by Memorial
Dr. on the north, Flat Shoals Pkwy. on the
south, Moreland Ave. on the west, and I–
20 on the east.

12 f-4
GARDEN HILLS

North of Ansley Park and south of Buckhead are the wooded lawns and charming houses of Garden Hills. The area
also has a core of both quaint and corporate retail and restaurant activity. Bordered by Lindberg Dr. on the south, E.
Wesley Rd. on the north, Peachtree Rd. on
the west, and Piedmont Rd. on the east.

15 g-8
GRANT PARK

An influx of the restoration-minded has
revived this Victorian neighborhood and
the mansions and bungalows that line
the streets surrounding the 100-acre
park. Bordered, roughly, by Hill St. on the
east, Boulevard Dr. on the west, Memorial
Dr. on the north, Atlanta Ave. on the
south.

15 d-2
HOME PARK

In the mid-1990s, this community was
hot property for houses of the handy-
man-special variety; now it's a renovated
jewel just on the other side of the free-
way from Midtown. Residents can enjoy
city views for a modest mortgage, and
the swanky restaurants are less than a
five-minute drive away. Bordered by
Northside Dr. on the west, I–75/I–85 on
the east, 14th St. on the north, and North
Ave. on the south.

14 a-4
INMAN PARK

Row upon row of marvelously renovated
Victorian mansions fill this neighborhood. The invitingly funky Little Five
Points retail district includes vintage-
clothing stores, appealing taverns, theaters, and coffeehouses. Bordered by
Ponce de Leon Ave. on the north, DeKalb
Ave. on the south, Highland Ave. on the
west, and Moreland Ave. on the east.

15 e-8
SUMMERHILL

A former slum that had been bulldozed
flat in the early 1970s, Summerhill has
undergone a true transformation. Most
of the shanty houses have been replaced
with new homes that seemed to pop up
overnight during the Olympic Games
boom of the mid-1990s. Because of the
almost-universal newness, the neighborhood manages a suburban feel only
minutes from downtown and within
walking distance of Turner Field. Bordered by I–20 on the north, Georgia Ave.
on the south, Hank Aaron Dr. on the west,
and Hill St. on the east.

14 a-2
VIRGINIA-HIGHLAND

Longtime residents and young professionals own the Craftsman-style bungalows and two-story traditional houses in
this desirable neighborhood. Its charming shops, eateries, and art galleries
make this one of the city's most inviting
dining and shopping districts. Bordered
by Monroe Dr. on the west, Briarcliff Rd.
on the east, Ponce de Leon Ave. on the
south, and E. Rock Springs Rd. on the
north.

15 a-8
WEST END

Unlike the famous London neighborhood after which it was named, this
West End fell into disrepair after it was
spliced by the construction of I–20 in
the 1950s. Today, however, it's been
enjoying a healthy comeback as its historic Queen Anne-style cottages—so
close to the city center—attract newcomers. Bordered by Ralph David Abernathy Blvd. on the west and south, I–20
on the north, and Lee St. on the east.

where to go

ARCHITECTURE

14 b-8

ABBEY MAUSOLEUM

(Harvey, Hellington and Day, 1943) This architectural oddity is little known because of its location inside antiquated Westview Cemetery, but don't let that keep you away. Built when legendary Coca-Cola entrepreneur Asa Griggs Candler died, the mausoleum holds a jaw-dropping 12,000 entombments, which were needed to alleviate overcrowding at Oakland Cemetery in the center of town. The massive structure, which is the final resting place not only of Candler but also of writer Joel Chandler Harris and former Atlanta mayor William B. Hartsfield, is built of coarsely cut granite, in the severe style of a medieval monastery—except that the eastern colonnade has a Spanish Revival motif. *Westview Cemetery, 1680 Ralph David Abernathy Blvd., West End, 404/755–6611. MARTA: West Lake.*

15 e-3

ACADEMY OF MEDICINE

(Philip Trammel Shutze, 1940) A neo-classic meeting place, library, and training center for Atlanta physicians, this is the work of one of the city's premier architects. Unfluted Doric columns support the central temple-style facade, and a low, squared tower with large lunette windows distinguishes this local landmark. Today, the lower level houses offices; the reception rooms and auditorium are used for weddings and other special events. *875 W. Peachtree St., Midtown, 404/874–3219. MARTA: Midtown.*

14 g-4

AGNES SCOTT HALL

(Bruce and Morgan, 1891) The premiere structure on the grounds of venerable Agnes Scott College, this is a steepled wonder of Romanesque Revival architecture. Sheathed in ornate brick below a severely angled roof line, the castlelike edifice takes your breath away with its elaborate Victorian accents. The building houses dormitories and administrative offices. *Agnes Scott College, 141 E. College Ave., Decatur, 404/638–6000.*

15 c-6

ALONZO F. HERNDON HOME

(William Campbell, builder, 1910; restoration Norman D. Atkins, 1982) Alonzo F. Herndon, Atlanta's most successful turn-of-the-20th-century African-American businessman, founded the Atlanta Life Insurance Company, which remains one of the largest black-owned businesses in the nation. With 15 rooms, gargantuan yet dignified exterior columns and porches, and elegant balustrades, his personal residence is testimony to his success and serves as a museum honoring his legacy. *587 University Pl., West End, 404/581–9813. MARTA: Vine City.*

15 e-6

ATLANTA CITY HALL

(G. Lloyd Preacher, 1930) The dramatic structure rises 14 stories above the former site of the home that served as General William T. Sherman's headquarters after the conquest of Atlanta. Designed by an Atlantan, the neo-Gothic building is filled with materials mined, harvested, or manufactured in Georgia. In the stunning main lobby, for instance, are abundant polished marble and a ceiling of gilded wood. A phoenix motif, symbol of Atlanta's rebirth after the Civil War, dominates the architecture of the second story. An addition was completed in 1988 and a complete renovation undertaken in 1989. *68 Mitchell St., Downtown, 404/330–6717. MARTA: Five Points.*

15 e-5

ATLANTA–FULTON COUNTY PUBLIC LIBRARY

(Marcel Breuer, Hamilton Smith Associated Architects, with Stevens & Wilkinson, 1969–80) Famed international architect Breuer teamed with Smith of New York and Stevens and Wilkinson of Atlanta to design this place, which recalls Breuer's Whitney Museum in New York City. The building was commissioned in 1969 and completed in 1980, replacing the stunning Beaux-Arts Carnegie Library (1902). *1 Margaret Mitchell Sq., Downtown, 404/730–1700. MARTA: Peachtree Center.*

15 e-5

ATLANTA MARKET CENTER

(Edwards and Portman, 1961; addition by John Portman and Associates, 1986) This wholesale service complex started out as a single building called the Atlanta Merchandise Mart, which was designed by John Portman, one of Atlanta's most noted 20th-century architects. Today, with more than 2 million square ft of showroom floor, the complex is more than triple its original size and encompasses the Atlanta Merchandise Mart, the Atlanta Apparel Mart, the computer-and-information-products Inforum (the only unit open to the public), and, on Spring Street, the Atlanta Gift Mart, which is perched atop one of Portman's 1960s-era parking garages. The complex's nondescript concrete exterior belies a stunning interior atrium brightened by skylights and surrounded by cascading balconies. *230, 240, and 250 Peachtree St., and 230 Spring St., Downtown, 404/220–3100. MARTA: Peachtree Center.*

 e-4

BANK OF AMERICA PLAZA

(Kevin Roche, Don Dinkeloo and Associates, 1992) An outstanding feature of Atlanta's modern profile, the Bank of America Plaza (formerly NationsBank Plaza) cuts a majestic outline against the sky. Its stone cladding and striking pyramidal roof with metal spire emulate the architectural accents crowning the Empire State Building in New York City. Also of note are the structure's beveled corners, which soften the edges of the building's horizontal thrust and create eight corner offices on each floor. The building is turned 45 degrees on its lot, so that it faces the surrounding streets at an angle; the result is better views from within and a more dramatic statement from without. *600 Peachtree St., Midtown. MARTA: North Ave.*

5 *c-2*

BARRINGTON HALL

(Willis Ball, 1842) One of the surviving antebellum gems built by Willis Ball, this temple-shape residence was commissioned by Roswell's manufacturing mogul of old, Barrington King. The pine, poplar, and brick used to construct the home came from King's own mills. *60 Marietta St., Roswell, 770/992–1665.*

15 *f-6*

BIG BETHEL A.M.E. CHURCH

(Architect unknown, 1891) Atlanta architecture enthusiasts have long bemoaned this church's loss of most of its exquisite Romanesque Revival detailing after a 1923 fire. The loss is especially tragic because it wasn't so much the fault of the flames as it was of the inattentive reconstruction. The church is now known for the illuminated "Jesus Saves" sign on its metal steeple, a favorite downtown landmark easily seen from the I–75/I–85 downtown connector. Big Bethel is also of historic interest, because it served as Atlanta's first school for African-American children. *250 Auburn Ave., Sweet Auburn, 404/659–0248, www.bigbethelame.org. MARTA: Five Points.*

15 *e-3*

BILTMORE HOTEL

(Shultze and Weaver, architects, Leonard Shultze, designer, 1924) In the early 1920s, when the city of Atlanta supported a booming hospitality industry, this hotel was built to accommodate guests with sophisticated tastes. Shultze was the natural choice to design the hotel, because he also designed the venerable Los Angeles Biltmore in California. The Atlanta Biltmore, along with its separate luxury apartment tower, the Biltmore Inn, enclosed an elaborate garden terrace until subsequent additions obliterated the garden. Set in pedimented arches and bookended by paired pilasters, the windows lining the top floor are of particular note, as are the broken-scroll pediments around the other windows and the massive porticoes with Corinthian columns at the main and back entrances. Though the interior was refurbished in the 1960s, urban blight in the neighborhood forced the hotel to close its doors in the early 1980s. In the 1990s, the buildings were completely renovated to house both commercial and loft residential space. *817 W. Peachtree St., Midtown. MARTA: Midtown.*

5 *c-2*

BULLOCH HALL

(Willis Ball, circa 1840) Uncomplicated yet courtly, Bulloch Hall is a stellar example of antebellum architecture. Built as the home of Major James Stephens Bulloch—Theodore Roosevelt's grandfather—the columned home sits in stately elegance at the end of a wooded cul-de-sac. The city purchased the building in the 1970s; it serves as a museum. *180 Bulloch Ave., Roswell, 770/992–1665.*

14 *b-3*

CALLANWOLDE FINE ARTS CENTER

(Henry Hornbostel, 1917–21) Built for the son of Coca-Cola mogul Asa Candler, this beautiful mansion might informally be called "neo-Tudor," but other than that it defies architectural categorization. The house's timberings, accented with a herringbone pattern, are too large for authentic Tudor architecture, and its unevenly stratified elevations also balk tradition. The result, though, is a gorgeous 27,000-square-ft masterpiece with an interior as rich in refreshingly innovative details as its exterior. Callanwolde houses the Fine Arts Center for the DeKalb County Recreation, Parks, and Cultural Affairs Department. *980 Briarcliff Rd., Druid Hills, 404/872–5338.*

15 *e-5*

CANDLER BUILDING

(Murphy and Stewart, 1906) One of the most visually interesting structures downtown, this 17-story, triangular neo-Renaissance wonder is named for Coca-Cola tycoon Asa Candler, who had it built as a testament to his success. State-of-the-art in its day, it was the tallest and most lavish office building in the city. The exterior, clad in white North Georgia marble, abounds with decorative flourishes, elaborate cornices, and lion-shape brackets in the style of sculptor B. F. Miles. Medallions in the exterior entrance bays depict the faces of famous men. Within, a monumental staircase is adorned with bronze birds and a snarling, winged griffin perched at the end of the marble banister; its frieze portrays local politicians and other Atlantans of note, including Candler's parents, Samuel and Martha. The building still houses offices. *127 Peachtree St., Downtown. MARTA: Peachtree Center.*

15 *e-5*

CARNEGIE BUILDING, DOWNTOWN

(G. Lloyd Preacher, 1926) The architect who designed City Hall also designed this triangular office structure next door to the Winecoff Hotel. Its facade, made of stone on the first floor and brick on the upper floors, is crowned with an ornate stone cornice. Rounded porticos bookend the entrance, at one tip of the triangle. *176 Peachtree St., Downtown. MARTA: Peachtree Center.*

15 *d-3*

CARNEGIE BUILDING, GEORGIA TECH

(Architect unknown, 1907) In the center of the campus's historic district, the Carnegie Building is rather small when compared with its neighbor, Georgia Tech's Administration Building. It has a Beaux-Arts–influenced portico and functions as an office building. *Georgia Tech, 223 Uncle Heinie Way, 404/894–5400. MARTA: North Ave.*

15 *f-2*

THE CASTLE

(Ferdinand McMillan, 1910; renovation and addition Surber and Barber, 1990) An anomaly among its looming, ultramodern neighbors in the heart of the Midtown business district, this curiosity is the creation of builder Ferdinand McMillan, who designed it as his home. McMillan's eccentric take on architecture comes across in the house's montage of mismatched features, including a turret of seeming Chinese influence. Planted atop a foundation of Stone Mountain granite, the Castle was a dilapidated eyesore for decades, until it was saved from demolition by forward-thinking preservationists in 1988. *87 15th St., Midtown. MARTA: Arts Center.*

14 *g-4*

CHARLES A. DANA FINE ARTS CENTER

(Edwards and Portman, 1965; renovation Bailey and Associates, 1989) The arts center provides an invigoratingly modern contrast to the Collegiate Gothic structures that define the campus of Agnes Scott College. Only one story tall, it features crisscrossing dormers that provide ample northern sunlight to the center's offices. *Agnes Scott College, 141 E. College Ave., Decatur, 404/638–6000.*

15 *f-2*

COLONY SQUARE

(Jova/Daniel/Busby, 1969, 1975) The first multiuse development built in the South was this giant office, retail, and hotel complex. In the center of the bustling Midtown business district, it originally had an ice-skating rink at its core, but retail shops and a food court replaced the rink in 1978. In addition to the shopping center, the complex includes a huge Sheraton (more than 450 rooms) and two office towers in which many of the floors have no central corridor, so that offices on these floors have views of both the eastern and western panoramas. *1175 and 1201 Peachtree St., Midtown, 404/881–6392. MARTA: Arts Center.*

 d-6

COUNSEL HOUSE

(Architect unknown, 1898; addition and renovation A. Ten Eyck Brown, 1924; restoration John Steinichen, 1983) Here is the most outstanding example of turn-of-the-20th-century architecture in the West End's historic Terminus District. The brick facade presents a beautiful row of arched windows, terra-cotta accents, and an ornamental cornice. Originally built as a feed-and-grain store, the structure has since housed myriad businesses over the years. *142 Mitchell St., Downtown. MARTA: Garnett St.*

15 *e-4*

FIRE STATION NO. 11

(Morgan and Dillon, 1907) The best-preserved turn-of-the-20th-century fire station in the city, this appealing neighborhood highlight stands around the corner from the landmark Fox Theatre. Still in service as a fire station, the quaint structure has an exterior of glazed white brick, with two large, arched, and molded entries to the fire-truck bays. *30 North Ave., Midtown. MARTA: North Ave.*

15 *e-3*

FIRST UNION PLAZA

(Heery Architects and Engineers, 1987) Though undeniably modern in construction, this tower evokes Art Deco glamour with its recessed silhouette and glittering marble facade. Its most interesting feature is the canopied entrance to the New Visions Gallery on the ground floor, which is considered a beautiful example of deconstructionist design. The 28-story office tower was built as the anchor of the ambitious Peachtree Place development. *999 Peachtree St., Midtown. MARTA: Midtown.*

15 *e-6*

FLATIRON BUILDING

(Bradford Gilbert, 1897; renovation Brisbon, Brook and Benyon, 1977–87) Eleven stories tall, this is the oldest extant skyscraper in Atlanta—and it predates the famous Flatiron Building (1901) in New York City. Situated on the sliver of a corner formed by Broad and Peachtree streets, the eccentric three-sided structure has a triangular footprint, and a very narrow one at that. Nonetheless, it has all the architectural accoutrements of an elegant turn-of-the-20th-century structure, such as bay windows and a colonnaded base. Its designer, New York–based Bradford Gilbert, built that city's Tower Building, America's first skyscraper. Originally called the English-American Building, the Flatiron still functions as an office building and often flies the flag of Canada, its current owner's homeland. *84 Peachtree St., Downtown. MARTA: Peachtree Center.*

15 *e-4*

FOX THEATRE

(Marye, Alger and Vinour, 1929) Otherworldly and onion-domed, this ornate edifice is one of Atlanta's most recognized landmarks. Planned as the headquarters for the local Arabic Order of the Nobles of the Mystic Shrine (a.k.a. the Shriners), the building was purchased by movie-house mogul William Fox when the order ran out of construction money. The Fox became a grand movie palace worthy of Hollywood's golden age and has since evolved into a venue for everything from classical recitals to traveling Broadway productions. *660 Peachtree St., Midtown, 404/881–2100. MARTA: North Ave.*

15 *g-7*

FULTON BAG & COTTON MILL

(Architect unknown, circa 1881; renovation Aderhold Properties, begun 1996, ongoing) A majestic example of exquisite turn-of-the-20th-century industrial architecture, the factory was a dilapidated architectural albatross until it was rescued by a private developer. Restored into a hive of fashionable residential lofts, it is now a major feature of historic, happening Cabbagetown. Especially appealing are the brick arcaded window bays, crowned by terra-cotta accents, that overlook Boulevard Drive. *170 Boulevard Dr., Cabbagetown, 404/526–9800. MARTA: King Memorial.*

15 *e-6*

FULTON COUNTY GOVERNMENT CENTER

(Rosser Fabrap International with Turner Associates, 1989) Filling an entire downtown city block, this complex encompasses the Fulton County Courthouse, a nine-story edifice built by A. Ten Eyck Brown, with Morgan and Dillon, Architects, in 1914. The postmodern design of the newer structure surrounds an atrium with several 3- to 10-story buildings. As at the City Hall annex (in a former Ford automobile factory in Poncey-Highland), the halls here are filled with fine art by contemporary artists. Free tours are conducted, but the schedule varies depending on staff availability. *141 Pryor St., Downtown, 404/730–8304. MARTA: Five Points.*

15 *e-6*

FULTON COUNTY JUDICIAL CENTER

(Rosser Fabrap International, 1993) This dramatic contemporary building houses superior- and state-court judges' offices and courtrooms, as well as a law library and the Fulton County sheriff's offices. Contemporary art in the building includes the figurative sculpture *Sardana, Dance of Peace* (1996) by Catalan artist Manuel Alvarez, which was a gift from the city of Barcelona, Spain. Tours of the center may be included with tours of the Fulton County Government Center. *185 Central Ave., Downtown, 404/ 730–4000. MARTA: Garnett St.*

12 *d-3*

GEORGIA GOVERNOR'S MANSION

(A. Thomas Bradbury and Associates, 1968) In appearance, the Georgia governor's home has more in common with a plantation house along the Mississippi River delta than with a Georgia-style antebellum mansion. The plain, rectangular residence is sheathed in redbrick and has a front porch with a two-story portico of white Doric columns. *391 W. Paces Ferry Rd., Buckhead, 404/261–1776.*

15 *e-5*

GEORGIA-PACIFIC CENTER

(Skidmore, Owings and Merrill, 1982) Opposite Margaret Mitchell Park, this grand 52-story granite skyscraper has a stepped silhouette that is a landmark on the city's skyline. It stands on the site of the Loew's Grand Theater, where *Gone With the Wind* premiered. The theater was demolished after a devastating fire, making way for the forestry company's

headquarters. *133 Peachtree St., Downtown. MARTA: Peachtree Center.*

15 *e-5*

GEORGIA RAILWAY & POWER BUILDING

(Morgan and Dillon, 1907; restoration Stang and Newdow, 1988) Flanked by the modern, flat-fronted Forty-One Marietta and Bank South buildings, this brick-and-stone structure stands in stark architectural contrast to its neighbors. Also known as Walton Place, it's a prime example of early 20th-century architecture. *75 Marietta St., Downtown. MARTA: Five Points.*

15 *e-7*

GEORGIA STATE CAPITOL

(Erdbrooke and Bernham, 1889) Perhaps the most recognizable element of the state capitol is its bright, golden dome, visible from quite a distance. Restored in 1981, the dome is gilded with gold from Dahlonega, Georgia, the site of the country's first gold rush (in the 1820s). To symbolize Georgia's restored allegiance to the Union after the Civil War, the glorious neoclassical exterior was designed to emulate that of the U.S. Capitol in Washington, D.C. Corinthian columns support a classical pediment four stories above the street, and a portico with large stone piers creates a grand entranceway. The facades are of Indiana limestone, while the interior makes lavish use of Georgia marble. On the surrounding grounds, monuments and statues honor local historical figures. *Capitol Sq., 206 Washington St., Downtown, 404/656–2844. MARTA: Georgia State.*

15 *d-5*

GEORGIA WORLD CONGRESS CENTER

(Thompson, Ventulett and Stainback, 1976, 1985) The convention and trade-fair facility was built in two phases and financed by the state. The second phase more than doubled the original square footage (for a total of 875,000 square ft) and added a dramatic entrance pavilion with a massive glass atrium and pedestrian concourse that opens directly onto International Boulevard. *285 International Blvd., Downtown. MARTA: Dome/GWCC/Philips Arena/CNN Center.*

e-4

GEORGIAN TERRACE

(William L. Stoddart, 1911; restoration and addition Smallwood, Reynolds, Stewart, Stewart and Associates, 1991) Touted as the South's answer to Parisian hotels, this was, when it opened, Atlanta's most lavish hotel. It welcomed Hollywood celebrities during the 1939 world premiere of *Gone With the Wind,* earning it a place in local legend. Almost unbelievably, the palatial building fell into disrepair and was closed in 1981. Frank Howington, a local developer with an eye for elegance, salvaged it in the early 1990s and converted it first to luxury apartments and then back into a hotel. With its cavernous, polished-marble lobby and the sweeping, columned terraces for which it is known, the hotel is one of the most courtly structures in the South. *659 Peachtree St., Midtown, 404/897–1991. MARTA: North Ave.*

 e-2

GLG GRAND

(Rabun Hatch and Associates, 1992) A striking skyscraper 50 stories high, the GLG Grand—with its tripartite construction, exterior terraces, and precast red-granite panels accented in bronze—is one of the reasons Midtown is known for outstanding development. The building's cascading horizontal silhouette is reminiscent of New York's Chrysler and Empire State buildings. The multiuse facility accommodates a hotel and commercial offices, as well as top-floor luxury apartments. *75 14th St., Midtown, 404/870–4900. MARTA: Arts Center.*

 e-6

GRANT-PRUDENTIAL BUILDING

(Bruce and Morgan, 1911; restoration and renovation Robert and Company, 1980) Fashioned from limestone and terra-cotta, the exterior of this office building is considered one of the city's finest examples of neo-Renaissance design. *44 Broad St., Downtown. MARTA: Five Points.*

 e-6

HEALY BUILDING

(Bruce and Morgan with Walter T. Downing, 1913; renovation Stang and Newdow, 1987) The inarguably beautiful office tower is notable for its Gothic-style facade with terra-cotta ornamenta-

tion. Its design typifies the height of early 20th-century architectural fashion, but it departs from the norm in the unique form of its street-level display windows, which project slightly from the facade. Another wonder is the elevator lobby facing Forsyth Street; the expansive rotunda with detailed and ornate molding is awash in sunlight from the many windows above. *47 Forsyth St., Downtown. MARTA: Five Points.*

 e-1

HIGH MUSEUM OF ART

(Richard Meier, 1983) No survey of Atlanta architecture is complete if it doesn't include the highly acclaimed High Museum. The contemporary-style feather in the city's cap sits with a kingly air on Peachtree Street, just north of the heart of the busy Midtown business district. Entirely clad in white panels of enameled steel, this impressively modern building is as much a work of art as the massive collection it encloses. When it was built, it was heralded by the *New York Times* as one of the best American architectural endeavors in a generation, and the American Institute of Architects placed it among the top 10 best-designed American buildings of the 1980s. An expansion has been planned. *1280 Peachtree Rd., Midtown, 404/733–4437. MARTA: Arts Center.*

 e-6

THE HURT BUILDING

(J.E.R. Carpenter, 1913, 1923) Designed to fit on a triangular lot, this building is named for Joel Hurt, the developer behind the Inman Park and Druid Hills neighborhoods. Hurt conceived the original design but brought in J.E.R. Carpenter from New York to finish the project. The stone foundation is supported by pilasters and Corinthian columns, and its front facade is recessed 30 ft to allow for more window space and a better view of the city. Renovated extensively in 1985, the building houses offices. *50 Hurt Plaza, Downtown. MARTA: Five Points.*

 e-5

HYATT REGENCY ATLANTA

(Edwards and Portman, 1967; additions John Portman and Associates, 1971, 1982, 1995) This blue-topped hotel tower is notable for two firsts: it was the first major hotel built in downtown Atlanta since the 1920s, and it was the prototype for the atrium hotels that the Hyatt chain has since built worldwide. The unassuming entrance gives no indication of the awesome atrium inside, and the dome, which houses a revolving lounge, no longer provides a panoramic view of the city's skyline (taller structures now surround the building). Extensive renovations and additions were completed in 1971, 1982, and 1995; a skywalk connects the hotel to Portman's adjacent Peachtree Center Mall. *265 Peachtree St., Downtown, 404/577–1234. MARTA: Peachtree Center.*

12 *d-3*
JAMES DICKEY HOUSE

(Hentz, Reid and Adler, 1917) One of the first homes to help make West Paces Ferry Road one of Buckhead's most opulent thoroughfares is also an anchor of one of Georgia's wealthiest neighborhoods. The wood-framed plantation-style house is the most massive home designed by Neel Reid; its towering front porch is braced by narrow Tuscan columns that evoke the portico at Mount Vernon, George Washington's Virginia home. It remains a private residence. *456 W. Paces Ferry Rd., Buckhead.*

7 *h-4*
LAKEWOOD FAIRGROUNDS EXHIBITION HALLS

(Edwards and Sayward, 1916) The two main halls in this quadrangle are exquisite examples of Spanish Colonial Revival architecture. Their tile roofs, terra-cotta accents, and mission-style stucco facades recall the buildings of the 1915 Panama-California exhibition in San Diego. *2000 Lakewood Ave., Southwest Atlanta, 404/622–4488.*

15 *e-5*
MACY'S

(Hentz, Adler and Shutze, 1927) This downtown treasure takes shoppers back to the days before the malls took over. Ensconced in two-story-high arched moldings, the display windows and store entrances woo customers with a grace rarely found in contemporary department stores. The coarse brick exterior, simple and unadorned except for a heavy cornice, was most likely inspired by the architecture of Italian palazzos. *180 Peachtree St., Downtown, 404/221–7221. MARTA: Peachtree Center.*

15 *f-4*
THE MANSION RESTAURANT

Prepare to lose yourself in another era as you enter this remarkably preserved example of Queen Anne–style architecture. Built in 1885, it was the home of the grandson of Richard Peters, who is credited with developing the Midtown business district. The interior is piled with period antiques. *179 Ponce de Leon Ave., Midtown, 404/876–0727. MARTA: North Ave.*

15 *e-5*
MARRIOTT MARQUIS

(John Portman and Associates, 1985) The biggest convention hotel in the Southeast (1,743 rooms), this tower has a soaring, sunlit atrium that reaches the amazing height of 50 stories. The balconies that overlook the atrium spiral down from the top floor in a cascade that lends the space an almost biomorphic feel. *265 Peachtree Center Ave., Downtown, 404/521–0000. MARTA: Peachtree Center.*

14 *g-3*
MARTA DECATUR STATION

(Edwards and Kelsey with Stevens and Wilkinson, Joint Venture Architects, 1978) Like all of MARTA's other rapid-rail stations, this one is designed to make a distinctive architectural statement. The entrance to the underground station is encased in a sculptural brick-and-steel structure in the shape of a beamed pyramid. The station's postmodernist presence is a refreshing counterpoint to Decatur's historic courthouse square, which lies just north of the pyramid. *Church St. and Sycamore St., Decatur. MARTA: Decatur.*

15 *e-6*
MARTA FIVE POINTS STATION

(Finch-Heery, Joint Venture, 1979) At the nexus of MARTA's north and south lines, this station pays homage to the building that was demolished to make way for it. Neoclassic arches from the Eiseman Building (Walter T. Downing, 1901), which once stood here, are incorporated into the modern design. *30 Alabama St., Downtown. MARTA: Five Points.*

15 f-2

THE MAYFAIR

(Smallwood, Reynolds, Stewart, Stewart and Associates, 1990) Near Midtown's Piedmont Park, this towering residential edifice contains apartments for well-heeled tenants. The eclectic building is crowned with four distinctive turrets and is studded with curious faux balconies. *199 14th St., Midtown, 404/607–9822. MARTA: Arts Center.*

14 d-1

MICHAEL C. CARLOS MUSEUM

(Michael Graves, 1993) The museum's architecture is notable not only as pure design but also as an excellent example of form that follows function. To house the museum's collection of thousands of ancient artifacts from Greece, Africa, Rome, and Egypt, Graves conceived a space with interior accents themed along classical and pre-classical lines. The 45,000-square-ft templelike structure of white and rose marble sits in the middle of the Emory University campus. *Emory University, 571 S. Kilgo St., Decatur, 404/727–4282.*

15 e-2 through g-3

MIDTOWN RESIDENTIAL DISTRICT

It's hard to believe that this well-to-do neighborhood was the epicenter of Atlanta's counterculture some three decades ago. But the area originated as an affluent one, its development spearheaded by Richard Peters, a streetcar builder who in 1849 bought 405 acres of choice land and laid out a streetcar network. Prosperous folk moved into the area and built the magnificent Victorian and Craftsman-style homes that crowd the residential streets. After World War II, however, the rise of the suburbs emptied Midtown of its wealthier denizens; urban blight set in and the neighborhood's homes fell into disrepair. As a low-rent district, Midtown attracted students, artists, hippies, and hangers-on in the 1960s, and anti-establishment protests often flared in Piedmont Park. But by the mid-1970s, forward-thinking home buyers became interested in this architecturally rich neighborhood close to the city's center. Before long, a new wave of home owners and entrepreneurs revitalized Midtown, and now street after street is lined with exquisitely renovated turn-of-the-20th-century

homes and bustling restaurants and taverns. *North Ave. to 14th St. between Peachtree St. and Monroe Blvd. MARTA: North Ave. or Midtown.*

5 c-2

MIMOSA HALL

(Willis Ball, circa 1940) Damaged by a fire soon after its construction, this residence lost its original wood exterior, which was replaced by striated stucco that gives the impression of bricks. Built by Civil War legend Major John Dunwoody, it later became the home of famed Atlanta architect Neel Reid. *127 Bulloch Ave., Roswell, 770/992–1665.*

15 e-6

MUSE'S BUILDING

(Philip Trammel Shutze, Hentz, Reid and Adler, 1921) Standing on the former site of a Confederate arsenal, this Italianate building with a limestone base is finished in plain beige brick and topped by a carved frieze. Once occupied by an upscale men's clothing store, which closed in 1992, it has been converted into an apartment building and contains the official residence of the president of Georgia State University. *52 Peachtree St., Downtown, 404/523–7344. MARTA: Five Points.*

15 f-6

ODD FELLOWS BUILDING

(William A. Edwards, 1912, and auditorium addition, 1914; tower restoration Stang and Newdow, Architects, 1988; auditorium restoration Perkins and Partners, Architects, 1991) As the headquarters of the Grand United Order of Oddfellows, this was the scene of vital business and social activity in Atlanta's black community in the early 20th century. The six-story building, with a turreted roofline and a pleasing facade of weathered brick with stone detailing, retains its turn-of-the-20th-century flavor. Busts of African-Americans adorn the exterior of this Sweet Auburn landmark. *250 Auburn Ave., Sweet Auburn. MARTA: King Memorial.*

15 e-2

ONE ATLANTIC CENTER

(John Burgee and Philip Johnson, 1987) The office tower punctuates the Midtown skyline with its unusual roof, on which a foundation of pink granite supports a pyramid of copper. Also known as the IBM Tower (because of its most prominent occupant), it exemplifies revivalist architecture in its evocation of early 20th-century Manhattan skyscrapers. *1201 W. Peachtree St., Midtown, 404/870–2929. MARTA: Arts Center.*

15 *e-4*

ONE GEORGIA CENTER

(Lamberson, Plunkett, Shirley and Woodall, 1968) An exterior of white marble sheathes this monolithic edifice. As the first major business structure built north of downtown, the 24-story office building was the cornerstone of commercial expansion into Midtown. *600 W. Peachtree St., Midtown. MARTA: Midtown.*

15 *e-5*

ONE-NINETY-ONE PEACHTREE TOWER

(John Burgee and Philip Johnson, 1990) Topped with two columned turrets, this modern take on the turn-of-the-20th-century skyscraper slightly resembles New York City's rose-granite, pediment-topped Sony Building (formerly the AT&T Building), which Johnson designed in 1984. The building's granite facade features a recessed central section that runs all the way to the top floor, visually bisecting the structure and creating the effect of two 50-story towers in one. A six-story atrium rises above retail space on the ground floor. *191 Peachtree St., Downtown. MARTA: Peachtree Center.*

15 *e-5*

ONE PEACHTREE CENTER

(John Portman and Associates, 1992) Designed to be a landmark on the Atlanta skyline, this 60-story office tower lives up to its expectations. Cased in varying shades of gray granite, the structure presents a facade whose vertical divisions give it a distinctive beveled appearance. Crowning the tower is a cluster of reflective glass in the shape of a stylized pyramid, which helps to make it one of the most identifiable buildings in the city. *303 Peachtree St., Downtown. MARTA: Peachtree Center.*

15 *e-5*

PEACHTREE CENTER MALL

(John Portman and Associates, 1973; addition 1979; renovation 1986) This retail complex unites four office towers—among them Portman's One Peachtree Center—via an inviting underground labyrinth of shops and courtyards. The mall includes a collection of specialty shops, restaurants, and a food court, which since an extensive 1986 renovation have been virtually invisible from the street level. A system of pedestrian walkways, reminiscent of that in New York City's Rockefeller Center, connects the mall to the surrounding buildings. *231 Peachtree St., Downtown, 404/524–3787. MARTA: Peachtree Center.*

12 *e-4*

PHILIP MCDUFFIE HOUSE

(Hentz, Reid and Adler, 1922) Developer of the exclusive Garden Hills district in Buckhead, Philip McDuffie built his home on an elevated plot of land overlooking Cherokee Road. Behind a stately facade of stone and red brick is a huge residence that attests to McDuffie's notable taste. Extremely detailed stone accents highlight the redbrick exterior, along with four Ionic pilasters that buttress the house's main entrance (which encases a massive stairway). The house is still a private residence. *7 Cherokee Rd., Buckhead.*

12 *h-2*

PHIPPS PLAZA

(FABRAP, 1969; renovation and addition Thompson, Ventulett, Stainback and Associates, 1992) Once a dowdy throwback overshadowed by the popular Lenox Square mall across the street, Phipps Plaza has, since a miraculous face-lift in the early 1990s, become what is arguably the most glamorous shopping center in Atlanta. *3500 Peachtree Rd., Buckhead, 404/261–7910. MARTA: Lenox or Buckhead.*

15 *e-4*

PONCE DE LEON APARTMENTS

(William L. Stoddart, 1913) The unusual 11-story structure, fondly known as the Ponce, was the first Atlanta apartment building designed specifically for the wealthy. It is distinguished by a curving facade, an elegant column-flanked entrance, and an elaborate balustrade atop the cornice. Today the units are privately owned condominiums. *75 Ponce de Leon Ave., Midtown, 404/873–1903. MARTA: North Ave.*

15 *e-2*

PROMENADE ONE

(Thompson, Ventulett, Stainback and Associates, 1981) This eye-pleasing mid-rise office complex is constructed of stone slabs. It consists of two sections that are offset from each other to maximize the flow of natural light through the windows. *1200 Peachtree St., Buckhead. MARTA: Arts Center.*

15 *e-2*
PROMENADE TWO
(Thompson, Ventulett, Stainback and Associates, 1990) A favorite silhouette along Atlanta's skyline, the gorgeous, Art Deco–influenced tower is clad in rose-color glass all the way from its Adoni granite base to its amazing, cascading-pyramid roof, which is crowned with a stately steel spire. *1230 Peachtree St., Midtown, 404/607–6700. MARTA: Arts Center.*

15 *e-1*
REID HOUSE
(Hentz, Adler and Shutze, 1924; remodeling Eugene E. Lowry, 1975) A commanding building constructed in the neo-Georgian style, this edifice today houses a collection of condominiums and apartments. A characteristic of special note is the Roman-influenced pediment with a medallion–and–bull's-head design. *1325 and 1327 Peachtree St., Midtown, 404/892–7416. MARTA: Arts Center.*

15 *e-6*
RHODES-HAVERTY BUILDING
(Pringle and Smith, 1929) The tallest structure in Atlanta until the Bank South Building dwarfed it in the early 1950s, this office building still calls for admiration. It is a fine example of Art Deco–influenced architecture, with Romanesque and Byzantine touches along the roofline. The interior lobby is worth a look for its ornately carved ceilings and beautiful elevator doors. *134 Peachtree St., Downtown. MARTA: Five Points.*

15 *e-1*
RHODES MEMORIAL HALL
(Willis F. Denny, 1904) This odd structure grabs your attention by revealing a new detail every time you drive by on Peachtree Street. Custom-built early in the 20th century as a dream home for the deep-pocketed Amos Giles Rhodes, a prosperous Atlanta furniture dealer, it is made entirely of rough-cut granite quarried at nearby Stone Mountain.

Rumor has it that the mansion was modeled after a German castle, and indeed, it includes a tower and a turreted roof. Inside, exquisite stained-glass windows representing Civil War scenes line a magnificent mahogany staircase. Today Rhodes Hall houses the Georgia Trust for Historic Preservation. *1516 Peachtree St., Midtown, 404/881–9980. MARTA: Arts Center.*

14 *a-3*
STILLWOOD CHASE
(Taylor and Williams, 1988) Unlike most other multifamily developments that sprouted throughout the 10 counties at the end of the 20th century, this one tries to fit in with the surrounding historic neighborhood. The residential complex is laid out in quirky condominium clusters with individualizing details such as clapboard exteriors, ornate latticework, and gazebos. The result is a community within a community, accessed via streets and sidewalks lined with plentiful preserved foliage. *Briarcliff Rd. at the By Way, Druid Hills.*

12 *e-3*
SWAN HOUSE
(Hentz, Adler and Shutze, 1926) One of Atlanta's finest examples of European–style architecture, this manor set on 25 sprawling acres of landscaped grounds is reminiscent of an 18th-century English country home. Its monumental entrance, Doric-column portico, and remarkable horseshoe staircase create a stunning mix of sophisticated design. The American Institute of Architects considers it the best work by the late, venerable Atlanta architect Philip Shutze. It is now part of the Atlanta History Center. *3101 Andrews Dr., Buckhead, 404/814–4000. MARTA: Buckhead.*

15 *e-4*
TECHWOOD HOMES
(Burge and Stevens, 1935) Born as a federally funded slum-clearance project—the first of its kind in the United States—Techwood Homes is not of much aesthetic value. It has the plain construction, large windows, and flat roof that typified early public housing, but it provided some groundbreaking modern amenities, such as electric stoves, bathtubs, and laundry rooms. The 25-acre complex, now attached to Georgia Tech University, houses student dormitories and rental apartments. *Cen-*

tennial Olympic Park Dr. at North Ave., Georgia Tech. MARTA: North Ave.

15 e-1

THE TEMPLE SYNAGOGUE
(Hentz, Reid and Adler, 1920) A prominent presence on Peachtree Street, this house of worship was commissioned by the Hebrew Benevolent Congregation. The block-shape building is an amalgam of Georgian-style architecture and historical Hebrew accents. Columns support a plain pediment atop the facade, and a wedding cake–like drum of white columns supports the dome of the roof. 1589 Peachtree St., Midtown, 404/873–1731. MARTA: Arts Center.

12 g-2

TOWER PLACE
(Stevens and Wilkinson, Architects, 1975) This visually arresting 29-story building was the first large business development in Buckhead, which has since sprouted an entire mini-downtown of commercial structures. The sharply beveled shape of the exterior affords an unusually high number of corner offices, and the structure is cloaked from top to bottom in reflective glass. A shopping mall, a movie theater, and a hotel flank the tower. 3340 Peachtree St., Buckhead. MARTA: Buckhead.

15 e-4

THE VARSITY
(Jules Grey, 1940, 1959, 1965) Atlanta's favorite fast-food institution popularized drive-in eating nationwide in the 1940s. To everyone's delight it still stands as an almost perfectly preserved example of Streamline Moderne architecture, a more cost-effective offshoot of Art Deco. The piano-shape curve of the southwest facade, the smooth enamel exterior, and the ocean liner–style porthole typify the look. 61 North Ave., Midtown, 404/881–1706. MARTA: North Ave.

15 e-6

WACHOVIA BANK OF GEORGIA BUILDING
(FABRAP with Emory Roth and Sons, architects, Cecil A. Alexander, designer, 1966) The tallest structure in the Southeast at the time of its creation, this tower (formerly known as the First National Bank Tower) is a typical 1960s International Style skyscraper. Marble columns run the entire height of the 41-story building's facade, in marked con-

trast to the bronzed aluminum spandrels. 2 Peachtree St., Downtown. MARTA: Five Points.

15 e-5

WESTIN PEACHTREE PLAZA HOTEL
(John Portman and Associates, 1976; renovation 1986) At 70 stories, the Westin Peachtree Plaza is the tallest hotel in the United States. Above its tremendous concrete base, the sleek cylinder of a building is completely covered with reflective glass. "Glass" elevators glide up the building's exterior in transparent tubes, to a revolving cocktail lounge offering one of the best cityscape vantages in town. 210 Peachtree St., Downtown, 404/659–1400. MARTA: Peachtree Center.

15 g-6

WIGWAM APARTMENTS
(Vincent Daley, 1940) One of the few examples of Streamline Moderne construction in Atlanta, this structure has flat roofs, stucco facades, cube-shape balconies, and wraparound windows. In the historic Old Fourth Ward, the apartments strike an architectural contrast to the shotgun shacks, row houses, and factories that surround them. 587–591 Auburn Ave. and 44–50 Randolph St., Sweet Auburn. MARTA: King Memorial.

4 h-6

WILDWOOD PLAZA
(I. M. Pei and Partners, 1991) Wrapped in smoky granite and reflective glass, these two 15-story office buildings are notable for their exquisite abstract design. Connecting the buildings is a stylized half-pyramid reminiscent of the pyramid Pei created to serve as the entrance to the Louvre museum in Paris. 3200 Windy Ridge Pkwy., Marietta.

15 e-6

WILLIAM-OLIVER BUILDING
(Pringle and Smith, 1930) Developer Thomas G. Healey named this building for his grandsons William and Oliver. Its red-granite base is topped by a limestone structure, with corner windows and Art Deco ornamentation on the upper two floors. Originally an office building, it has been converted to residential loft living. 32 Peachtree St., Downtown, 404/658–0047. MARTA: Five Points.

15 *e-6*

THE WORLD OF COCA-COLA PAVILION

(Thompson, Ventulett, Stainback and Associates, 1990) Though it serves a bubbly purpose as a museum of Coca-Cola memorabilia, the pavilion projects one of the most striking architectural outlines to be found downtown. Transparent walls and a covered courtyard connect its three pyramidal sections. A gargantuan, neon Coca-Cola sign adorns the four-story-tall entrance pavilion, which is open on two sides and has a single giant column supporting its ceiling. *55 Martin Luther King Jr. Dr., Downtown, 404/676–5151. MARTA: Five Points.*

15 *b-8*

WREN'S NEST

(Architect unknown, circa 1885; restoration W. Lane Greene, 1992) The former family home of Uncle Remus creator Joel Chandler Harris, this majestic home began as a simple, two-room clapboard cottage. Harris added to the structure over the years, creating the cavernous Queen Anne mansion that it is today. Some unusual accents include a funnel-lattice banister and fishtail shingles on the upper exterior. The house is now a museum. *1050 Ralph David Abernathy Blvd., West End, 404/753–7735. MARTA: West End.*

ART GALLERIES

14 *a-1*

ALIYA GALLERY

The light and airy gallery presents recent pieces by regional and national artists working in a variety of media. On Monday, it's open by appointment only. *1402 N. Highland Ave., Virginia-Highland, 404/892–2835, www.aliyagallery.com.*

12 *g-7*

ARTIST'S ATELIER OF ATLANTA

You can visit more than 20 individual artists in their studios at this cooperative. The media mix is eclectic. *800 Miami Cir., Suite 200, Buckhead, 404/231–5999. Closed Sun. MARTA: Lindbergh Center.*

3 *g-7*

A. R. WOOD STUDIO

This intriguing gallery on Buford's picturesque town square features an appealing collection of contemporary paintings. *9 E. Main St., Buford, 770/945–1660.*

14 *c-1*

BARBARA ARCHER GALLERY

The space offers a colorful odyssey of paintings, sculptures, and assemblages by self-taught artists from the South. *1123 Zonolite Rd., Druid Hills, 404/815–1545, www.barbaraarcher.com. Closed Sun.*

14 *b-3*

CALLANWOLDE FINE ARTS CENTER

This gorgeous Tudor mansion stands in stately serenity, far back from the street on 12 tree-studded acres. Constructed in 1917 for the oldest son of Coca-Cola mogul Asa Candler, the house was donated to DeKalb County in the early 1970s to house a nonprofit fine-arts center. The center contains artists' studios; offers classes in painting, drama, dance, pottery, creative writing, and photography; and presents gallery exhibitions. *980 Briarcliff Rd., Druid Hills, 404/872–5338, www.callanwolde.org. Closed Sun..*

12 *g-3*

CONNELL GALLERY

High-end crafts in an array of mediums—from clay to glass to wood—are the specialty at this visually pleasing space. The lighthearted work of Leo Sewell, "The King of Recycling," who creates playful life-size sculptures from society's castoffs, is shown here. *333 Buckhead Ave., Buckhead, 404/261–1712. Closed Sun.–Mon. MARTA: Buckhead or Lenox.*

15 *f-7*

EYEDRUM

For cutting-edge contemporary art, head for this arts center, which showcases the raw stylizations of some of Atlanta's most exciting young artists. Art openings often are set to original, atmospheric music installations. *290 Martin Luther King Jr. Ave., Suite 8, Downtown, 404/522–0655, eyedrum.memoryflux.com. MARTA: King Memorial.*

12 *h-4*

FAY GOLD GALLERY

Some of the most respected contemporary artists in the country are represented by this gallery. Paintings by the heralded

Tony Hernandez are shown here, as are exquisite displays of sculpture, photography, and glass works. The gallery represents, among others, the estates of Robert Mapplethorpe and Imogen Cunningham. *764 Miami Cir., Buckhead, 404/233–3843, www.faygoldgallery.com. Closed Sun.–Mon.*

12 *f-2*

GALERIE TIMOTHY TEW

On offer here is the work of American and European painters who give traditional motifs a bit of a twist. Featured painters include such nationally recognized artists as Leslie Bell, Laura Nothern, and Chuck Bowdish. *309 E. Paces Ferry Rd., Buckhead, 404/869–0511. Closed Sun.–Mon. MARTA: Buckhead or Lenox.*

5 *c-2*

HEAVEN BLUE ROSE GALLERY

A visual delight from the moment you walk through the doors, this artist-owned and -operated collective offers art in two- and three-dimensional media. *934 Canton St., Roswell, 770/642–7380. Closed Sun.–Mon.*

12 *g-3*

JACKSON FINE ART GALLERY

The display of 20th-century, vintage, and contemporary photography here is thought-provoking. *3115 E. Shadowlawn Ave., Buckhead, 404/233–3739. Closed Sun. MARTA: Buckhead or Lenox.*

12 *e-6*

KIANG GALLERY

The photographic collages of Lucinda Bunnen and the glazed ceramics of Archie Stapleton are part of the varied selection of contemporary works offered at this popular place. *TULA Arts Center, 75 Bennett St., Suite N-2, Buckhead, 404/351–5477. Closed Sun.–Mon. MARTA: Arts Center.*

5 *b-6*

KNOKE GALLERIES

A stroll through this local institution is an education in itself. Within its walls is one of the most complete collections of 19th- and 20th-century American folk art and pottery to be found anywhere. *5325 Roswell Rd., Sandy Springs, 404/252–0485. Closed Sun.*

15 *f-2*

LIVING ROOM GALLERY

From her Victorian-era home in Piedmont Park, well-known Atlanta art aficionado Ann Bassarab presents her homage to contemporary African and children's art—by appointment. Her collection includes an extraordinary display of Kenyan art, as well as the inspiring work of local and international African artists, among them the venerable Ethiopian artist Wosene Kosrof. *305 10th St., Midtown, 404/872–6608. MARTA: Midtown.*

12 *d-7*

LOWE GALLERY

Buckhead's Bennett Street is lined with shops and galleries, but this one stands out for its spacious loft and stock of works by some of Atlanta's most talented (living and dead) artists, including the paintings of an emerging local favorite, Honnie Goode. The gallery is visually impressive in every sense of the phrase. *75 Bennett St., Buckhead, 404/352–8114, www.lowegallery.com. Sun.–Mon. are by appointment only.*

12 *d-7*

MARCIA WOOD GALLERY

This Buckhead establishment is highly respected for its distinctive selection of well-seasoned contemporary artwork. Among the featured talent are the well-known mixed-media artists Daniel Troppca and Mary Engel. *1831 Peachtree St., Buckhead, 404/351–9390, www.marciawoodgallery.com. Closed Sun.–Mon.*

14 *a-1*

MODERN PRIMITIVE GALLERY

A storefront space in the heart of Virginia-Highland shows the colorful works of folk, outsider, and visionary artists. *1393 N. Highland Ave., Virginia-Highland, 404/892–0556, www.modernprimitive.com. Closed Mon.*

12 *d-7*

OPUS ONE GALLERY

Art-intensive Bennett Street in Buckhead is home to this gallery representing 30 local and international artists who create everything from abstract images to landscapes. Among other items, you can find the oil paintings of Deborah Bennett. Opus One is also a stained-glass studio that specializes in screens, windows, and custom designs. *75 Bennett St., Buckhead, 404/352–9727. Closed Mon.*

5 *c-2*

RAIFORD GALLERY

A bright and busy wonderland of original works by local and regional artists, this imaginative gallery—housed in a tremendous, airy cabin built from recycled wood—offers everything from ceramics, fiber art, and handmade paper to glass and even excitingly creative small furniture. *1169 Canton St., Roswell, 770/645–2050, www.jgossman. com/raiford_gallery.htm. Closed Sun.– Mon.*

12 *d-7*

ROBERT MATRE GALLERY

With a focus on figurative work, Robert Matre presents powerful contemporary paintings and sculptures by local and international artists. The gallery sits among the other shops and galleries of Buckhead's Bennett Street. *75 Bennett St., Buckhead, 404/350–8399. Closed Sun.*

12 *e-7*

SANDLER HUDSON GALLERY

The selection includes some of the best contemporary work the Southeast has to offer. *1831-A Peachtree Rd., Buckhead, 404/350–8480. Closed Sun.*

14 *g-3*

SHAWN VINSON FINE ART

This cache of sophisticated fine art highlights the work of European and American contemporary artists. *Marlo Building, 119 E. Court Sq., Suite 100, Decatur, 404/370–8008. Closed Sun.– Tues. MARTA: Decatur.*

12 *g-3*

TRINITY GALLERY

One of the most distinguished galleries in the city, Trinity offers an array of original paintings, sculptures, and works on paper, dating from the 17th century to the present. You can find the work of David Fraley, well known in Atlanta for his use of bold texture and classical imagery. *315 E. Paces Ferry Rd., Buckhead, 404/237–0370. Closed Sun.–Mon. MARTA: Buckhead or Lenox.*

12 *g-7*

UPSTAIRS GALLERY

Among other artwork, this gallery carries the massive color monoprints of Richard Gaskin, who creates images up to 8 ft in height using a handmade camera and pinhole optics. *800 Miami Cir., Suite 210, Buckhead, 404/237–2447. Closed Sun.– Mon. MARTA: Lindbergh Center.*

ART MUSEUMS

15 *e-5*

ATLANTA INTERNATIONAL MUSEUM OF ART & DESIGN

Not your ordinary yawn-fest of dusty relics, this place is all but guaranteed to pique the interest of even the most hardened museum resisters. Founded in 1989, the decisively welcome addition to the local museum scene takes you on a trip through time, using exhibits of folk art and design to chart the evolution of world culture. *285 Peachtree Center Ave., Downtown, 404/688–2467, www. atlantainternationalmuseum.org. Free. Weekdays 11–5. MARTA: Peachtree Center.*

15 *g-6*

ATLANTA LIFE INSURANCE COMPANY BUILDING

The current headquarters of this enterprise founded by Alonzo Herndon, a former slave, opened in 1980. Its lobby holds an excellent collection of works by black artists from the United States and Africa. *100 Auburn Ave., Sweet Auburn, 404/659–2100. Free. Weekdays 8:30–5. MARTA: Five Points.*

15 *e-2*

CENTER FOR PUPPETRY ARTS

At this interactive museum, you can see antique and modern puppets from around the world and attend puppet-making workshops. Performances, which include original dramatic works and classics adapted for the museum theater, are presented by professional puppeteers who leave youngsters spellbound. *1404 Spring St., Midtown, 404/ 873–3391, www.puppet.org. $5; special exhibits and programs extra. Mon.–Sat. 9–5, Sun. 11–5. MARTA: Arts Center.*

15 *g-4*

CITY GALLERY EAST

Don't be put off by its bureaucratic surroundings on the ground floor of

Atlanta's City Hall East annex: this gallery consistently offers some of the most sophisticated Southern-theme art to be found in the Southeast. Sponsored by the Office of the Mayor, the gallery is known for provocative exhibitions of works by a range of artists, from Atlanta city employees to such legendary folk artists as Thorton Dial. *675 Ponce de Leon Ave., Virginia-Highland, 404/817–6815 or 404/817–7956. Free. Weekdays 9–5.*

15 *b-8*

HAMMONDS HOUSE GALLERIES & RESOURCE CENTER OF AFRICAN AMERICAN ART

The only museum in Georgia solely dedicated to the preservation of African and African-American fine art and culture occupies an antebellum home in the historic West End district. The stunning collection includes hundreds of works by artists of local, regional, national, and international origin. Continuing lecture series and classes about African-American art are offered here, and scholars are welcome to use the facility's resource center (by appointment). Considered to be one of the oldest homes in the West End, the building once housed a kindergarten that is believed to have been Atlanta's first. *503 Peeples St., West End, 404/752–8730, www.hammondshouse.org. $2. Tues.–Fri. 10–6, Sat. 1–5. MARTA: West End.*

15 *e-1*

HIGH MUSEUM OF ART

There's no question that the High Museum of Art is one of the proudest examples of architecture the city of Atlanta has to offer. The sleek white structure is awesome outside and in, where a cascade of polished ramps surrounds a cavernous atrium. The best way to tackle the High is to take the elevator to the top and work your way downward on foot. Along the way you can admire the 10,000-piece permanent collection of contemporary and classical art from the Americas, Europe, and Africa. The museum mounts changing exhibits of major works from other collections, such as 1998's stunning "Picasso: Masterworks from the Museum of Modern Art" show. Part of the Woodruff Arts Center, the High Museum is affiliated with the Atlanta College of Art. Founded in 1928, the highly selective ACA has sculpture and photography studios, a large audito-

rium, darkrooms, and an expansive public art gallery for its student body of about 400. In the basement, the High Cafe with Alon's serves delicious sandwiches, soups, salads, and specialty coffees. *1280 Peachtree Rd., Midtown, 404/733–4437, www.high.org. $8. Tues.–Sat. 10–5, Sun. noon–5. MARTA: Arts Center.*

15 *e-5*

HIGH MUSEUM FOLK ART & PHOTOGRAPHY GALLERY

This extension of the High Museum is a treasure trove of changing folk-art and photography exhibits. One notable exhibition, "I made this jar . . . " The Life and Works of the Enslaved African American Potter, Dave," showcased ceramic jugs made by a slave who, unlike most other slaves, signed his work. Many of the haunting pieces were inscribed with Dave's simple yet poignant sayings. *30 John Wesley Dobbs Ave., Downtown, 404/577–6940, www.high.org. Free. Open Mon.–Sat. 10–5. MARTA: Peachtree Center.*

5 *h-3*

HUDGENS CENTER FOR THE ARTS

Juried shows, lectures, art classes, and major art shows and exhibits in all media are offered here. Formerly the Gwinnett Fine Arts Center, the center was renamed upon the completion of its highly anticipated Children's Arts Museum addition. Exhibitions at the center have included works by Ferdinand Rosa and Elizabeth Sheppell. *6400 Sugarloaf Pkwy., Duluth, 770/623–6002, www.hudgenscenter.org. $5. Hudgens Center Tues.–Fri. 10–5, Sat. 10–3; Children's Museum Tues.–Fri. 1–5, Sat. 10–3.*

14 *d-1*

MICHAEL C. CARLOS MUSEUM

One of the oldest museums in Georgia, this Emory University institution started out in 1919 as a library containing an odd assortment of curiosities, such as the fingernail of a Chinese Mandarin and a Dead Sea salt crystal that was labeled "part of Lot's wife." Housed in an expansive modern building designed by famed architect Michael Graves, the museum now mounts exhibitions ranging from "So Many Brilliant Talents: Art and Craft in the Age of Rubens" to "Mysteries of the Mummies" to "Uses of Photography in Contemporary Art." The collection still contains plenty of ancient artifacts of exquisite detail and beauty. Many of the artifacts were gathered in the early 1900s, during daring treks across treacherous terrain that was rife with bandits and warring tribes. A 1920 expedition, led by the fabled William Arthur Shelton of Emory's Candler School of Theology (who traveled across Egypt in an armor-plated Rolls-Royce equipped with a machine gun), added about 250 Egyptian, Babylonian, and other Near Eastern antiquities to the collection. *Emory University, 571 S. Kilgo St., Decatur, 404/727–4282, carlos. emory.edu. $3 suggested donation. Tues.– Wed. and Fri.–Sat. 10–5, Thurs. 10–9, Sun. noon–5.*

15 c-4
NEXUS CONTEMPORARY ART CENTER

Founded in 1973 as an artists' collective with severely limited funding, Nexus can today be counted among the most influential, cutting-edge arts institutions in Atlanta. Gutsy exhibitions, exciting openings, and galas dripping with local celebrities and artists keep the center in the spotlight. The huge, breathtaking renovation of historic warehouse space just west of the city's center holds artists' studios, a gallery with major bimonthly shows, an old-fashioned book press, and the spacious Performance Cafe. *535 Means St., Downtown, 404/688–1970, www.nexusart.org. $3. Tues.–Sat. 11–5.*

13 b-1
OGLETHORPE UNIVERSITY MUSEUM OF ART

This impressive museum provides metro Atlanta with its most comprehensive perspective on the figurative arts, with a focus on historical, mythological, and spiritual content. Opened in 1993 as the Oglethorpe University Art Gallery, it quickly became a cultural contender, with such highly acclaimed early exhibits as "The Family Photographs of Claude Monet in Giverny" and "Portraiture in Holography." Reborn as a museum in 1993, the facility now has two separate galleries. *Oglethorpe University, 4484 Peachtree Rd., Brookhaven, 404/364– 8555, museum.oglethorpe.edu. Free. Wed.–Sun. noon–5. MARTA: Brookhaven.*

5 d-5
SPRUILL CENTER FOR THE ARTS

Centered on a Victorian farmhouse sleekly restored into a state-of-the-art gallery and house museum, this sprawling arts complex includes the Spruill Center Gallery and the Spruill Education Center. The gallery presents a refreshing range of work by emerging as well as established regional artists, often featuring works by students at the education center. In addition to offering art exhibits, the Spruill Center provides a hefty dose of local heritage. It was established in 1975 by Geraldine Jameson Spruill on land donated by her family, members of the Atlanta aristocracy. Items on display in the house museum include a wall telephone with crank and a carved 1840s cradle, along with historic photographs of the Spruill family and the Dunwoody community. *5339 Chamblee-Dunwoody Rd., Dunwoody, 770/394–3447, www.spruillarts.org. Mon.– Thurs. 9–7, Sat. 9–5.*

BRIDGES

5 e-3
THE HALF-BRIDGE AT JONES BRIDGE

Within Jones Bridge Recreation Area is the babbling Jones Bridge Shoals, famous for its trout fishing, and this obscure landmark: a curious, wooden half-bridge that is as scenic as it is interesting. According to local lore, its missing half was stolen in the 1940s. *Jones Bridge Recreation Area, north of Holcomb Bridge Rd. on GA 140.*

4 e-7
NICKAJACK CREEK COVERED BRIDGE

About 2 mi northeast of Mableton on Concorde Road is this very old and very pretty bridge, which crosses Nickajack Creek on the way to Smyrna. Local folk say the covered bridge was built in 1872 because horses sometimes panicked at the sight of the creek's rushing water and refused to traverse an open bridge. Restored for safety late in the 20th century, the bridge is 133 ft long and handles approximately 9,500 vehicles daily. *Concorde Rd. between Mableton and Smyrna.*

3 a-2
POOL'S MILL BRIDGE

Considered the most neglected of Georgia's few surviving covered bridges, this antebellum structure has endured a history of such misfortune and folly that it's a wonder it still stands. First, a flood washed it away in 1901. Then, the local millwright commissioned to rebuild the bridge left his creation riddled with thousands of misdrilled holes and subsequently fled town. The bridge was restored to working order, but by the late 1980s it had fallen into severe disrepair and finally collapsed into the creek below. Today, thanks to community involvement, Forsyth County officials have again restored the bridge and transformed the surrounding grounds into a park. Most recently, an arsonist tried but failed to torch the structure, inflicting little damage. The bridge's freckling of misplaced auger holes is visible to this day. *Settendown Creek, near Heardsville in rural Forsyth County.*

 f-1

STONE MOUNTAIN PARK BRIDGE

The bridge on the grounds of Georgia's Stone Mountain Park was moved here from Athens, Georgia, in 1965. Constructed in 1891, the legendary span was dubbed "Effie's Bridge" in honor of a nearby bordello, which patrons could reach only by crossing the bridge. *U.S. 78, 5 mi outside (east) of I–285, Stone Mountain, 770/498–5690.*

CHILDREN'S MUSEUMS

5 *h-3*

CHILDREN'S ARTS MUSEUM

Part of the Hudgens Center for the Arts in Gwinnett County, the Children's Arts Museum introduces kids to the performing and visual arts, with interactive exhibits and art instruction. *6400 Sugarloaf Pkwy., Duluth, 770/623–4966, www.hudgenscenter.org. $5. Tues.–Fri. 1–5, Sat. 10–3.*

14 *c-3*

FERNBANK MUSEUM OF NATURAL HISTORY

This magnificent museum offers a plethora of surprisingly creative exhibits for children to enjoy. Among them are the Fantasy Forest and the Coca-Cola Georgia Adventure, which aim to give kids a hands-on experience of the earth's environment through clever experiments. Another museum feature is storyteller Ruth Manning, who conducts the popular Story Hour on the balconies outside the Discovery Room. Her program has proven remarkably effective at turning kids on to reading. Parents can find plenty to keep them busy while the kids listen to Ruth. *767 Clifton Rd., Emory, 404/929–6300, www.fernbank. edu. $12 adults, $10 children ages 12 and under. Mon.–Sat. 10–5, Sun. noon–5.*

14 *c-3*

FERNBANK SCIENCE CENTER

Kids happily set aside their Nintendo and Game Boys to witness the celestial wonder of the center's planetarium (Atlanta's largest), which comes complete with a real *Apollo* space capsule. Young naturalists can enjoy the hiking trail through acres of lush forest. *156 Heaton Park Dr., Emory, 404/378–4311, www.fernbank.edu. Free; planetarium show $2. Mon. 8:30–5, Tues.–Fri. 8:30 AM–10 PM, Sat. 10–5, Sun. 1–5.*

15 *f-4*

SCITREK SCIENCE & TECHNOLOGY MUSEUM OF ATLANTA

A favorite destination for kids of all ages, SciTrek is packed with fascinating exhibits that target youthful interests. A host of hands-on science displays introduces children to outer space, natural science, rocket science, chemistry, and more. The museum also presents exceptional seasonal programs, such as Holiday Express, which sets a collection of antique toy trains clattering around their tracks. Summer brings day camp as well as the popular overnights that give kids and their guardians an entire night to explore interactive exhibits. *395 Piedmont Ave., Downtown, 404/522–5500, www.scitrek.org. $7.50 adults, $6 children ages 3–17 and senior citizens. Mon.–Sat. 10–5, Sun. noon–5. MARTA: Civic Center.*

CHURCHES & SYNAGOGUES

5 *a-8*

ALL SAINTS METROPOLITAN COMMUNITY CHURCH OF ATLANTA

Reverend Ike Parker presides over a congregation that he describes as "progressive and multi-Christian." The church is the offspring of the Universal Fellowship of Metropolitan Community Churches, which was founded in Los Angeles by

Rev. Troy Perry with the goal of administering to the gay and lesbian community. *2352 Bolton Rd., Riverside, 404/605–7140, www.allsaintsmcc.com.*

15 *g-6*

BIG BETHEL A.M.E. CHURCH

Founded by slaves in 1843, this is one of the oldest African-American churches in the South. Soon after its inception, the congregation formed the Daughters of Bethel Benevolent Society, whose members tended to the welfare of ailing former slaves. In 1880, the church became the nation's first public school for African-American youth. *220 Auburn Ave., Sweet Auburn, 404/827–9707, www.bigbethelame.org. MARTA: Five Points.*

5 *c-5*

B'NAI TORAH SYNAGOGUE

A traditional congregation founded by Rabbi Juda Mintz in 1981, this small synagogue serves about 350 families. *700 Mt. Vernon Hwy., Sandy Springs, 404/257–0537, www.bnaitorah.org.*

12 *f-4*

CATHEDRAL OF ST. PHILIP

Luxuriant Buckhead is the perfect setting for this exquisite cathedral, which commands your gaze as you pass by on Peachtree Road. The congregation formed in 1847, making this Atlanta's first Episcopal church, and the cathedral was built in 1933. Though its Gothic home cuts an awesome—even intimidating—figure against the skyline, the congregation inside is known for being diverse and energetic. It participates in several community programs, including delivering meals to homeless shelters and building homes for low-income families through Habitat for Humanity. *2744 Peachtree Rd., Buckhead, 404/365–1000, www.stphilipscathedral.org.*

15 *e-6*

CENTRAL PRESBYTERIAN CHURCH

Founded in 1860, this church has a long history of social activism. The original building survived the Battle of Atlanta during the Civil War, but it was replaced by the current structure in 1967. Elegant yet inviting, the Victorian English-style church was designed by English-born Edmund G. Lind, who worked in Atlanta for about a decade. *201 Washington St., Downtown, 404/659–0274, www.centralpresbyterianatl.org. MARTA: Georgia State.*

12 *f-3*

CHRIST THE KING CATHEDRAL

A striking feature of this elegant Catholic cathedral is the massive pipe organ, built by the eminent Fratelli Ruffati, who came all the way from Padua, Italy, to install it when construction of the church was finished in 1937. At the time the cathedral was built, *Architectural Record* magazine considered this to be the most magnificent building in the city. *2699 Peachtree Rd., Buckhead, 404/233–2145, www.christtheking-atl.org.*

15 *e-3*

CHURCH OF THE REDEEMER

Built in the early 1950s, this Evangelical Lutheran church is an excellent example of the Deco phase of Gothic Revival. From its perch on a hill above Peachtree Street, it presents a towering exterior of coarsely cut stone bricks, decorated with medieval-style accents. *731 Peachtree St., Midtown, 404/874–8664, www.redeemer.org. MARTA: North Ave.*

15 *e-5*

CHURCH OF THE SACRED HEART OF JESUS

With its two imposing Gothic spires and sculpted tri-arch entry, Sacred Heart is an unmissable presence in the center of the city. Built in 1903, the Catholic church housed educational facilities established by the Marist fathers, lauded educators. *353 Peachtree Center Ave., Downtown, 404/522–6800. MARTA: Civic Center.*

14 *c-5*

CLIFTON PRESBYTERIAN CHURCH

Though the congregation is small in number, its heart is big. The church regularly converts its sanctuary into a shelter for homeless men. *369 Connecticut Ave., Decatur, 404/373–3253. MARTA: East Lake.*

14 *h-3*

CONGREGATION BET HAVERIM SYNAGOGUE

Billed as "Atlanta's only reconstructionist synagogue," this progressive congregation was founded in 1986 by members of the gay and lesbian community, though today the congregation is thoroughly diverse. Described by its members as open and welcoming, the synagogue is presided over by Rabbi Joshua Lesser. *Atlanta Friends Meeting House, 701 W. Howard Ave., Decatur (mailing address: Box 301, Decatur 30031), 404/607–0054, www.congregationbethaverim.org. MARTA: East Lake.*

7 g-8
CONGREGATION B'NAI ISRAEL
This Reform congregation is the only synagogue on the South Side. Rabbi Julie Schwartz describes her congregation as family-oriented and inviting. *90 Montego Cir., Riverdale, 770/471–3586, www.bnai-israel.net.*

15 g-6
EBENEZER BAPTIST CHURCH
In the heart of the legendary Sweet Auburn district stands a working monument to the memory of Martin Luther King Jr., who was born in the neighborhood and later preached at this church regularly before his assassination. A new sanctuary, designed by the firm Stanley, Love-Stanley, was completed in 1999. Its design is meant to recall a traditional African meetinghouse. *407 Auburn Ave., Sweet Auburn, 404/688–7263. MARTA: King Memorial.*

15 e-6
FIRST CONGRESSIONAL CHURCH
Founded in 1867, the First Congressional Church has earned a national reputation for its social activism on behalf of the African-American community. The church itself was built in 1908, with a profusion of archways, whimsical ornamentation, towers, columns, pediments, and stained-glass windows. The effect is eclectic and fanciful, revealing the influence of many architectural styles, including Romanesque, Spanish Mission, and even Victorian. *105 Courtland St., Sweet Auburn, 404/659–6255. MARTA: Georgia State.*

13 d-6
FIRST METROPOLITAN COMMUNITY CHURCH OF ATLANTA
The church serves a congregation of predominantly gay and lesbian members in a large former theater. *1379 Tullie Rd., Druid Hills, 404/325–4143, www.firstmcc.com.*

15 e-5
FIRST UNITED METHODIST OF ATLANTA
Here is the home of the oldest organized congregation in the city, founded in 1847. The present cathedral, built in 1903 with granite from nearby Stone Mountain, is a prime example of Gothic Revival architecture. *360 Peachtree St., Downtown, 404/524–6614, www.atlantafumc.org. MARTA: Civic Center.*

14 a-5
INMAN PARK METHODIST
Well suited to the charming, easygoing neighborhood in which it resides, this building resembles a simple English parish church. Influenced by Romanesque Revival design, it was built in 1898. *1015 Edgewood Ave., Inman Park, 404/522–9322, www.inmanpark.org/ipumc.html. MARTA: Inman Park.*

10 b-1
KING'S VINEYARD CHURCH
In addition to ministering to the local community, the multidenominational church also sends members to Mexico to help build churches in underdeveloped regions. *40 Mays Rd., Stockbridge, 770/389–1211.*

13 d-4
OR VESHALOM SYNAGOGUE
In 1915, 12 Sephardic Jews who had come to Atlanta from Turkey and Rhodes established this synagogue. It has thrived, retaining the distinctive Sephardic customs; since the 1960s Rabbi Robert Ichay has served the congregation. Architect Ben Hirsch designed the building, which incorporates skylights and dramatically varied ceiling heights. The synagogue welcomes Jewish immigrants from all over the world and prides itself on its ethnic and cultural diversity. *1681 N. Druid Hills Rd., Druid Hills, 404/633–1737.*

12 f-4
SECOND–PONCE DE LEON BAPTIST CHURCH
Along with Atlanta Community Ministries, this church organizes various community-outreach efforts, such as tutoring and neighborhood revitalization. The complex includes an education

annex and a 150-seat theater. *2715 Peachtree Rd., Buckhead, 404/266–8111, www.spdl.org.*

7 *g-4*

SHADY GROVE BAPTIST CHURCH

Under the auspices of Rev. Otis B. Burnett Jr., this in-town congregation prides itself on its youth programs; every April it hosts a weeklong festival titled "Youth and Young Adults Celebration." *1147 Osborne St., West End, 404/755–4332. MARTA: Lakewood/Fort McPherson.*

15 *e-6*

SHRINE OF THE IMMACULATE CONCEPTION

One of the few pre–Civil War structures left standing after the Union Army torched Atlanta, this mighty French Gothic Catholic church incorporates typical Victorian elements, such as two towers of unequal height, each with different ornamentation. The French Gothic influence is apparent in the rose window and the three-part entrance. The use of materials of varying colors is a feature of English High Victorian Gothic architecture. Damaged by fire in 1982, it has been beautifully restored. *48 Martin Luther King Jr. Dr., Downtown, 404/521–1866, www.archatl.com/icatl.htm. MARTA: Five Points.*

15 *e-5*

ST. LUKE'S EPISCOPAL CHURCH

A renovation completed in 2001 gave the majestic brick building a new bell tower. The church is well known for its community-outreach program, which includes community kitchen ministries and a soup kitchen. *435 Peachtree St., Downtown, 404/873–7600, www.stlukes-atl.org. MARTA: Civic Center.*

15 *f-3*

ST. MARKS UNITED METHODIST CHURCH

The visually spectacular church is the oldest among the cluster of churches along this stretch of Peachtree Street. Built in 1903, the structure is of neo-Gothic design with touches of the Victorian. Note the enormous, incandescent stained-glass window above the entrance. *781 Peachtree St., Midtown, 404/873–2636. MARTA: North Ave.*

2 *b-8*

ST. MICHAEL THE ARCHANGEL ROMAN CATHOLIC CHURCH

The doors of this church opened in 1995, to a congregation of 300 families. The 31,000-square-ft facility has a 700-seat sanctuary, a day chapel, and religious education offices. *490 Arnold Mill Rd., Woodstock, 770/516–0009, stmichaelthearchangelwoodstock.catholicweb.com/.*

4 *h-3*

TEMPLE KOL EMETH

Presided over by Rabbi Steven Lebow, this Reform synagogue is so popular that its sanctuary, which was built to accommodate 1,400 people, is nearly bursting. *1415 Old Canton Rd., Marietta, 770/973–3533, kolemeth.net.*

15 *e-1*

THE TEMPLE SYNAGOGUE

The Temple, home to a Reform congregation, has an impressive place in local lore: Bombed in 1958, the synagogue inspired the thriller *The Temple Bombing*, by Melissa Fay Green. It also made an appearance in the movie *Driving Miss Daisy*. The building's domed roof—coupled with its columns, which support a plain pediment—gives it a wedding-cake look. *1589 Peachtree St., Buckhead, 404/873–1731. MARTA: Arts Center.*

15 *g-6*

WHEAT STREET BAPTIST CHURCH

This primarily African-American church stands on Auburn Avenue, where Martin Luther King Jr. was born and raised. Founded in 1870, it has been one of the most influential institutions of the civil-rights movement. Its current stately building dates from 1920. *359 Auburn Ave., Sweet Auburn, 404/659–6820. MARTA: King Memorial.*

2 *b-8*

WOODSTOCK FIRST BAPTIST CHURCH

As the result of phenomenal residential development in the area, this congregation has grown rapidly in recent years, from 250 members in 1986 to more than 5,000 today. The church compound is so extensive that members use golf carts to shuttle around the grounds. Its facilities host numerous spiritual programs for residents. *777 Neese Rd., Woodstock, 770/926–4428, www.fbcw.org.*

COLLEGES & UNIVERSITIES

14 *g-4*

AGNES SCOTT COLLEGE

Established in 1889 as a female seminary, Agnes Scott College was named in honor of the mother of George W. Scott, a local benefactor, when it was transformed into a private liberal-arts college for women. It began as a single house on a small lot and has since expanded to 26 buildings and an apartment complex. The 105-acre campus is a beauty to behold, with wooded pathways and Victorian and Romanesque Revival architecture that make it one of the most engaging campuses in the South. The neo-Gothic McCain Library (Edwards and Sayward, 1936) is of special note for its interior reading room, which possesses an artful network of wood framing. In 2001, *U.S. News & World Report* listed the college as one of the top 20 "Great Schools at Great Prices" in the United States, a distinction that adds to its already respected academic standing. *141 E. College Ave., Decatur, 404/471–6000 or 800/868–8602, www.agnesscott. edu. MARTA: Decatur.*

 e-4

ART INSTITUTE OF ATLANTA

The institute's five-story, 115,000-square-ft structure offers state-of-the-art lab facilities as well as expanded class, conference-, and meeting-room space. Most of the college's 1,900 students are from Georgia, and many of them have returned to school to earn a second degree. At Creations, the teaching dining room, culinary students have the opportunity to feed the public. The Gallery, which hosts continually changing exhibits, is also open to the public. *6600 Peachtree-Dunwoody Rd., Dunwoody, 404/394–8300 or 800/275–4242, www.aia.artinstitute.edu. MARTA: Peachtree Center.*

15 *e-1*

ATLANTA COLLEGE OF ART

Founded in 1928, the Atlanta College of Art is the premier school of art and design in the Southeast, and it remains the only accredited four-year art college

in the nation to be located on a chunk of property that also houses a significant arts museum, theater company, and symphony orchestra. *Woodruff Arts Center, 1280 Peachtree St., Midtown, 404/733–5100 or 800/832–2104, www.aca.edu. MARTA: Arts Center.*

7 *g-4*

ATLANTA METROPOLITAN COLLEGE

A few minutes from downtown, this two-year, urban commuter campus offers affordable as well as accessible higher-education opportunities. Students pursue associate degrees designed for transfer to four-year colleges; applied associate's career programs; and joint programs with Atlanta Area Technical School. The student body, numbering nearly 2,000 strong, is primarily African-American; the average age is 25. *1630 Metropolitan Pkwy., Southwest Atlanta, 404/756–4004, www.usg.edu/inst/atmetro.html.*

15 *c-6*

CLARK ATLANTA UNIVERSITY

Two historically black institutions—Atlanta University and Clark College—combined to form Clark Atlanta University in 1988. Since then the university has experienced steady growth, with enrollment increasing to 5,000 students (4,000 of them undergraduate). More than 80 programs are offered in five schools: Arts and Sciences, Business Administration, Education, Library and Information Studies, and Social Work. *223 James P. Brawley Dr., Southwest Atlanta, 404/880–8000, www.cau.edu.*

14 *e-1*

EMORY UNIVERSITY

The university, which was founded in 1836 by the Methodist Church, has grown from a student body of 15 to a campus accommodating 11,300 students and 2,500 faculty members. In a wooded, stately area about 5 mi from Downtown, Emory University houses nine major academic segments, multiple centers for advanced study, and a legion of eminent, affiliated institutions. In addition to Emory College, the university includes a graduate school of arts and sciences, plus professional schools of medicine, theology, law, nursing, public health, and business. The satellite campus of Oxford College, a two-year undergraduate division, is on the original Emory University campus, in Oxford, Georgia. *1380 S. Oxford Rd., Decatur, 404/727–6123, www.emory.edu.*

15 *d-3*

GEORGIA INSTITUTE OF TECHNOLOGY

Founded more than a century ago, the Georgia Institute of Technology offers courses in technological research and education. The top-notch teachers, researchers, and consultants reflect Georgia Tech's position among the world's leading technology-oriented universities. Regularly listed in *U.S. News & World Report* as one the best 50 universities in the nation, Georgia Tech is also the South's largest industrial and engineering research agency. Industry and government studies consistently consult the Research Institute here, and Georgia Tech is also heralded for its athletics— football, basketball, golf, baseball, and women's volleyball. The 9-acre campus consists of numerous redbrick structures and is listed in the National Register. *225 North Ave., Midtown, 404/894– 2000, www.gatech.edu. MARTA: North Avenue.*

15 *e-6*

GEORGIA STATE UNIVERSITY

With 50 academic departments divided among six colleges, GSU is the largest urban university in the Southeast, but you wouldn't know it by looking at it. Even with its own MARTA rail station, the campus is almost completely camouflaged by the surrounding cityscape. The university counts some 24,000 students. Of particular architectural note is the Baptist Student Center, a stunning Queen Anne–style structure with an intricate roof line. Built in 1891, it originally served as the Coca-Cola Company's first bottling plant. *1 Park Pl., Downtown, 404/650–2000, www.gsu.edu. MARTA: Georgia State.*

15 *b-7*

MOREHOUSE COLLEGE

The nation's only all-male, primarily African-American, liberal-arts college has come a long way since its founding in 1867, when it was known as the Augusta Institute, in Augusta. The campus houses the Morehouse Research Institute and is the home of the *Journal of Negro History*. Its student body numbers

about 3,000; Dr. Martin Luther King Jr. and filmmaker Spike Lee count among its alumni. *830 Westview Dr., West End, 404/681–2800, www.morehouse.edu. MARTA: Ashby St.*

15 *c-6*

MORRIS BROWN COLLEGE

Established in 1885, the college got its start just 22 years after Abraham Lincoln signed the Emancipation Proclamation with a handful of students and teachers and a rickety wooden structure at the corner of Boulevard Drive and Houston Street. The event marked the opening of the first educational institution in Georgia under sole African-American patronage. Fully accredited by the Southern Association of Colleges and Schools, the college today offers majors in more than 30 areas of study and prides itself on its "institutional flexibility"—a directive based on serving the needs of any student with the passion and the potential to earn a college degree. Fountain Hall, a four-story Renaissance Revival structure built in 1882 has a monumental clock tower and a brick facade. *643 Martin Luther King Jr. Dr., West End, 404/ 220–0270, www.morrisbrown.edu. MARTA: Vine City.*

1 *e-4*

OGLETHORPE UNIVERSITY

In a small community called Midway, near Milledgeville, Georgia's former capital, Oglethorpe University began in 1838 with four faculty members and 25 students. The university closed during the Civil War: its students became soldiers, its endowment was lost in Confederate bonds, and its buildings were appropriated for barracks and hospitals. It was rechartered in 1915 and then established at its current location, on Peachtree Road in North Atlanta. In 1944 the university commenced a new approach to college education, called the "Oglethorpe Idea." Determined to provide a common learning experience for its students, it was a harbinger of the now-popular practice of developing a core curriculum. *4484 Peachtree Rd., North Atlanta, 404/261–1441 or 800/428– 4484, www.oglethorpe.edu. MARTA: Brookhaven/Oglethorpe University.*

15 *b-7*

SPELMAN COLLEGE

Founded as the Atlanta Baptist Female Seminary in 1881, Spelman Collage is the oldest surviving institution devoted to the education of African-American women. The college is named after Lucy Henry Spelman, the mother-in-law of John D. Rockefeller, the school's generous patron. Today, with more than 2,000 students, the college is highly regarded and thrives as a private, independent liberal-arts college. The historic campus spans 32 acres with 25 buildings about five minutes west of downtown. *350 Spelman La., West End, 404/ 681–3643, www.spelman.edu. MARTA: Vine City or Ashby St.*

GRAVEYARDS & CEMETERIES

4 *f-5*

MARIETTA CONFEDERATE CEMETERY

Thousands of unfortunate Confederate soldiers who perished in the Civil War have their final resting place in this old cemetery. Founded in 1863, the burial ground is on a hill overlooking Marietta Square. More than 500 boys and men in gray were buried here immediately following the bloody Battle of Kennesaw Mountain in 1864; 2,500 more were reinterred here after the Civil War ended, moved from battlefields around Georgia. Each grave marker simply notes the home state of the soldier buried there, and not much more. A distinguished headstone marks the grave of an unknown soldier, who is believed to have fallen in the Battle of Kennesaw. Buried by an artillery shell, his body remained where it fell until 1998, when it was discovered during a construction excavation. Identified as a Confederate infantryman by buttons marked "I" for infantry and by some remnants of a gray uniform, the unknown soldier was laid to rest in a hand-carved coffin. *West Atlanta St. and Cemetery St., Marietta.*

4 *g-4*

MARIETTA NATIONAL CEMETERY

The oldest grave here dates back to 1866, a year after the Civil War ended. In fact, more than half of the 18,410 headstones here belong to veterans of the Civil War—all of them Union, as opposed to Confederate, troops. The rest of the graves belong to veterans of the Spanish-American and Indian wars as well as both world wars. The cemetery reached full capacity in 1978 and

was closed to casket burials; it was closed to cremated remains in 1996. *Cole St. and Washington Ave. along Hwy. 120, Marietta, 770/428–5631.*

15 *g-7*

OAKLAND CEMETERY

Established in 1850—it's the oldest city-owned cemetery in Atlanta—this is an 88-acre wonderland of weathered headstones and mossy, ornate monuments to the long-dead. It has met the final needs of some of the city's most famous figures, among them author Margaret Mitchell, who penned the epic *Gone With the Wind.* The wooded burial ground is filled with reminders of the past, from the unmarked paupers' graves to the massive tombs of prominent citizens. Some of the thousands of Confederate soldiers buried here are said to haunt the site; their memory is honored by the statue *Lion of Atlanta. 248 Oakland Ave., Downtown, 404/688–2107. $3 adults, $2 senior citizens, $1 students and children. Guided tours Mar.–Oct., Sat. 10 AM and 2 PM, Sun. 2 PM. MARTA: King Memorial.*

14 *g-3*

OLD DECATUR CEMETERY

Some leading members of old Atlanta society are buried in this scenic graveyard, whose first burials date to 1827. Among the graves are those of Capt. William Towers, who fought with Andrew Jackson in the Battle of New Orleans; Capt. John Prather, who, 56 years before his death, fought on this very site in the 1864 Battle of Decatur; and Dr. Thomas Chivers, known as "the lost poet of Atlanta," who was a colleague of Edgar Allen Poe. *Church St. near Columbia Dr. and Ponce de Leon Ct., Decatur. MARTA: Decatur.*

6 *c-4*

OLD LAWRENCEVILLE CEMETERY

This atmospheric, worn-at-the-elbows bone-yard holds the remains of the pioneers of Gwinnett County, whose gravestones date back to the antebellum era. Many of the markers are choked with brush and some of them are weathered by decades of decay and algae, but the crumbling wonder of unkempt burial grounds like this holds definite charm for more than a few graveyard aficionados. *Bordered by Pike, Crogan, and Corbin Sts., Lawrenceville.*

5 *c-2*
OLD ROSWELL CEMETERY
In the heart of bustling downtown Roswell, this enchanting cemetery was first put into service in 1846, when its oldest grave was dug for a four-month-old girl. Though there are plenty of grand headstones, the most fascinating graves are the earliest, which are marked by simple fieldstones inscribed only with dates. *Woodstock Rd. and U.S. 19 (Alpharetta Rd.), Roswell.*

5 *c-2*
ROSWELL FOUNDERS CEMETERY
The site of Roswell's earliest recorded burial, in 1840, tiny Founders Cemetery counts the grandfather of President Theodore Roosevelt among its permanent residents. *Sloan St. near Atlanta St., Roswell.*

5 *b-5*
SANDY SPRINGS CEMETERY
In 1986, the Alfred Holt Colquit Chapter of the United Daughters of the Confederacy declared this charming cemetery an historic site. Though the cemetery has 550 graves, most of them remain unidentified because their original markers were simple fieldstones that went missing over the years, including that of an unnamed soldier who fought under Gen. Robert E. Lee. Today, only 195 of the graves possess identifiable markers. The cemetery is split in half by Mt. Vernon Hwy. *Mt. Vernon Hwy. and Lake Forest Dr., Sandy Springs.*

7 *h-4*
SOUTHVIEW CEMETERY
Back in 1886, a group of black Atlantans founded this graveyard in response to the overcrowding of Oakland Cemetery downtown and the segregation practices at Westview Cemetery in the West End. Reflecting the aesthetic values of the period's Rural Cemetery Movement, Southview sits on parklike grounds and contains beautiful examples of Victorian funerary architecture. Among the graves of prominent black citizens buried here is that of the Rev. Martin Luther King Sr. *1990 Jonesboro Rd., South Side.*

14 *b-8*
WESTVIEW CEMETERY
Established in 1884 to relieve the overcrowding of Oakland Cemetery, this 600-acre site is home to the massive Abbey Mausoleum, built for Coca-Cola founder Asa Candler. Legendary Atlanta citizens buried here include Joel Chandler Harris, author of the Uncle Remus stories. *1680 Westview Dr., West End, 404/755–6611. MARTA: West Lake.*

HAUNTED PLACES

12 *g-3*
ANTHONY'S
The popular restaurant is housed in the Pope-Walton House, an historic antebellum home that reportedly reveals its history to patrons and employees in strange ways. When you walk past the main staircase, you can supposedly hear children singing and can feel the presence of the house's former mistress. A boy once hanged himself from a big oak tree nearby, and to this day a mysterious light is said to jet occasionally about its branches. To investigate the ghostly rumors, a journalist spent a night in Anthony's in late 1998 and subsequently reported many unearthly occurrences, such as the incessant yet beautiful ringing of high-pitched bells and the sound of footsteps—accompanied by the sound of rustling skirts—approaching him throughout the night. You can't spend the night here, but you can come for dinner. *3109 Piedmont Rd., Buckhead, 404/262–7379, www.anthonysfinedining.com. MARTA: Buckhead.*

4 *f-6*
1848 HOUSE
A makeshift hospital for wounded soldiers during the Civil War, the 1848 House restaurant in Marietta has a haunted room. In the Scarlet Room, which was the hospital's operating room, guests and employees have reported sightings of a female ghost in a long dress looking in the window. The house also contains a mural depicting antebellum Marietta. *780 S. Cobb Dr., Marietta, 770/428–1848, www.1848house.com.*

4 *e-4*
KENNESAW MOUNTAIN NATIONAL BATTLEFIELD
In the bloody June 1864 battle at Kennesaw Mountain, more than 3,000 Union and Confederate soldiers were killed. At one point during the fight the Union general had to declare a truce in order to

clear the dead and wounded from the slopes of the "Dead Angle." To this day the battlefield is rumored to be haunted. Many ghost sightings have been reported, and photographs taken here show eerie apparitions, including the vague outlines of faces that the photographer did not see until the film was developed. Other apparitions include mysterious clouds of smoke, said to be ghost smoke from cannon fire, that appear in photographs taken on perfectly clear days. *Kennesaw Mountain National Battlefield Park, 905 Kennesaw Mountain Dr., Marietta, 770/427–4686, www.nps. gov/kemo. Free. Daily 8 AM–dusk.*

 g-7

OAKLAND CEMETERY

Nearly 4,000 Confederate soldiers who perished in the Civil War were hastily buried here in mass graves. Ghostly roll calls are said to echo through the night. *248 Oakland Ave., Downtown, 404/688–2107, oaklandcemetery.com. Free. Guided tours $5 adults; $3 senior citizens, students, and children. Daily dawn–dusk. Guided tours Mar.–Oct., Sat. 10 AM and 2 PM, Sun. 2 PM. MARTA: King Memorial.*

8 *e-1*

VILLAGE INN BED & BREAKFAST

A beautifully restored antebellum mansion that served as a Confederate hospital during the Civil War now houses this cozy B&B. Reportedly, guests are often treated to mysterious specters from the mansion's former life. Mischievous ghosts are said to sing gospel tunes, whistle, walk the halls, and relocate furniture and other items. *992 Ridge Ave., Stone Mountain, 770/469–3459 or 800/ 214–8385, www.villageinnbb.com.*

 e-1

WSB STUDIOS

Evidently there's an extra price to pay when you erect a $50 million television and radio station on the site of Confederate trenches used during the Battle of Atlanta. In WSB's case, that price came in the form of a playful ghost dubbed "The General." Staffers have reported hearing furniture rolling across the floor and papers shuffling when they were otherwise alone in the building, and one executive says the ghost teased her by flipping her hair from behind one night. Professional ghost hunters have confirmed, through instrument readings,

the presence of a spook, but perhaps most convincing to employees is one of the ghost hunters' snapshots. It shows an empty office, in which the misty outline of a skull wearing a Confederate cap is seen smiling at the camera. *1601 W. Peachtree St., Midtown, 404/897–7000. MARTA: Arts Center.*

HISTORIC STRUCTURES & STREETS

6 *f-3*

ALCOVY ROAD GRISTMILL

Legend has it that this mill's owner outsmarted Union troops during the Civil War by hiding his mules and valuables downstream on the Alcovy River. When the soldiers passed through, the story goes, they didn't deem the miller worthy of pillaging. Built between 1868 and 1879, the three-story, wood-frame gristmill was last used in 1986, but it remains in operating condition. *Alcovy Rd. between Lawrenceville and Dacula, 770/822–5174 (Gwinnett County Historical Society).*

15 *f-1*

ANSLEY PARK

Listed in the National Register of Historic Places, Ansley Park was the first Atlanta suburb built with the automobile—as opposed to the streetcar—in mind. Credited to civil engineer and landscape architect Frederick Law Olmsted, the 1904 neighborhood layout includes advanced (for the turn of the 20th century) features such as "pocket parks." The green spaces and the beautiful homes make the area a favorite place for strolls as well as one of the city's most desirable neighborhoods. *Peachtree St. to Piedmont Rd. between 14th St. and Monroe Ave. MARTA: Arts Center.*

9 *g-1*

ASHLEY OAKS MANSION

This virtual fortress was built with more than a million bricks in 1879. Understandably, it is one of the best-preserved examples of Greek Revival architecture in metro Atlanta. Tours are conducted Friday 10–4 and Sunday 1–5. *144 College St., Jonesboro, 770/478–8986. $5 adults, $2.50 children under age 12.*

`15` *e-6*

ATLANTA DAILY WORLD BUILDING

The simple two-story brick building, banded with a white frieze of lion's heads, was constructed in the early 1900s; since 1945 it has housed one of the nation's oldest black newspapers. Despite its title, the publication is not a daily, though it was for a period. Alexis Reeves, now publisher and CEO, is the granddaughter of William A. Scott II, who founded the paper as a weekly in 1928. *145 Auburn Ave., Downtown, 404/ 659–1110, www.atlantadailyworld.com. MARTA: Five Points.*

`15` *d-6*

ATLANTA JOURNAL–CONSTITUTION BUILDING

The *Atlanta Journal* and the *Atlanta Constitution*—to this day the two biggest newspapers published in Georgia—were rival publications as far back as 1883, until they were bought by media mogul James Cox in 1950. Since then they have combined to produce daily afternoon and morning editions. The lobby of the headquarters building showcases old front-page stories, an exhibit of antique typesetting techniques, and photographs of some more-famous staffers, among them Margaret Mitchell of *Gone With the Wind* fame and the venerable late humorist Lewis Grizzard. *72 Marietta St., Downtown, 404/614–2688. MARTA: Dome/GWCC/Philips Arena/CNN Center.*

`14` *h-3*

AVONDALE ESTATES

The picturesque community of Avondale Estates seems to pop out of the pages of a fairy tale, so beautiful is the area. The town was developed between 1924 and 1941 as part of the "new town" vision of entrepreneur George F. Willis. To this day it retains the charm and warmth of a bygone time. Throughout the wooded berg are homes that reflect a variety of architectural styles, such as Spanish Mission and Dutch Colonial, plus a smattering of Craftsman-style bungalows. *South of Avondale and Covington Rds. between Fairfield and Lakeshore Drs., to Avondale Lake. MARTA: Avondale.*

`15` *e-4*

BALTIMORE ROW

You may think you're in Yankee territory as you stroll this section of Midtown. Atlanta's first row-house development was built in 1886 to the specifications of J. S. Rosenthal, in honor of his Maryland hometown. *5–19 Baltimore Pl., Midtown. MARTA: North Ave.*

`15` *e-6*

BAPTIST STUDENT UNION AT GEORGIA STATE UNIVERSITY

In 1898, announcing to his shareholders that "it is sufficient for all the needs for all time to come," Asa Griggs Candler built this elegant Victorian structure as the first Coca-Cola bottling plant. Even visionaries, it seems, have their limitations. *125 Edgewood Ave., Downtown, 404/659–8726, www.gsu.edu. MARTA: Five Points or Georgia State.*

`4` *g-4*

THE BIG CHICKEN

This 56-ft-tall metal chicken was built in 1964 as a roadside oddity to attract customers to the Chick-Chuck-N'-Shake fast-food joint. When that enterprise went belly-up, a Kentucky Fried Chicken franchise bought the bird and its restaurant roost. The Big Chicken came close to extinction in 1993, after severe wind storms plucked it of all but a few of its sheet-metal feathers. KFC was reluctant to fork over the bucks to save the bird, but its plans to demolish the local treasure brought squawks of protest. Recognizing a public-relations disaster in the making, KFC decided not only to rescue the beloved local landmark but also to update its look by installing motors to animate its beak and eyes. Today, Marietta residents don't know how to give driving directions without mentioning the Big Chicken. If you can't follow directions from that point on, you can't maneuver around Marietta. *12 N. Cobb Pkwy., Marietta, 770/422–4716.*

`15` *g-7*

CABBAGETOWN

The engaging former mill village a few miles from the city's center is said to have earned its name when a cabbage cart overturned here. Now it's the site of a renovation rage among urban enthusiasts. The tiny houses, many of them simple shotgun shacks and cottages dating back to 1884, once served as housing for employees of the looming Fulton Bag and Cotton Mill, which itself has been turned into a hive of upscale loft apartments. The colorful community has many picturesque streets, including Savannah and Carroll streets, and is on the National Register of Historic Places. *Moreland to DeKalb Aves. between Boulevard Dr. and Chester Ave., www. cabbagetown.cc. MARTA: King Memorial.*

14 *a-5, b-5*

CANDLER PARK

Known for its charming collection of varied housing styles dating back to the late 1800s, Candler Park is full of exquisitely restored Eastlake-style cottages and Craftsman-style bungalows, with the occasional Victorian mansion thrown into the mix. The portion of Candler Park listed on the National Register of Historic Places is roughly bordered by Moreland, DeKalb, McClendon and Harold avenues, including Mathews Street and Clifton Terrace. *Bordered by Ponce de Leon Ave. on the north, DeKalb Ave. on the south, Moreland Ave. on the east, and Clifton Rd. on the west, www. candlerpark.org. MARTA: Edgewood/ Candler Park.*

15 *e-5*

CAPITOL CITY CLUB

Built in 1911, this stately edifice was designed by architect Donn Barber for an elite private club founded in 1883. Club members have included a Union general, Pennsylvanian John Randolph Lewis (later Atlanta's postmaster), Governor Joseph E. Brown (whose statue stands on the Capitol grounds), Coca-Cola founder Asa Candler, and unreconstructed rebel Robert Toombs, who was the Confederate Secretary of State. The club remains an exclusive spot, a favorite and lavish lunch setting for the city's leaders. The building's dignified facade includes a columned entrance and twin balconies. *7 Harris St., Downtown, 404/ 523–8221. MARTA: Peachtree Center.*

15 *d-5*

CENTENNIAL OLYMPIC PARK

The landscaped, 21-acre monument to Atlanta's role as host of the 1996 Olympic Games is rife with interesting sights. Inscriptions mark commemorative bricks purchased by Altantans before the games, artwork dots the grounds, and a fountain in the shape of the Olympic Rings is best described as a "water sculpture." *Marietta St. at International Blvd., Downtown. MARTA: Dome/GWCC/Philips Arena/CNN Center.*

15 *d-6*

COTTONGIM BUILDING

This classic example of turn-of-the-20th-century mill construction, built in 1890, is in the Terminus District, which was once a busy commercial center. Though somewhat dilapidated, the area has a historic air, since it has changed little since the early 1900s. The Cottongim Building, with wood joists and cast-iron columns, presently awaits restoration. *97 Broad St., Downtown. MARTA: Five Points.*

14 *b-3, c-2*

DRUID HILLS

Developer Joel Hurt commissioned Frederick Law Olmsted's firm to lay out Druid Hills. Eventually, Hurt had to sell the property because he was unable to garner financing for its completion, and none other than Coca-Cola mogul Asa Griggs Candler came to the rescue. Druid Hills premiered in 1908 as Atlanta's first effort at suburbia, attracting residents with its sprawling homes and beautiful churches. *N. Decatur Rd. and Ponce de Leon Ave. between Briarcliff and Lullwater Rds., www.fredericklawolmsted.com/druid. html.*

9 *g-1*

1869 JAIL/CLAYTON COUNTY HISTORY CENTER

The Gothic-style building was erected after the fabled 1864 Battle of Jonesboro. The interesting structure has since been renovated to showcase the relics of the Old South in Clayton County. *King St., Jonesboro, 770/473–0197 or 770/603– 0036, www.claytoncham.org. Donation requested. Wed.–Fri. 11–3:30.*

9 *e-4*

FAYETTE COUNTY COURTHOUSE

Built in 1825, this is the oldest courthouse in Georgia. Originally constructed as a simple brick building, it later acquired a gray stucco exterior and clock tower. *145 Johnson Ave., on the square, Fayetteville, 770/461–4703.*

15 *e-4*

FOX THEATRE

The Fox is no mere movieplex—it's a dramatic flashback to the times when ornamental excess was required for a glitzy night on the town. Built in 1929 as the headquarters for Atlanta's Arabic Order of the Nobles of the Mystic Shrine (a.k.a. the Shriners), the awesome conglomeration of curious but beautiful architecture changed hands before its completion. It was purchased by movie-house mogul William Fox, who turned it into the grand movie and performance palace it is today. *660 Peachtree St., Midtown, 404/881–2100, www.foxtheatre.org. MARTA: North Ave.*

15 *e-6*

GEORGIA RAILROAD FREIGHT DEPOT

Built in 1869, this redbrick, stone-accented depot originally stood three stories tall, but a fire in 1935 reduced it to its current single story. It remains the oldest extant building in downtown Atlanta. Beautifully restored, the Italianate structure is used today as a special-events and reception space. *65 Martin Luther King Jr. Dr., Downtown, 404/656–3850. MARTA: Five Points.*

15 *e-4*

GEORGIAN TERRACE

Heralded at the time of its construction in 1911 as the most lavish hotel in Atlanta, this is where Hollywood celebrities stayed during the 1939 world premiere of *Gone With the Wind*. The regal building fell into disrepair and was closed in 1981, and a decade later it was converted to luxury apartments. Since then, it has been resurrected as a hotel. Around a soaring central atrium, the interior is awash in polished marble; encircling the atrium are the columned terraces for which the hotel was named. *659 Peachtree St., Midtown, 404/897–1991, www.thegeorgianterrace.com. MARTA: North Ave.*

10 *e-4*

HENRY COUNTY COURTHOUSE

The little brick courthouse was built in 1897, with arched windows and a clock tower complete with turrets. It was designed to stand out in simpler times, when courtroom trials were the primary source of community entertainment. *1 Courthouse Sq., McDonough, 770/954–2121.*

14 *a-5*

INMAN PARK

In 1889, developer Joel Hurt began work on Inman Park, which today calls itself "Atlanta's First Suburb." Because of its roller-coaster ride in and out of prosperity over the years, the area encompasses a host of residential styles, from huge Victorian mansions to humble shacks. As the city expanded, the suburb became an in-town neighborhood. Its charm has made it one of the most popular neighborhoods in the city, home to Mayor Bill Campbell, among others. It is on the National Register of Historic Places. *Between Edgewood, Euclid, and Moreland Aves., www.inmanpark.org. MARTA: Inman Park/Reynoldstown.*

4 *f-4*

KENNESAW HOUSE

In 1993 this exquisite example of late Victorian architecture had a date with the wrecking ball, but citizens with a sense of history rallied to save it. The former hotel now houses office and retail space, as well as the Marietta Museum of History on the second floor. *1 Depot St., Marietta, 770/528–0431.*

15 *g-6*

MARTIN LUTHER KING JR. BIRTH HOME

Part of the Martin Luther King Jr. National Historic District, this modest Queen Anne–style bungalow is where King was born in 1929. On display are photographs and personal effects of the King family. To sign up for National Parks Service–led tours of the house, go to the fire station at 39 Boulevard Drive. *501 Auburn Ave., Sweet Auburn, 404/331–6922, thekingcenter.com. Free. Daily ½-hr tours every hr 10–5. MARTA: King Memorial.*

15 *g-6*

MARTIN LUTHER KING JR. NATIONAL HISTORIC DISTRICT

Administered by the National Parks Service, the Martin Luther King Jr. National Historic District occupies several blocks on Auburn Avenue, a few blocks east of Peachtree Street in the traditionally black business and residential community of Sweet Auburn. It includes the birthplace of Martin Luther King Jr. Across the street from the Martin Luther King Jr. Center for Nonviolent Social Change, the Parks Service operates a visitor center that contains a multimedia exhibit focused on the civil-rights movement and Dr. King's role in it. The Parks Service also leads tours of the district. *450 Auburn Ave., Sweet Auburn, 404/331–5190, thekingcenter.com. MARTA: King Memorial.*

2 c-4
OLD ROCK BARN
Picture horse-drawn buggies, harness racing, and small-town gossips, and you'll have a good idea of what Cherokee County's most familiar landmark was like at the turn of the 20th century, when horsebreeder Gus Coggins' barn was the most popular meeting place in the region. But in 1906, the racing stable was burned down by night riders who opposed Coggins' employment of black ranch hands, and several prized horses were lost in the blaze. Unintimidated, the determined horse breeder rebuilt the enormous barn in stone and continued to breed champion equines. Today the barn is a Canton city landmark. *GA 5 (Marietta Hwy.) near GA 140, Canton, 770/345–0400, www.rockbarn.org.*

12 g-3
POPE-WALTON HOUSE
Wiley Woods Pope started building this Classical Revival house in Washington, Georgia (117 mi east of Atlanta), early in the 19th century. After his death, the husband of his granddaughter, Annie Barnett, continued the construction, but while he was away fighting for the Confederacy during the Civil War, Gen. William Sherman's troops invaded Washington and plundered the mansion, even riding through the halls on horseback. In the end, though, they spared the house from their torches because its mistress was caring for a newborn child. In 1967, Anthony's restaurant bought the house and moved it, brick by brick, to its present location in Buckhead. Legend has it that the ghost of Annie Barnett was a stowaway on the journey and that she makes occasional appearances to the restaurant guests and staff. The move took three years, but the restoration is intricate and even the attic retains its original lumber and wooden pegs. *3109 Piedmont Rd., south of Peachtree Rd., Buckhead, 404/262–7379.*

5 c-2
ROSWELL MILL
Like most of Atlanta, this cotton mill withstood its dose of fire during the Civil War, but Gen. William Sherman was especially determined to destroy this particular site because it was used to manufacture uniforms for the Confederacy. Reportedly, Sherman deported the mill's 400 female seamstresses to the North, and to this day little is known of what became of them. The structure has been converted into a mall called Roswell Mill, which is full of upscale shops. *85A Mill St., Roswell, 770/640–3253.*

15 e-6
SHRINE OF THE IMMACULATE CONCEPTION
Built in 1848, Atlanta's oldest existing religious structure was one of the few buildings left standing by the Federal troops who burned Atlanta during the Civil War. The story goes that an Irish priest, Father Thomas O'Reilly, persuaded Gen. William Sherman that to destroy the building would cause a mutiny among the Union troops, many of whom were Irish Catholic immigrants. *48 Martin Luther King Jr. Dr., Downtown, 404/521–1866, www.archatl.com/icatl.htm. MARTA: Five Points.*

9 g-1
STATELY OAKS PLANTATION
The sprawling plantation house was built in 1839 with heart pine, considered the strongest timber available at the time. Even so, it's a wonder the mansion survived the torches of the Civil War. According to reports, Union soldiers camped on the property while its owner, a Confederate soldier, was away defending other parts of the South. For some reason they spared it the torch, and today the plantation is one of the few undamaged examples of antebellum architecture in the South. Tours are offered Thursday and Friday 11–3. *100 Carriage Dr., Jonesboro, 770/473–0197. $3 adults, $1 children under age 12.*

15 e-6
SWEET AUBURN
From the post–Civil War period in the late 1800s to about 1930, when segregation excluded blacks from the white business and social communities, Sweet Auburn served as Atlanta's "other" main street. It was in this thriving hub of

black commerce and cultural, religious, and political activity that Dr. Martin Luther King Jr. was born and raised. King got his start preaching at the neighborhood's Ebenezer Baptist Church. *Decatur St. to Ralph McGill Blvd. between Courtland and Randolph Sts.*

15 *e-6*

UNDERGROUND ATLANTA

On this site, Atlanta was born in 1837, with the original name of Terminus (it was the last stop on the Western & Atlantic rail line). Perhaps one of the most peculiar urban sites in the nation, this was originally an ordinary, street-level commercial district. The area was reduced to rubble during the Civil War, then restored to commercial use by the 1890s. Underground Atlanta was born in the 1920s, when the city built a system of viaducts to elevate the streets for automobile traffic. The original street level went underground, and businesses set up new entrances on the new street level. The lower level fell into disuse until 1968, when it became an entertainment and dining complex, but the development soon fizzled and in 1981 it shut down altogether. In 1989 the project reopened, with three levels of high-end shops and restaurants in the ornamental storefronts along the brick streets. As a shopping and entertainment complex, Underground Atlanta still struggles, but it remains a pleasant place to visit and is dotted with historical markers. *50 Upper Alabama St., Downtown, 404/523–2311, www.underatl.com. MARTA: Five Points.*

15 *b-8*

WEST END

Established in 1835 and incorporated into the city in 1894, this is Atlanta's oldest residential neighborhood. It prospered in the early part of the 20th century but entered a decline during World War II. The area began to turn around when home buyers discovered that the neighborhood's huge Victorian and Craftsman-style homes, though decidedly worn at the elbows, could be acquired and restored at bargain prices. *Lee to Langhorn Sts. between White St. and Westview Dr.*

15 *e-5*

WINECOFF HOTEL

Named for its builder and owner, William Fleming Winecoff, the hotel was designed by William L. Stoddart and built about 1913. It became nationally famous for a horrendous 1946 fire that killed 119 people—including Winecoff, who lived in the hotel. In the wake of the catastrophe, nationwide reforms in fire regulations were instituted. Since then, the building has served as a retirement home and an office building. The two upper floors are topped by a sharply dentiled cornice that stands in stark contrast to the brick below. *176 Peachtree St., Downtown. MARTA: Peachtree Center.*

15 *b-8*

WREN'S NEST

The fairy-tale look of Wren's Nest befits the former home of beloved children's book author Joel Chandler Harris, who is best known for *Uncle Remus: His Songs and Sayings.* A two-room cabin was built in 1885 and then was repeatedly enlarged, so that today it is a veritable mansion. The house got its name when a bird built a nest in Harris's mailbox. Now the property of the Joel Chandler Harris Memorial Association, the house is a museum. *1050 Ralph David Abernathy Blvd., West End, 404/753–7735. MARTA: West End.*

HISTORY MUSEUMS

15 *e-6*

AFRICAN-AMERICAN PANORAMIC EXPERIENCE

Contained within this museum is a stellar testament to black heritage. Start your visit with the introductory film, narrated by African-American celebrities, that chronicles Auburn Avenue's place in the history of black commerce and culture. Among other exhibits, a display of period artifacts accompanies the main-lobby display on the history of slavery in the South. *135 Auburn Ave., Sweet Auburn, 404/521–2749. $3 adults, $1.75 senior citizens and students; children free. Tues.–Sat. 10–5. MARTA: Five Points.*

15 *g-8*

ATLANTA CIVIL WAR MUSEUM

The museum spans two floors and includes hundreds of Civil War artifacts, including the locomotive *Texas. 800 Cherokee Ave., Grant Park, 404/624–1071 tickets; 404/658–7625 information, www.webguide.com/cyclorama.html. $5 adults,*

$4 senior citizens, $3 children ages 6–12. Labor Day–May, daily 9:30–4:30; June–Labor Day, daily 9:30–5:30. MARTA: King Memorial.

12 e-3
ATLANTA HISTORY CENTER

The Atlanta History Center is a pull-no-punches presentation of the history of this city. The good is presented with the bad—*Gone With the Wind* glamour alongside Ku Klux Klan racism. In the pulsing core of Buckhead, the center occupies 33 beautifully landscaped acres. The grounds contain the exquisite Swan House mansion, the Tullie-Smith Plantation, and McElreath Hall, an exhibition space and auditorium that houses the center's research library and archives. Tours are offered. *130 W. Paces Ferry Rd., Buckhead, 404/814–4000, www.atlhist.org. $12 adults, $10 senior citizens and students, $7 children ages 3–17. Mon.–Sat. 10–5:30, Sun. noon–5:30.*

5 c-2
BULLOCH HALL

On a sprawling lawn in a forested cul-de-sac is the stately Bulloch Hall, an antebellum mansion that was once the home of President Theodore Roosevelt's grandparents. Today it is the headquarters of the Roswell Historic Preservation Commission, which hosts demonstrations of old-time crafts, such as quilting and basketry, as well as historic reenactments in the magnificent home. *180 Bulloch Ave., Roswell, 770/992–1731. $5 adults, $3 children ages 6–16. Mon.–Sat. 10–3, Sun. 1–3.*

15 h-4
CARTER PRESIDENTIAL CENTER

From this hilltop, General William Sherman watched the bloody Battle of Atlanta in 1864. Now the site holds an institution dedicated not only to the career and administration of President Jimmy Carter but also to the issues of conflict resolution and human rights. The museum and archives are open to the public, but not the center, which sponsors foreign-affairs conferences and projects on such matters as world food supply. Designed in 1986 by Jova/Daniels/Busby with Lawton, Umemura and Yamamoto, the splendid building is set on a landscaped estate with meticulously tended Japanese-style gardens. From here you have a spectac-ular yet tranquil panorama of the cityscape. *One Copenhill, 441 Freedom Pkwy., Virginia-Highland, 404/331–3942, www.jimmycarterlibrary.org. $5 adults, $4 senior citizens, children free. Mon.–Sat. 9–4:45, Sun. noon–4:45.*

14 g-3
DECATUR HISTORICAL COURTHOUSE

Built in 1823, the Old Courthouse in Decatur is home to the DeKalb Welcome Center these days. The antique log cabin stands in the middle of the city's central square. *101 E. Court Sq., Decatur, 404/373–1088. MARTA: Decatur.*

15 e-2
FEDERAL RESERVE BANK

Within the walls of this building, a towering marble "monument to money" completed in 2001, resides an exhibit explaining the history of the U.S. banking system and of money as a medium of exchange. Items displayed include rare coins, uncut sheets of money, and a gold bar. *1000 Peachtree St., Midtown, 404/498–8764. Free. Weekdays 9–4. MARTA: Midtown.*

15 d-7
GEORGIA DEPARTMENT OF ARCHIVES & HISTORY

A little-known treasure trove of historical information, this agency maintains a plethora of records, photographs, and letters, both official and unofficial, that date back to the Revolutionary War. The windowless fortress encompasses 85,000 cubic ft of public material, including more than 65,000 reels of microfilm. It's a genealogy buff's dream come true. *330 Capitol Ave., Downtown, 404/656–2393, www.georgiaarchives.org. Free. Weekdays 8–4:45, Sat. 9:30–3:15. MARTA: Garnett St.*

8 f-1
GEORGIA'S STONE MOUNTAIN PARK

One of Georgia's most famous attractions, and certainly its most popular, this 3,200-acre park is best known for the giant Confederate Memorial carved into the side of the mountain. The park also contains a number of regional historical displays, among them the Road to Tara Museum, dedicated to everything and anything *Gone With the Wind*. At the Antebellum Plantation, more than a dozen authentic pre–Civil War buildings

moved here from across the state re-create life in the Old South. The park also
has three museums: Discovering Stone
Mountain, chronicling the geology of the
mountain and the story behind the
famous carving; Confederate Hall, trac-
ing the course of the Civil War in Georgia; and the Antique Car and Treasure
Museum, including a selection of vintage
autos, jukeboxes, and other interesting
artifacts from Georgia's past. The park
offers a nightly laser show during the
summer and a wide array of other events
throughout the year. There's a ton of
other stuff to do here, too, from riding
the Stone Mountain Railroad, the River-
boat, or the Skylift to visiting the Wildlife
Preserve and Petting Zoo or the Beach
and Waterpark to getting some exercise
at Stone Mountain Golf Course or the
International Tennis Center. If you plan to
visit the park several times a year, you
can save on admission by purchasing the
Rock, Stock, and Barrel Pass, which gives
you unlimited admission (excluding golf
and tennis) for a year; the pass costs $20
per person or $50 for a family of three. To
save on parking fees buy the $30 Classic
Rock Parking Permit for a year's worth of
unlimited parking. *U.S. 78 5 mi outside
(east) of I-285, Stone Mountain, 770/498-
5690, www.stonemountainpark.com.
Admission free; attractions $13 for Georgia
residents, $16 for nonresidents; parking $7.
Park daily 6 AM–midnight. Most attractions
open Sept.–May, daily 10–5; June–Aug.,
daily 10–8.*

6 e-4
GWINNETT HISTORIC COURTHOUSE

Built in 1885, this unusual example of
Romanesque architecture was last an
active courthouse in 1988. Now it
houses the Gwinnett County Historical
Society. The courthouse itself is hard
to miss, occupying an entire block in
the Lawrenceville town square. Dotting
the property are various monuments,
plus tables for picnickers and a gazebo.
*185 Crogin St., Lawrenceville, 770/
822–5450, www.gogwinnett.com/
gwinnethistoriccourthouse. Free.
Tues.–Fri. 10–4.*

15 e-2
MARGARET MITCHELL HOUSE & GONE WITH THE WIND MUSEUM

This shrine to Margaret Mitchell, her epic
novel *Gone With the Wind*, and the classic movie based upon it has everything
except Tara itself—including the famous
portrait of Vivien Leigh as Scarlet O'Hara
(which Clark Gable doused with liquor in
the movie). The museum documents the
making of the movie, its Atlanta premiere, and the movie's impact on society. Adjacent to the museum is the house
that Mitchell affectionately nicknamed
"The Dump." In this tiny hovel of a habitat, the famous writer penned what is
perhaps the most famous epic novel in
the world. Though the original structure
was all but destroyed by neglect, vandal-
ism, and fire, it was finally restored and
painstakingly refurbished with period furniture. On display are Mitchell's Reming-
ton portable typewriter as well as the
Pulitzer Prize she won for the novel. *990
Peachtree St., Midtown, 404/249–7015,
www.gwtw.org. $12 adults, $9 senior citizens and students, $7 children ages 6–11.
Daily 9:30–5. MARTA: Midtown.*

4 f-4
MARIETTA MUSEUM OF HISTORY

Enclosed in a beautiful former hotel, this
relative newcomer was established by
volunteers who renovated the space for
display. The exhibits, which chronicle the
history of Marietta, were donated by
longtime residents, and the collection
continues to expand as new artifacts
arrive. *1 Depot St., Marietta, 770/528–
0431, mariettasquare.com/history. Donations requested. Tues.–Sat. 10–4, Sun. 1–4.*

15 g-6
MARTIN LUTHER KING JR. CENTER FOR NONVIOLENT SOCIAL CHANGE

A tour of the center is essential if you
are seeking to understand the civil-
rights movement and the impact of the
life of Dr. King. His widow, Coretta Scott
King, established the center after his
assassination in 1968. On display are
personal items, such as King's Nobel
Peace Prize, Bible, and tape recorder,
along with memorabilia and photos
chronicling the civil-rights movement.
The center also includes an auditorium
and a gift shop. In the front courtyard is
King's white marble tomb. The surrounding portion of the Sweet Auburn
neighborhood, where King was born and
raised, is the Martin Luther King Jr.
National Historic District. *449 Auburn
Ave., Sweet Auburn, 404/524–1956, thek-
ingcenter.com. Free. Daily 9–5. MARTA:
King Memorial.*

15 *e-1*

RHODES MEMORIAL HALL

As massive as it is curious, the castlelike mansion built in 1904 for furniture mogul Amos G. Rhodes is as much a museum piece as the exhibits it now displays. The headquarters of the Georgia Trust for Historic Preservation, Rhodes Hall mounts exhibits on the history of Georgia architecture. Its interior is alight with nine elaborate stained-glass windows depicting scenes from the Civil War. *1516 Peachtree St., Buckhead, 404/885–7800, www.georgiatrust. org/rhodes.html. $5 adults, $4 senior citizens, $3 students, children under age 12 free. Weekdays 11–4. MARTA: Arts Center.*

5 *h-3*

SOUTHEASTERN RAILWAY MUSEUM

A virtual Shangri-la for railway aficionados, this huge collection of period railway curios includes more than 70 vintage locomotives (both steam and diesel), passenger and freight cars, along with thousands of items of railway memorabilia. *3595 Old Peachtree Rd., Duluth, 770/476–2013, www.srmduluth. org. $6 adults, $4 children ages 2–12 and senior citizens. Thurs.–Fri. 10–5, Sat. 9–5.*

4 *d-2*

SOUTHERN MUSEUM OF CIVIL WAR & LOCOMOTIVE HISTORY

A $5.5 million expansion has transformed the former Kennesaw Civil War Museum, which has a new name and a new structure. Shows are to feature traveling exhibits from the Smithsonian Institution, with which it is affiliated, as well as the famous "General," an old steam locomotive stolen by Union spies during the Civil War with the intent of blasting key bridges throughout the South. Its conductor relentlessly pursued the bandits on foot and by pushcart until the steam engine was recovered and the spies captured. The incident—the subject of two Hollywood movies—is depicted in a giant mural in the exhibition space. The museum tour includes a display of war artifacts and an interesting slide show. Call for admission and hours. *2829 Cherokee St., Kennesaw, 770/427–2117 or 800/742–6897, www.thegeneral.org.*

15 *e-6*

WORLD OF COCA-COLA

It's hard to believe that a simple soft drink could launch such an imposing corporate empire, but it's true, and the World of Coca-Cola is testimony to that fact. Displays in the modern, neon-lit facility chronicle the soft drink's rise from humble local specialty to the world's most popular refreshment. You can try to guess how many bottles move along the bottling line, sample Coke products, and view a film. Plan on one to two hours to see everything. A gift shop sells every imaginable item imprinted with the Coca-Cola logo. *55 Martin Luther King Jr. Dr., Downtown (near Underground Atlanta), 404/676–5151, www.woccatlanta.com. $6 adults, $4 senior citizens, $3 children ages 6–11. Weekdays 9–5, Sun. noon–6. MARTA: Five Points.*

LIBRARIES

15 *e-3*

ACADEMY OF MEDICINE

This grand neoclassic example is the work of Philip Trammel Shutze, who was one of the city's premier architects and a local leader in the field for generations. Stylized Doric columns support the central facade, and a low tower with large lunette windows distinguishes it as an Atlanta landmark. Today, the lower level houses offices, and the reception rooms and 230-seat auditorium are used for weddings, conferences, and other special events. Curious relics from the medical profession fill the small medical museum. *875 W. Peachtree St., Midtown, 404/874–3219. MARTA: Midtown.*

12 *f-3*

ATLANTA-FULTON PUBLIC LIBRARY SYSTEM, BUCKHEAD BRANCH LIBRARY

The design of this building was so ahead of its time that in the 1980s local residents couldn't grasp the concept put forth by the architectural firm of Scogin, Elam and Bray, who lobbied to have it quashed before it was even built. Luckily the plans survived the tumult, and the structure now stands as one of the prime examples of modernist architecture in the city. Its slate facade, jutting metal awnings, and glass panorama mark a proud figure in the neighborhood. *269 Buckhead Ave., Buckhead, 404/814–3500, www.af.public.lib.ga.us. Mon. and Wed. 10–8, Tues. and Thurs. 10–6, Sat. 11–6.*

15 *e-5*

ATLANTA-FULTON PUBLIC LIBRARY SYSTEM, CENTRAL LIBRARY

The city's best example of the Beaux-Arts style, this structure was the collaboration of famed international architects Marcel Breuer and Hamilton Smith of New York and the Stevens and Wilkinson firm of Atlanta. The facade is reminiscent of Breuer's Whitney Museum in New York City. The Georgia Local and Family History Department here includes genealogical resources as well as instruction on how to use them. The library system consists of 34 branches. *1 Margaret Mitchell Sq., at Forsyth and Peachtree Sts. and Carnegie Way, Downtown, 404/730–1700, www.af.public.lib.ga.us. Mon.–Thurs. 9–9, Fri.–Sat. 9–6, Sun. 2–6. MARTA: Peachtree Center.*

12 *e-3*

ATLANTA HISTORY CENTER

The archives here, founded in 1926, are a rich repository of primary source materials, including, among other things, maps, photographs, local family and neighborhood histories, business records, and Civil War items. The archives and research library are housed in McElreath Hall, which includes an exhibition space and auditorium. The exquisite Swan House mansion and the Tullie-Smith Plantation are also part of the 33-acre center. *130 W. Paces Ferry Rd., Buckhead, 404/814–4000, www.atlhist.org. $12 adults, $10 senior citizens and students, $7 children ages 3–17. Tues.–Sat. 10–5, Sun. noon–5:30.*

15 *h-4*

CARTER PRESIDENTIAL CENTER LIBRARY

Designed in 1986 by Jova/Daniels/Busby with Lawton, Umemura and Yamamoto, this splendid building is set on a landscaped estate with meticulously tended Japanese-style gardens. The library houses the presidential papers of the Carter Administration. *One Copenhill, 441 Freedom Pkwy., Virginia-Highland, 404/331–3942. www.jimmycarterlibrary.org. Free. Mon.–Sat. 9–4:45, Sun. noon–4:45.*

15 *d-7*

GEORGIA DEPARTMENT OF ARCHIVES & HISTORY

A windowless structure that juts up somewhat separately from the rest of the skyline, the Georgia archives building remains a mystery even to many of Atlanta's longtime residents. But the windowless facade is necessary to protect its fragile holdings—a plethora of records, photographs, and letters, both official and unofficial, that date to the Revolutionary War—from sunlight. *330 Capitol Ave., at Memorial Dr., Downtown, 404/656–2393, www.georgiaarchives.org. Weekdays 8–4:45, Sat. 9:30–3:15. MARTA: Garnett St.*

15 *b-8*

HAMMONDS HOUSE GALLERIES & RESOURCE CENTER OF AFRICAN AMERICAN ART

In a West End home thought to have been built in the second half of the 19th century, the Resource Center here holds extensive materials relating to the African diaspora—from books and publications to videos and slides. It's open by appointment only. Hammond House also offers lectures and workshops on art and related topics. *503 Peeples St., West End, 404/752–8730, www.hammondshouse.org. $2. by appointment Tues.–Fri. 10–6, Sat. 1–5. MARTA: West End.*

14 *g-4*

MCCAIN LIBRARY, AGNES SCOTT COLLEGE

The neo-Gothic McCain Library doubled its size in early 2001 with the addition of a wing housing a multimedia production facility and classrooms. The complex now includes a covered courtyard that encompasses a garden and offers a lovely respite for reading and research. Another special note is its interior reading room, which possesses an artful network of wood framing. *141 E. College Ave., Decatur, 404/471–6000 or 800/868–8602, www.agnesscott.edu. Weekdays 8–6, Sat. 9–6, Sun. 1–10:30. MARTA: Decatur.*

SCIENCE MUSEUMS & OBSERVATORIES

15 *g-1*

DOROTHY CHAPMAN FUQUA CONSERVATORY

Amid the lush landscape of the 30-acre Atlanta Botanical Garden stands this 16,000-square-ft shimmering glass home for exotic and endangered plant specimens from around the world. The conservatory's computer-controlled atmosphere is finely tuned for the cultivation of endangered desert and tropical plants. *1345 Piedmont Ave., Midtown, 404/876–5859, www.atlantabotanicalgarden. $7 adults, $5 senior citizens, $4 students and children ages 6 and up. Free Thurs. 3–closing. Apr.–Sept., Tues.–Sun. 9–7; Oct.–Mar., Tues.–Sun. 9–6. MARTA: Arts Center.*

14 *c-3*

FERNBANK MUSEUM OF NATURAL HISTORY

Housed in an ultramodern facility, this odyssey of exhibits and galleries details every aspect of Georgia's natural resources and beauty but also includes artifacts from around the world. The museum has an IMAX theater, which, for the price of a movie ticket, delivers a panoramic thrill ride. *767 Clifton Rd., Druid Hills, 404/370–0960; 404/370–0019 IMAX, www.fernbank.edu/museum. Museum $12 adults, $11 senior citizens and students, $10 children ages 3 and up. IMAX $10 adults, $9 senior citizens and students, $8 children ages 3 and up. Combination tickets $17 adults, $15 senior citizens and students, $13 children ages 3 and up. Mon.–Sat. 10–5 (Fri. IMAX 10–10), Sun. noon–5.*

14 *e-3*

FERNBANK SCIENCE CENTER

A dream come true for celestial enthusiasts, the Fernbank Science Center has one of the largest planetariums in the country. On clear nights you can climb to the observatory and peer through its colossal telescope at the zillions of stars shimmering light-years away. An astronomer is on duty to help you identify celestial phenomena. The extensive meteorite collection includes the Odessa meteorite, which was found in Texas in 1922, as well as a fragment from Mars. *156 Heaton Park Dr., Druid Hills, 404/378–4311, fsc.fernbank.edu. Free. Planetar-*

ium show $2 adults, free for senior citizens, $1 students and children ages 5 and up. Mon. 8:30–5, Tues.–Fri. 8:30 AM–10 PM, Sat. 10–5, Sun. 1–5.

15 *e-5*

SCITREK

Packed with 100 creative exhibits, it's no wonder this ranks among the top science museums in the country. The 96,000-square-ft facility overflows with innovative, hands-on introductions to all kinds of technology, such as multimedia and the Internet. The interactive excitement makes science anything but dull. *395 Piedmont Ave., Downtown, 404/522–5500, www.scitrek.org. $7.50 adults, $6 senior citizens and children ages 3–17. Mon.–Sat. 10–5, Sun. noon–5. MARTA: Civic Center.*

STATUES, MURALS, & MONUMENTS

15 *g-8*

ATLANTA CYCLORAMA

A huge, circular panoramic painting— the largest of its kind in the world—forever freezes in vivid color the calamitous 1864 Battle of Atlanta. The oil painting, created in 1885 by a team of German artists, is almost six stories tall, 358 ft in circumference, and weighs nearly 9,400 pounds. It's enclosed in a colossal, intricately designed exhibit space. *800 Cherokee Ave., Grant Park, 404/624–1071 tickets; 404/658–7625 information, www.webguide.com/cyclorama.html. $5 adults, $4 senior citizens, $3 children ages 6–12. Daily 9:30–4:30. MARTA: King Memorial.*

15 *e-6*

ATLANTA FROM THE ASHES

(Gambro Quirino, 1969) A stunning civic renovation that injects vitality into a formerly blighted section of downtown, Robert W. Woodruff Memorial Park is a tiny oasis amid bustling Little Five Points. At the southern entrance stands this blackened-bronze sculpture by Italian artist Gambro Quirino. Liberty, in the form of a woman, frees a captive bird, the mythical phoenix that rose from the ashes of its own destruction and is the symbol of Atlanta's rebirth after the infernos of the Civil War. *Peachtree St. between Edgewood and Auburn Aves., Downtown. MARTA: Five Points.*

15 *e-5*

CANDLER BUILDING

(F. B. Miles, 1906) The exterior of this 17-story office building built by Coca-Cola founder Asa Candler is encrusted with bas-relief medallion sculptures of famous men. Buffalo Bill Cody, William Shakespeare, Italian Renaissance painter Raphael, and industrialist Cyrus McCormick are among those depicted. *127 Peachtree St., Downtown. MARTA: Peachtree Center.*

15 *d-5*

CENTENNIAL OLYMPIC PARK

A legacy of the 1996 Olympic Games, this sprawling, urban green space is dotted with commemorative sculptures. The locally famous *Rings Fountain* (EDAW Inc., 1996) sprays water in the shape of the Olympic Rings and is a popular frolicking spot in the summer months. *Marietta St. at International Blvd., Downtown. MARTA: Dome/GWCC/Philips Arena/CNN Center.*

7 *g-6*

CONCOURSE E, HARTSFIELD ATLANTA INTERNATIONAL AIRPORT

In anticipation of the 1996 Olympic Games, a large group of Southern artists was commissioned to create permanent works for this airport concourse. The results are spectacular, reflecting whimsy and innovation with a distinctive folk-art flair. *Concourse E, Hartsfield Atlanta International Airport, I–85 at Camp Creek Pkwy. MARTA: Airport.*

8 *f-1*

CONFEDERATE MEMORIAL

(Gutzon Borglum, Augustus Lukeman, Walker Hancock, 1912–72) Hewn into the side of the promontory that gives Stone Mountain Park its name, this staggering bas-relief is 90 ft tall and 190 ft wide, making it the largest sculpture of its kind on earth. The monument to Confederate leaders depicts Jefferson Davis, Stonewall Jackson, and Robert E. Lee, all on horseback. Work on the carving began in 1912 and was finished 50 years later. To celebrate its unveiling, 20 prominent guests were treated to a formal lunch on General Lee's shoulder. *U.S. 78, 5 mi outside (east) of I–285, Stone Mountain, 770/498–5690, www. stonemountainpark.com. Free; attractions $13 for Georgia residents, $16 for nonresi-* dents, parking $7. Park daily 6 AM–midnight; most attractions Sept.–May, daily 10–5; June–Aug., daily 10–8.

15 *e-5*

FOLK ART PARK

Colorful whirligigs and other sculptures animate this formerly prosaic intersection on one of the city's busiest streets. Part of Atlanta's sprucing-up before the 1996 Olympic Games, the permanent display incorporates the diverse styles of a dozen U.S. (mostly Southern) folk artists. Passersby can enjoy a moment of beauty and whimsy at any time of day; indeed, in some ways nighttime is the best time to view the display, because traffic isn't so hectic. *Ralph McGill Blvd. at Courtland St., Baker St., and Piedmont Ave., Downtown. MARTA: Civic Center.*

15 *e-7*

GEORGIA STATE CAPITOL

On the manicured grounds of the Georgia State Capitol, amid lush oak and magnolia trees, is a collection of statues and monuments depicting everyone from Confederate general John B. Gordon (mounted on his horse) to Georgians who fought in the Spanish-American, Korean, and Vietnam wars. Among others honored are Civil War–era governor Joseph Brown and his wife, Elizabeth; President Jimmy Carter (depicted as a peanut farmer, with his sleeves rolled up); the late senator Richard B. Russell, and the 33 black legislators who were expelled from the State House in 1868. *206 Washington St., Downtown, 404/656–2844, www. georgiacapitolmuseum.org. Free. Weekdays 8–5, Sat. 10–4, Sun. noon–4. MARTA: Georgia State.*

15 *e-6*

HENRY GRADY STATUE

New York sculptor Alexander Doyle honored this visionary editor of the *Atlanta Constitution,* who called himself a booster of the post–Civil War New South, in this bronze piece that adorns Marietta Street in front of the newspaper's offices. In some ways Grady, a baseball fanatic, was a precursor to Ted Turner. Grady died of pneumonia in 1891 after giving his famous New South speech in Boston. *Corner of Marietta and Forsyth Sts., Downtown. MARTA: Five Points.*

14 b-8

JESSE PARKER WILLIAMS MEMORIAL

This piece of marble funerary art by Daniel Chester French represents an angel striding outward, away from the grave. It was erected in the early 20th century on the grave of Williams and his wife, Cora Beth Taylor. *Westview Cemetery, 1680 Westview Dr., Section 5, Lot 21, West End, 404/755–6611. MARTA: West Lake.*

15 g-5

JOHN WESLEY DOBBS PLAZA

Built as part of the effort to improve Atlanta's streets for the 1996 Olympic Games, the plaza is dominated by a life mask of John Wesley Dobbs, grandfather to Atlanta's first African-American mayor, Maynard Jackson. By looking through the eyes of the mask, visitors get a vision of Auburn Avenue, where Dobbs played a major role in the rise of Atlanta's Black Wall Street. Happily, the plaza has dressed up a formerly scruffy corner near the I–75/I–85 overpass. *Auburn Ave. adjacent to I–75/I–85 overpass, Sweet Auburn. MARTA: King Memorial.*

15 g-7

LION OF ATLANTA

(T. M. Brady, 1896) Among the ornate funerary pieces, headstones, and mausoleums of Oakland Cemetery is the striking *Lion of Atlanta,* a reproduction of the Lion of Lucerne memorial in Lucerne, Switzerland, to the soldiers who died there. Carved from a single solid slab of marble, this lordly mane-ruffed beast honors the scores of rebel soldiers who died in the Battle of Atlanta in 1864 and were laid to rest in the cemetery in minimally marked graves. *248 Oakland Ave., Downtown, 404/688–2107, oaklandcemetery.com. Free. Daily dawn–dusk. MARTA: King Memorial.*

15 g-6

MARTIN LUTHER KING JR. TOMB & PEACE PAVILION

At the Martin Luther King Jr. Center for Nonviolent Social Change, an eternal flame blazes in the plaza in front of Freedom Hall, before the Meditation Pool. King's tomb rises from the pool on a circular brick pad and bears the inscription FREE AT LAST! A chapel of all faiths stands at one end of the reflecting pool. Nearby, on the manicured grounds of the Peace Pavilion, King's vision of the future is represented in *Behold* (Patrick Morelli, 1986), a statue of a black man raising a child above his head. *501 Auburn Ave., Sweet Auburn, 404/331–6922, thekingcenter.com. Free. Guided ½-hr tours daily every hr 10–5. MARTA: King Memorial.*

15 e-8

OLYMPIC CAULDRON

(Cisiah Armajani, 1996) Iranian-born American sculptor Cisiah Armajani was chosen to design the cauldron to hold the Olympic Flame for the 1996 Centennial Olympic Games. The sculpture stands close to its original position, near Turner Field. *Fulton St. at Capitol Ave., Downtown, 404/522–7630. MARTA: Georgia State.*

15 e-4

SAMUEL SPENCE STATUE

(Daniel Chester French, 1910) American sculptor Daniel Chester French created this statue just before designing the Lincoln Memorial, and Spence's seated posture echoes the motif of that more famous monument. A gift to the citizens of Atlanta and Georgia, the likeness of the mayor of Atlanta and president of Southern Railroad was commissioned and paid for by company employees. In a peculiar twist of fate, Spence was killed in 1906 in a train wreck on his own railway. The sculpture, dedicated in 1910, sits on its original marble pedestal in the north end of Hardy Ivy Park, illuminated by the original gas lamps, now rewired for electricity. *Porter Pl. at W. Peachtree St., Downtown, 404/766–9049. MARTA: North Ave.*

4 e-2

SOUTHERN MUSEUM OF CIVIL WAR & LOCOMOTIVE HISTORY

The famous Civil War locomotive "The General" is not the only attraction here. Also of note is the huge mural that covers two entire walls of the large exhibit space. Finished in 1994 by local artist Terry Buchanan, the panoramic painting depicts a railway station from the Civil War era, with the Union spies who became notorious for stealing the massive locomotive, and the determined conductor who pursued them until "The General" was retrieved and the culprits punished. *2829 Cherokee St., Kennesaw, 770/427–2117, www.thegeneral.org.*

4 *f-6*

SUMMITVIEW MURAL
The mural in Marietta's 1848 House restaurant provides patrons a delightful glimpse of the community as it appeared before the calamitous destruction of the Civil War. *780 S. Cobb Dr., Marietta, 770/428–1848, www.1848house. com.*

VIEWPOINTS

15 *g-5*

BRIDGE AT PARKWAY DRIVE
Professional photographers favor this nondescript, concrete highway bridge, which hovers over the Freedom Parkway interstate on-ramp and offers one of the clearest, closest, and unobstructed views of the Atlanta skyline. *Parkway Dr. between Highland Ave. and Houston St., Downtown.*

4 *f-6*

BUCKHEAD BRANCH LIBRARY
Inside this architectural marvel is a virtual wall of glass that faces south, capturing a gorgeous view of the Midtown skyline. *269 Buckhead Ave., Buckhead, 404/814–3500.*

15 *h-4*

CARTER PRESIDENTIAL CENTER
From the hillcrest where this structure now stands, General William Sherman was able to monitor from a distance the Battle of Atlanta in 1864; you get to see a spectacular yet tranquil cityscape. *One Copenhill, 441 Freedom Pkwy., Virginia-Highland, 404/331–3942, www. jimmycarterlibrary.org.*

15 *f-2*

EINSTEIN'S
This popular restaurant is actually a string of creatively renovated bungalows linked with patios and porches, where the tables offer a rare, close-up view of Midtown. *1077 Juniper St., Midtown, 404/ 876–7925.*

1 *f-5*

GEORGIA'S STONE MOUNTAIN PARK
A network of hiking trails traverses the grounds along the Chattahoochie River in this 3,200-acre park. One of these

trails leads to the top of a ridge near Upper Overlook Park, where the lucky hiker can find a pair of viewing decks, one made of rock and the other of natural wood. The observation decks provide sweeping forest views that are particularly staggering come autumn. *U.S. 78, 5 mi outside (east) of I–285, Stone Mountain, 770/498–5690, www. stonemountainpark.com.*

4 *f-6*

PARKSIDE TAVERN
A favorite place to catch the Atlanta sunset, the patio of this eatery atop a hillock overlooks a tranquil expanse of grass along Piedmont Park as well as the highrise towers of Midtown. The colossal outdoor fireplace is a bonus. *500 10th St., at Monroe Dr., Midtown, 404/249–0001.*

4 *f-6*

ROBERT W. WOODRUFF PARK
Just off the Georgia State University campus, the park passes as a tranquil reprieve amid the very vortex of skyscrapers, traffic, and other related turbulence that makes up downtown. A huge wall-of-water fountain along one entire side of the park drowns out the city bustle with its continuous white noise, and the park's positioning atop a knoll gives you a wondrous close-up vantage of the skyline architecture. *Peachtree St. and Auburn Ave., Downtown. MARTA: Five Points.*

15 *e-5*

SUN DIAL RESTAURANT
Two floors from the top of the 73-story Westin Peachtree Plaza, the rotating Sun Dial has been the city's marquis observation point since it was built in 1973. An external glass-elevator ride (fee: $5) whisks you aloft and into the plush digs of the restaurant, where you can watch a 360-degree showcase of Atlanta's shimmering cityscape unfolding before you. *Westin Peachtree Plaza, 210 Peachtree St., Downtown, 404/659–1400. MARTA: Peachtree Center.*

15 *e-8*

TURNER FIELD
Built for the 1996 Olympics and now home of the Altanta Braves, Turner Field remains one of the city's proudest legacies from that event. The architects defied the inevitable and designed an

open-air coliseum with not a single bad seat in the house; the bleachers in the southern section of the stadium, facing north, provide a dazzling view of downtown. *755 Hank Aaron Dr., Downtown, 404/522–7630. MARTA: Five Points.*

guided tours

bus tours

`1` *f-4*

GRAY LINE OF ATLANTA
Tours begin with a drive down Piedmont Avenue, to highlight the wondrous Fox Theater and several of the majestic churches that withstood Sherman's torches during the Civil War. The home of author Margaret Mitchell is one of the many other landmarks featured. *705 Lively Ave., Norcross, 770/449–1806 or 800/593–1818, www.americancoachlines. com.*

specialized tours

LEGACY OF ATLANTA TOURS
Tours highlighting the life and work of Dr. Martin Luther King Jr. are the specialty of this operator, but general tours also are available. Itineraries can be tailored for large and small groups. *3960 LaSalle Way, Hapeville, 770/947–2179.*

walking tours

`15` *e-4*

ATLANTA PRESERVATION CENTER
The center began in 1980 as a citizen-based drive to increase public awareness of Atlanta's endangered architectural heritage and historic areas. Today it is one of the city's strongest advocates in support of its history. The walking tours, as popular with locals as with visitors, are an opportunity for leisurely strolls through old neighborhoods—Candler Park, West End, Cabbage Town, Inman Park, Grant Park, and downtown—with narration by knowledgeable volunteers. *537 Peachtree St., Midtown, 404/876–2041, www.preserveatlanta.com. MARTA: Midtown.*

`15` *g-6*

MARTIN LUTHER KING JR. NATIONAL HISTORIC DISTRICT
The National Parks Service leads tours of the Martin Luther King Jr. National Historic District, which it administers. The district encompasses several blocks of Auburn Avenue, a few blocks east of Peachtree Street in the traditionally black business and residential community of Sweet Auburn; it includes the birthplace of Martin Luther King Jr. Tours start at the visitor center across the street from the Martin Luther King Jr. Center for Nonviolent Social Change. *450 Auburn Ave., Sweet Auburn, 404/331–5190. MARTA: King Memorial.*

events

JANUARY

`15` *g-6*

KING WEEK
During this weeklong event at the end of January, people from all over the Southeast come together to honor the fallen Nobel laureate Dr. Martin Luther King Jr. The Center for Nonviolent Social Change, the event's major sponsor, offers various performances, religious services, seminars, and concerts. *404/524–1956, thekingcenter.com.*

FEBRUARY

`15` *g-6*

BLACK HISTORY MONTH
As the apex of the civil-rights movement, Atlanta hosts a moving Black History Month every year, with an affecting itinerary of events both educational and entertaining. For example, Big Bethel A.M.E. Church, famous for its role in civil-rights history, whirls with musical performances the entire month. Lectures and interactive programs are also featured. *404/524–1956.*

`12` *g-2*

TRINITY SPOTLIGHT ON SOUTHERN ARTISTS
The revered Trinity Gallery hosts this homage to Southern artists every year at the ritzy Swissôtel in Buckhead. The gala

culminates in a lively art auction, and it's possible to walk away with an original piece at an enviably low price. Auction admission includes a dinner buffet. *404/231–8100.*

MARCH

12 *f-3*
ST. PATRICK'S DAY
Every year the Hibernian Benevolent Society hosts a rousing St. Patrick's Day parade, which culminates in a massive celebration throughout the streets of Buckhead, the city's semi-official "party central" for the past few decades. The pubs are packed and the green-frocked are guzzling, but revelry isn't the only goal here; lectures on Irish heritage and Irish-music concerts are also featured. *770/594–7110, www.irishatlanta.com.*

APRIL

14 *g-2*
ATLANTA DOGWOOD FESTIVAL
Held every April in Piedmont Park, this arts festival observes the few weeks during which the dogwood trees are in lustrous bloom. The nine-day event is a celebration in the true sense, with hot-air balloon races, dog-Frisbee championships, parades, concerts, and plenty of food and drink to accompany the artwork displayed along the park pathways. *404/329–0501, www.dogwood.org.*

1 *d-6*
GEORGIA RENAISSANCE FESTIVAL
Deep in the woods in Riverdale, these impassioned performers and revelers celebrate their own perfectly re-created pocket of merry old England from late April to early June. Jugglers, minstrels, acrobats, and jousting knights frolic between 12 stages, featuring a constant stream of plays, music, and magic. There is plenty to see and do—and buy—with food and drink fit for a king. *770/964–8575, www.garenfest.com.*

14 *a-5*
INMAN PARK FESTIVAL
Quirky and thoroughly enjoyable, this is among Atlanta's oldest and favorite neighborhood festivals. Along Edgewood and Euclid avenues and the nearby streets, food, crafts, antiques, music, and a hilariously offbeat parade are among the highlights of the three-day event. The accompanying Inman Park Tour of Homes offers an inside glimpse of the neighborhood's most spectacular Victorian mansions. *770/242–4895, www.inmanpark.org.*

MAY

13 *b-1*
ATLANTA CELTIC FESTIVAL
Back after a hiatus in 2001 to accommodate the renovations of its host, Oglethorpe University, the two-day festival promises to be better than ever. Continuous performances on five stages, dances, music, arts and crafts, and plenty of food await festivalgoers. Sheepdog demonstrations and Gaelic football are also on the agenda—not your garden-variety festival. *No phone, atlanta.celticfestival.org.*

14 *g-3*
DECATUR ARTS FESTIVAL
Every May, Decatur's charming courthouse square comes vibrantly alive with this family-friendly two-day arts festival. Vendor booths offer a cornucopia of arts, crafts, and charming knickknacks, while others offer tasty food and drink. *404/371–9583, www.decaturga.com.*

JUNE

14 *c-5*
CANDLER PARK AND LAKE CLAIRE MUSIC & ARTS FESTIVAL
This breezy, easygoing neighborhood street party, along Clifton and McClendon avenues, involves plenty of art booths and musical events. Delectable food is central to the fair, especially since it takes place in front of two of Atlanta's favorite breakfast haunts: the Flying Biscuit and the Gato Bizco cafés. Festivities commence with a 5K run and an in-line skate race. *404/589–8777, www.candlerpark.org/festival.*

15 *h-2*
SUMMERFEST
The feel-good atmosphere at this cozy Virginia-Highland arts festival is hard to resist. For two days, music, interesting arts, beguiling crafts, handcrafted jew-

elry, food, and libations abound along Virginia Avenue. *404/222–8244, www. vahi.org.*

JULY

1 *f-5*

FANTASTIC FOURTH CELEBRATION

Stone Mountain Park bursts with excitement during this three-day salute to the United States. Major concerts, sports competitions, patriotic music, clogging, various contests, and the world's largest laser show spark the fun. On July 4 itself, metro Atlanta's most spectacular fireworks display is part of the celebration. *404/498–5633, www.stonemountainpark. com.*

15 *f-6*

NATIONAL BLACK ARTS FESTIVAL

Among the largest celebrations of African-American art and artists in the nation, this festival has hosted Atlanta Symphony Orchestra performances at historic Ebenezer Baptist Church, dance performances by the heralded African American Dance Ensemble, and energetic poetry readings and discussions about Africa with documentary filmmakers and Nobel laureates. Most events are free. *404/730–7315, www.nbaf.org.*

AUGUST

5 *g-5*

FOLKFEST

Festival founder Steve Slotin's motto is "folk art for all folks," and that's exactly what you find at this annual three-day folk-art extravaganza held at the North Atlanta Trade Center in Norcross. The selection is as plentiful and diverse as the genre itself, with more than 80 galleries and dealers showcasing the talent they represent. Past offerings have included works by such Southern folk-art stars as Howard Finster, R. A. Miller, Mary Klein, Ab the Flagman, and more. Prices are pleasing to the wallet. *770/ 932–1000, www.selftaughtart.com.*

1 *f-5*

LASERSHOW SPECTACULAR

August nights bring the mountain to life as Stone Mountain Park kicks its Laser-

show Spectacular into full gear. The face of the mountain is transformed into a 1-million-square-ft natural screen for the breathtaking laser-light show. Choreographed to music, the colorful laser beams and pyrotechnics re-create dramatic stories and historic tales and create comical characters and images. *404/ 498–5633, www.stonemountainpark.com.*

SEPTEMBER

4 *f-4*

ART IN THE PARK, MARIETTA

Every year, more than a hundred artists gather in quaint and peaceful Marietta Square to sell their creations out of festive tents and vendor booths. Attractions include silver jewelry, photography, metal sculpture, pottery, inlaid wood, and more. The festival is usually held on Labor Day weekend. *770/429–0832, mariettasquare.com.*

5 *h-3*

ARTS ON THE COURTHOUSE SQUARE

In front of Duluth's quaint courthouse, this merry neighborhood festival features a fun mix of arts, crafts, and entertainment that lasts two days. *770/822–5450, www.duluth-ga.com.*

5 *c-2*

ROSWELL ARTS FESTIVAL

The long-standing annual arts festival is one of the best in metro Atlanta. Held along historic streets lined with beautiful architecture and around lovely Roswell Square, with its cozy collection of storefronts, the two-day festival offers an astounding array of art and hand-crafted goods. *770/640–3253, www.cvb. roswell.ga.us.*

OCTOBER

15 *f-7*

HABITAT FOR HUMANITY BIRDHOUSE ARTFEST

The Atlanta arts scene is all aflutter during this nonprofit art gala showcasing birdhouses built with astounding creativity by top artists nationwide. Also featured are sculptures, quilts, paintings, and folk art with bird-related themes. Held at Phipps Plaza each year, it gives nearly 2,000 artists the opportunity to donate their works. All proceeds go to Habitat for Humanity, a nonprofit organization that builds homes for low-income families. *404/223–5180, www. atlanta-habitat.org.*

NOVEMBER

5 *c-2*

ROSWELL ARTISTS STUDIO TOUR

For three days late each November, one of metro Atlanta's most popular art events leads visitors through a labyrinth of beautiful artists' homes and studios on scenic Willeo Creek, north of historic Roswell Square. Dozens of vendors sell crafts from booths scattered along the trail, and virtually no aesthetic sensibility is left unsated. *770/645–2050.*

15 *h-4*

TELEPHONE FACTORY STUDIO TOUR

One of Atlanta's most coveted invitations is to this annual shindig, which runs from Thanksgiving to Christmas. The highly anticipated event transforms a studio complex into a three-floor arts odyssey, during which the many artists in residence roll out the red carpet, opening their lofts to the public. If you're lucky enough to score an invitation (you can't get in without one), you can get a look at some incredible original works, as well as a peek into the studios and homes in this converted Art Deco industrial complex. *404/577–0905.*

DECEMBER

12 *e-3*

ATLANTA HISTORY CENTER CANDLELIGHT TOURS

This annual holiday tradition includes 33 acres strewn with candlelit garden paths, holiday decorations in the 1926 Swan House mansion and rustic 1845 Tullie-Smith Farm, and storytelling by a cheery bonfire, in addition to the center's many wonderful exhibitions. *404/814–4000, www.atlhist.org.*

14 *g-3*

BEACON HILL ARTISTS STUDIO TOUR

Every December, arts patrons can get a glimpse of artists at work and look over a truckload of original crafts and artworks just in time for the holidays. On average each year, nine studios with as many as 12 guest artists present a festive collection of pottery, jewelry, paintings, weavings, and woodwork during the three-day event. *404/378–6602.*

14 *a-5*

EUCLID ARTS COLLECTIVE ARTISTS STUDIO TOUR

Nestled at the corner of Austin and Euclid avenues in the heart of Inman Park, the Little Five Points Community Center houses a cluster of artists' studios. The annual tour of the collective usually spans the first two weeks of December and always offers an interesting mix of artists and their creations, such as pottery, woodwork, paintings, and jewelry. *404/221–1530.*

chapter 5

ARTS, ENTERTAINMENT, & NIGHTLIFE

Whatever your age and interests, metro Atlanta delivers a good time.

Cultural capital of the Southeast, Atlanta has its own opera company as well as the country's oldest dance company. The internationally acclaimed Atlanta Symphony Orchestra, with numerous Grammy Awards to its credit, is making plans for a state-of-the-art performance hall. Meanwhile, the city's great strength in the performing arts is its dozens of theaters, which present all kinds of drama, from classic to experimental.

Metro Atlanta sizzles with popular music, too—from blues and jazz to rap and rock. Nationally recognized locals include the Indigo Girls and the members of the hip-hop group OutKast, Andre "Dré" Benjamin and Antwan "Big Boi" Patton. The thousands of up-and-comers who play around town hail from the 10 metro counties and beyond. Big names arrive from all over the world to give mega-concerts at venues like Philips Arena and Hifi Buys Amphitheatre. Midtown and Buckhead are the hottest spots; their dance clubs and trendy bars stay lively into the wee hours. And nearly every corner of town has a great place for socializing over a latte, a glass of wine, or a cold brew.

performing arts

For information on the fine arts, *see* Art Galleries and Art Museums *in* Chapter 4.

PERFORMANCE VENUES

8 *e-1*

ART STATION

The intimate 100-seat theater hosts professional performances of classic and original plays that reflect the Southern experience. In the heart of Stone Mountain Village, the Station has galleries with changing exhibits of local and international artists, plus a learning center, a dance studio, private music-rehearsal rooms, and a pottery studio. *5384 Manor Dr., Stone Mountain, 770/469–1105, www.artstation.org.*

15 *f-5*

ATLANTA CIVIC CENTER

Each year, the civic center hosts myriad arts performances and first-class touring shows, such as *Riverdance*. Its elegant, 4,600-seat auditorium, beautifully lit with chandeliers, is used by many Atlanta-area groups for arts-, church-, and education-related events. Although still not all they should be, the acoustics have been improved and upgraded in recent years. *395 Piedmont Ave., Midtown, 404/523–6275, www.atlantaciviccenter.com. MARTA: Civic Center.*

14 *b-3*

CALLANWOLDE FINE ARTS CENTER

The early 20th-century Tudor-style mansion, with its own built-in organ, was built for Charles Candler, son of Coca-Cola Company founder Asa Candler. As the performance venue for DeKalb County, it showcases recitals, choral presentations, and poetry readings. An art gallery is also here. *980 Briarcliff Rd., Druid Hills, 404/872–5338, www.callanwolde.org.*

5 *b-7*

CHASTAIN PARK AMPHITHEATRE

Chastain's 7,000-seat facility attracts renowned performers from every musical genre, whether it's Willie Nelson, Cassandra Wilson, or the Atlanta Symphony Orchestra. A festive mood usually takes hold as music lovers open picnic baskets, pour wine, and light candles. Unfortunately, some audience members are more interested in their table conversation than in the performance, interfering with the pleasure of those who want to hear the music. Performers complain, too, but they keep signing on. This is a great spot for the 4th of July, when there's a fireworks display and usually a performance by the Symphony. Chastain has no single box office; instead, you can receive information from the various groups that book the facility, including Atlanta Concerts (404/233–2227, www.atlantaconcerts.com) and the City of Atlanta's Bureau of Cultural Affairs (404/817–6815, www.bcaatlanta.org). *135 W. Wieuca Rd., Buckhead, no phone.*

4 f-5
COBB COUNTY CIVIC CENTER
Two buildings house a performing-arts theater where the Georgia Ballet, the Cobb Symphony, and visiting musical organizations perform. The center also has an exhibition hall that's mostly devoted to trade shows and conferences but that sometimes hosts large pop, rock, and gospel concerts as well as other performances. The theater seats 606, and the exhibition hall accommodates 3,000. Ticket prices run $15–$30, depending on the performance. *545 S. Marietta Pkwy., Marietta, 770/528–8450, www.co.cobb.ga.us.*

12 f-3
COCA-COLA ROXY THEATRE
A former movie theater, now tagged with the logo of Atlanta's most famous product, hosts rock, pop, blues, jazz, folk, reggae, and other concerts these days. There's an open dance floor (sometimes filled with reserved seating), a balcony with cushioned seats, two bars, and an extensive display of music memorabilia. Nearby are Buckhead's liveliest nightspots. *3810 Roswell Rd., Buckhead, 404/233–7699, www. atlantaconcerts.com/roxy.*

15 e-5
COTTON CLUB
A wide, shallow room with two balconies lets you get close to the stage at this small concert space, where you can hear all kinds of live music—everything short of classical, from Latin, jazz, and alternative to rock, pop, and heavy metal. Major national talent (Johnny Cash, Morphine, Lenny Kravitz), smaller national acts (Luscious Jackson, Lit, the Marvelous Three), and regional and local bands play here, and surprise guests sometimes perform impromptu sets. Four bars and an excellent sound-and-lighting system keep the party going. Tickets run $5–$17.50. Some shows require patrons be over 18, and you must present your photo ID for all events. Cotton Club occupies the space below the Tabernacle performance space. *152 Luckie St., Downtown, 404/688–1193. MARTA: Peachtree Center.*

15 e-1
EARTHLINK LIVE
Formerly the moribund Center Stage, this 1,035-seat performance hall received a high-tech makeover when it was resuscitated in 2001 by EarthLink, the Internet service provider that has headquarters nearby. Shows are primarily alternative, folk, blues, R&B, and jazz. *1374 W. Peachtree St., Midtown, 404/885–1365, www.earthlinklive.com. MARTA: Arts Center.*

14 d-1
EMORY UNIVERSITY
Musical artists from all over the world come to Emory each season to participate in jazz, classical, choral, and theatrical performances, and the university's theater, music, and dance departments mount sophisticated productions. All this activity takes place in several on-campus venues. Glenn Memorial Auditorium (1652 N. Decatur Rd.), in a campus church, is where world-renowned soprano Cecilia Bartoli gave her sold-out Atlanta debut in 1995; Cannon Chapel (515 Kilgo Cir.) is a small venue perfect for chamber concerts; and the Performing Arts Studio (1804 N. Decatur Rd.) seats 200–250. The Mary Gray Munroe Theater in Dobbs University Center (605 Asbury Cir.) showcases classical and contemporary theater, as well as dance performances. Plans for the Donna and Marvin Schwartz Center for the Performing Arts (1700 N. Decatur Rd.)—at this writing slated to open in late 2002—include a 825-seat concert hall with orchestra pit and choral balcony, a 135-seat experimental theater, and a 135-seat dance studio. Film screenings, including those of the Silent Film Society of Atlanta, take place in White Hall (480 Kilgo Cir.), which is equipped with state-of-the-art equipment. *1804 N. Decatur Rd., Decatur, 404/727–5050 box office, www.emory.edu/ARTS.*

15 f-2
14TH STREET PLAYHOUSE
Part of the Woodruff Arts Center, this three-theater complex is a locus of diversity and innovation in Atlanta theater. Many respected local performing-arts groups work here, including the theater's resident companies: Art Within (770/558–8169), a theater company that highlights Christian themes; Atlanta Classical Theatre (404/685–8861); multiShades Atlanta (404/377–8158 or 800/861–4952), a woman-focused group that blends film and theater; Jomandi Productions, Onstage Atlanta, and Theatre Gael (*see* Theater, *below*); and Several

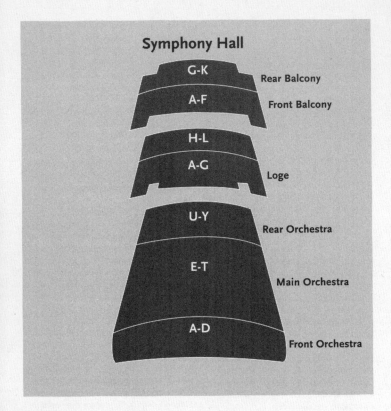

Symphony Hall

G-K — Rear Balcony

A-F — Front Balcony

H-L

A-G — Loge

U-Y — Rear Orchestra

E-T — Main Orchestra

A-D — Front Orchestra

Dancers Core (*see* Dance, *below*). The Playhouse also houses the offices of the Atlanta Coalition of Performing Arts (404/873–1185) and Georgia Citizens for the Arts (404/876–1720). *173 14th St., Midtown, 404/733–4750 box office; 404/733–4754 administrative offices. MARTA: Arts Center.*

15 *e-4*

FOX THEATRE

The only word for the Fox Theatre is . . . *breathtaking*. This faux Moorish landmark from the 1920s has a grand stage used for everything from concerts, recitals, and opera to movie premieres and Broadway shows. The splendid Egyptian Ballroom and the Grand Salon are opulent facilities equipped for catering and entertaining. An attempt to raze the theater and replace it with the brutalist office tower that now rises behind it provoked a massive community response that led to its being declared a National Historic Landmark in 1976. The Atlanta Preservation Center conducts tours of the Fox (*see* Chapter 4). *660 Peachtree St., Midtown, 404/881–2100 box office. MARTA: North Ave.*

9 *b-6*

FREDERICK BROWN JR. AMPHITHEATRE

Seating about 2,000, this bowl nestled among woods hosts everything from pops to contemporary music to drum-and-fife concerts. Tickets to most events range from $20 to $35, plus a $3 handling fee. *191 McIntosh Trail, Peachtree City, 770/631–0630.*

6 *b-3*

GWINNETT CIVIC & CULTURAL CENTER

A quality arts venue in the northeast metro area, the Civic Center hosts trade and commercial exhibitions, while the Performing Arts Center—part of the Cultural Center—hosts events ranging from Trisha Yearwood to the Boston Ballet. The Gwinnett Philharmonic, the Gwinnett Ballet, and other local groups also perform in the 700-seat Center, which has excellent stage lighting. The Children's Arts Museum, devoted to introducing the performing and visual arts to children, is on the grounds. *6400 Sugarloaf Pkwy., Duluth, 770/623–4966, ext. 3, box office, www.gwinnettciviccenter.com.*

7 *h-4*

HIFI BUYS AMPHITHEATRE

Pops, rock, blues, country, and gospel play at this outdoor venue at Lakewood Fairgrounds, which seats about 20,000. The acoustics are good and the reserved seating is fairly comfortable. You can't bring food or drink inside, though you can tailgate before the show; refreshments are available inside. Call MARTA (404/848–4711) for information on shuttles from the Fort McPherson rail station. *Lakewood Fairgrounds, 2002 Lakewood Way, Lakewood Heights, 404/443–5090, www.hifibuysamp.com. MARTA: Lakewood/Fort McPherson*

4 *e-2*

HOWARD LOGAN STILLWELL THEATER

In 1990, Kennesaw State University built this intimate 321-seat theater as a venue for college- and community-based artists as well as visiting stars, such as soprano Marilyn Horne and jazz pianist Marian McPartland. The theater hosts Classic Theatreworks, the university's theatrical group. The Kennesaw Jazz Ensemble, composed of students and local musicians, performs here, usually twice a semester. Admission to most music events at the theater is free, but some special events—such as the Premier Series, in which well-known stars from various musical genres perform throughout the academic year—cost up to $45. Theater events usually cost $10. *1000 Chastain Rd., Kennesaw, 770/423–6151.*

15 *d-6*

RIALTO CENTER FOR THE PERFORMING ARTS

This well-equipped and acoustically superb space is the home stage of the Georgia State University School of Music. In the Rialto, Downtown has a first-class venue for jazz, blues, rock, and classical musicians; local and national dance companies; and theatrical troupes. The 900-seat facility, in the historic Fairlie-Poplar district, was created from the old Rialto movie theater, which in turn was a conversion of a theater built in 1916. *80 Forsyth St., Downtown, 404/651–4727, www.rialtocenter.org. MARTA: Five Points.*

15 *c-3*

ROBERT FERST CENTER FOR THE ARTS AT GEORGIA TECH

On the Georgia Tech campus, this 1,200-seat performing-arts center brings renowned classical musicians, dancers, and vocalists to Midtown. Named for its benefactor, who was a major contributor to Georgia Tech, the center also houses galleries and a student-run theater. *Georgia Institute of Technology, 349 Ferst Dr., Midtown, 404/894–9600, www.ferstcenter. gatech.edu. MARTA: North Ave.*

15 *e-1*

ROBERT W. WOODRUFF ARTS CENTER

Atlanta's best-established theater, music, and art institutions—including the Atlanta Symphony Orchestra, the Alliance Theatre Company, and the High Museum of Art—all call this venue home. Symphony Hall seats close to 1,800, with wheelchair and companion seats available. The Alliance has several stages here. Light lunches and sweets are served during the day (except Sunday) at an outpost of Alon's Bakery Café, on the terrace level of the High Museum. On Thursdays, Fridays, and Saturdays prior to ASO Master Season Performances, buffet dinners are available at FanFare, on the lobby mezzanine (404/733–4275; reservations recommended). The 14th Street Playhouse, nearby, is also part of Woodruff. *1280 Peachtree St., Midtown, 404/733–5000, www.woodruffcenter.org. MARTA: Arts Center.*

5 *c-2*

ROSWELL CULTURAL ARTS CENTER

Seating 600 in an orchestra-plus-balcony configuration, this intimate suburban space hosts the Georgia Ensemble Theatre, a professional company with adult and youth conservatory programs. Orchestra Atlanta, an amateur 63-musician orchestra, also performs here. The community makes extensive use of this facility for high school graduations, dance recitals, and concerts. *950 Forrest St., Roswell, 770/594–6232, www.roswell. ga.us/cac.*

8 *b-7*

SPIVEY HALL

Cathedral ceilings and wonderful acoustics make this an elegant venue.

The centerpiece of the 400-seat hall is the Albert Schweitzer Memorial Organ, a 4,413-pipe wonder with accents of marble and gold leaf. Nationally and internationally renowned artists, primarily small orchestral groups and individual classical-music performers and the occasional jazz stylist, appear here. *Clayton State College and University, N. Lee St. (Clayton State Blvd.), Morrow, 770/961–3683, www.spiveyhall.org.*

14 *a-5*

VARIETY PLAYHOUSE

Concerts of all kinds, from Cajun and Celtic to jazz, rock, and blues, draw massive crowds to this small theater, where the seating ranges from 500 to 1,000, depending on the show. Plan ahead and arrive early if you want a seat. A bit worn about the edges, the theater is nonetheless popular with audiences and entertainers alike. Shows have featured the bands Stereolab and the North Mississippi AllStars, flamenco guitarist Ottmar Liebert, traditional Irish musicians Tommy Makem and the Clancy Brothers, and blues guitarist Tinsley Ellis. You can buy snacks, beer, and wine at the small bar and, if you're lucky, grab one of the tables along the sides of the room. *1099 Euclid Ave., Little Five Points, 404/521–1786, www.variety-playhouse. com. MARTA: Inman Park.*

5 *c-2*

VILLAGE PLAYHOUSES OF ROSWELL

With two stages and a theater-in-the-round, this 10-year-old community theater includes the Village Center Playhouse (the main stage), Storybook Theater (the children's theater), and Roswell Village Theater (a proscenium theater). Comedies, uplifting dramas and musicals, and seven children's productions a year are the draws. Tickets usually go for $8–$16. *633 Holcomb Bridge Rd., Roswell, 770/998–3526.*

CONCERTS IN CHURCHES

12 *e-4*

CATHEDRAL OF ST. PHILIP

At the neo-Gothic seat of the Episcopal archdiocese of Atlanta, concerts that coincide with religious seasons are frequent events. An ongoing free concert series of organ and choral recitals follows Sunday afternoon evensong. Other concerts are ticketed and cost $10–$20. Artists who have appeared here include the Inman Piano Trio, a local jazz ensemble, and the Winchester Cathedral Choir, from the United Kingdom. *2744 Peachtree Rd., Buckhead, 404/365–1000, www.stphilipscathedral.org.*

5 *f-7*

EMBRY HILLS UNITED METHODIST CHURCH

The Sacred and Performing Arts Series here includes concerts by the church's choir as well as other artists. Acoustics are excellent. The Atlanta Baroque Orchestra also gives frequent performances, sometimes with name guest performers. Ticket prices range from free to about $15. *3404 Henderson Mill Rd., Chamblee, 770/938–0661.*

5 *c-5*

LUTHERAN CHURCH OF THE APOSTLES

At special events and concerts, the Chancel Choir, the New Life Singers, and the Bell Choir perform traditional and contemporary Christian music. Appalachian storytellers and musicians, the Atlanta Sacred Chorale, AmerCord, the Atlanta Singers, and the National Lutheran Choir are also frequent performers. The church holds an annual Scandinavian musical festival the third Sunday in May. Many church members are professional or semi-professional musicians, and the Members Recital, usually held the last Sunday before Lent, is a fun "Preludes, Pipes, and Pizza" evening. Most concerts are free. *6025 Glenridge Dr., Sandy Springs, 404/255–8668, www.atlantaapostles.org.*

5 *c-2*

ROSWELL UNITED METHODIST CHURCH

"Sounds of the Spirit," the 2,000-seat church's concert series, presents choral and instrumental music that ranges from classical to inspirational throughout the year. The annual Roswell Patriotic Celebration (June) and Christmas Festival Concerts (December) have become community traditions. Nationally known ensembles and guest artists fill out the series. Performances are open to the public; a donation is requested. *814 Mimosa Blvd., Roswell, 770/594–0512, www.rumc.com.*

DANCE

companies

15 *e-2*

ATLANTA BALLET

Founded seven decades ago by the extraordinary Dorothy Alexander, this is the oldest continuously operating dance company in the United States. Since taking over as artistic director in November 1994, John McFall has presented four world premieres and steered the company toward innovative, boundary-crossing projects like the 2001 collaboration with local folk rockers the Indigo Girls. The Ballet's Centre for Dance Education instructs youths and adults alike in ballet, jazz, modern, flamenco, hip-hop, yoga, tai chi, and other creative movement. *1400 W. Peachtree St., Midtown, 404/873–5811, www.atlantaballet.com. MARTA: Arts Center.*

5 *c-5*

Centre for Dance Education, Chastain Square, 4279 Roswell Rd., Sandy Springs, 404/892–3303.

5 *e-3*

ATLANTA DANCE UNLIMITED

The company presents ballet, jazz, modern, and tap at festivals and at locations throughout Atlanta, primarily at the Roswell Cultural Arts Center. World-class choreographers from around the United States create arrangements for ADU, which is the performance arm of the Dancer's Studio/Backstage. *8560 Holcomb Bridge Rd., Suite 118, Alpharetta, 770/993–2623, www.dancers-backstage. com.*

7 *f-5*

BALLETHNIC DANCE COMPANY

Traditional ballet is blended with other influences, particularly African-American, to create exciting and unique performances. Founded in 1990 by dancers Nena Gibreath and Waverly Lucas of the Dance Theatre of Harlem and Atlanta Ballet, this is Atlanta's first and only professional black ballet company. The company performs at the Rialto Center and the Robert Ferst Center for the Arts, and elsewhere. It also offers classes through the Ballethnic Academy. *2587 Cheney St., East Point, 404/762–1416, www.ballethnic.org.*

BEACON DANCE COMPANY

This innovative contemporary dance ensemble performs site-specific works, at venues all over the area. It's a principal sponsor of and participant in both the Fringe Festival of Contemporary Dance and Performance Art and the Decatur Arts Festival dance program. *Box 1553, Decatur 30030, 404/377–2929, www.beacondance.org.*

FULL RADIUS DANCE

The organization's focus is "physically integrated dance," bringing together professional dancers with and without physical disabilities; half the company uses wheelchairs. It maintains a busy performance schedule, usually at 7 Stages, including fall and spring repertory seasons. Classes are offered for children with disabilities and in physically integrated dance technique for professionals. *Box 54453, 30308, 404/724–9663, www.fullradiusdance.org.*

4 *f-4*

GEORGIA BALLET

Founded in the 1960s, Georgia Ballet is made up of a professional company, often joined by dancers of national and international acclaim, and a children's ballet school with an enrollment of 275. Performances are usually held at the Cobb County Civic Center. Georgia Ballet's outreach programs aim to expose children in metro area to the magic of ballet. *31 Atlanta St., 3rd floor, Marietta, 770/425–0258, www.georgiaballet.org.*

6 *c-7*

GWINNETT BALLET THEATRE

Artistic Director Lisa Sheppard leads a nonprofit dance troupe and ballet school. Performances, mostly in the traditional vein, are at the Gwinnett Civic and Cultural Center. *2204 Fountain Square, Snellville, 770/978–0188.*

15 *h-8*

MOVING IN THE SPIRIT

Operating on the principle that the universal language of dance can break down racial, ethnic, and cultural barriers in order to teach values and life skills, MITS sponsors programs for metro Atlanta youth in schools, public housing, inner-city shelters, and community centers. The new works and occasional classics are performed mainly at the company's own community theater, called the Beam. Admission to these events is by donation. *750 Glenwood Ave., Grant Park, 404/627–4304, www. mitsdance.org.*

11 *h-6*

SEVERAL DANCERS CORE

The professional organization's innovative approach to contemporary dance often involves improvisation. Founded in 1980, the group operates in Houston as well as Atlanta. It also collaborates with other arts and social-service organizations; the resulting network of shared resources helps the groups reach a culturally and ethnically diverse audience. Performances are at the 14th Street Playhouse, classes at the company's studio on the Decatur square. *Studio: 133 Sycamore St., Decatur, 404/373–4154, www. severaldancerscore.org.*

SOWETO STREET BEAT DANCE THEATRE

Isabelle Ngcobo, a cofounder of this African-dance and musical-production company, hails from South Africa. The history and culture of the Zulu Nation are central to the performances of the group, which began in Soweto in 1989. *Box 5049, 30302, 770/435–4691, www. sowetostreetbeat.com.*

FILM

programs & theaters of note

15 *e-6*

CINEFEST

This Georgia State University film society treats fellow students and other Atlanta residents to fascinating documentaries, black-and-white classics, and independent films that they might not be able to view anywhere else in the metro area. A nominal admission is charged for the screenings in the University Center Building. *Georgia State University, 66 Courtland St., Downtown, 404/651–2463, www15.brinkster.com/ cinefest. MARTA: Georgia State.*

15 *f-2*

GOETHE INSTITUTE ATLANTA

From fall to spring, this German cultural and information center presents classic and contemporary German films, some-

times dubbed in English, sometimes in German with subtitles. Free for members, the screenings are in the institute's auditorium and open to the public ($4). *400 Colony Sq., Midtown, 404/892–2388, www.goethe.de/uk/atl/enpfilm.htm. MARTA: Arts Center.*

15 *e-2*

HIGH MUSEUM OF ART

Year-round, the museum exhibits films of artistic merit. The program, which includes recent independents, classics, and foreign-language films, is screened in the Rich Auditorium of the Woodruff Arts Center. Students and senior citizens receive a discount of $1 off the $5 general admission. *Woodruff Arts Center, 1280 Peachtree St., Midtown, 404/733–4570, www.high.org/inframeexhibits.htm. MARTA: Arts Center.*

12 *d-7*

IMAGE FILM/VIDEO CENTER AT THE TULA ARTS CENTER

IMAGE (Independent Media Artists of Georgia, Etc.) is one of the most respected nonprofit media-arts centers in the nation. It seeks to enhance public awareness of film and video as art forms and to help independent media artists produce and exhibit their films and videos. The center presents a great deal of offbeat and experimental material that otherwise might not find an audience. Screenings are held at various venues around town. Tickets generally cost $3–$6 but are free to members (annual membership is $75). *75 Bennett St., Buckhead, 404/352–4225, www.imagefv.org.*

12 *f-4*

LEFONT THEATRES

The Lefont theater chain is alone among metro Atlanta's commercial movie promoters in specializing in classic and fine contemporary films, both American and foreign. The consistently high quality of its presentations makes its theaters popular with Atlanta's serious cineastes, who tend to mind their manners and watch the screen rather than hoot and chat. Garden Hills Cinema is one of the few spacious, single-screen movie houses left. The art-deco style Plaza, however, did not escape the ax; its balcony was sectioned off to make a small second auditorium. *Garden Hills Cinema, 2835 Peachtree Rd., Buckhead, 404/266–2202.*

`14` *a-4*

Plaza Theatre, 1099 Ponce de Leon Ave., Virginia-Highland, 404/873–1939.

PEACHTREE FILM SOCIETY

This membership organization of film buffs (annual dues are $25) holds monthly screenings around town of off-beat and foreign films, including frequent programs of shorts. *Box 550442, 30355, no phone, www.peachtreefilm.org.*

SILENT FILM SOCIETY OF ATLANTA

The SFSA celebrates European and American silent films, letting Atlanta audiences see wonderful works that might otherwise be forgotten. The monthly screenings open with an introduction by Bill Eggert, who launched the organization in 1990. The introductions give background not only on the film being shown but on the first 30 years of filmmaking. The society exhibits films at various locations, including Emory University's White Hall, and hosts an annual festival of silent films, usually in early March. *Box 25435, 30322, 404/885–1787, www.silentfilmatlanta.com.*

festivals & special events

`15` *c-6*

AFRICAN FILM FESTIVAL

Clark Atlanta University presents this cavalcade of the latest, mostly independent film productions from Africa and elsewhere. During July in even-number years, it's a part of the National Black Arts Festival; in odd-number years, it's held in April. Screenings conclude with panel discussions by notable local and international filmmakers. *Clark Atlanta University, 223 James P. Brawley Dr., West End, 404/880–6143. MARTA: Ashby.*

ATLANTA FILM & VIDEO FESTIVAL

Since 1976 the IMAGE Film and Video Center has presented innovative, independent works, emphasizing those from southeastern artists. More than 150 films are screened each May or June at various venues throughout the metro Atlanta area. Tickets cost $5–$15. *404/352–4254, www.imagefv.org.*

DOWNSTREAM INTERNATIONAL FILM FESTIVAL

This annual event seeks to rescue the idea of the "independent" film by con-

centrating on under-recognized film and video makers. The festival also aims to be inclusive, showing as many works by female directors as male. At this writing Downstream is scheduled for July, with films screened about 45 minutes north of metro Atlanta, in Gainesville. *Mailing address: 915 Saddle Ridge Court, Roswell 30076, 770/998–2288, www. downstreamfest.com.*

`15` *e-2*

LATIN AMERICAN FILM FESTIVAL

The Latin American Art Circle of the High Museum of Art produces this much-anticipated film festival each fall. Film students and other aficionados flock to the screenings, which are often followed by receptions attended by the actors and filmmakers. Screenings are $5. *Woodruff Arts Center, Rich Auditorium, 1280 Peachtree St., Midtown, 404/733–4570, www.latinfilm.org. MARTA: Arts Center.*

`12` *d-7*

OUT ON FILM: THE ATLANTA GAY & LESBIAN FILM FESTIVAL

Begun in 1987 by the IMAGE Film and Video Center, Out on Film brings to the screen gay-themed movies and videos that range from romance and comedy to drama and suspense. The screenings are shown for four days in the fall. Admission is $5–$10. *75 Bennett St., Suite N-1, 30309, 404/352–4254, www. outonfilm.com.*

`14` *d-1*

SILENT HEAVEN

The festival, named in honor of the silent film *Seventh Heaven* (1927), is held annually, usually in March. Co-sponsored by Emory University's film studies department, it brings silent classics to the Emory University campus. Admission is free. *Emory University, White Hall, 480 Kilgo Cir., Decatur, 404/885–1787, www.silentfilmatlanta.com.*

OPERA

companies

`15` *e-3*

ATLANTA OPERA

The Atlanta Opera produces four operas a year, usually the classics but occasionally some modern works. All productions are in the Fox Theatre, where a supertitles screen above the stage translates the libretto. To promote understanding of and appreciation for opera, the Atlanta Opera Studio presents operas and workshops in schools throughout the state. *728 W. Peachtree St., Midtown, 404/881–8801, www. atlantaopera.org.*

ORCHESTRAS & ENSEMBLES

performing groups

ATLANTA CHAMBER PLAYERS

The city's first chamber-music ensemble, established in 1976, has a repertoire that goes from traditional masterpieces of Brahms and Beethoven to contemporary classics of George Crumb and Shostakovich. The players have also commissioned and premiered works by such composers as John Harbison and Anne LeBaron. A three-instrument core of piano, violin, and cello is sometimes joined by instruments from the wind, string, and brass families. Concerts are held at the Rialto Center, the Woodruff Arts Center, and elsewhere around Atlanta. *Box 56834, 30343, 770/242–2227, www.mindspring.com/~acplayers.*

ATLANTA POPS ORCHESTRA

Since the mid-20th century, Paris native Albert Coleman and his 55-member orchestra have put on free concerts in public venues such as Centennial Olympic Park. The group specializes in George Gershwin's compositions, romantic favorites, and the classics. *Box 723172, 31139, 770/435–1222.*

15 *e-2*

ATLANTA SYMPHONY ORCHESTRA

Atlanta's symphony is under the direction of Robert Spano, former music director of the Brooklyn Philharmonic. Donald Runnicles, music director of the San Francisco Opera, serves as principal guest conductor. ASO has long performed at the Woodruff Arts Center, but plans are being drafted for a new symphony hall. Concerts featuring name artists frequently sell out well ahead of time. *Woodruff Arts Center, 1280 Peachtree St., Midtown, 404/733–5000, www. atlantasymphony.org. MARTA: Arts Center*

ATLANTA VIRTUOSI

Under the direction of Atlanta Symphony Orchestra violinist Juan Rubín Ramírez, who founded the group in 1977, this chamber ensemble pursues an active performance schedule. Most of its members also play in the ASO; in this format they appear in local churches, shopping malls, and even private homes. The group sometimes debuts commissioned works; it mounts a free series of concerts for children and also sponsors an annual Hispanic Festival of the Arts. *Box 77047, 30357, no phone, www.atlantavirtuosi.org.*

4 *f-5*

COBB SYMPHONY ORCHESTRA

Playing at the Jennie T. Anderson Theatre in the Cobb Civic Center, and other Cobb Country venues, this long-established symphony presents programs with classical, operatic, and pops pieces, as well as free children's concerts and an annual holiday concert. The season runs from October through May, although the community and professional musicians that make up the group also present occasional summer concerts. *548 S. Marietta Pkwy., Marietta, 770/528–8490, www. cobbsymphony.org.*

14 *d-1*

EMORY CHAMBER MUSIC SOCIETY OF ATLANTA

In residence at Emory University, the Society is one of the premier professional musical organizations in Atlanta. There are no gimmicks, just musical integrity from high-caliber musicians who generally also perform solo and as part of the Atlanta Symphony Orchestra. Guest artists have included cellist Yo-Yo Ma, the Lark String Quartet, and violinist William Preucil. Most performances, in both free and ticketed series, are held at Emory. *1804 N. Decatur Rd., Decatur, 404/727–5050 box office, www.emory.edu/ MUSIC/ecms1.htm.*

6 *b-3*

GWINNETT PHILHARMONIC

Conductor and director Monte Nichols, a longtime Gwinnett resident, founded the philharmonic in 1995. Made up of 65 principal musicians, the orchestra presents concerts from fall to spring, plus special events. Performances are at the Gwinnett Civic Center's Performing Arts Center and cost $15–$25. *Box 920159,*

Norcross 30010, 770/418–1115, www.
gwinnettphilharmonic.org.

LANIER TRIO

In 1979 Decaturites Dorothy and Cary
Lewis (a cellist and a pianist, respectively) teamed up with violinist William
Preucil, former concertmaster of the
Atlanta Symphony Orchestra. The trio
performs works by Dvorak, Mendels-
sohn, and the like, appearing at local
venues such as the Rialto and across the
country. 404/636–6265, www.laniertrio.
org.

MUSES GARDIN

Performing early music for soprano,
harp, lute, and viola da gamba on repli-
cas of period instruments, this ensemble takes its name from an influential
musical collection, The Muses Gardin for
Delights (1610). Performances are given
at various venues around town. 770/
638–8760.

 c-2

ORCHESTRA ATLANTA

The 63-member orchestra performs
under the direction of Thomas Ludwig,
former music director of the Atlanta Ballet. During its season, November to May,
the orchestra performs classical music
in the Roswell Cultural Arts Center. Tickets run $20–$30. 1000 Holcomb Woods
Pkwy., Suite 112, Roswell 30076, 770/992–
2559, www.orchestraatlanta.com.

THAMYRIS

Named after a poet who challenged the
Muses of Greek mythology and lived to
regret it, Thamyris plays 20th- and 21-
century music. Since 1999 its members
have been the ensemble-in-residence at
Emory University, where most performances take place. Having commissioned more than 50 new works since it
began in 1987, the ensemble is a major
player in Atlanta's new-music scene.
404/522–1608, www.thamyris.org.

classical music festivals
& special events

15 e-2

ATLANTA SYMPHONY
ORCHESTRA HOLIDAY
CONCERTS

What better way to reenergize after
shopping than to take in a relaxing
evening of beautiful musical perfor-

mances? Don't miss the favorite
"Gospel Christmas" concerts. Woodruff
Arts Center, 1280 Peachtree St., Midtown,
404/733–5000, www.atlantasymphony.org.
MARTA: Arts Center.

5 c-2

CHRISTMAS
FESTIVAL CONCERT

Each Christmas season, the Roswell
United Methodist Church presents a cel-
ebratory program that varies widely
from year to year. Processional
pageantry, familiar carols, choral and
instrumental music, and drama and
scripture readings make up the event.
The show is free, but complimentary
tickets, available at the church a month
in advance, are strongly recommended,
as the sanctuary usually fills for this
event. 814 Mimosa Blvd., Roswell, 770/
594–0412 music office, www.rumc.com.

5 e-6

HISPANIC FESTIVAL
OF THE ARTS

Founded in 1990, this festival organized
by the Atlanta Virtuosi celebrates Hispanic heritage through traditional and
classical music, art exhibitions, folk
dance, and lectures about Hispanic culture. Performances take place at the
Embry Hills United Methodist Church.
Box 77047, 30357, 770/938–8611, www.
atlantavirtuosi.org.

5 c-2

ROSWELL PATRIOTIC
CELEBRATION

An annual tradition in Roswell, this
"star-spangled spectacular" of narration, ceremony, and traditional patriotic
music is presented at the end of June in
the Roswell United Methodist Church.
The show is quite popular so be sure to
get the complimentary tickets in
advance; they're available at the church
a month before the concert. 814 Mimosa
Blvd., Roswell, 770/594–0412 music office,
www.rumc.com.

THEATER

companies

15 c-3

ACADEMY THEATRE

Now headquartered in a renovated glass
warehouse, Academy was the first racially

integrated professional theater company in Georgia. It mounts community-oriented productions and has premiered some 350 plays since its founding in 1956. Its programs include a drama camp for children ages 8–13. *501 Means St., Northwest Atlanta, 404/525–4111, academytheatre.home.mindspring.com.*

15 *b-2*

ACTOR'S EXPRESS

The troupe's goal is "to produce plays that sweep us off our feet, fill us with a sense of wonder, and leave us dizzy"— and it certainly accomplishes that. Performing both classical and contemporary pieces in an intimate space, the group is energetic, physical, and adventurous. Actor's Express also runs an acting school and an internship program. *King Plow Arts Center, 887 W. Marietta St., Suite J-107, Northwest Atlanta, 404/607–7469, www.actorsexpress.com.*

15 *e-3*

AGATHA'S— A TASTE OF MYSTERY

Agatha's is the crème de la crème of dinner theater in Atlanta. Delightful and absurd mysteries are staged by professional actors; audience members are enlisted to participate in, and solve, the mysteries. Amid the gasps and laughter, an excellent five-course meal with wine and beverages is served. The inclusive price ranges from $42.50 to $50. *693 Peachtree St., Midtown, 404/875–1610, www.agathas.com.*

15 *e-2*

ALLIANCE THEATRE COMPANY

Without a doubt, this is one of the largest and most revered resident theaters in the South. On the main Alliance Stage and the 200-seat Hertz Stage, it produces the works of renowned playwrights, reaching an audience of more than 300,000 each season. (Occasional productions are staged at the 14th Street Playhouse.) An integral part of the Atlanta arts community, the Alliance trains actors and runs a delightful children's theater program, with performances that appeal to both the young and the young at heart. *Woodruff Arts Center, 1280 Peachtree St., Midtown, 404/733–5000, www.alliancetheatre.org. MARTA: Arts Center.*

15 *e-4*

ATLANTA SHAKESPEARE TAVERN

Truly the place to eat, drink, and be merry, this theater-cum-tavern stages lively productions of Shakespeare on a small stage, in the middle of what resembles an old English pub. The tavern also presents works by other classic European dramatists, including Molière and Shaw. The pub-fare menu includes such items as Cornish pasties and shepherd's pie. Guinness, Harp, and Bass are offered on tap. Tickets are in the $20–$25 range. *499 Peachtree St., Downtown, 404/874–5299, www.shakespearetavern.com.*

6 *a-3*

AURORA THEATRE

The semi-professional theater company brings drama, comedy, and musical productions to the North Gwinnett suburbs. Selections are mainly modern American classics, including dramas by Tennessee Williams and comedies by Neil Simon. *3087B Main St., Duluth, 770/476–7926, www.auroratheatre.com.*

15 *e-1*

CENTER FOR PUPPETRY ARTS

Here's a magical theater experience that offers powerful and thought-provoking entertainment, and not just for kids; the annual New Directions series (fall–winter) has serious puppet drama for adults. The largest puppetry center in the United States, this institution has three theaters and a museum with interactive displays of antique and modern puppets from all over the world. *1404 Spring St., Midtown, 404/873–3391 or 404/873–3089, www.puppet.org. MARTA: Arts Center.*

15 *h-5*

DAD'S GARAGE

One of the city's most innovative young theaters takes on everything from comedy to musicals, but it's best known for its wacky audience-participation improvs. Dad's also offers snacks and beverages. Admission runs up into the teens at most. *280 Elizabeth St., Suite C101, Inman Park, 404/523–3141, www.dadsgarage.com. MARTA: Inman Park.*

5 *c-2*

GEORGIA ENSEMBLE THEATRE

During its season, roughly September–April, this professional company mounts five productions at the Roswell Cultural Arts Center. Its comedies, dramas, and musicals appeal to a broad audience. The theater also has a children's and adults' conservatory. Ticket prices are $22–$31; there are sometimes discounts for senior citizens and students. *950 Forrest St., Roswell, 770/641–1260, www.get.org.*

14 *a-5*

HORIZON THEATRE COMPANY

An intimate 200-seat theater in Little Five Points is where this troupe produces its dramas, comedies, and satires. Focusing on contemporary plays, Horizon also sponsors programs such as the Teen Ensemble and the Senior Citizens Ensemble, which aim to cultivate broader public interest in theater. *1083 Austin Ave., Little Five Points, 404/584–7450, www.horizontheatre.com. MARTA: Inman Park.*

5 *e-5*

JEWISH THEATER OF THE SOUTH

Several productions each year bring what's new in Jewish theater to the 253-seat Morris & Rae Frank Theatre. The proscenium hall is equipped with assisted listening devices for the hearing impaired. *5342 Tilly Mill Rd., Dunwoody, 770/395–2654, www.atlantajcc.org/artent.htm#JTS.*

JOMANDI PRODUCTIONS

Founded in 1978, this nonprofit group is the oldest and largest professional African-American theater company currently producing plays in Georgia. Featuring local and regional talent, particularly black playwrights, the production company stages challenging works of ethnic significance. The company usually performs at the 14th Street Playhouse. *Office: 675 Ponce de Leon Ave., 8th floor, 30308, 404/870–0629, www.jomandi.com.*

15 *f-2*

ONSTAGE ATLANTA

Founded in 1971, this professional company produces an eclectic mix of live theater, including Broadway, off-Broadway, and regional work. The actors like to be close to their audience, so they prefer the intimate stages 2 and 3 at the 14th Street Playhouse. Stage 3, for instance, may be configured to seat only 58 patrons. Abracadabra! Children's Theatre, part of Onstage Atlanta, produces classics adapted to the stage, such as *Beauty and the Beast, Cinderella,* and *Sleeping Beauty.* Tickets are $7–$10 for the children's theater, $16–$22 for Onstage productions. *Box 54178, 30308, 404/897–1802, www.onstageatlanta.com.*

13 *b-7*

PUSHPUSH THEATER

Housed in a warehouse-district workshop space, this company develops and

---

CULTURE WITH THE KIDS

Having fun and exploring the arts need not be mutually exclusive experiences for the younger members of your family. Atlanta is full of exciting activities and events that turn kids on to the arts.

Atlanta Ballet (Dance)
Who doesn't love Tchaikovsky's Nutcracker during holiday season? And that's not the only children's programming at the Atlanta Ballet, so keep an eye on the schedule.

Atlanta Opera (Opera)
At holiday time, the AO performs Menotti's interpretation of the familiar story Amahl and the Night Visitors. The one-act production, sung in English and starring a young boy, is an easy introduction to opera.

Center for Puppetry Arts (Theaters)
Puppet plays, a fine exhibition of puppets, and workshops help make boring, rainy Saturday afternoons fun.

Gwinnett Civic and Cultural Center (Performance Venues)
Here, at the Children's Arts Museum, young audiences have a great time at the workshops, performances, and exhibits, which introduce them to the visual and performing arts.

Robert W. Woodruff Arts Center (Performance Venues)
Myriad activities at the center are designed to attract young people, from acting lessons to performances by the Atlanta Youth Symphony.

premieres plays and presents productions of everything from contemporary works to rarely seen works of Henrik Ibsen. PushPush enables playwrights from Atlanta's theater scene to explore new territory and perhaps take risks not always possible at more-commercial companies. The theater presents an annual festival of new American plays and sometimes hosts other local groups. *Floataway Bldg., 1123 Zonolite Rd., off Briarcliff and Johnson Rds., Northeast Atlanta, 404/892–7876, www. pushpushtheater.com.*

14 *a-5*

7 STAGES THEATRE & PERFORMING ARTS CENTER

The passionately nonconformist theater has been bringing provocative, modern performance to Atlanta since 1978. Committed to the avant-garde, the company specializes in contemporary twists on old themes, as in a recent reprise of the Faust legend. Smaller companies perform in the 90-seat black box Backstage theater, in the rear of the facility. There's an art gallery and bistro in the lobby. *1105 Euclid Ave., Little Five Points, 404/523–7647, www.7stages.w1.com.*

15 *f-2*

THEATRE GAEL

Founded in 1985, this professional company is dedicated to performing plays, poetry, music, and storytelling from the Celtic tradition. The company's arts-education programs target children throughout Georgia, with workshops and exercises that deal with human rights and conflict resolution. Theatre Gael sometimes commissions new work. Performances take place at the 14th Street Playhouse. *Box 77156, 30357, 404/876–1138, www.arthouse.com/gael.*

4 *f-4*

THEATRE IN THE SQUARE

Second only to the Alliance Theatre in annual attendance, this professional company works in a former cotton warehouse that's been converted to a 225-seat theater. The group isn't afraid to take a few risks, striving to produce works that are as stimulating as they are entertaining. *11 Whitlock Ave., Marietta, 770/422–8369, www.theatreinthesquare.com.*

festivals & special events

5 *d-7*

GEORGIA SHAKESPEARE FESTIVAL

The neo-Gothic architecture of Oglethorpe University's campus is the perfect backdrop for this annual June–November season of plays. In addition to works by Shakespeare, the company produces other classics from time to time. The thrust-stage theater seats 509 and has walls that swing open to the outdoors in pleasant weather. *Oglethorpe University, 4484 Peachtree Rd., Brookhaven, 404/264–0020, www. gashakespeare.org. MARTA: Brookhaven.*

TICKETS

ATLANTA COALITION OF THEATRES

Half-price theater tickets are available on the day of the show through the group's AtlanTIX Info line. The group represents theaters in eight metro Atlanta counties. Its Web site posts the show calendars of all 112 members, with links to their sites. The telephone information line also has a fax-on-demand service that sends a year-at-a-glance show calendar to callers. *770/772–5572 AtlanTIX Info line, www. atlantatheaters.org.*

TICKETMASTER

The service offers tickets to all kinds of metro Atlanta performing-arts events. To use it, you must have a charge card. A service fee is added to the price of your tickets. *404/279–6400, www.ticketmaster.*

nightlife

BARS & LOUNGES

5 *c-5*

AMERICAN PIE

Boisterous and usually packed, this casual gathering spot is hugely popular with young singles. The outdoor deck is always open during the summer. In addition to pool tables and dartboards, there's a dance floor with a DJ spinning popular dance music most nights. Saturday afternoons, you can listen to live music on the deck. There are 52 TVs and two wide-screeners, usually tuned to sporting events. The menu favors burgers and salads. *5840 Roswell Rd., Sandy Springs, 404/255–7571.*

B *d-1*

THE AQUARIUM

An upscale, suburban, mostly African-American crowd comes to this club. Media personalities, such as local radio name Porsche Foxx, who shows up for "Sexy Saturday" with a live R&B band, often host events here. Cover varies; dress to impress. *Atrium Plaza, 5471 Memorial Dr., Stone Mountain, 404/508–4599.*

14 *b-8*

THE FLATIRON

Neighborhood denizens surround the U-shape bar in this classic old building. Nachos, sandwiches, and similar bar fare are available, but food isn't the focus. Instead, the young patrons gather for conversation, drinks, and plain old camaraderie. *520 Flat Shoals Ave., East Atlanta, 404/688–8864.*

15 *a-8*

FOUNTAINHEAD LOUNGE

The younger set fills this lively spot, gathering around the bar opposite the entrance or lounging at the tables scattered around the room. Although slightly scruffy, the Fountainhead might almost qualify as a wine bar. The wine list is impressive, with lots served by the glass—in good glassware to boot. Some appetizers are offered, but mostly it's drinks and chatter that bring 'em in. Fountainhead is open late (3 AM on weekdays, 4 AM on weekends). *485A Flat Shoals Ave., East Atlanta, 404/522–7841.*

15 *e-2*

THE LEOPARD LOUNGE

Live jazz and swing music make this joint jump every Friday and Saturday night. On other nights (except Sunday), recorded music—from rock to house—brings bodies to the dance floor. To refuel, pizzas are served into the wee hours. After 10 PM Friday and Saturday, the cover is $10, but women typically get in free. Dress nicely, and leave the sports gear at home. *84 12th St., Midtown, 404/875–7562. MARTA: Midtown.*

12 *f-3*

TONGUE & GROOVE

A chic crowd fills this dance floor and comes for occasional live performances.

Wednesday is Latin Night; on other nights, a DJ plays American and European pop and R&B. The dress code for this 25- to 45-year-old crowd prohibits jeans and T-shirts, and the beautiful people here always seem to look their best. Most nights, the club is open 9 PM–4 AM, Saturday until 3 AM. It's closed Sunday. *3055 Peachtree Rd., Buckhead, 404/261–2325. MARTA: Buckhead.*

5 *c-3*

WHISKERS DUNWOODY TAVERN

A real neighborhood bar, Whiskers has pool and TV sports, plus bands five nights a week. Terrific live blues and rock from some of Atlanta's best local groups, including Motor City Josh, begin around 10. The lunch and dinner menu focuses on steaks and burgers. There's no cover. *8371 Roswell Rd., Dunwoody, 770/992–7445.*

BILLIARDS

Metro Atlanta has more billiards tables than you can shake a (cue) stick at. Almost any sports bar is a popular spot to shoot some pool. Multiple tables can also be found at places like American Pie (*see* Bars & Lounges, *above*), Churchill Arms (*see* Pubs & Taverns, *below*), Dave & Buster's (*see* Fun, *below*), Scrooges Lounge *see* Pubs & Taverns, *below*), and the Last Great Watering Hole (*see* Pop/Rock, *below*). For hard-core billiards parlors, *see* Chapter 3.

BLUES

4 *h-4*

BAYOU ROOM

The 350-seat music club, attached to Mama Mae's Louisiana Kitchen, has a rotating music menu. There's blues every Thursday, and zydeco and jazz acts other nights. Regular performers include Heaven Davis, the Eric Austin Band, and Andrew Black and the Believers. A light Cajun menu is available until the early hours. *2217 Roswell Rd., Marietta, 770/971–2343.*

14 *a-3*

BLIND WILLIE'S

The small, nationally renowned club packs a blues wallop with live blues from Chicago, New Orleans, and everyplace in between. Local bands—including the house outfit, House Rocker Johnson and the Shadows—as well as national performers are featured. The music starts at 10 but the bar opens at 8, and a limited bar menu is available. Crowds jam the place every night and parking is scarce in this neighborhood, so get here early and come by taxi, or grab the first parking space that catches your eye—don't be fussy. Reservations aren't accepted, and only those 21 and older are admitted (with I.D.). The cover charge varies. It's closed Sunday. *828 N. Highland Ave., Virginia-Highland, 404/873–2583.*

2 *b-8*
BLUE PIG
At this suburban music and barbecue spot, you can here serious blues on Friday and Saturday nights, beginning at 9. A clean-cut crowd fills the tables and packs the bar to listen to local and regional bands. First-class 'cue with homemade sides is served daily. There's no cover charge. *9770 S. Main St., Woodstock, 770/517–2583.*

4 *f-4*
BLUE RACCOON
The funky, friendly, lively spot off the Marietta square offers a light bar-food menu, a dance floor, and live music every night. You'll mostly hear blues from popular performer locals like Sean Costello and Bill Sheffield. It's open Tuesday–Saturday until 2 AM. *188 Garrison Rd., Marietta, 770/426–6400.*

CHIPS BAR & GRILL
Although outside the 10-county area, this spot's worth the trip if you want to hear important regional blues and rock acts try out new material. Music is typically featured each Friday and Saturday as well as two Sundays a month; it starts relatively early (about 9 PM; 4 PM on Sunday). You can grab a bite from a menu of burgers and barbecue. Cover charges run from $3 for local acts to $25 for nationally known acts, with most shows in the middle of the range. *655 Patrick Mill Rd., Winder, 770/307–2840.*

15 *f-7*
DADDY D'Z
The funky cinder-block barbecue joint, in a rapidly gentrifying industrial neighborhood, is the real deal for both ribs and the blues. Great and often unknown local musicians tune up every Friday and

Saturday night around 9. There's no cover. *264 Memorial Dr. SE, Grant Park, 404/222–0206. MARTA: King Memorial.*

4 *h-4*
DARWIN'S
Musicians from in town and "outta town" bring the blues to the northside. Located 1 mi east of the Big Chicken, a 50-ft-tall Kentucky Fried Chicken that's impossible to miss, Darwin's has won the respect of a blues-knowledgeable crowd. Shows start at 9 on weeknights, 9:30 on weekends. When there's a cover charge, it's usually $5–$10. Light fare, like the New Orleans's muffaletta sandwich, is served. *1598 Roswell Rd., Marietta, 770/578–6872.*

12 *g-7*
FAT MATT'S RIB SHACK
This little barbecue place is a stage for great local blues players, who pack in an early crowd eager to hear some good music. Decent ribs, sandwiches, barbecued chicken, side dishes, and plenty of beer define the menu. Outdoor seating accommodates anyone who'd rather keep the music in the background. Credit cards aren't accepted. *1811 Piedmont Ave., Midtown, 404/607–1622.*

15 *e-2*
FRONT PAGE NEWS
A journalistic theme prevails in this space, where owner Josh Sagarin decorates the walls with headlines collected from newspapers. On the menu, creole-style food is the order of the day. Musically, there's a little of everything, from zydeco and blues to jazz. Performances by some good artists are usually free. Sunday jazz brunch, served outside when weather permits, is another hit, with some performers showcasing original compositions. *1104 Crescent Ave., Midtown, 404/897–3500. MARTA: Midtown.*

13 *b-4*
FUZZY'S PLACE
A smoky music venue sits at one end of the long bar here, a restaurant televising sports events at the other end. The music side fills early as regulars stake out seats, even though the show doesn't start until 9 on weeknights and 10 on Friday and Saturday. Local talents, such as vocalist Francine Reed or Nancy Nagle with Cold Chills, grace the stage. Although the place really comes alive to the blues, the music varies, with rock

some nights and a more contemporary sound on others. The full menu of well-prepared creole fare, available 11–11, makes this a very popular lunch spot for workers from nearby offices. There's a $5 cover on weekends. *2015 N. Druid Hills Rd., North Druid Hills, 404/321–6166.*

5 *e-4*

LAGNIAPPE ON THE BAYOU

Savor Cajun fare and stick around for classic New Orleans jazz, blues, or swing—and sometimes even R&B. Friday and Saturday are the nights to come, beginning around 9:30. There's no cover. During the week, the restaurant also serves lunch. *1412 Dunwoody Village Pkwy., Dunwoody, 770/671–9777.*

15 *b-2*

NORTHSIDE TAVERN

Every night of the week this full-blooded blues club attracts big-name performing legends. The music usually starts at 10, and the tavern closes between 2 and 3 AM. You can order any imaginable drink, but food is limited to chili, except for Wednesday, when what's offered is at the whim of the cook. Here you can meet die-hard blues fans, as well as some of the best blues players around. *1058 Howell Mill Rd., Northwest Atlanta, 404/874–8745.*

4 *h-5*

POPPER'S

Regional blues acts perform in this casual, low-key club, which has photos of great blues artists on its walls. A full menu, served until late at night, includes fare like burgers and cheese sticks. Monday is karaoke night, Wednesday is open-mike night, and Tuesday and Thursday are set aside for jam sessions. There's a $5 cover charge (more if a major national band performs) on weekends only. *2555 Delk Rd., Marietta, 770/953–8779.*

festivals

ATLANTA BLUES SOCIETY FESTIVAL

Begun in 1999, this intense one-day musical blowout has brought regional and national talent to town. Past shows have included D.C. Bellamy, the Electromatics, and the duo Liz Melendez and Donna Hopkins. With a ticket price under $20, it's a blues bargain. *404/237–9595, www.atlantablues.org.*

MONTREAUX ATLANTA INTERNATIONAL MUSIC FESTIVAL

See Jazz, *below.*

WRFG BLUES BBQ

The city's community radio station, Radio Free Georgia, is a major blues force in the city. It holds an annual blues fest and picnic every Labor Day, with local and national talent. This is a fundraiser, so despite the station's nickname it's not free; if you contribute to the station, though, you can get a discount on tickets. *404/523–3471, www.wrfg.org.*

BREWPUBS & MICROBREWERIES

15 *e-1*

ATLANTA BREWING COMPANY

Numerous bars around town sell this brewery's products, which include Red Brick (a traditional amber ale), Peachtree Pale (a pale ale), and Laughing Skull (a Bohemian-style pilsner). On Friday from 5:30 PM until 7:30 there are $5 tours of the plant, plus live music by local bands—a worthy happy-hour alternative. *1219 Williams St., Midtown, 404/892–4436. MARTA: Arts Center.*

12 *f-3*

BUCKHEAD BLOCK

Eight house brews, from light lagers to stout, are on tap at this nightlife multiplex. On the patio, there's usually live acoustic music. The indoor lounge, where amplified bands play, can get loud. The dining area is lower key; the menu runs to standard bar fare. *3013 Peachtree Rd., Buckhead, 404/261–9898.*

10 *b-1*

BUCKHEAD BREWERY & GRILL

A log-finished exterior outlined in lights frames large windows that reveal the gleaming copper brew tanks within. Impressive hunt trophies hang on the walls, and a copper-hooded firebox in the center of the room waits for cold weather. This large brewpub and grill has two levels designed for family dining and a bar that's usually filled with single guys watching sports on TVs. Some half dozen brews are available at any time, plus a decent root beer; the wheat beer and the Hop Island Indian Pale Ale are the richest tasting. The pub grub includes a beer-cheese soup and quite good buffalo shrimp. It's open daily. *1757 Rock Quarry Rd., Stockbridge, 770/389–8112.*

12 *a-8*

DOGWOOD BREWING COMPANY

A pale ale, a wheat beer (hefeweizen), and a stout are brewed here year-round. In season you can also try the Dogwood Summer Brew, a Belgian-style white beer; Dogwood Winter Ale, made with barley, oats, wheat, rye, and a smoked malt; Octoberfest, a German-style lager; and Dogwood Bock, available around town in spring. Free brewery tours are given Thursday at 5:30 PM (proper I.D. required), and there are occasional live music concerts on the site. *1222 Logan Cir., Northwest Atlanta, 404/367–0500, www.dogwoodbrewing.com.*

15 *e-3*

GORDON BIERSCH BREWERY & RESTAURANT

Big, sleek, and somewhat corporate, this outpost of a California-based chain is inside a building designed to resemble a 19th-century brewery. The loft-like open interior and patio with a skyline view make it airier than many other pubs. Three German-style lagers are produced on site: a crisp, hoppy pilsner; an auburn, slightly sweet märzen; and a malty dunkles (a dark kind of beer less heavy than stout or bock). Following centuries-old German purity laws, the brewery makes its beer from just hops, barley, yeast, and water. There are full menus for lunch, dinner, and weekend brunch, but the place really gets rocking at happy hour. *848 Peachtree St., Midtown, 404/870–0805. MARTA: Midtown.*

12 *f-3*

JOHN HARVARD'S BREW HOUSE

Rich woods and gleaming brew tanks, visible inside the entrance, make this seem like a neighborhood pub. It's better suited to group gatherings than to romantic dating. The beer's decent, and the food ranges from appetizers like hummus or pepper Jack nachos—served in portions large enough for sharing—to entrées like ale-and-mustard chicken or Cajun salmon. The Stout Mud Slide Pie is made with real stout. *3041 Peachtree Rd., Buckhead, 404/816–2739, www.johnharvards.com.*

5 *d-3*

1564 Holcomb Bridge Rd., Roswell, 770/645–2739.

15 *e-5*

MAX LAGER'S

Busy every day of the week, Downtown's brewpub has rough-hewn interior brick walls and seating on an outdoor patio, which offers a view of the urban landscape. Order a tasting of the current brews and some of the great gumbo. The veggie pita and grilled chicken are good choices, too. For nondrinkers, the house-made root and ginger beers are refreshing and lively. *320 Peachtree St., Downtown, 404/525–4400. MARTA: Civic Center.*

15 *g-2*

PARK TAVERN & BREWERY

Overlooking Piedmont Park and the Midtown skyline, this bar has one of the best views in town. Friendly to park visitors, the staff tolerates patrons who show up wearing in-line skates and lunch guests in sometimes scanty exercise garb. It's even been known to provide water dishes and doggie biscuits for pets. The brewery creates pleasing hand-crafted beers, including a pilsner, a pale ale, an amber, a porter, and usually a couple of specialty items, such as a Scottish ale. There are two full bars with a Western-lodge look and giant leather chairs for lounging in three "comfy" areas. The Park is open for lunch Friday–Sunday, for brunch on Sunday, and until 2 AM most days. There are occasional live music and DJ events. *500 10th St., Midtown, 404/249–0001, www.parktavern.com. MARTA: Midtown.*

1 *b-5*

PECKERHEAD BREWERY

This microbrewery is also a coffee shop, a full-service restaurant with a Southern menu, and a full bar. Local and regional blues musicians perform on Friday and Saturday evenings. The various ales and lagers, in European and American styles, are made on site. Peckerhead's German-style koltzh (a light, crisp ale) is also bottled and sold at other area bars. *8514 Hospital Dr., Douglasville, 770/947–8788, www.peckerheadbrewery.com.*

12 *g-3*

ROCK BOTTOM BREWERY

There's an extensive menu and a good list of well-made suds at this neighborhood brewpub. Six quite good house-made brews are on tap at all times, plus a couple of specialty brews that vary with the season. With the food running toward the spicy, a brew is almost a required part of a meal here. *3242 Peachtree Rd., at Piedmont Rd., Buckhead, 404/264–0253.*

5 *e-1*

U.S. BORDER BREWERY CANTINA

Good Tex-Mex fare and from 8 to 10 fine brews are on offer at this pub. From pilsner to stout, amber ale to porter, the beer selection is wide; the Sun Salsa is so popular it's sold at local grocery stores. Live acoustic music—folk, pop, rock, contemporary, country, whatever—plays on Friday and Saturday nights, when the Cantina closes around midnight. The rest of the week, closing is at 10 PM. *12460 Crabapple Rd., Alpharetta, 770/772–4400.*

CAJUN & ZYDECO

13 *a-5*

ATLANTA CAJUN DANCE ASSOCIATION

On select Friday and Saturday evenings (call for the schedule), aficionados of Louisiana culture transform the local Knights of Columbus Hall into a dance club. The musicians come from Cajun country as well as from the local scene; Atlanta Swamp Opera and Hair of the Dog perform when out-of-state groups are, well, out-of-state. Festive evenings open at 7 PM with an hour's lesson in the art of the two-step and other forms of Cajun dance. Don't fret if you don't have a partner—everybody mixes. Wear comfortable, loose-fitting clothes and soft-sole shoes. You can grab a bite from the limited menu of Cajun food and wash it down with beer from the cash bar (wine and the hard stuff are not available). Depending on who's performing, covers run $10–$15. Parking is horribly tight, so come early or find a spot across the street. *Knights of Columbus Hall, 2620 Buford Hwy., at Lenox Rd., Northeast Atlanta, 770/451–6611, www.mindspring.com/~atlcajundance.*

14 *f-3*

YA YA'S

Every night they pull back the tables and chairs at this Cajun restaurant in preparation for dancing to bands like Big Hat and the Zydeco Kings. Tuesday the music is acoustic, Wednesday it's a blues invitational, on Friday and Saturday you can hear rockabilly and country zydeco, and on Sunday it's country. The cover depends on the act. Dancing starts around 9 and lasts till the bands stop rocking. The kitchen stays open till after midnight. *426 W. Ponce de Leon Ave., Decatur, 404/373–9292.*

CIGAR BARS

12 *g-3*

BELUGA MARTINI BAR

Live piano music and a vast drink menu full of wines and martinis are what set Beluga apart. The two humidors hold a selection of about a dozen cigars. Come to smoke, drink, and chill, but note that food isn't served. *3115 Piedmont Rd., Buckhead, 404/869–1090. MARTA: Buckhead.*

12 *g-3*

GOLDFINGER

This fun martini and cigar bar offers excellent drinks and a humidor full of Montecristos, Cohibas, Macanudos, and other premium cigars. On James Bond (shaken, not stirred) theme nights, 007 movies are shown continuously downstairs in the Red Room. A good place to kick back and relax, it's open Tuesday–Saturday. *3081 E. Shadowlawn Ave., Buckhead, 404/627–8464.*

15 *e-2*

MARTINI CLUB

Locally famous for the 101 varieties of martini it offers, the Martini Club is decorated in art-deco style. Its fully stocked walk-in humidor holds 30 or so different kinds of cigars, including Cohibas, Arturo Fuentes, and Macanudos. On the weekends, the house tobacconist oversees the cigar sales. Each of the dishes on the light menu, including a Brie selection and chocolate fondue with fresh fruit and pound cake, is served in a martini glass. Live jazz is heard on Wednesday and Friday, and a DJ spins on Saturday. The bar is closed Sunday; there is no cover or minimum. *1140 Crescent Ave., Midtown, 404/873–0794. MARTA: Midtown.*

COFFEEHOUSES

14 *a-4*

AURORA COFFEE
The house blend at this local roaster and hangout is medium dark and mild. The house crowd, by contrast, appears less meek—pierced, tattooed, dreadlocked, and dyed. With a deck and a spacious neo-industrial interior, Aurora's a great respite from the surrounding neighborhood's often wild street scene. *468 Moreland Ave., Little Five Points, 404/523–6856. MARTA: Inman Park.*

14 *a-3*

992 N. Highland Ave., Virginia-Highland, 404/892–7158.

12 *g-8*

1572 Piedmont Rd., Morningside, 404/607–9994.

15 *h-4*

INNOVOX CONNECTIVITY LOUNGE
The subterranean location, at the bottom of a former auto factory converted to loft apartments, suits the glamour-free scene at Innovox. Proprietor Jeff Ford's commitment is to community space, and all kinds of groups have their meetings here. There are homey arrangements of thrift-shop furniture to lounge on, computers to rent time on, offbeat publications on the news rack, and a big welcome for all. *699 Ponce de Leon Ave., Poncey-Highland, 404/872–4482.*

12 *g-2*

JOE MUGGS NEWSSTAND
It's bright and comfortable at this coffeehouse and magazine store, where the upholstered seating is arranged in friendly conversation groups. It's a meeting place for locals, who enjoy coffee from Atlanta's own J. Martinez and pastries from the excellent Buckhead Bread Company. The place opens at 6 AM daily and stays open late. *3275 Peachtree Rd., Buckhead, 404/364–9290. MARTA: Buckhead.*

14 *b-8*

SACRED GROUNDS
This onetime neighborhood pioneer pairs the usual caffeinated beverages and tasty bakery items with wacky, tempting tchotchkes and "recycled" furniture. The second branch transplants the same postmodern sensibility to a new looks-old loft building in downtown's Fairlie-Poplar district. *510 Flat Shoals Ave., East Atlanta, 404/223–0089.*

15 *e-5*

123B Luckie St., Downtown, 404/588–0666. MARTA: Peachtree Center.

14 *a-2*

SAN FRANCISCO COFFEE ROASTING COMPANY
In a restored brick storefront, this longstanding, locally owned outfit roasts its own coffee and sells good pastries. It's a great place for a date. Folks often bring along board games for an evening of friendly competition. There's also occasional live music. *1192 N. Highland Ave., Virginia-Highland, 404/876–8816.*

COMEDY

5 *b-5*

THE PUNCH LINE
Recognized comics from all over the United States have played this renowned club. Local yuckster Jeff Foxworthy made his name here; others of national note who have appeared here include Henry Cho and Bobcat Goldthwait. The menu of finger food includes chips, dips, sandwiches, and salads, and of course there's a full bar. Reservations are recommended on weeknights and required for weekend shows. Some shows are no-smoking. *280 Hilderbrand Dr., Sandy Springs, 404/252–5233.*

12 *e-6*

UPTOWN COMEDY CORNER
No reservations are necessary: just show up and laugh. Local and national stand-up talent is featured, and on Tuesday night Blacktop Circus Improv Group takes the stage in a show that encourages audience involvement. On Sunday's open-mike nights, you can enjoy the antics of amateurs or give stand-up a whirl yourself. Appetizers—catfish nuggets and chicken wings—are available to accompany the drinks you can order from the full bar. The club is open Tuesday–Sunday, and shows start at 9. Tickets are $5–$15, depending on the night of the week. *2140 Peachtree Rd., Buckhead, 404/350–6990.*

15 *e-2*

WHOLE WORLD THEATRE
Improvisational comedy flourishes in this intimate 120-seat theater. This is some of the city's most reasonably priced comedy, with admission of $15–$17.50. Shows sell out at least a week in advance so make reservations. If you do miss out, you can see the show for free, via a video simulcast in the café next door. (The small bar there serves beer and wine and is an outlet for Rocky's Brick Oven Pizza.) Shows are on Thursday at 8 PM, Friday and Saturday at 8 and 10:30 PM. *1214 Spring St., Midtown, 404/817–0880, www.wholeworldtheatre.com. MARTA: Arts Center.*

COUNTRY & WESTERN

4 *e-3*

COWBOYS CONCERT HALL
"Atlanta's Premier Honky-Tonk" offers live country music nightly and C&W dance lessons on Monday, Wednesday, Saturday, and Sunday evenings. If you think you need exercise after a night of line dancing, you've been doing more watching than dancing. Wednesday is Ladies' Night, when a balloon drops cash and prizes onto the dance floor. Sunday is family day—alcohol isn't served, but the $10 admission includes a buffet and dance lessons. Most days the club opens at 6:30 and closes between 2 and 3 AM. The cover charge is usually $7, unless the evening's headliner is a major national act. *1750 N. Roberts Rd., Kennesaw, 770/426–5006.*

6 *e-3*

FLYING MACHINE
At the edge of a runway at Gwinnett County airport, this aviation-theme spot delivers country bands like local performers Hokey Sloan and Jenna Lee Rose, as well as pop/contemporary music. There's entertainment Monday–Saturday beginning at about 7 PM, with no cover. The restaurant serves three meals daily, mostly steaks, burgers, and sandwiches, and creative specials on the weekend. *510 Briscoe Blvd. (South Terminal at Briscoe Field), Lawrenceville, 770/962–2262.*

8 *d-2*

MAMA'S COUNTRY SHOWCASE
The mammoth Mama's, 32,000 square ft in all, has one of the largest dance floors in Atlanta, a vast 3,000 square ft. A powerful sound system serves not only the dance floor but also six full-service bars, a diner (for when the munchies strike), and spaces that hold seven pool tables, a slew of video games, and one mean hydraulic bull. The occasional bikini contest has large cash prizes. Thursday evening brings a free buffet and line-dancing lessons. Women get in free on Friday. Open to the late hours from Thursday through Saturday, it's closed the rest of the week. *3952 Covington Hwy., Decatur, 404/288–6262, www.mamascountryshowcase.com.*

DANCE CLUBS

12 *f-3*

BELL BOTTOMS
A big dance floor, spinning mirrored balls, a light show, a fog machine, a life-size cutout of John Travolta, and loud music pumping away—all the best disco touches are here. Favorite tunes from the 1970s and 1980s keep the crowd grooving; you can request your favorite dance hit by simply walking upstairs to the DJ booth and asking. There are even a couple of cages to dance in. The cover charge is minimal ($5), but you must be 21 (with ID) to enter. *225 Pharr Rd., Buckhead, 404/816–9669.*

8 *c-3*

CLUB MIRAGE
Popular with African-Americans, this club is packed on the weekends, when well-known DJs spin house music for enthusiastic club goers. On Ladies' Night each Thursday, the Black Chippendales dance, and there's a free buffet; cover Thursday is $10 after 8 PM and $15 after 10. On other nights, it's $10. The club is open Tuesday–Sunday; nice dress is required. *3843 Glenwood Rd., Decatur, 404/286–1313.*

12 *f-3*

COBALT LOUNGE
High-energy dance and alternative music shake this Buckhead hangout. There are two levels: upstairs, DJs spin heat in the dance club, while lounge lizards inhabit the lower level. You can

order from a civilized bar menu (baked Brie, smoked salmon, crab cakes) until 3 or 4 AM. Some private party rooms are available. *265 E. Paces Ferry Rd., at Bolling Way, Buckhead, 404/760–9250.*

15 *e-2*

CRESCENT ROOM

DJs play deep house music for those who like to work it on this Midtown club's dance floor. DJs play Wednesday–

MOVE TO THE MUSIC

If sitting around watching performances is beginning to spread you, well, not so thin, get up and move to the music. Don't know how to dance? Maybe it's time to learn!

Atlanta Cajun Dance Association (Cajun & Zydeco)
For a hopping evening that will set your toes to tapping, there's nothing like an evening of Cajun dancing. Let the good times roll!

Chattahoochee Country Dancers (Folk Dancing)
Line up or circle 'round: either way, you'll get a real workout, make some new friends, and hear some fine traditional bluegrass.

City Lights Dance Club (Social & Ballroom Dancing)
Learn to dance with a partner, whether you want to waltz or lambada. That's what it's all about at this smoke- and alcohol-free nightclub.

Cowboys Concert Hall (Country & Western)
There's no way to resist the rhythm of live country music, so you might as well take one of the free line-dancing lessons here. You'll wear yourself a smile at the end of the night.

Hoedown's (Gay and Lesbian Bars & Clubs)
This country-and-western bar teaches line dancing to songs spun by DJs. It's mostly a guy thing, but the place does its best to attract women, especially on Thursday and Sunday nights. You're welcome as long as you're willing to kick it up.

Sanctuary Latin Nightclub (Latin)
Surrounded by Latin energy and glamour, learn tango, salsa, and merengue.

Saturday, and on the weekends there's a live percussionist, too. Dress is funky and hip. The club opens nightly at 10, and the cover is $5–$10. *1136 Crescent Ave., Midtown, 404/875–5252. MARTA: Midtown.*

12 *h-7*

DEUX PLEX

This two-story complex has a spacious lounge upstairs; downstairs a 7,500-square-ft dance club with a sunken floor can hold about 600 people, who can get comfortable on modern furniture arranged in intimate groupings. World-class DJs work the massive sound system. Friday is Latin Night, and Sunday is Industry Night. Cover is generally $10. *1789 Cheshire Bridge Rd., Northeast Atlanta, 404/733–5900.*

12 *f-3*

EUPHORIA

The multilevel club, with a rooftop deck, plays an eclectic mix of popular dance music and casts itself as a bit more grown-up than some of its neighbors. Thursday is College Night, followed by Fashion Forward Friday—dress to impress. Saturday brings a DJ from Q100. Dress is classy casual, and the cover is $10. *208 Pharr Rd., Buckhead, 404/233–6583.*

12 *f-3*

FUEL

It's all about attitude at this industrial-loft-look club decorated with futuristic art. If you're not somehow connected to the entertainment industry, you can't even get in the door on "Secret Mondays." There are four bars—two in the upstairs VIP area—and a patio. Wednesday there's live music for "Soul Lounge"; Thursday is "So-So-Def Night," named after the local hip-hop record company. The cover is $5–$15. *3073 Peachtree Rd., Buckhead, 404/262–9111, www.fuelatlanta. com. MARTA: Buckhead.*

12 *f-3*

HAVE A NICE DAY CAFÉ

Across from the Roxy, this very retro spot rocks with the music of the 1980s on Thursday night, which is also Ladies' Night (no cover for women). Friday and Saturday are 1970s Dance Party nights, and Wednesday is College Night, when the club opens to everyone age 18 and up. It's closed Monday and Tuesday.

3095 Peachtree Rd., Buckhead, 404/261–8898. MARTA: Buckhead.

12 *f-3*

MAKO'S

Dripping with tacky, colorful strings of beads, this club sets out to throw a party as awesome as "Mardi Gras—365 Days a Year." Top 40 hits raise the pulse on the lively dance floor. There's also a cigar and martini lounge and a Cajun menu. Mako's is closed Sunday, and you must be 21 to enter. *3065 Peachtree Rd., Buckhead, 404/846–8096, www. anythinggoesatmakos.com. MARTA: Buckhead.*

15 *h-4*

THE MASQUERADE

A good place to check out local bands, this club is popular with a college-age crowd. Each of the three floors has its own name and function: Heaven, a rocking concert hall, headlines local bands during the week and on some weekend nights. Hell is where DJs, flashing lights, and lots of sweaty bodies add up to a massive dance party. Purgatory is the game room, where you can chill out with pool and other diversions. From Wednesday through Saturday each night has a theme; during the summer months, Friday is the "Freaky Foam Party," when 500 partyers play in foam. The club opens on Monday and Tuesday only if a national band is booked. The cover runs $5–$8. *695 North Ave., Poncey-Highland, 404/577–8178; 404/577–2007 band and ticket info, www.masq.com.*

15 *e-2*

NOMENCLATURE MUSEUM

This funky place is an art parlor, a nightclub, and more. What will you find here? A discotheque where world-renowned DJs spin house music, for one thing. There's also a mini avant-garde theater that showcases what the club calls bizarre performance art. Then there's an outdoor patio, the Comatose Den (for chillin' out), and, of course, that art gallery. Cover varies from $3 to $7 depending on performers. *44 12th St., Midtown, 404/874–6344. MARTA: Midtown.*

4 *6*

VEGAS NIGHTS

Think Las Vegas glamour when you get dressed to come dancing here—no jeans, athletic gear, baseball caps, or sneakers, please. Standard bar food is always available, but there's a free buffet 6–8 PM on Friday, when the music starts with jazz and then moves on to old school. Saturday is for hip-hop. The club even has a swimming pool and hot tub, with a poolside grill. You must be 21 years old to enter. *1830 S. Cobb Pkwy., Marietta, 770/612–9112, www.vegas-nights. com.*

15 *f-2*

VELVET ROOM

Cosmopolitan folk in their thirties people this nightclub, which has three VIP sections and is furnished with comfortable groupings of chairs and couches in— what else?—velvet. Tuesday is for hip-hop and R&B, Wednesday for a gay and lesbian crowd, and on Friday and Saturday big-name DJs spin. The cover is usually $10. *1021 Peachtree St., Midtown, 404/876–6275, www.velvetroomatlanta.com. MARTA: Midtown.*

DINING & DANCING

12 *f-3*

CELEBRITY ROCK CAFE

Don't let the name fool you—this place doesn't tend to draw celebrities, and it's not just a rock-and-roll joint. Instead, a diverse thirtysomething crowd dines from a full menu of bar food such as quesadillas, burgers, and hot wings and dances to live music. Latin rhythms energize Wednesday night; a seven-piece house band playing '70s, '80s, and '90s dance music takes over Thursday–Saturday nights. The club is closed the rest of the week. There's no cover Thursday; otherwise it's $10. *56 E. Andrews Dr., East Andrews Square, Buckhead, 404/262–7625.*

2 *h-8*

1848 CAFE

Here are several operations in one: first, there's a long bar with bar seating and high tables. To one side is a performance space that's basically devoted to rock, while upstairs the fine restaurant presents jazz, comedy, and occasional wine-tasting events. The menu downstairs has an extensive selection of typical American bar food—burgers, sandwiches, grilled chicken, pasta—and sometimes adds a Peruvian touch. *29 S. Main St., Alpharetta, 770/751–5954.*

5 b-7
JOHNNY'S HIDEAWAY

A large and accommodating bar, music from the 1930s through the 1960s, a dance floor for all kinds of dancing, and a full menu that includes steaks, seafood, burgers, and appetizers make this a favorite of the 40-plus crowd, although younger and older patrons come, too. Some folks dress formally and some casually. The Sinatra Room is worth a visit; it houses more than 100 pieces of Frank memorabilia. "King's Corner" is devoted to Elvis memorabilia and photos. The club is open daily. Instead of a cover, there's a two-drink minimum. *3771 Roswell Rd., Buckhead, 404/233–8026, www.johnnyshideaway.com.*

15 e-2
KAYA BISTRO & NIGHTCLUB

From Tuesday through Sunday, Atlanta's finest DJs spin dance music ranging from reggae to hip-hop to house at this multifunctional nightspot. The biggest crowd gathers on Friday, when V-103's Frank Ski hosts "Northern Exposure." The bar-food menu carries wings, mozzarella sticks, sandwiches, and salads. Cover charge varies, and women enter free before 11 PM. *1068 Peachtree St., Midtown, 404/874–4460, www.kayaclub.com. MARTA: Midtown.*

5 f-6
PREMIER CLUB

This isn't your run-of-the-mill dance club. Indian cuisine is the specialty in the kitchen, and Indian pop, Bhangra, and European and American pop are on the DJ play list. On some special occasions, live Indian music is presented. In addition to the dance floor, there is also karaoke, pool tables, and a full-service bar. The club is closed Monday, and there is no cover. *2100 Park Lake Dr., Tucker, 770/493–7159.*

5 d-5
RENDEZVOUS

Inside this spacious club, DJs spin a mix that ranges from rock to high-energy dance music for a thirtysomething crowd. A dinner menu is available until 11 on weekdays and midnight on weekends, in case you need to fuel up. Weekend cover is $5. *4711 Ashford-Dunwoody Rd., Dunwoody, 770/901–9995, www.rendezvousatlanta.com. MARTA: Dunwoody.*

FOLK & ACOUSTIC

12 f-3
BUCKHEAD SALOON & SWEET RIVER TAVERN

Live acoustic music, from folk to popular, plays here Wednesday–Saturday beginning at 5:30. Casually dressed folks in their mid- to late twenties meander in and out of the bar, and much of the time there are performances on the covered deck. There's no cover or drink minimum. *3107 Peachtree Rd., Buckhead, 404/261–7922. MARTA: Buckhead.*

14 b-8
THE EARL

The name stands for "East Atlanta Restaurant and Lounge," and this laid-back room is both a decent, casual eatery and one of the most intimate places in town for hearing live music. There's an enlightened bar-food menu—in addition to burgers you can have a salmon BLT, a tuna burger, or a good salad. The eclectic music goes from country to grunge rock. *488 Flat Shoals Ave., East Atlanta, 404/522–3950, www.badearl.com.*

14 g-3
EDDIE'S ATTIC

You can hear internationally known musicians as well as struggling locals here. Eddie, the proprietor, has helped to give many talented performing songwriters, such as the Indigo Girls, their first break. There are regular open-mike showdowns, and the space occasionally serves as a gallery for local visual artists. A full menu of burgers, chicken sandwiches, pasta, and salads, plus bar nibbles such as wings and stuffed mushrooms, is available. Doors open at 4 daily and covers run $3–$10, depending on who's playing. *515B N. McDonough St., Decatur, 404/377–4976, www.eddiesattic.com.*

15 g-2
REDLIGHT CAFE

Open to the early morning hours, this pioneering cybercafé (it opened in 1994) has live music that includes jazz, blues, bluegrass, rock, and acoustic. Wednesday is open-mike night, so there's no cover. Thursday is devoted to bluegrass ($3 cover). Friday–Sunday brings local and national acoustic acts, with covers ranging from $5 to $25; jazz is featured occasionally. On Tuesday, patrons bring board games and just hang out. The café offers a simple menu of appetizers (quesadillas, Brie and baguette, garlic-cheese bread), salads, sandwiches, pasta, and desserts, along with beer and wine. It's closed Monday. *553 Amsterdam Ave., Virginia-Highland, 404/627–0875, www.redlightcafe.com.*

FOLK DANCING

12 *g-7*

CHATTAHOOCHEE COUNTRY DANCERS

Morningside Baptist Church's gym was hardly designed as a dance club, but when this group puts on its Friday-night contra dances, you'd never know the difference. The evening starts at 7:30 with a half hour of lessons upstairs, at which you can learn the earliest versions of line and circle dancing. There's always a live band and live caller. Wear comfortable, loose clothing and flat, soft-sole shoes. And you don't have to bring a partner, as mixing's the thing at these friendly shindigs. There's a $5 cover, unless a special band is playing. For information, call Atlanta Dance Hotline (404/634–2585). *Morningside Baptist Church, 1700 Piedmont Ave., Morningside, no phone, www.contradance.org.*

14 *e-5*

ENGLISH COUNTRY DANCE ATLANTA

Think of the party scenes in all the Jane Austen movies you've seen, subtract the costumes, and you'll have a picture of English country dancing, which saw its heyday from the 16th to the 18th centuries. A called form of dancing, it's always done to live music. The people here are into truly social dancing, not posing or performing, and meet most second Sundays of the month. Wear comfortable, soft-sole shoes. There's a $5 cover; call Atlanta Dance Hotline (404/634–2585) for the schedule. *Oakhurst Baptist Church, 222 Eastlake Dr., Decatur, no phone. MARTA: East Lake.*

ROYAL SCOTTISH COUNTRY DANCE SOCIETY, ATLANTA BRANCH

The international organization is devoted to teaching and preserving the traditional ballroom dancing of Scotland. The graceful, sprightly steps of the form, also known as Scottish country dancing, are the focus of classes and social events.

Activities take place at various venues all over town. For schedules, call the Atlanta Dance Hotline (404/634–2585). *Box 33905, Decatur 30033, no phone, www.mindspring.com/~atlbrnch.*

FUN

4 *h-5*

DAVE & BUSTER'S

For game players, this is the ultimate hangout: you can play video games, pinball, virtual-reality games, skee-ball, table hockey, and pool. Families get in on the fun, too, often on the midway, where slot machines and other games pay off in tickets that can be exchanged for toy prizes. There is a full-service bar and a restaurant that serves decent American fare. The place is open daily from about 11 AM until late. *2215 D&B Dr., Marietta, 770/951–5554.*

6 *a-3*

4000 Venture Dr., Duluth, 770/497–1152.

12 *f-3*

JELLYROLL'S DUELING PIANOS & SING-A-LONG

Atlanta's only rock-and-roll dueling piano bar makes you laugh and sing out loud. Four pianists take turns dueling with each other while goading the audience into the fray. It's too much fun to ignore. Music is the focus, but the place can get crazy and wild. The bar is open Wednesday–Saturday 7 PM–3 AM, and the show begins at 8 (food isn't served). You must be 21 to enter. The cover is $3 on Thursday, $6 on Friday and Saturday; no cover Wednesday. *295 E. Paces Ferry Rd., Buckhead, 404/261–6866.*

GAY AND LESBIAN BARS & CLUBS

15 *f-4*

ATLANTA EAGLE

Very proudly gay-owned and -operated, this Levis-and-leather bar is a fun, tolerant (women are welcome) place to dance. There are regularly scheduled contests and leather fests, and various organizations meet and hold charity events here. There's also a shop for leather clothing and paraphernalia. *306 Ponce de Leon Ave., Midtown, 404/873–2453, www.atlantaeagle.com. MARTA: North Ave.*

15 *e-3*

BACKSTREET

Dance to house, pop, and techno and then catch the fabulous drag show, *Charlie Brown's Cabaret,* at this 24-hour club. What is probably Atlanta's best-known gay space welcomes all kinds—gay and straight, male and female, the freakier the better—and a veritable crush of folks shows up. Everyone must show I.D., no matter your age, to get in. This is a members-only club, with dues costing $10 per quarter; membership entitles cardholders to free entry Sunday–Thursday and $5 admission on Friday and Saturday. Take a taxi if you can, as parking ($10 on the weekends) is a real nuisance and very limited. *845 Peachtree St., Midtown, 404/873–1986, www.backstreetatlanta.com. MARTA: Midtown.*

15 *g-1*

BURKHART'S PUB

Dark wood paneling, redbrick floors, a patio full of lush plants, and carefully selected artwork are what makes up this warm and friendly bar, where gay men and their friends mix and mingle. This is a pub and then some, with pool tables, frequent karaoke nights, and concerts every Sunday evening by the locally famous Gospel Girls. If it's too crowded for you at Burkhart's, you can step across the parking lot to one of three other gay-oriented bars. Imbued with a spirit of community involvement, the bar is proud of being the largest corporate sponsor in Atlanta for HIV/Aids Services. *1492F Piedmont Rd., Ansley Square, Midtown, 404/872–4403, www.burkharts.com.*

12 *g-7*

CLUB RARITY

Once the Otherside, this complex contains a patio with a marbleized stage for shows. Inside are VIP rooms, piano bar, martini bar, and a champagne balcony. There's something happening every night, including "Sin Nite for the Service Industry" on Monday and a body-parts contest on Thursday. *1924 Piedmont Rd., Midtown, 404/875–5238.*

15 *g-3*

HOEDOWN'S

DJs aren't the only ones doing the spinning at this country-music venue. It's predominantly a men's bar but everyone is welcome. Line-dance lessons are offered Tuesday, Wednesday, and Thursday beginning at 8 PM and Sunday at 4 PM. Also on Sunday, there's a free buffet 6–8. Hoedown's charges a cover only on New Year's Eve, and it's closed Monday. *931 Monroe Dr., Midtown Promenade, 404/876–0001, www.hoedownsatlanta. com.*

14 *g-4*

MY SISTERS' ROOM

Tucked away on a slip of a street near Agnes Scott College, this gathering spot for lesbians of all sorts—especially couples—is a comfortable haven for an evening out. A large patio covered by a domed canvas roof holds table seating; just beyond lies a garden. Within is sofa seating, a bar, and a juke box. From time to time, live entertainment by regional and national women singers draws large crowds. The limited menu mostly sticks to bar food—mozzarella sticks, sandwiches, fries, with occasional homemade specials. Curb-side parking is extremely limited. The bar is open late and serves brunch on Sunday. *222 E. Howard Ave., Decatur, 404/370–1990.*

15 *f-2*

OUTWRITE BOOKSTORE & COFFEEHOUSE

A coffeehouse and bookstore catering to the gay and lesbian community, Outwrite is casual, comfortable, and civilized. Printed matter, and very good coffee with pastries (cakes, brownies, and bagels), is the order of the day. A comfortable seating area doubles as a venue for author readings, poetry slams, and the like, and the little balcony overlooking the gay-central intersection of 10th and Piedmont is a favorite hangout. It's open Sunday–Thursday 9 AM–11 PM and weekends 9 AM–midnight. *991 Piedmont Ave., Midtown, 404/607–0082, www.outwritebooks. com. MARTA: Midtown.*

15 *h-4*

TOWER II

An unpretentious nightspot in a quiet residential neighborhood, tower II welcomes all lesbians. There's a pool room, a "Rainbow Room" for special events, and music every night of the week until late. Lip-sync shows are every Saturday. A $5 cover is in effect only for the occasional special events. *735 Ralph McGill Blvd., Poncey-Highland, 404/523–1535.*

HOTEL BARS

For hotel sports bars, *see* Sports Bars, *below*.

6 *a-4*

BUTTONS LOUNGE

Buttons takes its name from Button Gwinnett, a signer of the Declaration of Independence. The bar serves a light menu along with good libations. A dance floor beckons in the evening, and a DJ plays popular tunes on Friday and Saturday. *Gwinnett Marriott Hotel, 1775 Pleasant Hill Rd., Duluth, 770/923–1775.*

15 *e-5*

FANDANGLES

The after-work set hasn't quite discovered this plush bar in the downtown Sheraton, so it's still a mellow place to unwind. Two snuggly curtained-off zones provide an extra bit of privacy. You can nibble from a tapas menu. *Sheraton Atlanta Hotel, 165 Courtland St., Downtown, 404/659–6500. MARTA: Peachtree Center.*

12 *g-2*

GRAND HYATT LOBBY LOUNGE

A quiet spot, this cigar-friendly lounge has crystal chandeliers, a waterfall and Japanese garden outside tall windows, and a short bar menu of delectables. The specialty of the house is the Grand Supreme Martini, made with pear cognac, vodka, and lime. *Grand Hyatt Hotel, 3300 Peachtree Rd., Buckhead, 404/365–8100. MARTA: Buckhead.*

9 *a-6*

HUNT LOUNGE

A gathering spot for southsiders, this busy hotel bar can get really jammed. Live music on the weekends draws a diverse crowd, from the 20s on up, that's ready for dancing. Music ranges all over the keyboard. There's a simple bar menu. *Wyndham Peachtree City Conference Center, 2443 GA 54 W, Peachtree City, 770/487–2000, ext. 7538.*

15 *d-5*

LATITUDES

This lobby bar has one of the city's prettiest and most engaging urban views. You can look out over Centennial Olympic Park, with its dazzling light towers and fountains, toward a skyline backdrop—but from an intimate, third-floor level, not from way up. A light bistro menu is available. *Omni Hotel, 100 CNN Center, Downtown, 404/818–4452. MARTA: Omni.*

15 *e-2*

PARK 75 LOUNGE

Cushy upholstered seating, a large bar, and the lilt of piano music make for a genteel and relaxing evening. Whether you prefer to read a book in a corner wing chair or chat with friends around a table, you can find pure comfort here. Thursday–Saturday the piano music is live. Lovely tapas are occasionally served at cocktail hour, and the bar menu has appetizers, soups, salads, pasta, and similar light fare. *Four Seasons Atlanta Hotel, 75 14th St., Midtown, 404/881–9898. MARTA: Arts Center.*

12 *h-21*

RITZ-CARLTON, BUCKHEAD, LOBBY LOUNGE

Besides the inviting bar, this large space has a fireplace and very comfortable seating. Live piano entertainment keeps the room harmonious all day long. On the weekends there's dancing to light jazz, sometimes with fine vocalists. Afternoon tea is served daily, or order from the appetizer and martini menus. *Ritz-Carlton, Buckhead, 3434 Peachtree Rd., Buckhead, 404/237–2700. MARTA: Buckhead or Lenox.*

7 *d-2*

RODNEY'S

You can take to the Ramada Inn's dance floor for everything from Top 40 to oldies to country and western. Live bands perform popular rock-and-roll hits Friday and Saturday nights. Bar food is available, or you can order from the adjoining restaurant's full menu. The bar is open daily until the early hours. *Ramada Inn, 4225 Fulton Industrial Blvd., Northeast Atlanta, 404/696–2728.*

5 *c-5*

SAVU

The lavish W Atlanta @ Perimeter Center includes a casual yet upscale bar that's as good for after-work gatherings as it is for leisurely unwinding. Plush seating, a cool white-and-gray color scheme, and low lighting create the mood. There's a bar menu for quick bites. *W Atlanta @ Perimeter Center, 111 Perimeter Center W, off Ashford-Dun-*

woody Rd. at I–285, Dunwoody, 770/396–6800. MARTA: Sandy Springs.

JAZZ

clubs

5 *c-5*

CAFÉ 290

A favorite place for friends who want to hang out, the café presents decently prepared American food and live jazz Tuesday–Sunday. The talent is often local, and it never fails to be top notch. Music starts at 9:30 PM and keeps going until 4 AM; on Sunday the crowds thin out. The cover is $7. *290 Hilderbrand Dr., Sandy Springs, 404/256–3942.*

15 *e-3*

CHURCHILL GROUNDS

The menu of light appetizers is perfect for the accompanying straight-ahead jazz that is performed live Tuesday–Sunday, beginning about 9:30 PM. Cover runs from $5 to $25, as some of the performers are major national and international artists. Pastries and espresso are lovely. This is a good spot for a quick bite before events at the Fox Theatre, next door. *660 Peachtree St., Midtown, 404/876–3030. MARTA: North Ave.*

5 *e-2*

COMEAUX'S LOUISIANA BAR & GRILL

A Cajun-creole restaurant, oyster bar, and jazz-blues club, this is a rock-solid suburban performance venue. The dining room is family friendly, but couples are comfortable here, too. Live music begins as early as 4 PM, with a second group taking over at 10 PM. There's no cover. *9925 Haynes Bridge Rd., Alpharetta, 770/442–2524.*

12 *g-2*

DANTE'S DOWN THE HATCH

Hot fondue and cool jazz (except on Monday) in nautical surroundings are what this place is all about. The Paul Mitchell Trio entertains regularly, along with visiting guitar players and folk singers. There's an extensive wine list. Diners who wish to sit in the jazz area pay a $6 cover; if you want the chocolate fondue, order it when you make your reservations. It's open daily. *3380 Peachtree Rd., Buckhead, 404/266–1600,* www.dantesdownthehatch.com. MARTA: Buckhead.

12 *f-2*

HIGH NOTE JAZZ CLUB

With 350 seats and great acoustics, this sprawling club is a serious jazz venue. The Blue Room (also know as the Ice Cave) and the Japanese Room give customers a place to talk and get bar service, leaving the Main Room for the listener who doesn't appreciate chatter during performances. It's open Wednesday–Saturday 8 PM–2 AM. The cover charge is $10. There's a nightly complimentary buffet with such fare as finger sandwiches, fruit, cheese, and desserts. *3259 Roswell Rd., Buckhead, 404/239–0202.*

5 *a-6*

RAY'S ON THE RIVER

Overlooking the Chattahoochee, this restaurant draws fans with live jazz in the bar on Tuesday–Saturday nights, beginning at 8 PM Tuesday–Thursday and 9 PM Friday and Saturday. The restaurant serves dinner daily, lunch on weekdays, and brunch on Sunday. There's no cover. *6700 Powers Ferry Rd., Marietta, 770/955–1187,* www.raysontheriver.com.

12 *g-3*

SAMBUCA JAZZ CAFÉ

After dinner, well-dressed jazz fans queue up to get into this club, so get here early if you want a seat. Hard-core music enthusiasts dive for the center tables, while those who like to chat gather around the large bar. The food's not the forte here, but if you get a good seat the music may be worth some mundane munchies. Open daily, the café starts its shows at 8 PM. There's a $10 cover in the bar on Friday and Saturday and a $17 per person minimum at dinner (exclusive of alcohol). *3102 Piedmont Rd., Buckhead, 404/237–5299,* www.sambucajazzcafe.com.

festivals

ATLANTA JAZZ FESTIVAL

Sponsored by the city, this festival celebrates homegrown as well as national and international jazz talent. Concerts are held in Grant and Piedmont parks throughout Memorial Day weekend, with free outdoor "side" concerts on the city's streets during the week preceding the event. *404/817–6815.*

MONTREAUX ATLANTA INTERNATIONAL MUSIC FESTIVAL

Atlanta throbs during the week before Labor Day, when internationally renowned ensembles perform at clubs and public venues throughout the metro area. The weekend brings three days of free jazz, blues, and a bit of reggae to Piedmont Park. *404/817–6815, www.atlantafesitvals.com.*

LATIN

12 *f-3*

HAVANA CLUB

Here you can dance to straight-up Latin salsa until 1 or 2 AM from Monday through Saturday. True to its name, Havana is also a cigar bar, complete with walk-in humidor. The mixologists specialize in martinis, and a free buffet is served at Salsa Sunday, the weekly Latin disco. A private VIP lounge is available for private events. Covers are charged only for special events. *247 Buckhead Ave., East Village Square, Buckhead, 404/869–8484.*

12 *f-3*

SANCTUARY LATIN NIGHTCLUB

The dance floor here swings to sizzling Latin rhythms on Friday and Saturday, and on the first and third Sunday of the month it's taken over by the tango fanatics (*see* Tango Dances, *below*). The mature, sharp-dressing crowd of professionals doesn't begin to gather until around 10 PM, and the club stays open way past bedtime. Don't worry if you want to salsa but don't know a rumba from a samba: lessons are complimentary. The cover is $10. *128 E. Andrews Dr., Buckhead, 404/262–1377, www.sanctuarynightclub.com.*

TANGO DANCES

Several groups of Argentine tango enthusiasts give lessons around town, and all get together regularly for open dances. You need not bring a partner. Dances are held on the first and third Sunday of each month at Sanctuary (404/262–1377), in Buckhead, with a $10 cover; on the first Thursday at Après Diem, in Midtown (404/872–3333), with no cover; and on Friday at changing venues. *404/634–2585 Atlanta Dance Hotline, www.tango-atlanta.com or www.tango-rio.com.*

PIANO BARS

5 *b-7*

CARBO'S

For more than 20 years, Carmen and Bob Mazurek have dished out American contemporary food in their full-service restaurant. You can start or end your evening in the piano bar, where you can hear live solo piano music nightly beginning at 8 PM. It's closed Sunday and Monday. *3717 Roswell Rd., Buckhead, 404/231–4433.*

12 *g-3*

MCKINNON'S LOUISIANE

At the back of the bar of this popular Cajun-creole restaurant, patrons gather around a piano before or after dinner, on Friday and Saturday evenings. *3209 Maple Dr., Buckhead, 404/237–1313. MARTA: Buckhead.*

5 *d-5*

PARK PLACE

At one of the city's most comfortable piano bars, pianists perform nightly, beginning in the late afternoon. Across from Perimeter Mall, it's perfect for an after-shopping chill. A happy-hour buffet starts at 5 PM on weeknights. The bar is closed Sunday. *4505 Ashford-Dunwoody Rd., Park Place, Dunwoody, 770/399–5990. MARTA: Dunwoody.*

5 *d-4*

TRATTORIA VARKETTA'S & PIANO BAR

The bar presents live music Thursday–Saturday: Bobby B. begins to play on the baby grand at 7 PM. Lots of hardwood and brick makes the place seem warm. The casual trattoria serves substantial Italian cuisine. Everything from pizza to pasta and salad to veal graces the ample menu. Monthly wine dinners with jazz are a deal for about $45 for a five-course meal. The bar is open daily. *Shoppes of Dunwoody, 5486 Chamblee-Dunwoody Rd., Dunwoody, 770/396–0335.*

POP/ROCK

bars & clubs

12 *f-3*

CJ'S LANDING

In the concert hall at this rocking multiplex, top regional and national bands are the draw. Acoustic cover acts perform on the climate-controlled deck. Upstairs, the classy Tango Bar is a place to lounge and drink. There's an extensive, if standard, bar-food menu to soak up the suds. *270 Buckhead Ave., Buckhead, 404/237–7657, www.cjslanding.com.*

14 a-3
DARK HORSE TAVERN
Local, and sometimes national, bands rock downstairs while diners enjoy a good meal upstairs. You have to pay a cover to see the show, which usually begins around 9 PM, Wednesday–Saturday. The bar is open nightly until the very early hours. *816 N. Highland Ave., Virginia-Highland, 404/873–3607.*

14 b-8
ECHO LOUNGE
Live music every night—primarily contemporary pop and rock—has made the Echo a significant player on Atlanta's music scene. Most shows welcome anyone over 18 (though you must prove you're 21 to drink) and begin at 9 PM. There's a different act every day. *551 Flat*

Shoals Ave., East Atlanta, 404/681–3600, www.echostatic.com.*

5 g-7
THE LAST GREAT WATERING HOLE
On weekends, mostly local rock-and-roll bands take the fairly large stage. During the week, however, this totally guy joint draws locals to its seven pool tables; tournaments are frequent events. The menu is mostly bar bites—fries, sandwiches, and the like—although substantial steaks at great prices are a major menu draw. There is no cover. *4341 Hugh Howell Rd., Tucker, 770/270–5571.*

12 f-3
METROPOLITAN PIZZA BAR
This place offers a rare thing: a casual, budget-friendly evening of entertainment in Buckhead. In addition to terrific pizzas, calzones, and sandwiches, rock and roll and R&B are served until the early-morning hours. Local bands play on Friday and Saturday, with no cover charge. Karaoke rules Tuesday, while DJs take care of Wednesday and Thursday. It's closed Sunday and Monday. *3055 Bolling Way, Buckhead, 404/264–0135, www.metropolitanpizza.com.*

12 g-8
SMITH'S OLDE BAR
At this venue for local and regional musicians, contemporary electric and alternative music heats up the upstairs area; cool jazz, folk, light rock, and acoustic sounds mellow the downstairs on occasion, usually in the spring on Tuesday nights. Bar food, such as chicken wings, burgers, and Philly cheese steak sandwiches, is served in the downstairs restaurant. There's a cover, generally $5–$10, for upstairs shows only. Smith's is open daily until the very early hours. *1578 Piedmont Ave., Ansley Park/Morningside, 404/875–1522.*

14 a-4
STAR COMMUNITY BAR
The popular bar in the colorful Little Five Points district has funky live music every day of the week. Usually, it's a rock or pop band, but the acts change frequently. While here, step downstairs to check out another bar, the Little Vinyl Lounge, or go up to the Grace Vault, a shrine to Elvis Presley. *437 Moreland Ave., Little Five Points, 404/681–9018. MARTA: Inman Park.*

NIGHTTIME NOSHES

There's nothing like a tasty bite to eat while you're grooving to some music or sipping a cocktail. Keep yourself fueled up into the wee hours of the morning.

Blue Pig (Blues)
It's hard to decide whether to come for the music or for the ribs. Hmm . . . ribs—now there' an idea! But the music is first-rate, so it's a win-win situation.

Fuzzy's Place (Blues)
So what if it's a bit scruffy? The food's good, the blues are superb, and everything's funky. Better be smoke tolerant, though.

Park 75 Lounge (Hotel Bars)
Settle into a comfy chair with a glass of champagne and savor the delicious small dishes. The piano music, low and mellow, allows conversation with a friend or lover.

Savu (Hotel Bars)
Coolly sophisticated, the bar at the sleek W Atlanta @ Perimeter Center draws its appetizer menu from the hotel restaurant, which prepares elegant Pacific Rim fare.

concert venues

CHASTAIN PARK AMPHITHEATRE
See Performance Venues, under Performing Arts, *above*.

COBB COUNTY CIVIC CENTER
See Performance Venues, under Performing Arts, *above*.

COCA-COLA ROXY THEATRE
See Performance Venues, under Performing Arts, *above*.

COTTON CLUB
See Performance Venues, under Performing Arts, *above*.

EARTHLINK LIVE
See Performance Venues, under Performing Arts, *above*.

HIFI BUYS AMPHITHEATRE
See Performance Venues, under Performing Arts, *above*.

 f-5

INTERNATIONAL BALLROOM
A run-down former warehouse out in the suburbs makes an appropriately funky venue for such hard-hitting acts as acid-jazz band Jamiroquai, grunge rockers the Deftones, and occasional oddball events like the X-Files Expo. It also frequently hosts Latin dance bands, which draw throngs from the immigrant enclaves of Doraville and nearby Chamblee. *6616 New Peachtree Rd., Doraville, 770/936–0447.*

RIALTO CENTER FOR THE PERFORMING ARTS
See Performance Venues, under Performing Arts, *above*.

15 *e-5*

THE TABERNACLE
Rehabbed into a performance venue for the 1996 Olympics, this huge, five-level former church showcases top local bands as well as national acts: everything from Memphis blues to hard-core rock and roll. Acts and show times vary from day to day. Because of the raked floor, no seat is more than 40 yards from the stage. The Cotton Club is downstairs. If you catch a show here, look for the black-and-white photos of the "Preachers of Rock and Roll," semi-

nal musicians of the 20th century. *152 Luckie St., Downtown, 404/659–9022, www.atlantaconcerts.com/tabernacle. MARTA: Peachtree Center.*

VARIETY PLAYHOUSE
See Performance Venues, under Performing Arts, *above*.

festivals

MIDTOWN MUSIC FESTIVAL
Some of the industry's top performers—including Santana, Lucinda Williams, and Al Green—attend this weekend festival in early May. Beer and food booths abound. *404/872–1115, www.musicmidtown.com.*

PUBS & TAVERNS

14 *a-4*

BREWHOUSE HOUSE OF BREWS
In addition to resident locals, Brits hang out at this lively establishment with a distinctive neighborhood feel to it. The extensive menu includes bangers and mash, fish-and-chips, and similar pub grub, along with familiar chicken dishes and burgers and some lighter fare. There's patio seating in good weather. Of course, there are beers a-plenty: 22 on tap and 24 by the bottle. Brewhouse closes at 3 AM Monday–Saturday and at 1 AM Sunday. *401 Moreland Ave., Little Five Points, 404/525–7799. MARTA: Inman Park.*

5 *c-3*

CHAPLINS
The place has many personalities: It's a restaurant with a full menu of steaks and seafood. It's a sports bar with TVs and a big screen to show the game. It's a casual tavern with a heated outdoor deck where folks can lounge, munch, and converse. And, on Saturday nights, it's a full-tilt karaoke bar with contests and prizes. Chaplins is near the entrance to the Old Southern Mill in historic Roswell; it's open daily. *555 S. Atlanta St., Roswell, 770/552–1147.*

12 *f-3*

CHURCHILL ARMS
Small groups of friends chat around a roaring fireplace, while another bunch warbles around a piano. In the next

room, billiards and darts are the draw. Meanwhile, in the center of it all, an attentive gentleman dispenses drinks at the bar. Come for the camaraderie. *3223 Cains Hill Pl., Buckhead, 404/233–5633.*

15 *h-3*

DUGAN'S TAVERN

A raft of beers and some singularly odd-sounding drinks complement a good-size menu that's heavy on bar food. The Virginia-Highland tavern seems a bit rowdy, while the Stone Mountain version is more sedate and has a somewhat more extensive menu. The Virginia-Highland Dugan's also serves as a neighborhood sports bar, attracting locals who enjoy sports events on the more than 30 TVs. *777 Ponce de Leon Ave., Virginia-Highland, 404/885–1217.*

8 *e-1*

5922 Memorial Dr., Stone Mountain, 404/ 297–8545.

14 *a-5*

EUCLID AVENUE YACHT CLUB

The laid-back bar has served good food and every kind of beer imaginable—including 20 on draft—since the mid-1980s. It has a TV, but people don't come here to watch the tube; they come to hang with friends and neighbors. The club is open from noon (12:30 on Sunday) until sometime after 2:30 AM, depending on the night. Ask the owners (they do frequent the place) the origin of the bar's name. *1136 Euclid Ave., Little Five Points, 404/688–0163. MARTA: Inman Park.*

12 *f-3*

FADÓ

Step inside this popular Buckhead after-work bar, the first in the chain, and you'd swear you took a plane to the Auld Sod itself. Dark-wood paneling divides the space into intimate areas, and rough-hewn furnishings provide seating. Friends gather to hoist a pint and watch delayed-play rugby and Irish football matches on the large-screen TV. Good Irish food includes the house-made soda bread and boxty, the classic filled potato pancake. Some evenings offer live Celtic music. On Sunday, come for the Irish breakfast. There's brunch on Saturday and Sunday. *3035 Peachtree Rd., Buckhead, 404/841–0066. MARTA: Buckhead.*

5 *g-7*

FLANIGAN'S THERE GOES THE NEIGHBORHOOD

Neighbors come to this watering hole offering fair food and friendly staffers to watch TV on the numerous screens, including one big-screener. The large bar anchors the establishment, and booth seating lines the opposite wall. Food ranges from fish-and-chips and fried chicken to steaks and crab legs. But the real reason to come here is the conviviality. Live music events include reggae on Wednesday and various bands on Friday and Saturday, including the Irish band The Charms at least twice a month. *4092 Lawrenceville Hwy., Tucker, 770/270–0001.*

14 *b-8*

GRAVITY PUB

Pool tables, foosball, pinball, videos games, and a jukebox are all in this funky neighborhood pub's basement. On Tuesday nights, there's a trivia quiz, and on the last Wednesday of the month, it's "Kodac Harrison's Blue Plate Special," featuring acoustic music and a poetry slam. The menu has standard bar food; brunch is served on Sunday. *1257 Glenwood Ave., East Atlanta, 404/627–5555, www.thegravitypub.com.*

14 *a-3*

HAND IN HAND

Here's a pretty convincing facsimile of an English pub, with a wonderful lattice-shaded terrace outside and lots of dark wood paneling and velvet and tapestry-covered booths and stools within. The menu includes English standards (fish-and-chips, Welsh rarebit, shepherd's pie) plus bar food ranging from wings to hummus. There's also a Sunday brunch. *752 N. Highland Ave., Virginia-Highland, 404/872–1001.*

15 *f-2*

JOE'S ON JUNIPER

A neighborhood bar with a good menu and easygoing charm, Joe's is filled with locals, mostly singles. The food tends toward quality burgers and sandwiches. About 30 good beers are on tap, with more than 150 brews (including micros) sold by the bottle. The sidewalk patio out front is a good spot for enjoying supper, a snack, or some people-watching. Last call is at 1:40 AM. *1049 Juniper St., Midtown, 404/875–6634.*

14 *a-3*

LIMERICK JUNCTION

Local Celtic bands and singers transport patrons from this pub to the Old Country every night. The traditional music goes well with the clinking of glasses and the hoisting of pints. This is a neighborhood kind of place that draws suburbanites as well as locals with families, so it never gets rowdy. A small cover is sometimes charged, and the bar stays open until 3 AM on weekends. *822 N. Highland Ave., Virginia-Highland, 404/874–7147.*

15 *h-4*

THE LOCAL

The mostly youngish upscale locals who gather here do so more for the conversation than for the classic bar fare, which includes an extensive selection of sandwiches and burgers. Barbecue is house-made, with mustard sauce available, and served with hush puppies. Opening time is 5 PM. If customers hang around, closing isn't until about 4 AM, but the bar can shutter as early as 1:30 AM if it's not busy. *758 Ponce de Leon Ave., Poncey-Highland, 404/873–5002.*

14 *a-4*

MANUEL'S TAVERN

The quintessential neighborhood pub by which all others in town are measured began more than 50 years ago. Politicians (including one former president and his wife), reporters, students, and young attorneys and accountants make up the crowd. Large-screen TVs make watching Braves and Falcons games plenty of fun, and the food's quite good, too. The steak sandwich and chicken wings are especially worthy. *602 N. Highland Ave., Poncey-Highland, 404/ 525–3447.*

12 *f-3*

MCDUFF'S IRISH PUB

From Wednesday through Saturday this little pub shakes with live folk, pop, and acoustic tunes. Despite the name, Celtic music is featured only occasionally. The full menu of bar fare includes chicken and buffalo tenders, potato skins and potato soup, nachos, salads, sandwiches, and a house-made chicken curry. You can have a drink at the full bar and enjoy some friendly conversation before the show. McDuff's is open daily to the early hours. *56 E. Andrews Dr., E. Andrews Sq., Buckhead, 404/816–8008.*

14 *h-1*

MELTON'S APP & TAPP

Here are two operations, really—a restaurant appended to a classic neighborhood pub. On the pub side, there's a TV for sports devotees, who cluster around the bar. Friendly personnel keep track of patrons, firmly excluding anyone whose behavior doesn't measure up to standards. There are great burgers and buffalo tenders, and fantastic beer–cheese soup, when the kitchen makes it. *2500 N. Decatur Rd., Decatur, 404/634–9112.*

12 *f-3*

MIKE 'N' ANGELO'S

Buckhead's authentic neighborhood tavern, this place has plenty of regulars who come throughout the week for the warmth and friendly service. A standard bar menu is offered, plus a daily special, which might be steak, meat loaf, or stir-fry. There's rock and roll on the speakers and a game room with two pool tables. The bar is open daily until the very early morning hours. *312 E. Paces Ferry Rd., Buckhead, 404/237–0949.*

14 *a-2*

MOE'S & JOE'S BAR & GRILL

Now more than a half century old, Moe's & Joe's draws locals and Emory students to its personable environment. A long Formica-topped bar, booths, and tables give it a homey, old-fashioned character. There's beer and wine only. *1033 N. Highland Ave., Virginia-Highland, 404/873–6090.*

13 *e-1*

NAUGHTY'S GOOD TIME EMPORIUM

A game of pool, a few brews, some munchies, and a football game on the TV add up to an ideal evening for the Buford-Clairmont area folks who come to this friendly place. It's open daily until after midnight. *3747 Buford Hwy., Northeast Atlanta, 404/320–6999.*

5 *g-5*

OLDE PECULIAR PUBLIC HOUSE

You can relax and talk without the blare of TVs at this warm-and-fuzzy old-style pub. There's a fireplace, a large deck, and lots of beers on tap. It serves bangers and mash and fish-and-chips— your typical British pub fare. Traditional

Irish music is scheduled on some weekend nights and on the second Wednesday of the month. There's sometimes an acoustic open mike on Tuesday beginning around 9 PM. There's no cover. *29 Jones St., Norcross, 678/291–9220, www.oldepeculiar.com.*

PADDY'S IRISH PUB

Snuggled up against the main building of Château Elan, Georgia's largest winery, stands this Irish pub. Paddy's furnishings are imported from Ireland, as are the recipes on the menu (e.g., shepherd's pie) and the tunes played by live musicians on the weekends. Rather than sipping wine, you can enjoy good lagers, ales, and stouts. Paddy's is open daily.

BEST BEER BARS

Churchill Arms
At what could be a cozy English pub, the selection on tap includes Whitbread, Bass, Guinness, and Harp.

Euclid Avenue Yacht Club
One of Atlanta's most eclectic and entertaining haunts has suds like Red Hook, Paulaner, Staropramen, Bass, and Guinness on tap. The bottle selection is even better, and there's a good dart alley and dependable bar food.

Fadó
It's like a step across the Atlantic to the quintessential Irish pub—or pubs. Designed by the Irish Pub Co. (a business partner of Guinness), the pub has areas resembling a Victorian pub, a Gaelic pub, and others.

Limerick Junction
Come for the beer and stay for the popular sing-alongs that begin after 9 PM. Guinness, Bass, Paulaner Hefe-weizen, and Harp lager are on tap, plus a good bottled selection.

Melton's App & Tapp
This lively, neighborhood-style Decatur bar has a great microbrew selection and decent food to go with it.

Prince of Wales
Since it's an expat hangout, no surprise that the selection of imported drafts here stands out: Guinness, Bass, Newcastle, Watney's Cream Stout, Celis White, Paulaner Hefe-weizen; and Atlanta's own Red Brick, too, plus a top-notch bottle list.

---

100 Tour de France, Braselton, 770/932–0900 or 800/233–9463.

12 *f-3*

PARK BENCH

Antique wood bars, comfortable booths, and live music make the branches of this minichain popular places to relax after work. Local talent performs live acoustic and popular music Thursday–Saturday nights; on Wednesday night there's an open mike (at Buckhead and Emory). The menu runs to New York–style pizza, burgers, and hot wings. The Buckhead bar is open until 3 AM nightly and is closed Sunday except during football season. Dunwoody and Emory, which offer lunch, are open daily—Dunwoody until around 11 PM and Emory until the wee hours. There are no covers and no drink minimums. *256 E. Paces Ferry Rd., Buckhead, 404/264–1334, www.theparkbench.com.*

5 *d-4*
Dunwoody Hall, 5592 Chamblee-Dunwoody Rd., Dunwoody, 770/804–1000.

14 *d-2*
1577 N. Decatur Rd., Emory Village, 404/377–8888.

5 *f-4*

POOR RICHARD'S PUB & PORCH

A sports bar as well as a pub, this neighborhood hangout has 11 TVs, including one big screen. Live music, from blues to rock and roll to jazz, is featured on Friday; Sunday is open-mike night. The food runs to steaks and sandwiches, and there's a free happy-hour buffet (with the purchase of a beverage) weekdays 5:30–7. You can choose from more than a dozen beers on tap, most of them imports. *3330 Peachtree Corners Cir., Norcross, 770/447–1776.*

15 *f-2*

PRINCE OF WALES

As close to an English pub as you'll get in Atlanta, this place is home-away-from-home for a lot of nostalgic Brits. Among other atmospheric touches, soccer trophies won by the amateur-league clubs that gather here are scattered about. Dimly lit and paneled in dark wood, the pub is a perfect place to refresh and refuel after a Piedmont Park outing. The food is strictly pub grub, including really good fish-and-chips and bread pudding. *1144 Piedmont Ave., Midtown, 404/876–0227. MARTA: Midtown.*

5 *e-5*

SCROOGES LOUNGE

A rustic neighborhood hangout with loyal regulars, Scrooges has four pool tables, two large projection TVs, and a few smaller tubes, which are usually tuned to the game. The joint serves lunch and offers a full menu with daily specials and weekend buffets. The lemon-pepper wings are famous. Daily specials concentrate on Southern and American dishes. You can play pool free on Sunday and Monday nights. The bar is open very late. *4480 Winters Chapel Rd., Doraville, 770/448–8394.*

SOCIAL & BALLROOM DANCING

5 *b-6*

ATLANTA BALLROOM DANCE CENTRE

Ballroom, Latin, and swing rule at this popular smoke-free spot, where private lessons and parties devoted to ballroom dancing are held every Thursday 9–11 PM. On Saturday it's open 8:30–11, and the cover is $10 per couple. *6125 Roswell Rd., Suite 104A, Sandy Springs, 404/847–0821, www.atlantadancecentre.com.*

5 *f-6*

CITY LIGHTS DANCE CLUB

The smoke- and alcohol-free nightclub has one of the largest open dance floors in the city. The crowd runs from teenagers to senior citizens, with most folks in the thirties to fifties age group. It's decorated in a basic manner, but that doesn't make it any less fun. Most forms of social dancing—ballroom, swing, and Latin—are taught here, on a rotating schedule that changes monthly. Lessons start as early as 6 PM during the week and run all day Saturday and Sunday. Friday and Saturday nights are open dances, with a cover of $10 when recorded music plays and $12 when there's a band. *Embry Hills Shopping Center, 3539 Chamblee-Tucker Rd., Embry Hills, 770/451–5461, www.citylightsdanceclub.com.*

SPORTS BARS

7 *f-6*

BENTLEY'S LOUNGE

The casual, relaxed sports bar at the Airport Marriott has 15 TVs, some video games, and bar food. The lounge is open daily. *Airport Marriott, 4711 Best Rd., College Park, 404/766–7900, ext. 6663.*

15 *e-5*

CHAMPIONS

Large-screen TVs, pool tables, and video games bring a fun-loving crowd to this bar. The kitchen serves burgers, sandwiches, wings, salads, and the like. The hotel is frequented by sports celebrities, so you might just bump into one here. The bar is open daily 11:30 AM–2 AM. *Atlanta Marriott Marquis, 265 Peachtree Center Ave., Downtown, 404/521–0000. MARTA: Peachtree Center.*

12 *e-6*

CHEYENNE GRILL SPORTS BAR

Buckhead's liveliest sports bar has 27 TVs, including 3 big screen TVs. Its famous buffalo-wing sauce supposedly comes from the Anchor Bar in Buffalo, New York, where some say the spicy wings were invented. The place offers nine beers on draft and tons of bottled brews. In good weather there's patio dining. *Peachtree Battle Shopping Center, 2391 Peachtree Rd., Buckhead, 404/842–1010.*

13 *e-6*

FAMOUS PUB & SPORTS PALACE

Popular with Emory students, this bar has 30 TVs tuned to sports, 12 pool tables, 5 dartboards, lots of video games, and dancing to popular recorded tunes. Burgers, wings, and steaks are served with beer, wine, and other libations. *2947 N. Druid Hills Rd., Northeast Atlanta, 404/633–3555.*

2 *c-8*

FIREHOUSE GRILL

Although a sports bar with the usual collection of TVs, pool tables, and video games, this place also has a full menu of bar food, sandwiches, pastas, fish, and steaks. Open daily, the grill offers inexpensive weekday lunch specials. Tuesday and Thursday are karaoke nights, and perhaps not coincidentally there's also a special on draft beer then. On weekends, live music attracts crowds. *12195 GA 92 (at Trickum Rd.), Woodstock, 770/924–5594.*

5 b-6

FRANKIE'S FOOD, SPORTS & SPIRITS

Sports fans of all stripes and ages come to this rather spiffy spot. It also attracts members of Atlanta's pro teams and visiting competitors, who try to blend in with the crowd. Everybody enjoys the 175 TVs and the enclosed outside deck, which also has TVs. Live acoustic music begins at 6 PM on Friday, but there's no cover. *The Prado, 5600 Roswell Rd., Sandy Springs, 404/843–9444.*

15 d-6

JOCKS & JILLS

Four satellite dishes and more than 100 TVs anchor the Downtown location of this sports-bar minichain. The branch is a favorite with sports celebrities. Sports mementos decorate the bar, including a pair of Evander Holyfield's boxing gloves and a ball from a Braves no-hitter. (The Norcross branch is plastered with the pennants of various teams from the past 50 years.) The all-American menu lists hamburgers, salads, seafood, pizza, and similar casual fare. Each of the bars has occasional live music; a DJ spins dance music on Friday. All the branches are open daily. *1 CNN Center, Downtown, 404/688–4225. MARTA: Dome/GWCC/ Philips Arena/CNN Center.*

5 g-2

9775 Medlock Bridge Rd., Duluth, 770/ 495–9113.

4 h-7

Galleria Specialty Mall, 2569 Cobb Pkwy., Smyrna, 770/952–8401.

15 e-2

112 10th St., Midtown, 404/873–5405. MARTA: Midtown.

5 c-7

4046 Peachtree Rd., Sandy Springs, 404/ 816–2801.

10 a-1

PENALTY BOX

Even though it's in a suburban shopping center, this establishment substantially enlivens the southside after-hours scene and is very much a neighborhood joint; it's open to 2 AM Wednesday–Saturday, midnight other nights. A huge U-shape bar adorned with neon beer signs nearly fills the place. There's a patio, and 37 TVs, including 3 big-screen TVs. Appetizers, pizzas, burgers, sandwiches, and salads make up the fare. *3570B GA 138, Stockbridge, 770/389–3551.*

4 g-4

ROCCO'S PUB

About 2 mi east of the Big Chicken (the huge Kentucky Fried Chicken restaurant), this sports haven keeps its 20 TVs—including a couple of big screens—tuned to the big events. The kitchen dishes up burgers, sandwiches, salads, and such. The house-made chili is especially popular; in fact, Rocco's is the sponsor of the Georgia State Chili Cook-Off. The pub is open daily. *Town and Country Shopping Center, 1393 Roswell Rd., Marietta, 770/971–8806.*

8 d-6

SPORTS OASIS

The only sports bar within 10 mi, this is a fan's oasis, where everybody knows everybody. Several TVs, video games, a jukebox, and a big-guy menu (steaks, ribs, and other meat) keep the crowd happy. The bar presents live music, from country and western to rock and oldies, usually on Friday and Saturday nights. The Oasis is closed Sunday. *1792 Panola Rd., at Flakes Mill Rd., Five Points Crossing, Ellenwood, 770/593–9505.*

12 f-4

THREE DOLLAR CAFÉ

Favored by a younger crowd, this chain keeps its numerous TVs permanently tuned to sports, and some locations have giant screens. The Buckhead, Marietta, and Sandy Spring branches present live music on the outside decks most weekends during the summer. Best known for its hot wings, the menu also offers steaks, sandwiches, salads, and appetizers. The bars are open 11 AM to midnight from Sunday through Thursday, until 1 AM Friday and Saturday. *3002 Peachtree Rd. (at Pharr Rd.), Buckhead, 404/266–8667. MARTA: Buckhead.*

5 c-3

8595 Roswell Rd., Dunwoody, 770/992– 5011.

4 f-3

Town Center, 423 Ernest Barrett Pkwy., Kennesaw, 770/426–6566.

4 g-5

2580 Windy Hill Rd. (at I–75), Marietta, 770/850–0868.

5 *b-5*

5825 Roswell Rd., Sandy Springs, 404/235–2380.

5 *e-3*

TJ'S SPORTS BAR & GRILL

With 54 regular TVs and six big-screen TVs, this place is likely to be showing a game you want to see. While you watch the game, you can chow down on some surprisingly healthful eats. In addition to nachos and porterhouse steaks, you can try sandwiches, turkey burgers, a Porto-bello burger, and chicken grills. TJ's is open daily. *Holcomb Center, 2880 Holcomb Bridge Rd., Alpharetta, 770/552–7700.*

WINE BARS

12 *h-4*

ECLIPSE DI LUNA

Authentic Spanish tapas for $3.25 a plate and glasses of wine for only $5.95 (or $20 a bottle) a pour keep this high-energy bar packed with young couples. The wine list is constantly being changed and updated, as management seeks new labels and good values. There are lots of Spanish wines, but also Californian, Australian, Chilean, South African, and the occasional French wine. Outdoor seating is available. *764 Miami Cir., Buckhead, 404/846–0449.*

15 *e-3*

ENO

At this Mediterranean restaurant, a savory menu of small dishes is designed to go with wine, and has wine suggestions to match. There are about 100 unusual vintages by the taste size (2-ounce pours) and by the glass, as well as by the bottle. In addition, a fine list of excellent grappas adds depth to the tasting experience. With ample windows that face the street, the welcoming space has a long bar and numerous tables. Eno is perfect for a drink or a quick bite before going on to the Fox Theatre nearby. *800 Peachtree St., at 6th St., Midtown, 404/685–3191. MARTA: North Avenue.*

12 *f-4*

LO SPUNTINO

This chic Tuscan-inspired wine bar and food shop is the work of Vicki and Sam Sebastiani of the California wine-producing family. At any time, they're pouring 15 wines from around the world. While sipping, you can enjoy small dishes of California-Mediterranean-style fare. Vicki's special recipes, such as a sun-dried-tomato aioli, are among the products sold in the shop, where you also can buy wine by the bottle. Lo Spuntino is closed Sunday. *3005 Peachtree Rd. (Pharr Rd.), Buckhead, 404/237–5724. MARTA: Buckhead.*

12 *f-4*

VINO!

At this Spanish restaurant you can order wines by the "flight," which gives you three 2-ounce pours. Sample, for instance, three contrasting Spanish reds, or three sauvignon blancs, for $9.50—$1 of which is donated to the Atlanta Ballet. The tapas—especially the mussels and octopus—are among the best reasons to come here. *The Peach Shopping Center, 2900 Peachtree Rd., Buckhead, 404/816–0511.*

14 *f-3*

WATERSHED

Primarily a restaurant, Watershed also includes a wine bar and a well-stocked wineshop. Carefully selected fine wines, many served by the glass, lend themselves to quiet conversation at the bar, either during cocktail hour or at the end of the evening, with a scrumptious dessert. Part-owner Emily Saliers, of Indigo Girls fame, often does sommelier duty at the bar, pouring wines and discussing them knowledgeably with the wine-savvy patrons. In the restaurant, the varied menu focuses on updated versions of American (mostly Southern) home-style fare. *406 W. Ponce de Leon Ave., Decatur, 404/378–4900.*

12 *h-2*

WINE BAR
AT THE RITZ-CARLTON

The focus at this hushed area off the Buckhead Ritz-Carlton's bustling lobby lounge is on wines of the New World—that is, everywhere but Europe. Sips are made to shine by matching "flights" of exquisite nibbles—three each, either seafood, meat, cheese, or vegetarian. Plug your laptop in at tableside to surf wine sites. The bar is open Tuesday–Saturday 5:30–10:30. *3434 Peachtree Rd., Buckhead, 404/237–2700. MARTA: Buckhead or Lenox.*

chapter 6

HOTELS

Atlanta has made a booming industry out of that famous Southern calling card, hospitality. Its reputation for excellence in the hospitality trade was secured fairly recently, with the 1980s-era construction of two Ritz-Carlton hotels, which for a time made this the only city in the world with more than one of the luxury properties. Since then, and even since the 1996 Olympic Games, hotel development here has not abated. Old properties, such as the Georgian Terrace Hotel, are being renovated, and all-suites hotels aimed at the business traveler are being built. Many of the newer properties, such as the Four Seasons Hotel, operate high-end restaurants that showcase some of the world's finest chefs.

The metro area also has gained a number of fine bed-and-breakfasts, which are especially popular among locals for romantic weekend getaways but also appeal to business travelers with a hankering for homey accommodations for a change. For both audiences, they combine intimacy and historic charm with convenience and comfort.

PRICE CATEGORIES

CATEGORY	COST*
Very Expensive Lodgings	over $210
Expensive Lodgings	$150–$210
Moderately Priced Lodgings	$90–$150
Budget Lodgings	under $90

*All prices are for a standard double high-season room, excluding 13% tax and service.

VERY EXPENSIVE LODGINGS

CHÂTEAU ÉLAN

A 16th-century-style "château," built in the early 1980s, is the heart of this resort. The complex includes a winery, the Inn (in the "château"), a European health spa with 14 suites, and the 80-room lodge. Complimentary winery tours and tastings, 63 holes of golf, a tennis center, an equestrian center, and a variety of restaurants help to keep you busy. Nature trails invite leisurely strolling or vigorous hiking through well-landscaped grounds. The resort, off I–85 at Exit 126, hosts several concerts and special events, including monthly horse shows, throughout the year. *Inn:* 100 Rue Charlemagne, Braselton 30517, 678/425–0900 or 800/233–9463, fax 678/425–6000; Spa: Haven Harbour Dr., Braselton 30517, 678/425–6064 or 800/233–9463, fax 678/425–6069; Lodge: 2069 Hwy. 211, Braselton 30517, 770/867–8100 or 800/233–9463, fax 770/867–3236; www.chateauelan.com. 332 rooms, 35 suites. 5 restaurants, café, pub, 1 indoor and 1 outdoor pool, spa, 9-hole golf course, 3 18-hole golf courses, 6 tennis courts, hiking, pro shop, baby-sitting, children's program (ages 4–12), meeting rooms, free parking. AE, D, DC, MC, V.1

5 *f-2*
FOUR SEASONS HOTEL, ATLANTA

The luxury hotel occupies the first 19 floors of a 50-story building also housing residences and offices. The grand staircase in the soaring lobby leads up to the hotel's well-regarded Park 75 restaurant and an intimate lounge with a mahogany bar and high-back chairs. Rose-hue marble is used liberally in the public spaces. Guest quarters are traditional in style and include marble bathrooms with extra-large soaking tubs as well as brass chandeliers and those famously comfortable mattresses. In-room fax machines are available upon request. 75 14th St., 30309, Midtown, 404/881–9898 or 800/332–3442, fax 404/873–4692, www.fourseasons.com. 226 rooms, 18 suites. Restaurant, bar, in-room data ports, in-room safes, minibars, no-smoking rooms, room service, indoor pool, health club, laundry service, business services, meeting rooms, parking (fee). AE, D, DC, MC, V. MARTA: Arts Center.

15 *e-5*
HILTON ATLANTA

One of the city's largest hotels, this Hilton occupies an entire square block and has five dining establishments, including the world-class Nikolai's Roof on the 30th floor. Guest rooms are spacious and have two two-line telephones. Executive-level rooms are more luxurious, with a third phone, speaker-phone capability, full-size desks, and in-room fax machines. 255 Courtland St., 30303, Downtown, 404/659–2000 or 800/445–8667, fax 404/221–6368, www.hilton.com.

1,140 rooms, 60 suites. 3 restaurants, 2 lounges, coffee shop, deli, in-room data ports, in-room safes, minibars, no-smoking rooms, room service, pool, 4 tennis courts, basketball, health club, jogging, billiards, baby-sitting, laundry service, concierge, business services, convention center, meeting rooms, parking (fee). AE, D, DC, MC, V. MARTA: Peachtree Center.

15 d-5
OMNI HOTEL AT CNN CENTER

Adjacent to the headquarters of Ted Turner's Cable News Network, the Omni welcomes you with a combination of old-world and modern decor. Amid the marble floors, Oriental rugs, and exotic floral and plant arrangements of the lobby are closed-circuit monitors that show unedited CNN film, bloopers and all. Rooms have large windows and contemporary-style furniture, including a sofa in each room. When you stay here you have access to the CNN health club. The hotel has 15 large meeting rooms and a ballroom with a capacity of 2,000. It's handy to Philips Arena, the Georgia World Congress Center, Centennial Olympic Park, and the Georgia Dome. 100 CNN Center, 30335, Downtown, 404/659–0000 or 800/843–6664, fax 404/525–5050, www.omnihotels.com. 467 rooms, 12 suites. 2 restaurants, lobby lounge, in-room data ports, no-smoking rooms, room service, hair salon, children's programs, dry cleaning, concierge, business services, meeting rooms, parking (fee). AE, DC, MC, V. MARTA: Dome/GWCC/Philips Arena/CNN Center.

15 e-5
RITZ-CARLTON, ATLANTA

Behind this New Orleans–style facade, amid hunt-theme sculptures and paintings from a simpler age, is a sanctuary from life's hurly-burly. Stroll past the 17th-century Flemish tapestry near the Peachtree Street entrance and take a seat in the intimate, sunken lobby, where a traditional afternoon tea is served beneath an 18th-century chandelier. Upstairs, the most luxurious guest rooms have marble writing tables, plump sofas, four-poster beds, and white marble bathrooms. Atlanta Grill, a contemporary American restaurant, offers excellent casual dining on a veranda overlooking Peachtree Street. 181 Peachtree St., 30303, Downtown, 404/659–0400 or 800/241–3333, fax 404/688–

0400, www.ritzcarlton.com. 441 rooms, 22 suites. Restaurant, bar, lobby lounge, in-room data ports, in-room safes, minibars, no-smoking rooms, room service, massage, health club, baby-sitting, laundry service, business services, meeting rooms, parking (fee). AE, D, DC, MC, V. MARTA: Peachtree Center.

12 h-2
RITZ-CARLTON, BUCKHEAD

The public spaces of this elegant gem, a flagship of the chain, are replete with 18th- and 19th-century antiques. Film stars, politicos, and performers have been spotted in the lobby, where shoppers from nearby Lenox Square mall and Phipps Plaza often revive over afternoon tea or cocktails in the richly paneled lounge. The guest rooms, outfitted with reproductions of antique furniture, are

---

FINE HOTEL DINING

Some of the city's best restaurants are in its hotels, where chefs drawn from all over the world hold court in the kitchen. See Chapter 1 for reviews of these stars.

Four Seasons Hotel, Atlanta (very expensive)
Park 75, a favorite among national food critics, offers inventive and substantial cuisine, excellent American farmstead cheeses, house-baked breads, and a notable wine list.

Grand Hyatt Atlanta (expensive)
Kamogawa is the most elegant Japanese restaurant in the city and the restaurant of choice for Japanese visitors when they entertain local guests.

Hilton Atlanta (very expensive)
At Nikolai's Roof, a 30th-floor view of the city's architectural splendor—most dramatic at night—enhances contemporary Continental dining.

Ritz-Carlton, Buckhead (very expensive)
Exceptional food, service, and ambience are the hallmarks of the Dining Room, where chef Bruno Ménard earns global recognition for his French-Asian cuisine.

Swissôtel (expensive)
An outpost of the venerable New York steak house, the Palm serves up the best in beef to Atlanta's power crowd.

spacious and have decadent white marble baths. In-room fax machines are available upon request. The view of Buckhead from the hotel's club floors confirms Atlanta's reputation as a city of trees. The Dining Room is a world-class restaurant; the Café is an early morning option that serves lunch and dinner as well. The hotel also has elegant spaces for special-occasion functions and meetings. *3434 Peachtree Rd., 30326, Buckhead, 404/237–2700 or 800/241–3333, fax 404/239–0078, www.ritzcarlton.com. 524 rooms, 29 suites. 2 restaurants, bar, coffee shop, lobby lounge, in-room data ports, in-room safes, minibars, no-smoking rooms, room service, indoor lap pool, hot tub, massage, sauna, health club, baby-sitting, laundry service, concierge, business services, meeting rooms, parking (fee). AE, D, DC, MC, V. MARTA: Lenox.*

15 *e-5*

WESTIN PEACHTREE PLAZA

Sometimes it seems that every photograph of Atlanta's skyline taken since 1990 features this cylindrical glass tower, the tallest hotel in North America. Designed by John Portman, the hotel has a five-story atrium; a narrow glass elevator, made famous in the film *Sharkey's Machine*, slithers up the building's exterior. Suites have minibars, and rooms on select floors have fax machines and data ports. For great views of Atlanta, you can have a drink or meal in the revolving, multilevel Sun Dial Restaurant & Lounge atop the hotel. Perfect for casual dining, the street-level Savannah Fish Company is known for its smoked-bluefish dip and fresh fish dishes. *210 Peachtree St., at International Blvd., 30303, Downtown, 404/659–1400 or 800/228–3000, fax 404/589–7424, www.starwood.com/westin. 1,020 rooms, 48 suites. 3 restaurants, 3 bars, in-room safes, minibars (some), no-smoking rooms, room service, indoor-outdoor pool, health club, laundry service, concierge, business services, parking (fee). AE, D, DC, MC, V. MARTA: Peachtree Center.*

EXPENSIVE LODGINGS

5 *d-5*

CROWNE PLAZA–RAVINIA

An anchor of Perimeter Center, the hotel is about 17 mi from downtown but near several Fortune 500 companies; many shopping and dining options are close at hand, too. The lobby offers a splendid view of lush atrium gardens and has a nice bar. La Grotta, which also has a fine view of the gardens, draws fans from all over the metro area with its northern Italian cuisine and well-chosen wine list. Elegant furnishings fill the guest rooms. *4355 Ashford-Dunwoody Rd., 30346, Dunwoody, 770/395–7700 or 800/2CROWNE (800/227–6963), fax 770/392–9503, www.sixcontinentshotels.com/crowneplaza. 495 rooms, 43 suites. 2 restaurants, food court, lobby lounge, in-room data ports, in-room safes, minibars, no-smoking rooms, room service, indoor pool, hot tub, massage, sauna, tennis court, basketball, health club, coin laundry, concierge, business services, meeting room, free parking. AE, D, DC, MC, V. MARTA: Dunwoody.*

12 *g-2*

EMBASSY SUITES–BUCKHEAD

This all-suites modern high-rise is a few blocks from the Phipps Plaza and Lenox Square malls. The suites all have either double or king-size beds, a kitchen area with a microwave oven and a small refrigerator, and a living-dining area with a sofa bed and overstuffed chairs. Some suites can accommodate conferences. Rates include afternoon cocktails; a complimentary shuttle travels to points within 1 mi of the property. *3285 Peachtree Rd., 30326, Buckhead, 404/261–7733 or 800/EMBASSY (800/362–2779), fax 404/261–6857, www.embassy-suites.com. 317 suites. Restaurant, in-room data ports, in-room safes, kitchenettes, no-smoking rooms, room service, 1 indoor and 1 outdoor pool, gym, laundry service, business services, meeting rooms, parking (fee). AE, D, DC, MC, V. MARTA: Buckhead.*

15 *e-3*

GEORGIAN TERRACE

Enrico Caruso and the Metropolitan Opera stars once lodged in this 1911 hotel, as did the *Gone With the Wind* stars attending the film's 1939 Atlanta debut. Indeed, this fine all-suites hotel—on the National Register of Historic Places—still counts the rich and famous among its clientele. The suites are generous in size and, because the building at one point had been transformed into plush apartments, have kitchens or kitchenettes and washer-dryers. The ground floor offers retail services and a 5,500-square-ft conference center. *659 Peachtree St., 30308, Midtown, 404/897–*

1991 or 800/651–2316, fax 404/724–9116, www.thegeorgianterrace.com. 326 suites. 2 restaurants, in-room data ports, kitchenettes, minibars (some), no-smoking rooms, room service, pool, laundry service, meeting rooms, parking (fee). AE, D, DC, MC, V. MARTA: North Ave.

12 *g-2*

GRAND HYATT ATLANTA

The lobby of this towering hotel has a high ceiling and faces a courtyard with a Japanese garden and a 35-ft waterfall. The dramatic look gives way to a softer elegance elsewhere. Guest rooms have spacious marble bathrooms, three telephones, a fax machine, and plush bathrobes; the palette is pale and includes gold accents. The two ballrooms, three boardrooms, 16 meeting rooms, and three spacious outdoor terraces can accommodate a variety of events and special occasions. The Kamogawa and Cassis restaurants serve, respectively, Japanese and Mediterranean cuisines. *3300 Peachtree Rd., 30305, Buckhead, 404/365–8100 or 800/233–1234, fax 404/233–5686, www. atlanta.hyatt.com. 417 rooms, 20 suites. 2 restaurants, bar, in-room data ports, in-room fax, minibars, no-smoking rooms, room service, pool, health club, laundry service, meeting rooms, parking (fee). AE, D, DC, MC, V. MARTA: Buckhead.*

15 *e-5*

HYATT REGENCY ATLANTA

Easily identified at night by its brightly lighted blue bubble dome, this remains one of Atlanta's more unusual-looking hotels. This Hyatt, with its cavernous 23-story lobby, was architect John Portman's first atrium-centered building and became the model for his other hotels, including the Atlanta Marriott Marquis. The Hyatt stands across from the Merchandise Mart and Peachtree Center, both Portman designs; a skywalk connects it to the latter. Three towers house the guest rooms, which have upholstered and wood furnishings. Business Plan rooms offer in-room fax machines and data ports and off-hours access to supplies and services. *265 Peachtree St., 30303, Downtown, 404/577–1234 or 800/233–1234, fax 404/588–4137, atlanta.hyatt. com. 1,206 rooms, 58 suites. 3 restaurants, bar, snack bar, in-room data ports, in-room safes, minibars, no-smoking rooms, room service, pool, gym, baby-sitting, dry cleaning, laundry service, business services, convention center, meeting rooms, parking*

(fee). AE, D, DC, MC, V. MARTA: Peachtree Center.

 c-2

INN AT EAGLES LANDING

Championship golf and a relaxing atmosphere are two of the draws at this European-style inn 20 minutes south of Atlanta. You have full club privileges for Eagles Landing Country Club, including use of an 18-hole private championship golf course designed by Tom Fazio (greens fees apply), a pool, and a spa. In addition, you can play tennis on the hotel's two hard-surface and four lighted clay courts. The rooms open onto either terraces or balconies. Continental breakfast and an innkeeper's afternoon reception are served in the living room daily. *425 Country Club Dr., Stockbridge 30281, 770/389–3118 or 800/7–THEINN (800/784–3466), fax 770/389–0928, www. eagleslandinginn.com. 53 rooms, 4 suites. Dining room, in-room data ports, in-room safes, minibars, golf privileges, 6 tennis courts, gym, baby-sitting, laundry service, concierge, business services, meeting rooms, free parking. AE, D, DC, MC, V.*

12 *h-2*

JW MARRIOTT HOTEL LENOX

Lenox Square mall is connected to this modern 25-story hotel, where reproduction antiques are set amid brass and crystal accents. The hotel's large windows provide expansive views of Buckhead. Irregularly shaped rooms have spacious baths with separate shower stall and tub. Nightly jazz plays in Ottley's lounge. Meeting rooms are large and well equipped, and a MARTA stop is across the street. *3300 Lenox Rd., 30326, Buckhead, 404/262–3344 or 800/228–9290, fax 404/262–8689, www.marriott. com. 371 rooms, 4 suites. Restaurant, coffee shop, lobby lounge, in-room data ports, minibars, no-smoking rooms, room service, indoor pool, barbershop, hair salon, hot tub, sauna, health club, baby-sitting, laundry service, concierge, business services, meeting rooms, car rental, parking (fee). AE, D, DC, MC, V. MARTA: Lenox.*

15 *e-5*

MARRIOTT MARQUIS

Immense and coolly contemporary, the lobby of the Marquis goes on forever as you stand under a huge fabric sculpture that appears to float from below the sky-lighted roof some 50 stories above. Glass-enclosed elevators glide noiselessly through this expanse. Each guest room opens onto the atrium, a signature element in architect John Portman's hotel design. For the best view, request a room above the 10th floor; face north to see the city, south to view the airport. *265 Peachtree Center Ave., 30303, Downtown, 404/521–0000 or 800/ MARRIOTT (800/627–7468), fax 404/ 586–6299, www.marriott.com. 1,675 rooms, 68 suites. 3 restaurants, lounge, pub, in-room data ports, in-room safes, no-smoking rooms, room service, indoor-outdoor pool, hair salon, health club, laundry service, concierge, business center, meeting rooms, parking (fee). AE, D, DC, MC, V. MARTA: Peachtree Center.*

15 *e-2*

REGENCY SUITES HOTEL

In Atlanta's business and financial district, this nine-story European-style all-suites hotel combines personalized hospitality with such special amenities as valet parking. Some of the suites have a kitchenette. The rate includes a Continental breakfast buffet, and Monday–Thursday, dinner. Meeting facilities are available for groups up to 40 people. *975 W. Peachtree St., 30309, Midtown, 404/876–5003 or 800/642–3629, fax 404/817–7511, www.regencysuites.com. 99 suites. Dining room, in-room data ports, kitchenettes (some), minibars, no-smoking rooms, room service, gym, baby-sitting, coin laundry, meeting rooms, parking (fee). AE, D, DC, MC, V. MARTA: Midtown.*

4 *h-7*

RENAISSANCE WAVERLY–GALLERIA

One of the most luxurious hotels in northwest Atlanta, the Waverly is adjacent to Cobb Galleria Centre and Galleria Mall and offers easy access to the nearby convention center. Bold contemporary art decorates the public spaces; all rooms include plush upholstery, three telephones, a desk area, and nightly turndown service. In-house conference facilities include 50,000 square ft of meeting-banquet space. There are more-moderate Renaissance properties downtown and near the airport. *2450 Galleria Pkwy., 30339, Northwest Atlanta, 770/953–4500 or 800/HOTELS1 (800/ 468–3571), fax 770/953–0740, www. renaissancehotels.com. 497 rooms, 24 suites. 2 restaurants, café, coffee shop, lounge, pub, in-room data ports, no-smoking rooms, room service, 1 indoor and 1*

outdoor pool, sauna, steam room, health club, racquetball, laundry service, concierge, business services, meeting rooms, free parking. AE, D, DC, MC, V.

15 *f-2*

SHERATON MIDTOWN ATLANTA AT COLONY SQUARE

A bold color scheme sets off blond-wood sleigh beds and other unfussy furnishings at this high-rise hotel, which anchors the Colony Square office-residential-retail complex. Piano music filters through the dimly lighted atrium lobby, which is brightened with fresh flowers. The hotel is two blocks from the Woodruff Arts Center and the High Museum of Art. *188 14th St., 30361, Midtown, 404/892–6000 or 800/325–3535, fax 404/872–9192, www.sheraton.com. 464 rooms, 3 suites. Restaurant, lobby lounge, no-smoking rooms, room service, pool, gym, laundry service, concierge, business services, meeting rooms, car rental, parking (fee). AE, D, DC, MC, V. MARTA: Arts Center.*

12 *g-2*

SWISSÔTEL

Sleek and efficient, this favorite of business travelers has a glass-and-white tile exterior with curved walls and sophisticated Biedermeier-style interiors. Exquisite modern art fills its halls and public spaces. Complimentary car service is available within a 3-mi radius of the hotel, which is handy to Lenox Square mall, a prime shopping and dining destination. The hotel restaurant, the Palm, is noted for its steaks. *3391 Peachtree Rd., 30326, Buckhead, 404/ 365–0065 or 800/253–1397, fax 404/365– 8787, www.swissotel.com. 349 rooms, 16 suites. Restaurant, lobby lounge, in-room data ports, in-room fax, minibars, no-smoking rooms, room service, indoor pool, hair salon, massage, spa, health club, concierge, business services, meeting rooms, parking (fee). AE, D, DC, MC, V. MARTA: Buckhead.*

5 *c-5*

W ATLANTA @ PERIMETER CENTER

The W, within sight of Perimeter Mall, keeps rates relatively low without giving up designer aesthetics. The contemporary minimalism and cool colors suggest Japanese design and a refreshingly with-it environment. Rooms offer luxury-caliber sheets and comforters, oversize desks, CD players, and such in-room business amenities as two-line cordless speaker phones and high-speed Internet access. Savu, the wildly popular restaurant, serves light Asian-fusion fare and caters to the beautiful people as well as the business throngs. *111 Perimeter Center W, off Ashford-Dunwoody Rd. at I–285, 30346, Dunwoody, 770/396–6800 or 877/WHOTELS (877/946–8357), fax 770/399–5514, www.starwood.com. 252 rooms, 22 suites. Restaurant, lobby lounge, snack bar, in-room data ports, minibars, no-smoking rooms, room service, pool, hot tub, sauna, gym, concierge, business services, meeting rooms, car rental, free parking. AE, D, DC, MC, V. MARTA: Dunwoody.*

MODERATELY PRICED LODGINGS

15 *e-1*

BEST WESTERN/ SUITE HOTEL

Built in 1924 as apartments, this three-story Spanish colonial–style hotel is a charming focal point in Midtown. It's one block from the High Museum of Art and 10 mi from the airport. The rate includes a hearty breakfast buffet, an evening cocktail on weekdays, and shuttle service within a 3-mi radius. Some suites have whirlpool baths; apartments have kitchens. *1302 W. Peachtree St., 30309, Midtown, 404/876–6100 or 800/548–5631, fax 404/875–0502, www.bestwesterngeorgia.com. 30 rooms, 70 suites, 3 apartments. In-room data ports, no-smoking rooms, room service, gym, laundry service, business services, meeting rooms, parking (fee). AE, D, DC, MC, V. MARTA: Arts Center.*

15 *e-5*

BEST WESTERN INN AT THE PEACHTREE

A courtyard offers an escape from urban mayhem at this downtown property within two blocks of MARTA. A short walk also brings you to the gift and merchandise marts, Peachtree Center Mall, Centennial Olympic Park, and numerous restaurants. King rooms have microwaves and coffeemakers; suites have kitchens. The fifth floor is a penthouse suite. A full, hot buffet breakfast is included, and complimentary cocktails are served evenings Monday–Thursday. *330 W. Peachtree St., 30308,*

Midtown, 404/577–6970 or 800/242–4642, fax 404/659–3244, www.bestwestern.com. 104 rooms, 8 suites. No-smoking rooms, refrigerators (some), room service, gym, coin laundry, dry cleaning, business services, meeting rooms, parking (fee). AE, D, DC, MC, V. MARTA: Civic Center or Peachtree Center.

3 *d-5*

COMFORT SUITES

Lake Lanier is 7 mi from this all-suites chain property; stores, restaurants, and entertainment venues are nearby, too. Rooms deliver all the basics and include microwaves and refrigerators; Continental breakfast is included. *905 Buford Rd., Cumming 30041, 770/889–4141 or 800/517–4000, fax 770/781–9294, www.choicehotels.com. 71 suites. In-room data ports (some), no-smoking rooms, refrigerators, pool, meeting rooms, free parking. AE, D, DC, MC, V.*

URBAN ESCAPES

Even when it's only a few miles from home, the right hotel can take you far away from your day-to-day life, if only for a day. Try these for relaxation and romance.

Château Élan (very expensive)
 Nature trails, golf, fine food, and frequent concerts make a weekend at the inn or the spa, both set among pine trees and vineyards, a favorite Atlanta getaway.

Renaissance PineIsle Resort (moderate)
 Whisk your honey away for a night of dining, dancing, and relaxing in one of the hot-tub suites; wake up to a day of golf and water sports.

Serenbe Bed & Breakfast Inn (moderate)
 You can restore your equanimity with a taste of the country life just beyond the city. Meander through the fields, curl up with a book, or admire the exceptional garden.

Village Inn at Stone Mountain (moderate)
 Near historic Stone Mountain Village and Stone Mountain Park is this reasonably priced retreat. Each room has a hot tub to wash away your cares.

5 c-5

DOUBLETREE GUEST SUITES ATLANTA–PERIMETER

Off I–285 and GA 400 and 1 mi from Perimeter Mall, this all-suites property in Dunwoody draws extended-stay and business travelers. Two televisions, speaker phones, wet bars, work desks, and whirlpool baths are some of the pluses here. *6120 Peachtree-Dunwoody Rd., 30328, Dunwoody, 770/668–0808 or 800/222–8733, fax 770/668–0008, www. doubletree.com. 224 suites. Restaurant, lounge, in-room data ports, no-smoking rooms, refrigerators, indoor-outdoor pool, hot tub, sauna, gym, coin laundry, laundry service, concierge, business services, meeting rooms, free parking. AE, D, DC, MC, V. MARTA: Dunwoody.*

12 g-2

DOUBLETREE HOTEL ATLANTA BUCKHEAD

The Lenox Square and Phipps Plaza malls, as well as many of the city's favorite eateries, are steps from this hotel; a complimentary shuttle service whisks you to and from the hot spots. Guest rooms and suites offer ergonomic work centers and luxe marble baths. State-of-the-art fitness equipment, along with an indoor pool, fills the 10,000-square-ft health club. *3342 Peachtree Rd., 30326, Buckhead, 404/231–1234, fax 404/231–3112, www.doubletree. com. 230 rooms. Restaurant, in-room data ports, no-smoking rooms, room service, indoor pool, health club, free parking. AE, D, DC, MC, V. MARTA: Buckhead.*

5 a-7

EMBASSY SUITES HOTEL–GALLERIA

The Galleria Convention Centre and Office Complex is within walking distance of this all-suites hotel; two major shopping centers and many restaurants are nearby. The suites, which open onto an enclosed atrium, have separate living and bedroom areas, wet bars, large work desks, refrigerators, two TVs, and two phones. The rate includes cooked-to-order breakfasts. *2815 Akers Mill Rd., Marietta 30339, 770/984–9300 or 800/ EMBASSY (800/362–2779), fax 770/955–4183, www.embassy-suites.com. 261 suites. Restaurant, lounge, no-smoking rooms, refrigerators (some), pool, gym, free parking. AE, D, DC, MC, V.*

14 d-1

EMORY CONFERENCE CENTER HOTEL

Emory University's tree-filled campus provides the hotel's beautiful surroundings. Rooms are comfortable and have sitting areas and dual telephone lines. Come to the club room or take a dip in the hot tub for a bit of pampering. If you're feeling more energetic, you can use Emory's Physical Education Center or the hotel's outdoor lighted tennis and basketball courts. The ballroom can accommodate up to 450 guests or be divided into five separate rooms. State-of-the-art multimedia technology is available for presentations. *1615 Clifton Rd., Decatur 30329, 404/712–6000, fax 404/712–6235, www.emoryconferencecenter. com. 198 rooms. Dining room, in-room data ports, no-smoking rooms, indoor pool, hot tub, sauna, steam room, tennis court, basketball, gym, free parking. AE, D, DC, MC, V.*

15 e-5

HAMPTON INN & SUITES DOWNTOWN

A few blocks from the marts, the Georgia Dome, CNN Center, and Centennial Olympic Park, this stunning renovation of a 1920s office building is on the National Register of Historic Places. Light floods the art deco–style lobby atrium. Guest rooms are dressed in neutral tones with honey-blond, deco-style furnishings; suites have kitchens, good work desks, and sleeper sofas. The rate includes Continental breakfast. *161 Spring St., 30303, Downtown, 404/589–1111 or 800/HAMPTON (800/426–7866), fax 404/589–8999, www.hamptoninn. com. 77 rooms, 42 suites. In-room data ports, kitchenettes, no-smoking rooms, gym, coin laundry, dry cleaning, meeting rooms, business services, parking (fee). AE, D, DC, MC, V. MARTA: Peachtree Center.*

5 f-4

HILTON ATLANTA NORTHEAST HOTEL

The Technology Park Hilton serves Gwinnett County's high-tech industry. A beautiful interior of marble and mahogany and substantial multipurpose meeting space are standout features. Guest rooms have cherrywood furnishings; suites are spacious and comfortable, with full-size desks, wet bars, and whirlpool tubs. Some rooms have data ports. *5993 Peachtree Industrial Blvd., Norcross 30092, 770/447–4747 or 800/*

774–1500, fax 770/448–8853, www.hilton.com. 234 rooms, 38 suites. Restaurant, bar, in-room data ports (some), refrigerators, 1 indoor and 1 outdoor pool, sauna, golf privileges, gym, business services, meeting rooms, free parking. AE, D, DC, MC, V.

14 g-3

HOLIDAY INN SELECT ATLANTA–DECATUR HOTEL & CONFERENCE CENTER

Convenient to historic Decatur and its business district, this striking postmodern hotel offers good value and is walking distance to a MARTA stop. Interiors of dark green, rust, and burgundy recall a men's club. Meeting rooms here are ideal for small to midsize gatherings. 130 Clairemont Ave., Decatur 30030, 404/ 371–0204 or 800/225–6079, fax 404/377– 2726, www.hiselect.com. 184 rooms, 4 suites. Restaurant, lounge, in-room data ports, no-smoking floor, refrigerators, indoor pool, hair salon, gym, baby-sitting, coin laundry, dry cleaning, laundry service, concierge, business services, meeting rooms, parking (fee). AE, D, DC, MC, V. MARTA: Decatur.

5 d-1

HOMEWOOD SUITES

You have a choice of one or two bedrooms at this all-suites property off GA 400 and Mansell Road. The hotel is close to Alpharetta's business district and to many company headquarters, shops, and restaurants. Suites have living rooms and full kitchens; some have balconies. The rate includes full breakfast and, Monday–Thursday, a social hour with complimentary beer and wine. 10775 Davis Dr., Alpharetta 30004, 770/ 998–1622 or 800/CALLHOME (800/ 225–5466), fax 770/998–7834, www. homewood-suites.com. 112 suites. Breakfast room, in-room data ports, no-smoking rooms, refrigerators, pool, hair salon, gym, coin laundry, laundry service, business services, meeting rooms, free parking. AE, D, DC, MC, V.

5 e-2

LA QUINTA INN & SUITES

Sunlight brightens the lobby of this contemporary chain property near North Point Mall and minutes from northern Fulton County's business district. Rooms have large desks and the rate includes Continental breakfast buffet. 1350 North Point Dr., Alpharetta 30022, 770/754–7800 or 800/687–6667, fax 770/ 754–9242, www.laquinta.com. 125 rooms, 6 suites. In-room data ports, no-smoking rooms, pool, gym, laundry service, free parking. AE, D, DC, MC, V.

4 g-4

MARIETTA CONFERENCE CENTER & RESORT

Minutes from Marietta and Kennesaw National Battlefield is this 132-acre resort with an 18-hole championship golf course and lighted tennis courts. The lobby is decked out in marble floors and chandeliers. The rooms, dressed in autumn colors, include oversize desks. Extensive conference and meeting space is available. 500 Powder Springs Rd., Marietta 30064, 770/427–2500, fax 770/ 429–9577, www.mariettaresort.com. 189 rooms, 11 suites. Restaurant, pub, in-room data ports, pool, hot tub, sauna, 18-hole golf course, 2 tennis courts, health club, concierge, business services, meeting rooms, free parking. AE, D, DC, MC, V.

5 c-5

QUALITY HOTEL DOWNTOWN

This quiet, older (but renovated) downtown hotel two blocks off Peachtree Street has modestly proportioned rooms. Its marble lobby, with a sofa and a grand piano that you can play, is inviting. Because of its proximity to the World Congress Center and the gift and merchandise marts, the place is very popular during conventions, and prices go up when groups are in town. 89 Luckie St., 30303, Downtown, 404/524– 7991 or 800/228–5151, fax 404/524–0672, www.choicehotels.com. 75 rooms. No-smoking rooms, gym, meeting rooms, parking (fee). AE, D, DC, MC, V. MARTA: Peachtree Center.

1 g-2

RENAISSANCE PINEISLE RESORT

In a majestic, 1,200-acre pine forest in the foothills of the Blue Ridge Mountains 45 minutes from downtown Atlanta sits this spectacular lake-front paradise. The many recreational facilities include a water park and outdoor and indoor tennis courts. The hot-tub suites, with king beds, private lanais, comfortably furnished sitting areas, and splendid views, are ideal for romance. Conference and meeting facilities are extensive. To get here, take Exit 8 off I–985, near the South Carolina border. 9000 Holiday Rd.,

Lake Lanier Islands 30518, 770/945–8921 or 800/HOTELS1 (800/468–3571), fax 770/945–0351, www.renaissancehotels. com. 226 rooms, 28 suites. 3 restaurants, lounge, in-room data ports, in-room safes, pool, 18-hole golf course, 7 tennis courts, sauna, gym, meeting rooms, free parking. AE, D, DC, MC, V.

3 *a-8*

RESIDENCE INN BY MARRIOTT–ALPHARETTA

This all-suites hotel 3 mi from North Point Mall offers many of the comforts of home, a big draw for anyone planning an extended stay. The suites all have separate living and work areas, bedrooms, and full kitchens; some have fireplaces. *5465 Windward Pkwy. W, Alpharetta 30004, 770/664–0664 or 800/ MARRIOTT (800/627–7468), fax 770/ 664–7781, www.residenceinn.com. 103 suites. In-room data ports, no-smoking rooms, refrigerators, pool, hot tub, sauna, tennis court, gym, coin laundry, laundry service, meeting rooms, free parking. AE, D, DC, MC, V.*

1 *c-7*

SERENBE BED & BREAKFAST INN

In south Fulton County, this B&B complex is on a 350-acre farm that includes walking trails, streams, and a lake, as well as an assortment of animals. The rooms are in a guest house and a converted barn, which has excellent American contemporary and folk art and a patio with a fireplace; a cottage holds a suite with two double rooms, a living room, and a kitchen. The look is country casual with a few frills. A full breakfast is served in the restored farmhouse, which houses a small conference center that can hold up to 35 people; teleconferencing is available. *10950 Hutcheson Ferry Rd., Palmetto 30268, 770/463–2610, fax 770/463–4472, www.serenbe.com. 7 rooms, 1 cottage suite. Breakfast room, pool, hot tub, meeting rooms. No credit cards.*

15 *f-3*

SHELLMONT BED & BREAKFAST

Named for the shell motif that appears throughout the 1891 house, the Shellmont is an architectural gem with curved and arched windows, exquisitely detailed stained glass, Victorian-style stenciled interiors, and a delightful garden. Fine American Victorian antiques

fill the guest rooms, which receive nightly turndown service with chocolates. The renovated carriage house has a hot tub for two. A full breakfast is served daily. Children over age 12 are welcome. *821 Piedmont Ave., 30306, Midtown, 404/872–9290, fax 404/872–5379, www.shellmont.com. 3 rooms, 3 suites. Dining room, library, laundry service, free parking. AE, DC, MC, V.*

15 *e-5*

SHERATON ATLANTA HOTEL

An angular tent-like awning welcomes you to the lobby of this well-designed 12-story hotel. The courtyard pool—a world of plants and flowers—has a retractable roof and poolside service. Executive Tower rooms, which have access to a club lounge and a small meeting room, are aimed at the business traveler. The health club is open around the clock. *165 Courtland St., 30303, Downtown, 404/659–6500 or 800/833–8624, fax 404/ 524–1259, www.sheratonatlantahotel.com. 734 rooms, 31 suites. 2 restaurants, bar, deli, lounge, in-room data ports, in-room fax, minibars, no-smoking rooms, room service, indoor-outdoor pool, health club, concierge, business services, meeting rooms, car rental, parking (fee). AE, D, DC, MC, V. MARTA: Peachtree Center.*

12 *h-2*

SHERATON BUCKHEAD

This modern and well-maintained eight-floor hotel is one block from the Lenox Square and Phipps Plaza malls. Jewel-tone furnishings punch up the contemporary decor. Complimentary transportation is available around the Buckhead area. *3405 Lenox Rd. NE, 30326, Buckhead, 404/261–9250 or 800/ 241–8260, fax 404/848–7391, www. sheraton.com. 369 rooms, 7 suites. Restaurant, bar, in-room data ports, no-smoking rooms, room service, gym, concierge, business services, meeting rooms, car rental, parking (fee). AE, D, DC, MC, V. MARTA: Lenox.*

5 *c-7*

SIERRA SUITES BROOKHAVEN

The Brookhaven MARTA station is adjacent to this all-suites hotel about 1½ mi from the Lenox Square and Phipps Plaza malls. The studio suites are small but uncluttered and neat and have fully equipped kitchens. *3967 Peachtree Rd., 30319, Brookhaven, 404/237–9100 or 800/*

4–SIERRA (800/474–3772), fax 404/237–0055, www.sierrasuites.com. 92 suites. In-room data ports, kitchenettes (some), no-smoking rooms, pool, gym, coin laundry, dry cleaning, free parking. AE, D, DC, MC, V. MARTA: Brookhaven.

4 f-4

STANLEY HOUSE

Marietta's historic district surrounds this carefully restored 1895 three-story Queen Anne structure two blocks from Marietta Square. A wraparound porch and courtyard welcome you. Antiques fill the five guest rooms. One bedroom has a loft that's appropriate for an older child; another has a four-poster canopy bed and old-fashioned claw-foot tub. Full breakfast is included. 236 Church St., Marietta 30060, 770/426–1881, fax 770/426–6821, www.thestanleyhouse.com. 5 rooms. Free parking. AE, D, MC, V.

5 c-5

SUMMERFIELD SUITES HOTEL–ATLANTA PERIMETER

One- and two-bedroom suites with full kitchens and large work areas are available at this all-suites hotel 1 mi from Perimeter Mall and the Perimeter business district. Some of the two-bedroom suites have two bathrooms. 760 Mount Vernon Hwy., 30328, Sandy Springs, 404/250–0110 or 800/833–4353, fax 404/250–9335, www.wyndham.com/summerfield. 122 suites. In-room data ports, in-room safes, no-smoking rooms, refrigerators, pool, gym, coin laundry, meeting rooms, free parking. AE, D, DC, MC, V. MARTA: Dunwoody.

14 g-3

SYCAMORE HOUSE BED & BREAKFAST

This B&B offers a romantic, peaceful getaway within the city. Large rooms and generous windows give the circa-1905 house an airy feel. Rooms blend antiques with contemporary furniture and art. The suite includes a sitting area with fireplace. You can take refuge in the secluded garden, which has a waterfall and a heated pool with a hot tub. Breakfast is served whenever you wish. A MARTA station, restaurants, galleries, and entertainment are a five-minute walk away. Note that innkeepers Ren and Judy Manning have dogs and cats that stay in the house. 624 Sycamore St., Decatur 30030, 404/378–0685, fax 404/373–6631, www.city-directory.com/sycamorehouse. 2 rooms, 1 suite. Pool, hot tub, free parking. No credit cards. MARTA: Decatur.

6 a-8

VILLAGE INN AT STONE MOUNTAIN

The inn, less than 1 mi from the entrance to Stone Mountain Park, opened in the 1820s and served as a Confederate hospital during the Civil War before becoming a private residence; it was turned into an inn in 1995. All rooms have telephones and two-person hot tubs; three rooms have gas fireplaces and two have balconies. A garden, a video library, and in-room coffeemakers are among the amenities. Innkeepers Christy and Earl Collins serve a full Southern breakfast. The inn is said to be haunted, but it's a favorite wedding and honeymoon spot nevertheless. 992 Ridge Ave., Stone Mountain 30083, 770/469–3459 or 800/214–8385, fax 770/469–1051, www.villageinnbb.com. 5 rooms, 1 suite. Dining room, in-room data ports, in-room VCRs, free parking. AE, D, MC, V.

1 e-4

WESTIN ATLANTA NORTH AT PERIMETER CENTER

The hotel is within walking distance (or a short shuttle ride) of one of the region's favorite shopping complexes, Perimeter Center. Each room is outfitted with such plush comforts as sitting areas with overstuffed chairs, roomy bathrooms, and thick comforters; some rooms offer a tranquil view of a private lake. 7 Concourse Pkwy., 30326, Dunwoody, 770/395–3900 or 800/241–8260, fax 770/395–3935, www.westin.com. 351 rooms, 17 suites. Restaurant, bar, no-smoking rooms, refrigerators, room service, concierge, business services, meeting rooms, parking (fee). AE, D, DC, MC, V. MARTA: Lenox.

4 f-4

WHITLOCK INN

An elegant, architectural jewel, this Victorian inn has spindled verandas, a rooftop porch, pocket doors, hardwood floors, and lead-glass windows in the reception parlor. Rooms are equipped with cable TV and private phones; breakfast is Continental and may include quiche, muffins, and breads. An addition has space for receptions and meetings. Children over age 12 are welcome.

57 Whitlock Ave., Marietta 30064, 770/
428–1495, fax 770/919–9620, www.
whitlockinn.com. 5 rooms. Dining room,
no-smoking rooms, meeting room, free
parking. AE, D, MC, V.

15 *e-5*

WYNDHAM ATLANTA

You can walk to the CNN Center, the gift
and merchandise marts, and Centennial
Olympic Park from this star in downtown's lodging firmament. The hotel's
atrium lobby is spacious; guest rooms
are business-friendly and have large
desks. Caliterra, the restaurant, has
established itself as a notable dining
destination. The bar, with a good view of
the street, frequently hosts live entertainment. 160 Spring St., 30303, Downtown,

---

BEST FOR BUSINESS

*Atlanta is indubitably a grand city of
commerce, an international player on
the world economic stage. Most of its
hotels cater to business travelers, but
these stand out.*

Hilton Atlanta (very expensive)
 *With its own convention center, plus
 meeting rooms and a business center, this giant is ready to meet business needs on every scale. Rooms are
 equipped with multiple two-line
 telephones and voice mail; some
 have fax machines.*

**Holiday Inn Select Atlanta–Decatur
Hotel and Conference Center
(moderate)**
 *A conference center with lots of
 meeting rooms makes this an excellent choice for small gatherings.*

Hyatt Regency Atlanta (expensive)
 *You can get business supplies at off-
 hours, as well as 24-hour access to
 printers and copiers. Business Plan
 rooms have in-room faxes and extra-
 large desks with high-end chairs and
 ample lighting.*

Marriott Marquis (expensive)
 *Ergonomically correct desk chairs
 and desks that open up into large
 work surfaces are just two of the
 pluses.*

Quality Hotel Downtown (moderate)
 *This small hotel is Atlanta's premier
 value for lodging when you're here
 to attend events at the nearby Georgia World Congress Center.*

404/688–8600 or 800/WYNDHAM
(800/996–3426), fax 404/524–5543, www.
wyndham.com. 286 rooms, 8 suites.
Restaurant, bar, in-room data ports, no-
smoking rooms, room service, pool, gym,
laundry service, concierge, business services,
meeting rooms, parking (fee). AE, D, DC,
MC, V. MARTA: Peachtree Center.

9 *a-5*

WYNDHAM PEACHTREE
CITY CONFERENCE CENTER

About 25 minutes from Hartsfield
Atlanta International Airport and 35 minutes from downtown, this complex
offers city conveniences in a tranquil
wooded atmosphere laced with trails.
Resort facilities such as a tennis center
and a health club offer ample opportunity for relaxation; you also have access
to an 18-hole championship golf course.
Rooms have private balconies and large
work areas. 2443 GA 54, Peachtree City
30269, 770/487–2000 or 800/WYND-
HAM (800/996–3426), fax 770/487–
4428, www.wyndham.com/peachtree. 250
rooms, 6 suites. 2 restaurants, bar, in-room
data ports, no-smoking rooms, room service, 1 indoor and 1 outdoor pool, hot tub,
massage, sauna, steam room, golf privileges, 3 tennis courts, health club, jogging,
laundry service, concierge, business services, meeting rooms, free parking. AE, D,
DC, MC, V.

BUDGET
LODGINGS

5 *e-2*

AMERISUITES

Designed for extended stays, this comfortable all-suites property ¼ mi from
North Point Mall has separate living and
sleeping areas, a microwave oven, iron
and ironing board, VCR, and a work
space with a two-line telephone. The
rate includes Continental breakfast buffet. 7500 North Point Pkwy., Alpharetta
30022, 770/594–8788 or 800/833–1516,
fax 770/594–1977, www.amerisuites.com.
126 suites. In-room data ports, no-smoking
rooms, refrigerators, pool, laundry service,
business services, gym, free parking. AE, D,
DC, MC, V.

6 *a-4*

AMERISUITES
ATLANTA–GWINNETT

The suites at this Duluth property, adjacent the Gwinnett Place mall and 2 mi

away from the Gwinnett Civic Center, have separate sitting and sleeping areas, microwaves, wet bars, and desks. Buffet breakfast is included. *3530 Venture Pkwy., Duluth 30096, 770/623–9699 or 800/833–1516, fax 770/623–4640, www. amerisuites.com. 125 suites. Lounge, in-room data ports, no-smoking rooms, refrigerators, pool, gym, coin laundry, meeting rooms, free parking. AE, D, DC, MC, V.*

 b-8

BEST WESTERN INN—STONE MOUNTAIN

Stone Mountain Park and the village are a few minutes' drive from these economical accommodations, on the outskirts of the metro area. Rooms are clean and include a microwave oven and a sizable bathroom. *1595 E. Park Pl., Stone Mountain 30087, 770/465–1022 or 800/528–1234, fax 770/465–9089, www. bestwestern.com. 60 rooms. Restaurant, lounge, in-room data ports, in-room safes, no-smoking rooms, refrigerators, hot tub, pool, meeting rooms, free parking. AE, D, DC, MC, V.*

2 *e-2*

COMFORT INN

A mile from downtown Canton, the hotel is an easy walk from local shopping. Rooms are comfortably furnished in contemporary style and include microwave oven, mini-refrigerator, and wet bar. Continental breakfast is included. *138 Keith Dr., Canton 30114, 770/345–1994 or 800/228–5150, fax 770/345–1994, www.comfortinncanton.com. 47 rooms, 3 suites. Breakfast room, in-room data ports (some), no-smoking rooms, refrigerators, pool, gym, laundry service, business services, meeting room, free parking. AE, D, DC, MC, V.*

5 *e-6*

COMFORT INN & CONFERENCE CENTER

This Comfort Inn delivers great amenities 15 minutes away from major shopping and business districts. A free shuttle takes you to the Doraville MARTA station. Guest rooms, which open into interior corridors, are comfortable, with a contemporary decor. The conference facilities can hold 500 people. *2001 Clearview Ave., Doraville 30340, 770/455–1811 or 800/228–5150, fax 770/451–6795, www.comfortinn.com. 228 rooms, 6 suites. Restaurant, bar, no-smoking rooms, pool, laundry service, meeting*

rooms, free parking. AE, D, DC, MC, V. MARTA: Doraville.

5 *e-2*

COUNTRY INN & SUITES

Standard rooms at this franchise include ironing boards, coffeemakers, and cable TV; suites have, in addition, king-size beds, separate sitting areas, microwave ovens, refrigerators, and work space. The business center is self-service but is accessible around the clock. Continental breakfast is included. *2950 Mansell Rd., Alpharetta 30022, 770/552–0006 or 800/456–4000, fax 770/993–3541, www.countryinns.com. 51 rooms, 11 suites. In-room data ports, no-smoking rooms, refrigerators (some), indoor pool, hot tub, gym, business services, meeting rooms, free parking. AE, D, DC, MC, V.*

4 *g-5*

COURTYARD ATLANTA DELK ROAD

Here's a clean and affordable, if pleasantly pasteurized, option to the costly accommodations in the area. The rooms are spacious and include a comfortable sitting area, a large work desk, and cable TV. You can walk to many chain eateries from here. *2455 Delk Rd., Marietta 30067, 770/956–1188 or 800/321–2211, fax 770/933–0489, www.courtyard.com. 134 rooms, 12 suites. Breakfast room, lounge, in-room data ports, no-smoking rooms, pool, hot tub, gym, coin laundry, dry cleaning, laundry service, meeting rooms, free parking. AE, D, DC, MC, V.*

7 *c-2*

DAYS INN AT SIX FLAGS

You can walk to Six Flags amusement park from this inexpensive two-story hotel, and downtown Atlanta is about 10 mi away. The basic rooms have double beds (some rooms have three of them) and offer no surprises—a definite plus in this price range. *95 S. Service Rd., Austell 30168, 770/941–1400 or 800/325–2525, fax 770/819–9988, www.daysinn.com. 96 rooms. Breakfast room, no-smoking rooms, pool, free parking. AE, D, DC, MC, V.*

7 *b-2*

FAIRFIELD INN ATLANTA AT SIX FLAGS

Comfortable, basic accommodations are the draw at this budget chain 3 mi from the Six Flags amusement park. Pluses include work desks, in-room movies, and complimentary local calls and Continental breakfast. Limited business facilities are available. *976 West Pointe Ct., Lithia Springs 30057, 770/739–2800 or 800/228–2800, fax 770/739–2800, www. fairfieldinn.com. 64 rooms, 17 suites. In-room data ports, no-smoking rooms, hot tub, indoor pool, laundry service, meeting room, free parking. AE, D, DC, MC, V.*

1 *b-5*

HOLIDAY INN EXPRESS

Accommodations at this budget chain property about 7 mi from Six Flags are simple and without surprises. Rooms are large and clean and free local calls

---

LUXE LOUNGES

A good hotel bar is both a convivial spot where you can unwind after a hectic business day and an intimate boîte where you can woo your special someone. See Chapter 5 for more on these standouts.

Four Seasons Hotel, Atlanta (very expensive)
The huge, well-stocked bar beckons irresistibly as you enter the Park 75 Lounge from a plant-filled terrace. Sink into cushy seating grouped around low tables, and let the soft lighting, piano music, and complimentary cocktail buffet work their magic.

Grand Hyatt Atlanta (expensive)
While you sip your cabernet or Cosmopolitan at the Lobby Lounge, set aside your cares and enjoy the sight of the serene, Japanese-style rock garden and the sound of its burbling waterfall.

Ritz-Carlton, Buckhead (very expensive)
The Lobby Lounge attracts imbibers to high tea in the afternoon and to the cocktail hours of the evening, which are sometimes backed by live jazz. In winter a fireplace chases away the chill.

Westin Peachtree Plaza (very expensive)
High atop one of Atlanta's most distinctive towers, the slowly spinning Sun Dial Restaurant & Lounge takes in exquisite views of the city's architecture.

---

are included. *5479 Westmoreland Plaza, Douglasville 30134, 770/949–5730 or 800/465–4329, fax 770/949–2619, www. holiday-inn.com. 46 rooms, 4 suites. No-smoking rooms, pool, business services, free parking. AE, D, DC, MC, V.*

4 *g-5*

RAMADA LIMITED SUITES

Three blocks west of I–75 and 1 mi from the Marietta business district, this value-oriented motel offers typical chain rooms with cable TV and complimentary Continental breakfast. The location is within headache-free highway distance of the city. *630 Franklin Rd., Marietta 30067, 770/919–7878 or 888/298–2054, fax 770/514–0824, www.ramada.com. 46 rooms. In-room data ports, kitchenettes, no-smoking rooms, refrigerators, pool, gym, free parking. AE, D, DC, MC, V.*

15 *f-5*

TRAVELODGE–DOWNTOWN

Some staffers have been working at this family-owned motel near the civic center since it opened in 1964. Rooms are well maintained; the executive rooms are a little more plushly furnished than the standard rooms. Designed especially for children, "Sleepy Bear Dens" have special decor and an adjoining bedroom for the grown-ups. Complimentary doughnuts and coffee are provided each morning. *311 Courtland St., 30303, Downtown, 404/659–4545 or 800/578–7878, fax 404/659–5934, www.travelodge.com. 71 rooms. In-room data ports, in-room safes, no-smoking rooms, pool, laundry service, free parking. AE, D, DC, MC, V. MARTA: Civic Center.*

3 *h-6*

WHITWORTH INN

This white dormered building on a pretty landscaped property is popular with business travelers as well as with families visiting Lake Lanier. Rooms are simple and bright and have TVs; baths are strictly functional. A full breakfast is included. *6593 McEver Rd., Flowery Branch 30542, 770/967–2386, fax 770/967–2649, www.whitworthinn.com. 10 rooms. Dining room, no-smoking rooms. AE, MC, V.*

5 *f-4*

WINGATE INN PEACHTREE CORNERS

Rooms at this business-oriented inn, part of a small chain and one of the best values in the area, are spacious and have microwave ovens, separate work areas with cordless telephones, Web TV, and free high-speed Internet access. Suites have hot tubs. A cold Continental breakfast is included. This location is handy to metro Atlanta's numerous technology parks and also is close to the Deer Valley and River Pines golf ranges. *5800 Peachtree Industrial Blvd., Norcross 30071, 770/263–2020 or 800/228–1000, fax 770/263–2022, www.wingateinns.com. 114 rooms, 4 suites. In-room data ports, in-room safes, no-smoking rooms, refrigerators, lap pool, hot tub, gym, coin laundry, laundry service, business services, meeting rooms, free parking. AE, D, DC, MC, V.*

HOSTELS & YMCAS

15 *f-4*

BUTLER STREET YMCA

Founded in 1894 in the basement of Wheat Street Baptist Church, this YMCA provided first a stomping ground and then a stage for Dr. Martin Luther King Jr. In fact, local civil-rights activist groups have been meeting at this location since before 1920, when the original YMCA building was erected for and by African-Americans. The YMCA now stands across the street and provides beds and other basic facilities for men. *22 Butler St., 30303 Downtown, 404/659–8085 or 404/659–0915, fax 404/589–8444, www.ymca.net. 50 rooms with shared baths. Free parking. AE, D, MC, V. MARTA: North Ave.*

15 *f-4*

HOSTELING INTERNATIONAL ATLANTA

Atlanta's only youth hostel sits in the center of bustling Midtown. Dormitory-style rooms house four to six beds each ($18 per bed nightly); bathroom facilities are shared. Coffee and doughnuts are served in the morning. The hostel office is open 8–noon and 5–midnight. You must show a photo ID when checking in. *223 Ponce de Leon Ave., 30308, Midtown, 404/872–1042, fax 404/870–0042, www.hostel-atlanta.com. 8 rooms, 80 beds. Free parking. AE, D, MC, V. MARTA: North Ave.*

HOTELS NEAR THE AIRPORT

7 *f-6*

ABBETT INN

Built in the 1880s, this Queen Anne Victorian is the scene not only of weekend getaways but of weddings, reunions, even murder-mystery parties. The large house stands on a large, wooded lot in a quiet neighborhood 10 minutes from downtown Atlanta. Innkeepers Donald Taylor-Farmer and John W. Hoard renovated the house to a contemporary level of comfort but retained the old bathtubs. Four of the rooms have private baths, and each floor has a kitchen for guests. Complimentary transportation is available to and from the airport and the nearby MARTA station. *1746 Virginia Ave., College Park 30337, 404/767–3708, fax 404/767–1626, www.abbettinn.com. 6 rooms, 4 with bath. Dining room, in-room data ports, no-smoking rooms, airport shuttle, free parking. AE, D, MC, V. MARTA: College Park. Moderate.*

7 *f-6*

AMERISUITES— ATLANTA AIRPORT

This well-priced chain property about 1½ mi from the airport offers suite accommodations with separate living and sleeping areas. Computer-ready desks, wet bars, and microwaves are some of the amenities. *1899 Sullivan Rd., College Park 30337, 770/994–2997 or 800/833–1516, fax 770/994–8626, www.amerisuites.com. 125 suites. In-room data ports, no-smoking rooms, refrigerators, pool, gym, coin laundry, meeting rooms, airport shuttle, free parking. AE, D, DC, MC, V. Budget.*

7 *h-8*

COMFORT INN—AIRPORT

Six miles from Hartsfield Atlanta International Airport and 12 mi from downtown, this motel offers convenience and comfort for the budget-conscious. All rooms are decorated in a straightforward contemporary style and have microwaves; Continental breakfast is included. *6370 Old Dixie Hwy., Jonesboro 30236, 770/961–6336 or 800/228–5150, fax 770/961–0946, www.comfortinns.com. 67 rooms. No-smoking rooms, refrigerators, pool, free parking. AE, D, DC, MC, V. Budget.*

7 *f-6*

COMFORT INN–
ATLANTA AIRPORT

This soundproof six-story building is convenient to the Georgia International Convention and Trade Center as well as to the airport, which is about ½ mi away. Guest rooms open onto an interior corridor. The inn has 1,700 square ft of meeting space. *4601 Best Rd., College Park 30337, 404/761–6500 or 800/228–5150, fax 404/763–3267, www.comfortinns. com. 160 rooms. Restaurant, no-smoking rooms, pool, gym, business services, meeting rooms, airport shuttle, free parking. AE, D, DC, MC, V. Budget.*

7 *f-6*

COURTYARD ATLANTA
AIRPORT SOUTH

Courtyard repeats its successful formula for the busy traveler 1 mi from the airport. Rooms are spacious. Express check-in and check-out help your stay to go smoothly, as can the services of the concierge. At the end of the day, you can relax in the hot tub or over a cocktail. *2050 Sullivan Rd., College Park 30337, 770/997–2220 or 800/321–2211, fax 770/994–9743, www.courtyard.com. 132 rooms, 12 suites. Restaurant, lounge, in-room data ports, no-smoking rooms, refrigerators, room service, indoor pool, hot tub, gym, coin laundry, concierge, meeting rooms, airport shuttle, free parking. AE, D, DC, MC, V. Moderate.*

7 *g-5*

CROWNE PLAZA–
ATLANTA AIRPORT

A full range of facilities and superb accommodations and service are available at this 12-story hotel 1 mi from Hartsfield Atlanta International Airport and six minutes from downtown. Rooms are large, equipped with a well-lit work area and two telephones with voice mail. Public areas include 16,000 square ft of meeting space. *1325 Virginia Ave., East Point 30344, 404/768–6660 or 800/2CROWNE (800/227–6963), fax 404/766–6121, www.crowneplaza.com. 376 rooms, 2 suites. Restaurant, lounge, in-room data ports, no-smoking rooms, pool, gym, coin laundry, dry cleaning, concierge, business services, meeting rooms, airport shuttle, free parking. AE, D, DC, MC, V. Moderate.*

7 *f-7*

FAIRFIELD INN
BY MARRIOTT–
ATLANTA AIRPORT

This link in Marriott's more-budget-minded chain offers health-club privileges to guests. Rates include Continental breakfast and a shuttle service (5 AM–midnight) with a 5-mi radius that includes the airport. The inn is handy to Fort McPherson and Six Flags, among other points of interest. *2451 Old National Pkwy., College Park 30349, 404/761–8371 or 800/228–2800, fax 404/559–3483, www.fairfieldinn.com. 132 rooms. No-smoking rooms, pool, laundry service, airport shuttle, free parking. AE, D, DC, MC, V. Budget.*

7 *f-6*

HILTON ATLANTA
AIRPORT & TOWERS

Accommodations at this contemporary hotel 1½ mi north of the airport are fresh and comfortable. The location just on the outskirts of the normal flight patterns at Hartsfield International provides a bit of a buffer to the noise factor. Rooms include a spacious work area, triple-paned windows, and two phone lines. *1031 Virginia Ave., Hapeville 30354, 404/767–9000 or 800/774–1500, fax 404/768–0185, www.hilton.com. 499 rooms, 5 suites. 3 restaurants, bar, in-room data ports, 1 indoor and 1 outdoor pool, sauna, tennis court, gym, billiards, laundry service, concierge, business services, meeting rooms, airport shuttle, free parking. AE, D, DC, MC, V. Very expensive.*

7 *f-6*

MARRIOTT–
ATLANTA AIRPORT

The hotel sits amid 14 landscaped acres. Guest rooms here offer the familiar Marriott amenities; 141 of the rooms are designed with the business traveler in mind. Meeting facilities offer 21,000 square ft of flexible space. *4711 Best Rd., College Park 30337, 404/766–7900 or 800/MARRIOTT (800/627–7468), fax 404/209–6808, www.marriott.com. 628 rooms, 10 suites. 2 restaurants, lounge, in-room data ports, no-smoking rooms, 1 indoor and 1 outdoor pool, hair salon, 2 tennis courts, health club, laundry service, business services, meeting rooms, airport shuttle, free parking. AE, D, DC, MC, V. Moderate.*

7 *f-6*

RENAISSANCE CONCOURSE– ATLANTA AIRPORT

The airport is five minutes from this hotel with an 11-story atrium; golf and tennis facilities are also nearby. Rooms have inviting sitting areas and spacious bathrooms. A club level occupies the upper floors, but all guests have access to the hotel's business center and secretarial services. A multilingual staff and foreign-currency exchange help to make international visitors feel welcome. There is 34,000 square ft of meeting space. *1 Hartsfield Centre Pkwy., College Park 30354, 404/209–9999 or 800/ HOTELS1 (800/468–3571), fax 404/209– 7031, www.renaissancehotels.com. 370 rooms, 17 suites. Restaurant, lounge, in-room data ports, minibars, no-smoking rooms, 1 indoor and 1 outdoor pool, massage, sauna, health club, business services, meeting rooms, travel services, airport shuttle, free parking. AE, D, DC, MC, V. Expensive.*

7 *f-6*

RESIDENCE INN BY MARRIOTT– ATLANTA AIRPORT

This all-suites hotel 1½ mi from Hartsfield Atlanta International Airport is designed for extended stays. Each of the suites has a full kitchen, separate living and sleeping areas, and a large work space. *3401 International Blvd., Hapeville 30354, 404/761–0511 or 800/MARRIOTT (800/627–7468), fax 404/761–0650, www.residenceinn.com. 126 suites. Restaurant, in-room data ports, kitchenettes, no-smoking rooms, pool, hot tub, gym, coin laundry, dry cleaning, free parking. AE, D, DC, MC, V. Moderate.*

7 *f-6*

SHERATON GATEWAY HOTEL–ATLANTA AIRPORT

Adjoining the Georgia International Convention Center, this Sheraton offers easy access to downtown. The hotel has 10,000 square ft of meeting space. *1900 Sullivan Rd., College Park 30337, 770/ 997–1100 or 800/833–8624, fax 770/991– 5906, www.sheraton.com. 383 rooms, 12 suites. Restaurant, 2 lounges, no-smoking rooms, indoor-outdoor pool, hot tub, gym, meeting rooms, airport shuttle, free parking. AE, D, DC, MC, V. Expensive.*

7 *f-7*

TRAVELODGE– ATLANTA AIRPORT

Rooms at this comfortable and affordable full-service hotel in the Phoenix Office Park complex, 1½ mi from the airport, open onto an interior corridor. Continental breakfast is included. Access to the major freeways into the city is easy, putting you about a 10-minute drive from Downtown and Turner Field. *1808 Phoenix Blvd., College Park 30349, 770/991–1099 or 800/578– 7878, fax 770/991–1076, www.travelodge. com. 193 rooms. Bar, lounge, in-room data ports, no-smoking rooms, pool, gym, laundry service, airport shuttle, free parking. AE, D, DC, MC, V. Budget.*

7 *f-6*

WESTIN HOTEL– ATLANTA AIRPORT

Five minutes from Atlanta Hartsfield International Airport and 15 minutes from downtown, this hotel is also near a MARTA line; a free shuttle runs to the airport and to the station. Rooms in the 10-story glass building surround a central atrium. All include desks and spacious, polished bathrooms; plush down pillows and comforters top the luxuriously comfortable mattresses. Some rooms also provide speaker phones, basic office supplies, and fax machines with printer and copier functions. *4736 Best Rd., College Park 30337, 404/762– 7676 or 800/228–3000, fax 404/559– 7388, www.starwood.com. 462 rooms, 33 suites. Restaurant, in-room data ports, no-smoking rooms, indoor-outdoor pool, hot tub, sauna, health club, basketball, meeting rooms, airport shuttle, free parking. AE, D, DC, MC, V. Expensive. MARTA: Airport.*

B&B RESERVATION SERVICES

BED & BREAKFAST ATLANTA

These folks can help you make B&B reservations, arrange home stays, rent corporate apartments, and find alternative lodging gems. *1608 Briarcliff Rd., Suite 5, Decatur 30306, 404/875–0525 or 800/967–3224, fax 404/875–8198, bbon-line.com.*

GEORGIA BED & BREAKFAST COUNCIL

An affiliate of the Georgia Hospitality and Travel Association, the council publishes a directory that you can request by telephoning or by visiting the Web site. *600 W. Peachtree St., 30308, Downtown, 404/873–4482, www.stay-in-ga.com.*

GREAT INNS OF GEORGIA

This private marketing consortium publishes a brochure listing member inns. For a copy, call and leave your name and address. *404/843–0471 or 404/851–1585.*

chapter 7

CITY SOURCES

getting a handle on the city

basics of city life

BANKS

atms
Cirrus Cash Machine Locator *800/307–7309.*

Plus ATM Locator *800/843–7587.*

major institutions
The following are full-service banks, members FDIC. In addition, Atlanta has a plethora of small banks, many with only one or a few locations, that offer service with a small-town feel. But they might not offer all the services the large banks do. Most banks are open week-days 9–4, with exceptions noted at the appropriate listings; the majority of branches have ATMs.

Bank of America Formerly NationsBank, until its absorption by Bank of America in 1999, this bank has 46 branches in the Atlanta area, with numerous loca-tions in Kroger grocery stores. Weekday hours are 10–8 in the Kroger stores, 9–4 in the freestanding banks; 20 locations are open Saturday (some just drive-through), with hours varying from 9 to noon or 1, while the Kroger locations are open 10–5. *800/299–BANK customer ser-vice.*

Citizens Trust Bank With more than 75 years of service to Atlanta's African-American community, CTB has a dozen branches chiefly downtown and on the south side of Atlanta. Some are open Saturday 9–noon. *404/659–5959 main office.*

Colonial Bank Its 11 branches are princi-pally in the north and west metro area. Those open Saturday chiefly have drive-through service only 9–noon; Dun-woody, Mableton, Wade Green, and Windy Hill offer full-service banking dur-ing those hours. *877/502–2265 customer service.*

Fidelity National Bank The Decatur-based bank offers full-service banking at 19 branches, with Saturday service 9–noon at all branches. *404/639–6500 main office; 888/248–5466 customer service.*

First Union A merger of several well-respected Atlanta area institutions, this large bank has branches throughout the metro area. All are open Saturday 9–noon. Service is available in Spanish. *800/801–0714 or 800/ASKFUNB 24-hour customer service.*

Regions National Bank This small but growing regional bank has about 20 branches, chiefly located in the north and west metro area, although there's one in East Point. Selected banks are open Sat-urday 9–noon. *800–REGIONS customer service (dial 0 for personal attention).*

SouthTrust With more than 140 branches throughout the Atlanta area, it offers Saturday services 9–noon at about half of its locations. *770/956–0634 or 800/239–6919 customer service.*

Summit National Bank It's small, with five branches scattered around the north and west, and specializes in the banking needs of the Asian and Latino communi-ties' business owners. The bank's Asian Banking Center (3490 Shallowford Rd., Chamblee, 770/455–1772) has Saturday hours 9–1. *770/454–0400.*

SunTrust With 79 branches, 50 of them in Publix supermarkets, SunTrust is now one of the largest bank holding compa-nies in the United States. *404/230–5555 24-hour service or 800/432–4932.*

Tucker Federal Bank Serving mostly the north and east sides, this metro-area bank touts itself as "Not too big. Not too small. Just right." Tucker Federal has 13 branches around Atlanta, 7 of which are open 9–noon on Saturday. *770/908–6400 or 800/277–4075 customer service.*

United Americas Bank N.A. Specializing in the financial needs of the Hispanic community, this young bank has extended Friday hours (9–6) and is open Saturday 9–1. Besides its main branch (3789 Roswell Rd., Buckhead), the bank has two other locations (one at the intersection of Buford Hwy. and Chamblee-Tucker Rd., the other in Mari-etta). *404/240–0101.*

Wachovia Based in Charlotte, North Car-olina, this large bank—part of First Union—has 92 branches all over the metro Atlanta area, including Clayton and Fayette counties. Hours at most locations are Monday–Thursday 9–5, Friday 9–6. However, the downtown branch does business 8:30–5 only. *800/922–4684 24-hour customer service.*

DRIVING

Like most other modern American cities, Atlanta is difficult to negotiate without a motor vehicle. The city's extensive sprawl forces most residents to rely on major highways to get around, even when it's just to take the kids to soccer practice. Encircling metro Atlanta and cutting through its principle counties (DeKalb, Fulton, Cobb) is I–285. Crossing it are I–75 from the northwest and I–85 from the northeast; the two merge into the infamous "Downtown Connector" only to split again and head south to Florida (I–75) or west through the middle of Georgia to Alabama (I–85). Crossing this network from east to west is I–20. Running south from I–285 East is I–675, which provides a shortcut to Henry County and reconnects to I–75 near McDonough. Atlanta's only toll road, GA 400 is a northbound highway that starts near Lenox Square in Buckhead; it heads toward Roswell and Alpharetta, ending near Dahlonega.

The speed limit on interstate highways in the metro Atlanta area is 55 mph. On GA 400 and U.S. 78 (another east–west limited-access highway that goes to Stone Mountain), the speed limit is 65 mph. On I–285 especially, 55 mph is nearly impossible to maintain, as most drivers exceed that substantially. While the local traffic-enforcement authorities seem to have thrown their hands up in resignation, occasionally they do crack down and pull over the most flagrant speeders. By and large, they won't bother you until you hit 65 mph. Rule of thumb? Go with the flow, not faster.

On secondary streets, posted speed limits average about 35 mph, depending on the number of lanes. In school zones 25 mph is the norm when the blinker light is flashing, and the limit is often vigorously enforced by radar-toting police posted nearby. Right turns on red are permitted following a complete stop.

Except in downtown and Midtown, Atlanta's streets lack any semblance of an orderly grid pattern. Midtown is the most gridlike zone, with east–west streets bearing numbers running from 4th to 27th. City streets are often one-way, especially in downtown and Midtown, where narrow roadways make two-way traffic impractical. Street signs are difficult to see, especially at night, and sometimes are missing altogether. On newer, wide streets and major thoroughfares, street signs are often suspended overhead, making them easy to spot well before you need to make a turn. Some streets change names in the mid-course, apparently without any rhyme or reason. For instance, North Druid Hills Road—which goes nowhere near Druid Hills—becomes Valley Brook Road at Lawrenceville Highway. Downtown's streets are named for notable citizens, so as one leader falls from grace and another comes into favor, the city renames at will. For newcomers, a good street atlas, available at most office-supply stores, is essential.

Georgia law requires drivers and front-seat passengers to wear seat belts while the vehicle is in operation, and children 4 and younger must be buckled into appropriate safety seats in the rear. Children 5 to 12 years old must sit in the rear seat if the vehicle is equipped with air bags. Georgia law dictates that drivers who fail to use the proper child-safety restraints incur one point on their driving record for the first offense and two points for second and subsequent offenses. Violators also pay a fine of $50 for the first offense and $100 for the second and subsequent offenses.

In Georgia, vehicles, not the individual drivers, must have liability insurance; failure to maintain proper insurance usually results in a six-month license suspension. Most of the 10 counties require an emissions inspection every two years for most newer-model vehicles. If the model year of your vehicle is an odd year you must have it inspected every odd year; even-year models must be inspected every even year. Georgia drivers who accumulate 15 points on their license for moving violations or any other infractions within a 24-month period are subject to suspension of their license.

licenses & registration

Georgia requires first-time drivers to pass a written test covering traffic rules and road signs, an eye exam, and a driving test. Drivers with an expired out-of-state license or a Georgia license that expired more than two years ago must pass an eye test and a driving test. License renewals may be obtained as much as 150 days in advance of expiration and require an eye exam. New permanent residents of the state must obtain a Georgia driver's license within

30 days of moving here; those who are 18 years old or older and who surrender a valid license from another state when applying for a Georgia license need to pass only an eye exam. New residents must present their social-security cards and evidence of residence (a utility bill, bank statement, or lease or contract of sale), and all drivers under age 18 must present proof that they've attended an approved drug-and-alcohol course. Non-U.S. citizens must present proper INS documentation when they apply for a Georgia driver's license.

The license fee is $15 and the license is good for four years, expiring on the holder's birthday of the renewing year. Veterans and active-duty National Guard members receive their licenses free. You can get your new Georgia driver's license at any of the posts of the **Georgia State Patrol** (404/657–9300, www.ganet.org/dps) scattered throughout the metro area. If you are renewing, you can also do so at an office in your local Kroger grocery store. When you obtain or renew your driver's license, you may indicate your desire to be an organ donor and you may register to vote. Georgia also issues nondrivers' photo ID cards at any driver's license examination office at a cost of $10.

If you change your address you must apply for a new license—one with your correct address—within 60 days of moving. Be sure to bring evidence of your new address, such as a utility bill or bank statement. If you change your name by marriage or otherwise, you also must obtain a new license within 60 days. Either change may be made at any of the Kroger locations. A replacement license, valid for the current renewal period, is issued once in any four-year period, free of charge.

New, permanent Georgia residents are required to obtain Georgia tags within 30 days of moving to the state. Prior to issuing tags, some jurisdictions require that certain vehicles have emissions-inspection certification. You can have your vehicle tested at myriad locations around the metro area for a nominal fee. When you apply for tags, bring your original title documents, previous registration, proof of insurance, and (if required) emissions-inspection certification.

DEPARTMENT OF MOTOR VEHICLES

Each county maintains its own motor-vehicle division, and satellite offices are usually scattered around each county. The motor-vehicle office of the county in which you reside can provide further information.

Cherokee County DMV *100 North St., Canton, 770/479–0523; 7545 N. Main St., Woodstock, 770/924–4099.*

Clayton County DMV *Courthouse Annex Three Bldg., 121 S. McDonough St., Jonesboro, 770/477–3331; Clayton Commons Shopping Center, 5389 Jonesboro Rd., Lake City, no phone.*

Cobb County DMV *700 S. Cobb Dr., Marietta; Government Service Center, 4400 Lower Roswell Rd., Marietta; Market Square Shopping Center, 2950 Canton Hwy., Marietta; Government Service Center, 4700 Austell Rd., Marietta; 770/528–8247 24-hour help line.*

DeKalb County DMV *4380 Memorial Dr., Decatur; 1358 Dresden Dr., Brookhaven; 1 South DeKalb Mall, I–20 at Candler Rd., Decatur; 404/284–8901.*

Douglas County DMV *8700 Hospital Dr., Douglasville, 770/949–2309.*

Fayette County DMV *140 W. Stonewall Ave., Suite 109, Fayetteville, 770/461–3611.*

Forsyth County DMV *110 E. Main St., Cumming, 770/781–2112.*

Fulton County DMV *Fulton County Bldg., 141 Pryor St., Room 1106, Downtown, 404/730–6100 (all Fulton County locations); 7741 Roswell Rd., Roswell; Kroger, Haynes Bridge Shopping Center, 3000 Old Alabama Rd., Alpharetta; 11913 Wills Rd., Alpharetta; 5600 Stonewall Tell Rd., College Park; Hightower Station shopping center, 2636 Martin Luther King Jr. Dr., Suite 12, Southwest Atlanta; 677 Fairburn Rd., Southwest Atlanta (for senior citizens only and only open Mon.–Wed. 10–3); 6500 Vernon Woods Dr., Sandy Springs (for senior citizens only and only open Tues.–Thurs. 9–3).*

Gwinnett County DMV *Gwinnett Justice Administration Center, 750 S. Perry St., Lawrenceville, 770/822–8801 24-hour information (all locations) or 770/822–8818; 5030 Georgia Bell Ct., No. 1030, Norcross; Interlochen Village, 5270 Peachtree Pkwy., Peachtree Corners; 2280 Oak Rd., Snellville.*

Henry County DMV *345 Phillips Dr., McDonough, 770/954–2471; 130 Berry St., Stockbridge, 770/389–7820; Court Council/Police Station, 20 E. Main St. S, Hampton, no phone (open only Thurs.); City Hall, 3644 GA 42, Locust Grove, no phone (open only Tues.).*

tolls

Atlanta's only toll road is GA 400. If you access or exit the highway near Lenox Square, the toll is 50¢, but you can exit or enter at I–285 and not pay the toll. Wisdom dictates avoiding GA 400 at peak rush hours. If you drive GA 400 daily, you may wish to obtain a "Cruise Card" from the **Georgia Department of Transportation** (Piedmont Center, 3525 Piedmont Rd., Bldg. 7, Suite 205, 30305, Buckhead, 404/365–7790). Applications may be requested by mail or picked up at the office; renewals may be paid for with a credit card supplied at the time of application. The "Cruise Card" ($40 paid in advance) enables drivers to zip through the toll plaza without stopping to plunk exact change into the basket. Each time you use the cruise lane a scanner reads the electronic device decal mounted on your windshield and 50¢ is automatically deducted from your account. If you use the cruise lane without a "Cruise Card," the fine is $25.50 per occurrence.

traffic

Traffic jams have become as rampant around Atlanta as in any other large city. During rush hours (6–9 AM and 3–7 PM), I–285 can be absolutely infuriating as traffic moves at a crawl. Similarly, GA 400, a major conduit from the northern 'burbs to Buckhead, is a solid strip of vehicles during rush hours. If you live in a northern area and have a plane to catch, allow at least one additional hour of travel time to reach Hartsfield Atlanta International Airport during those hours.

Complicating the flow of traffic in metro Atlanta is the apparent failure of every municipality to synchronize traffic lights with speed limits. It was rumored at the time of the 1996 Centennial Olympic Games that a system governing traffic-light changes would be established, but the games are long over, and it hasn't happened. You often can find, as a result, that you leave one newly changed-to-green traffic light only to watch the very next one turn red, while the one after that is green, and so forth, creating a string of Christmas lights ahead of you. At some intersections equipped with turn arrows, the interval is curiously brief, so it's important to be ready to go when they change. Making all this worse is the bad habit Atlanta drivers have of not using their turn signals to indicate what they have on their minds.

At any time—including 3 AM—metro Atlanta's highways are likely to become traffic-jammed. When traffic is backed up, it's a good idea to use secondary roads, although lately even these have proven to be clogged at peak hours. Major surface thoroughfares, such as Northside Drive, DeKalb Avenue from downtown to Decatur, and Roswell Road just south of Roswell, have switch lanes that function as inbound lanes in the morning and outbound lanes in the afternoon. Instructional lighting over these lanes indicates their direction at any given moment. What you see is either a green arrow or a red "X".

GAS STATIONS

Georgia has one of the lowest state gasoline taxes in the United States, so filling your tank is relatively inexpensive. Most gas stations in the 10 counties pump fuel and sell groceries, maps, and automotive supplies. Self-service is the norm, although for an extra few cents per gallon you can get full service, which means an attendant pumps your gas and should check your fluids and clean your windshield. Old-fashioned, full-service, 24-hour stations are few and far between in the metro area. **BP-Northlake Car Care Center** (4121 LaVista Rd., Tucker, 770/938–1174), at exit 28 of I–285, is one full-service station in the area. It's not exactly a 24-hour station, as it won't work on cars at 2 AM, but the mechanics will check your coolant and the air in your tires.

GEOGRAPHY

Atlanta was founded on a ridge that now runs the length of Peachtree Street downtown and forms a watershed divide between the Gulf of Mexico and the Atlantic Ocean. The city lies at an elevation of 800 ft to more than 1,400 ft above sea level, with the lower areas on the south side of town and the higher to the north, toward the Blue Ridge Mountains. Rolling, wooded terrain in the residential north gives way to level land in the south, where Hartsfield Atlanta International Airport stands.

From its urban center, Atlanta fans out toward the neighborhoods. Several downtown-style areas, with their own high-rise office and apartment buildings, encircle downtown proper. Among these is Midtown, framed by North Avenue to Pershing Point, where Peachtree Road intersects with West Peachtree Street. Peachtree continues north to Buckhead, another cluster of commercial and residential towers. Beyond Buckhead, the outer perimeter has started developing its own set of high-rise clusters, at U.S. 41 and I–285 (known as Galleria) in Northwest Atlanta and at Peachtree-Dunwoody Road and I–285 in Dunwoody.

To the east of downtown and Midtown lie Virginia-Highland, Poncey-Highland, and Inman Park.

Decatur, to the immediate east of the city of Atlanta, was founded in 1823 and retains its villagelike charm and character. Historic towns such as Marietta, Roswell, and Jonesboro, which saw its own Civil War battle, have been integrated into the metroplex while retaining their traditions and character.

HOLIDAYS

During the holidays listed here, all city and county government offices in metro Atlanta are closed, as are banks and sometimes other businesses. In addition, state offices are closed for Confederate Memorial Day and some businesses also close for Christmas Eve.

New Year's Day January 1.

Martin Luther King Jr. Day Third Monday in January.

Presidents' Day Third Monday in February.

Confederate Memorial Day April 26.

Memorial Day Last Monday in May.

Independence Day July 4.

Labor Day First Monday in September.

Columbus Day The Monday closest to October 12.

Thanksgiving Day Fourth Thursday in November.

Christmas Day December 25.

LIQUOR LAWS

Packaged alcohol may be sold from 8:30 AM until midnight in Georgia jurisdictions that permit its sale. Not all do; the state still has many dry counties and cities. Package stores may sell all alcoholic beverages, and grocery stores may sell beer and wine but not liquor. Neither type of outlet may sell alcohol on Sunday, though restaurants in much of the metro area can serve it. However, local jurisdictions are empowered to set their own standards and may prohibit all alcohol sales on Sunday, as is the case in Henry County. To avoid confusion or disappointment, check well in advance of any planned events that may fall on a Sunday. Cities and counties may also prohibit the sale of beverage alcohol on election day, because once upon a corrupt time some politicians bought votes with shots of whiskey. In addition, state law generally prohibits direct shipments of wine to Georgia residents and makes the shipper a felon on second offense.

You must be at least 21 years old—and be able to prove it with proper ID—to buy alcohol in Georgia. The city of Alpharetta, in Fulton County, requires businesses to card anyone who wishes to purchase alcohol, no matter how old he or she may appear. If you do not have a valid driver's license, you should carry a state-issued photo ID card if you plan on buying a cocktail or a six-pack.

NO-SMOKING

Georgia's local jurisdictions regulate smoking in public places via a variety of ordinances. Throughout the 10 counties, smoking isn't permitted in most stores and public buildings. Hospitals are no-smoking, and so is most of Hartsfield Atlanta International Airport, which has special areas set aside for smokers. Restaurants usually designate entire rooms as smoking sections; however, some establishments are too small to do so and instead prohibit smoking entirely. But some restaurants don't maintain separate spaces for nonsmokers. Bed-and-breakfast inns customarily restrict smoking to common areas such as porches and sitting rooms, although some larger B&Bs and most hotels and motels reserve guest rooms and sometimes entire floors for smoking patrons. If you cannot tolerate tobacco smoke or if you can't enjoy yourself without a cigarette, check with these businesses in advance.

PARKING

Downtown, Midtown, and Buckhead are becoming parking nightmares, and it's very difficult to find parking on the street. Parking in Virginia-Highland and Little Five Points is a veritable horror, and only a few lots are available to accommodate visitors. Atlanta, Decatur, and other municipalities have metered curb parking, but there is often a limit on how long you may park. Times vary on street meters, and some accept only quarters. In Marietta, Lawrenceville, Tucker, and similar small towns throughout the metro area, municipal street parking is first come, first served, with no meters.

In the city of Atlanta, valet parking isn't allowed during the day, but it is available at night at most of the better restaurants and hotels. Be aware, however, that a few charge for the service. If you're coming into town for an evening's entertainment, you'll find that lots fill early in the evening. In both downtown and Midtown, parking for events, especially at the Fox Theatre and Woodruff Arts Center, can get expensive—about $6 or $7. But just a block or two away from major venues, charges are more reasonable. For sporting events at Turner Field, the Georgia Dome, and Philips Arena, parking costs about $10, depending on the event. MARTA, if you can take it, is the best way to get to Woodruff Arts Center, which has Arts Center Station, a connected stop that's accessible via a covered passageway. MARTA is also a great way to get to Philips Arena, where the station (Dome/GWCC/Philips Arena/CNN Center) is practically inside the complex.

rules & enforcement

Metro-area parking regulations vary. Within Atlanta city limits, drivers encounter numerous street signs that forbid parking, limit duration for on-street parking, or restrict parking to certain hours. Residential neighborhoods off Peachtree Street have become sensitive to the abuse of street parking in their tree-shaded areas, and many of these streets, such as 17th Street near Peachtree Street, restrict parking. Parking isn't allowed along curbs painted yellow, and blue paint restricts those spaces to vehicles for people with mobility problems. White curbs indicate that parking is permitted. For obvious reasons, you may not park in marked fire lanes; violations can result in fines or in some cases towing.

You can pay parking fines by mail, using the envelope left on your windshield by the ticketing officer. Fines for parking violations vary throughout the metro area. In the city of Decatur, for instance, they range from $15 to $50, the latter being the charge levied for parking in a fire lane. In all localities, the fine for parking in a handicap-reserved space can run as high as $500. In most jurisdictions the actual amount is set by a judge, so parking in one of these spaces also means a day in court. The most aggressively enforced parking regulations are at Hartsfield Atlanta International Airport, where foot-patrol officers vigorously—and with alacrity—write tickets for people who leave their vehicle in front of a terminal for any length of time.

If your car is towed from the street, you must contact the authorities of the jurisdiction that's doing the towing. Fines vary from one jurisdiction to another, and additional charges for storing your vehicle may apply as well. If you've parked on private property, such as in a business parking lot but without doing business at that location, the property owner is the one to contact to locate your vehicle. Businesses in Virginia-Highland guard their spaces with particular zeal and are quick to tow violators.

parking lots

Major commercial zones include numerous parking garages—often attached to banks, hotels, and office buildings—where the public may park for a fee. If you're doing business or dining in the connecting establishment, your parking may be complimentary if you have your ticket validated before leaving. Shopping centers and malls have extensive lots and garages where shoppers can park for free; some, such as Lenox Square and Phipps Plaza, offer valet parking for $3–$5.

Downtown and Midtown have a fair number of pay parking lots, which may or may not be attended. In those that are unattended, you insert the required amount of cash into a metal box that has numbered slots corresponding to specific parking spaces. Be sure to remember your space number and put your money in the correct slot. Occasionally, scurrilous characters loiter in unattended lots claiming to be attendants, in order to take your fee. Legitimate parking attendants should be able to give you a receipt and perhaps also place a ticket on the windshield. Don't pay anyone collecting parking fees in self-park lots without proper ID.

Here are several convenient parking garages in the more-congested areas of metro Atlanta's shopping, business, and entertainment districts.

BUCKHEAD

Lenox Marketplace 3535 Peachtree Rd., 404/760–1370 security. **Phipps Plaza** 3500 Peachtree Rd., 404/261–7910, ext. 63. **Sheraton Buckhead Hotel** 3405 Lenox Rd., 404/261–9250, ext. 471. **Swissôtel** 3391 Peachtree Rd., 404/365–6455. **Tower Place** 3340 Peachtree Rd., 404/262–1587.

DOWNTOWN ATLANTA

Central Parking System (valet parking only) 55 Marietta St., at Forsyth St., 404/688–6492; 55 Park Place Bldg., 55 Park Pl., 404/523–3163; 42 Auburn Ave., at Peachtree Center Ave. (behind the building), 404/577–1968; 45 John Wesley Dobbs Ave., 404/523–4661. **CNN Center Decks** 30 Spring St. (entrance on Centennial Olympic Park Dr.), 404/521–0691. **Georgia Pacific Center** 60 John Wesley Dobbs Ave., 404/524–1909. **Peachtree Center** 227 Courtland St., 404/681–0415. **Standard Parking** 75 Piedmont Ave., at Auburn Ave., 404/522–2713. **System Parking Inc.** (across the street from Rialto Theatre) 102 Cone St., 404/222–9497. **Underground Atlanta** 75 Martin Luther King Jr. Dr., 404/577–2202.

MIDTOWN ATLANTA

Fox Theatre (event parking only) 711 W. Peachtree St. or 222 14th St., 404/876–2571. **Georgian Terrace hotel** 459 Peachtree St., across from Fox Theatre, 404/881–6076. **Medical Arts Building** 384 Peachtree St., 404/522–2068. **Midtown Bell South Building** (lot across the street) 662 W. Peachtree St., near Fox Theatre, 404/847–3600. **Midtown Exchange Building** 730 Peachtree St., at 4th St., 404/685–9170.

DECATUR

Holiday Inn Towne Center II 130 Ponce de Leon Ave., 404/377–9959.

PERSONAL SECURITY

As in any urban area, you should exercise a reasonable level of caution in order to stay safe in metro Atlanta. At night, in particular, know where you're going and how you expect to get there. Downtown Atlanta's reputation as a dangerous neighborhood is somewhat exaggerated, but on the street you should nevertheless be alert to who's around you and what's going on. Most major downtown streets are well lit and patrolled by uniformed police officers; most good bars and music clubs have security; and MARTA employs its own security force. In preparation for the 1996 Olympic Games, the city trained "ambassadors" to roam downtown beats and assist visitors who may be lost or in distress. The program remains in place; ambassadors may be identified by their uniforms and pith helmets. These smiling people help ward off panhandlers and will happily conduct the lone damsel to her hotel.

PUBLIC TRANSPORTATION

Metro Atlanta's public-transportation system, the Metropolitan Atlanta Rapid Transit Authority (MARTA), is limited to the two major metro counties: DeKalb and Fulton. Cobb and Henry counties have some public transportation; Cobb's ties into MARTA, but Henry's does not. Cherokee, Clayton, Douglas, Fayette, Forsyth, and Gwinnett counties don't have public transportation.

MARTA comprises two components, bus and rapid rail, which are linked; riders can transfer between the bus system and the rapid-rail system. However, cross-town travel—from Emory University to Northlake Mall or to Buckhead, for instance—requires a lot of transferring. The fare to ride on MARTA's rapid-rail and bus systems is $1.50, paid using tokens purchased from machines at each MARTA rail station or from a MARTA Ride store.

MARTA Ride *Hartsfield Atlanta International Airport (near baggage claim), 404/848–3498, daily 7 AM–10 PM; 30 Alabama St., Five Points, 404/848–3205, daily 7 AM–6 PM; Lenox Square in Lenox Station, across from Lenox Square mall and Marriott, 404/848–3327, daily 8 AM–4 PM; 2424 Piedmont Rd., at Lindbergh Station, across from MARTA headquarters, 404/848–4100, daily 8 AM–4 PM.*

bus

Cobb Community Transit CCT connects with MARTA at the Arts Center station on 14th Street. Other limited connections operate weekdays between midtown Atlanta and the Marietta area. Service is generally available from East and South Cobb. The fare on CCT buses is $1.25; a 10-ride pass costs $11.25 and a monthly pass $45. *450 N. Cobb Pkwy., Marietta, 770/427–4444 or 770/427–2222 (customers with disabilities).*

Henry County Transit The free service is designed to aid Henry County residents who have transportation difficulties and who are elderly or have disabilities. Transportation is available only to points within the county; most riders use it to go to the grocery store and to medical appointments. If you need a ride, call to make arrangements a week in advance. The system doesn't operate before 9 AM, and return trips should be scheduled for just after lunch. *45 Work Camp Rd., McDonough, 770/954–2033.*

MARTA The bus system serving Fulton and DeKalb counties has more than 100 routes traversing metro Atlanta. Bus frequency depends on the day of the week, time of day, and route and ranges from 8 to 55 minutes. The fare is $1.75 one-way; transfers between buses and to MARTA rapid rail are free. A weekly pass costs $13, a monthly $52.50. *2424 Pied-mont Rd., Buckhead, 404/848–4711; 404/848–5389 people with disabilities; 404/848–5662 TDD Spanish-language information available for all.*

rapid rail

MARTA Under constant expansion, the rapid-rail system has a north–south line and an east–west line. The two lines cross at Five Points station downtown. The south line goes directly to Hartsfield Atlanta International Airport. On weekdays, trains start running shortly after 4:30 AM from Hartsfield, Dunwoody, Indian Creek, and Hamilton Holmes; the last trains depart around 1:30 AM. On weekends, they run 5 AM–1 AM. Most MARTA rail stations have generous free short-term parking, but the Bankhead, Civic Center, Decatur, and North Avenue stations have no parking at all, and the Arts Center station and Midtown stops offer only severely limited parking. Long-term parking in secured areas ($3 per day) is available at the Brookhaven, College Park, Doraville, Dunwoody, Lenox, Lindbergh, and Medical Arts stations. Transfers between trains and to buses are free. The one-way fare is $1.50; a weekly pass costs $12 and a monthly $45. *2424 Piedmont Rd., Buckhead, 404/848–4711; 404/848–5389 passengers with disabilities; 404/848–5662 TDD (Spanish-language information available).*

taxi

Taxi companies in the metro area have an unfortunate reputation for shabby vehicles and unprofessional, badly dressed drivers. Many seem to have a calculated habit of not carrying change, even for small bills, so if you're taking a taxi, have small bills on hand. Many drivers are foreign nationals who may not speak English well or know the city as well as they should, although they often try very hard to provide good service.

Buckhead Safety Cab The service area of this one consistently good taxi company is limited to Buckhead, Midtown, downtown, and Hartsfield. With 24 hours' notice it will arrange a pickup anywhere within reasonable distance from Buckhead ($20 limit) to go to the airport. *2541 E. Paces Ferry Rd., Buckhead, 404/233–1152.*

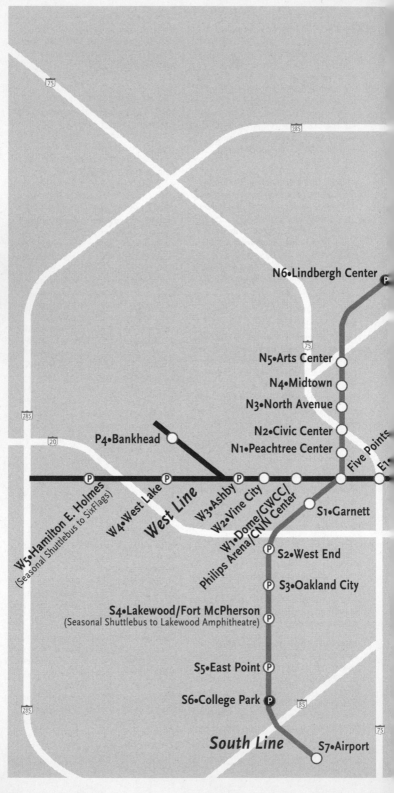

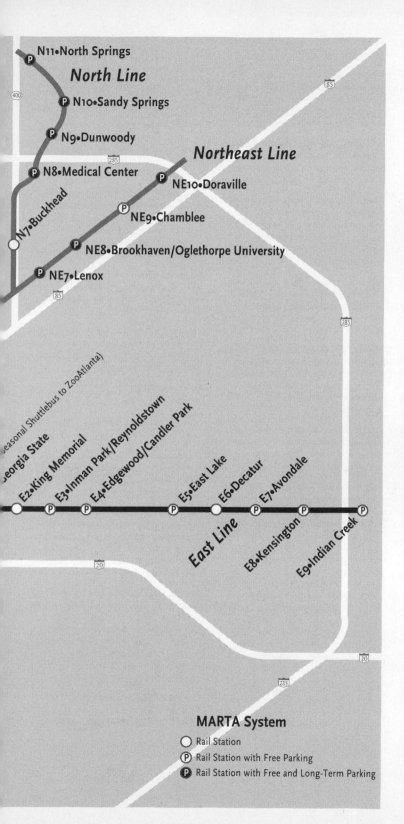

PUBLICATIONS

Art & Antiques The glossy monthly is devoted to the fine and decorative arts, including graphic arts, and also covers homes of collectors. *815/734–1162 subscriptions; 770/955–5656 local number.*

Art Papers This highly regarded tabloid, published six times a year, presents in-depth articles on art and prints critiques of local exhibitions. *404/588–1837.*

Atlanta Business Chronicle Appearing every Friday, this substantial, business-oriented weekly newspaper is a must-read for anyone interested in the metro area's commercial life. *404/249–1010 subscriptions.*

Atlanta Citymag Appearing eight times a year, this glossy publication (formerly called *Dossier*) focuses on the businesses and lifestyles of entrepreneurial Atlantans. *404/231–5433 subscriptions.*

Atlanta Daily World Despite its title, this respected voice of Atlanta's African-American community appears only a few times a week. It's one of the nation's oldest black-owned and -published newspapers. *404/659–1110.*

Atlanta Homes & Lifestyle This glossy monthly focuses on area residential design and local lifestyle and personalities. *404/252–6670 subscriptions.*

Atlanta Journal-Constitution The city's chief daily newspaper is a combination of two papers that in past decades were published independently. They maintain separate editorial boards but share news and feature staff. On weekdays, the *Constitution* appears in the morning and the *Journal* in the evening. On weekends and holidays, they combine to publish a single edition. For information on current cultural and special events, see the Friday "Weekend" section, appearing in both papers, and the Saturday "Leisure" section. Other sections concentrate on suburban and neighborhood issues and news. *404/522–4141 subscriptions.*

Atlanta Magazine The city's glossy monthly covers everything from politics, education, and the arts to dining, sports, and lifestyle. *404/872–3100 subscriptions.*

Atlanta Now The bimonthly magazine is available free through Atlanta Convention and Visitors Bureau centers and at hotels and attractions around the city. *404/521–6600 or 800/ATLANTA.*

Atlanta Sports & Fitness The free monthly magazine covers local recreation opportunities and is available at sporting-goods stores and other area locations. *404/843–2257.*

Atlanta Tribune Issues and news of interest to the city's upscale African-American community are the focus of this well-designed monthly magazine. *770/587–0501 subscriptions.*

Atlanta Wine Report A monthly publication available free at package stores, restaurants, wine shops, and other selected outlets, the report lists tastings and special wine-focused events throughout the metro area. *678/985–9494.*

Business to Business The city's Fortune 500 companies are the main audience of this monthly magazine. *404/888–0555 subscriptions.*

Catalyst This bimonthly business magazine is aimed at the metro area's young professionals and entrepreneurs. *404/888–0555 subscriptions.*

Creative Loafing Entertainment takes center stage in this free popular weekly paper; it's available in boxes at nightclubs, bars, bookstores, and restaurants. *404/688–5623.*

Dunwoody Crier The local weekly publication is free and focuses on news and personalities in Dunwoody and the surrounding areas. *770/451–4147.*

Five Points: A Journal of Literature and Art Based at Georgia State University's Department of English, this national tri-annual publication focuses on art and literature. *404/651–0071 subscriptions, www.webdelsol.com/Five_Points.*

Georgia Magazine Published monthly by Oglethorpe Power, this is Georgia's only statewide lifestyle magazine. Residents of the west metro area—in parts of Cobb County, for instance—may receive it gratis if they get their power from an electrical membership cooperative. *770/270–7071 subscriptions.*

Georgia Trend The monthly publication surveys business issues around the state but is decidedly Atlanta-centric. *770/931–9410 subscriptions.*

Gwinnett Daily Post Gwinnett County news and lifestyle are the meat of this suburban daily. *770/339–5845 subscriptions.*

The Hudspeth Report This free tabloid publication covers developments in dining and nightlife and lets readers know what's closing and what's opening. *404/255–3220.*

Jewish Times Atlanta's Jewish community keeps in touch not only with local news but also national and international items of interest through this weekly newspaper. *404/252–1600, ext. 205, subscriptions.*

Jezebel Fashion, entertainment, and lifestyle are the topics covered in this glossy monthly magazine about and for upscale Atlantans. *404/870–0123.*

Knife and Fork A monthly newsletter devoted to reviews of local restaurants—sometimes with tips about out-of-town dining—keeps Atlanta up to date on what's new, what's good, and what's not in the opinion of its French-born publisher, Christiane Lauterbach. *404/387–2775 subscriptions.*

Marietta Daily Journal The newspaper highlights the goings-on in Marietta and Cobb County, with a focus on the jurisdiction's politics, often to the dismay of its elected officials. *770/795–2300 subscriptions.*

Mundo Hispánico A Spanish-language newspaper in business since 1980, this free weekly covers chiefly local events of interest to the Atlanta Hispanic community but also includes some global news. *770/590–0881 subscriptions.*

Museums & Galleries This digest-size bimonthly, available free at galleries and other places, reports the happenings in Atlanta's myriad art galleries. *770/992–7808.*

The Neighbor newspapers The North Fulton edition of these weeklies reports on that area only, and the DeKalb *Neighbor* features events in that county. *770/428–9411 subscriptions.*

Our Kids Issues related to children and parenting dominate this monthly magazine. *404/256–4477.*

Presenting the Season The Atlanta social season is the reason for this glossy quarterly. *770/998–1118 subscriptions.*

Southern Voice The South's most widely read gay and lesbian weekly newspaper offers information on events and topics of special interest to the community. It's available free in boxes at package stores, bookstores, nightclubs, restaurants, and other locations throughout the city. *404/876–1819.*

Style The Atlanta lifestyle-and-arts bimonthly is published in partnership with the Woodruff Arts Center. *404/252–1600, ext. 206.*

Where Atlanta Shopping and dining, special events and nightclubs, and the arts and entertainment: this monthly covers all these subjects, and more. Available free at selected outlets—mostly hotels, bars, and restaurants that advertise in the publication—it may also be ordered by subscription. Its free digest-size semiannual, *Dining Out*, is available at the same venues. *404/843–9800 information and subscriptions.*

RADIO STATIONS

am
550 WDUN News, talk

590 WDWD Children's programming

610 WPLO Spanish

640 WGST News, talk

680 WCNN Sports talk

750 WSB News, talk

790 WQXI Sports talk

860 WAEC Christian talk

920 WAFS Contemporary Christian music and ministry

1010 WGUN Christian ministry and information

1050 WPBS Gospel

1060 WKNG Traditional country, news

1080 WFTD Southern Gospel and ministry

1100 WWWE Christian music, ministry, news, and weather in Spanish

1190 WGKA Classical, jazz, arts, CNN news

1240 WGGA Music of the 1950s and '60s

1270 WYXC Country, news, sports, weather

1290 WCHK News, talk

1330 **WBTR** News, talk

1340 **WALR** Gospel

1380 **WAOK** Gospel, talk

1480 **WYZE** Gospel and ministries

fm

88.5 **WRAS** College

89.3 **WRFG** Public radio/folk, Celtic, reggae, jazz, blues

90.1 **WABE** NPR news, classical and jazz

91.1 **WREK** College

91.9 **WCLK** Blues and jazz, African-American issues

92.1 **WBTR** Country

92.5 **WEKS** Country

92.9 **WZGC** Classic rock

94/94.1 **WSTR** Contemporary hits

94.9 **WPCH** Easy listening, contemporary rock

95.5 **WYAP** Top 40

96.1 **WKLS** Rock

97.1 **WFOX** Rock-and-roll oldies

97.5 **WHTA** Hip hop, rap

98.5 **WSB** Adult contemporary

99.7 **WNNX** New rock

100.1 **WNSY** Oldies

100.7 **WGHR** Alternative, urban, and electronic

101.5 **WKHX** Country, talk

102.7 **WCKS** Adult contemporary

102.9 **WMJE** Adult contemporary

103.3 **WVEE** Urban rhythm and blues, hip hop

104.1 **WJZF** Jazz

104.7 **WALR** Urban rhythm and blues

105.5 **WYAI** Country and news

105.7 **WGST** News and talk, simulcast on 640 AM

106.7 **WYAY** Country, talk

107.5 **WAMJ** Rhythm-and-blues oldies

RECYCLING

Most jurisdictions in the 10 counties don't require recycling or separation of cans and bottles (Georgia doesn't have a bottle-deposit law) from garbage and newspapers. The City of Atlanta offers optional recycling and will supply can-collecting bins to home owners. **BFI** (404/792–2660), a private trash-garbage collection company, picks up recyclable material.

In unincorporated DeKalb County, home owners must separate lawn clippings from other trash into special biodegradable paper bags (sold at grocery stores, hardware stores, and other locations). Alternatively, yard clippings may be placed in a separate garbage can with the lid off. Clippings are collected in designated trucks by the county sanitation department on a schedule that varies from street to street. On the first pick-up day of the week in DeKalb County, **DeKalb Sanitation** (404/294–2900) collects aluminum cans bagged in plastic grocery bags. Newspapers, packed in brown grocery bags or stacked and tied, are collected on the week's second pick-up day.

Some jurisdictions have found creative ways of coaxing home owners into recycling. Believing that an ordinance would be difficult to enforce and too costly to monitor, the City of Decatur gives citizens an economic incentive to recycle. City residents must dispose of trash in 8- to 33-gallon "pay-as-you throw" bags, which cost anywhere from 30¢ to $1 depending on size. The more you throw away, the more you pay. Ten retail outfits, city hall, and various stores (Kroger, Publix, Winn-Dixie) sell the bags. The **City of Decatur Department of Sanitation** (404/377–5571) can provide information about Decatur recycling.

Despite these efforts, most metro-area recycling is done by private individuals and groups. You can find recycling stations at community clubs, grocery stores, and similar locations. Some counties have "Clean and Beautiful" organizations that can provide recycling information. Otherwise, you can contact the sanitation department of the city, county, or jurisdiction in which you live. For-profit recycling has also arrived.

Wise Recycling Centers *3382 Shallowford Rd., Chamblee, Tues.–Sat. 9:30–5; 3655 Memorial Dr., Decatur, weekdays 9:30–*

4:30, Sat. 9:30–3; 5922 Fairburn Rd., Doraville, weekdays 9:30–5, Sat. 9:30–3; 3400 Hamilton Blvd., Hapeville, open weekdays 8–5, Sat. 8–12:30; 404/761–2318 or 800/851–1190.

TAX & TIP

sales tax & beyond

Sales tax in the metro area is generally 7%, but in some jurisdictions it's as low as 5% (Cobb). Sales tax in Gwinnett County is 6%. Hotel-motel taxes range from 5% in Henry and Clayton counties to 14% in Fulton County. Cities may charge additional hotel-motel taxes. Ad valorem taxes likewise vary widely, with the more populous Fulton and DeKalb counties charging more than suburban jurisdictions. Property taxes are highest in the city of Atlanta and lower away from the central city core.

tipping

In restaurants, tip 15%–20% depending on the quality of the service, less if service has been inadequate. However, if service was fine but you are disappointed with the food, don't take it out on the waitstaff. For large parties (more than six or eight diners) most restaurants automatically add a 20% service charge. If you have brought your own wine and paid a corkage fee, you may add the value of the wine to the total bill and pay the gratuity on that basis, or you may prefer to tip the sommelier directly.

Tip taxi drivers 15% and porters $1–$2 per bag, whether at the airport or at hotels. Valet parking attendants should receive at least $1, depending on the value of your vehicle and how closely they have watched it.

TELEVISION

cable

28 Learning Channel

37 Fox News Channel

39 Fox Family Channel

44 Discovery Channel

50 MTV

52 History Channel

55 Lifetime Network

57 Food Network

59 Home and Garden Network

60 Sci-fi Channel

62 Cartoon Network

63 Nickelodeon

66 American Movie Classics

network

Channel 2 WSB (ABC)

Channel 5 WAGA (Fox)

Channel 11 WXIA (NBC)

Channel 30 WPBA (PBS/AT)

Channel 33 Local access

Channel 46 WGNX (CBS)

Channel 63 WHSG (TBN)

VOTER REGISTRATION

U.S. citizens who live in Georgia may register to vote when they obtain their driver's license. Otherwise, register at the courthouse of the county in which you live; or, in more populous counties, check with the chief administrator's office, as the county may have auxiliary offices open elsewhere for voter registration. Voter-registration applications also may be obtained on-line, on the State of Georgia Web site (www.sos.state.ga.us); you can fill one out electronically, print it out, add your signature, and mail in the application to the Secretary of State's office or to your local county board of registrars office. (Voter-registration lists are no longer the source from which jurors' names are drawn; now you may be called for jury duty if you have registered a motor vehicle.)

Cherokee County Board of Elections and Voter Registration *130 E. Main St., Suite 106, Canton 30114, 770/479–0407.*

Clayton County Board of Registrars *148 Courthouse St., Jonesboro 30236, 770/477–3372.*

Cobb County Board of Elections and Voter Registration *47 Waddell St., Bldg. F, Marietta 30090, 770/528–2581.*

DeKalb County Board of Elections and Voter Registration *4830 Memorial Dr., Suite 300, Decatur 30032, 404/298–4020.*

Douglas County Board of Registrars *8700 Hospital Dr., Room A-1003, Douglasville 30134, 770/920–7217.*

Fayette County Board of Elections and Voter Registration *140 W. Stonewall Ave., Suite 208, Fayetteville 30214, 770/460–5730.*

Forsyth County Board of Elections and Voter Registration *110 E. Main St., Suite 200, Cumming 30040, 770/781–2118.*

Fulton County Board of Elections and Voter Registration *141 Pryor St. SW, Suite 4065, Downtown, 30303, 404/730–7020.*

Gwinnett County Board of Elections and Voter Registration *75 Langley Dr., Lawrenceville 30245, 770/822–8787.*

Henry County Board of Registrars *34 Covington St., McDonough 30253, 770/954–2021.*

Secretary of State *1104 West Tower, 2 Martin Luther King Dr. SE, Downtown, 30334, no phone.*

WEATHER

Without doubt, the most glorious of the metro area's four distinct seasons is spring, when the azaleas and dogwoods bloom, lining Atlanta's thoroughfares with pinks, whites, and blazing reds. But fall is fabulous, too, and rivals spring for color. In between, summer is green with hardwoods and pines. Summer humidity percentages can match the high temperatures, making hot weather seem much hotter. Evenings, however, usually are noticeably cooler. Mercifully short, winter usually gets really cold only in January and February, but March can go out like a lion, sometimes giving the city its most memorable blizzards. Most Atlantans are poorly equipped to deal with the rare snowstorm: drivers don't have snow tires or chains and the towns don't have snow-removal equipment. Besides, those who learned to drive in the South have no clue about how to handle snow in an automobile, so when the white stuff comes down, they stay home.

Annual rainfall in Atlanta is about 48 inches, much of which (or so it seems) falls in wintertime, although August downpours are legendary. Average temperatures range between 52°F (11°C) during the day and 36°F (2°C) at night in January, and 88°F (31°C) daytime and 70°F (21°C) at night in July. Rarely do temperatures drop below 20°F (-6°C) or exceed 100°F (38°C), and then not for very long.

Time & Temperature *770/455–7141 or 770/387–1666.*

Weather Channel *770/226–0000.*

Weather Channel Connection *900/932–8437 (95¢ per minute from a Touch-Tone phone).*

resources for challenges & crises

BABY-SITTING SERVICES

A Friend of the Family You can find a live-in nanny or a Saturday-night baby-sitter through this agency, which serves private, hotel, and convention clients. In business since 1984, the agency charges an initial $75 registration fee and an $11 referral fee per day, each time you use the service to find a sitter; this referral fee is $25 if you give less than 24 hours' notice and $16 for Saturday evenings after 5 PM. The caregiver/sitter charge is $9–$12 per hour for a minimum of four hours. *880 Holcomb Bridge Rd., Roswell, 770/643–3000 permanent help; 770/725–2748 temporary help, www.afriend.com.*

CATERING

In addition to private caterers, many restaurants also cater events. Metro Atlanta's larger caterers include the following:

Chef William Neal Preparations include gourmet and Southern fare for weddings, theme parties, and corporate events. *690 Dalrymple Rd., Sandy Springs, 770/392–0822.*

Jimmy's Smokehouse Bar-B-Q Among the city's busiest caterers, Jimmy Lee Stokes and his wife, Thelma, whip up superior pork barbecue with sauce, potato casserole, and other side dishes. *Corner Scenic Hwy./GA 124 and Everson Rd., Snellville, 770/972–1625.*

Linda Easterlin This outfit specializes in private home catering. *3832 W. Nancy Creek Ct., North Atlanta, 404/255–5146.*

Louisiana's Cajun Cookin' Pete Sellers and his family fire up Louisiana-style barbecue, including deep-fried whole turkeys for Thanksgiving and Christmas. Stop by their shopping-center kiosk for a taste. *5025 Winter's Chapel Rd., Doraville, 770/522–8866.*

Lowcountry Barbecue Catering South Carolina–style barbecue is the focus of this service. Preparations include whole-pig barbecue, low-country shrimp boils, and wild game. (You can get some to go at Lowcountry Barbecue Catering Express, 1281 Collier Rd., Buckhead, 404/352–1121.) On-site holiday cooking and corporate events are specialties. *2000 S. Pioneer Dr., Smyrna, 404/799–8049, www.lowcountrybarbecue.com.*

The Preferred Caterer This kosher caterer specializes in weddings, bar and bat mitzvahs, and other special occasions. *Shops of Buckhead, 2221 Peachtree Rd., Buckhead, 404/872–2466.*

Proof of the Pudding The long-established caterer can handle both private events and corporate affairs. *2039 Monroe Dr., Buckhead, 404/892–2359.*

Tuohy's Catering Although the company works in various culinary styles and offers great desserts for private parties and corporate events, Mediterranean-style fare is its specialty. *442 Armour Cir., Midtown, 404/875–3885.*

The Varsity Jr. All of the menu items of the popular Atlanta landmark are available for catering at children's parties. *1085 Lindbergh Dr., Midtown, 404/261–8843.*

CHILD CRISIS

ChildKind This nonprofit agency specializes in helping children with AIDS. *828 W. Peachtree St., Suite 201, Midtown, 404/882–8313.*

Children's Healthcare of Atlanta at Egleston The children's hospital has its main site on the campus of Emory University, but it also operates a number of satellite clinics in metro Atlanta. In 1999 it forged a partnership with Scottish

Rite, another children's hospital. *Emory University, 1405 Clifton Rd., Emory, 404/325–6000; 404/325–6400 24-hour nurse advice line.*

Children's Healthcare of Atlanta at Scottish Rite A premier children's hospital, now in partnership with Emory-based Egleston, this provider has satellite clinics all over the Atlanta area, in addition to its major hospital in Dunwoody. *1001 Johnson Ferry Rd., Dunwoody, 404/256–5252; 404/250–5437 24-hour nurse advice line.*

Hughes Spalding Children's Hospital Serving children throughout the metro area, this children's hospital is affiliated with Grady Health Systems and Grady Memorial Hospital. Grady Health Systems also has 10 neighborhood health centers around the metro Atlanta area that focus on the needs of inner-city children. *35 Butler St., Downtown, 404/616–6600.*

COAST GUARD

Coast Guard Auxiliary Operations Center The center, at Lake Lanier, is open only during boating season, mid-May to mid-September. *770/967–2322.*

CONSUMER PROTECTION

Better Business Bureau of Metropolitan Atlanta *101 Edgewood Ave., Downtown, 30303, 404/688–4910.*

Governor's Office of Consumer Affairs *Sloppy Floyd Bldg., 2 Martin Luther King Jr. Dr., Plaza Level East, Suite 356, Downtown, 404/651–8600 or 800/869–1123.*

COUNSELING & REFERRALS

aids advice

AIDS Legal Project This is a project of the Atlanta Legal Aid Society and is staffed Monday through Thursday. *151 Spring St., Midtown, 404/524–5811.*

Project Open Hand Services are provided chiefly within the I–285 perimeter and in Clayton, Gwinnett, and Cobb counties. The project also publishes a booklet of key contacts in the metro area and throughout the state. *176 Ott-*

ley Dr., Midtown, 404/872–8089, www.
projectopenhand.org.

alcoholism treatment

Alcoholics Anonymous Chapters meet
throughout the metro area—in
churches, community-service centers,
and social halls, among other locations.
127 Peachtree St., Suite 1310, Downtown,
404/525–3178, www.atlantaaa.org.

Charter Treatment Centers The centers
specialize in substance-abuse treatment
and suicide prevention. Outpatient and
inpatient care is available for all ages. To
determine which facility has the program you need, call 800/242–7837
(800/CHARTER). 204 Church St.,
Decatur, 404/377–5300; 2151 Peachford
Rd., Dunwoody, 770/455–3200; 5454 York-
town Dr., off Riverdale Rd., Hapeville,
770/991–6044; 811 Juniper St., Midtown,
404/881–5800; 934 Briarcliff Rd., Virginia-
Highland, 404/888–7860.

Ridgeview Institute Founded in 1976,
this fully accredited private nonprofit
hospital specializes in inpatient and out-
patient chemical-dependence and psy-
chiatric treatment services for all ages.
3995 S. Cobb Dr., Smyrna, 770/434–4567.

crime victims

Crime Victims Advocacy Council The
council sponsors support groups
throughout the metro area for victims of
all kinds of crime. 3101 Paces Mill Rd.,
Vinings, 770/333–9254.

domestic violence

Men Stopping Violence The organization's goal is to help end men's violence
against women though training, education, and other assistance. 1020 DeKalb
Ave., Suite 25, Inman Park, 404/688–
1376, www.menstoppingviolence.org.

drug-abuse treatment

Charter Treatment Centers 800/CHAR-
TER (800/242–7837).

Cocaine Anonymous; Cocaine Hotline
404/255–7787.

DeKalb Addiction Clinic 455 Winn Way,
Decatur, 404/508–6430.

Focus on Recovery This nationwide, 24-
hour hot line for drug- and alcohol-
abuse programs is staffed by counselors
and recovered addicts. 800/237–0420.

Narcotics Anonymous Atlanta 404/672–
6621 or 404/708–3219.

Narcotics Anonymous Chamblee 404/
672–7647.

Narcotics Anonymous Douglasville 770/
577–0809.

Narcotics Anonymous Marietta 770/421–
8881.

Narcotics Anonymous North Atlanta
770/451–7373.

Narcotics Anonymous Smyrna 770/421–
8881.

Narcotics Anonymous South Atlanta
404/362–8484.

**Northside Recovery Center Northside
Hospital** 1100 Johnson Ferry Rd., Suite
190, Dunwoody, 404/851–8961.

Ridgeview Institute 3995 S. Cobb Dr.,
Smyrna, 770/434–4567.

West Paces Medical Center 3200 Howell
Mill Rd., Buckhead, 404/350–4450.

mental-health
information & referral

Some referral services operate around
the clock.

**Cherokee County Georgia Highlands
Center** 191 Lamar Haley Pkwy., Canton,
770/704–1600.

**Clayton County Clayton Response Cen-
ter** 409-A Arrowhead Blvd., Jonesboro,
770/603–8222.

**Cobb and Douglas Counties Cobb/Dou-
glas Community Services Boards Access
Center** 6043 Prestley Mill Rd., Suite D,
Douglasville, 770/422–0202.

**DeKalb County DeKalb Community Ser-
vice Board** 404/892–4646.

Forsyth County Lakewinds 472 S. Enota
Dr., Gainesville, 800/347–5827.

**Fulton County Department of Mental
Health** 141 Pryor St., Suite 4035, Downtown, 404/730–1600.

**Gwinnett County Mental Health Emer-
gency Line** 770/985–2494.

**Henry County Mental Health Counsel-
ing Center** 139 Henry Pkwy., McDonough,
770/898–7400.

Mental Health Association of Georgia *620 Peachtree St., Downtown, 404/875–7081.*

Mental Health Intake *11 S.W. Upper Riverdale Rd., Riverdale, 770/991–8500 or 770/996–4357.*

Ridgeview Institute *3995 S. Cobb Dr., Smyrna, 770/434–4567.*

rape crisis

Clayton County Family and Children Services *770/477–2177.*

DeKalb Rape Crisis Center *404/377–1428.*

Georgia Network to End Sexual Assault *404/659–6482, www.gnesa.com.*

Grady Memorial Hospital Rape Crisis Center *80 Butler St., Downtown, 404/616–4861.*

Gwinnett Sexual Assault Center *770/476–7407.*

DOCTOR & DENTIST REFERRALS

Atlanta Medical Center *303 Parkway Dr., Downtown, 404/265–4000 or 800/541–9637.*

Chiropractic Information Bureau *404/294–4900.*

Fayette Community Hospital *1255 GA 54 W, 770/541–1111.*

Georgia Dental Association *7000 Peachtree-Dunwoody Rd., Dunwoody, 770/668–9093.*

Grady Healthcare System Advice Line *404/616–0600.*

Greater Atlanta Sports Medicine *3200 Downwood Cir., off W. Paces Ferry Rd., Buckhead, 404/350–0007.*

Henry Medical Center *1133 Eagle's Landing Pkwy., Stockbridge, 770/389–2242.*

Medical Association of Atlanta/Academy of Medicine Information & Referral Service *875 W. Peachtree St., Midtown, 404/881–1714.*

Millennium Healthcare *4370 Georgetown Sq., Dunwoody, 770/390–0012.*

North Fulton Regional Hospital *3000 Hospital Blvd., Roswell, 770/751–2600.*

Northlake Regional Medical Center *1455 Montreal Rd., Tucker, 770/270–3330.*

Northside Hospital Doctor Matching *1000 Johnson Ferry Rd., Dunwoody, 404/851–8817.*

Piedmont Hospital Physician Referral *1968 Peachtree Rd., Buckhead, 404/541–1111.*

St. Joseph's Hospital Physician Referral *5665 Peachtree-Dunwoody Rd., Dunwoody, 404/851–7312.*

FAMILY PLANNING

Planned Parenthood of Georgia *100 Edgewood Ave., Downtown, 404/688–9300; Cobb Center: 617 Roswell St., Marietta, 770/424–1477; Gwinnett Center: 950 Indian Trail-Lilburn Rd., Lilburn, 770/451–2741.*

GAY & LESBIAN CONCERNS

Atlanta Gay & Lesbian Center The center serves as a clearinghouse for information about organizations throughout the metro area. The office is open Monday through Thursday 2–9. There also is a clinic (828 W. Peachtree St.) that's open Monday through Thursday 5:30 PM–9 PM. *71 12th St., Midtown, 404/876–5372; 404/892–0661 help line.*

GOVERNMENT

Beyond the city of Atlanta itself, the metro area is split into jurisdictions of all sizes, each with its own ordinances and bureaucracies. The notion of merging all these fragmented governments into a single entity, much discussed in the past, has been getting less and less air time as the years go by. Thus, residents must identify—and communicate directly with—the local authorities that control their public and legal lives. The Bell South White Business Pages list government phone numbers in the blue pages found at the end of the book. Boards of Commissioners control counties, while city councils and mayors or city managers govern municipalities large and small. Sometimes these entities overlap, as in that part of the city of Atlanta that lies in unincorporated areas of DeKalb County. When they do, it can be unclear which entity provides which services.

complaints

City of Atlanta, Dead-Animal Removal
*404/659–6757 weekdays; 404/523–0632
Sat. and holidays.*

City of Atlanta, Trees Down in the Street
*404/817–5813 6 AM–6 PM weekdays; 404/
658–6666 nights, weekends, and holidays.*

DeKalb County Traffic-Signal Malfunction *404/297–3947.*

DeKalb Peachtree Airport-Noise Abatement *770/936–5442.*

Fulton County Airport–Brown Field Noise Hotline *404/699–8900.*

Fulton County Rat Control *404/730–1322.*

Hartsfield Atlanta International Airport Noise Abatement *404/209–0931.*

city-government resources

City of Alpharetta 24-hour Information Line *678/297–6015.*

City of Atlanta Mayor's Office *404/330–6100.*

City of Decatur, City Manager's Office *404/370–4102.*

City of Marietta, City Manager's Office *770/794–5611.*

City of Roswell Mayor's Office *770/641–3727.*

county-government resources

Cherokee County Board of Commissioners *770/479–0400.*

Clayton County Board of Commissioners *770/477–3208.*

Cobb County Board of Commissioners *770/428–3315.*

DeKalb County Board of Commissioners *404/371–2886.*

Douglas County Board of Commissioners *770/920–7266.*

Fayette County Administrator's Office *770/460–5730.*

Forsyth County Board of Commissioners *770/781–2101.*

Fulton County Board of Commissioners, Chairman's Office *404/730–8206.*

Gwinnett County Commissioners *770/822–7000.*

Henry County Board of Commissioners *770/954–2400.*

education boards

Atlanta City Schools *210 Pryor St., Downtown, 404/827–8000.*

Cherokee County *110 Academy St., Canton, 770/479–1871.*

Clayton County *120 Smith St., Jonesboro, 770/473–2700.*

Cobb County *14 Glover St., Marietta, 770/426–3300.*

Decatur City Schools *320 N. McDonough St., Decatur, 404/373–8532.*

DeKalb County *3770 N. Decatur Rd., Decatur, 404/297–1200.*

Douglas County *9030 GA 5, Douglasville, 770/920–4000.*

Fayette County *210 Stonewall Ave., Fayetteville, 770/460–3535.*

Forsyth County *101 School St., Cumming, 770/887–2461.*

Fulton County *786 Cleveland Ave., Southwest Atlanta, 404/768–3600.*

Henry County *396 Tomlinson St., McDonough, 770/957–6601.*

Marietta City School *250 Howard St., Marietta, 770/422–1389.*

HOMEWORK-HELP HOT LINES

Homework Hotline The free service, initiated by the Atlanta public-school system, is staffed by teachers Monday through Thursday 4–9 PM. *404/827–8620.*

HOUSECLEANING-HELP AGENCIES

Brittany Maids The agency can provide a variety of services on a schedule customized to your needs. *1687 Tullie Cir., Suite 117, Northeast Atlanta, 404/633–5152.*

INTERIOR DESIGNER & ARCHITECT REFERRALS

American Institute of Architects *231 Peachtree St., Downtown, 404/222-0099.*

American Society of Interior Designers *Atlanta Decorative Arts Center, 351 Peachtree Hills Ave., Buckhead, 404/321-3938.*

American Society of Landscape Architects *605 Tuxworth Cir., Decatur, 404/633-9828.*

International Interior Design Association *Atlanta Decorative Arts Center, 351 Peachtree Hills Ave., Buckhead, 404/233-4432.*

LANDLORD-TENANT ASSISTANCE

Georgia law favors the rights of landlords over tenants, although the courts in each jurisdiction will assist aggrieved tenants. The **Atlanta Legal Aid Society** (151 Spring St., between Luckie and Williams Sts., Downtown, 404/524-5811) can help with landlord-tenant issues.

LEGAL SERVICES

American Civil Liberties Union of Georgia The ACLU assists in issues of free speech, free press, free assembly, freedom of religion, and due process of law. *142 Mitchell St., Suite 301, Downtown, 404/523-5398.*

Atlanta Legal Aid Society The group offers assistance with landlord-tenant issues, consumer issues, and divorce. *151 Spring St., between Luckie and Williams Sts., Downtown, 404/524-5811; 246 Sycamore St., Suite 120, Decatur, 404/377-0701.*

Cobb County Legal Aid The organization offers a full line of legal services for those citizens below a certain minimum income. *32 Waddell St., near the Square, Marietta, 770/528-2565.*

LOST & FOUND

at airlines & airports
Hartsfield Atlanta International Airport *404/530-2100.*

on other public transportation
MARTA Items are claimed at Five Points Station. *404/848-3208.*

lost animals
Most jurisdictions require pet owners to tag their animals (cats and dogs). On the tag, you must indicate the county in which Fido or Fifi is registered and list phone numbers for the county and for the registering agency. The tag also must indicate the year of your pet's most recent rabies vaccination and the year the license was issued. Veterinarians usually dispense rabies tags when they give vaccinations, but it's up to you to register your furry loved one with the county. Registration makes it easier to recover lost pets, because if the information on file is up-do-date, the county will know how to find you. For further information about pets, *see* Pets, *below.*

Atlanta Humane Society *404/875-5331, www.atlhumane.org.*

Chamblee Animal Control *770/986-5019.*

Cherokee County Animal Control *770/345-7270, www.cchs.cherokee.ga.us.*

Clayton County Animal Control *770/477-3509.*

Cobb County Animal Control *770/590-5610, www.cobbanimalcontrol.org.*

DeKalb County Animal Control *404/294-2996.*

Fayette County Animal Control *770/487-6450.*

Forsyth County Animal Control Shelter *770/888-2500.*

Fulton County Animal Control *404/794-0358.*

Gwinnett County Animal Control *770/339-3200, www.gwinnettanimalcontrol.com.*

Henry County Animal Control *770/954-2100, www.co.henry.ga.us/animalcontrol.htm.*

lost credit cards

American Express/Optima 800/327–2177.

AT&T Universal Card 800/423–4343.

Citibank 800/843–0777.

Dillard's 800/643–8276.

Diners Club/Carte Blanche 800/234–6377.

Discover 800/347–2683.

JCB 800/736–8111.

MasterCard 800/307–7309.

Nordstrom 800/964–1800.

Parisian 800/832–2455.

Visa 800/847–2911.

lost traveler's checks

American Express 800/528–4800.

Citibank 800/645–6556.

Thomas Cook 800/223–7373.

MEDICAL EMERGENCIES

ambulance

Dial 911.

hospital emergency rooms

Metro Atlanta is full of hospital emergency rooms and trauma centers. Here is a partial list of the ones most likely to be of use.

Children's Healthcare of Atlanta at Egleston 1405 Clifton Rd., Decatur, 404/325–6400.

Children's Healthcare of Atlanta at Scottish Rite 1001 Johnson Ferry Rd. NE, Dunwoody, 404/250–2007.

DeKalb Medical Center 2701 N. Decatur Rd., Decatur, 404/501–5350.

Emory-Adventist Hospital 3949 S. Cobb Dr., Smyrna, 770/434–0710.

Grady Health System This place is famous for its burn-care and neonatal-emergency-care units. 35 Butler St., Downtown, 404/616–6200.

Hughes Spalding Children's Hospital 35 Butler St., Downtown, 404/616–4373.

North Fulton Regional Hospital 3200 Hospital Blvd., Roswell, 770/751–2555.

Northside Hospital 1000 Johnson Ferry Rd., Dunwoody, 404/851–8937.

Piedmont Hospital/Promina 1968 Peachtree Rd., Buckhead, 404/605–3297.

Rockdale Hospital 1412 Milstead Ave., Conyers, 770/918–3000.

St. Joseph's Hospital of Atlanta 2701 N. Decatur Rd., Dunwoody, 404/851–7001.

Southern Regional Medical Center 11 Upper Riverdale Rd., Riverdale, 770/991–8188.

Southwest Hospital & Medical Center 501 Fairburn Rd., Southwest Atlanta, 404/505–5680.

WellStar Kennestone Hospital 677 Church St., Marietta, 770/793–5000.

poison-control center

Georgia Poison Center 404/616–9000; 800/282–5846; 404/616–9287 TDD.

suicide prevention

Also see Mental-Health Information & Referral, above.

National Hope Line Network 800/SUICIDE (800/784–2433).

PETS

adoption & rescue

Pets can be adopted from area humane societies with ID, proof of address, and, if you rent, a copy of a lease showing that your landlord allows animals. Fees vary by animal type, age, facility, and range generally from $30 to $75. The organizations listed here may also be able to help you in locating a lost pet.

Atlanta Humane Society 981 Howell Mill Rd., Northwest Atlanta, 404/875–5331, www.atlhumane.org.

Cherokee County Humane Society 131 Chattin Dr., Canton, 770/928–5115, www.cchumanesociety.org.

Clayton County Humane Society 810 N. McDonough St., Jonesboro, 770/471–9436, www.claytoncountyhumane.org.

Cobb County Humane Society 8 Fairground St., Marietta, 770/428–5678, www.humanecobb.org.

DeKalb Humane Society 5287 Covington Hwy., Decatur, 770/593–1155, www.dekalbhumanesocietyinc.org.

Douglas County Humane Society 770/942–5961.

Fayette County Humane Society 770/487–1073, www.fayettehumane.org. Adoptions: Petsmart, 101 Pavillion Pkwy., Fayetteville, 770/719–4444.

Forsyth County Humane Society 4440 Keith Bridge Rd., Cumming, 770/887–6480, www.forsythpets.com.

Gwinnett Animal Control Shelter 632 High Hope Rd., Lawrenceville, 770/339–3200.

Gwinnett Humane Society Box 750, Lawrenceville, 30046, 770/798–7711, www.gwinnetthumane.com. Adoptions: 3724 Hwy. 29, Lawrenceville.

Henry County Animal Shelter 46 Work Camp Rd., off Phillips Dr., McDonough, 770/954–2100.

Henry County Humane Society 770/914–1272, www.henrycounty.petfinder.com. Adoptions: Petsmart, 1986 Mt. Zion Rd., Morrow, 770/478–0860.

dog-walking services

Pawsitively Pets This in-home pet-sitting service has been around for more than a decade. 3421 Ivy's Walk, Pleasantdale. 770/723–0255.

Tall Tails Pet Sitting The service offers customized pet care, whether it be for midday walks or during extended vacations. 2804 Asbury Heights Rd., Decatur, 404/286–6569.

grooming

Petsmart 3221 Peachtree Rd., Buckhead, 404/266–0420; 3803 Venture Dr., Duluth, 770/813–8400; 128 Perimeter Center W, Dunwoody, 770/481–0511; 875 Lawrenceville–Suwanee Rd., Lawrenceville, 770/432–8250; 2540-B Hargrove Rd., Smyrna, 770/432–8250; 2150 Paxton Dr., Snellville, 770/985–0469; 4023 LaVista Rd., Tucker, 770/414–5033.

sitting & boarding

Critter Sitters 2266 Ridgemore Rd., Buckhead, 404/377–5475.

training

Alpha Academy of Dog Training 710 Ponce de Leon Ave., Midtown, 404/874–5224.

Camp Paradise Pet Resort 1774 Smyrna Rd., Conyers, 770/483–4738.

Comprehensive Pet Therapy 7274 Roswell Ave., Dunwoody, 770/442–0280.

veterinary hospitals

Cat Clinic of Cobb 2635 Sandy Plains Rd., Marietta, 770/973–6369.

Fair Oaks Veterinarian Clinic 2142 Austell Rd., Marietta, 770/432–7155.

For Pet's Sake Mimi Shepherd, DVM, and Ken Slossberg, DVM, treat only reptiles, birds, and other exotic mammals. 3761 N. Druid Hills Rd., Decatur, 404/248–8978.

Lafayette Center Animal Hospital 105 Marquis Dr., Fayetteville, 770/460–0090.

Pharr Road Animal Hospital 553 Pharr Rd., Buckhead, 404/237–4601.

veterinarian referrals

Friends of Animals The clinic maintains a toll-free number that provides information on low-cost spaying and neutering. 534 Medlock Rd., Decatur, 404/378–2053 or 800/321–7387.

Hawk's Crest Equine Services Dr. Ron Dawe specializes in chiropractic and acupuncture for horses. 3141 Paddock Rd., Covington, 770/554–0455.

PHARMACIES OPEN 24 HOURS

CVS 5446 Peachtree Industrial Blvd., Chamblee, 770/457–4401; 2438 N. Decatur Rd., Decatur, 404/508–2456; 300 Powder Springs Rd., Marietta, 770/422–1413; 5095 Peachtree Pkwy., Norcross, 770/209–9299.

Kroger The supermarket chain has pharmacies in more than a dozen stores in the 10 counties. 404/222–2024.

POLICE

For nonemergencies, call the police department operating in your jurisdiction—do not dial 911, which should be used only in an emergency.

city police departments

Atlanta Police Department If you live in Atlanta proper, you can find out how to reach your precinct by contacting the department. *675 Ponce de Leon Ave., Midtown, 404/853–3434.*

Canton Police Department *221 E. Marietta St., 770/479–5316.*

Chamblee Police Department *3518 Broad St., 770/986–5005.*

Cumming Police Department *301 Old Buford Rd., 770/781–2000.*

Decatur Police Department *420 W. Trinity Pl., 404/377–7911.*

Douglasville *6730 W. Church St., 770/920–3010.*

East Point Police Department *2727 E. Point St., 404/761–2177.*

Fayetteville Police Department *105 Johnson Ave., 770/461–4357.*

Jonesboro Police Department *1715 Main St., 770/478–7407.*

Lawrenceville Police Department *405 S. Clayton St., 404/963–2443.*

Marietta Police Department *150 Haynes St., 770/794–5300.*

McDonough Police Department *43 Lawrenceville St., 770/957–1218.*

Roswell Police Department *39 Hill St., 770/640–4100.*

Stockbridge Police Department *131 Burke St., 770/389–7850.*

Woodstock Police Department *400 E. Main St., 770/479–3117.*

county police departments

Cherokee Sheriff's Office *90 North St., Canton, 770/479–3117.*

Clayton County Police Department *7346 N. McDonough St., Jonesboro, 770/477–3747.*

Cobb County Police Department *140 N. Marietta Pkwy., Marietta, 770/499–3911.*

Cobb County Sheriff's Office *185 Roswell St., Marietta, 770/499–4600.*

DeKalb Center Precinct *3630 Camp Cir., Decatur, 404/294–2643. East Precinct: 2484 Bruce St., Lithonia, 770/482–0300. North Precinct: Perimeter Mall, 4453 Ashford-Dunwoody Rd., Dunwoody, 404/294–2375. South Precinct: 1616 Candler Rd., Decatur, 404/286–7911.*

DeKalb County Police Chief *4415 Memorial Dr., Decatur, 404/298–8000; 404/298–8331 TDD.*

Douglas County Sheriff's Department *6840 W. Church St., Douglasville, 770/942–2121.*

Fayette County Sheriff's Department *155 Johnson Ave., Fayetteville, 770/461–6353.*

Forsyth County Sheriff's Department *202 Old Buford Rd., Cumming, 770/781–2222.*

Fulton County Police Department *130 Peachtree St., Downtown, 404/730–5700. Northside Precinct: 7741 Roswell Rd., North Annex, Sandy Springs, 770/551–7600. Southside Precinct: 5600 Stonewall Tell Rd., South Annex, College Park, 770/306–3005. Southwest Precinct: 4121 Cascade Rd., Southwest Atlanta, 404/505–5780.*

Fulton County Sheriff's Office *185 Central Ave., Northeast Atlanta 404/730–5100.*

Gwinnett County Sheriff's Office *2900 University Pkwy., Lawrenceville, 770/822–3100.*

Gwinnett Police Department *770 High Hope Rd., Lawrenceville, 770/513–5100.*

Henry County Police Department *100 Henry Pkwy., McDonough, 770/754–2900.*

POSTAL SERVICES

united states postal service, atlanta district

Main Post Office *3900 Crown Rd., South Atlanta, 404/765–7518 or 800/275–8777.*

Akers Mill Station *2997 Cobb Pkwy., 31139.* **Ben Hill Station** *2260 Fairburn Rd., 30331.* **Briarcliff Station** *3104 Briarcliff Rd. NE, 30345.* **Broadview Station** *740 Morosgo Dr., 30324.* **Brookhaven Station** *3851 Peachtree Rd., 31119.* **Buckhead Station** *1 Buckhead Loop Rd., 31126.* **Cascade Heights Station** *2414 Herring Rd. SW,*

30311. **Central City Finance Station** *183 Forsyth St. SW, Downtown,* 30302. **Chamblee Branch** *3545 Broad St., Chamblee,* 30341. **Civic Center Station** *570 Piedmont Ave. NE, Midtown,* 30308. **CNN Center Station** *1 CNN Center, Downtown,* 30303. **College Park Station** *3799 Main St., College Park* 30337. **Cumberland Mall Station** *1101 Cumberland Mall Dr., Vinings* 31139. **Doraville Station** *4700 Longmire Ext., Doraville,* 30340. **Druid Hills Station** *1799 Briarcliff Rd.,* 30333. **Dunwoody Station** *1551 Dunwoody Village Pkwy.,* 30338. **East Atlanta Station** *1273 Metropolitan Ave. SE,* 30316. **East Point Station** *2905 E. Point St., East Point* 30344. **Eastwood Station** *1926 Boulevard Dr. SW,* 30317. **Embry Hills Station** *3579-A Chamblee Tucker Rd.,* 31141. **Gate City Station** *486 Decatur St. SE, Cabbagetown,* 30312. **Glenridge Station** *5400 Glenridge Dr., Dunwoody,* 30342. **Greenbriar Mall Station** *Greenbriar Mall, 2841 Greenbriar Pkwy., East Point,* 30331. **Hapeville Station** *650 S. Central Ave., Hapeville* 30354. **Howell Mill Postal Store** *1984 Howell Mill Rd., Buckhead,* 30325. **Industrial Station** *5686 Fulton Industrial Blvd., Southwest Atlanta,* 30336. **Lakewood Station** *1590 Jonesboro Rd. SE,* 30315. **Little Five Points Station** *455 Moreland Ave. SE,* 31107. **Martech Finance Station** *794 Marietta St., Downtown,* 30318. **Midtown Station** *1072 W. Peachtree St.,* 30309. **Morris Brown Station** *50 Sunset Ave. SW, West End,* 30314. **North Atlanta Station** *1920 Dresden Dr. NE,* 30319. **North Highland Station** *1190 N. Highland Ave. NE, Virginia-Highland,* 31106. **North Springs Station** *7527 Roswell Rd. NE,* 31156. **Northlake Station** *3212 Northlake Parkway,* 31145. **Northridge Station** *1185 Hightown Trail, North Springs,* 30350. **Old National Station** *2385 Godby Rd., Southwest Atlanta,* 30349. **Peachtree Center Station** *240 Peachtree St. NW, Downtown,* 30343. **Perimeter Center Station** *4707 Ashford-Dunwoody Rd., Dunwoody,* 31146. **Pharr Road Station** *575 Pharr Rd. NE, Buckhead,* 30355. **Sandy Springs Postal Store** *227 Sandy Springs Pl., Sandy Springs,* 30328. **West End Station** *848 Oglethorpe Ave.,* 30310.

fedex

To find the location closest to you or to schedule pickups, call 800/463-3339.

City of Atlanta *49 W. Paces Ferry Rd., Buckhead; 100 Peachtree St., Downtown; 229 Peachtree St., Downtown; 340*

Peachtree Rd., Midtown; 401 Windsor St., Downtown; 1201 W. Peachtree St., Midtown; 2441 Cheshire Bridge Rd., North Druid Hills; 1255 Executive Park Dr., North Druid Hills; 100 Galleria Pkwy. NW, Vinings; 1715 Howell Mill Rd., Buckhead; 425 Fulton Industrial Blvd. W, Southwest Atlanta.

Cobb County *1890 N. Cobb Pkwy., Kennesaw; 2049 Franklin Way, Marietta; 4880 Lower Roswell Rd., Marietta; 3000 Windy Hill Rd., Marietta.*

DeKalb County *1117 Perimeter Center W, Dunwoody; 5901 Peachtree-Dunwoody Rd., Dunwoody.*

Fayette County *100 N. Peachtree Pkwy., Peachtree City.*

Fulton County *3600 Zip Industrial Blvd., College Park; 1000 Abernathy Rd., Sandy Springs; 710 Morgan Falls Rd., Sandy Springs; 5948 Roswell Rd., Sandy Springs.*

ups

For pickups, call 800/PICKUPS. Service centers, which don't have published phone numbers, are generally open weekdays 8:30 AM–7 PM.

City of Atlanta *1240 Toffee Terr., near Hartsfield Atlanta International Airport, Hapeville.*

Clayton County *255 Southfield Ct., Forest Park.*

DeKalb County *3930 Pleasantdale Rd., Doraville.*

Fulton County *1300 Old Ellis Rd., off Mansell Rd., Roswell; 270 Marvin Miller Dr., Southwest Atlanta.*

SENIOR-CITIZEN SERVICES

American Association of Retired Persons The national membership organization provides information; acts as an advocate on legislative, consumer, and legal issues; and offers a wide range of benefits, products, and services for its members. *999 Peachtree St., Midtown, 404/888-0077.*

Cobb Senior Center If you're 55 or older, you can sign up for continuing-education classes and programs here. *1885 Smyrna–Roswell Rd., Smyrna, 770/438-2988.*

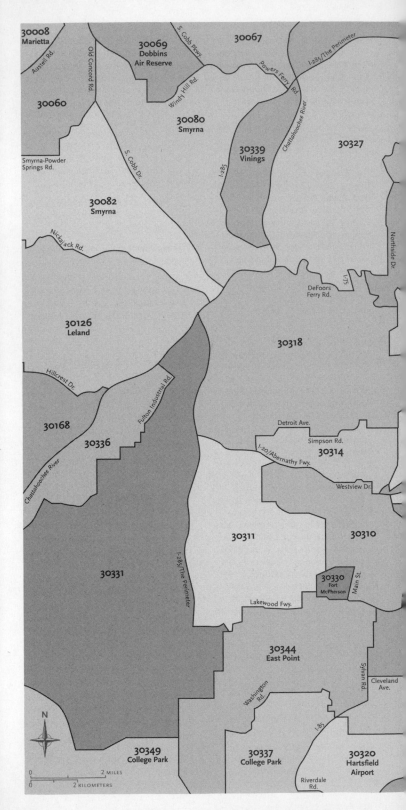

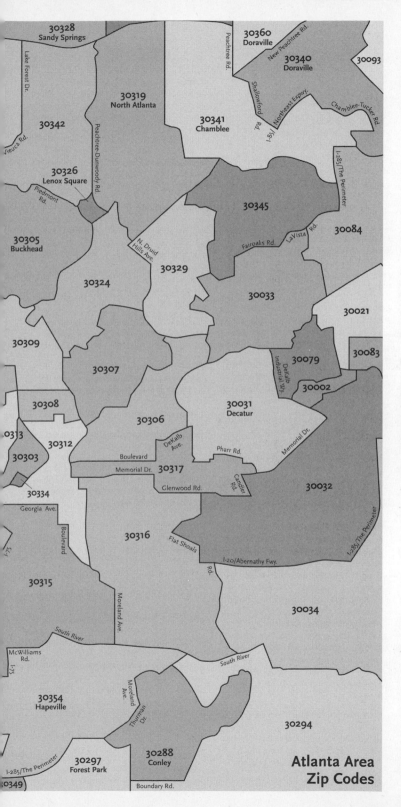

Atlanta Area Zip Codes

Fulton County Council on Aging The council is responsible for the "Each One Reach One" program, which is designed to get housing-repair services for low-income senior citizens. *236 Forsyth St., Downtown, 404/523–5027.*

Meals on Wheels The volunteer-based organization brings nutritious meals to homebound individuals who are 60 and older and can't prepare meals for themselves. *1615 Peachtree St., Midtown, 404/873–1345, ext. 26; 1705 Commerce Dr., Midtown, 404/352–9303; 202 Nelson Ferry Rd., Decatur, 404/370–4081.*

Senior Citizen Services of Metropolitan Atlanta From meal preparation to computer training to companionship, this places offers senior citizens a slew of services. *1705 Commerce Dr., Midtown, 404/351–3888.*

Soapstone Center for the Arts Painting, line-dancing, and tai chi classes are available for senior citizens here. *1 S. DeKalb Center, Decatur, 404/241–2453.*

Southeast Arts Center You can find arts classes here. *John C. Birdine Neighborhood Center, 215 Lakewood Way, Southeast Atlanta, 404/658–6036.*

YMCAs In the metro area, many special classes and programs for senior citizens—including arthritis-therapy classes (chiefly aquatic) and walking clubs—are available at local Ys. The Centennial Place Family YMCA focuses on art. For YMCA listings, *see* Chapter 3.

elder sitting services

A Friend of the Family You can hire temporary and permanent in-home elder-care from this agency. In business since 1984, the agency charges an initial $75 registration fee and an $11 referral fee per day, each time you use the service to find a caregiver; this referral fee is $25 on less than 24 hours' notice and $16 for Saturday evenings after 5 PM. The caregiver/sitter charge is $9–$12 per hour for a minimum of four hours. *880 Holcomb Bridge Rd., Roswell, 770/643–3000 permanent help; 770/725–2748 temporary help.*

Kadan Corporation The firm specializes exclusively in sitting services for older clients with nonmedical needs. *Dunwoody Club Center, 2494 Jett Ferry Rd., Suite 201, Dunwoody, 770/396–8997.*

SERVICES FOR PEOPLE WITH DISABILITIES

Center for the Visually Impaired In- and out-patient services include Braille instruction and job placement. *763 Peachtree St., Downtown, 404/875–9011.*

Georgia Interpreting Services Network Interpreting services are offered for almost any situation for people who are deaf. *44 Broad St., Suite 503, Downtown, 404/521–9100.*

Shepherd Spinal Center Spinal-cord and brain-injury patients may receive rehabilitation and physical therapy here but only by physician referral. *2020 Peachtree Rd., Buckhead, 404/352–2020.*

TELEVISION-CABLE COMPANIES

Numerous cable companies deliver service in the 10 counties.

AT&T Broadband It serves most of metro Atlanta. *678/545–2289 signing up; 678/545–2455 billing questions; 678/545–6683 moving or changing service; 678/545–7372 service and repair.*

BellSouth Metro Atlanta is the service area. *770/360–4999.*

InterMedia The company covers the south metro area, including south Fulton County, south Atlanta, Peachtree City, and Fayetteville. *770/487–5011.*

Time Warner Cable If you live in Cobb and south Cherokee counties, the company can hook you up. *770/926–0334.*

UTILITIES

gas & electric

Atlanta residents must choose their supplier from among approximately 18 natural-gas marketers. If you don't select one, a gas marketer is chosen for you. Some problems have arisen from this system: the Georgia Public Service Commission has been investigating the practice of "slamming," in which your gas company is changed without your consent. The Atlanta Gas Light Company can provide a list of certified marketers.

Atlanta Gas Light Company *770/994–1946; 770/907–4231 emergency service.*

Austell Natural Gas Serves west and south Cobb County. *770/948–1841.*

Fairburn Electric Serves the city of Fairburn. *770/964–2244.*

Georgia Power Company Provides electric services for the state of Georgia, including the entire Atlanta area. *888/660–5890 24-hour customer service; 800/870–3942 in Spanish.*

Marietta Power Supplies power within the city limits of Marietta. *770/794–5150.*

Palmetto Only residents of the Palmetto, in south Fulton County, have access to this utility service. *770/463–3377.*

telephone

BellSouth Local and regional service. *404/780–2355 residential; 404/780–2800 business.*

BellSouth Mobility Cellular-phone services. *404/847–3600.*

water

Water, sanitation, and sewer services in the 10 counties are often provided by small municipalities as well as larger municipalities and counties.

Atlanta Water Department Serves metropolitan Atlanta and communities, such as Sandy Springs, in unincorporated Fulton County. *404/658–6500.*

Austell Water Department *770/944–4300.*

Ball Ground Water Dept. Serves northeast Cherokee County. *770/735–2123.*

Canton Water Department *770/704–1500.*

Cherokee County Water Authority *770/479–1813.*

Clayton County Water Authority *770/951–2130.*

Cobb County Water & Sewer Department *770/423–1000.*

Cumming Water Department *770/781–2020.*

DeKalb County Water & Sewer Customer Service *404/378–4475.*

Douglasville Water & Sewer Authority Also serves Douglas County. *770/949–7617.*

East Point Water Department *404/765–1008.*

Fairburn Water & Sewer *770/964–2244.*

Fayette County Water System *770/461–1146.*

Forsyth County Water & Sewer Department *770/781–2160.*

Fulton County Water Department Serves Alpharetta and north Fulton County. *404/730–6830.*

Gwinnett County Public Utilities *770/822–8811.*

Henry County Water & Sewer Authority *770/957–6659.*

Kennesaw (City of) Water Department *770/424–8274.*

Lawrenceville Utilities *770/963–2414.*

Marietta Water & Sewer *770/794–5230.*

McDonough Water Department *770/898–1505.*

Palmetto Public Works *770/463–3322.*

Riverdale Public Works Department *770/996–3397.*

Roswell Water Department *770/641–3715.*

Smyrna Utility Services *770/319–5338.*

Stockbridge Water Department *770/389–7901.*

Woodstock Water & Sewer Maintenance *770/592–6036.*

VOLUNTEERING

how to

United Way The resource center, open around the clock, provides information for volunteer opportunities, such as work in shelters, community clinics, public schools, and senior-citizen centers throughout the metro area. *100 Edgewood Ave. NE, Downtown, 404/614–1000.*

organizations

Big Brothers Big Sisters of Metropolitan Atlanta Volunteer opportunities include one-on-one mentoring for children ages 6–12 from single-parent households and one-on-one mentoring for specific groups of at-risk teenagers. *100 Edgewood Ave. NE, Suite 710, Downtown, 404/527–7600, www.bbbsatl.org.*

Friends of the Atlanta Opera Volunteers supply office and production assistance throughout the season. *728 W. Peachtree St., Midtown, 404/881–8801, www. atlantaopera.com.*

Friends of Zoo Atlanta The program offers zoo membership and "Adopt an Animal" programs. *800-A Cherokee Ave., Grant Park, 404/624–WILD or 404/624– 9453, www.zooatlanta.org.*

Habitat for Humanity Atlanta You can help build homes for low-income families. *1125 Seabord Ave., Reynoldstown, 404/223–5180, www.atlanta-habitat.org.*

Hands on Atlanta After participating in a short orientation meeting, residents can become members of this organization and receive a monthly newsletter profiling volunteer opportunities. *1605 Peachtree St., Midtown, 404/872–2252, www.handsonatlanta.org.*

Project Open Hand Volunteers help cook, package, and deliver meals daily to people with AIDS. *176 Ottley Dr., near Briarcliff and Johnson Rds., Northeast Atlanta, 404/872–6947, www. projectopenhand.org.*

WASTE-REMOVAL SERVICES

Most metropolitan jurisdictions provide waste-removal services, which you pay for when you pay your water bill. Some jurisdictions, however, require you to contract with a private service.

All South Robertson *678/432–1670 Henry County.*

BFI Waste Systems *404/792–2660 north Fulton and Cobb counties; 770/339–9393 Gwinnett County.*

ZONING & PLANNING

Atlanta Department of Planning, Development and Neighborhood Conservation *404/330–6070; 404/330–6175 zoning enforcement.*

Cherokee County Planning and Zoning *770/479–0504.*

Clayton County Community Development *770/477–3678.*

Cobb County Community Development *770/528–2199 planning; 770/528–2035 zoning.*

Cumming Planning and Zoning *770/ 781–2024.*

Decatur Building Inspections *404/370– 4104.*

DeKalb County Department of Planning *404/371–2155.*

Douglas County Planning and Zoning *770/920–7241.*

Fayette County Planning Department *770/460–5730.*

Fayetteville Planning *770/461–6029.*

Forest Park Planning, Building and Zoning *404/608–2300.*

Forsyth County Planning and Development *770/781–2115.*

Fulton County Planning and Zoning *404/730–8094 planning; 404/730–7814 zoning.*

Gwinnett County Planning and Development Department *770/822–7500.*

Henry County Planning and Development *770/954–2457.*

Marietta Planning and Zoning Department *770/794–5440.*

McDonough Planning and Zoning *770/ 957–3915.*

Peachtree City Planning Department *770/487–7657.*

learning

ACTING SCHOOLS

Alliance Theatre Acting Program All age groups are welcome. The program also provides in-school classes and teacher training. *Woodruff Arts Center, 1280 Peachtree St., Midtown, 404/733–4700.*

ADULT EDUCATION

Clayton State College & University Day and evening classes cover all areas of continuing education, from computers to health care to lawn care. *5900 N. Lee St., Morrow, 770/961–3556.*

Emory University Its Evening at Emory program offers a wide range of courses, from beginning language to home renovation and wine appreciation. *Emory University, 1560 Clairemont Rd., Emory, 404/727–6000.*

Oglethorpe University, University College Classes in accounting, business administration, humanities, psychology, social sciences, and other disciplines are available. *4484 Peachtree Rd., Brookhaven, 404/364–8383.*

Senior University Retired professors teach classes to senior citizens that might include such topics as Mozart's operas, Dante's *Divine Comedy,* the Civil War, health, the Supreme Court, Central Asia, investing, and contemporary Georgia politics. *Emory University, 1560 Clairemont Rd., Emory, 404/727–6000; Mercer University, 3001 Mercer University Dr., Chamblee, 770/986–3109*

ART SCHOOLS

American College Four-year degree programs in fashion and graphic and interior design are offered. *3330 Peachtree Rd., Buckhead, 404/231–9000.*

Art Institute of Atlanta Continuing-education and four-year-degree programs in all artistic fields are options here. *6600 Peachtree-Dunwoody Rd., Dunwoody, 770/394–8300 or 800/275–4242.*

A R T Station You can take basic and intermediate-level visual-art, writing, and crafts classes at this arts center, which also runs a community theater program. *5384 Manor Dr., Stone Mountain, 770/469–1105.*

Atlanta College of Art Painting, sculpture, advertising, interior design—you can pursue these and other art-related subjects via four-year-degree and continuing-ed programs. *Woodruff Arts Center, 1280 Peachtree St., Midtown, 404/733–5001.*

Callanwolde Fine Arts Center Community classes include painting, music, theater, and meditation. *980 Briarcliff Rd., Decatur, 404/872–5338.*

Chastain Arts Center The wide variety of art classes encompasses pottery, painting, stained glass, and printmaking for adults and children over age four. *Chastain Park, 135 W. Wieuca Rd., Buckhead, 404/252–2927.*

Creative Circus Here you can receive professional training in advertising, graphic design, photography, and illustration. *812 Lambert Dr., Buckhead, 404/607–8880.*

Georgia State University School of Art and Design Traditional disciplines (sculpture, painting, photography) as well as professional disciplines (graphic design, interior design) are covered here. *Art & Humanities Bldg., 10 Peachtree Center Ave., Room 117, Downtown, 404/651–2257.*

Portfolio Center The center offers professional training in photography, graphic design, illustration, and advertising. *125 Bennett St., off Peachtree St., Buckhead, 404/351–5055.*

Soapstone Center for the Arts Senior citizens may sign up for painting lessons here. *1 S. DeKalb Center, Decatur, 404/241–2453.*

Southeast Arts Center Classes cover jewelry, pottery, printmaking, and black-and-white photography. Youth weekend programs are available. *John C. Birdine Neighborhood Center, 215 Lakewood Way, Southeast Atlanta, 404/658–6036.*

Spruill Center for the Arts Community arts classes include literary, performing, and visual-arts topics. *5339 Chamblee-Dunwoody Rd., Dunwoody, 770/394–3447.*

CHILDREN'S EDUCATION PROGRAMS

Centennial Place Family YMCA After-school programs and various drama, sports, and other classes are available. *555 Luckie St., Downtown, 404/724–9622.*

Covington YMCA It offers swimming lessons and other classes and runs after-school programs at some area elementary schools. *2140 Newton Dr., Covington, 770/787–3908.*

Kid Connection The staff here provides transportation from school to after-school programs and supervises field trips and similar activities for private schools. *3260 U.S. 78, Snellville, 770/978–2849.*

Prime Time at Waller Park This program for high-risk, low-income children ages 5–12 runs 2:30–6:30 PM on school days. Snacks, homework time, and crafts activities are included. *250 Oak St., Roswell, 770/642–4963; or 770/664–1220, ext. 128 (ask for Franklin Hamilton).*

South DeKalb YMCA Childcare Academy
The after-school program includes
snacks and homework time. *2575-A
Snapfinger Rd., Decatur, 770/987–4666.*

Southeast YMCA Family Place All-day
day care for pre-school age children is
available. *3482 Flat Shoals Rd., Decatur,
404/243–9662.*

Southwest YMCA After-school programs
here include such options as karate,
swimming, and gymnastic lessons,
along with snacks and homework help.
*22 Campbellton Rd., off Lakewood
Fwy./Langford Pkwy., Southwest Atlanta,
404/753–4169.*

COMMUNITY COLLEGES

Georgia Perimeter College *Clarkston Campus: 550 N. Indian Creek Dr., Clarkston,
404/299–4000. Decatur Campus: 3251
Panthersville Rd., Decatur, 404/244–5090.
Dunwoody Campus: 2101 Womack Rd.,
Dunwoody, 770/551–3000. Lawrenceville
Campus: 1201 Atkinson Rd., Lawrenceville,
770/995–2191. Rockdale Campus: 1115 West
Ave., Conyers, 770/785–6970.*

COMPUTER CLASSES

Computer Learning Centers Classes
cover software engineering, computer
programming, and systems analysis.
*2359 Windy Hill Rd., Marietta, 770/226–
0056; 5678 Jimmy Carter Blvd., Norcross,
678/966–9411.*

Georgia State University The Department of Computer Information Systems
has degree programs and evening
classes in programming, system design
and analysis, and related computer-science topics. *35 Broad St., Downtown,
404/651–3880.*

Micro Center Computer Education Desktop design, computer programming, and
Web-site design are available. *1221 Powers Ferry Rd., Marietta, 800/562–0058.*

COOKING SCHOOLS

Culinary Institute of Atlanta Housed in
the Art Institute, the school has degree
programs in culinary arts and runs
weekend workshops for casual cooks.

6600 Peachtree-Dunwoody Rd., Dunwoody, 770/394–8300 or 800/275–4242.

CPR & FIRST-AID CERTIFICATION

The American Red Cross gives CPR and
first-aid training at a number of locations in and around Atlanta.

DeKalb/Rockdale Service Center *3486
Covington Hwy., Decatur, 404/296–0505.*

Fulton Service Center *Lindbergh Plaza,
2581 Piedmont Rd., Buckhead, 404/262–
7010.*

Gwinnett Service Center *550 Hi Hope
Rd., off GA 316, Lawrenceville, 770/963–
9208.*

Northwest Metro Service Center *324 Victory Dr., Marietta, 770/428–2695.*

South Metro Service Center *1115 Mt.
Zion Rd., Suite H, Morrow, 770/961–2552.*

DANCE CLASSES

ballet
Atlanta Ballet Centre for Dance Education *1400 W. Peachtree St., Midtown,
404/873–5811; Chastain Square, 4279
Roswell Rd., Buckhead, 404/303–1501.*

Rotaru International Ballet School *6000
Peachtree Industrial Blvd., Norcross, 770/
662–0993.*

Ruth Mitchell Dance Studio *81 Church
St., Marietta, 770/426–0007.*

Soapstone Center for the Arts Children
only. *1 S. DeKalb Center, Decatur, 404/
241–2453.*

ballroom & latin
Arthur Murray Dance Centers *7256
Roswell Rd., Sandy Springs, 770/396–
9444; 2468 Windy Hill Rd., Marietta, 770/
951–8811.*

Atlanta Ballroom Dance Centre *120
Northwood Dr., Suite B8, West Terrace
Level, Sandy Springs, 404/847–0821.*

Atlanta Dance World *2200 Northlake
Pkwy., Suite 270, Tucker, 770/604–9900.*

Dance City Ballroom *Lindbergh Plaza,
2581 Piedmont Rd., Buckhead, 404/266–
0166.*

Fred Astaire Dance Studios *1170 La Vista Rd., at Cheshire Bridge Rd., Midtown, 404/321–0306.*

Locurto's Ballroom DanceSport Studio *Toco Hills Shopping Center, 2991-D N. Druid Hills Rd., North Druid Hills, 404/636–7433.*

Tango/Atlanta *133 Sycamore St., Decatur, 404/378–6985.*

folk & social

Atlanta Dance Hotline This general resource number has information on all kinds of recreational and folk dancing, from Cajun to contra. *404/634–2585.*

Chattahoochee Country Dance Association The group offers information about contra dance. *Morningside Baptist Church, 1700 Piedmont Ave., Morningside, 404/634–2585.*

Metro Atlanta Square Dancers Association The Internet home page of this group includes addresses and schedules for area square-dancing clubs. *www.geocities.com/~jgraser.*

Soapstone Center for the Arts Senior citizens can participate in in-line dancing here. *1 S. DeKalb Center, Decatur, 404/241–2453.*

DRIVING SCHOOLS

Clarkston Driving Academy *4765 Memorial Dr., Decatur, 404/294–9007.*

Cool Driving *2453 Coronet Way NW, Riverside, 404/327–8760.*

Taggart's Driving School *3566 Lawrenceville Hwy., Tucker, 770/934–2144.*

LANGUAGE SCHOOLS

esl

Georgia State University The university offers certification in teaching English as a second language, as well as a variety of languages and traditional academic language programs and classes for nonmatriculated auditing students. *Department of ESL and Applied Linguistics, University Plaza, Downtown, 404/651–3650.*

french

Alliance Française Language instruction classes as well as literature and cultural classes are offered. *1360 Peachtree St., Midtown, 404/875–1211.*

german

Friends of Goethe All types of language and cultural classes are offered. *Colony Square, 1197 Peachtree St., Midtown, 404/724–9390.*

japanese

Japan America Society In addition to general language courses, the society offers classes in business Japanese and Japanese culture. *2222 Harris Tower, Peachtree Center, 233 Peachtree St., Downtown, 404/524–7399.*

other

Inlingua Private lessons and some group classes cover all European languages and many Asian languages, including Japanese and Vietnamese. *Lenox Center, 3355 Lenox Rd., Buckhead, 404/266–2661.*

LIBRARIES

Auburn Avenue Research Library on African-American Culture and History This is a noncirculating library. *101 Auburn Ave., Downtown, 404/730–4001.*

Cobb County Main Library *266 Roswell St., Marietta, 770/528–2318.*

DeKalb County Main Library *215 Sycamore St., Decatur, 404/370–3070.*

Douglas County Library *6810 Selman Dr., Douglasville, 770/920–7125; 7100 Junior High Dr., Lithia Springs, 770/944–5931.*

Fayette County Library *Heritage Park Way, Fayetteville, 770/461–8841.*

Forsyth County Library *585 Dahlonega Hwy., Cumming, 770/781–9840.*

Fulton County Main Library *1 Margaret Mitchell Sq., Downtown, 404/730–1700 or 404/730–4636.*

Georgia State Archives *330 Capitol Ave., Downtown, 404/656–2393.*

Gwinnett County Library *Library Headquarters 1001 U.S. 29, Lawrenceville, 770/822–4522.*

Jimmy Carter Library This noncirculating research library is part of the Carter Center complex. *1 Copenhill Ave., Poncey-Highland, 404/331–0296.*

National Archives & Records *1557 St. Joseph Ave., East Point, 404/763–7477.*

MUSIC SCHOOLS

Atlanta Music Center Children age three and up can receive Yamaha-method instruction in all instruments; instrument rental is available. *5509 Chamblee-Dunwoody Rd., Dunwoody, 770/394–1727; 1205 Johnson Ferry Rd., Marietta, 440/ 977–0003; 4051 U.S. 78, Lilburn, 770/ 979–2887.*

Ken Stanton Music Private instruction in percussion, piano, strings, and wind instruments for adults and children is offered. Instrument rental is available. *777 Roswell St., Marietta, 770/427–2491;627 Holcomb Bridge Rd., Roswell Village, Roswell, 770/993–8334; South Pointe Center, 1105 Parkside La., Woodstock, 770/ 516–0805; Scenic Square Center, 1977-B Scenic Hwy., Snellville, 770/979–0736.*

Maple Street Guitars Owner George Petsch, a classical guitarist, sells electric and acoustic guitars and gives lessons in classical and rock styles. *3199 Maple Dr., Buckhead, 404/231–5214.*

Neighborhood Music Schools, Georgia State University School of Music The program provides instruction of many instruments for all ages at numerous area locations. *404/651–1111.*

Rotaru International Ballet School Primarily a dance school, Rotaru also gives private piano lessons. *6000 Peachtree Industrial Blvd., Norcross, 770/662–0993.*

Southern Keyboards Voice, piano, guitar, and banjo lessons for children and adults are available. *1898 Leland Dr., Suite B, Marietta, 770/953–0938.*

Steinway Piano Galleries Whatever your age, you can take piano lessons here. Piano sales and rentals are available. *6650-B Roswell Rd., Sandy Springs, 404/ 351–0550.*

WINE PROGRAMS

Alliance Française The delights of French wine are taught by Labe Mell. *1360 Peachtree St., Midtown, 404/875–1211.*

Anita L. Laraia's Wine School Designed for both professional and nonprofessional students, the six-week basic diploma course ($240) includes course book and wine tastings. *Box 52723, 30355, 770/901–9433.*

Evening at Emory Wine 101 is taught in several sections by faculty associated with the *Atlanta Wine Report. Emory University, 1560 Clairemont Rd., Decatur, 404/727–6000.*

Friends of Goethe Don Reddicks, a well-known specialist in German wines, teaches occasional courses in German wine. *Colony Square, 1197 Peachtree St., Midtown, 404/724–9390.*

vacation & travel information

AIRLINES

major carriers

American *800/433–7300.* **Continental** *800/525–0280.* **Delta** *800/221–1212.* **Northwest Airlines** *800/225–2525.* **United** *800/241–6522.* **US Airways** *800/428–4322.*

smaller carriers

Air Canada *800/776–3000.* **AirTran** *770/ 994–8258 or 800/247–8726.* **American** *800/433–7300.* **American Eagle** *800/433– 7300.* **Atlantic Southeast/Delta Connection** *800/221–1212 or 800/282–3424.* **ComAir** *800/221–1212.* **Continental Express** *800/525–0280.* **Midway** *800/ 446–4392.* **Midwest Express** *800/452– 2022.* **Southwest** *800/435–9792.*

AIRPORTS

The only commercial airport in the 10 counties is the Hartsfield Atlanta International Airport. Metro Atlanta also has several small general aviation airports that serve corporate clients and recreational pilots.

hartsfield atlanta international airport

6000 N. Terminal Pkwy., Hapeville, 404/ 530–6830; 404/530–6674 ground transportation; 404/530–6725 airport parking;

404/530–2100 lost and found; 404/635–6800 traffic; 404/486–1133 weather.

GETTING THERE BY PUBLIC TRANSPORTATION

Hartsfield Airport lies within the elbow of I–85 and I–285 in the south part of metro Atlanta, straddling Fulton and Clayton counties. The amount of luggage you're carrying and whether you're traveling with small children will likely determine what kind of transportation you take to reach the airport. Taxis and shuttles are by far the most expensive options.

MARTA provides very easy access to Hartsfield, especially if you don't have a lot of luggage. Trains go directly into the airport, and each MARTA car has designated luggage space. What's more, at $1.75, this deal can't be beat. The airport sits at the end of the north–south line, so if you board MARTA along the east–west line you have to change trains at Five Points. You can park at certain MARTA stations (North Springs, Sandy Springs, Brookhaven, Doraville, Chamblee, Lenox Square, Lindbergh, Dunwoody/Medical Center, and College Park) in secured areas for $3 a day. North–south trains run from Doraville and North Springs to the airport every 8–10 minutes weekdays, every 15 minutes after 9:30 PM and on weekends. When returning to Doraville or North Springs, make sure to get on the destination-designated train, as not all northbound trains go as far as Doraville, and not all deviate to the North Springs station.

Taxi service to the airport is costly. From downtown, the fare is $18 per person; from Buckhead, the per-person fare is $28. The farther out you are, the more expensive the trip. A trip from Sandy Springs to the airport, for instance, costs about $45–$50.

Numerous shuttle services operate between suburban points and Hartsfield.

Atlanta Airport Shuttle Licensed by the city of Atlanta, this outfit provides door-to-door service to and from the airport. One-way fares range from $38 (from College Park) to $65 (from Alpharetta). You can save money if you board at the shuttle's Roswell or Marietta terminal. The fare from Roswell is $20 one-way, $32 round-trip; the fare from Marietta is $20 one-way, $30 round-trip. For door-to-door and terminal service, book your reservation at least 24 hours in advance.

359 Whitehall St., Downtown, 404/768–7600; 10930 Crabapple Rd., Roswell, 770/998–1893; 200 Interstate North Pkwy., Marietta, 770/952–1601.

Atlanta Airport Superior Shuttle On the northside, this service picks up from hotels and residences within a 50-mi radius of the airport, although it may travel up to 200 mi. On the southside, only residential pickup is available. The service requires one week's notice for groups and 24 hours' notice for individuals. A typical one-way fare is $50 from Alpharetta. 1945 Savoy Dr., Chamblee, 770/457–4794.

Park 'N Fly From this terminal/parking lot, continuous 24-hour shuttle service runs to the airport every three to five minutes. The lot has 24-hour security; you pay $66 per week or $11 per day to park your car, but the shuttle is free. 3950 Conley St., College Park, 404/768–8582.

Park 'N Fly Plus A shuttle leaves for the airport every three to five minutes around the clock. Additional services include ticketing at the Delta terminal, car wash, and auto detailing. Daily parking rates range from $10.25 (self-park) to $15 (covered valet parking), but the shuttle is included. 2525 Camp Creek Pkwy., College Park, 404/761–6220.

Park 'N Go Park your car in this secured lot and take the shuttle, which leaves every three to five minutes around the clock, to Hartsfield. Parking ranges from $8.25 (uncovered) to $9.50 (covered) per day. The shuttle ride is free. 3151 Camp Creek Pkwy., East Point, 404/669–9300.

Park 'N Ticket Uncovered parking and a shuttle service to Hartsfield are available for $9 a day (covered parking is under construction). The shuttle leaves every 7–10 minutes, 24 hours a day. 3945 Conley St., College Park, 404/669–3800.

Woodstock Airport Shuttle You must reserve 24 hours in advance for pickup from residences or offices. The one-way fare from Woodstock is $34.98; round-trip is $62.54. Prices are a little higher from Canton. 1340 Bells Ferry Rd., Marietta, 770/425–4090.

GETTING THERE BY CAR

From the north, take GA 400 to I–285; then drive east to I–85 and take it south to the airport. Airport exits are clearly marked, leaving no doubt as to when you should turn off the highway. Or you

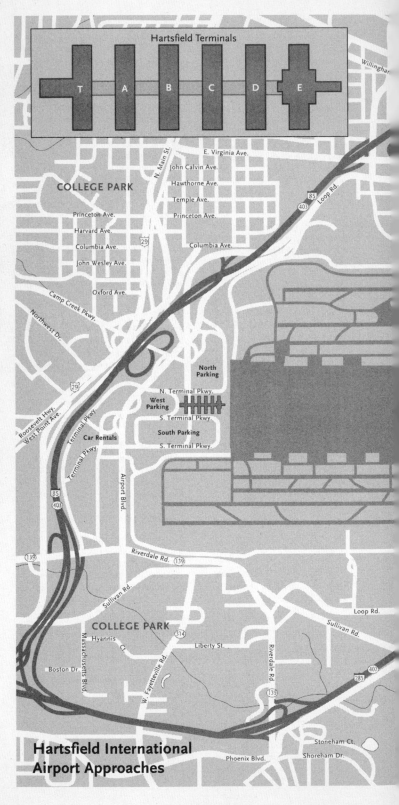

**Hartsfield International
Airport Approaches**

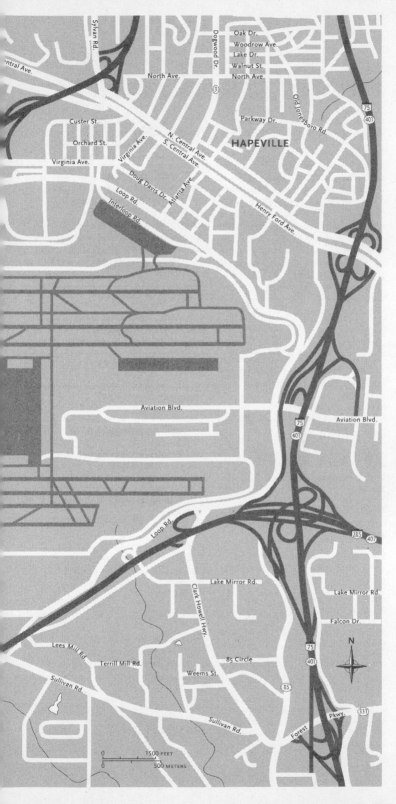

Sylvan Rd.

Dogwood Dr.

Oak Dr.
Woodrow Ave.
Lake Dr.
Walnut St.
North Ave.

North Ave.

③

75
401

Central Ave.

Custer St.

Orchard St.

Virginia Ave.

Parkway Dr.

Old Jonesboro Rd.

N. Central Ave.
S. Central Ave.

HAPEVILLE

Virginia Ave.

Doug Davis Dr.

Atlanta Ave.

Loop Rd.

Interloop Rd.

Henry Ford Ave.

Aviation Blvd.

Aviation Blvd.

75
401

Loop Rd.

285 401

Lake Mirror Rd.

Lake Mirror Rd.

Clark Howell Hwy.

Falcon Dr.

Lees Mill Rd.

Terrill Mill Rd.

85 Circle

Weems St.

N

75
401

Sullivan Rd.

Sullivan Rd.

85

Forest Pkwy.

331

0   1500 FEET
0   500 METERS

can continue east along I–285 and take exit 44 to I–85 north; the airport exit is the first one off I–85. If you live in west metro, take I–285 to I–85 north, and then follow the signs to the airport exit. From the south, take I–85 north to the airport. If you live in the east, travel west on I–20, take I–285 south, and then exit 44 to I–85 north, first exit to the airport.

Once you reach Hartsfield you have several parking options, depending on the strength of your legs and the size of your wallet. The hike from the long-term uncovered parking lot ($5 per day in economy) to the terminal is fairly long. It's a bit easier to negotiate if you find an abandoned SMART luggage cart. Less strenuous is the park-and-ride off the South Terminal, where uncovered parking costs $6 per day ($1 per hour short-term). From here, you get to the terminals via shuttles that run every few minutes in both directions. Keep your parking stub so you know which shuttle to take back to your parking lot and space. Daily parking in a covered deck costs $12. Hourly short-term parking is available directly across from North and South terminals in covered and uncovered decks. The rate here is $1 for 1–3 hours, $2 for 3–6 hours, $24 for 6–24 hours, and $48 for subsequent days or fractions thereof.

other airports

DeKalb Peachtree Airport 2000 Airport Rd., Chamblee, 770/936–5440.

Fulton County Airport–Brown Field 3952 Aviation Cir., Carol Heights, 404/699–4200.

Gwinnett County Airport–Briscoe Field 770 Airport Rd., Lawrenceville, 770/822–5196.

Peachtree City–Falcon Field 7 Falcon Dr., Peachtree City, 770/487–2225.

McCollum Airport 1723 McCollum Pkwy., Kennesaw, 770/422–4300.

CAR RENTAL

All the big national agencies have concessions at Hartsfield and other locations, but local agencies abound, often providing good rentals at less expensive rates. These may not have access to airport property per se but usually are nearby. They typically provide pick-up and drop-off service. Rates at national

car-rental chains vary slightly between the airport branches and the city locations; luxury and full-size autos generally are more expensive at the airport, but rates for economy or compact cars are about the same.

major agencies

Alamo 2045 Car Rental Row, College Park, 404/768–4161 or 800/327–9633, www.alamo.com.

Avis Rent a Car 800/331–1212, www.avis.com; 4225 Car Rental Row, College Park, 404/530–2700; 281 S. Main St., Alpharetta, 770/619–3275; 143 Courtland St., Downtown, 404/659–4814; 4975 Jimmy Carter Blvd., Norcross, 770/921–3395; 933-4 S. Hairston Rd., Stone Mountain, 770/469–2579.

Budget 800/527–0770, www.budget.com; 4150 Car Rental Row, College Park, 404/767–2566; 6952 Tara Blvd., Jonesboro, 404/530–3000; 1110 Northchase Pkwy., Marietta, 770/305–1990.

Dollar 800/800–4000, www.dollar.com; 4003 Main St., College Park, 404/766–0244; 2200 Northlake Pkwy., Tucker, 770/939–5280.

Enterprise Rent A Car 800/736–8222 in-town rentals; 800/325–8007 out-of-town rentals, www.enterprise.com; 3907 Main St.–Atlanta Airport, College Park, 404/763–5220; 3088 Piedmont Rd. NE, Buckhead, 404/261–7337; 2742 N. Decatur Rd., Decatur, 404/299–3385; 303 Courtland St., Downtown, 404/659–6050; 6189 Roswell Rd., Sandy Springs, 404/255–3873; 4205 Jonesboro Rd., Union City, 770/969–5654.

Hertz 800/654–3131, www.hertz.com; 3920 Main St.–Atlanta Airport, College Park, 404/530–2925; 1954 Airport Dr.–DeKalb Peachtree Airport, Chamblee, 770/986–8908; 3050 Satellite Blvd., Duluth, 678/417–5237; 10915 Hwy. 92 E, Woodstock, 678/445–4159.

National Car Rental 800/227–7368, www.nationalcar.com; 4010 Main St.–Atlanta Airport, College Park, 404/530–2800; 2560 Shallowford Rd., Chamblee, 770/458–0049.

Thrifty Car Rental 800/847–4389, www.thrifty.com; 4708 Riverdale Rd.–Atlanta Airport, College Park, 770/996–2350; 100 Courtland St. NE, Downtown, 404/524–2843; 461 W. Pike St., Lawrenceville, 770/682–2711; 277 Marietta Pkwy., Marietta, 770/421–0729.

local agencies

All Star Rent-a-Car *1199-B Roswell Rd. NE, Marietta, 770/429–9999.*

Atlanta Rent-a-Car *3185 Camp Creek Pkwy., East Point, 404/763–1110.*

Payless Car Rental *1931 Roosevelt Hwy., College Park, 404/788–2120.*

Rent-a-Wreck *5222 Old Dixie Rd., Forest Park, 404/363–8720.*

CONSULATES

Consulate General of Argentina *Marriott Marquis Tower I, 245 Peachtree Center Ave., Suite 2101, Downtown, 404/880–0805.*

Consulate General of Belgium *Peachtree Center, 235 Peachtree St., Suite 850, North Tower, Downtown, 404/659–2150.*

British Consulate General *Marriott Marquis Tower I, 245 Peachtree Center Ave., Suite 2700, Downtown, 404/836–0301.*

Canadian Consulate General *100 Colony Sq., Suite 1700, Midtown, 404/532–2000.*

Chilean Consulate *2876 Sequoyah Dr., Buckhead, 404/350–9030.*

Consulate General of Colombia *5780 Peachtree-Dunwoody Rd., Suite 250, Dunwoody, 404/255–3038.*

Consulate of the Czech Republic *2110 Powers Ferry Rd., Suite 220, Marietta, 770/859–9402.*

German Consulate General *Marriott Marquis Tower II, 285 Peachtree Center Ave., Suite 901, Downtown, 404/659–4760.*

Consulate of Greece *Tower Place, 3340 Peachtree Rd., Suite 1670, Buckhead, 404/261–3313.*

Consulate General of Iceland *20 Executive Park W, Suite 2023, North Druid Hills, 404/321–0777.*

Consulate General of Israel *Selig Center, 1100 Spring St., Suite 440, Midtown, 404/487–6500.*

Italian Consulate *755 Mt. Vernon Hwy., Suite 270, Dunwoody, 404/303–0503.*

Consulate General of Japan *100 Colony Sq., Suite 2000, Midtown, 404/892–2700.*

Consulate General of the Republic of Korea *Peachtree Center, 229 Peachtree St., Suite 500, International Tower, Downtown, 404/522–1611.*

Consulate General of Mexico *2600 Apple Valley Rd., Brookhaven, 404/266–0777.*

Consulate of the Netherlands *Ronstadt Bldg., 2015 S. Park Pl., Downtown, 770/937–7123.*

Panamanian Consulate and Trade Commission *229 Peachtree St. NE, International Bldg., Suite 1209, Downtown, 404/522–4114.*

Swedish Consulate *Bank of America Plaza, 600 Peachtree St., Suite 2400, Downtown, 404/815–2250.*

Swiss Consulate General *1275 Peachtree St. NE, Suite 425, Midtown, 404/870–2000.*

Thailand Consulate Office *3333 Riverwood Pkwy., Suite 520, Vinings, 770/988–3304.*

Turkish Honorary Consulate *7155 Brandon Mill Rd., Roswell, 770/913–0900.*

CURRENCY EXCHANGE

The currency-exchange offices listed here buy and sell travelers' checks and foreign currency, though it's best to call ahead to verify availability, especially if you require special denominations or large amounts of currency. Most banks also can execute currency exchanges with several days' advance notice (sometimes as much as two weeks), depending on the size of the bank's international department.

American Express You can get the major currencies here, including travelers' checks in other currencies, on a moment's notice. Less commonly exchanged currencies require a few days' advance notice. *800/461–8484; 7855 Northpoint Pkwy., Alpharetta, 770/625–3900; Lenox Plaza, 3384 Peachtree Rd., Buckhead, 404/262–7561.*

Thomas Cook Both branches are at Hartsfield Atlanta International Airport. Less commonly exchanged currencies must be ordered two weeks ahead of time. *800/287–7362; Hartsfield Atlanta International Airport, Concourse E, Gate 26, 404/761–6332. Customs branch: Hartsfield Atlanta International Airport, downstairs from main office in Concourse E, 404/761–1406.*

INOCULATIONS, VACCINATIONS, & TRAVEL HEALTH

Centers for Disease Control and Prevention Information about other countries' immunization requirements, U.S. Public Health Service recommendations, and other health guidance, including risks in particular countries, is available here. *888/232–3228 24-hour hot line; 888/232–3299 automated fax-back service, www. cdc.gov.*

PASSPORTS

The nearest U.S. Passport Agency is in Miami, but a number of local facilities— courthouses, post offices, and municipal offices—may accept your paperwork. You must apply for a passport in person if you haven't previously applied or if your passport was lost or stolen. A new passport costs $60, a renewal $40. Passport application forms are available from designated post offices, clerks of court, county and municipal offices, and travel agencies, or by calling the National Passport Information Center (900/225–5674; 35¢ per minute). If you have Internet access and a printer, the forms also are available at the State Department's Consular Affairs Web site (travel.state.gov), which has extensive information about passport applications. In addition to the forms, you must produce two recent, identical photos; proof of U.S. citizenship; and valid photo identification. Average wait time is six weeks; if you can't wait that long, you can pay an additional $35 for expedited service.

Passport renewal is handled most easily through the mail. Obtain the necessary forms as explained above and either mail them in or drop them at the nearest passport acceptance facility. These are the facilities in the metro area:

Federal Information Center *800/688–9889.* **Howell Mill Postal Store** *1984 Howell Mill Rd., Buckhead, 404/605–0526.* **Sandy Springs Postal Store** *227 Sandy Springs Pl., Sandy Springs, 404/255–9643.* **U.S. Post Office–Briarcliff Station** *3104 Briarcliff Rd. NE, Briarcliff, 800/325–0497.* **U.S. Post Office–Brookhaven Station** *3851 Peachtree Rd., Brookhaven, 404/816–8058.* **U.S. Post Office–Buckhead Station** *1 Buckhead Loop, Buckhead, 404/816–9486.* **U.S. Post Office–Central City Finance Station** *183 Forsyth St.,* *Downtown, 404/521–9843.* **U.S. Post Office–Doraville Station** *4700 Longmire Ext., Doraville, 770/216–8475.* **U.S. Post Office–East Point Station** *2905 E. Point St., East Point, 404/766–0553;* **U.S. Post Office–Midtown Station** *1072 W. Peachtree St., Midtown, 404/521–9843;* **U.S. Post Office–Pharr Road Station** *575 Pharr Rd. NE, Buckhead, 404/869–4413.*

passport photos

Charles Baker Photography & Fine Art *5217 Memorial Dr., Stone Mountain, 404/294–3616.*

Fast Foto *2887 N. Druid Hills Rd. NE, Toco Hills, 404/633–9800.*

Mail & Package Center *4155 Lawrenceville Hwy., Lilburn, 770/925–0300.*

Metro Color Lab *1693 Washington Rd., East Point, 404/768–1298.*

Passport Fast Photos *566 Pharr Rd., Buckhead, 404/261–2900.*

Perfect Photo *3466 Holcomb Bridge Rd., Norcross, 770/441–0303.*

A Quick Passport & Visa *316 Hammond Dr. NE, Sandy Springs, 404/255–0341.*

ROUTING SERVICES FOR U.S. TRIPS

Automobile Association of America The local AAA affiliate, Auto Club South, offers travel-agency services and free guidebooks to members. Also, AAA can map out your trip with customized routing maps called TripTiks®. If you're an AAA member, you can get a TripTik® by visiting or calling one of the club's offices or by visiting the Web site (www.aaa.com). Just enter your postal code, click on "Travel," and follow the prompts. *Norcross World Travel, 5450 Peachtree Pkwy., Norcross, 770/448–7024; Tara Travel, 696 Mt. Zion Rd., Jonesboro, 770/961–8085.*

TOURIST INFORMATION

for local information

Airport Area Chamber of Commerce *600 S. Central Ave., Suite 100, Hapeville, 404/209–0910.*

Atlanta Convention & Visitors Bureau
*233 Peachtree St., Suite 2000, Downtown,
404/222–6688 or 800/847–4842; Underground Atlanta, 50 Upper Alabama St.
SW, Downtown, 404/577–2148.*

**Cherokee County Chamber of Com-
merce** *3605 Marietta Hwy., Canton, 770/
345–0400.*

**Clayton County Convention & Visitors
Bureau** *104 N. Main St., Jonesboro, 770/
478–4800 or 880/662–STAY.*

Cobb Chamber of Commerce *240 Interstate North Pkwy., Northwest Atlanta,
770/980–2000.*

DeKalb Chamber of Commerce *750 Commerce Dr., Suite 201, Decatur, 404/378–
8000.*

DeKalb Convention & Visitors Bureau
*750 Commerce Dr., Decatur, 404/378–
2525 or 800/999–6055.*

Douglas County Chamber of Commerce
*2145 Slater Mill Rd., Douglasville, 770/
942–5022.*

Fayette County Chamber of Commerce
*200 Courthouse Sq., Fayetteville, 770/
461–9983.*

Forsyth County Chamber of Commerce
*Forsyth Professional Bldg., 110 Old Buford
Rd., Suite 120, Cumming, 770/887–6461.*

**Georgia Department of Industry, Trade
and Tourism** *Marriott Marquis Tower II,
285 Peachtree Center Ave., Suite 1000,
Downtown, 404/656–3590 or 800/847–
4842.*

Gwinnett Chamber of Commerce *5110
Sugarloaf Pkwy., Lawrenceville, 770/513–
3000.*

Henry County Chamber of Commerce
*1310 GA 20 W, McDonough, 770/957–
5786.*

Marietta Welcome Center *4 Depot St.,
Marietta, 770/429–1115 or 800/835–0445.*

Metro Atlanta Chamber of Commerce
*235 International Blvd., near Centennial
Olympic Park, Downtown, 404/880–
9000.*

**North Fulton County Chamber of Com-
merce** *1025 Old Roswell Rd., Roswell, 770/
993–8806.*

Roswell Visitors Center *617 Atlanta St.,
on the Square, Roswell, 770/640–3253 or
800/776–7935.*

TRAVELER'S AID

**Traveler's Aid Society of Metropolitan
Atlanta** *Hartsfield Atlanta International
Airport (near baggage claim and general
airport-information booth), 404/766–4511;
477 Henry Dr., Marietta, 770/428–1883;
828 W. Peachtree St., Midtown, 404/817–
7070.*

U.S. CUSTOMS

Port of Atlanta *4341 International Pkwy.,
Suite 600, across from Hartsfield Atlanta
International Airport, 404/675–1300.*

VISA INFORMATION & TRAVEL ADVISORIES

U.S. Department of State Complete visa
information, current travel warnings and
advisories, and information for visiting
or immigrating foreign nationals is
available from the department. *Visa Services, U.S. Department of State, Washington, DC 20522, 202/647–5226; 202/663–
1225 information for foreign nationals,
www.travel.state.gov.*

DIRECTORIES

restaurants by neighborhood

ALPHARETTA

Altobeli's Italian Restaurant & Piano Bar, 33
Atlanta Bread Company (café), 14
Cabernet (steak), 56–57
California Pizza Kitchen, 35, 48
Canyon Cafe (southwestern), 54–55
Comeaux's Louisiana Bar & Grill (Cajun/Creole), 16, 250
Di Paolo Cucina (Italian), 34
Ippolitos's Family Style Italian Restaurant, 35
Killer Creek Chop House (steak), 57
La Paz (southwestern), 35, 55
P.F. Chang, A Chinese Bistro, 19
Vinny's on Windward (Italian), 38

ANSLEY PARK

Agnes & Muriel's (American), 2–3
Fat Matt's Rib Shack (barbecue), 11, 238
King and I (Thai), 60
Piccadilly Classic American Cooking (southern), 53

AUSTELL

Longhorn Steaks, 57
Wallace Barbecue, 13

AVONDALE ESTATES

Skip's Hot Dogs (American/casual), 9

BRASELTON

Fleur-De-Lis (French), 30
Le Clos at Château Élan (French), 30
Paddy's Irish Pub, 33, 256

BROOKHAVEN

Bajarito's (eclectic), 13, 25
Mellow Mushroom (pizza), 48–49
Original Pancake House (American/casual), 9

BROOKWOOD

Cafe Sunflower (vegetarian & macrobiotic), 61
Houston's (American/casual), 9
R. Thomas Deluxe Grill (American/casual), 9

BUCKHEAD

Abruzzi (Italian), 33
Anis (French), 29
Annie's Thai Castle (Thai), 59–60
Anthony's (continental), 22, 203
Antica Posta (Italian), 33
Aria (eclectic), 25
Atlanta Fish Market (seafood), 49, 91
Basil's Mediterranean Café, 41
Blue Ridge Grill (American), 3
Bluepointe (eclectic), 20, 25
Bone's (steak), 56
Brasserie Le Coze (French), 29
Bread Market (Café), 14
Bridgetown Grill (Caribbean), 17–18
Buckhead Bread Company & Corner Café, 14
Buckhead Brewery & Grill (American), 3, 239–240
Buckhead Diner (American), 3
Café Intermezzo, 14–15
Café Tu Tu Tango (eclectic), 25–26, 35
California Pizza Kitchen, 35, 48
Casa Grande (Tex-Mex), 59
Cedars (Mediterranean), 42
Chequers Seafood Grill, 50
Chops (steak), 57
Ciao Bella (Italian), 34
Coca-Cola Café, 15
Coco Loco (Cuban), 23
Dining Room, The Ritz-Carlton, Buckhead (contemporary), 20–21
Eclipse di Luna (Latin), 40, 259
Fadó (Irish), 33, 254, 256
Fishbone Piranha Bar (seafood), 50
Fogo de Chao (Brazilian), 14
Fratelli di Napoli (Italian), 34
Georgia Grille (southwestern), 55

Goldberg's (delicatessen), 24
Grappa (Mediterranean), 42
Hal's (Cajun/Creole), 17
Horseradish Grill (contemporary), 21
Houston's (American/casual), 8
Huey's (Cajun/Creole), 17
Imperial Fez (Moroccan), 35, 46
Kamogawa (Japanese), 38
La Fonda Latina (Latin), 40
La Grotta Ristorante Italiano, 35
Landmark Diner (American), 6
Longhorn Steaks, 57
Maggiano's Little Italy (Italian), 36
Malaya (Pan-Asian), 46
McKinnon's Louisiane (Cajun/Creole), 17, 251
Meritage (contemporary), 21, 28
Morton's of Chicago (steaks), 58
Nava (southwestern), 55
Nickiemoto's (Pan-Asian), 46
Nona's Italian Kitchen, 36
Oh!...María (Mexican), 45
OK Café (southern), 52–53
Outback Steakhouse, 58
Palm (steak), 58
Pano's and Paul's (continental), 20, 22
Piccadilly Classic American Cooking (southern), 53
Portofino (Mediterranean), 42–43
Pricci (Italian), 37
Prime (steak), 58
Rajah (Indian), 32
Rib Ranch (barbecue), 12
Ritz-Carlton, Buckhead (tea), 59
Rock Bottom Brewery (American), 9, 240–241
Rocky's Brick Oven Pizza & Italian Restaurant, 49
Ruth's Chris Steak House, 58–59
Satay Ria (Malaysian), 41
Seeger's (contemporary), 20, 21
Soleil (French), 30
Soto (Japanese), 39
Swan Coach House (tea), 59
Tomtom, A Bistro (eclectic), 28

DULUTH

Athens Pizza House (Greek), 31
Bugaboo Creek Lodge & Bar (steak), 56
Carrabba's Italian Grill, 34
Ciao Bella (Italian), 34
Corky's Ribs & Bar-B-Q, 11
El Taco Veloz (Mexican), 44
Georgia Diner (American/casual), 8
Hal's (Cajun/Creole), 17
Kurt's (continental), 22
Poona (Indian), 32
Romano's Macaroni Grill (Italian), 37
Sia's, 7
Stoney River (steak), 59
Thai Chilli, 60
Vreny's Biergarten (German), 31

DUNWOODY

Café Nordstrom, 15
California Pizza Kitchen, 35, 48
Canyon Cafe (southwestern), 54–55
Chequers Seafood Grill, 50
Don Taco (Mexican), 13, 43
E. 48th Street Italian Market (delicatessen), 24, 91
Goldberg's (delicatessen), 24
Goldfish (seafood), 50
Houston's (American/casual), 8
La Grotta Ravinia Ristorante Italiano, 35
La Strada (Italian), 35–36
McKendrick's (steaks), 58
Mellow Mushroom (pizza), 48–49
Mi Spia (Italian), 36
Oscar's Villa Capri (Italian), 36
P.F. Chang, A Chinese Bistro, 19
Romano's Macaroni Grill (Italian), 37
Savu (Moroccan), 47, 249–250
Villa Christina (Italian), 38

EAST ATLANTA

Grant Central Pizza and Pasta, 48
Pastificio Cameli (Italian), 37
Zesto Drive-In (American/casual), 10

EAST ATLANTA VILLAGE

Heaping Bowl & Brew (American), 5

FAYETTEVILLE

Du Roc Café (barbecue), 11

FOREST PARK

Zesto Drive-In (American/casual), 10

GAINESVILLE

El Taco Veloz (Mexican), 44

GRANT PARK

Grant Central Pizza & Pasta, 48
Ria's Bluebird (American), 6

HAPEVILLE

Café at the Corner, 14
Grecian Gyro (Greek), 31
Original Dwarf House (southern), 53

INMAN PARK

Fritti (Italian), 34
Son's Place (southern), 54
Sotto Sotto (Italian), 37
Virginia's (eclectic), 28

JONESBORO

Dean's (barbecue), 11
Harold's (barbecue), 12
Longhorn Steaks, 57

KENNESAW

Bell's (barbecue), 11
Carrabba's Italian Grill (Italian), 34
Ippolito's Family Style Italian Restaurant, 35
Outback Steakhouse, 58
Romano's Macaroni Grill (Italian), 37
Varsity (American/casual), 10, 13

LAWRENCEVILLE

Original Pancake House (American/casual), 9

LILBURN

Kalamata Greek Restaurant and Pizza, 31
Mellow Mushroom (pizza), 48–49
Spiced Right (barbecue), 13

LITTLE FIVE POINTS

Bang (French), 29
Bridgetown Grill (Caribbean), 17–18
La Fonda Latina (Latin), 40
Savage Pizza, 49
Vortex (American/casual), 10
Zesto Drive-In (American/casual), 10

MARIETTA

Baldinos Giant Jersey Subs (delicatessen), 24
Basil's Neighborhood Café (Mediterranean), 41–42
Carey's Place (American/casual), 7
Cherokee Cattle Co. (steak), 57
Crazy Cuban, 23
Don Taco (Mexican), 13, 43
1848 House (southern), 51
Haveli (Indian), 31–32
Houck's Steak & Seafood (American), 6
Houston's (American/casual), 8
La Strada (Italian), 35–36
Mellow Mushroom (pizza), 48–49
Provence (French), 30
Ray's on the River (American), 6, 250
Rib Ranch (barbecue), 12
Sukothai (Thai), 60
Williamson Brothers (barbecue), 13

MCDONOUGH

O. B.'s (barbecue), 12

MIDTOWN

Abbey (continental), 21–22, 28
Andaluz (Spanish), 56
Après Diem (eclectic), 25, 43
Baraonda (Italian), 33
Bridgetown Grill (Caribbean), 17–18
Cherry (eclectic), 26
Churchill Grounds (café), 15, 250
Einstein's (American), 4, 43, 217
Eno (Mediterranean), 42, 259
F.R.O.G.S. Cantina (Mexican), 44

index

CITY NOTES

CITY NOTES

CITY NOTES

CITY NOTES

CITY NOTES